15
5
005
7
5
6

D0414677

The Medieval Landscape
of Wessex

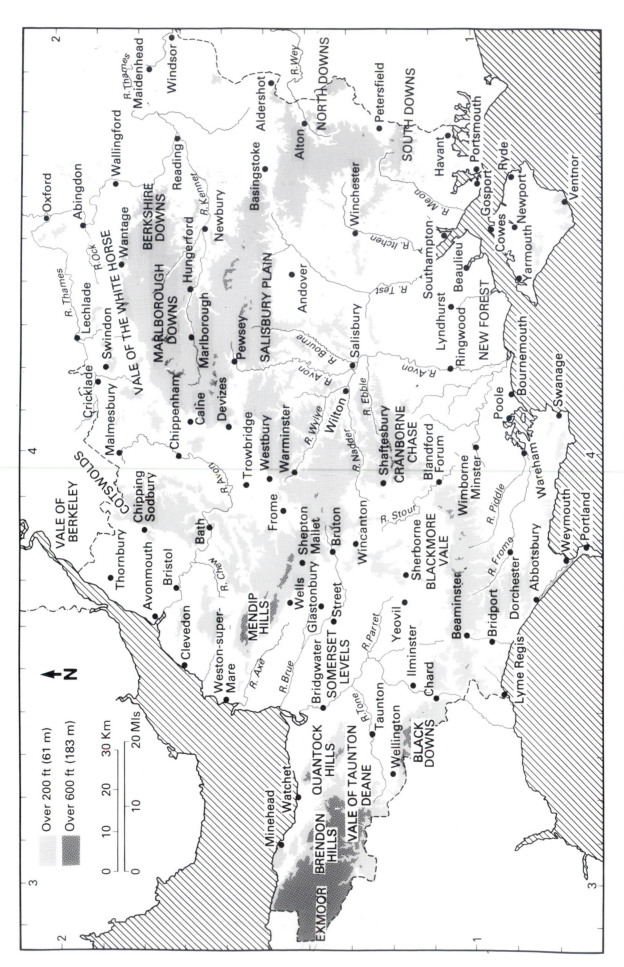

The Wessex Region (Map showing main places in the book area).

The Medieval Landscape
of Wessex

Edited by
Michael Aston and Carenza Lewis

Oxbow Monograph 46
1994

Published by
Oxbow Books, Park End Place, Oxford OX1 1HN

© Oxbow Books, 1994

ISBN 0 946897 78 6

This book is available direct from
Oxbow Books, Park End Place, Oxford OX1 1HN
(Phone: 0865-241249; Fax 0865-794449)

The production of this volume was supported by grants from the University of Bristol
Department for Continuing Education and the Royal Commission on the Historical
Monuments of England (RCHME)

Printed in Great Britain by
The Short Run Press, Exeter

Contents

List of Contributors

MICHAEL ASTON
Dept for Continuing Education
University of Bristol
8–10 Berkeley Square
Bristol BS8 1HH

JAMES BOND
2 Stone Edge Batch
Tickenham
Clevedon
Avon BS21 6SF

MICHAEL COSTEN
Dept for Continuing Education
University of Bristol
8–10 Berkeley Square
Bristol BS8 1HH

ROBERT CROFT
Dept of Environment and Planning
Somerset County Council
County Hall
Taunton TA1 4DY

BRUCE EAGLES
RCHME
Kemble Drive
Swindon
Wiltshire SN2 2GZ

JOHN HARE
Peter Symonds College
Winchester
Hampshire SO22 6RX

PATRICK HASE
20 Tenth Street
Hong Lok Yuen
Tai Po
New Territories
Hong Kong

DAVID HINTON
Dept of Archaeology
University of Southampton
Highfield
Southampton SO9 5NH

DELLA HOOKE
Dept of Geography and Geology
Cheltenham and Gloucester College
  of Higher Education.
Francis Close Hall
Swindon Road
Cheltenham
Gloucestershire GL50 4AZ

MICHAEL HUGHES
Hampshire County Planning Dept
The Castle
Winchester SO13 8UE

CARENZA LEWIS
RCHME
Kemble Drive
Swindon
Wiltshire SN2 2GZ

STEPHEN RIPPON
Dept of Archaeology
University of Reading
Whiteknights
Reading RG6 2AA

CHRISTOPHER TAYLOR
13 West End,
Whittlesford,
Cambridge CB2 4LX

Preface

When I am living in the Midlands.
Which are sodden and unkind,
I light my lamp in the evening
And the dark is left behind;
Then the great hills of the South Country
They come into my mind;
The great hills of the South Country
That stand along the sea ...

Hillaire Belloc, *The South Country*

With that curious respect for the accident of longevity which characterises the young and the mere middle-aged, the two editors have invited this veteran to intervene for a moment between the reader and their pages. Thus, with the gift of a set of page proofs I – a mere Mercian by birth and upbringing – can glory for a short while in the privilege of being one of the three best-informed people in the world on the history of the medieval landscape of Wessex: the other two being the editors themselves. Then, after publication, I look forward to ceding that privileged position with grace, with pleasure, and with enthusiasm so that a procession of reader after reader can pass on to find answers to their questions on landscape history and to find questions to which there are (as yet) no answers.

The price to be paid for my privilege is this short preface, to which no brief was supplied other than 'Something about Wessex and you ...'. Anyone who knows me from the printed page or who studies my various occupations in *Who's Who* will know that by and large Wessex and I have passed each other by, certainly for workaday activities even though holidays were a different matter. My parents were regular in their conviction that Wessex was the place for the annual seaside holiday, and for long – the 'twenties and most of the 'thirties – 'Wessex' to me was the name of the express train which left Birmingham New Street and plunged past the Cotswolds into Wessex. I am a survivor of the passengers on that delicious line, long put out to grass, which by-passed Bristol to steam chestily up the incline out of Bath into the Mendips on its way to Dorset, Wiltshire and Hampshire. (It was a shameful error of taste which prevented me entering the Wessex of Thomas Hardy until I was nearly fifty).

No one would have had reason to be surprised if I had declined to contribute a Preface with an autobiographical tone, although I suppose that the demands of friendship and my admiration of the work of the editors and authors within could have produced something between a eulogy and a critical review. But should not prefatory eulogies be confined to publishers' blurbs? will not more informed and objective reviewers than I soon be getting to work? and is not a reader looking for an overview already well provided for in the editors' Introduction which follows?

It was at this stage in compositional activity that I recalled the lines from Belloc that I have placed at the head. Sometime about 1931 our grammar school English Literature class was set to learn Belloc's poem by rote, and although Sutton Coldfield, despite its name, was not always sodden and unkind I can see how the contrast with the hills of the holiday counties (which Memory bathes in perpetual July sunshine) and which provided an annual escape from a flat landscape of Midland suburbia, made my mind respond to Belloc's sentiments, more so than the now-forgotten Keats, Shelley and Wordsworth. His lines must have been etched firmly in my subconscious, ready just now to be resurrected as a text for me, to stimulate me to emphasise how I – and, I believe, subsequent decades of landscape historians – must see this collection of essays on the Wessex countryside; a significant step forward in the context of English landscape studies that I have seen develop over my lifetime.

For there is no doubt that, partly by accident, English landscape history has been dominated hitherto by the Midland image. One accident was the location of the historians' workplaces. Well before 1939, after a brief spell of what he described as 'incarceration' in Brad-

vii

ford, William Hoskins was by day lecturing in economic history at the University College of Leicester, and by night to adult students at Vaughan College in the city. His leisure was spent in archives and in the field, and increasingly his Vaughan lecture courses moved to a mixture of field archaeology and landscape history. Naturally, both for exploration as well as exposition, his material lay in a Midland Landscape. His first book was *The Heritage of Leicestershire*, followed by (what I personally regard as his best) *Midland England*. When this canvas was fully extended to *The Making of the English Landscape* it was still very much a Midland England. Another side of William was, of course, the Devonian which found expression in his massive *Devon* and in *Devonshire Studies* but in pursuing that interest he had taken a giant knight's move, stepping over the Wessex counties. In the uncompleted series of county-by-county *Makings ...* which he commissioned it was counties of the Midland kind that came off best.

I must plead guiltily that much of my own work has been similarly conscripted. Critics of *Medieval England: an Aerial Survey* rightly pointed out that the selection of sites was unkind to the south-west, as well as to the north-west. No doubt some of this bias was due to the flight-base being in East Anglia; but also to the distance between my own home and county record offices in the south-west, so that in all honesty the defence would have been, as with Dr Johnson, "pure ignorance, madam". With so much at hand nearer to home, and by no means repititious, it was tempting to take what was handiest.

At that time I was living in Leeds, but by first base was employment in Rugby, Warwickshire, at the junction of Felden and Arden but still Midland. Differences between Arden and Felden were important enough to receive attention from Harry Thorpe and his pupils and were the basis of many studies: perhaps we were too self-satisfied, having discovered one pair of differences, so that champion-bocage too easily served as conceptual compartments elsewhere.

I regard my own experience after moving from Rugby to Yorkshire as instructive. The great surprise, as the process of self-education from my new base proceeded (for there were no text books), was the discovery that as far as medieval landscapes were concerned, Midland England extended all up the eastern plain as far as the Scottish Border. The first suspicion must have come from the open-field maps long in print in the *Northumberland County History* and then from the abundance of pre-enclosure plans in archives; then from the wide survival of ridge and furrow in the grasslands; and then from the depopulated village sites similar to those in the Midlands, even in their density.

That was a long time ago: and what has happened down in Wessex – and note the inadvertent condescension – is immediately apparent from the subject matter of these essays; from the excavation reports recorded in their footnotes; from the mapped record of field-work; and from local aerial photography. (James Bond is unnecessarily apologetic (p. 151) that illness has prevented him from shortening his contribution, it stands as a remarkable record of research.)

Indeed it is characteristic of this volume that it is so solidly based on research, and – as the dates in the bibliographies show – such recent research, and some of that unpublished. Future historiographers will certainly note two influences on the developing output of landscape studies, so well exemplified in the large- and small-scale work reported here: the role of the adult education classes organised by the WEA and the Universities' Extra-Mural Departments; and, closely connected, the role played in the progress of field work by the amateur, often first recruited in such a class with collective projects initiated by the lecturer. Many such contributions lie behind the studies in this book, and there are many other amateurs in Wessex and surrounding counties who, as I have seen for myself, have been introduced not just to a pastime but to active participation in scholarship through the many classes of all sorts conducted in the last decades by the indefatiguable towsled imp who goes under the name of Michael Aston, just as sixty years ago a young lecturer in Leicester began to teach his class members to follow him, not only in learning how to get mud on their boots but how to look over fence and hedge to decipher the Making of a Landscape.

It is in the nature of landscape history to have a role for an accumulated record of single and small observations which can be so easily be combined with outdoor recreation; it has been the good fortune of my lifetime that curiosity about the countryside and its works has grown so much, facilitated by increased leisure but stimulated by general and specialised publications. In historical research one generation stands on the shoulders of another, and this volume will both inform and stimulate future work in Wessex and beyond.

Introduction

Michael Aston and Carenza Lewis

This collection of papers explores the history of the Wessex countryside in the middle ages. This part of southern England, which formed the heartland of Alfred the Great's kingdom, was a vital political and military force in the later Saxon period, and continued to wield immense economic power in the following centuries with many extensive and wealthy royal and ecclesiastical estates. This must have had an immense impact on the countryside, whence much of the wealth of the region was derived and where most of the population lived. It is perhaps surprising then, that compared with other parts of England, Wessex is not an area which has featured prominently in recent medieval settlement studies. This volume seeks to redress this imbalance, by bringing together some of the work that has been undertaken recently to provide both a review of what is known and a stimulus for future work.

The Wessex Region

In the Anglo-Saxon period Wessex was a separate kingdom along with Sussex, Kent, Mercia, and more distantly, others such as East Anglia, Lindsey and Northumbria. Wessex in the tenth century annexed and controlled much of southern England, but the counties which made up its heartland were always Dorset, Hampshire, Somerset and Wiltshire, with Devon and Berkshire on the periphery (Hill 1981). This is the core area discussed in this volume (see Frontispiece). It is easy to associate the Wessex region, both geologically and topographically, with the chalk downland of southern England and indeed much of the centre of the region is dominated by these gentle rolling hills and clear stream valleys. But this landscape is surrounded by a rich variety of other terrains, including the rugged uplands of Exmoor in the far west, through the marshes of the Somerset Levels and the wooded regions of Selwood in Wiltshire and Hampshire, to the lowland heaths of the New Forest and Dorset. This Wessex heartland extends from the English Channel in the south to the Bristol Channel in the north, and is bounded by the more elevated regions of Dartmoor to the west, the Cotswolds to the north and the Sussex Downs to the east. Of all the rivers which rise within the region, only the Thames flows to the sea outside it.

Medieval Rural Settlement Studies in Wessex

Medieval rural settlement archaeology is a relatively young subject, but while research has forged ahead in much of the midlands and north of the country it has lagged behind in Wessex. This partly reflects the interests of those working in the area. When Chris Taylor was working in Dorset, ideas about settlement origins and development were in their infancy, but were given considerable stimulus by his analytical account of the evolution of the landscape and settlement of Whiteparish in Wiltshire (Taylor 1967). When he moved away from the region, it was to the benefit of the east midlands, but to the disadvantage of Wessex.

Such comments are in no way intended to belittle the work that has been carried out in the region. A number of important excavations have taken place in the region, ranging from the Saxon palace at Cheddar (So), the trading centre at Hamwic (Ha), the rural settlement of Chalton (Ha), the medieval village of Gomeldon (Wi) and town of Winchester (Ha). Other studies of related interest have been carried out, such as Desmond Bonney's discussion of the origins of chalkand parish boundaries (Bonney 1979), which have proved of lasting value to researchers in Wessex and beyond. However, despite the county-wide work of Michael Aston in Somerset (see Aston this volume), Michael Hughes in Hampshire (see Hughes this volume) and RCHME in Dorset (see Taylor this volume), little progress has been made in drawing together and developing our perception of the processes and patterns involved in the development of medieval rural settlement in this part of the country.

This is surprising because Wessex has great potential for the study of medieval rural settlement. Firstly, the area has an abundance of documentary evidence. There is a wealth of early charter material and other Anglo-Saxon records, partly as a result of the political prominence of Wessex in the later part of that period. The distribution maps of David Hill (1981) and the work of Ann Goodier (1984) show how many of the charters, the estates mentioned in them and their bounds, occur in Wessex. From the tenth century onwards there is an even greater quantity of documentary material including writs, leases and wills, much of it, of course, associated with the vast tracts of land owned and exploited by the large ecclesiastical establishments such as Glastonbury Abbey and the bishopric of Winchester. These bureaucratic landlords maintained very detailed records, many of which have survived in extensive archives. Comparable areas only exist elsewhere in Worcestershire, the Thames Valley, Kent and the Fens. This mass of material has been at once a help and a hindrance. It can tell us much about early estates, land use and rural settlement, but it demands very specialised expertise to utilise fully the potential contained in such documents. Without modern translations and re-evaluations their true value cannot be appreciated. Herein lies the nub of the old problem of combining archaeological and historical research.

Secondly, Wessex is of value for medieval settlement studies because it has a wide variety of landscape types. Although often considered to be a region of nucleated villages, national surveys of village-type settlements (Thorpe 1964; Roberts 1977, 1987) show that only the centre of the region (eastern Somerset, north and south Dorset, south Wiltshire and parts of Hampshire) are in fact dominated by nucleated villages. Other areas are characterised by more dispersed settlement patterns. Much of east Devon and west Somerset is characterised by a profusion of hamlet settlement with occasional villages and many isolated farms, and the same is true for central Dorset, parts of Wiltshire and most of Hampshire. This pattern continues east into Surrey and Sussex. Only recently have archaeologists and historians turned their attention to dispersed settlement patterns, recognising that an understanding of these areas, where villages do not occur, is vital if we are to understand why they do appear in other areas. Wessex, with its mixed settlement patterns, is really on the edge of the English 'village belt', and is consequently an ideal region for studying both nucleated and dispersed settlements and the relationship between these different types.

Wessex has further potential for unravelling the history of the medieval rural landscape because it has much better evidence for settlement in the preceding centuries, and particularly the Roman period, than many other parts of the country where medieval settlement studies have hitherto focused. It is increasingly being recognised that an understanding of the exploitation of the landscape in the Roman period, and perhaps earlier, is vital to the study of the later centuries, as evidence for the abandonment of some sites is countered by evidence for the continued use of other rural and urban settlements and ritual or administrative foci. Furthermore, in Wessex the presence of early monuments and boundary features and their relationship with parish and township boundaries can be used to discuss the continued use of elements of estate structures.

The fourth factor which enhances the value of Wessex for medieval settlement studies is the fact that the region experienced very different political circumstances to those in the east of the country in those years which are now seen as critical in the emergence of nucleated villages. It spanned the divide between Anglo-Saxon and Celtic Britain, it was the heart of Alfred's kingdom, it never lay within the Danelaw, and was not fought across in the course of the 'reconquest'. The evidence of Domesday Book suggests that it suffered less from the Viking raids of the early eleventh century, and it is notable for the relatively low numbers of manors recorded as 'waste' in 1086. There is no obvious historical context, such as the Wessex reconquest of the Danelaw or the Harrying of the north, which can be cited to explain the large-scale reorganisation of settlement into nucleated villages. For these reasons it has great potential as both a 'control' and test-bed for ideas about the causes of nucleation developed from settlement research in other parts of the country.

The History of Wessex

The papers in this volume consider many aspects of the evolution of the countryside of Wessex in the middle ages. The following summary of the archaeology and history of Wessex is intended to provide a general context for these papers, particularly for those readers unfamiliar with the region. It summarises briefly what is currently known, and reviews some of the main themes to emerge from the new research which is represented by the papers in this volume.

Prehistoric Wessex

The prehistoric archaeology of the Wessex region is immensely rich and many of its monuments rank among the most impressive in the country. These have often dominated research into British prehistory, and have certainly overshadowed the archaeology of the medieval period: Wessex was indeed in many respects the cradle of British prehistory. The prominent place occupied by Wessex in the early study of British prehistory is demonstrated in the earliest phase of the British neolithic (4,500–2,000 BC), which is named after the causewayed enclosure at Windmill Hill (Wi). Long barrows, such as Waylands Smithy (Be), are mostly concentrated in Wessex, and from the later neolithic the stone circles and henges of Avebury (Wi) (Fig. 1) and Stonehenge (Wi) are internationally renowned. That neolithic activity is widespread throughout Wessex is apparent in the evidence for extensive occupation and exploitation of such diverse landscapes as the Somerset Levels and the Mendips (So).

In the early and middle bronze age (2,000–1,600 BC)

Fig. 1 *Avebury, Wiltshire. This site spans 4000 years of human activity in Wessex: within the encircling bank and ditch of the neolithic henge can be seen the present village of Avebury. Between the houses and the henge ditch can be seen earthwork remains of former croft boundaries and building platforms. (Photo: Mick Aston)*

round barrows are found extensively across much of the region and Wessex contains the densest concentration of such structures in Europe. By the later bronze age (1,600–800 BC), querns, grain impressions on pottery and settlements associated with field systems and linear ditches which may have been stock enclosures are all found in the region and point to a healthy mixed arable and pastoral economy in which sheep in particular become prominent in the archaeological record.

The iron age in Wessex has been extensively studied for the chalklands, although, as with all periods, less so further west. Extensive field systems survive on the downland, particularly on Salisbury Plain, although other upland areas such as Dartmoor appear to be virtually abandoned. It is clear that land was carefully managed and was divided up by extensive linear boundaries. Some settlements lay within enclosures, and hillforts stand out as a distinctive type of settlement for the period. Some occupy the sites of earlier enclosures, such as Maiden Castle, and there is a tendency towards increasing ostentatious complexity in hillfort construction over the period. The late iron age is also characterised by the development of some very large nucleated settlements which bear many of the characteristics of urban settlement, such as Hengistbury Head in Dorset. By the eve of the Roman conquest, we can seek to reconstruct tribal divisions in the region from contemporary texts and from coinage: the core counties of Wessex were occupied by the Atrebates in eastern Hampshire and Berkshire, the Belgae in parts of western Hampshire and Wiltshire, the Durotriges in Dorset and east Somerset, the Dumnonii in west Somerset and Devon and the Dobunni to the north-west in Avon.

Roman Wessex

At the Roman conquest, much of Wessex was rapidly brought under imperial control, helped by the establishment of the client kingdom of the Atrebates in the east. The frontier, which was for a while marked by the Fosse Way extending from Exeter north-east via Ilchester and Cirencester, was soon pushed even further north-west into Wales. The impact of the conquest on the rural economy of Wessex is difficult to assess. Certainly many of the large nucleated settlements of the late iron age are occupied in the Roman period, although demonstrating continuity is more difficult and it appears that some may be abandoned or less intensively occupied in the early Roman period. However, the extensive exploitation and careful management of arable and pasture resources characterised in the late iron age is an even stronger feature of the Roman period. Generally it is apparent that the

Fig. 2 *Malmesbury, Wiltshire. This town is on the site of a possible Iron Age hillfort, Roman settlement, and a monastery founded in the eighth century. The site occupies a natural spur, and the plan of the ninth-century burh founded by Alfred is still visible in the central street which runs the length of the town, and the regularly spaced toft boundaries which extend perpendicular to it. (Photo: Mick Aston)*

Roman period saw a considerable expansion in the rural economy, with an increase in the number and size of both rural and urban settlements. These range from rigidly planned towns, through nucleated settlements, also with a regularity suggestive of planning, high status villas, to small farmstead-type settlements. The period saw the extensive industrial exploitation of all types of landscape including wooded areas such as the New Forest with its fine pottery industry; lead and stone quarries in the Mendips and around Box in Wiltshire, and extensive drainage and land reclamation in coastal and wetland areas such as the Somerset Levels. Much of this activity must have been organised within the framework of large villa estates, and the sites of villas are turning up with increasing frequency in areas such as the chalkland valleys. In other areas, such as the more heavily wooded pastoral landscapes, the situation is more difficult to interpret as there is less evidence, but even here, the ubiquity of Roman pottery attests to the widespread and dense settlement of most of Wessex by the third century AD, and new sites are being discovered all the time. The practice of Christianity is evident in the region from the fourth century, and by the end of that century there were a number of churches and shrines associated with the regional *civitas* capitals.

Saxon Wessex

The history of Wessex from the fifth century to the Norman Conquest is, as elsewhere in the country, generally more obscure and only slightly illuminated by archaeological evidence. The limited amount of work that has been carried out in this period is beginning to show evidence for continued occupation of some Roman sites in the sub-Roman era, particularly towns and villages. There is good evidence for the continued use of religious sites, particularly in the west. Other sites, including the large nucleated settlements on Salisbury Plain and some villas, particularly those in the east, appear to have been abandoned. Anglo-Saxon cultural traditions permeated westwards across the region from the fifth century onwards, and only in the far west did this influence fail to penetrate. Wessex has little of the archaeological wealth of the Kentish pagan graves, and it is only with the appearance of documentary records that we can identify the earliest existence of the kingdom of the West Saxons. This appears to have been first established in the southeast of the region in the early sixth century, and had expanded to include Dorset and south Somerset by the late seventh. Its rise from these apparently humble beginnings followed an erratic course, and was frustrated by the strength of the kingdom of Mercia to the north in the seventh and eighth centuries and the invasions of the Vikings in the ninth and tenth centuries, but it grew eventually to encompass much of southern England. In the ninth and tenth centuries the region was dominated by a number of able kings, most notably Alfred (849–899), who established royal centres, minster churches and important monasteries (Hinton 1977). The *burhs*, founded by Alfred in the ninth century, ensured the security of the kingdom and laid the foundations for later prosperity at most of these sites (Fig. 2). The itineraries of the Saxon kings show that they spent most of their time in the heartland of Wessex (Hill 1981), and royal palaces in the region include Cheddar (So) in the west and Winchester (Ha) in the east, with others at Wilton (Wi), Chippenham (Wi) and elsewhere. By the tenth century the region was dominated by wealthy, powerful and influential ecclesiastical establishments. There were bishops in dioceses based at Winchester, Wells (So), Sherborne (Do), Ramsbury (Wi) and Exeter (De). Major monasteries existed at Glastonbury (So), Athelney (So), Cerne (Do), Milton (Do), Cranborne (Do) and Winchester (Ha). Major Anglo-Saxon nunneries existed at Shaftesbury (Do), Amesbury (Wi), Wilton, Romsey (Ha), Wherwell (Ha) and Nunnaminster (Ha). The wealth of these as major

landowners is well demonstrated in Domesday Book. The cultural and social importance of the region in the late Saxon period, eloquently illustrated by the craftsmanship of the Alfred Jewel found near North Petherton (So), is unfortunately not reflected in research into rural settlement, which has been very limited to date. The region has not yet benefitted from the sort of extensive field-walking projects carried out in the east which have revealed a settlement pattern of small dispersed farmstead units, replaced sometime after the ninth century by a smaller number of nucleated villages associated with regular open fields. Whether this disjunction is also present in the history of rural settlement in Wessex, with its very different late Saxon historical circumstances, is difficult to ascertain, although it seems that there is evidence here for a higher degree of continuity of estate integrity, and that settlement evolution may have been characterised more by gradual shift than sudden change.

Post-Conquest Wessex

By the Norman Conquest, Wessex was a politically important and wealthy part of England, and a number of castles were built at the Conquest to ensure the stability of the area (Fig. 3), including those at Dunster (So),

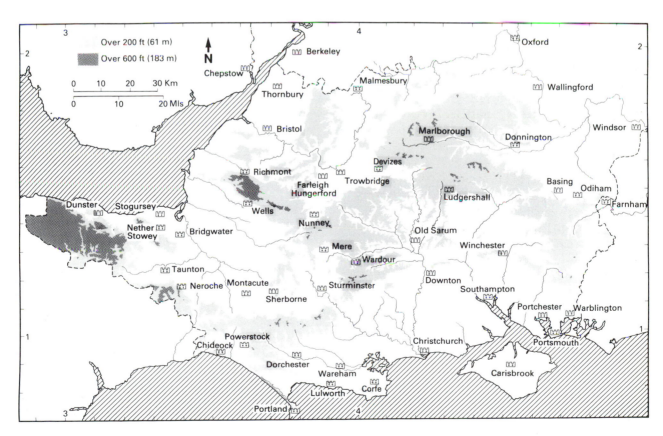

Fig. 3 *Castles in Wessex.*

Fig. 4 *The hillfort of Old Sarum, near Salisbury in Wiltshire. Inside the hillfort lie the remains of a Norman royal castle and the first site of Salisbury cathedral. (Photo: Roy Canham)*

Fig. 5 *The hall at Clarendon Palace, Wiltshire. The site is now overgrown, but was once an opulent palace favoured by Henry II. It lies within the deer park at Clarendon, east of Salisbury. (Photo: Mick Aston)*

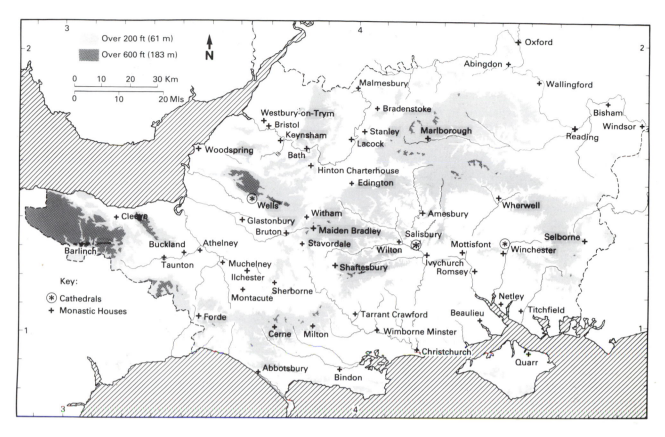

Fig. 6 *Monastic sites in Wessex.*

Montacute (So) and Corfe (Do). Royal castles were built at Old Sarum (Wi) (Fig. 4), Winchester, Southampton (Ha), Porchester (Ha) and Sherborne (Do). Houses of the king, often associated with hunting forests and parks, were at Cheddar, Gillingham (Do), Poorstock (Do), Bere (Do), Cranborne, Clarendon (Wi) (Fig. 5), Hurstbourne (Ha), Freemantle (Ha), Wolverton (Ha) and Tidgrove (Ha). Itineries of Norman kings demonstrate the continued emphasis on Wessex, showing the frequency with which they visited the region (Hindle 1982). Winchester, the largest of the Alfredian *burhs*, was one of the wealthiest and most powerful centres in the country, second only to London, with an episcopal palace and a royal mint. While most of the *burhs* founded by Alfred achieved market status and continued to prosper, many new towns were also founded across the region during the twelfth to fourteenth centuries (Beresford 1967). Wessex was one of the major centres for the cloth industry, which brought great wealth to the region in the later medieval period. Based initially on monastic estates and in towns such as Winchester and Marlborough, the industry in the thirteenth century moved gradually out into the country, notably along the river Frome on the border between Somerset and Wiltshire.

The importance of the ecclesiastical and monastic establishments (Fig. 6) was enhanced in Wessex, as elsewhere, by an increase in the number of new establishments. The new orders were never overwhelmingly represented in Wessex, but there are nevertheless houses of most orders in the region. For monks, Cistercians were established at Bindon (Do), Beaulieu (Ha), Netley (Ha), Quarr (Ha), Cleeve (So), and Stanley (Wi). The two earliest Carthusian monasteries were founded in Somerset at Witham and Hinton. Houses of canons were not as numerous in this area as elsewhere but there were Augustinians in Hampshire, Wiltshire and Somerset, Gilbertines at Marlborough (Wi), Premonstratensians at Titchfield (Ha), and Bonshommes at Edington (Wi). The friars settled in Winchester, Southampton (Ha), Salisbury, Dorchester, Ilchester (So) and Bridgwater (So), and the military orders had a house in each county. Bishops had important residences in the region. The bishop of Winchester had palaces at Wolvesey in Winchester, Bishops Waltham and Taunton and the bishop of Salisbury held Sherborne Castle. The bishop of Wells had a moated fortified palace at Wells itself as well as other establishments at Wiveliscombe, Banwell and elsewhere.

Much of the conflict of the Civil War between Stephen (1135–54) and Matilda raged across Wessex, with two of Matilda's strongest supporters holding castles at Bristol and Gloucester (Robert of Gloucester) and Sherborne, Malmesbury, Salisbury and Devizes (Roger of Salisbury). Many other unlicensed castles sprang up during the conflict, both to hold territory and to besiege other castles. While the impact of the fighting on rural life is difficult to ascertain, either in the archaeological record or the documentary sources, it certainly marked the beginning of the end of the political prominence of Winchester, which ceased to be a royal capital soon after peace was restored. There is, as elsewhere in the country, evidence for considerable expansion in the rural economy between the eleventh and late thirteenth centuries, although this may not have been steady and sustained throughout the period. Work is still in progress on pottery production in the region, which took place in Wiltshire at Minety and Laverstock, among other places, and at Donyatt in Somerset (Coleman-Smith and Pearson 1988; Gerrard 1987). The Black Death, which entered the country through Weymouth, sharply reduced the population on many manors, although left others relatively unscathed. The consequent acceleration in the move away from labour rents, and also towards large-scale sheep farming had a considerable impact on life in the countryside and much arable land which was turned over to pasture has remained so ever since. Retrenchment is detectable also in parochial provision, with the amalgamation of some parishes in the fourteenth and fifteenth centuries. Although the counties of Wessex were less involved with day-to-day trade with the increasingly dominant capital city of London than others nearer the capital, the region benefited from foriegn trade through ports in the English and Bristol Channels. Wessex, although it never regained the nationally prominent political and social position it had occupied in the ninth to twelfth centuries, was still a comfortably prosperous region at the end of the middle ages.

It is evident from this brief summary that Wessex was an important region in the history of England in the middle ages, but its interest for this period has been overshadowed by the wealth of prehistoric archaeology, and research has tended to focus on this evidence to the detriment of the later periods. This is a great pity as Wessex is an ideal area for the study of the medieval rural landscape, not least because of its wealth and importance to the crown and aristocracy in the middle ages.

This Volume

This volume is not, however, concerned with the establishments built and used by members of the upper end of the medieval social hierarchy. Rather, it examines the settlements where the mass of the population, the peasants and freeman farmers, lived and worked, and about whom traditional historical sources tell us much less. A number of themes which have emerged in this collection of papers will now be reviewed.

Settlement Origins

Several of the papers in this volume consider the evidence for the rural landscape of fifth to eleventh century Wessex. Bruce Eagles, in a wide ranging paper, reviews the evidence in the fifth to seventh centuries for the presence of Anglo-Saxons in each county against the background of a persistence of Romano-British population. Clearly, there is an increasing volume of archaeological evidence from these early post-Roman centuries to counter the reliance on historical frameworks which has persisted for so long. The difficulties of identifying territories at this date are considered by Eagles, and this theme is taken up by Della Hooke and Michael Costen in papers covering later estates and place names. Hooke's paper covers a wide geographical area, from Cornwall eastwards, and considers high status places as well as ordinary settlements. She makes it clear that attempts to define hierarchies in settlement patterns and the economic links between them are fruitful lines of research in pre-Conquest Wessex. Costen considers the evidence for settlements and land use which can be derived from charters and the place names recorded in them. This approach is proving increasingly successful in locating early abandoned sites whose earlier existence in indicated by habitative elements in field names, and also is reconstructing the land use of contemporary landscapes.

Other contributors debate the likely dates for the origin of settlements which they have studied. Many see the centuries before the Norman Conquest as the critical period for village creation; these are often seen to replace, or develop alongside, a more dispersed pattern of hamlets and farmsteads. This dispersed pattern is argued to be at least late Saxon in origin, while speculation ranges over the possibilities that it might be post-Roman (Rippon), Romano-British (Lewis) or even late prehistoric (Aston) in origin in different parts of the region. Such ideas leave little room for conventional explanations of a socio-economic collapse accompanied by widespread abandonment of settlement and productive land in the post-Roman period. They argue rather for a great measure of continuity in both territory and land use, with a more erratic continued use of individual settlement sites. There are problems in testing these ideas: several authors refer to the problems posed by the likely existence of settlements on a site long before they are first recorded in documentary sources, and equally that many recorded names which are not habitative in form may not record early settlement but reflect merely the increasingly bureaucratic nature of state and manor. Archaeological evidence often fails to provide a solution to these problems, particularly in the fifth to eleventh centuries, as David Hinton points out. Post-Roman pottery is very sparse in the region with only a limited number of high status imports from the Mediterranean and a little chaff-tempered ware elsewhere. The region was beyond the range of wares from the eastern production centres of St Neots, Ipswich, Stamford and elsewhere. There appears to be little else in the traditional archaeological armoury with which to identify the settlements of the period, but Michael Aston's paper suggests a way forward using new techniques such as geophysical and geochemical prospection for finding sites that would otherwise be invisible to archaeology or history. If these can be used to locate sites in larger numbers, it would be possible to take further the question whether much of the settlement pattern in the region, which appears in the documentary record only in the thirteenth century, really does represent new colonisation at that date. Several authors discuss this problem, including Stephen Rippon, who examines the evidence for the medieval reclamation of parts of the Somerset Levels.

Settlement Form

Several authors discuss the form of settlements in specific areas. This approach has been neglected in the past in this region and more work still needs to be done. There are difficulties, however, as many settlements are large and complex with intricate plans, while elsewhere much of the settlement pattern is dispersed, and the study of this form of settlement in any part of the country is still in its infancy. Nevertheless progress is being made, as Chris Taylor shows in his careful re-examination of many deserted medieval villages and hamlets in Dorset, which reveals evidence of regular planned settlement elements similar to those seen in the east and north.

A clear description of the settlement pattern provides a sound basis for further study. This approach has been developed and applied in the north and the midlands (Shepherd 1974, 1976; Roberts 1987, 1989; Lewis *et al.* forthcoming) but, with the exception of Somerset (Roberts 1987, 182–3), has not been tried for Wessex. Carenza Lewis here successfully applies these ideas to Wiltshire, and it is clear that the same is now needed for the other counties of the Wessex region. In general, however, Maitland's comments of nearly a hundred years ago, 'the science of village morphology is still very young', still holds true for Wessex.

Settlement Desertion

By contrast there has been much more research into the demise of settlements, stimulated initially by the work of the Deserted Medieval Village Research Group (DMVRG), now the Medieval Settlement Research Group (MSRG). Large numbers of deserted and shrunken medieval settlements have been identified in the region (Fig. 7), ranging in size from substantial villages down through small hamlets to individual farm sites, many of which are moated. Further work on these sites, together with consideration of economic factors which may have been

Fig. 7 Deserted settlement and gardens at Richardson on the chalklands of north Wiltshire. (Photo: Roy Canham)

involved in their collapse, is discussed here, particularly in Wiltshire and Hampshire by John Hare and Michael Hughes. These papers among others make it clear that the abandonment of settlements was usually the end result of a complex process rather than a single event, and which, although more common at some dates than others, occurred throughout the period from the late Roman to the nineteenth century. In most cases, and this is certainly true in Wessex, we cannot establish exactly when a settlement was finally abandoned and usually we are left ignorant as to the reasons why. While we are now aware that gradual social and economic changes hold the key, this tells us little about the mechanisms involved.

Society and Economy

Socially created factors which influence the development of settlement in the landscape are even more difficult to identify than economic ones. Patrick Hase provides a panoramic review of the development of the Christian church and the parochial system from the Roman period onward which shows, among other things, the strong element of continuity inherent in this most powerful of social institutions. The creation of areas of restricted access and rights within forests and parks is another socially determined factor which constrained and shaped the medieval countryside, and is considered here by James Bond. We can see in both these papers that decisions about where and how to live are often predicated on grounds other than the simply economic, and they furnish a vital background to many of the more specifically settlement oriented papers. It is clear from many of the studies which make up this volume that we need to know much more about the demographic changes of the last two thousand years: most contributors seem to feel that greater knowledge of the size and make up of the population would help in their understanding of the processes of settlement evolution, expansion, colonisation and abandonment.

Aspects of the economy of the region, from the Anglo-Saxon to the later medieval, are discussed by several contributors, including Bruce Eagles for the fifth to the seventh centuries, David Hinton for the eighth to twelfth centuries, and John Hare for the thirteenth to fifteenth. The area was, of course, famous for the breeding of sheep and the production of large quantities of wool which were exported through such ports as Southampton on the south coast and Bristol on the north. There was also a home woollen cloth industry based in the larger medieval towns in the region, such as Salisbury and Winchester. From the late fourteenth century onwards the region developed a very important rural woollen cloth industry, particularly around north-east Somerset and north-west Wiltshire and continuing north into Gloucestershire, taking advantage of the fast-flowing streams in that area. This industrial activity helped partly to offset the demographic decline seen in other parts of the region following successive poor harvests and plagues in the fourteenth century, as labour was taken up in the expanding cloth towns and villages of Castle Coombe (Wi), Pensford (Av), Bradford on Avon (Wi) and elsewhere (Baker 1976; Mann 1987). The archaeology of the early years of this industry has hardly begun to be studied, but field evidence of the management of the sheep flocks is discussed by John Hare, who draws attention to the presence of numbers of sheepcotes still preserved on the pasture downland. Hare also considers the other major downland economy, the farming of rabbits in man-made warrens, which also survive as archaeological features on the chalk downs of Wiltshire and Hampshire. A close examination of other rural industrial activities falls beyond the scope of this volume, but are known to include pottery manufacture and ironworking.

Urban Development

Several of the papers in this volume include discussion of the development of towns and urbanism in the region. Wessex saw the re-establishment of towns in the Anglo-Saxon period, rather earlier than in many other parts of the country: Hamwic, the forerunner to Southampton, is discussed here by David Hinton, while David Hill and others have elsewhere drawn attention to the rich late Saxon heritage of towns in this region (Hill 1981; Haslam 1984). By the Norman Conquest there were more towns in this part of England than anywhere else in the British Isles. Each of the Wessex counties has had some appraisal in the recent past (see Penn 1980; Hughes 1976; Aston and Leech 1977; Haslam 1976,), although some of these now need updating. Michael Hughes in this volume looks at the growth and decline of various towns and rural settlements in Hampshire, where it is evident that there is considerable similarity in processes such as planning and in the factors which determined the success or stagnation of both rural and urban settlements. As is evident from this and other papers, an understanding of the interaction between town, market place, rural settlements and the countryside is crucial to our understanding of the development of all settlements. Critical re-examination of the documents would help in this endeavour, as would a comparison of environmental material from both rural and urban excavated sites, which would together provide a wealth of comparative and interrelated material.

Future Research

It is hoped that this collection of papers will achieve two purposes. Firstly, we hope that it conveys a fair and useful appraisal of the current state of research into medieval settlement in one part of Britain – the area of southern England formerly called Wessex. It demonstrates that a great deal of research is being carried out in the region and, in drawing some of it together, provides an indication of what we know at present. Nowhere is this comprehensive, but it shows that most aspects of medieval settlement studies at present of interest to archaeologists, historians and historical geographers are being pursued currently somewhere in the region, and we have tried to ensure that most of the region is considered from one or other academic perspective.

Secondly, we hope that this volume will show the limitations of our present state of knowledge and point out useful directions for future research. It would be possible to draw up a long and complex list of research priorities, but a number seem to us to be of particular interest. Most obviously, we need to increase our understanding of the archaeology of settlements and their contemporary landscapes in the pre-Conquest period, to complement both studies on other regions of England and the state of research into the documentary evidence. So few sites have been identified, let alone excavated, that we still have very little idea of their siting, organisation or length of occupation for much of the region. In Somerset, for example, we know of only one settlement for the entire period 400–1100 AD which has been excavated, that of Eckweek in Peasedown St John parish. Such a lack of settlement evidence for a seven hundred year period can really only be mirrored in parts of the prehistoric period. Yet this is the period when the foundations of many of the institutions and settlements which determined the pattern of the later medieval landscape were established. It is crucial to our understanding of the whole period. These sites will not be found easily, but the potential of new and developing techniques of geophysical and geochemical prospection offer exciting possibilities which should be exploited.

A second priority for future research concerns those medieval settlements which are still occupied today as villages or hamlets. In most cases we still have very little idea of how or why they developed into their present form. Much of the problem lies in the lack of widespread plan analysis which has been carried out elsewhere in the country, the basis for which is provided by Brian Roberts. The recent work funded by the Leverhulme Trust (Lewis *et al.* forthcoming) in the east midlands provides a model for the collection of basic data over a wide area so that the many factors involved in the establishment and occupation of settlements can be compared. This approach needs to be extended into Wessex. Alongside this work there is clearly the need for more intensive work on smaller groups of settlements: here the work at Shapwick in Somerset may provide a model for the investigation of parishes elsewhere in the region. We hope that this collection of papers on medieval Wessex may stimulate the inception of these or other research projects in the future.

Acknowledgements

Many people have helped in the production of this volume, both in giving encouragement and advice in the planning stages, and in providing practical asistance as it approached publication. In particular, we thank Maurice Beresford for writing the preface and Joe Bettey for permission to reproduce his maps. At Oxbow Books we are grateful to David Brown for publishing this book, and to Val Tomlin for her enormous effort in bringing it to fruition. Penelope Wenham helped with proof reading, and Carinne Allison with compiling the index. Most importantly, we must acknowledge our debt to all those, whether named in this volume or not, whose research into aspects of the medieval landscape of Wessex has contributed to the sum of our knowledge today, and without whom this volume could not have been attempted.

References

Aston, M. *et al.* (eds) 1989: *The rural settlements of medieval England* (Oxford).

Aston, M. and Leech, R. 1977: *Historic Towns in Somerset* (Bristol).

Baker, A. R. H. 1976: 'Changes in the Later Middle Ages', in H. C. Darby (ed.), *A New Historical Geography of England before 1600* (Cambridge) 186–247.

Beresford, M. 1967: *New Towns of the Middle Ages* (London).

Bonney, D. 1979: 'Early Boundaries and Estates in Southern England, in Sawyer, P. (ed.), *English Medieval Settlement* (London).

Coleman-Smith, R. and Pearson, T. 1988: *Excavations in the Donyatt Potteries* (Chichester).

Gerrard, C. 'Trade and Settlement in Medieval Somerset'. Unpublished PhD thesis, University of Bristol.

Goodier, A. 1984: 'The formation of Boundaries in Anglo-Saxon England: a Statistical Study', in *Medieval Archaeology* 28, 1–21.

Haslam, J. 1976: *Wiltshire Towns – The Archaeological Potential* (Devizes).

Haslam, J. 1984: *Anglo-Saxon Towns in Southern England* (Chichester).

Hill, D. 1981: *An Atlas of Anglo-Saxon England* (Oxford).

Lewis, C., Mitchell Fox, P. and Dyer, C. C. (forthcoming): *Medieval settlement in the East Midlands* (Manchester).

Hindle, B. P. 1982: *Medieval Roads* (Aylesbury).

Hinton, D. 1977: *Alfred's Kingdom: Wessex and the South 800–1500* (London).

Hughes, M. 1976: *The Small Towns of Hampshire* (Southampton).

Man, J. De L. 1987: *The Cloth Industry in the West of England from 1640 to 1880* (Oxford).

Penn, K. J. 1980: *Historic Towns in Dorset* (Dorchester).

Roberts, B. K. 1977: *Rural Settlement in Britain* (Folkestone).

Roberts, B. K. 1987: *The making of the English Village* (Harlow).

Roberts, B. K. 1989: 'Nucleation and Dispersion: Distribution Maps as a Research Tool' in Aston *et al.*

Sheppard, J. 1974: 'Metrological Analysis of Regular Village Plans in Yorkshire', in *Agricultural History Review* 22, 118–35.

Sheppard, J. 1976: 'Medieval village planning in Northern

England: Some Evidence from Yorkshire', in *Journal of Historical Geography* 2(1), 3–20,

Taylor, C. 1967: 'Whiteparish: a Study of the Development of a Forest-Edge Parish', in *Wilts. Archaeol. & Nat. Hist. Mag.* 52, 79–102 (Devizes).

Thorpe, H. 1964: 'Rural Settlement', in J. W. Watson and J. B. Sissons (eds) *The British Isles: A Systematic Geography* (London) 358–379.

1. The Archaeological Evidence for Settlement in the Fifth to Seventh Centuries AD

Bruce Eagles

The first sections of this paper are concerned with a presentation of the evidence for the origins of Anglo-Saxon settlement in Wessex in the fifth century and its subsequent intensification and expansion. Wansdyke, together with the later phases of Bokerley Dyke belong, it is suggested, to the immediate post-Roman period and relate to the borders of already established territories. A theme of this chapter is the interaction of the British and English elements of the population, hints being provided from the archaeological point of view through settlements, cemeteries and certain classes of artefacts. Place-names and personal names in the literary sources afford other and important evidence of this cultural intermingling in this period in Wessex.

For the purpose of the issues which are addressed in this paper, the area of Wessex which is encompassed includes Somerset east of the River Parrett, Dorset, Wiltshire, Hampshire and parts of southern Berkshire. In the period under discussion, much of Berkshire from the fifth century onwards was closely associated with the pattern of settlement in the Thames valley, a subject only touched upon here but important in its own right and one which has benefited from a recent overall survey (Hawkes 1986).

Anglo-Saxons in the Fifth Century

Dorset

Two of the earliest Anglo-Saxon objects yet found in the heartland of Wessex (the counties of Hampshire, Wiltshire and Dorset) were recovered recently in central Dorset from a location immediately below the hillfort of Hod Hill at Stourpaine, on the River Stour; the site is also close to that of a Roman building, probably a villa (RCHM 1970b, 104, Hanford (5)). The artefacts in question are an equal-armed brooch with animal-headed terminals and part of a cruciform brooch; neither is likely to date to later than the middle of the fifth century. The same site has also produced a number of silver coins of the seventh and eighth centuries and a gilded roundel with interlace design, probably of eighth-century date (Eagles and Mortimer forthcoming; fifth-century Anglo-Saxon sites in Wessex are tabulated on p. 15 below, where additional references to those cited in the text are given; sites in Dorset, Hampshire and Wiltshire are also mapped on Fig. 1.1). The only other item of pagan Saxon date from the locality is a spearhead (in the Durden Collec-tion in the British Museum) from within the hillfort. It is of Swanton's type H1, which dates to between the mid fifth and mid sixth centuries (pers comm., Dr H. Härke; all subsequent references to spearheads are to Swanton 1973 and 1974 unless specific mention is made other-wise). A button brooch is known from near Blandford, which lies some 5km south east of Hod Hill, but it is not more precisely provenanced; it may date to the sixth, rather than the fifth century (Avent and Evison 1982, 99–100, 117).

Wiltshire

Germanic objects of fifth-century manufacture are known from a group of sites, all of them cemeteries, around Salisbury (Fig. 1.1). The ancient *Sorviodunum* lay close to a major junction of Roman roads and immediately below the hillfort of Old Sarum from which the place in part took its name. A Frankish warrior was buried at Winterbourne Gunner (Musty and Stratton 1964), together with his traditional throwing axe, the *francisca*, and a strap-end with distinctive animal ornament (the stamped pottery sherds, usually regarded as of sixth-century date, included in the grave group were recovered from the fill of this shallow grave and it is doubtful whether they should be used to date the burial itself (Mr N. Moore, formerly on the archaeological staff of Salisbury Museum, drew my attention to this point); there is also in any case some doubt about the actual date of the potsherds, cf. Eagles 1979 (i), 98, 121). The site lies a short distance south of the Portway, the Roman road from Old Sarum to Silchester. At Petersfinger there were both west-east and

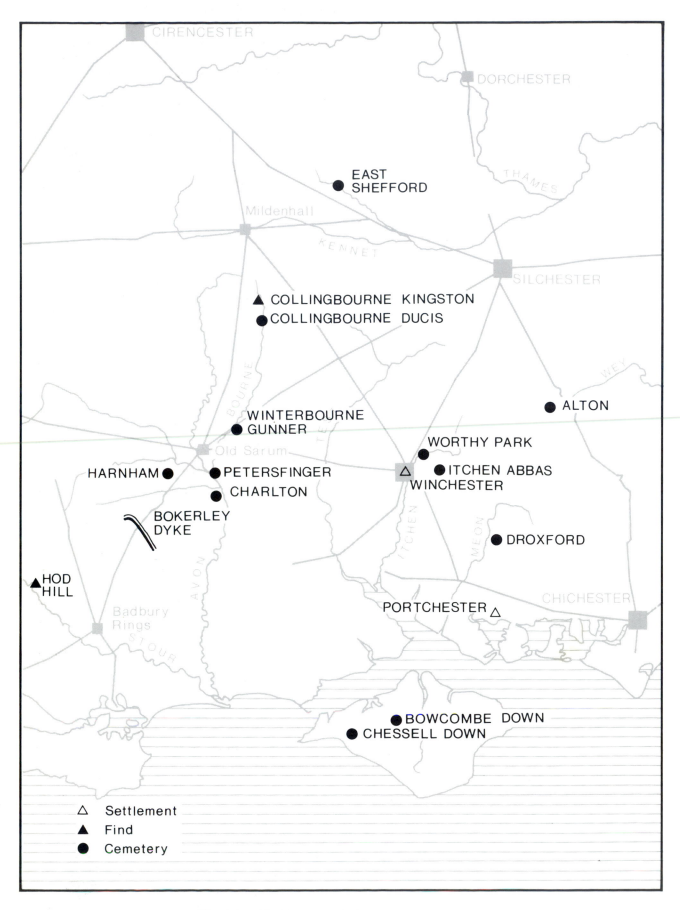

Fig. 1.1 *Fifth-Century Anglo-Saxon Sites in Wessex.*

Fifth-Century Anglo-Saxon Sites in Wessex (Fig.1.1)

Dorset
1. Hod Hill | casual finds | in private hands Eagles and Mortimer (forthcoming)

Wiltshire
2. Petersfinger | inhumation cemetery | west-east group, graves 21, 29. Evison 1965, 38–9; Böhme 1986, 509, 564. south-north grave 63. Evison 1965, 39.

3. Harnham | inhumation cemetery | grave 40. Evison 1965, 38; Avent and Evison 1982, 92, 109–10, 121.

4. Winterbourne Gunner | inhumation cemetery | grave VI. Evison 1965, 39, 60–1, 67.

5. Charlton | inhumation cemetery | Davies 1984; Ager 1990, 154.

6. Collingbourne Ducis | inhumation cemetery | e.g. graves 6, 11, 20, 23. Evison 1977, 133; 1978, 266–8; Böhme 1986, 548, 571–2.

7. Collingbourne Kingston | casual finds | in Devizes Museum

Hampshire
8. Winchester | pottery and triangular bone comb from excavs | refs. given above

9. Itchen Abbas | mixed cemetery | refs. given above

10. Worthy Park | mixed cemetery | refs. given above

11. Alton | mixed cemetery | Evison 1988

12. Droxford | inhumation cemetery | Aldsworth 1978

13. Portchester | occupation site | refs. given above

Isle of Wight
14. Chessell Down | mixed cemetery | Evison 1965, *passim*; Arnold 1982, c. 1.

15. Bowcombe Down | mixed cemetery | Evison 1965, *passim*; Arnold 1982, c. 11.

Berkshire
6. East Shefford | inhumation cemetery | Evison 1965, *passim*; Böhme 1986, 548, 572.

north-south oriented burials, in almost equal numbers (Leeds and Shortt 1953). Graves of probable late fifth-century date occur in both groups and it is possible that there were originally two adjacent cemeteries, which served two distinct communities. Among the west-east group, grave 21 was that of a warrior with, in particular, a fine Frankish sword, a spearhead of group H1 and a buckle plate set with a garnet and glass. At Harnham, excavated in the nineteenth century and with only a minimal record, burial also appears to begin in the fifth century. Finally, the cemetery at Charlton in the Avon valley began in the fifth century. This site was discovered during road widening (Davies 1984). The earliest objects there include a small quoit brooch from burial 12 and tubular belt-slides with burials 9 and 24. The latter are also typical of assemblages associated with the Quoit Brooch Style, which has its origin in late Roman metalwork and is widely distributed in south-eastern Britain in the second half of the fifth century (Evison 1965, 51; Ager 1990). Frankish connections are again evident here from a shield-on-tongue buckle and a kite-shaped rivet with burial 8. A pair of disc brooches with ring-and-dot decoration with burial 17 are also likely to date to the fifth century, although some examples of the type are known from sixth-century contexts (Dickinson 1979).

Another cemetery with origins in the fifth century has been excavated at Collingbourne Ducis, some 32km north of Salisbury and 3km east of the Roman road between *Sorviodunum* and *Cunetio* (Mildenhall), in the upper valley of the south-flowing Bourne, a tributary of the Avon (Gingell 1975/76). Among a number of notable objects there is an oval buckle inlaid with transverse silver wires, in grave 11; inlaid metalwork is otherwise known in this region only at Salisbury (Evison 1965, Map 2). Recent casual finds at Collingbourne Kingston, the parish immediately to the north of Collingbourne Ducis, comprise a fragmentary 'pair' of very worn tinned or silvered disc brooches with ring-and-dot decoration and a gilded copper-alloy saucer brooch decorated with five spirals, a type whose origins also lie in the fifth century but which was also in use in the sixth century (Evison 1981, 137; Dickinson 1991, 55).

South-West Berkshire and Hampshire

An inhumation cemetery in use in the fifth century is known at East Shefford, which lies in Berkshire in the valley of the River Lambourn, a tributary of the Kennet, and some 2.5km to the north of the Roman road between Silchester and Cirencester. The former existence of extensive tracts of woodland on the sands, clays and gravels in and to the south of the Kennet valley, and possibly further afield, is noted below (p. 22).

In the Roman period Winchester, *Venta Belgarum*, was the capital of the large *civitas* of the Belgae and a focus of the road system (Fig. 1.1). As at other Roman towns, excavations (which have covered only some 2%

of the walled area) have recorded major changes after the middle of the fourth century, when town houses were demolished and their sites cleared and turned over to industrial or other purposes; timber buildings were allowed to encroach upon the streets. Throughout the walled area itself there developed a deposit of black earth which contained fourth-century pottery and iron-working debris. Such soils have been identified on many Romano-British town sites and elsewhere. Recent micromorphological analysis of such 'dark earth' layers (in London, but of general applicability) makes it clear that they came about through the continual deposition and redeposition of decayed timber or the remains of less substantial buildings and the associated domestic waste, a process accentuated by later gardening activities (Courty, Goldberg and MacPhail 1989, 261–8). In Winchester, a decorated triangular bone comb of the fifth century has been found in the Roman forum and fifth-century Germanic pottery in Lower Brook Street (Biddle 1972, figs 3, 4). At Southgate a bastion was added to the town wall in the fourth century. The gateway there subsequently collapsed; its debris littered the street but traffic continued to pass and indeed the road was twice resurfaced. Later still, the route was cut by a ditch, whose fill contained Roman ware and 'two sherds of fifth-century pagan Saxon pottery'; above the fill lay two unburied bodies (Biddle 1972, 1983). The extra-mural cemetery at Lankhills remained in use into the early fifth century. Graves there of the second half of the fourth century included some of males with cross-bow brooches; such brooches were worn by Roman officers and civil servants, all *milites,* but burial in dress was not a Roman custom and the burials are likely to be those of soldiers serving in the Roman army but of barbarian descent (Clarke 1979, 377–403, but see also page 262 that wide distribution and local variation suggest unofficial use; and cf. Baldwin 1985). At Itchen Abbas, in the Itchen valley and some 6km to the north east of Winchester, site evaluation and rescue excavation have identified some sixty burials, which include cremations placed inside penannular ditches and both east-west graves without goods and others aligned north-south, one of the latter a fifth-century burial with artefacts which included a sword, late Roman belt-fittings and a type K1 spearhead (Youngs 1985, 180–1; Hawkes 1989, 92; McCulloch 1992). This technically sophisticated form of spear with a broad leaf-shaped blade, of stepped section, hardly lasted in use after *c.* 500 (Hawkes 1986, 80). The spear type is also known from another nearby cemetery, that at Worthy Park, which during its period of usage contained both cremation and inhumation burials; the Quoit Brooch Style is also represented here in grave 50 (Swanton 1973, 206, fig. 83f; for later Anglo-Saxon sites around Winchester see p. 26 below). Spearheads of type K1 are also recorded at Alton (Evison 1988, 5) and Droxford (Aldsworth 1978) in Hampshire and from Petersfinger and Marlborough in Wiltshire. At Alton there are both fifth-century cremations and inhumations. Among

fifth-century graves at Droxford is one (35) which contained a firesteel with possible bird-headed terminals and spiral-coil wire inlay. Finally, occupation within the late Roman Saxon shore fort at Portchester appears to date to the second half of the fifth century (Cunliffe 1976, 301). On the Isle of Wight, the cemeteries at Bowcombe Down and Chessell Down, both of them on the Upper Chalk, indicate fifth-century settlement there.

The Expansion of Anglo-Saxon Settlement in the Sixth and Seventh Centuries

The great wave of Germanic immigration into England in the fifth century appears to have greatly receded in the sixth – it is certainly the case that from the sixth century a wide range of artefacts show strong insular development (Hawkes 1986, 81).

Hampshire and Wiltshire

The evidence for sixth-century occupation is widespread throughout Berkshire, Hampshire and much of Wiltshire. It would appear likely, therefore, that there was some expansion from existing settlements, although there must also have been newcomers and it has been suggested furthermore that the distribution also reflects the adoption by the Britons of the dress, burial and other customs of the ascendant Anglo-Saxons (see e.g. Dickinson 1982, 52; Scull 1992, 14). The great majority of known sites of this period are cemeteries. Most of them have not been the subject of extensive modern excavation. In most cases fewer than a dozen burials have been recorded but it is not clear whether these sites are parts of large burial grounds or are indeed small ones which served only the needs of individual families. An example of a large cemetery which has recently been excavated is that at Blacknall Field (Black Patch) in the Pewsey Vale in Wiltshire; three cremations and 102 inhumations, the earliest of which date to the late fifth century, were recorded there (information from the excavator, Mr K. Annable: see also *Wilts Archaeol. and Nat. Hist. Mag.* 65 (1970), 206; 66 (1971), 189–90; 67 (1972), 175; 68 (1973), 135–6).

In the chalklands, which are so extensive in these two counties, the distribution of many burial sites tends to be related to the rivers and to mirror the later pattern of settlement in this type of terrain. An early settlement in such a location is that partially uncovered at Abbots Worthy in the Itchen valley; it is considered to have begun in the late sixth century and to have continued throughout the seventh century. Several sunken-featured buildings but no halls were identified in the limited area which was available for excavation (Fasham and Whinney 1991). However, significant settlement remains have also been excavated on high chalkland at Chalton and Cowdery's Down in Hampshire (p. 21). At Chalton it has been pointed out that this location may be a secondary one, away from an earlier site on lower ground; its marginal position may have been a factor in its relatively short life (Champion 1977, 369).

In Hampshire, the Chalk is bounded both to north and south by great extents of Tertiary sands, clays and gravels. These deposits produce soils which are inhospitable to long-lasting agriculture and in the early Anglo-Saxon period it is clear that many of them were covered by expanses of woodland (p. 22 below). In the area of the New Forest, as elsewhere, this type of environment supported an important Roman pottery industry, which probably depended upon an abundant local timber supply. There is little enough sign of English settlement on these soils in the period under review. It is of particular note, therefore, that a keystone garnet disc brooch, of the late sixth or early seventh century and of Kentish type, was found in 1980 on the Bagshot Sands at Ampfield, north east of Romsey; there were no other finds and no sign of a burial (Denford 1986). A point of a different kind but of particular interest in this connection may be made in regard to the brickearths of the lower Test valley, which are at their greatest extent around Romsey, where they are for the most part bounded on the east by the sands and clays of the Bracklesham Beds. The fertile brickearths have been farmed, it now appears, since at least the middle bronze age and they were worked extensively in the Roman period; in recent times they have been used intensively for horticulture and this activity appears to have destroyed any evidence for post-Roman farming. Certainly, a programme of watching briefs carried out by the Test Valley Archaeological Trust in this area over some twenty years has produced little indication of early Anglo-Saxon settlement.

In Wiltshire, pagan Anglo-Saxon style burial extends to the limits of the Chalk in the south west. The pattern on the clays and limestone in the northern and north-western parts of the county is markedly sparse and ceases altogether at the River Avon. Some sites are, however, known in this region, notably at Swindon (Canham and Phillips n.d.) and Highworth (Collins 1986) and a cemetery at Purton (Grinsell 1957, 98) on the limestone. A settlement beyond the Avon is discussed below, p. 21.

Dorset

The early Anglo-Saxon pattern of settlement in eastern Dorset may have been influenced by the deterrence offered by the east-facing Bokerley Dyke, an earthwork whose general course marked a boundary of some significance perhaps as early as the bronze age and which is followed today by the county boundary with Hampshire (Bowen 1990). In the area immediately west of Bokerley Dyke only one burial appears to date even as early as the sixth century. It was found on Oakley Down in the parish of Wimborne St Giles and its accompaniments included a button brooch and amber beads (Hoare 1812, 236–7; Avent and Evison 1982, 99, 107). A stray find of a sixth-century harness mount is recorded at Wor Barrow (Pitt Rivers 1898, pl. 258. 15).

The construction of a discrete and massive ditch, the Rear Dyke, on the Bokerley alignment, severed Ackling Dyke, the Roman road from Old Sarum to Badbury Rings and Dorchester. The road was soon re-opened and the Rear Dyke slighted. The Fore Dyke was then built and the road was permanently blocked. Bokerley Dyke was also built to massive proportions well to the south of the Roman road, most notably at Blagdon Top, and as far as the Epaulement, whence it was only subsequently united with the sector at Ackling Dyke. There were, therefore, several significant phases in the final development of the Dyke and these are likely to reflect the major role which it may be presumed to have served. Although these last phases have been argued to have occurred in late Roman times, it was clear to Pitt Rivers himself, and it still remains the case, that the Roman material recovered from the earthworks (in the main where the Dyke crosses the late Roman roadside settlement at Woodyates (Bokerley Junction)) only dates their construction to the Roman period or later and a post-Roman date appears more probable.

Signs of sixth-century occupation are also very sparse and widely scattered elsewhere in the county. Near the coast in west Dorset, sixth-century burials were excavated on Hardown Hill (Evison 1968). At two other places the evidence relates to hillforts. At Badbury, there is a record of a surface find of an EI spearhead, which was acquired by the British Museum in 1892 (information from Leslie Webster); it belongs to the fifth or sixth century (cf. T. M. Dickinson in Rahtz *et al.* 1992, 119). At Spetisbury, on the Stour and only 5km to the west, spearheads of types BI (not closely datable within the pagan period), C1 (probably sixth century), E1 and E2 (of the sixth or seventh century) were found last century when the railway line was constructed. The cemetery at Bargates, Christchurch, began in the late sixth century (Jarvis 1983). It was sited, on the south coast, on fertile gravels near the confluence of the Stour and Avon, although the area generally is characterised by uncultivated heath. Two bronze age ring ditches were the focus of a partly excavated mixed cemetery of four cremations in urns and more than thirty inhumations. Eleven male burials were accompanied by weapons. The evidence from Spetisbury and Christchurch suggests that Saxons were now penetrating Dorset along the Stour – a possible route, too, for their predecessors at Hod Hill in the fifth century (p. 13). Anglo-Saxon advances at this time may provide a context for the final refurbishment, of late Roman or subsequent date, of the east-facing Combs Ditch, a linear earthwork some 5km to the west of the Stour (RCHM 1970b. 313, Winterborne Whitechurch (19)).

Otherwise, pagan style burials belong to the seventh century. They are known from a number of sites, most of them centring upon Dorchester. 'The Trumpet Major' cemetery is in the town itself (Green 1984, 149–52).

Others are close outside (Bradford Peverell, in the Frome valley 4km north west – Keen 1977, 120; 1978, 112; 1979, 133; Hawthorne 1981, 126: Maiden Castle, 3km south west – Wheeler 1943, 78–9: and Mount Pleasant, less than 2km to the east – Schwieso 1979, 181–3). Other cemeteries are recorded at Long Crichel (Cook 1982) and Hambledon Hill, immediately north of Hod Hill (Mercer 1980, 53–5). It is of interest to note that Mount Pleasant is a neolithic henge and that the hillforts at Maiden Castle and Hambledon Hill were also major centres of neolithic activity.

Somerset

The archaeological evidence for Anglo-Saxons in Somerset before the seventh century is of a very limited nature. It may be noted that the earliest Saxon object appears to be the spearhead from Worle, at Weston-super-Mare. The spearhead belongs to type L, most of which date to the later fifth or earlier sixth century. It can only be surmised why the piece should be found in the very west of the county. Conditions on the coast may have been exceptional. Certainly in the later fourth century insecurity near the Bristol Channel was a matter of major concern (Bird in Aston and Iles (eds) n.d., 69). There is also an Anglo-Saxon shield boss of fifth- or sixth-century date from Ham Hill hillfort (Burrow 1981, 273, fig. 34). A pair of disc brooches with ring-and-dot decoration and a square-headed brooch from Ilchester are likely in this area to date to the sixth century (Evison 1968, 238). The occurrence of a pair of brooches suggests that they had been worn in the Saxon fashion. There are also other Anglo-Saxon items from South Cadbury (p. 19 below).

Otherwise the information points entirely to the seventh century and generally the east of the county (Rahtz *et al.* 1992, fig. 1). At Camerton, near a Roman settlement on the Fosse Way, there is a seventh-century Anglo-Saxon cemetery which is known to have contained more than a hundred graves (Horne 1928, 1933). Four burials, which appear to be Anglo-Saxon and of the late seventh century, were found at Compton Pauncefoot, 1km east of South Cadbury (Taylor 1967). There is another seventh-century cemetery at Buckland Dinham (Horne 1926). A grave at Queen Camel is reported to have contained an Anglo-Saxon sword (Anon. 1946). All these sites are east of the Fosse Way. West of the road, in the Parrett valley to the north west of Ilchester, there is an inhumation with a pair of bronze tweezers at Wearne, Huish Episcopi, which is also likely to be that of an Anglo-Saxon (Leech 1976). Finally, an Anglo-Saxon gold pendant, beads and bone fragments have been found at Burnett, near Keynsham, between the River Avon and Wansdyke (Bulleid 1922; Leighton 1937, 244–5).

The British Population

In recent years there has been a growing recognition of the significance of hand-made organic-, often grass- or chaff-tempered pottery in the immediate post-Roman period. Such locally produced wares occur both in sub-Roman contexts, where they provide one of the few pointers to the British population, as for example in places in Gloucestershire where the occupation shows no sign of Saxon influence, and elsewhere on Anglo-Saxon sites, as in fifth- to eighth-century deposits at Portchester.

In Wessex probable sub-Roman contexts are known in the Avon valley south of Salisbury, where this type of pottery has been recorded at Romano-British sites at Bickton. In the same area at South Charford, however, grass-tempered sherds and part of an allegedly sixth-century long brooch were found together, which might be thought to indicate Anglo-Saxon occupation. These finds were made in the course of an extensive programme of field-walking. This is an example of the way in which even slight traces of new sites may be identified in locations which have responded poorly to aerial photography (Light 1985). Further south, on the gravels in the same valley at Hucklesbrook, limited rescue excavation uncovered a possible Anglo-Saxon sunken-featured building; associated pottery included grass-tempered wares (Davies and Graham 1984). Elsewhere in the area vegetable-tempered pots have been recovered from Anglo-Saxon burials at Ford (Musty 1969), Petersfinger and Winterbourne Gunner. Sherds of this type are also known from Mumworth (information from David Algar), a lost settlement at the confluence of the Avon and the Bourne and near the Petersfinger cemetery. Finally, a grass-tempered pot was found at the hillfort at Whitsbury, where there was also some indication of post-Roman refurbishment of the ramparts but no sign of Anglo-Saxon usage (Ellison and Rahtz 1987).

On the Downs in Oxfordshire, a short distance to the north of the border with Berkshire, another field-walking project in the Vale of the White Horse produced grass-tempered pottery, much of it from the foot of the chalk escarpment; a few sherds were also recovered from the site of a Romano-British settlement, which was occupied until at least the late fourth century, on the down at Knighton Bushes (Tingle 1991, 68). In Hampshire, the excavation of the Anglo-Saxon site at Church Down, Chalton (p. 21 below) followed surface collection of grass-tempered pottery over an extensive area; it also occurred on nearby late Roman settlements (Cunliffe 1972).

British Settlement Sites

Dorset

The recent excavation of a settlement at Poundbury has provided unique information in Wessex about a British community immediately after the end of the Roman period. The settlement, which was preceded on the same site by a Romano-British one which itself continued in use into the fifth century and also overlay part of the late Roman cemetery, was occupied from the fifth until, probably, the early seventh century. In the first, fifth-century, phase there were a minimum of five rectangular timber buildings. Remnants of the Roman cemetery, including mausolea, were incorporated into the new arrangements. Grain driers were identified and provided important evidence of the cereal crops which were grown (p. 21 below). Radiocarbon dates obtained from charred grain from the driers provide a mean value of cal AD 529–621 (442–635) at the 68% (95%) confidence level (for this and other radiocarbon dates quoted in this chapter see note below on p. 29 under Acknowledgements). The limits of occupation were defined by shallow ditches, which appear to have enclosed about 0.8 hectares (2 acres). It is suggested that the second phase occurred in the sixth and early seventh centuries. The settlement was again set within a boundary ditch, on a different orientation, which now encompassed some 0.7 hectares (1.8 acres). Three rectangular timber buildings could certainly be assigned to this period, and two grain driers may be contemporary. The excavators noted the general irregularity of the timber buildings in comparison with those at Anglo-Saxon sites discussed below. There were also irregular enclosures with sunken-featured buildings elsewhere in the area defined by the ditch. Among the finds, Dr Tylecote drew particular attention to the sophisticated metalworking techniques as evidenced by the iron knives, which had specially hardened edges. These technically advanced artefacts, except one from the filling of drier 4, were from the latest occupation. Hone types also differed from those in use in the Roman settlement. It is pertinent to notice that the excavation produced only two sherds of hand-made pottery, both of them vegetable – tempered. In one place it was noted that there were quantities of Romano-British sherds with fresh breaks in and near structures characteristic of the post-Roman phase. At the end of the settlement, some buildings, at least, were burnt down (Green 1987).

Somerset

Excavation took place at the hillfort at South Cadbury between 1966 and 1970, when the sequence of the fortifications and some 6% of the interior were examined (Alcock 1982). There was probably a late Roman temple within the defences. At some later date, apparently, the innermost rampart was refortified. The new defence was some 4–5m wide and 1200m long, with a ragged dry stone front revetment with timber framework, which would have required 20,000m of planks and beams. Roman building materials were re-used in the core of the rampart. There was an elaborate gateway, with two double doors and possibly a tower above, at the south west. The rear face of the rampart was subsequently refurbished in dry masonry. A repair made to a metalled road through the gate sealed a late sixth-century silver ring. The ring

itself is of great interest for its form is at present unparalleled but it carries Germanic Salin Style I decoration, which perhaps suggests some degree of British and Anglo-Saxon cultural assimilation. A button brooch was also recovered from the site (Avent and Evison 1982, 100, 107).

Following geophysical survey, excavation uncovered traces of a post-Roman timber hall. This has been interpreted as a structure measuring 19m by 10m, with slightly bowed end walls, a chamber at the east end and two longitudinal inner aisles. Imported BI amphorae sherds (datable to between the fourth and early seventh centuries, see below) were found in the filling of one wall-slot. Imported pottery is generally widely scattered on the site but there were concentrations in and around this building and at the gate. Another building, measuring 4m by 2m, was identified some 4m from the hall; an amphora sherd was recovered from a wall trench.

Examination of the pottery imported from the Mediterranean suggests that occupation continued through much of the sixth century (phase 11). The absence of Class E ware of the seventh and eighth centuries may point to a cessation of use before that time, although it has been noted that this pottery is generally absent in central and eastern Dumnonia (Thomas 1981, fig. 50), or to a change in the nature or status of the settlement.

Cadbury Congresbury hillfort has been the focus of an important excavation, carried out on some 5% of the interior, between 1968 and 1973. This work has added greatly to our knowledge of Somerset in the immediate post-Roman period. The hillfort is less than half the extent of South Cadbury and it has far weaker defences. It faces west, towards the Bristol Channel, which was within easy reach along the River Yeo.

In the area examined, at least three periods of post-Roman occupation, recorded as subdivisions of Phase 3, were identified. Dating the successive stages, and indeed the sequence overall, presents many problems, in spite of the wealth of datable artefacts recovered. Thus a considerable amount of post-Roman glass, reported on by Dr J. Price, was recovered but none of it was found in a primary archaeological context. This glass included a minimum of eight Kempston type cone beakers of the fifth to mid sixth centuries, whose source lay in the Anglo-Saxon east of England. Other glass, from conical beakers and bowls, is not paralleled there and is probably of Continental origin, although there is the possibility that it was produced in western Britain. Altogether, there is glass from some sixty vessels from the hillfort. Pottery from the Mediterranean further underlines the status of the occupation. It includes Phocaean (one vessel of the late fifth but most of the early to mid sixth century) and African Red Slip Ware (including a stamped dish of the second and third quarters of the sixth century); and East Mediterranean amphorae (class BI, fourth to early seventh century; BII, early fifth to mid seventh century; and BIV, probably late fourth to sixth century). The excavators suggest occupation occurred between either *c.* 450 and 650 or *c.* 480 and 580. Imported Class E ware is absent, which in this area suggests that the former date bracket is correct.

The first of the three periods was characterised by the excavators as 'ultimate Roman', before the arrival of imported pottery and glass but at a time, perhaps the later fifth century, when Roman artefacts and building-materials were available for salvage, although Roman building techniques, such as the use of mortar, were no longer current (the filling of one deep pit or quarry showed a clear horizon between deposits with Roman and with imported material). Burning traced under the 'Diagonal Bank' of period II may mark the clearance of scrub. The 'Diagonal Bank' also partly sealed the possibly domestic Structure VI, of irregular but partially rectilinear outline, and a nearby hearth. The rectilinear Structure I, the very large, rounded, Structure III and a series of rock-cut platforms also belong to this initial period.

The second period, which possibly followed very closely on the first but is characterised by the presence of imports (as is the third period), is thought to date to the late fifth or early sixth century. The construction of the 'Diagonal Bank' now divided the hilltop into two parts; the excavation exposed the entrance through it. The 'Diagonal Bank' make-up itself produced only a few sherds of Roman pottery. The penannular Structure II was now built – a sherd of Class BII amphora was found in its wall trench; a northern entrance was inserted in Structure III; and the apparently substantial Structure V belongs to this phase. This period is seen as marking a major change from the previous one in building style, which was now more massive, regular and accomplished.

The third period is dated to the sixth century. Some features, notably foundation wall(s) inside Structure VII and the 'apron' of stones by the 'Diagonal Bank' and partly underlying VII were possibly integrated at some stage into the bank. Structure VII itself, which had a stone base, lay athwart the 'Diagonal Bank'; it was considered a defence or status feature, and possibly a successor to the foundations and the 'apron'. The superstructure of the 'Diagonal Bank' suffered intense burning. The small penannular Structure IV, with evidence of craft working and with which a full range of imports was associated, was located so as, apparently, to block the entrance through the 'Diagonal Bank', which was now therefore presumably an irrelevance; Structure VIII occupied a similar position outside, that is to the east of, the 'Diagonal Bank'. The latest features recorded include a deposit which is notable for a variety of hand-made pottery not recorded elsewhere (Rahtz *et al.* 1992).

British Cemeteries

Dorset

A cemetery of more than fifty inhumations, oriented west-east and arranged in north-south rows, was excavated at

Ulwell, near Swanage in the Isle of Purbeck, in 1982. Some of the burials were in stone cists, others defined by kerbstones; one grave contained an iron knife. Radiocarbon dating indicated use of the site throughout the seventh century (Cox 1988). There are other indications that Purbeck retained a distinctive British culture until long into the Anglo-Saxon period (p. 28) and, indeed, the absence of pagan Anglo-Saxon burials there has already been noticed (p. 17). The latest phase of the Roman cemetery at Poundbury, outside Dorchester, may be similarly marked by cists and stone-lined graves (A. Woodward in Farwall and Molleson 1993, 235–7).

Somerset

At a cemetery at Cannington, just beyond the River Parrett, most graves were lost in quarrying but some 500 were excavated in 1962–3. The graves, on an east-west orientation and some of them slab-lined, belonged to men, women and children. Two infant burials were accompanied by a variety of dress items, including a silver bracelet, penannular G brooches (Dickinson 1982), beads, and a pierced Roman coin. Amongst the potsherds were pieces imported from the Mediterranean and hand-made pottery from Cornwall; these objects and radiocarbon dates suggest a usage from perhaps the fourth to the early eighth centuries (Rahtz 1969: Rahtz and Fowler 1972, 200 and fig. 24, plan). Another British cemetery is known nearby, at Wembdon (Langdon 1986; Croft and Woods 1987; Croft 1988; Hollinrake 1989). There are also several other probable British cemeteries (Rahtz and Fowler 1972, 199): these are known at Wint Hill, Banwell (with perhaps hundreds of graves, some of them cut through a Roman villa); Brean Down, in a sandcliff (one grave contained a triangular knife – this site produced a radiocarbon date of cal AD 650–800 (595–895) at the 68% (95%) confidence level (Burrow 1976)); Portishead; and near Romano-British temples at Henley Wood and at Lamyatt Beacon, the latter with radiocarbon determinations of cal AD 545–712 (429–811) at the 68% (95%) confidence level and cal AD 774–969 (677–1010) at the 68% (95%) confidence level (Leech 1986, 270). The continued use of another temple, that at Pagans Hill, is clear from the discovery there in the well of a pail and an almost complete Anglo-Saxon blue glass squat jar of the seventh century (Rahtz and Watts 1989). The burial with a knife at Evercreech (Dobson 1935) and others, without grave goods except for one with a knife, at Saltford (Keynsham) (Crook 1938) are as likely to be those of Britons as Saxons.

Anglo-Saxon Settlement Sites

Hampshire

There have been few major excavations of early Anglo-Saxon settlements in Wessex. One of the most important took place over some 2 hectares (5 acres) on the top of

Church Down, Chalton, on the Chalk in Hampshire, between 1970 and 1976. The excavation uncovered sixty-one definite structures and in one part of the site identified four phases of occupation, which included two successive fenced farm units, within which the contemporaneity of some buildings may be suggested by their regular arrangement. Elsewhere few buildings were found to intersect each other. The largest structures were some 11m by 6m and characterised by opposing central doorways in their long sides and, with one exception, transverse internal partitions near the east end. Where a relationship could be identified, those of post-built construction were earlier than those erected using a post-in-trench technique. Some buildings were laid out end-on and in these cases their relative sequence was often problematical. Only four sunken-featured buildings, one of them of exceptionally small size and another, where loomweights were found, unexpectedly large, were identified on the site. It is difficult to discern any planned layout to the settlement as a whole. Chronologically diagnostic finds indicate occupation in the seventh century; they include bronze pins and an escutcheon from a hanging-bowl. Among the others, oyster shells, glass, quernstones and wheelthrown pottery are of particular interest (Addyman, Leigh and Hughes 1972; Addyman and Leigh 1973; Champion 1987).

A second excavation, from 1978 to 1981, of considerable significance for our knowledge of early Saxon settlement morphology, was carried out at another site in the Hampshire chalklands on Cowdery's Down, above the River Loddon, near Basingstoke. A minimum of three phases of occupation were identified here. Finds were few and generally of little help in dating, which depends upon calibrated radiocarbon dates of 580±67 for phase A and 609±57 for phase C, at the 68% confidence level. In each of the first two periods there were two farms with long, rectangular buildings and fenced enclosures. Spaced posts were used in the framework for the buildings. The subsequent arrangement, partly overlying the others, comprised in addition a number of larger halls; trench-built construction was used for all of the buildings of this phase. There were also two sunken-featured buildings, and again enclosures with fences (Millett with James 1983).

In regard to the purpose of the sunken-featured buildings, it seems that their frequent use was for weaving and other economic functions and that the population dwelt in large halls nearby. The site at Old Down Farm, Andover, in Hampshire appears to be an exception. There the excavators uncovered, with little doubt, the whole settlement which comprised only six of these sunken-featured structures. They were thought to have been used for only a short period (Davies 1980). It may be noted that the term 'sunken-floored' is often applied to these buildings but it may be a misnomer in most cases. Excavation followed by careful reconstruction at West Stow in Suffolk has shown that at least some of them had raised,

boarded floors (West 1985, 113–21; cf. Welch 1992, 21–5). The deep layer of rubbish which excavators often find in the pit itself may derive either from debris which has fallen through the floorboards or, more probably in most cases, from subsequent filling during levelling of the site after final demolition. Hearths have been recognised on the floor of the pit in some places but they may relate only to a subsequent re-use of the site.

Wiltshire

At Foxley, on the Corallian limestone and near the River Avon west of Malmesbury in north-west Wiltshire, aerial photography has revealed, and magnetic survey and limited excavation have subsequently confirmed, traces of a substantial settlement, with a timber 'hall' (Hinchliffe 1986, building 'B'), of two phases, a building (probably a church) with an apse at the east end in its own enclosure, and some twenty other large structures, together with fenced closes. No floor remains survived within the buildings. The excavations showed that the post-in-trench technique of construction was used for many buildings. The walls of the 'hall', in its first, but not its second phase, were supported by external posts. There were very few finds, and these not particularly diagnostic, but oak charcoal from a wall trench produced a date of cal AD 555–665 (430–760) at the 68% (95%) confidence level – the only radiocarbon date available from this site.

Arable Farming and Livestock in a British Context

At Poundbury, in Dorset, the numbers of corn driers indicate the large scale of cereal production in the post-Roman settlement. Wheat, barley and cultivated oats are represented in the record, with a particular and new emphasis here on a free-threshing bread wheat (*Triticum aestivo-compactum*), although this variety is recorded in a number of late Roman contexts in Wessex. The free-threshing form certainly involved less intensive processing, thereby releasing labour for other tasks. The kilns were probably used for drying the grain rather than malting, although it was noted that parallels elsewhere suggest they are likely to have served several functions during their useful life (Monk 1987, 132–7).

In regard to livestock at this site a comparison with the late Roman period showed that there was a significant post-Roman increase in the numbers of sheep and their contribution to the meat diet, although cattle remained dominant and continued to provide meat at the same level as before. There was also a fall in the numbers of fully grown cattle and sheep, but it was noted that the fragmentary state of the bones limited the data available on the size of the animals. No young horses were identified and it has been suggested (Harcourt 1979) that horses were not bred but that animals were selected and trained following a round-up, which would imply land available for wild horses to run free, although not necessarily in the immediate area. An extension of woodland in late Roman times is suggested both by increases in red and roe deer and in the continued importance of fully matured pig in the economy (Buckland-Wright 1987, 129–32).

Arable Farming in an Anglo-Saxon Context

The study of plant remains provides invaluable information on which to base some assessment of farming and the environment in early Anglo-Saxon Wessex. However, many of the relevant data remain unpublished and not easily accessible. The nature of the evidence varies, inevitably, both in quantity and quality from site to site and it is still difficult to make inter-site comparison which would allow a broad picture to emerge. Thus the presence of, say, significant quantities of barley from the chalkland at Shavards Farm, Meonstoke (information from F. J. Green) and in analysed samples at Chalton (Green 1991) does not allow the conclusion that the crop was necessarily a major component of the overall economy of those settlements. In another case, at Cowdery's Down, the evidence is altogether slight as only the foundation trenches of the buildings were sampled (Green 1983). It is also not legitimate to assume that because a particular crop is known to be especially suited to a certain soil type, the crop most probably predominated there in an ancient economy.

Attention may be drawn to recent work carried out in Hampshire. Important environmental evidence has recently been gained from a sunken-featured building and ditches at King's Somborne in the Test valley (Scott 1991). Wheat, barley and oats were important in that order; rye was absent from the samples (information from F. J. Green). At two other places, exceptional environmental conditions have played an important role in the recovery of evidence. At Shavards Farm, Meonstoke, mineralised preservation has allowed identification of a wider range of plants, including pea and grape – possibly cultivated locally – than has been recorded elsewhere. The recent evaluation of the plant remains from Abbots Worthy (p. 16 above), where some deposits may have been at least periodically waterlogged, has indicated a wide range of species, although in many cases it is not possible to say whether they were cultivated or not. The list there includes *T aestivo-compactum*, mentioned above in connection with Poundbury; elderberry; sloe; apple; blackberry/raspberry; pea; hazelnuts; horse bean, possibly for animal fodder; carrot; celery; and cabbage/turnip/mustard (Carruthers 1991).

The Environment

Our knowledge of the vegetational cover of Wessex in the early Anglo-Saxon period is at present very limited. On the Chalk the lack of suitable sites for pollen analysis

has always been a controlling factor, in addition to the general one of the interpretation of pollen dispersal. Attention, however, may be drawn to one piece of research which is of particular interest (Waton 1982). A core taken through the peat fen at Winnall Moors, near Winchester in the Itchen valley, showed an uninterrupted accumulation there since the Boreal period. Between 1000 BC and AD 1000 cereal pollen remains significant at 1–4%, herbs increase and arboreal and shrub pollen are constant at 20–30%. *Cannabis* type (hemp and hops) and *Secale* type (rye) pollen are also present in the second half of the period. It is likely that more than 50% of the pollen derives from chalkland plants. The overall picture is one of permanently open conditions, with considerable evidence for arable cultivation, together with pasture and areas of woodland – whether scrub or managed copses or even continuous dense woodland at a distance is unknown. However, the attraction of the higher chalk downland for arable cultivation may have been considerably less in the early Saxon period than in former times. The work of Dr Martin Bell has drawn attention to the decreasing fertility of downland soils which had been exploited for agriculture over very long periods (discussed in Welch 1985, 21–2). The extent of pasture, here or elsewhere, in the post-Roman period would have been the greater if the ancient system of farming known as foggage had been in operation. Under this regime, which is particularly suited to an economy where manpower is scarce, extra grassland is made available for winter feed. The hay crop on the additional areas is not taken off but is left long and finally dies on the plants. The cattle then feed off this less nutritious grass (information from Dr M Robinson).

Place-names too provide important evidence of early woodland. Berkshire owes its name to that of the forest of Barroc. The exact location of this wooded area is uncertain but it has been suggested that it stretched from Enborne to Hungerford, its heart on the clays in the region of Kintbury (Hooke 1988, 150 (following Peake)). Romano-British pottery kilns at Kintbury and Hamstead Marshall, as those at Savernake and in the New Forest, point to woodland at that time (Swan 1984, 6–8). It seems likely, therefore, that Savernake Forest and that of Barroc were almost continuous. Extensive woodland cover in south-west Berkshire in the early Anglo-Saxon period would probably have discouraged newcomers to the area, and indeed few sites of the pagan period are known there. Furthermore, study of the place-names has pointed to a marked survival of Brittonic names, which include that of Barroc itself, in that part of the county (Gelling 1976, 801–5). It may be noted that Savernake too is a pre-English name (Gover *et al.* 1939, 15; Jackson 1953, 294). In regard to forest names, it is also pertinent to draw attention to Chute and Melchet, also of Brittonic derivation, which occur on the border between Hampshire and Wiltshire (Gelling 1984, 190; Coates 1989, 115). The retention of these British names for forests may give some

Fig. 1.2 The Wansdyke at All Cannings in Wiltshire. (Photo: Roy Canham)

indication of the great extent of the woodland; the names of these major features of the landscape were known to communities over a wide area, just as those of rivers, and they were for this reason less subject to change.

Linear Earthworks

The significance of Bokerley Dyke has been discussed above (p. 17).

Wansdyke

The Wansdyke falls into two parts, the West Wansdyke and the East Wansdyke, both of which face north (Clark 1958; Fox and Fox 1958). West Wansdyke begins at the hillfort of Maes Knoll in Somerset and extends, though apparently not continuously, eastwards to Bath; its course also incorporates a second hillfort, that of Stantonbury. The earthwork is in places some 26m across; overall but reliable information about its structure remains very limited (Iles 1988).

West Wansdyke is separated from the eastern dyke

by a 22km stretch of the Roman road across lower ground between Bath and Mildenhall. The East Wansdyke (Fig. 1.2) begins on Morgan's Hill, some 10km west of the Ridgeway, and extends eastwards to New Buildings, less than 1.5km west of the present edge of Savernake Forest. Pitt Rivers had shown that at Brown's Barn, Bishop's Cannings, the East Wansdyke was built in the Roman period or later. A and C. Fox demonstrated that at Morgan's Hill it blocked the Roman road from Mildenhall to Bath. Green (1971) at New Buildings showed its construction there to be post-Roman. Both dykes are recorded in various charters from the ninth century onwards. In chalk country the dyke is a massive barrier (up to 30m across) to incursions from the north east, but on the mixed soils east of Shaw House, which is less than 1.5km east of the Ridgeway, the Wansdyke is of much smaller dimensions.

Dr A. J. Clark, *in litt.*, has made the following observations:

A date for East Wansdyke at the end of the Roman period is especially suggested by evidence from the 'Brown's Barn' Section II (Pitt Rivers 1892, 258–65, 270–6), which was located close to a Romano-British ditched enclosure partly buried by the dyke. The distribution of pottery within and beneath the bank showed that there was little time for worm action to take place between the cessation of deposition and the building of the dyke. Charles Darwin (1883) demonstrated that burial by worms takes place at an average rate of 4cm in ten years, so that pottery dropped on the surface would reach a depth of 20cm in fifty years. This process would be upset by ploughing, but the darkness of the old soil underlying the bank at Brown's Barn is in keeping with an undisturbed turf. Pottery sherds are scattered at all depths throughout this layer; otherwise they are almost completely confined to a mould deposit higher in the bank, probably consisting mainly of turf derived from the excavation of the ditch. In particular, an iron sandal cleat, of a type found by Pitt Rivers in Romano-British contexts, was discovered lying on the old ground surface, and a fourth-century mortarium type was present.

This evidence indicates that Wansdyke was built not earlier than the fourth century and soon after the dropping of Romano-British pottery on the surface of the site, with an upper limit of about forty years. If the cleat was associated with the site, its position suggests a much shorter interval; if it was lost by one of the builders of the dyke, it supports the likelihood that they were Roman or sub-Roman.

Defining Ancient Territories

In the late Roman period, the area that was later to become Wessex was divided for the purposes of Roman civil administration between several self-governing *civitates*, which were centred upon Silchester, Winchester, Dorchester (Dorset) and Ilchester. These units, which were for the most part of tribal origin, were themselves subdivided into *pagi*, about which little is yet known. The Roman name *Durocornovium*, which was given to a settlement on Ermine Street and beside the Dorcan stream (a Brittonic name (Bonney 1973, 482)) near Wanborough in north Wiltshire, however, appears to mean the 'fort of the Cornovii', who perhaps occupied one of these lesser territories (Rivet and Smith 1981, 350; Gelling 1988, 46; Burnham and Wacher 1990, 160–4).

Although it is not possible to reconstruct the boundaries of these late Roman units, there are hints of them at certain places. Thus in the Roman period part of the eastern boundary of the Durotriges, whose capital was at Dorchester, is likely to have followed the line of Bokerley Dyke, which today is part of the county division between Dorset and Hampshire. Recent work has shown that there had been a boundary on the Bokerley line since, probably, the middle bronze age (p. 17 above). Martin, the name of one of the parishes adjacent to the Dyke on the Hampshire (formerly Wiltshire) side, probably means 'the boundary settlement' (Cole 1991–92). A hint of another possible point on the eastern boundary of the Durotriges is provided by the British place-name Teffont, which means 'the *funta* on the boundary', in Wiltshire (Gelling 1988, 86); there is a probable Roman temple site there

(information in the National Monuments Record, RCHME).

The results achieved by his excavations at Bokerley Dyke focused the attention of Pitt Rivers on the other great linear earthwork in Wessex, the Wansdyke. The two dykes, but in particular, Bokerley and the East Wansdyke, as seen today, may indeed belong to the same historical phase, soon after the end of Roman rule in Britain. Just as Bokerley relates to the canton of the Durotriges, so East Wansdyke may be thought to lie close to the boundary between the Belgae, to the south, and the Atrebates and the Dobunni, to the east and north. At the east, Wansdyke ended against the forest (p.23; in the same way, the forest of Selwood stood between the Belgae and the Durotriges (Stenton 1971, 65–6)). The only hints of the boundary with the cantons to the north in this area are the possible Romano-British temples at the villa at Brown's Farm, west of Mildenhall (recently discovered from aerial photography), and at Mother Anthony's Well, Bromham (information respectively from Mark Corney and Dr Paul Robinson). To the north west, the temple complex at Nettleton Shrub on the Fosse Way has been thought to mark the division between the Belgae and the Dobunni (Rivet 1958, 141) and the intermediate temple at Studley might therefore also lie on this boundary (for a suggested allocation of individual Romano-British sites to *civitates* see Frere *et al.* 1983). Changes may have taken place in the early post-Roman period. The Anglo-Saxon Chronicle (Whitelock *et al.* (eds) 1961) records the defeat in 577 of three named British kings at Dyrham (in Avon) and the capture of three cities, one of them Bath – although it is not certain that the kings and the towns are to be directly associated (Sims-Williams 1983, 33). However, Bath was claimed as Belgic by Ptolemy, and if the Chronicle does indeed imply that a territory based upon the city was a separate entity and had become independent of the former Belgic canton, it may provide a clue to the siting of West Wansdyke. This dyke too could have been part of the northern defences of the Belgae, but here set against a new kingdom centred on Bath and in control of the River Avon. West Wansdyke does not match its eastern counterpart and follow a sound defensive course and its alignment may rather relate closely to a tribal boundary (cf. Myres 1986, *passim*, which sets Wansdyke in a rather different context). The locations of temples elsewhere in Wessex provide hints of some other boundaries between Romano-British cantons in the region. For instance, a possible line dividing the Durotriges from the Belgae to their north may be indicated by the shrines at Cold Kitchen Hill and Lamyatt Beacon (Leech 1980, 336). It is known that some temples were sited on pre-Roman bounds in Gaul, where they served a variety of inter-tribal needs (Rivet 1958, 134).

Early Anglo-Saxon kings were not always sole rulers and they might share power, even if one of them was pre-eminent. Examples of 'pairs' of kings are Cerdic and his son, or grandson according to one version of the genealogy, Cynric. In some cases there appears to have been a territorial division of authority. Literary sources and place-names provide some indications of the extent of the territories of some early Anglo-Saxon groups and kingdoms in Wessex (Yorke 1990, 142–6). However, none of them has a clear archaeological identity, in spite of various valiant attempts over the years to provide them with one.

The Jutes' name is preserved in *Ytene*, the New Forest; *Ytingstoc*, Bishopstoke on the River Itchen (Coates 1989, 34, 122); and also in *Ytedene*, 'the valley of the Jutes', a settlement name near East Meon by the Sussex border (Yorke 1989, 90). These places may hint at the limits, respectively in the west, north and east, of Jutish authority (probably, but not certainly, a royal one (Yorke 1989, 91)). Winchester appears to have lain outside their lands (p. 26) but it is unknown whether this tract of country along the south coast had been a separate subdivision (*pagus*) of the Belgae, ceded to or conquered by the Jutes, or was an entirely new political creation from whatever lands had been wrested from the British. The reference to Portchester in the Chronicle may indicate that the place played some administrative role in the Jutish province. The separate mention by Bede (Colgrave and Mynors (eds) 1969, hereafter H.E.) iv. 13) of the *Meanware*, together with the evidence of the place-name *Ytedene* cited above, suggests that they were a distinct group within Jutish territory; the cemetery at Droxford, with its origins in the fifth century (p. 2) perhaps relates to an early focus of this people (Stenton 1971, 293–4). Bede (H.E. i. 15; iv. 16) records that the Isle of Wight was also Jutish and was ruled by kings at the time of Caedwalla.

Turning to the northern frontier of Wessex, the Anglo-Saxon Chronicle says that in 648 Cenwalh entrusted to his relation Cuthred 'three thousands', an ancient unit here denoting a province (Stenton 1971, 66), at Ashdown (the Berkshire Downs). This was a strategically important area, traversed by the Ridgeway, where, the Chronicle relates, Wulfhere in 661 began his campaigns which led to Mercian domination of a part of Hampshire, Wight and Sussex. There are numerous pagan period sites and objects from various locations beside the Ridgeway (see also p. 27). They include, on Lowbury Hill (on Ashdown), a seventh-century warrior burial, with goods which included a hanging-bowl. It has been suggested that this warrior could have been Cuthred's man, perhaps of *Gesith* rank (Hawkes 1986, 91).

Finally, according to a monastic tradition, elements of which may date to the seventh century, that was preserved by Abingdon Abbey (Stenton 1913, 8–19), the *subregulus* Cissa, claimed to have been a predecessor of Caedwalla (685?–8), was also said to have ruled Wiltshire and the greater part of Berkshire from his 'metropolis' at Bedwyn and stronghold at Chisbury ('Cissa's burh, either the hillfort (Gover *et al.* 1939, 334–5) or his own 'fortified dwelling' (Haslam 1976, 23; 1980, 63)).

Another point of particular note in connection with Bedwyn is that it was later recorded as the centre of a hundred hide royal estate (Darlington 1955, 97), a primitive unit of assessment for the payment of the king's *feorm* (Stenton 1971, 298–301; see also Eagles forthcoming).

Roads, Boundaries and Anglo-Saxon Burials

A matter of interest concerning the siting of early Anglo-Saxon burials is the proximity of some, often richly-furnished, seventh-century graves to main Roman roads. This is a phenomenon which is widespread in many parts of England but which has not yet been satisfactorily explained. An example, under a barrow, in Wessex is that on Salisbury Racecourse (Evison 1963) which lies beside the route from Old Sarum to Dorchester – and at a point where three parishes meet, although none of their boundaries coincides with the line of the Roman road itself. Such coincidence is in fact most noticeable in areas little developed in the iron age, where the road may be taken to have been a new feature in the landscape; conversely the roads ignore the parishes in places where there is known to have been a concentration of pre-Roman settlement. Anglo-Saxon routes appear to have been regarded in a similar way to the Roman roads. The elaborately furnished female burial, secondary in a bronze age round barrow, at Swallowcliffe was both near a *herepath* and on the parish boundary; the barrow itself was named *Posses Hlaewe* in a tenth-century charter (Speake 1989). In regard to another major linear feature of the Wessex landscape, the East Wansdyke, the demonstration that it ignores parish bounds – in notable contrast to Bokerley Dyke, p. 17 above – has brought the suggestion that the parishes predate the construction of the dyke (Bonney 1972). Thus it may be argued that the Wansdyke is unlikely to have followed, certainly in any precise way, an existing boundary (cf. p. 24 above). The possibility of the continuity of some land units since the iron age is made the more likely by the recognition of the continuing use of the pre-Roman Grim's Dyke on Grovely Ridge, near Wilton, as a manorial boundary. There are many examples of the occurrence of pagan Saxon graves on or very close to parish boundaries (Bonney 1966).

Archaeology and the Literary Traditions

Entries in the Anglo-Saxon Chronicle purport to provide an historical framework for the conquest of Wessex by the house of Cerdic. The value and accuracy of these annals have been much debated (Yorke 1993). Discussion has centred upon a variety of issues which include observable differences, both of lengths of reign and the succession itself, between extant versions of royal genealogies and king lists (Dumville 1985); the duplication of some annals (Harrison 1971); and the earliest date that the information passed from an oral tradition to a written form. It has also become increasingly evident that the early material in the Chronicle was manipulated during the compilation of the present version, apparently in c. 890, to suit the propaganda needs of Alfred himself (Nelson 1991). There are only limited means of checking the entries in the Annals from independent sources; in this connection Bede provides important information, such as that for Caedwalla (H.E. iv. 15–16; v. 7).

The Chronicle refers to events in various parts of Wessex where they impinge upon the careers and reigns of successful leaders and kings. An inevitable consequence of this historical selection is that large parts of the region receive no mention at all and their early Anglo-Saxon history is often almost wholly lost to us.

Southern Hampshire and the Wiltshire Avon near Salisbury

It has been reasonably suggested that some of the earliest entries relate to the kingdom of the Jutes, the extent of whose territory has been referred to above (p. 24) and that these 'Jutish annals' could have been adopted by the Cerdicings following their savage conquest of the Isle of Wight in the reign of Caedwalla. Southern Hampshire, it seems likely, fell to them at the same time; Jutish independence was at an end. The significance of this victory would have been underlined by Caedwalla's adoption of a novel title, *Rex occidentalium Saxonum*, in recognition of his new wider authority, now no longer limited to the Gewisse (Yorke 1989, 93). The importance of the Solent for the future development of Wessex is seen clearly in the foundation of the port at Hamwic, near Southampton, possibly in the reign of Caedwalla's successor, Ine (Morton (ed.) 1992, 28). These momentous events in the history of Wessex would provide background enough for the West Saxon absorption of Jutish royal traditions – which in any case could hardly have been ignored in West Saxon claims to rule as their heirs.

The entry in the Chronicle for 501 does not mention Cerdic but records the success of other newly arrived Saxons, under their leader Port at Portsmouth. In 514, it is said, there was another landing, at the unidentified *Cerdicesora*, and Stuf and Wihtgar, 'kinsmen' of Cerdic and Cynric, were also successful against the Britons. The account in the Anglo-Saxon Chronicle of the landing in 495 by Cerdic and Cynric at *Cerdicesora*, their defeat in 508 of Natanleod which allowed them to gain control of territory as far as Charford, and finally the entry for 530 that Cerdic and Cynric took control of Wight, all appear to have been designed to link the traditions of the Gewisse and the Jutes. The primacy given to Cerdic and Cynric in 495 may be pure invention, in order to emphasise the later domination of the region by the house of Cerdic. It is notable that, apparently, no genuine names of Jutish kings survive in the Chronicle; and that the leaders' names in the saga are noticeably fictitious, especially Port, Wihtgar and Natanleod (a name which apparently has to

do with the English place-name Netley on the west bank of Southampton Water (Coates 1989, 121; Sims-Williams 1983, 29–30)). It is as if the Jutish royal house were expunged from the record (Yorke 1989). Archaeological evidence which has been cited above (p. 16) provides confirmation of the very early, if not indeed primary, importance of Portchester and the Isle of Wight in the Germanic settlement of the Solent.

The West Saxon conquest of the Jutes followed a period of Mercian aggression and penetration, which had culminated in their control of the Isle of Wight and the lands of the *Meanware*, now placed in the hands of the South Saxons under Mercian overlordship (H.E. iv, 13). Cenwalh's establishment very soon afterwards, in c. 662, of the new see at Winchester, transferred from Dorchester-on-Thames, reflects increasing West Saxon interest in the region. Reference has been made above to the situation at Winchester in the late Roman period and the fifth century (pp. 15–16). It has been argued that Winchester continued to play an important, though ill-defined, role thereafter. Attention has been drawn in particular to the presence at a variety of locations within and without the walls of vegetable-tempered pottery, some of which is of sixth- or seventh-century date; to a rich female burial of the mid to later seventh century, with gold and garnet pendants, and one of four excavated in the Lower Brook Street area (Hawkes *et al.*, in Biddle 1990); and finally to the existence of several sixth- and seventh-century Anglo-Saxon cemeteries nearby (a grave at Oliver's Battery contained a hanging bowl and in others at Winnall were found garnet jewellery and silver pins and rings) (Biddle 1972, 1983).

Identifiable place-names which do seem to refer to Cerdic are Charford and *Cerdices beorg*, near Hurstbourne Tarrant (Ha); both places lie outside the Jutish kingdom, although Charford may be close to its boundary (Yorke 1989, fig. 6.1). Annals recount the conquest by Cerdic and his son Cynric of the Avon valley and the Salisbury area, which was said to have been ultimately achieved following a victory at Charford in 519 (there is grass-tempered pottery and a brooch fragment, reputedly sixth-century, from Charford, p. 18 above). In 527 the Chronicle records that Cerdic and Cynric fought the British at *Cerdicesleag*, which is unknown. Other annals state that Cerdic died in 534, and that Cynric defeated the Britons at Old Sarum in 552. It has been shown above (p. 13) that the archaeological evidence makes it clear that there was a Germanic presence around Salisbury as early as that on the Solent. The archaeological pattern well suits an interpretation of the Chronicle which points to distinct areas of primary settlement, originally under different political control.

Central and Northern Wiltshire

The Anglo-Saxon Chronicle, under the annal for 556, introduces Ceawlin and records that in that year he and

Cynric fought alongside each other against the British at *Beranbyrg*, identified as Barbury, a hillfort on the Ridgeway 11km to the north of the Wansdyke. It may be noted that there is an Anglo-Saxon single-edged battle-knife from Barbury (in Devizes Museum; the two spear-heads listed by Swanton are of iron age date – information from Dr P. H. Robinson). None of the events of Ceawlin's remarkable career – he is the only West Saxon king to appear in Bede's list of great overlords (H.E. ii. 5) – takes place south of Wansdyke. His fighting along-side Cynric has been taken to indicate joint action for the first time by Anglo-Saxon kingdoms based on the Thames and in southern Wessex (Hawkes 1986, 86–7; Sims-Williams 1983, 28, however, that the sources do not present Ceawlin other than as a Cerdicing). The bound-ary between these kingdoms, marked militarily, it may be suggested, by Wansdyke, may have been established in the Roman period, when it served to divide tribal can-tons (p. 24). The events reported for 556 may also mark a decisive point towards the ultimate achievement of a single Wessex kingdom. There is no further mention of Cynric. In 560 the Chronicle states that Ceawlin suc-ceeded to the kingdom of Wessex; he fights alongside members of his own family, which may indicate that one or more of them was put in charge of the southern West Saxons on his behalf. The result of the great battle at Woden's Barrow (the long barrow called 'Adam's Grave' just to the south of the Wansdyke, see below) in 592 was that Ceawlin 'was driven out'. This entry, which does not specify the combatants, has always been difficult to understand but the battle may have been fought between Ceawlin and Saxons south of Wansdyke who now re-gained their independence. Ceawlin died in 593.

Ceawlin's career indicates clearly the importance of the Ridgeway; the battle at Barbury has already been mentioned and at the hillfort at Liddington Castle, ap-proximately 6.5km further to the north east, limited ex-cavations have shown some refurbishment of the ram-parts, although this activity can be dated no more closely than to the Roman period or later (Hirst and Rahtz 1976). 'Woden's barrow' itself lies 1.5km south of the point, at Red Shore, Alton Priors, where there is the only original passage yet identified through East Wansdyke (Green 1971); the record of another battle here in 715 empha-sises the strategic significance of the place. It may be noted that the use of Woden in place-names may crystal-lise only in the Christian missionary period (Gelling 1988, 148).

Conclusion

It has been shown that the evidence for the first presence of Saxons in Wessex, in the fifth century, is not concen-trated in one particular area but is to be found at a number of widely distributed locations in Hampshire and Wilt-shire, and also at one place, Hod Hill, in central Dorset. The distribution is mapped on Fig. 1.1 and the places

listed summarily on p. 15.

It could be argued that the earliest of all these sites is that at Hod Hill, where Saxons had arrived by the mid fifth century. The Anglo-Saxon finds there could well derive from a British context. They are isolated from other Anglo-Saxon material and Dorset, protected it seems by Bokerley Dyke, appears as a whole to have resisted Germanic settlement on any scale until the seventh cen-tury. The fifth-century objects from Hod Hill may have belonged to the families of Saxon warriors in British employ (Gildas (Winterbottom (ed.) 1978) 23.5 uses of-ficial late Roman billeting terms). The Saxons themselves could have reached Hod Hill direct from the coast along the Stour, the next major river west from the Wiltshire Avon, from Hengistbury Head. Gildas (25.1) refers to British strongholds on the tops of hills and it is worth noting that these defended positions would have been as useful during civil wars between the British (Gildas cc. 19, 21) as in warfare against the Anglo-Saxons.

It is also noticeable that there are clusters of sites around Winchester and Old Sarum, both nodal points in the Roman road network and the former a *civitas* capital. The earliest of these sites, probably around the middle of the fifth century, appear to be those at the Roman forum at Winchester and at Winterbourne Gunner, where the warrior burial is likely to belong to this phase. This Germanic presence, as at Hod Hill, may well have come about at a time when the British were still in control in these places. Other fifth-century material in these groups may for the most part relate to the latter part of the cen-tury; it is likely to indicate new settlement, whose con-text might have been, perhaps, a deliberate policy by the Anglo-Saxons to target British centres and subjugate them. It is pertinent to note that the Roman name for Winchester, *Venta*, passed directly into Old English as *Wintanceaster* and that the British name for the hillfort at Old Sarum clearly appears to be the ultimate source of that, *Searobyrg*, given to the place by the Anglo-Saxons (Gelling 1988, 54–5).

The sixth-century Anglo-Saxon finds noted above from various sites, particularly hillforts, in Dorset and Somer-set may also indicate that the newcomers served some British leaders in purely native struggles. Anglo-Saxon warriors formed a personal bond with their lord, a rela-tionship which entailed mutual obligations. Bede (H.E. iii. 14) records that young nobles from many different places attached themselves to the successful king Oswine of Deira. In the same way, it is possible that some Saxon warriors owed allegiance to some British rulers.

A further clue to British involvement in the earliest phases of English settlement is provided by names in the genealogies of the West Saxon kings. The names Cerdic, Ceawlin, Caedwalla and Cenwalh are of British origin (Hawkes 1986, 76; Coates 1989–90; Yorke 1990, 138–9). Presumably, unless they represent English name borrow-ing from the Britons, a matter of interest in its own right, they reflect intermarriage with the Britons at the highest social level. British names also occur in the genealogies of other kingdoms; they were not always those of members of local families but their recurrence in Wessex makes this more likely. Such dynastic marriages would have been one means by which new territories were brought under English control.

In 577 the battle of Dyrham, if the entry in the Chronicle is to be believed and is not merely a later West Saxon attempt to bolster its territorial claims in the struggle with Mercia (Sims-Williams 1983, 33–4), brought about the submission of most of Gloucestershire, together with Avon, to West Saxon rule, a state of affairs which appears to have been maintained until 628 when Wessex and Penda of Mercia 'came to terms' at Cirencester. The background to a battle at Bradford-on-Avon (Wi) in 652 is particularly obscure, as it is variously recorded as fought against the British or as civil war in different sources (Whitelock *et al.* (eds) 1961, 20, n. 2). It is therefore not at all clear that it relates to a further onslaught against British territory. The first unambiguous reference to a West Saxon advance westwards is that in the Chronicle which records the battle of *Peonnan*, usually taken to be Penselwood (So), in 658 when the Britons were driven back to the River Parrett. It has been noted above (p. 24) that Selwood lay near the border of the Durotriges and the Belgae. In 705, when the bishopric of Sherborne (Do) was established, it provided for those living 'west of the wood'. The battle in 658 may, therefore, have opened up Dorset and Somerset to the West Saxons.

The archaeological evidence is difficult to relate to this particular problem. It is clear that pagan Saxon burials of the seventh century spread to the western limits of the chalklands of Wiltshire and some way beyond, but apparently not into the limestone in the north west of the county; that they also occur in Dorset, although many of them there are concentrated around Dorchester, and that they exist in east Somerset, particularly to the east of the Fosse Way. There has been no recent overall assessment of this archaeological evidence and further study may provide some indication of the relative sequence of the sites. The reassessment needs to be carried out in the light of the important new work, discussed above, on British sites occupied after the end of the Roman period.

Attention has been drawn to notable groups of names which appear to imply continuing English recognition of a British population in particular localities and areas (Gelling 1988, 90). It would be of great interest, though clearly beyond the scope of the present study, to look at such areas closely from both the British and the English vantage point. Relevant names are particularly evident in south Hampshire, most of them within Jutish territory. They include Wickham (in the Meon valley); Boarhunt, Funtley, Havant and Mottisfont; and Portsmouth (Gelling 1988, fig. 2). It is also thought probable that Solent and the river names Itchen and Test were given before the Anglo-Saxons arrived (Coates 1989). There is other information, of a different kind, about the survival of a flourishing British community in the Isle of Purbeck in south Dorset. Five memorial inscriptions to Britons – on re-used Roman stones – were found in 1840 built into the fabric of the church of Lady St Mary, Wareham. They appear to date to between the seventh century and, at the latest, the early ninth; they provide evidence for traditions kept alive through an active British church (RCHM 1970a, 308, 310–2; Hinton 1992). Other burial evidence has been cited above (p. 20) for the presence of Britons elsewhere on Purbeck in the seventh century and it is notable that there is no information about an early Saxon presence, in spite of the location on the south coast. In regard to Sherborne, it is of great interest to note that there appears to have already been a British church there, which was known as Lanprobus. Cenwalh had links with the place, for he is listed among benefactors to the church at Sherborne, and there is a charter in his name, the witness list of which suggests a date of 670–2 (Finberg 1964, 98–9; Barker 1980, 107). It has also been pointed out that a man with a British name, Catwali, was ruling an abbey in Dorset long after the Saxons had taken control (Finberg 1964, 85).

There was possibly an Irish monastery in the mid seventh century at Malmesbury (Wi) (Campbell 1987, 338). If so, its influence may help to explain the presence of certain high status artefacts found in Wiltshire graves. At Swallowcliffe, the grave goods included a silvered-bronze sprinkler, which has only one parallel, from a ninth-century Viking grave in Norway, which carries Celtic decoration apparently of the seventh century. The mount on the satchel in the Swallowcliffe grave utilised silver and gold repousseé foils which exhibited both Celtic and Anglo-Saxon styles of ornament. A grave at Roundway Down contained a pin-suite with a gold roundel with a blue glass setting in the form of a cross, of probable Irish workmanship, and possibly of Christian significance (Meaney and Hawkes 1970, 48–9).

There are some other signs of contact between the Britons, archaeologically largely invisible as they may be, and the English. Attention may be drawn, for instance, to the substantial amounts of Anglo-Saxon glass which reached Cadbury-Congresbury in the far west of Somerset – although it is also true that imported pottery from the Mediterranean and elsewhere shows a markedly western and apparently distinct trading network away from Anglo-Saxon centres; the spread eastwards of penannular class G brooches; and the occurrence at Poundbury of sunken-featured buildings normally associated with Anglo-Saxon sites (see also James, Marshall and Millett 1984 for the adoption of British building techniques in the construction of Anglo-Saxon timber halls). As evidence continues to accumulate from a wide variety of sources, the extent, range and complexity of the links become ever more clear. It is against this background that the period of bilingualism, during which the British inhabitants adopted English speech (Jackson 1953, 241–6), should be set. The overwhelming number of place-names, however, are of English, not British, origin and this, it has been persuasively argued, indicates both that the immigrants were relatively numerous and that they included a large body of peasants who worked the land (Gelling 1976, 201–3; Gelling 1993).

Acknowledgements

I am most grateful to many friends and colleagues who have willingly provided information and advice on numerous occasions during the preparation of this paper. I would like to thank in particular: Ken Annable, Mark Corney (who also drew the map), Nick Griffiths, Dr Heinrich Härke, Dr Catherine Mortimer, Dr Mark Robinson, Leslie Webster, Dr Barbara Yorke and Susan Youngs. My appreciation is also due to Frank Green, who very kindly allowed me to refer to the results of new work contained in a forthcoming paper, and to Dr Paul Robinson, who drew my attention to recent and other finds in Devizes Museum and who also kindly made available a copy of the typescript interim note by S. Hirst and P. Rahtz on the Liddington Castle excavations. Dr Anthony Clark, in addition to many helpful comments, generously offered to calibrate radiocarbon dates which are quoted in another form in published reports; this has provided an overall consistency and allows comparison between the dates for the first time (University of Washington Quarternary Isotope Laboratory Radiocarbon Calibration Program 1987 (Rev. 2.0), based on the high precision calibration curves published in Radiocarbon 28, no. 2B, 1986). Dr Andrew David provided further information about the radiocarbon date from Foxley. I have also benefited considerably from discussions with my immediate colleagues in the National Monuments Record.

References

Addyman, P. V. and Leigh, D. 1973: 'The Anglo-Saxon village at Chalton, Hampshire: second interim report', *Medieval Archaeol* XVII, 1–25.

Addyman, P. V., Leigh, D. and Hughes, M. J. 1972: 'Anglo-Saxon houses at Chalton, Hampshire', *Medieval Archaeol* XVI, 13–31.

Ager, B. 1990: 'The alternative quoit brooch: an update', in *Anglo-Saxon Cemeteries. A Reappraisal.* (Proceedings of a conference held at Liverpool Museum 1986), ed. E. Southworth, 153–61. Stroud.

Alcock, L. 1982: 'Cadbury-Camelot: a fifteen-year perspective', *Procs British Academy* LXVIII, 355–88.

Aldsworth, F. R. 1978: 'The Droxford Anglo-Saxon cemetery, Soberton, Hampshire', *Procs Hants Field Club and Archaeol. Soc.* 35, 93–182.

Anon, 1946: 'Accessions to Museum', *Procs Somerset Archaeol. and Nat. Hist. Soc.* 92, 47–8.

Arnold, C. J. 1982: *The Anglo-Saxon Cemeteries of the Isle of Wight.*

Avent, R. and Evison, V. I. 1982: 'Anglo-Saxon button brooches', *Archaeologia* CVII, 77–124.

Baldwin, R. 1985: 'Intrusive burial groups in the late Roman cemetery at Lankhills, Winchester – reassessment of the evidence', *Oxford Journal of Archaeology* 4(1), 93–104.

Barker, K. 1980: 'Early ecclesiastical settlement in Dorset: a note on the topography of Sherborne, Beaminster and Wimborne Minster', *Dorset Proceedings* 102, 107–12.

Biddle, M. 1972: 'Winchester: the development of an early capital', in *Vor- und Frühformen der europäischen Stadt im Mittelalter* (Bericht über ein Symposium in Reinhausen bei Göttingen vom 18. bis 24. April 1972, Abhandlungen der Akademie der Wissenschaften in Göttingen), eds H. Jankuhn, W. Schlesinger and H. Steuer, Teil I, 229–61. Göttingen.

Biddle, M. 1983: 'The study of Winchester: archaeology and history in a British town, 1961–1983' (Albert Reckitt Archaeological Trust Lecture), *Procs British Academy* LXIX, 299–341.

Bird, S. in Aston, M. and Iles, R. (eds) n.d.: 'Roman Avon', in *The archaeology of Avon. A review from the Neolithic to the Middle Ages,* 53–71 (Bristol).

Böhme, H. W. 1986: 'Das Ende der Römerherrschaft in Britannien und die angelsächsische Besiedlung Englands im 5 Jahrhundert', *Jahrbuch des Römisch – Germanischen Zentralmuseums* 33, 469–574.

Bonney, D. J. 1966: 'Pagan Saxon burials and boundaries in Wiltshire', *Wilts Archaeol. and Nat. Hist. Mag.* 61, 25–30.

Bonney, D. J. 1972: 'Early boundaries in Wessex', in P. J. Fowler (ed.) 1972, 168–86.

Bonney, D. J. 1973: 'The pagan Saxon period *c.* 500 – *c.* 700', in *VCH Wilts* I, part 2, 468–84.

Bowen, H. C. 1990: *The Archaeology of Bokerley Dyke*, ed. B. N. Eagles. Royal Commission Hist. Mons England. London.

Buckland-Wright, J. C. 1987: 'The animal bones', in Green, C. S. 1987, 129–32.

Bulleid, (A.) 1922: 'Saxon gold pendant from Somerset', *Antiq. J.* II, 383.

Burnham, B. C. and Wacher, J. S. 1990: *The 'Small Towns' of Roman Britain.* London.

Burrow, I. C. G. 1976: 'Brean Down hillfort, Somerset, 1974', *Procs University Bristol Spaeleological Soc.* 14, part 2, 141–54.

Burrow, I. 1981: *Hillfort and hill-top settlement in Somerset in the first to eighth centuries A.D.* (British Archaeol. Reports, British Series 91). Oxford.

Campbell, J. 1987: 'The debt of the early English Church to Ireland', in *Irland und die Christenheit: Bibelstudien und Mission*, eds P. Ní Chatháin and M. Richter, 332–46. Stuttgart.

Canham, R. and Phillips, B. n.d.: *The archaeology of Old Swindon Hill* (Swindon Archaeol. Society Report No. 1).

Carruthers, W. J. 1991: 'The plant remains', in Fasham and Whinney 1991, 67–75.

Champion, T. 1977: 'Chalton', *Current Archaeology* 59, 364–9.

Clark, A. J. 1958: 'The nature of Wansdyke', *Antiquity* 32, 89–96.

Clarke, G. 1979: *The Roman cemetery at Lankhills (Pre-Roman and Roman Winchester, part 2)* (Winchester Studies 3). Oxford.

Coates, R. 1989: *The place-names of Hampshire.* London.

Coates, R. 1989–90: 'On some controversy surrounding *Gewissae/Gewissei, Cerdic* and *Ceawlin*', *Nomina* XIII, 1–11.

Cole, A. 1991–92: 'Distribution and use of the Old English place-name *mere-tūn*', *Journal of the English Place-Name Society* 24, 31–41.

Colgrave, B. and Mynors, R. A. B. (eds) 1969: *Bede's Ecclesiastical History of the English People*. Oxford.

Collins, M. D. H. 1986: *Haresfield Estate Highworth* (Archaeol. Report 1975–81), 28–32. Privately printed.

Cook, A. M. 1982: 'Appendix 11: the Saxon secondary burials', in C. Green, F. Lynch and H. White, The excavation of two round barrows on Launceston Down (Long Crichel 5 and 7), *Dorset Proceedings* 104, 56–8.

Courty, M. A., Goldberg P. and MacPhail, R. 1989: *Soils and micromorphology in archaeology* (Cambridge Manuals in Archaeology). Cambridge.

Cox, P. W. 1988: 'A seventh century inhumation cemetery at Shepherd's Farm, Ulwell near Swanage, Dorset', *Dorset Proceedings* 110, 37–47.

Croft, R. A. 1988: 'Bridgwater, Wembdon Hill', *Procs Somerset Archaeol. and Nat. Hist. Soc.* 132, 221.

Croft, R. A. and Woods, H. M. 1987: 'Wembdon, Wembdon Hill', *Procs Somerset Archaeol. and Nat. Hist. Soc.* 131, 215.

Crook, M. 1938: 'Saxon cemetery at Saltford', *Procs University Bristol Spaeleological Soc.* 5(1), 90.

Cunliffe, B. W. 1972: 'Saxon and medieval settlement-pattern in the region of Chalton, Hampshire', *Medieval Archaeol.* XVI, 1–12.

Cunliffe, B. W. 1976: *Excavations at Portchester Castle. II. Saxon* (Research Report Soc. of Antiquaries of London 33). Oxford.

Darlington, R. R. 1955: 'Introduction to the Wiltshire Domesday', *VCH Wilts* II, 42–112.

Darwin, C. 1883: *Vegetable mould and earth-worms*. London.

Davies, S. M. 1980: 'Excavations at Old Down Farm, Andover. Part 1: Saxon', *Procs Hants Field Club and Archaeol. Soc.* 36, 161–80.

Davies, S. M. 1984: 'The excavation of an Anglo-Saxon cemetery (and some prehistoric pits) at Charlton Plantation, near Downton', *Wilts Archaeol. and Nat. Hist. Mag.* 79, 109–54.

Davies, S. M. and Graham, A. H. 1984: 'Evidence of prehistoric and Anglo-Saxon settlement found during gravel extraction near Hucklesbrook, in the Avon valley, Hampshire', *Procs Hants Field Club and Archaeol. Soc.* 40, 127–30.

Denford, G. T. 1986: 'A keystone garnet disc brooch from Ampfield', *Procs Hants Field Club and Archaeol. Soc.* 42, 160–1.

Dickinson, T. M. 1979: 'On the origin and chronology of the early Anglo-Saxon disc brooch', *Anglo-Saxon Studies in Archaeology and History* I, eds. S. C. Hawkes, D. Brown and J. Campbell (British Archaeol Reports, British Series 72), 39–81.

Dickinson, T. M. 1982: 'Fowler's Type G penannular brooches reconsidered', *Medieval Archaeol.* XXVI, 41–68.

Dickinson, T. M. 1991: 'Material culture as social expression: the case of Saxon saucer brooches with running spiral decoration', *Studien zur Sachsenforschung* 7, 39–70.

Dobson, D. P. 1935: 'A Saxon burial at Evercreech', *Procs University Bristol Spaeleological Soc.* 4, part 3, 268.

Dumville, D. N. 1985: 'The West Saxon genealogical Regnal List and the chronology of Wessex', *Peritia* 4, 21–66.

Eagles, B. N. 1979: *The Anglo-Saxon settlement of Humberside* (British Archaeol. Reports, British Series 68, parts i and ii). Oxford.

Eagles, B. N. forthcoming: 'The area around Bedwyn in the Anglo-Saxon period', in E. Hostetter and T. N. Howe (eds), *The Romano-British villa at Castle Copse, Great Bedwyn*. Bloomington, Indiana, USA.

Eagles, B. N. and Mortimer, C. forthcoming: 'Early Anglo-Saxon artefacts from Hod Hill, Dorset', *Antiq. J.* LXXIII.

Ellison, A. and Rahtz, P. 1987: 'Excavations at Whitsbury Castle Ditches, Hampshire, 1960', *Procs Hants Field Club and Archaeol. Soc.* 43, 63–81.

Evison, V. I. 1963: 'Sugar-loaf shield bosses', *Antiq. J.* XLIII, 38–96.

Evison, V. I. 1965: *The fifth-century invasions south of the Thames*. London.

Evison, V. I. 1968: 'The Anglo-Saxon finds from Hardown Hill', *Dorset Proceedings* 90, 232–40.

Evison, V. I. 1981: 'Distribution maps and England in the first two phases', in V. I. Evison (ed.), *Angles, Saxons and Jutes. Essays presented to J. N. L. Myres*, 126–67. Oxford.

Evison, V. I. 1988: *An Anglo-Saxon cemetery at Alton, Hampshire* (Hants Field Club and Archaeol. Society: Monograph 4).

Farwell, D. E. and Molleson, T. I. 1993: *Excavations at Poundbury 1966–80. Volume II: the cemeteries* (Dorset Nat. Hist. and Archaeol. Society: Monograph 11).

Fasham, P. J. and Whinney, R. J. B. 1991: *Archaeology and the M3* (Hants Field Club and Archaeol Society: Monograph 7).

Finberg, H. P. R. 1964: *Lucerna. Studies of some problems in the early history of England*. London.

Fowler, E. 1963: Celtic metalwork of the fifth and sixth centuries A.D., *Archaeol. J.* 120, 98–160.

Fowler, P. J. (ed.) 1972: *Archaeology and the landscape. Essays for L. V. Grinsell*. London.

Fox, A. and Fox, C. 1958: 'Wansdyke reconsidered', *Archaeol. J.* 117, 1–48.

Frere, S. S. *et al.* 1983: *Tabula Imperii Romani. Condate-Glevum-Londinium-Lutetia*. London.

Gelling, M. 1976: *The place-names of Berkshire. Part III* (The English Place-Name Society. Volume LI) Cambridge.

Gelling, M. 1984: *Place-names in the landscape*. London.

Gelling, M. 1988: *Signposts to the past. Place-names and the history of England*. Second edition. Chichester.

Gelling, M. 1993: 'Why aren't we speaking Welsh?', *Anglo-Saxon Studies in Archaeology and History* 6, 51–6.

Gingell, C. J. 1975–76: 'The excavation of an early Anglo-Saxon cemetery at Collingbourne Ducis', *Wilts Archaeol. and Nat. Hist. Mag.* 70/71, 61–98.

Gower, J. E. B., Mawer, A. and Stenton, F. M. 1939: *The place-names of Wiltshire* (The English Place-Name Society. Volume XVI) Cambridge.

Green, C. S. 1984: 'Early Anglo-Saxon burials at the "Trumpet Major" public house, Alington Avenue, Dorchester', *Dorset Proceedings* 106, 149–52.

Green, C. S. 1987: *Excavations at Poundbury. Volume I. The settlements* (Dorset Nat. Hist. and Archaeol. Soc. Monograph Series 7).

Green, F. J. 1983: 'The plant remains', in Millett with James 1983, 259–61.

Green, F. J. 1991: 'Landscape archaeology in Hampshire: the

Saxon plant remains', in J. M. Renfrew (ed.), *New light on early farming. Recent developments in palaeoethnobotany*, 363–77. Edinburgh.

Green, H. S. 1971: 'Wansdyke, excavations 1966 to 1970', *Wilts Archaeol. and Nat. Hist. Mag.* 66, 129–46.

Grinsell, L. V. 1957: 'Archaeological gazetteer. A. General gazetteer, arranged under parishes', in *VCH Wilts* I, part 1, 21–131.

Harcourt, R. 1979: 'The animal bones', in G. J. Wainwright, *Gussage All Saints: an Iron Age settlement in Dorset* (Dept of Environment Archaeological Report 10), 150–60. London.

Harrison, K. 1971: 'Early Wessex annals in the Anglo-Saxon Chronicle', *English Hist. Review* 86, 527–33.

Haslam, J. (with Edwards, A.) 1976: *Wiltshire towns: the archaeological potential*. Devizes.

Haslam, J. 1980: 'A middle Saxon iron smelting site at Ramsbury, Wiltshire', *Medieval Archaeol.* XXIV, 1–68.

Hawkes, S. C. 1986: 'The early Saxon period', in G. Briggs, J. Cook and T. Rowley (eds), *The archaeology of the Oxford region*, 64–114. Oxford.

Hawkes, S. C. 1989: 'The south-east after the Romans: the Saxon settlement', in V. A. Maxfield (ed.), *The Saxon Shore. A handbook.* (Exeter. Studies in History No. 25, produced for 15th International Congress of Roman Frontier Studies, Canterbury).

Hawkes, S. C. *et al.* 1990: 'The Anglo-Saxon necklace from Lower Brook Street', in M. Biddle, *Object and economy in medieval Winchester* (Winchester Studies 7.ii, part 2), 621–32. Oxford.

Hawthorne, J. 1981: 'Bradford Peverell', in *Dorset Proceedings* 103, 126.

Hinchliffe, J. 1986: 'An early medieval settlement at Cowage Farm, Foxley, near Malmesbury', *Archaeol. J.* 143, 240–59.

Hinton, D. A. 1992: 'The inscribed stones in Lady St Mary Church, Wareham', *Dorset Proceedings* 114, 260.

Hirst, S. and Rahtz, P. 1976: *Liddington Castle. Wiltshire, England* (a typescript distributed by the excavators).

Hoare, R. Colt 1812: *The ancient history of Wiltshire*. Vol I. London.

Hollinrake, C. and N. 1989: 'Bridgwater, Wembdon Hill', *Procs Somerset Archaeol. and Nat. Hist. Soc.* 133, 171.

Hooke, D. 1988: *Anglo-Saxon settlements*. Oxford.

Horne, E. 1926: 'Saxon cemetery at Buckland Denham, Somerset', *Antiq. J.* VI, 77–8.

Horne, E. 1928: 'Saxon cemetery at Camerton, Somerset', *Procs Somerset Archaeol. and Nat. Hist. Soc.* 74, 61–70.

Horne, E. 1933: 'Anglo-Saxon cemetery at Camerton, Somerset. Part II', *Procs Somerset Archaeol. and Nat. Hist. Soc.* 79, 39–63.

Iles, R. 1988: 'West Wansdyke: recent archaeological research and future prospects', *Bristol and Avon Archaeology* 7, 6–10.

Jackson, K. 1953: *Language and history in early Britain. A chronological survey of the Brittonic languages. First to twelfth century A.D.* Edinburgh.

James, S., Marshall, A. and Millett, M. 1984: 'An early medieval building tradition', *Archaeol. J.* 141, 182–215.

Jarvis, K. S. 1983: *Excavations in Christchurch 1969–1980* (Dorset Nat. Hist. and Archaeol. Soc. Monograph Series 5).

Keen, L. 1977: 'Dorset archaeology in 1977', in *Dorset Proceedings* 99, 120.

Keen, L. 1978: 'Dorset archaeology in 1978', in *Dorset Proceedings* 100, 112.

Keen, L. 1979: 'Dorset archaeology in 1979', in *Dorset Proceedings* 101, 133.

Langdon, M. 1986: 'Wembdon, Wembdon Hill', *Procs Somerset Archaeol. and Nat. Hist. Soc.* 130, 151.

Leach, P. J. 1990: 'The Roman site at Fosse Lane, Shepton Mallet', *Procs Somerset Archaeol. and Nat. Hist. Soc.* 134, 47–55.

Leech, R. H. 1976: 'Romano-British and medieval settlement at Wearne, Huish Episcopi', *Procs Somerset Archaeol. and Nat. Hist. Soc.* 120, 45–50.

Leech, R. H. 1980: 'Religion and burials in south Somerset and north Dorset', in W. Rodwell (ed.), *Temples, churches and religion in Roman Britain* (British Archaeol Reports, British Series 77, part i), 329–66. Oxford.

Leech, R. H. 1986: 'The excavation of a Romano-Celtic temple and a later cemetery on Lamyatt Beacon, Somerset', *Britannia* XVII, 259–328.

Leeds, E. T. and Shortt, H. de S. 1953: *An Anglo-Saxon cemetery at Petersfinger, near Salisbury, Wilts.* Salisbury.

Leighton, W. 1937: 'The manor and parish of Burnett, Somerset', *Trans Bristol and Gloucestershire Archaeol. Soc.* 59, 243–85.

Light, T. 1985: 'Avon valley', *Archaeology in Hampshire* (Hants County Council Planning Dept, Annual Report for 1983), 74–5.

McCulloch, P. C. 1992: 'Itchen Abbas Anglo-Saxon cemetery – major discoveries', *Winchester Museums Service Newsletter* 12, 6–7.

Meaney, A. L. and Hawkes, S. C. 1970: *Two Anglo-Saxon cemeteries at Winnall, Winchester, Hampshire* (Soc. Medieval Archaeol. Monograph 4).

Mercer, R. 1980: *Hambledon Hill. A Neolithic enclosure.* Edinburgh.

Millett, M. with James S. 1983: 'Excavations at Cowdery's Down, Basingstoke, Hampshire, 1978–81', *Archaeol. J.* 140, 151–279.

Monk, M. 1987: 'The botanical remains', in C. S. Green 1987, 132–7.

Morton, A. D. (ed.) 1992: *Excavations at Hamwic. Volume 1: excavations 1946–83, excluding Six Dials and Melbourne Street* (Council for British Archaeology Research Report 84). London.

Musty, J. 1969: 'The excavation of two barrows, one of Saxon date, at Ford, Laverstock, near Salisbury, Wiltshire', *Antiq. J.* 49, 98–117.

Musty, J. and Stratton, J. E. D. 1964: 'A Saxon cemetery at Winterbourne Gunner, near Salisbury', *Wilts Archaeol. and Nat. Hist. Mag.* 59, 86–109.

Myres, J. N. L. 1986: *The English settlements*. Oxford.

Nelson, J. 1991: 'Reconstructing a royal family: reflections on Alfred, from Asser, chapter 2', in I. N. Wood and N. Lund (eds), *People and places in northern Europe 500–1600. Essays in honour of Peter Hayes Sawyer*, 47–66.

Pitt Rivers, A. 1892: *Excavations in Bokerly and Wansdyke, Dorset and Wiltshire 1888–1891, with observations on the human remains*. Vol III. London.

Pitt Rivers, A. 1898: *Excavations in Cranborne Chase near Rushmore on the borders of Dorset and Wiltshire 1893–1896*. Vol IV. London.

Rahtz, P. A. 1969: 'Cannington hillfort 1963', *Procs Somerset Archaeol. and Nat. Hist. Soc.* 113, 56–68.

Rahtz, P. A. and Fowler, P. J. 1972: 'Somerset AD 400–700', in P. J. Fowler (ed.) 1972, 187–221.

Rahtz, P. A. and Watts, L. 1989: 'Pagans Hill revisited', *Archaeol. J.* 146, 330–71.

Rahtz, P. A. *et al.* 1992: *Cadbury Congresbury 1968–73. A late/post-Roman hilltop settlement in Somerset* (British Archaeol. Reports, British Series 223). Oxford.

Rivet, A. L. F. 1958: *Town and country in Roman Britain.* London.

Rivet, A. L. F. and Smith, C. 1981: *The place-names of Roman Britain.* London.

Royal Commission on Historical Monuments (RCHM) 1970a: *An Inventory of Historical Monuments in the County of Dorset. Vol Two. South-East.* Part Two. London.

Royal Commission on Historical Monuments (RCHM) 1970b: *An Inventory of Historical Monuments in the County of Dorset. Vol Three. Central Dorset.* London.

Schwieso, J. 1979: 'The Anglo-Saxon burials', in G. J. Wainwright, *Mount Pleasant, Dorset: excavations 1970–1971* (Reports of Research Committee of Soc of Antiquaries of London XXXVII), 181–3.

Scott, I. R. 1991: 'King's Somborne – County Primary School', in *Archaeology in Hampshire* (Hants County Council Planning Dept, Annual Report for 1990), 38.

Scull, C. J. 1992: 'Before Sutton Hoo: structures of power and society in early East Anglia', in M. O. H. Carver (ed.), *The age of Sutton Hoo. The seventh century in north-western Europe.* Woodbridge.

Sims-Williams, P. 1983: 'The settlement of England in Bede and the *Chronicle*', *Anglo-Saxon England* XII, 1–41.

Speake, G. 1989: *A Saxon bed burial on Swallowcliffe Down. Excavations by F. de M. Vatcher* (English Heritage Archaeol. Report no. 10). London.

Stenton, F. M. 1913: *The early history of the abbey of Abingdon.* Reading.

Stenton, F. M. 1971: *Anglo-Saxon England.* Third edition. Oxford.

Swan, V. G. 1984: *The pottery kilns of Roman Britain* (Royal Commission on Historical Monuments. Supplementary Series: 5). London.

Swanton, M. J. 1973: *The spearheads of the Anglo-Saxon settlements* (The Royal Archaeological Institute). London.

Swanton, M. J. 1974: *A corpus of pagan Anglo-Saxon spear-types* (British Archaeol. Reports, British Series 7). Oxford.

Taylor, R. F. 1967: 'An Anglo-Saxon cemetery at Compton Pauncefoot', *Procs Somerset Archaeol. and Nat. Hist. Soc.* 111, 67–9.

Tingle, M. 1991: *The Vale of the White Horse survey* (British Archaeol. Reports, British Series, 218). Oxford.

Thomas, C. 1981: *Christianity in Roman Britain to AD 500.* London.

Waton, P. V. 1982: 'Man's impact on the chalklands: some new pollen evidence', in M. Bell and S. Limbrey (eds), *Archaeological aspects of woodland ecology* (Symposium of the Association for Environmental Archaeology No. 2), 75–91 (British Archaeol. Reports, International Series 146). Oxford.

Welch, M. G. 1985: 'Rural settlement patterns in the early and middle Anglo-Saxon periods', *Landscape History* 7, 14–25.

Welch, M. G. 1992: *Anglo-Saxon England.* London.

West, S. E. 1985: *West Stow. The Anglo-Saxon village.* Vols 1 and 2 (East Anglian Archaeol. Report No. 24).

Wheeler, R. E. M. 1943: *Maiden Castle, Dorset* (Reports of Research Committee of Soc. of Antiquaries of London XII). Oxford.

Whitelock, D. *et al.* (eds) 1961: *The Anglo-Saxon Chronicle. A revised translation.* London.

Winterbottom, M. (ed.) 1978: *Gildas. The Ruin of Britain and other works* (History from the sources. General Editor: J. Morris). Chichester.

Yorke, B. 1989: 'The Jutes of Hampshire and Wight and the origins of Wessex', in S. Bassett (ed.), *The origins of Anglo-Saxon kingdoms* (Studies in the early history of Britain) 84–96. Leicester.

Yorke, B. 1990: *Kings and kingdoms of early Anglo-Saxon England.* London.

Yorke, B. 1993: 'Fact or fiction? The written evidence for the fifth and sixth centuries AD', *Anglo-Saxon Studies in Archaeology and History* 6, 45–50.

Youngs, S. M. *et al.* 1985: Medieval Britain and Ireland in 1984, *Medieval Archaeol.* XXIX, 158–230.

2. The Archaeology of Eighth- to Eleventh-Century Wessex

David A. Hinton

The development of Wessex into a powerful kingdom can be recognised in the archaeological evidence of a more exploitative agricultural regime and progressively more organised trading systems. The kingdom had ceased to have autonomous functions by the end of William the Conqueror's reign.

Introduction

Considerable attention has been paid in recent years to the formation of the early Anglo-Saxon kingdoms, both by historians and by archaeologists (e.g. Bassett (ed.) 1989; Carver (ed.) 1992). The later Saxon period has not been a focus for so much debate and there have been fewer new approaches. Historians tend still to give a lead to archaeologists, rather than being their equal partners. There are fewer uncertainties over the exactitude of chronicled dates, and on whether recorded events actually occurred; the narrative framework is much less open to challenge. Furthermore, there is less diversity in some parts of the archaeological record after the end of the seventh century: burials become more uniform, social hierarchies seem more clearly apparent in the often limited settlement evidence, at least so far as enclosed residences and castles show, and exotic objects are less frequently found. After the volatility of kingdom establishment, there seems less room for manoeuvring over interpretation. There are, of course, new developments, a reflection of different sorts of complexity; the early Anglo-Saxon period may be called one of 'early complex societies', or 'chieftainships', but there is no equivalent phrase for what follows, not least because Europe is almost alone in having developed from an 'early' phase, so that 'feudalism' tends to be applied to any state system with an element of strong central control, rather than to be used in its more restricted sense, involving vassalage and personal service.

Kings, Coins and the Church

Despite the seventh-century developments, it remains difficult to establish precisely how strong was kings' control at the beginning of the eighth century. The most obvious way in which this question first arises is through interpretations of what were, for southern England at least, new economic systems, using coinage and regulated places for some forms of exchange. It is virtually beyond dispute that in the tenth century the central authority issued the former and took an interest in the latter: it is indisputable because documents like law-codes make express statements. This is not true of the eighth century, in the area that it is by then correct to call Wessex (Yorke 1990, 131–2, 137–8): King Ine's law-code of 688x96 makes no mention of minting rights, and its only direct reference to traders is that they should have witnesses to transactions 'in the countryside' (Whitelock 1955, 367). This seems as likely to have been intended to prevent bloody wrangling over property as to promote an economic system by which merchants brought their goods to the king ('directional trading'), although Whitelock took 'in the countryside' to mean that use of a *port* was already a viable alternative (*loc. cit.* n.4). As they were foreigners, overseas or non-Wessex traders would have been under royal protection, but the value of their *wergilds* is unfortunately not stated. The possibility that one early form of the silver coins usually called *sceattas*, Series W, was minted in Wessex has recently been mooted on the basis of its distribution (Metcalf 1993, 154–7) and could reflect inland trading at a limited level, perhaps using old hill-forts as occasional *ports*.

Most of the early eighth-century coins do not have inscriptions identifying where or by whom they were issued. Nevertheless, it is very likely that there was a mint in Wessex at Hamwic (Saxon Southampton) during the eighth century, because it is there that most of the Series H *sceattas* of Types 39 and 49 have been found (Metcalf 1993, 4). Series H coins are otherwise few in number and Type 49 is all but confined to Wessex (*ibid.* 22). Other *sceattas*, from other kingdoms, are also found, but in small numbers after the early eighth century (Fig. 2.1). It is not clear, therefore, whether those non-Wessex

Fig. 2.1 *Sceattas', probably of the first two thirds of the eighth century, excavated in Saxon Southampton. Top: Series X Type 81, perhaps an English imitation of a series thought to have been minted in Denmark, called by numismatists the 'Woden/Monster' type; the obverse has a face surrounded by hair and beard, the reverse a cross. Diameter 11mm. Bottom: Series W Type 54, one of the very few Southampton coins from a grave, found close to a skull and quite possibly deliberately deposited rather than dropped in accidentally as the grave was refilled; obverse, a half-length figure holding two long-shafted crosses; reverse, a cross-crosslet (i.e. with transverse lines through the tops of the arms) with a saltire cross. Diameter 11mm.*

coins are few because they were deliberately excluded – by a central authority anxious to exercise a monopoly – or if they are few because there was little use of or demand for any coins in Wessex outside Southampton, or if Wessex was suffering from an unfavourable balance of trade. Indeed, it is not known if the coinage was already regulated by Wessex kings, or merely tolerated by them, with the issuers being merchants or churchmen (*ibid.* 15–17). Although Metcalf inclines to the view that royal control is the more probable, it cannot be taken for granted that what happened in Wessex was the same as in other areas, where the evidence of royal involvement is just a little stronger. Similarly, it cannot be assumed that, because kings' interest in London and its toll revenues can be demonstrated from extant charters, a king

was also interested in Hamwic, at least until well into the ninth century (Morton 1992, 27).

Morton's careful re-assessment of all the available evidence has suggested that the foundation of Hamwic need have been no earlier than the beginning of the eighth century, despite the presence in it of a few objects that may be of seventh-century manufacture (Morton 1992, 28). It grew rapidly, to cover some 42 hectares or more (*ibid.* 29). This implies a considerable influx of people, and an organised system of food supply to sustain them is suggested by the animal-bone evidence (Bourdillon 1979, 185). Again, royal control is a plausible explanation. With Wessex newly enlarged by conquest, and the profits of the Isle of Wight to be exploited, who better than the king to set all these developments in train (e.g. Yorke 1990, 140)? The answer could, of course, be the Church: although there is no particular evidence to favour that suggestion, it is worth emphasising that we do not know whether King Ine would have had the slightest idea of what a *mercimonium* was, or would have understood that it would be a good thing to have.

That the Church should have been a catalyst for economic as well as for religious developments was almost inevitable, given its requirement for endowments to support its priests and its institutions. Although much of the produce of its estates could be consumed by its own members, it could not be self-sufficient in everything. The Church in Wessex may not have had very profitable dealings with the outside world, however. The seventh-century church at Winchester was a substantial stone structure and it received some augmentation before the tenth century, although full details are not yet available. It seems to have had glazed windows (Biddle and Hunter 1990, 352–7). Glastonbury, too, was a large stone church, apparently enlarged in the eighth century (Radford 1981, 117–8), and there was perhaps another at Wareham (RCHM 1970, 309–10). Almost nothing that can certainly be attributed to this period survives at such establishments as Wimborne, Sherborne or Malmesbury, despite their fame. Recent discoveries at church sites in eastern England suggest a level of material culture (e.g. Webster and Backhouse (eds) 1991) more opulent than anything found in Wessex attributable to the eighth century: the excavations in Winchester included areas near to the minster, but very few artefacts were revealed (Biddle 1990), and other such sites have been no more fruitful. In the same way, Wessex has no de luxe manuscripts ascribed to it. Nor is there much evidence of commercial prosperity: Hamwic has its coins, and glass, but little else that suggests either wide-scale, long-distance or prestigious trading. The imported pottery seems mostly to have come from northern France (Hodges 1991). Despite its westwards expansion, Wessex has none of the E-ware pottery, thought to be from south-west France, which ought to reveal trade with southern Europe (Thomas 1990, 20–21). Apart from a single Islamic dirham of *c.* 765–814 from Hamwic (Brown 1988, 25–6), there is nothing to suggest any such contacts, let alone regular exchange. Wessex was perhaps unable to share to a great extent in the main English commerce of the eighth century, which was dominated by the Frankish-Frisian-southern Scandinavian nexus. Geographically, it was a little isolated: politically, it was repressed by and perhaps sometimes paying tribute to Mercia after the death of King Ine in 726 (Yorke 1990, 140–2; the Tribal Hidage (*ibid*. 9–12) may be a record of such payments).

Rural Settlement

Yorke points out that, despite political problems, the post-Ine period may have been one of consolidation in Wessex (1990, 141): the archaeological record provides evidence of this not only in the continued (if perhaps fluctuating) use of Hamwic, but also by economic developments in the countryside. The discovery of iron-smelting evidence is becoming almost a pattern: to Ramsbury, Wiltshire (Haslam 1980), can now be added two Dorset sites, Gillingham (Heaton 1992) and Worgret (Hinton 1992). Dendrochronology at the latter produced a date of between AD 664 and 709 for a structure, perhaps a mill, filled with slag and furnace residues. Archaeomagnetic dating of ovens at Gillingham suggests the eighth century (radiocarbon suggests the seventh, but such dating is often too early). Other sites with slag of similar type include Wimborne, Dorset, where it is not precisely dated, and Romsey, Hampshire (McDonnell 1992). All these sites may have had royal or church associations, which suggests that these major land-owners were setting out to increase the profitability, or at least the productive capacity, of their estates.

None of these iron-producing sites, except Ramsbury, has yielded pre-Conquest artefacts, even sherds of pottery that can certainly be attributed to a date earlier than the twelfth century. At Ramsbury, the sherds were all chaff-tempered types (also known as grass- or organic-tempered); it is one of the major frustrations of the archaeology of this period that there are so few sites that produce any pottery at all, and that when it is found, it has such a wide date range, with Ramsbury taking chaff-tempered ware into the ninth century (Haslam 1980, 30–1). Hamwic was using other indigenous wares (Timby 1988, 80–90), and examples occur elsewhere in Hampshire (*ibid*. 110), but apparently in very few other Wessex counties. Nor do they get recovered in field-walking, even when it is as systematically and rigorously conducted as the work by the Avon Valley Archaeological Research Group (Light *et al.* forthcoming). A number of sites on the Avon's river terraces have been identified from chaff-tempered pottery, but this only means deposition at some time between the fifth and ninth centuries: a more precise pattern of abandonment and foundation of sites cannot yet be established in Wessex as it can be further east, where Ipswich-type wares at least indicate sites with seventh-century or later use (e.g. Newman 1992).

One recently published site, Abbots Worthy in the Itchen valley (Fig. 2.2; Fasham and Whinney 1991), epitomises some of the problems. Firstly, the Anglo-Saxon features lay deeply buried by a build-up of colluvium, presumably eroded – by ploughing? – from the slopes on either side, and could not have been located either by field-walking, by geophysics or by air photography. Secondly, most of the artefacts that were recovered came from the infill of a single sunken-featured building, whereas the only other sunken-featured building contained very few, as did pits. This means that there was a bias in the data towards a single feature, the parallels to the pottery from which pointed to a sixth-century date. That would probably have become the accepted century for the settlement as a whole if pottery had been all that was recovered. Fortunately, a few bone and metal artefacts suggested at least eighth-century dates, and that the area was in use for a minimum of 200 years, though not necessarily continuously, and with occupation scattered over a distance of 140 metres or more. There may be many other such sites hidden in valley bottoms.

Just as there is uncertainty over the length of use of chaff-tempered ware, so too it remains unknown for how long the use of sunken-featured buildings continued: what that use may have been is considered above by Eagles (chapter 1). There is no evidence that they outlasted the eighth century in Wessex, but because there are so few rural sites that can be positively dated until pottery becomes considerably more prolific, in the twelfth century, later examples may yet be found. An important contribution to this discussion has been made by the site at Trowbridge, Wiltshire, where traces of earlier occupation underlay a cemetery, church and castle (Fig. 2.4; Graham and Davies 1993). Here, there was a sunken-featured building and, apparently of the same period, there were some ground-level buildings, of beam-slot construction, succeeded by others of post-hole type. The pottery in the fill of the sunken-featured building was not chaff-tempered, though there was pottery of this type on the site. Its absence from the fill may be fortuitous, its presence in later levels caused by residuality: but it may be that it was a late arrival here, not in use until the ninth century or even later. With only twelve sherds being found, the sample is too small for any firm conclusions to be drawn (Mepham 1993, 102–4). Because of such problems, it is not certain that the site remained in continuous use before a church was built, in or after the middle of the tenth century. In the eleventh, a manorial enclosure indicates high-status occupation, as do coins, a brooch and other artefacts, and this is confirmed by its subsequent use as a castle site. It would not, however, be possible to take that interpretation of its status back to the pre-church occupation with any certainty: Graham and Davies compare the site's location and the size of its buildings to Cowdery's Down, Hampshire, but are right to leave open whether it already had the status ascribed to the final phase of the large enclosure at that Hamp-

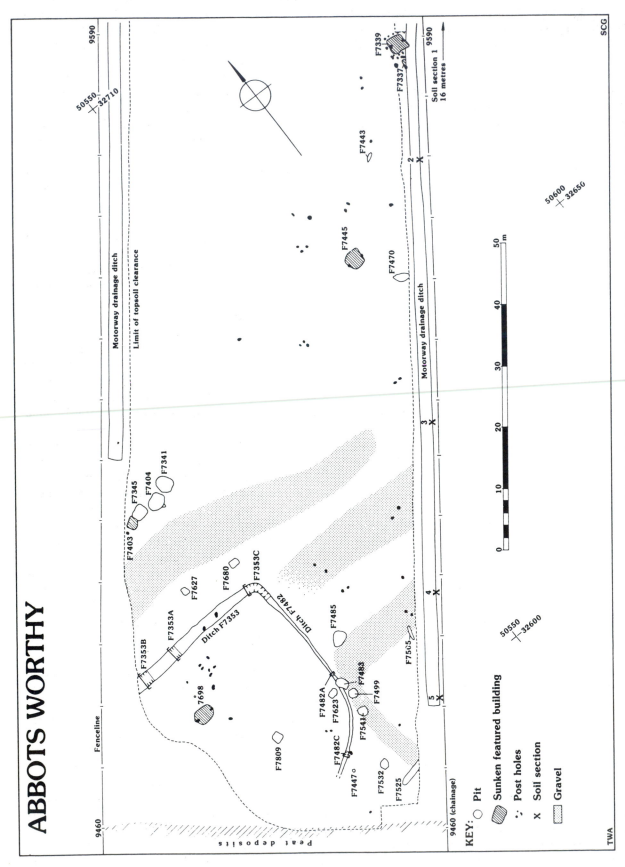

Fig. 2.2 Abbots Worthy (Ha). General plan of the excavations of the Anglo-Saxon settlement found during top-soil stripping for the M3 motorway east of Winchester. Copyright Wessex Archaeology, reproduced by permission.

shire site, or whether Trowbridge was initially no more than a typical rural settlement.

There is such a dearth of mid and late Saxon rural settlement excavation in Wessex that there are inadequate criteria by which to judge a site like Trowbridge which yields limited, albeit extremely welcome, information. But it also shows that sites where evidence is even more vestigial cannot be reliably placed in any precise chronological framework: the post-Roman occupation west of the River Avon at Whitsbury Castle is an example, where chaff-tempered pottery and a bone pin-beater could be an example of fifth-/sixth-century re-use of a hillfort, or the eighth-/ninth-century beginnings of a small settlement later to be provided with a church, half a mile away (Ellison and Rahtz 1987, 65, 75, 80). Similar problems arise with another Avon Valley site, Downton, where a large pit containing chaff-tempered and other pottery also floats between the fifth and the ninth centuries (Rahtz 1964). Downton, the site of a Roman villa, went on to become a hundred centre and an estate of the bishops of Winchester. Rather like Ramsbury, it may have been an important eighth-/ninth-century focus, but the archaeological evidence is imprecise. There is no clear sequential path from settlement to settlement-with-church to village: Cowage Farm, Wiltshire, which apparently goes no further along that route than settlement-with-church, shows that a steady chronological sequence of development cannot be assumed (Hinchliffe 1986). For reasons like this, it seems better not to draw into the discussion any site from which the available evidence has yet to be published, even though at one end of Wessex that precludes consideration of the exciting work recently done by Hughes in the Meon Valley (rightly lauded by Hamerow 1991, 15), and at the other of the large excavations outside Dorchester at Alington Avenue (Davies *et al.* 1985, 108–10), at which various structures may turn out to belong to the period after the West Saxon conquest of Dorset, by which time Poundbury had perhaps gone out of use (see Eagles, above).

It is another difficulty of Wessex's early medieval archaeology that there is an imbalance between evidence from coastal sites in Hampshire and from the Isle of Wight and Dorset. Although both the latter have important Roman sites in the inter-tidal zone, it is not possible to point to equivalents not only to Hamwic, but to a fringe of sites around Portsmouth Harbour, like Fareham (Holmes 1978, 46, 53–4), presumably exploiting marine resources such as salt and fish, as well as locally fertile land. Within Christchurch Harbour, the Bargates cemetery at Christchurch remains isolated, apart from an enigmatic oven cut by a Saxo-Norman ditch and a scatter of stray finds (Jarvis 1983, 17 and 37). It is most unlikely that Poole Harbour was not being used, but the direct evidence is still lacking; even Wareham has produced little to match the importance of its church – a few pottery sherds and an inadequately-provenanced eighth-century *sceatta* (Rigold and Metcalf 1977, 49 – though its provenance is

better than Dorset's only other coastal coin of the *sceatta* type, which might be from Weymouth and might be Roman (*ibid.*)!). More than anything else, the 150 of these coins (found by 1987: Metcalf 1988, 17) make Hamwic so exceptional. Their number becomes even more remarkable when contrasted to the other Hampshire coastal site which has yielded really substantial material, Portchester Castle, where no *sceattas* were found despite a sequence of pits, wells and structures, some of which fall within the eighth century (Cunliffe 1976, 122–3). Since the land there was owned by the Bishop of Winchester in 904, there is a presumption that it was an episcopal estate for some time before that, although there is nothing to define a particular episode to mark its acquisition. Nor is there anything in its archaeology to give a clear indication of its function in the eighth century: an Islamic glass fragment which may be eighth century (Harden 1976) and a possible Breton sherd (Hodges 1976, 192–3) are not enough to indicate that the bishops were using Portchester as a landing-place on any regular basis. Potentially, the site is of great interest as an example of an estate centre with a supplementary role: in practice, it is difficult to establish what activities were taking place within it. The use of pits to dispose of rubbish, instead of spreading it as manure upon neighbouring fields, might have seemed a useful pointer to an interpretation of the site as having been somewhat isolated from its immediate surroundings, receiving foodstuffs but not being involved in their production. But this can no longer be regarded as tenable, since there were pits ultimately at least used for cess disposal, and others of uncertain use, at Abbots Worthy (Fasham and Whinney 1991, 76). Whatever they were for, it would be difficult to maintain that that site was not part of the local agricultural regime.

It is from the fills of pits such as these, and from those of sunken-featured buildings, that some of the best environmental data are derived. At Abbots Worthy, a mixed agricultural economy seems to have been practised: the local calcareous soils were especially suitable for barley, which was the cereal most represented by surviving grains, with wheat about half as frequent; there were a few oats, a single grain of rye, and legumes such as peas and beans (Carruthers 1991). Similar results are reported from other Hampshire sites, with barley always predominant (Green 1991). Farm animals were cows, sheep, pigs and a few horses (Coy 1991). There was little sign of reliance upon wild resources – no deer bones, a few hedge fruits. Overall, the evidence is in harmony with the only pollen sample from the area, from Winnall Moors, which shows no total break in cereal production – but is not accompanied by a sequence of radiocarbon dates; it could be that a period of cereal decline is early post-Roman – with rye and hemp or hops being added to the cultivar assemblage; a change to a higher grass component could indicate more emphasis on local sheep-rearing in the later Middle Ages (Waton 1982). The other rural site which has yielded a reasonable amount of fairly securely dated environmental evidence for the eighth and ninth centuries is Ramsbury, where deer bones were present in some numbers, presumably reflecting local woodlands and the iron-makers' capacity to exploit them (Coy 1980, 49–51). Most other rural assemblages, such as they are, are either earlier in date or have a wide date range, such as The Mount, Glastonbury, where there were also relatively large numbers of deer bones (Darvill and Coy 1984/5). Deer were also a significant component at Portchester, but in other respects the bones from that site show the high quality of the local agricultural regime, rather than any special selection of preferred joints for consumption by an elite group (Grant 1976, 286). By far the largest assemblage, however, is that from Hamwic, where reliance upon food supplies from outside the settlement's own terrain was essential, and which shows the region's ability to supply large amounts of agricultural surplus (Bourdillon 1988).

Environmental assemblages such as these caution against over-ready acceptance of one aspect of the 'multiple estate' model that is sometimes propounded; that there were large estates, comprising many different occupation sites, can be demonstrated (e.g. for the upper Itchen valley, Klingelhöfer 1990), but this does not mean that each unit specialised to any very great extent upon a particular crop or stock. Abbots Worthy shows how such a view can develop from examination of a too-narrow range of deposits; there were significant differences between the pit and the sunken-featured building fills so far as ratios of surviving animal bones were concerned (Coy 1991, 61), and peas were found in only a single pit (Carruthers 1991, 72–3). The local environment, with its calcareous soil, biased its farmers towards barley, but theirs was seemingly a mixed regime, as it probably was elsewhere, with self-sufficiency as the main goal for each unit. At the same time, some surpluses were passed on to landlords; the readiness with which Hamwic was supplied suggests that surpluses were not inconsiderable. Similarly, a scale of production beyond a domestic norm is suggested by the Gillingham ovens, which are interpreted as being for cereal processing operated at the behest of a large land-owner (Heaton 1992). The Worgret structure may have been a mill for both iron and grain; the reappearance of mills for cereal-grinding is another example of larger-scale production processes, involving landlord investment and control (Hinton 1992).

Material Prosperity

The domination of an elite becomes more recognisable through the evidence of greater material prosperity in the ninth than in the eighth century. The ninth-century assemblage at Portchester is noticeably different from that of the eighth: there are three coins, one a gold imitative *solidus* (Pagan 1976), and two silver objects (Hinton and Welch 1976, 214–6), though no more glass. This prosperity is echoed elsewhere in ninth-century Wessex:

the Laverstock gold ring (Wilson 1964, no. 31) and the Sevington silver hoard, both from Wiltshire (*ibid.* nos 67–79), are assuredly ninth-century because of the former's inscription with the name of King Æthelwulf (828–58) and the latter's association with coins of *c.* 850: other objects are less securely dated, though probably of the period (e.g. Webster and Backhouse (eds) 1991, nos 200 and 256). Other kingdoms are able to show comparable objects, but it is as though Wessex had emerged from being a relative backwater and could now acquire considerable wealth. The most famous object of the period is the Alfred Jewel, which may have been a royal gift to a church; the Bowleaze Cove 'mount' could have had the same function, even if not the same distinguished patron (*ibid.* nos 260 and 258). Wessex still does not seem to have produced lavishly decorated manuscripts, nor are there large church buildings positively attributable to the ninth century; there are, however, sculptures such as the Britford panels, the Colerne cross, some of the Ramsbury fragments and the Codford cross (*ibid.* p. 187 and no. 108), for which dating is stylistic, but for which the ninth century seems appropriate, and general opinion would incline to see the Winchester reliquary as rather earlier in the century than was originally proposed (*ibid.* no. 136). It is difficult for an archaeologist not to fall back upon the bayonet of historical texts at this point and to explain the new prosperity as a reaction to political events – King Egbert's conquests, King Æthelwulf's Frankish relations, and King Alfred's fight to his near-death with the Vikings. There may, of course, be other explanations: population increase, although there is no worthwhile demographic evidence, or climatic improvement, difficult though it is to date and unlikely as it is to have had much effect on lowland Wessex.

Hamwic's fortunes do not seem fully to correspond with these developments: there is a gold coin very similar to Portchester's (Pagan 1988, 71–2), but the ninth-century silver pennies from the excavations are considerably fewer than their predecessors, there being eighteen English and three Carolingian (Fig. 2.3; Metcalf 1988,

Fig. 2.3 Silver penny of Charles the Bald, 843–77, minted in Toulouse, from the Saxon Southampton excavations. A rare coin in France, and even more unusual in England. Diameter 21mm.

Fig. 2.4 *Trowbridge (Wi), phase plan of the Saxon features with (upper left) a sunken-featured building, structure 4, and traces of contemporary structures, and (lower right) the pre-castle manorial enclosure with the church, structure 17, external to it. Copyright Wessex Archaeology, reproduced by permission.*

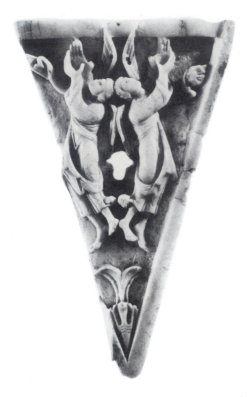

Fig. 2.5 *An ivory panel, perhaps from a casket or reliquary-shrine, found at St Cross, Winchester, showing two flying angels with outstretched arms. Late tenth or early eleventh century. Height 76mm. Copyright City of Winchester Museums, reproduced by permission.*

52–5). Morton (1992, 71–8) discusses the problem of nineteenth-century records that tell of many tenth-century pennies in hoards (Pagan 1988, 64–70) and opts for the view that transfer of activity to the Test-side site on the Southampton peninsula was a discontinuous process from *c.* 850 onwards, affected, but not mortally, by Viking raids and disruptions. It is not easy to reconcile this view with the proposal that there was a wholesale population shift to Winchester in the aftermath of raids in 840 and/or 842 (e.g. Kjølbye-Biddle 1992, 224).

King Alfred's defence of Wessex against the Vikings is well, or at least quite lengthily, recorded in the Anglo-Saxon Chronicle and elsewhere. For an archaeological manifestation, it is natural to turn to the *burhs* of the Burghal Hidage (Hill and Rumble, forthcoming). Suffice it to say that of those places mentioned in that document, few would be recognised from their archaeology as having been built, or brought back into use, in the late ninth or early tenth century. The similarity between Wareham, Wallingford and Cricklade might have been observed, but for the most part the banks and ditches that have been excavated at various *burhs* would float as awkwardly in chronologies as does Wansdyke. Indeed, many of them should still do so, for when Asser says of Wareham that the Vikings in 876 went to a 'fortified site', it suggests an already existing *burh* in contrast to,

for example, Reading, where in 871 they 'constructed a rampart' after their arrival (Keynes and Lapidge 1983, 78, 82 and *contra* 245). The development of some of the *burhs* into towns, and of other places taking the same path, has also been much discussed (summaries include Clarke and Ambrosiani 1991), and their emergence as a significant and stable element during the tenth and eleventh centuries is to be seen as a physical manifestation of a different system of exchange, increasingly using regular markets and coinage, but with the latter at least as much required to make tax payments as to purchase goods, since Domesday Book makes clear that rents were paid in cash, as well as in kind and by service, depending upon conditions of tenure.

The profits of lordly exactions, and perhaps an increasing wish to be seen as clearly distinct from the rest of the population, seem to be evidenced by a number of enclosures which probably had aristocratic status: that at Trowbridge is in the classic manorial position next to a church (Fig. 2.4; Graham and Davies 1993, 324–6) and was succeeded by a castle, from which the town developed by the end of the twelfth century. Its high eleventh-century status is also shown by three English silver pennies, two most unusual pennies from Dublin and a coin-brooch (Robinson 1993, 78–80), as well as a silver pin and gold thread (Mills 1993a, 81). It also yielded some iron slags, a crucible used in copper-alloy production (McDonnell 1993) and implements used in textile manufacture. It thus joins the other published Wessex late Saxon royal and aristocratic sites which were production centres: Faccombe Netherton, Hampshire (Fairbrother 1990), Cheddar, Somerset (Rahtz 1979) and Portchester (Cunliffe 1976). In their various ways, these sites show that the craft and industrial functions which are associated with medieval towns were not as closely confined to them as they were to be in the twelfth century. Their aisled and other halls (for which see also Waltham: Lewis 1985), with near-by churches or internal chapels, suggest relatively lavish life-styles for their owners when they visited, with a nucleus of servants to turn agricultural products into food, and visiting craftsmen making ornaments.

Craftsmen were also of course working in the service of the Church, as were clerics who were scribes and illuminators. The later tenth century saw the Reform movement, and a number of decorated books produced in consequence of it; the Benedictional of St Aethelwold is the most lavish (Backhouse *et al.* (eds) 1984, no. 37), and its dedication and some of its pictures tie its production to Winchester, as does the subject matter of the New Minster Charter and the same house's *Liber Vitae* (*ibid.* nos 26 and 62). A number of other attributions to Winchester, notably those of pre-Reform manuscripts, do not stand up to scrutiny by modern palaeographers (Dumville 1992, 60–88 and 97–98), although it remains likely that the great majority are products of the south of England. Nor can it be assumed that the magnificent embroideries made to the order of Aelfflaed for Bishop Frithestan were made in Winchester just because Frithestan was the bishop there and the Nunnaminster was a house under royal patronage where there could have been the necessary skills (*ibid.* 87). Objects found in Winchester need not have been made there (Fig. 2.5). Nevertheless, their findspots show that it was there that they were used, and it must have been there that Frithestan wore his robes. The ability of the place to display such fineries, and its major churches, two newly founded, testify to its tenth-century wealth and prestige.

Apart from Winchester, there were other new foundations and enlargements, notably Glastonbury (e.g. Radford 1981). There is a wider range of sculptures, the East Stour cross fragment being an outstanding example (Backhouse *et al.* (eds) 1984, no. 23). As is examined elsewhere in this volume, it is a period in which many new churches were founded, some of which cost their patrons or owners considerable sums. Around 1100, even a relatively minor church like Wareham's St Martin could have fine wall-paintings illustrating stories and ideas only recently come into circulation (Park 1990). Considerable expansion of the economy is implied by such expenditure, and should perhaps be seen as part of the more general expansion that took the Wessex dynasty to the kingship of the whole of England.

Production and Markets

Economic developments included various sorts of production as well as those attested in aristocratic residences and the new towns. For obvious reasons, salt had to be extracted from coastal environments where there were no restrictions on space to inhibit the spread of debris (Keen 1991, 22–4: Hampshire and Wight need comparable evaluations). In Wessex, unlike other parts of England, pottery seems to have been largely a non-urban craft: for Hampshire, kilns at Michelmersh are known, and suspected in Boarhunt; no glazed Winchester-type ware kilns have been located, but green-glazed pottery may have been made in Southampton, where wasters occur; no production sites have been found in Dorset; the suggestion that a French potter worked at Castle Neroche, Somerset, has been discredited; in Wiltshire, Domesday Book refers to potters in Westbury (references in McCarthy and Brooks 1988) – the place-name Potterne, 'the workshop of the potters', may not mean that pottery was made there in the Middle Ages, but that the prolific Bronze Age site now known there had been recognised and was well-enough known to be used as an appellative (Parsons 1991, 7–8). Metal extraction and stone quarrying may have been practised, but on a scale too small to be of much significance: the iron ores smelted are likely to have been superficial deposits, collected when required, augmented by steel from unknown sources (Tylecote 1990, 140–4). Smithing probably took place fairly widely, as slags would show: lack of evidence from

rural, non-aristocratic sites may well be due to paucity of excavation, not of production. That is probably a contrast to copper-alloy and precious-metal working, which was certainly practised in urban Winchester, as it had been at Hamwic, and is likely to have been too specialised to be a rural craft (Bayley and Barclay 1990), although as Trowbridge and other sites show, itinerants were probably also visiting particular places. Weaving was still practised on vertical looms, though the horizontal type, with its call on specialists, was coming into use, boosting towns like Winchester (Keene 1990, 203–5) and taking that craft out of the countryside.

The development into towns of many places within Wessex is part of a wider European phenomenon of the tenth and eleventh centuries and the programme of work at Winchester is an important contribution to its study (e.g. Biddle (ed.) 1976; Biddle 1990). Excavations there show dense use in the pre-Norman period, with buildings, pits and craft evidence (e.g. Scobie 1991, 34–9), and streets such as the intra-mural one which was remetalled nine times before being sealed by the castle (Biddle and Keene 1976, 278). Other Wessex towns have revealed less substantial evidence. A new review of the late Saxon Test-side settlement at Southampton is awaited, but the most recent synopsis indicates patchy rather than prolific use (Holdsworth 1984). Wareham seems to have grown slowly, with a little tenth-century material (Hinton and Hodges 1977). In Bath, black-earth deposits continued to build up in some areas until perhaps as late as the eleventh century, but that occupation near-by was causing these accumulations is shown by pottery that includes two organic-tempered sherds probably pre-dating the tenth century; pottery becomes much more prolific from the late tenth onwards, however (Davenport (ed.) 1991; Vince 1991, 43, 48, 70, 102). It is probably a coincidence rather than a sign of concentrated militarism that both these Burghal Hidage *burhs* have yielded late Saxon swords (Hinton and Okasha 1977; Watkins and Brown 1991). Bristol's rapid growth in the eleventh century is shown by the coins issued from its mint and by mentions of it in Domesday Book, with the Irish slave trade an important factor not directly recognizable in the archaeological record. Neither at Ilchester nor at Taunton is there structural evidence, but pottery of the type known as Cheddar E, dated to the late tenth century, has been found at both (Vince 1991, 70). At the former, there was also a late tenth-century coin (Leach n.d. *c.* 1982, 12–13, 176–7, 240), at the latter three late Saxon objects (Leach (ed.) n.d. *c.* 1986 – the object published in fig. 48, 3 would now be seen as a late Saxon stirrup attachment: Robinson 1992).

Ilchester and Taunton are two of a number of places in Somerset and Wiltshire which, despite their small size, had urban status attributed to them by the location of a mint within them. This cannot be because of general economic expansion, or there would have been many more small mints in other areas. Hill's explanation that they were all on royal estates which had been reduced in extent, causing the king to create mints to offset his declining incomes (1978, 222), is less attractive than one which sees them as royal estate centres where there was a special requirement to turn food renders into cash for tax purposes; this is partly supported by the Axbridge Chronicle (Neale 1976), which suggests deliberate location of small markets close to royal residences where surplus produce could be sold; a mint would be an additional facility. A minster might be another factor in creating a parcel of functions at different locations within an estate, with centralisation as a later development (Aston 1986). The archaeological evidence and the later history of such places as Taunton shows that minting was not a major economic motor, however. The numbers of known coins issued from the Somerset and Wiltshire mints is very small (tables in Metcalf 1981, 68–78). Winchester is the only Wessex mint ever to have produced more than 10% of the various issues of coins made between *c.* 973 and *c.* 1066. For two issues, Wilton was responsible for over 3% of the known total; for three, Ilchester achieved over 2%. No other mint appears ever to have reached 2% – not even Bath, despite its proximity to Charterhouse, lead from which has been suggested as a source of wealth (Maddicott 1989, 48–50; *id.*, 1992, 184–5).

Expansion of the rural economy is no easier to chart from direct archaeological evidence. Indeed, landscape and settlement studies rely upon charters, church locations, place-names and Domesday Book rather than upon field-walking and excavation. Hedgerow dating by species count is occasionally possible within very broad limits (e.g. Roseaman 1991), but such research is confirmatory rather than predictive, since so much depends upon local environment. On Purbeck, for instance, the species count varies according to the geology (Moore *et al.* 1967, 206). The division of large estates into smaller units is discussed elsewhere in this volume (Hooke, chapter 4), and it is pointed out that reorganisation's effects eventually begin to show in such things as deer bones. Dated changes to field systems remain elusive to discover from physical survival. Even more frustrating is the absence of excavated farmstead or village house sites. The other contributors to this volume cannot look to evidence from them in their discussions of such matters as hamlet origins or village planning before the twelfth century. Wessex does not have a single site to compare to the Thames Valley's Wraysbury, where a model is suggested of tenth-century ridge-top development from a ninth-century nucleus, followed by partial abandonment and resettlement – a pattern of fluctuation (Astill and Lobb 1989).

Churches and Aristocrats

At Wraysbury, the proximity of the present church to the Saxon occupation makes it likely that the 13th-century building had a much earlier predecessor (Astill and Lobb 1989, 84). It is often the case that, once established, a church became a permanent feature, even if the settlement which it served did not thereafter remain stable in its occupation zones. Nevertheless, the structure at Cowage Farm suggests that early churches were not invariably to have long histories; presumably if a principal residence was abandoned, its church or chapel might not be maintained (above; for the relationship between minsters and lesser churches, see Hase, chapter 3). Cowage Farm does not seem to have had a graveyard, however, which might have been a major reason for retaining a church on a particular site. The survival of both a church and a graveyard at Trowbridge, even though this involved incorporation within the castle in the twelfth century, shows the strength of feeling which might be involved (Graham and Davies 1993, 63–74).

From cemeteries like Trowbridge's comes information about the later Anglo-Saxon and Norman population. Where details are available, the health and vigour of the people seem to have been quite good; at Trowbridge, mean heights were little different from to-day's; there were some cases of *cribra orbitalia* which may be inherited or may be caused by anaemia in childhood; several infections were severe enough to have affected bones, and there were several healed fractures – a fairly tough life-style is also indicated by osteo-arthritis, and lack of furniture to sit upon by squatting facets (Jenkins 1993). Similar facets were observed in the late Saxon/early Norman skeletons at Portchester (Hooper 1976, 242). Despite the anaemia possibility, reasonably robust skeletons indicate adequate food resources; if the population was growing, as is generally supposed, with the new towns absorbing at least part of the rural surplus, it is not possible to recognise any particular difficulty in supplying the increased numbers. A reduction in the size of cattle has been observed at some Wessex sites (Bourdillon 1993, 129) but, in general, animal-bone evidence, such as that from Trowbridge, suggests robust stock, albeit roughly treated (*ibid*. 136). Domesday Book implies high carrying capacities, with large sheep flocks, though both over and understocking on Abbotsbury Abbey's estates have been demonstrated from the Exon records (Keene 1991, 11–113); such variation may have been widespread, but the Exchequer Domesday does not enable it to be revealed.

Cemeteries also give some idea of contemporary attitudes to the dead, and belief in an after-life. That burial in churchyards had become universal by the ninth century is taken for granted, although Morton has shown that there are examples in Hamwic where no church or chapel has been found and burial seems to have taken place more or less anywhere within the town, although presumably licences of some sort were required (1992, 48–51). Even in late Saxon Winchester, two graves were found in the Brooks which may not have any connection to one of the very many churches (Scobie 1991, 37, 39; Kjølbye-Biddle 1992, 226, 233). It is interesting that there is a wide range of different burial methods known, in-

Fig. 2.6 *Corfe Castle (Do), from the west. The earliest surviving element, the eleventh-century hall, is incorporated within the bailey wall to the right; the wall towers are an addition by King John. The tall keep is of c. 1100. The castle is on a natural hill between two gaps in the chalk ridge.*

cluding the use of charcoal packing for some apparently important people (*ibid.* 228–33), yet at Trowbridge there was no sign of this, despite the presence of a richer element, demonstrated by grave slabs (Mills 1993b, 98). Charnel practices seem also to have varied, with re-interment being quite carefully done, at least of skulls, in several Trowbridge graves (Graham and Davies 1993, 67–70), whereas in Winchester pits seem to have been used. There is also a variety of different ways of lining graves, and supporting heads, which could reflect different local practices.

Trowbridge now joins Portchester as a second well-demonstrated example in Wessex of a Saxon manorial enclosure later converted into the site of a castle; Neroche in Somerset may be another, but its early earthwork may be prehistoric (Higham and Barker 1992, 49). At Corfe, Dorset, the remains of a substantial hall with herring-bone masonry may pre-date 1066, and the stories that accrued around the murder of Edward the Martyr imply a tenth-century royal residence in Corfe (despite use of its name in Domesday Book, Kingston, in the same parish, should perhaps be seen as an outlier rather than as

the original focus of the estate: RCHM 1970, 57–9 and 69–70; Bourne 1984/5). In 1066, the site of Corfe Castle was owned by the Abbess of Shaftesbury, so any royal hall may briefly have been in her hands. William the Conqueror's anxiety to acquire the site is probably testimony to its splendid setting in the midst of good hunting country rather than to its strategic significance (Fig. 2.6). Other castles which he built, like Winchester, or which were probably begun in his reign, like Portchester, had a more obvious national role.

Various studies have been made of the castles of Wessex, which in general serve to show a wide variety of reasons for choice of location: Marlborough's good communication links being contrasted to Ludgershall's convenient position for hunting in Chute Forest, for instance (Stevenson 1992). Although mottes were probably more frequently used, enclosures without mottes are common enough – in Hampshire, there were ten of the former to nine of the latter (Hughes 1989, 56), although such figures are not 'absolute' since excavations like Goltho have shown how sites could be transformed by removal (or addition) of a motte. Most of the smaller sites have no surviving buildings and are undocumented; precise dating is difficult and a particular owner's decision may be the initiating factor rather than any particular national emergency, such as the aftermath of the White Ship disaster in 1120 or the Anarchy of 1139–54; illicit castles were a constant problem (Pounds 1990, 29). In a few cases, castles are so close together that rivalries between neighbouring estate owners may be signalled, although more mundane explanations such as abandonment of one site for the other are equally possible (e.g. Lewis 1989). The effect of castles upon the landscape and its settlement patterns is considered by other contributors, as is that of the institutions of the Norman-period and later Church.

Perhaps more obviously than any other class of monument, castles bring Wessex into a European ambit, both politically and in terms of constructional features. These wider contacts can be seen, however, as part of a continuum, which began at the end of the seventh century with the kingdom's initial expansion and grew further with the success of its ruling dynasty in the ninth and tenth centuries. There was nothing ineluctable about that dynasty's progression from their original territory to control of a unit that was to become a recognisable state, for it was exceptional within a fragmented Europe largely composed of small kingdoms and petty duchies. Any cohesion which the old kingdom may have retained in the eleventh century under the great earldom of Wessex was finally lost after the Norman Conquest. The last vestiges of 'chieftainship' were eradicated, and a shire-based but ultimately coherent English kingship was achieved. Domesday Book does not even pay lip-service to the Wessex of Ine and Alfred. The subsequent archaeology of the area may sometimes point towards economic regionalism, but only within a national political and social structure.

References

Andrews, A. (ed.) 1988: *The Coins and Pottery from Hamwic*, Southampton, City Museums.

Astill, G. G. and Lobb, S. J. 1989: 'Excavation of prehistoric, Roman and Saxon deposits at Wraysbury, Berkshire', *Archaeological Journal*, 146, 68–134.

Aston, M. 1986: 'Post-Roman central places in Somerset', 49–77 in Grant (ed.).

Backhouse, J., Turner, D. H. and Webster, L. (eds) 1984: *The Golden Age of Anglo-Saxon Art, 966–1066*, London, British Museum Publications.

Bassett, S. (ed.) 1989: *The Origins of Anglo-Saxon Kingdoms*, Leicester, University Press.

Bassett, S. (ed.) 1992: *Death in Towns. Urban Responses to the Dying and the Dead*, Leicester, University Press.

Bayley, J. and Barclay, K. 1990: 'The crucibles, heating trays, parting sherds and related material', 175–98 in Biddle.

Bell, M., and Limbrey, S. (eds) 1982: *Archaeological Aspects of Woodland Economy*, Oxford, British Archaeological Reports International Series, 146.

Biddle, M. (ed.) 1976: *Winchester in the Early Middle Ages*, Winchester Studies 1, Oxford, Clarendon Press.

Biddle, M. 1990: *Object and Economy in Medieval Winchester*, Winchester Studies 7ii, Oxford, Clarendon Press.

Biddle, M. and Keene, D. J. 1976: 'Winchester in the eleventh and twelfth centuries', 241–448 in Biddle (ed.).

Blair, J. and Ramsay, N. (eds) 1991: *English Medieval Industries*, London/Rio, Hambledon Press.

Bourdillon, J. 1979: 'Town life and animal husbandry in the Southampton area, as suggested by the excavated bones', *Proceedings of the Hampshire Field Club and Archaeological Society*, 36 (1979), 181–92.

Bourdillon, J. 1988: 'Countryside and town: the animal resources of Saxon Southampton', 177–95 in Hooke (ed.).

Bourdillon, J. 1993: 'Animal bone', 127–36 in Graham and Davies.

Bourne, J. 1984/5: 'The castles of Marlborough and Ludgershall in the Middle Ages', *Wiltshire Archaeological and Natural History Magazine*, 85, 70–9.

Bowden, M., Mackay, D. and Topping, P. (eds) 1989: *From Cornwall to Caithness*, Oxford, British Archaeological Reports British Series, 209.

Carr, J. 1984/5: 'Excavations on the Mound, Glastonbury, Somerset, 1971', *Proceedings of the Somerset Archaeological and Natural History Society*, 129, 37–62.

Carruthers, W. 1991: 'The plant remains', 67–75 in Fasham and Whinney.

Carver, M. (ed.) 1992: *The Age of Sutton Hoo*, Woodbridge, Boydell.

Cather, S., Park, D. and Williamson, P. (eds) 1990: *Early Medieval Wall Painting and Painted Sculpture in England*, Oxford, British Archaeological Reports British Series, 216.

Clarke, H. and Ambrosiani, B. 1991: *Towns in the Viking Age*, Leicester, University Press.

Coy, J. P. 1980: 'The animal bones', 41–51 in Haslam.

Coy, J. P. 1991: 'The animal bones', 60–7 in Fasham and Whinney.

Cunliffe, B. 1976: *Excavations at Portchester Castle Vol. II: Saxon*, London, Society of Antiquaries.

Darvill, T. C. and Coy, J. P. 1984/5: 'Report on the Faunal Remains from the Mount, Glastonbury', 56–61 in Carr.

Davenport, P. (ed.) 1991: *Archaeology in Bath 1976–1985*, Oxford, University Committee for Archaeology, Monograph 28.

Davies, S. M., Stacey, L. and Woodward, P. J. 1985: 'Excavations at Alington Avenue, Fordington, Dorchester 1984/85: interim report', *Proceedings of the Dorset Natural History and Archaeological Society*, 107, 101–10.

Dumville, D. N. 1992: 'The Anglo-Saxon Chronicle and the origins of English square minuscule script', 55–139 in Dumville.

Dumville, D. N. 1992: *Wessex and England from Alfred to Edgar*, Woodbridge, Boydell Press.

Ellison, A. and Rahtz, P. 1987: 'Excavations at Whitsbury Castle Ditches, Hampshire, 1960', *Proceedings of the Hampshire Field Club and Archaeological Society*, 43, 63–81.

Fairbrother, J. R. 1990: *Faccombe Netherton*, London, British Museum Ocasional Paper 74, Department of Medieval and Later Antiquities.

Fasham, P. J. and Whinney, R. J. B. 1991: *Archaeology and the M3*, Trust for Wessex Archaeology, Hampshire Field

Club and Archaeological Society Monograph 7.

Graham, A. H. and Davies, S. M. 1993: *Excavations in Trowbridge, Wiltshire, 1977 and 1986–1988*, Salisbury, Wessex Archaeology Report 2.

Grant, A. 1976: 'The animal bones', 262–87 in Cunliffe.

Grant, E. (ed.) 1986: *Central Places, Archaeology and History*, Sheffield, Department of Archaeology and Prehistory.

Green, F. J. 1991: 'Landscape archaeology in Hampshire: the Saxon plant remains', 363–77 in Renfrew (ed.).

Harden, D. B. 1976: 'The glass', 232–4 in Cunliffe.

Hamerow, H. F. 1991: 'Settlement mobility and the 'middle Saxon shift': rural settlements and settlement patterns in Anglo-Saxon England', *Anglo-Saxon England*, 20, 1–17.

Haslam, J. 1980: 'A middle Saxon iron smelting site at Ramsbury, Wiltshire', *Medieval Archaeology*, 24, 1–68.

Haslam, J. (ed.) 1984: *Anglo-Saxon Towns in Southern England*, Chichester, Philimore.

Heaton, M. J. 1992: 'Two mid-Saxon grain driers and later medieval features at Chantry Fields, Gillingham, Dorset,' *Proceedings of the Dorset Natural History and Archaeological Society,* 114, 96–126.

Higham, R. and Barker, P. 1992: *Timber Castles*, London, Batsford.

Hill, D. 1978: 'Trends in the development of towns during the reign of Ethelred II', 213–26 in Hill (ed.).

Hill, D. (ed.) 1978: *Ethelred the Unready*, Oxford, British Archaeological Reports British Series, 59.

Hill, D. H. and Rumble, A. R. forthcoming: *The Defence of Wessex: The Burghal Hidage and Anglo-Saxon Urbanisation*, Manchester, University Press.

Hinchliffe, J. 1986: 'An early medieval settlement at Cowage Farm, Foxley, near Malmesbury, Wiltshire', *Archaeological Journal*, 143 (1986), 240–59.

Hinton, D. A. 1992: 'Revised dating of the Worgret structure', *Proceedings of the Dorset Natural History and Archaeological Society*, 114, 258–60.

Hinton, D. A. and Hodges, R. 1977: 'Excavations in Wareham, 1974/5', *Proceedings of the Dorset Natural History and Archaeological Society*, 42–83.

Hinton, D. A. and Okasha, E. 1977: 'The Wareham sword', 80–1 in Hinton and Hodges.

Hinton, D. A. and Welch, M. 1976: 'The finds', 195–221 in Cunliffe.

Hodges, R. 1976: 'A preliminary petrological examination of a selection of the early Saxon pottery', 191–4 in Cunliffe.

Hodges, R. 1991: 'The 8th century pottery industry at La Londe, near Rouen, and its implications for cross-channel trade with Hamwic, Anglo-Saxon Southampton', *Antiquity*, 65 (no. 249), 882–7.

Holdsworth, P. 1984: 'Saxon Southampton', 331–44 in Haslam (ed.).

Holmes, A. G. 1978: 'Excavations at 33 High Street, Fareham, Hants.', *Rescue Archaeology in Hampshire*, 4, 44–59.

Hooke, D. (ed.) 1988: *Anglo-Saxon Settlements*, Oxford, Blackwell.

Jarvis, K. S. 1983: *Excavations in Christchurch 1969–1980*, Dorset Natural History and Archaeological Society, Monograph 5.

Hooper, B. 1976: 'The human burials', 235–61 in Cunliffe.

Hughes, M. 1989: 'Hampshire castles and the landscape, 1066–1216', *Landscape History*, 11, 27–60.

Jenkins, V. 1993. 'Human bone', 120–7 in Graham and Davies.

Keen, L. 1991: 'An introduction to the Dorset Domesday', *The Dorset Domesday*, London, Alecto Historical Editions.

Keene, D. 1990: 'The textile industry', 200–14 in Biddle.

Keynes, S. and Lapidge, M. 1983: *Alfred the Great*, Harmondsworth, Penguin Books.

Kjølbye-Biddle, B. 1992: 'Dispersal or concentration: the disposal of the Winchester dead over 2000 years', 210–47 in Bassett (ed.).

Klingelhöfer, E. 1990: 'Anglo-Saxon manors of the Upper Itchen Valley: their origin and evolution', *Proceedings of the Hampshire Field Club and Archaeological Society*, 46, 31–9.

Leach, P. n.d. *c.* 1982: *Ilchester Volume I. Excavations 1974–5*, Bristol, Western Archaeological Trust Excavation Monograph 3.

Leach, P. (ed.) n.d. *c.* 1986: *The Archaeology of Taunton*, Bristol, Western Archaeological Trust Monograph 8.

Lewis, C. 1989: 'Paired mottes in East Chelborough, Dorset', 159–71 in Bowden *et al.* (eds).

Lewis, E. 1985: 'Excavations in Bishop's Waltham 1967–78', *Proceedings of the Hampshire Field Club and Archaeological Society*, 41, 81–126.

Light, A. *et al.*, forthcoming: *Field Research in the Avon Valley*.

McCarthy, M. R. and Brooks, C. M. 1988: *Medieval Pottery in Britain A.D. 900–1600*, Leicester, University Press.

McDonnell, G. 1992: 'The slag', 141–3 in D. Coe and J. W. Hawkes, 'Excavations at 29 High Street: Wimborne Minster, Dorset, 1992', *Proceedings of the Dorset Natural History and Archaeological Society*, 114, 135–44.

McDonnell, J. G. 1993: 'Metalworking residues', 92–4 in Graham and Davies.

Maddicott, J. R. 1989: 'Trade, industry and the wealth of King Alfred', *Past and Present*, 123, 3–51.

Maddicott, J. R. 1992: 'Trade, industry and the wealth of King Alfred. Reply', *Past and Present*, 135, 164–88.

Mepham, L. N. 1993: 'Pottery', 101–14 in Graham and Davies.

Metcalf, D. M. 1981: 'Continuity and change in English monetary history, *c.* 973–1086', *British Numismatic Journal*, 51, 52–90.

Metcalf, D. M. 1988: 'The coins', 17–60 in Andrews (ed.).

Metcalf, D. M. 1993: *Thrymsas and Sceattas in the Ashmolean Museum, Oxford Vol. 1*, London, Royal Numismatic Society and Ashmolean Museum.

Mills, J. M. 1993a: 'The metalwork', 81–92 in Graham and Davies.

Mills, J. M. 1993b: 'Sepulchral stones', 98–9 in Graham and Davies.

Moore, N. W., Hooper, M. and Davis, B. N. K. 1967: 'Hedges I: introduction and reconnaissance', *Journal of Applied Ecology*, 4, 201–20.

Morton, A.D. (ed.) 1992: *Excavations at Hamwic: Volume 1*, London, Council for British Archaeology Research Report 84.

Neale, F. 1976: 'The relevance of the Axbridge Chronicle', 10–12 in Rahtz.

Newman, J. 1992: 'The late Roman and Anglo-Saxon settlement pattern in the Sandlings of Suffolk', 25–38 in Carver.

Pagan, H. E. 1976: 'The coins', 230–1 in Cunliffe.

Pagan, H. E. 1988: 'The older coin finds from Southampton' and 'The imitative Louis the Pious solidus', 60–72 in Andrews (ed.).

Park, D. 1990: 'Anglo-Saxon or Anglo-Norman? Wall paintings at Wareham and other sites in southern England', 224–47 in Cather *et al.* (eds).

Parsons, D. 1991: 'Stone', 1–28 in Blair and Ramsay (eds).

Pounds, N. J. G. 1990: *The Medieval Castle in England and Wales*, Cambridge, University Press.

RCHM 1970: Royal Commission on Historical Monuments, *An Inventory of Historical Monuments in the County of Dorset Volume Two, South-East*, London.

Radford, C. A. R. 1981: 'Glastonbury Abbey before 1184: interim report on the excavations, 1908–64', *Conference Transactions for the Year 1978*, British Archaeological Association, 110–34.

Rahtz, P. A. 1964: 'Saxon and medieval features at Downton, Salisbury', *Wiltshire Archaeological and Natural History Magazine*, 59, 124–9.

Rahtz, P. 1979: *The Saxon and Medieval Palaces at Cheddar*, Oxford, British Archaeological Reports British Series 65.

Renfrew, J. M. (ed.) 1991: *New Light on Early Farming*, Edinburgh, University Press.

Rigold, S. E. and Metcalf, D. M. 1977: 'A check-list of finds of English sceattas', *British Numismatic Journal*, 47, 31–52.

Robinson, P. 1992: 'Some late Saxon mounts from Wiltshire', *Wiltshire Archaeological and Natural History Magazine*, 85, 63–9.

Robinson, P. H. 1993: 'The coins', 78–81 in Graham and Davies.

Roseaman, J. 1991: 'An archaeological study of field and parish boundaries in North Newnton', *Wiltshire Archaeological and Natural History Society Magazine*, 84, 71–82.

Scobie, G. D. 1991: 'Saxon and medieval topography; Tenement 365/6', 34–54 in Scobie *et al.*

Scobie, G. D., Zant, J. M. and Whinney, R. 1991: *The Brooks, Winchester*, Winchester, Museums Service.

Stevenson, J. H. 1992: 'The castles of Marlborough and Ludgershall in the Middle Ages', *Wiltshire Archaeological and Natural History Magazine*, 85, 70–9.

Thomas, C. 1990: "*Gallici Nautae de Galliarum Provinciis*' – A sixth/seventh century trade with Gaul, reconsidered', *Medieval Archaeology*, 34, 1–26.

Timby, J. 1988: 'The middle Saxon pottery', 73–122 in Andrews (ed.).

Tylecote, R. F. 1990: 'Scientific examination and analysis of iron objects', 140–60 in Biddle.

Watkins, S. and Brown, D. 1991: 'A Viking period sword from Upper Borough Walls', 1–5 in Davenport (ed.).

Waton, P. V. 1982: 'Man's impact on the Chalklands; some new pollen evidence', 75–91 in Bell and Limbrey (eds).

Webster, L. and Backhouse, J. (eds) 1991: *The Making of England: Anglo-Saxon Art and Culture AD 600–900*, London, British Museum Publications.

Vince, A. 1991: Pottery reports in Davenport (ed.), *passim.*

Whitelock, D. 1955: *English Historical Documents Volume I, c. 500–1042*, London, Eyre and Spottiswoode.

Yorke, B. 1990: *Kings and Kingdoms of Early Anglo-Saxon England*, London, Seaby.

3.   The Church in the Wessex Heartlands

P. H. Hase

The local church is an essential part of local society, and the history of the local church is, therefore, essential to English settlement history in general. Ecclesiastical conservatism means, in fact, that the local church often gives better clues to settlement history than anything else.

Local churches began to appear in the Wessex heartlands in late Roman and sub-Roman times, and the early Medieval church, at least in Somerset and Dorset, grew from these beginnings.

After the conversion of the West Saxons, mother churches were founded by the kings on the royal estates around which the districts into which the Kingdom was divided were formed. These royal estates were the local judicial, economic, and social centres, and the establishment of churches at these royal estates increased West Saxon local royal authority, as well as providing a good structure for local evangelisation. These mother churches were founded particularly during the reign of King Ine.

This system of mother churches, each responsible for a district, broke down in the later Saxon and Norman period, with ever more churches being founded responsible for just one manor. However, many West Saxon mother churches retained wide parochial districts covering many settlements.

After about 1175 the tightening dominance of the Canon Law led to a fossilisation of the local church, which thereafter failed to develop in line with other, secular, developments, until the Victorian period. A tendency for local oratories to be founded in the later Medieval period to fill in the gaps in local church provision as inherited from before 1175 was ended by the Reformation, when most such oratories were closed as chantries.

Before Birinus: The Roman and Sub-Roman Church

(a) The Roman Church, to 450

Christianity probably came to the lowlands of Britain at about the same time that it came to northern Gaul, that is, by the late third or early fourth century at the latest, but it is a matter of debate as to how much this Roman Christianity imparted to the Anglo-Saxon and later church and society in England.

There is little archaeological evidence for early Christianity in the Wessex region. The Christian cemetery at Poundbury, Dorchester, has its origins in the very early fourth century, however, and this may also be true of the far more exiguous Christian part of the cemetery at Lankhills, Winchester.[1] Just outside the area, the Cirencester Christian cemetery has burials beginning in the third century, and that city may well have had a bishop who attended the Council of Arles (314). The probable house-church at St Mary de Lode, Gloucester, is likely to date from the early fourth century, as also the possible house-church at Caerwent. There were certainly Chris-

tians at Caerleon in the third century, since Gildas mentions the martyrs Aaron and Julius who suffered there then.[2] It can be assumed that there were congregations of Christians to be found throughout the region before the Peace of the Church in 313.

It is, however, perhaps unlikely that the Christian component of most of the early fourth century southern British *civitates* was very large. Nonetheless, the church and baptistry at Silchester seem to have been built within a generation of 313, on land which was probably communally owned by the *civitas* as part of the forum complex, and may be associated with deliberate destruction and Christianisation of pagan shrines elsewhere in the city.[3] Here, the Christian element in the population must have been quite significant.

The Roman Empire was officially Christian from the 360s and the public practice of paganism was banned from 391–2. Magistrates who had previously sacrificed to the gods in the course of their official duties now found they had to attend a Christian liturgy. Any *civitas* without a church would have found itself embarrassed in the third quarter of the fourth century, and acutely embar-

47

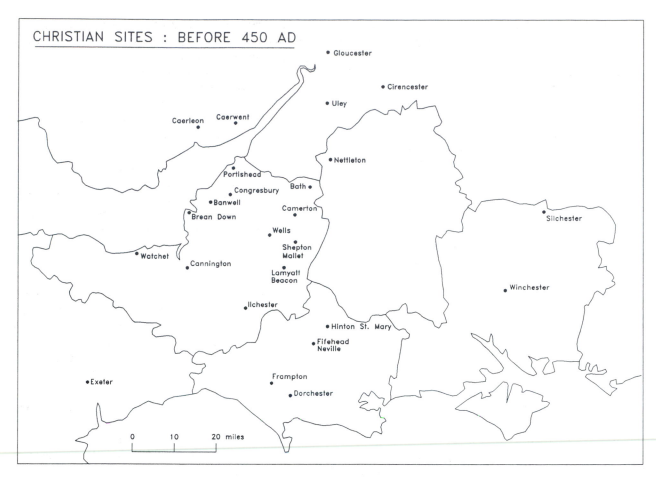

Fig. 3.1 Christian sites: Before 450 AD.

rassed at the end of the century. It is probably in these circumstances that we see churches being built into forum complexes and rural shrines being Christianised, in the later fourth century.

The best example of conversion of part of a forum complex to Christian uses in the general Wessex region is Exeter. Recent excavations there have shown that the church of St Mary Major, founded by the West Saxons about 680–700, was preceded by use of the immediately adjacent forum area as a sub-Roman church and cemetery, from about 390.[4] The forum here had been repaired in the mid fourth century, and again a few decades later, but was then demolished and the space used as a Christian cemetery. It is likely that there was a church somewhere within the site, either built following the demolition of the forum, or else using a few old rooms patched up for the purpose.

The larger rural shrines in Roman Britain may have been owned by the *civitates*. This may be the reason why many such shrines were Christianised in the mid or late fourth century. The best attested archaeologically is Uley, in Gloucestershire,[5] but within the Wessex region, Lamyatt Beacon near Bruton, Nettleton Shrub, Brean Down, and probably Henley Wood near Congresbury were Christianised.[6] These shrines were in the remote,

often hill-top, sites where the gods had been worshipped since Iron Age times.

In Dorset, three villas (Hinton St Mary and Fifehead Neville, near Sturminster Newton, and Frampton, near Dorchester) are known archaeologically to have been Christian from the mid fourth century and to have had chapels. Some rural settlements must have been Christian from about then, too, since their cemeteries were Christian: Cannington, in Somerset, is the clearest case. Camerton, Wint Hill at Banwell, Portishead, the recently discovered cemetery at Shepton Mallet, and Daw's Castle at Watchet, with the cemeteries which developed around the Christianised shrines at Lamyatt Beacon, Brean Down, Henley Wood, and Nettleton Shrub, are other cases in point: most of these cemeteries probably originated in the early fifth century.[7]

Thus, there were Christian congregations before 400–450 in Dorchester, Silchester, Exeter, Cirencester, Caerleon/Caerwent, Gloucester and probably Winchester, as well as in some of the rural areas. To these places should be added Bath, where it was almost certainly Christians who desecrated the pagan cult centre in the middle of the fourth century,[8] and Ilchester, where there are hints of Christianity in the later history of the town cemetery (late fourth–early fifth century).[9] The history of Wells also begins with a Christian mausoleum, probably of the fifth century,[10] around which the later minster was built (see Fig. 3.1).

The most telling evidence for the growth of Christianity in the fourth century, however, is the disappearance of paganism. Many pagan shrines were, as noted above, Christianised in the second half of the fourth century. Some, however, remained pagan until the end of the century, including the shrine on Pagan's Hill in Somerset, the shrine at Maiden Castle near Dorchester, the great temple at Bath, and the healing-cult centre at Lydney: some, indeed, were rebuilt or extended during the second half of the fourth century.[11] Few, if any, however, remained functioning much after 400–420: mid fifth-century evidence of continuing pagan worship in Britain is very slight. Certainly St Patrick, writing probably in the third quarter of the fifth century, could take it as an unanswerable debating point that all the inhabitants of Britain were Christian, and should behave as such.[12] St Germanus, visiting Britain some decades earlier, found heresy a problem among the *Brittani*, but not paganism.[13]

(b) The Sub-Roman Church, 450–650

If St Patrick and St Germanus suggest that lowland Britain was, at least nominally, Christian in the mid fifth century, this becomes more certain in the succeeding, sub-Roman period. About a century after St Patrick, St Gildas, in his impassioned attack on the sins of the rulers of Britain, does not mention paganism or infidelity to Christian truth, and specifically says that the ordinary citizens of Britain 'trusted first of all in God'. The royal sins which Gildas demands repentence for are mostly specifically Christian crimes (divorce, breach of an oath made to God, disrespect for sanctuary, disrespect for Holy Orders). His kings accepted Christianity but, to Gildas, did not measure up to the Christian way of life.[14] The evidence of Gildas, therefore, supports the inferences to be drawn from St Patrick and St Germanus: from the mid fifth century the whole of the Wessex region was basically Christian.

However, the churches in that region in about 450 seem to have been few, small, to a large extent ill-located on remote hill-top sites, and poorly constructed.[15] The rich Christian families of the Dorset villas disappeared during the earlier fifth century and their villas were, by the mid century, in ruins. The new aristocracy of the emergent sub-Roman kingdoms was less cultured and more violent, less likely to act as the leaders of a specifically Christian society, than those of a century before, as Gildas demonstrates. The *civitas* capitals, where the larger churches had been founded, and the *pagus* towns, where there may have been a few public churches under the local bishop's direction, were, in the mid fifth century, becoming empty of people and were no longer the obvious central places of what was developing as an exclusively rural population. The Christianity of most of the population in the mid fifth century may well have been shallow and corrupt. Christianity may have been, by that date, a veneer. That Christianity did not disappear was due to developments in the church in the century following St Patrick.

There was a major revitalisation of Christianity in Britain during the later fifth, and particularly the sixth and early seventh, centuries. This was based on a new asceticism manifested in monasticism. This movement began, as far as northern Europe was concerned, with St Martin of Tours at the very end of the fourth century, and with St Germanus of Auxerre in the early fifth. This movement reached Britain by the mid fifth century, which is the most likely date for the establishment of the monastery founded by St Illtyd in a Roman villa at Llanilltyd Fawr in Glamorgan. Illtyd's contemporaries, St Piran and St Cadoc, and slightly later, in the early and mid sixth century, St David, St Teilo, St Samson, St Gildas, and St Dyfrig, were all also working in this new ascetic tradition.[16] The new ways required the building of monasteries in rural areas. Evangelisation was accepted as a duty by these reformers: preaching stations and subordinate churches appeared in the areas around the new monasteries.

We know most about the situation in Erging and Gwent, where it seems certain that Dyfrig and his successors had established at least a skeleton of rural churches by 600.[17] By 650, few areas of these kingdoms were more than an hour or two's walk from a church. Further west, in present day Glamorgan and Dyfed, the developments seem to have been very similar.

In Cornwall the vital period also seems to have been the late fifth and sixth centuries. The critical figures here were St Piran, St Petroc and St Samson.[18] Monasteries were established at suitable coastal locations; subordinate preaching stations, in due course replaced by small rural churches, grew up around them.

In South Wales and Cornwall, most of our evidence for the revitalization of the church in the late fifth and sixth centuries comes from hagiography, which was transmitted orally for many centuries before being committed to writing. In areas where the oral tradition was interrupted by the influx of the Anglo-Saxons, this hagiography has mostly been lost. Nonetheless, the scraps of surviving hagiography associated with the names of St Nectan of Hartland and St Congar of Congresbury suggest that the evangelisation in depth of Somerset and North Devon was also accomplished by itinerant mid sixth-century monks. The Somerset dedications to St Kea (Street, previously known as 'Lantocai', 'Church of Kea'), St Decuman (Watchet), St Kew (Kewstoke), and St Carantoc (Carhampton) may imply that those saints founded the churches which bear their names. All these saints seem to have flourished in the mid or late sixth century. As in South Wales and Cornwall, Somerset too must have had at least a skeleton of rural churches by 600–650.[19]

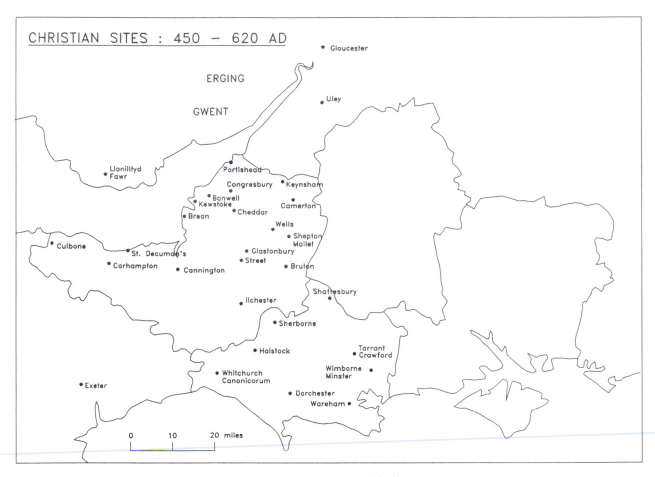

Fig. 3.2 Christian sites: 450–62 AD.

In a few places these late fifth and sixth century monks used old villa sites for their churches, as St Illtyd had at Llanilltyd Fawr. On present evidence, use of villa sites in this way seems to be more typical of the western half than the eastern half of the Wessex region. This may be due to no more than archaeological chance, but seems more likely to represent choice by British monks: Anglo-Saxon churches were normally built in very close proximity to royal *burhs*, and the Anglo-Saxon kings seem to have preferred to build away from villa ruins. However, in Somerset, Banwell, Keynsham and Cheddar churches are built on top of, or immediately alongside, villas: in Dorset, Halstock, Beaminster, Whitchurch Canonicorum and Tarrant Crawford are, while Wimborne Minster stands over a 'substantial Roman building'. Most of these churches were important Middle Saxon churches and their siting over Roman buildings can tentatively be considered as suggesting pre-Anglo-Saxon foundation.[20]

Sixth-century foundation is more certain at Wareham, where several sixth-century Celtic inscribed stones have been found near St Mary's church,[21] and at Glastonbury, Shaftesbury and Sherborne. Glastonbury seems to have originated as a monastic community on top of the Tor somewhere about 500: this community moved down to the foot of the hill, possibly in about 600.[22] Shaftesbury

seems to have had abbots with British names in the years after the Saxon conquest of the area, suggesting that it was an old British foundation.[23] The British name of Sherborne ('Lanprobus': 'Church of St Probus') is known, and the church was important enough to attract the interest of the kings of Dumnonia even after the Saxon Conquest:[24] there can be little doubt that Sherborne was a major ecclesiastical centre well before Aldhelm's date.

Within the western half of Wessex, therefore, enough evidence survives for the sub-Roman church for it to be at least clear that there was, before 650, a significant number of rural churches. The churches known or suspected to have been Christian centres in this period are mostly built on flat land near streams in the centre of fertile areas: these areas can be assumed to have been the most densely populated of the sub-Roman kingdoms of the region (see Fig. 3.2). Knowledge of the sixth- and early seventh-century church of this area will continue to increase as further archaeological evidence is uncovered.

(c) The Continuing Influence of the Roman and Sub-Roman Church

The Anglo-Saxons did not conquer Wessex all at one time. The earliest Anglo-Saxon settlers in the region can be traced archaeologically from about 450 in the middle Thames valley near Abingdon and Dorchester-on-Thames, and in Wiltshire south of Ashdown: at that date these settlers must have been subject to some sub-Roman polity. By 500, the society of Wiltshire south of Ashdown was probably predominantly Anglo-Saxon. In Hampshire, early Anglo-Saxon settlement is less well attested. There are several early Anglo-Saxon cemeteries immediately outside the walls of Winchester, and others at Andover and Alton,[25] but there are no signs of early Anglo-Saxon settlement in a zone between two and about twelve miles from Winchester: this area must have remained essentially Celtic for some time, but under steadily increasing Anglo-Saxon domination.

Central Hampshire, Wiltshire south of Ashdown, and probably the middle Thames valley, became the West Saxon kingdom about 520. Any remnant Celtic population in central Hampshire would thereafter have been part of an Anglo-Saxon kingdom. This West Saxon kingdom conquered the Upper Thames Valley, (including Wiltshire north of Ashdown), and the Avon Valley north of the Mendips, in the 570s.[26] The conquest of Dorset, however, was a matter of the second half of the seventh century, following the battle *æt Peonnum* in 658.[27] The conquest of Somerset south of the Mendips was no earlier than that of Dorset.

The implications of this long history of piecemeal conquest for the church in Wessex is that, for those areas not under Anglo-Saxon political control until after 600, the effects of the monastic reform movement of the fifth and sixth centuries should have had time to make an impact before the conquest: in such areas the Anglo-Saxons are likely to have taken over districts with a resident church of some vigour and with rural churches to provide pastoral care. Where the Anglo-Saxons took over between about 520 and 600, the continuing existence of the church through the years is less likely, and where the Anglo-Saxons became dominant before about 520, it is unlikely. In Wessex we should, therefore, expect the sub-Roman church in Dorset and Somerset (conquered after the West Saxons were officially Christian) to have survived the conquest more or less intact, and we might expect some continuation of tradition in Wiltshire north of Ashdown, and perhaps just possibly in Central Hampshire. The chances of survival of any Christian institutions in Wiltshire south of Ashdown, however, are definitely poor.

As can be seen from Figs 3.1 and 3.2, the evidence for survival of the sub-Roman church in Somerset and Dorset is indeed substantial, while that for survival in Wiltshire and Hampshire is currently non-existent. The Middle Saxon church in the west of the region must have been based almost entirely on a sub-Roman foundation: to the east on predominantly or wholly new bases.

However, the Middle Saxon church in the two areas seems more or less the same in its organisation, and in its relationship with the Anglo-Saxon kings: the Celtic and Saxon districts seem to have developed a broadly similar ecclesiastical structure. Almost all the places in Somerset and Dorset where evidence of sub-Roman Christian activity from the period 450–650 survives continued as major churches into the Middle and Later Saxon periods: the victorious West Saxons clearly felt no need to make any substantial changes to the system they found. Aldhelm's foundations (Bradford-on-Avon, Bruton, Sherborne, Wareham, Frome) should be seen either as refoundations (Wareham), relocations (Bruton, in place of the inconveniently located Lamyatt Beacon or its successor church; and Sherborne), or as filling in gaps in the system inherited by him (Bradford-on-Avon, Frome).[28] The implications are clear: the basic structure of society that faced the sixth- and early seventh-century Celtic monks in Somerset and Dorset was basically the same as that found in the lands to the east in the eighth century. The ecclesiastical structure felt to be natural to those monks was one that felt natural, too, to Middle Saxon kings.

The Roman church was public. The episcopal church was in the *civitas* capital and the subordinate churches were built by the bishop in the *pagus* towns. In Britain, however, the structure of *civitas* and *pagus* had broken down by 450, to be replaced by local kingdoms which were without towns of any sort. The monastic reformers of the sixth and early seventh centuries looked firstly to the central places of the new kingdoms as the sites for their new churches – the royal estates – and thereafter to the smaller villages subordinate to those royal estates.

This is probable for South Wales and Cornwall and is a reasonable inference for Somerset and Dorset. It may be assumed that the victorious West Saxon kings would have taken for themselves the estates the kings of Dumnonia had previously occupied, rather than undertake a full-scale reorganisation of land-holdings. Certainly, almost all of the places in Somerset and Dorset where suggestions of sub-Roman Christianity have survived to the present are royal estates after the Saxon conquest – Congresbury, Brean, Banwell, Keynsham, Cheddar, Cannington, Carhampton, Bruton, Watchet, Ilchester, Wareham, Wimborne, Dorchester, Sherborne, Shaftesbury, Camerton, Halstock and Whitchurch Canonicorum. Only Glastonbury, Wells, Portishead, Shepton Mallet, Kewstoke and Tarrant Crawford are not known to have been royal in Saxon times, and of these, Glastonbury and Wells were held in ecclesiastical hands from so early a date as to make surviving evidence of Saxon royal ownership perhaps unlikely. Portishead and Shepton Mallet were also in ecclesiastical hands at the date of the earliest surviving evidence.

There has been considerable discussion of the origins of the Middle Saxon and later 'Multiple Estate', and whether it can be assumed to have originated from a Celtic system, the ancestor of the later Welsh Multiple Estate.[29] That the church developed structures very similar in both the Celtic east and the Saxon west of Wessex in the seventh and eighth centuries suggests that the local economic and social systems of the two societies, sub-Roman and Anglo-Saxon, were very similar. Both, it would appear, were dominated by royally-held central places which, in a purely agricultural society, must each have been supported by a substantial rural estate, and in both it must have appeared natural to plant local churches one to each such estate.[30]

It seems clear, therefore, that the sub-Roman church did impart a good deal to the later West Saxon church – Congar and Carantoc were as much the evangelisers of Wessex as Birinus. Furthermore, the ecclesiastical evidence must also be seen as implying some continuing influence of the sub-Roman local political, social and economic structures on the later West Saxon systems.

The Middle Saxon Period: Establishment of the Mother Church System

(a) The West Saxon Multiple Estate and its Church

The West Saxons inherited from their sub-Roman predecessors a land without towns or a market economy, or even coinage. In this entirely agricultural milieu, their political and social systems had to be based on self-reliance and subsistence. This was achieved by local military, political, social and economic systems being managed through a network of central places which were also the places from which the king drew the food and other supplies on which he and his Court subsisted. The Celtic kingdoms operated through similar systems, as did the other Anglo-Saxon kingdoms.

It would be wrong to assume that these systems were identical everywhere: they were not. The Kentish system differed from the West Saxon system, which in turn differed from the Mercian.[31] All these systems were, however, similar and operated in ways which tended to differ only in detail.

The essential factor was the division of the kingdom into districts, *regiones*. Within each *regio* the central place was a *burh*, a defended house, the centre of a royal estate, the *villa regalis*. Here lived the king's reeve. In Wessex there seems to have been such a *villa regalis* every six to eight miles, on average. It seems likely that everywhere in Wessex lay within the area of responsibility of one reeve or another.[32]

Around the reeve's house was a farm, managed by the reeve, which was expected to produce a significant surplus, especially of grain, cheese, animals for slaughter, bacon, beer, mead and honey, to store it until the king called for it, and to have it carried to wherever the king called for it.[33] This farm was worked by the king's slaves, and his semi-free adscripted dependents. This farm would have been marked by barns, cheese-stores, beer-stores, smoke houses and so forth, since the surplus had to be able to be stored for up to a year, depending on the king's needs.

Many, perhaps most, reeves would also have had a special duty to provide a special surplus – horses, salt, worked iron, blankets, wearing cloth, hounds, hawks, or whatever – and to manage the stores where such surpluses could be kept against need.[34] Often, such specialist tasks were carried out, under the reeve's supervision, at a berewick, a separate settlement, detached from the main farm. The reeve's first duty, therefore, was to supervise a farm, to provide for the king's subsistence needs, and to defend the stores against bandits or rebel warbands.[35]

Among the reeve's other important duties were the need to manage the wastes of the area for the king's hunting (see Figs 3.4–5, 3.8–11), to supervise the rural markets to check cattle rustling, theft, use of false weights and so forth, and to act as the president of the district court of free-holders, and to hang felons on its behalf. The ancient duties of unpaid labour on necessary works (which would in due course become the *trinoda necessitas*) were managed through the reeve, who could call on the free men of his district as needed. In many areas, the unpaid work the reeve could demand included assistance in bringing in the king's harvests. The reeve would also have lead the free men of the district in arms when called on to do so.

The king's farm needed quite a lot of workers: without them it could not have produced the large surpluses the system demanded. As a result, at the gates of the *burh* there was often a nuclear village – these were perhaps the only nuclear villages of the period.[36] A mile or two away were small dependent settlements where the essential specialist craftsmen of the estate, the carters, message riders and carriers, essential to carrying the surplus to where the king wanted it and to receiving and despatching the king's orders, and other free tenants of the king, grew the food they subsisted on. These small settlements were part of the king's lands: granted out to free men who were, however, required to serve the king's needs on the estate and who were not able to sell the land or withdraw their services. These dependencies were, in many cases, ancient land units, but most would have had only one or two resident households in Middle Saxon times.

Around the *burh* and the dependencies of the *villa regalis* were other settlements which owed various services to the king through the reeve, but which were not part of the royal lands in the same way as the *burh* and its dependencies. These places paid grain or other rent, or *vectigal* or other dues paid not as rent but as *feorm*, to the reeve. All this grain paid to the reeve went to increase the stored surplus for the king.[37] There were probably yet other lands which were merely required to support the reeve in arms when called on, or to assist him when the king required other specified duties. These other lands, owing only more or less dues to the reeve, might be held by alodiaries, who had inherited their lands, and who might in some circumstances have been able to devise them, or by *duguth* royal thegns holding land from the king in return for their services in arms. In many areas, the *burh* and its dependendencies occupied only a minority of the productive land of a district, the bulk lying in these small settlements of free men owing to the reeve only the various services appropriate to free men.

This somewhat lengthy description of the system of *regiones* is needed as the development of the parochial system in England is intimately bound up with it. The Christian religion had a great deal to offer the kings of Anglo-Saxon England. With the new religion came concepts of law, fidelity, obedience and the sacred nature of duly constituted authority which were of great value to kings wishing to widen their power base. Christian theology gave the king a very exalted role and the king, supported by his bishop, had access to sources of power and prestige that the pagan kings did not. There can be little doubt that it was this which lead to the speed of the conversion, and to the fact that almost everywhere the kings were the first converts.

However, the value of Christianity to the kings was not only at this high level. At the local level Christianity also brought great advantages to the kings. A reeve who had a church would be able to force the free men of that *regio* to come to the gates of his *burh* for their marriages, for the christening of their children and the burial of their dead. In the church the free men would hear the priest preach the importance of obedience and loyalty, under the immediate eye of the reeve. Christianity brought new obligations binding on all men: these new duties would have been enforced by the reeve, thus increasing his public profile and power. The priest would support the reeve at the local court, not least by providing religious awe to the ordeals presided over by the reeve. The reeve alone of the laymen of the *regio* would have had access to written documents if needed. The priest's spiritual power assisted the reeve, while the reeve's authority supported the priest. At the local, as well as the national level, there was a natural alliance between Church and State, and their close co-operation lead to marked advantages for both. The reeve with a church had a further, and powerful, organ of control over his *regio*.

It was, therefore, probably inevitable that the kings founded churches on their estates as soon as the conversion was accomplished. In Wessex it looks as if there was a conscious policy to ensure that every *regio* had a church, a royal church (see Fig. 3.3). Such a policy ensured that every settlement was clearly in some specific

Fig. 3.3 West Saxon mother churches.

regio and *parochia*, so that every settlement was subject to a specific royal reeve, advised and assisted by a specific, and almost equally royal, priest. At the local level, political, social, economic and religious life would thus have been controlled by royal agents, subject to a king advised by a close-knit group of ældormen and bishops. This would have given Middle Saxon kings as much power as was possible in the circumstances. As noted above, the Celtic kings seem to have followed a similar course, although probably not so systematically. The reign of Ine (688–726) seems to be the period when this system was fully established in Wessex.

(b) Mother Churches, Sites

It is often said that the early Anglo-Saxons had a predilection for founding their churches within ancient hillforts, or within the enceinte of Roman enclosures. These general statements require to be checked kingdom by kingdom: in Wessex they seem to be quite mistaken. In Wessex, only Malmesbury of known Middle Saxon churches is believed to be built within an ancient hillfort, although it is a possibility that an iron-age fort underlies the later defences at Shaftesbury.[38] Avebury, where the church lies across the ditch of a neolithic henge, is *sui generis* and cannot be treated as forming part of any 'normal' practice. At Congresbury and Bruton churches were moved from hill-top sites within or adjacent to hillforts, either in the last sub-Roman, or the first Anglo-Saxon century.

In a number of places, the Anglo-Saxons seem to have deliberately avoided using hillforts. In some places, such as Tatchbury and Winklebury in Hampshire, hillforts had been used to set out the Roman roads: at some, such as Badbury Rings in Dorset and Old Sarum in Wiltshire, Roman towns developed at the road junction outside the fort (see Figs 3.4–7, the exact line of some Roman roads in the areas of these maps is unknown: the most likely line is shown). At all four places, the Anglo-Saxons founded their churches on low ground, near streams, a mile or two from the hillforts. Tatchbury and Winklebury are both low-lying and would seem to have been eminently usable for a church – the former now houses a public hospital, the latter a school. Other examples of apparent deliberate avoidance of hillforts are Andover (see Fig. 3.8), Amesbury (where the large hillfort stands on low-lying land on the west bank of the Avon, and the church immediately opposite, on the east bank) and Bradford-on-Avon (where the church seems to have been built immediately outside a hillfort).[39] Wessex has more hillforts than anywhere else in England: in these circumstances, the few early churches to be found in hillfort enclosures suggests that the Anglo-Saxons in this part of England deliberately *avoided* such places when they founded their churches:[40] it is interesting to note that Malmesbury was founded by an Irish pilgrim and not by a West Saxon.

Much the same conclusion has to be reached where Roman enclosures are in question. We have seen that villas were used as church sites in Dorset and Somerset, probably by the Celtic monks in the sixth or early seventh century. Where larger Roman sites are in question, the most normal reaction of the early West Saxons seems to have been to found a church immediately *outside* the enclosure, not within it. Thus, churches were built immediately outside Dorchester, Ilchester and the Roman fort at Carisbrooke. The siting of St Mary Extra Southampton should be regarded as another example with regard to Bitterne (see Figs 3.11–13 and Fig. 3.4). The only exception is a few of the major Roman cities, where churches were established in a corner of the enclosure, away from the main through roads.[41] No early West Saxon church is known to occupy a Roman enceinte in the way that Reculver, Dover, and Bradwell-on-Sea do.[42]

In the present state of knowledge, general statements as to church foundation practice in Middle Saxon times, drawn from a handful of examples from all over England, should be avoided. No-one would consider assuming that practice in twelfth-century Wiltshire was identical to practice in twelfth-century Northumberland, or twelfth-century Kent, but Bede's statements as to practice in eighth-century Northumbria, or the deductions drawn from eighth-century Kentish texts are frequently assumed to be generally applicable to the whole of England, including eighth-century Wessex. Yet, in the twelfth century, a single strong monarchy ruled the whole of England, with a nobility which all had interests in many parts of England: in the eighth century, West Saxon noblemen are unlikely to have had interests outside Wessex, and it is surely likely that West Saxon kings would have decided on policies taking into account only what they thought was best for their own lands. Middle Saxon church foundation practices need to be studied at the local level before any general statements as to practices common to the whole of England are formulated. It is likely that, once this has been done, significant regional variations will be found.

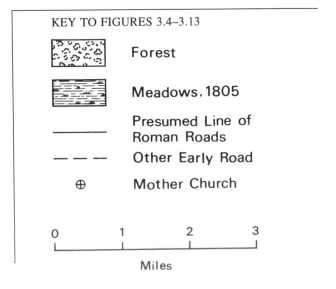

KEY TO FIGURES 3.4–3.13

Forest

Meadows, 1805

Presumed Line of
Roman Roads

Other Early Road

⊕   Mother Church

0   1   2   3

Miles

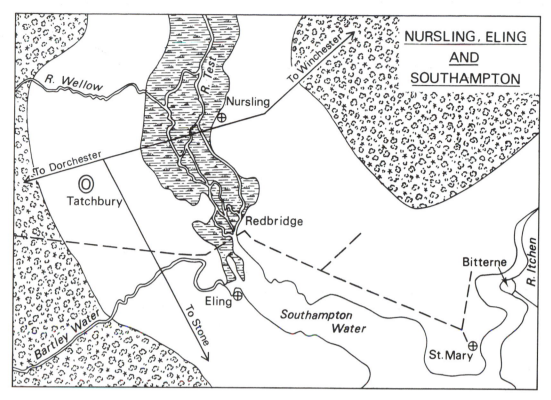

Fig. 3.4 *Mother church siting and location map for Nursling, Eling and Southampton.*

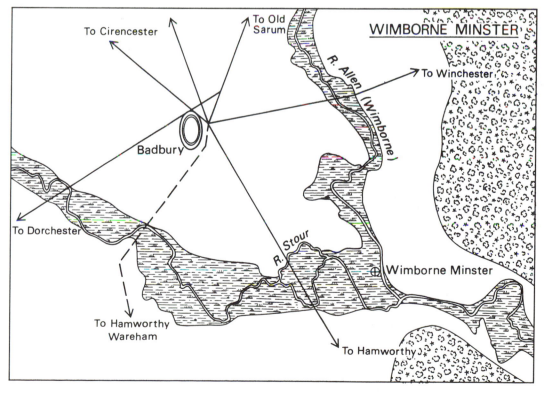

Fig. 3.5 *Mother church siting and location map for Wimborne Minster.*

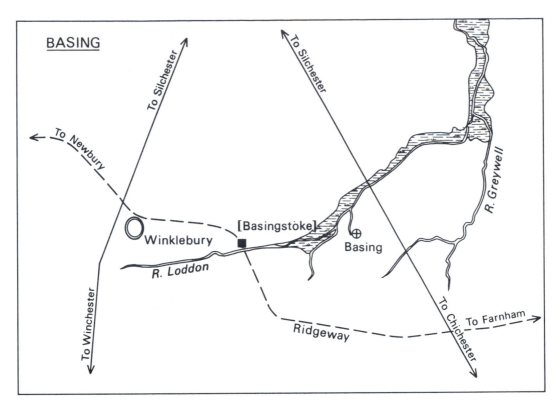

Fig. 3.6 *Mother church siting and location map for Basing.*

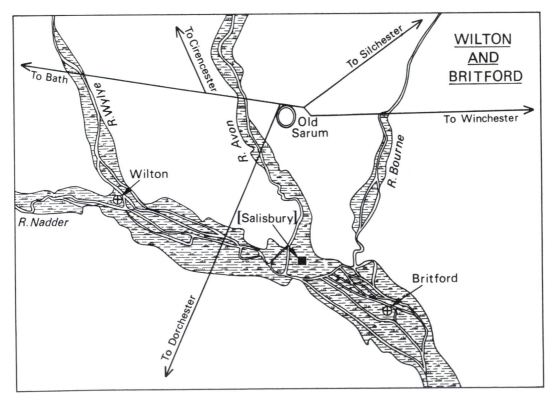

Fig. 3.7 *Mother church siting and location map for Wilton and Britford.*

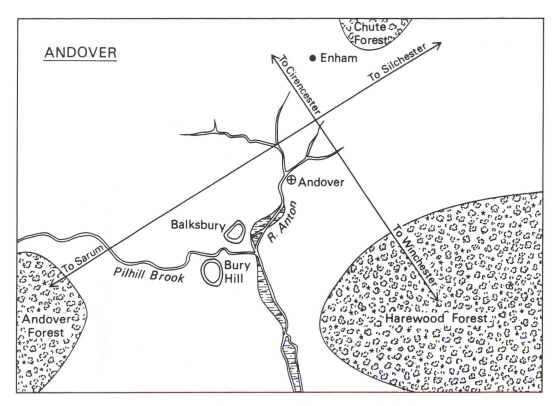

Fig. 3.8 *Mother church siting and location map for Andover.*

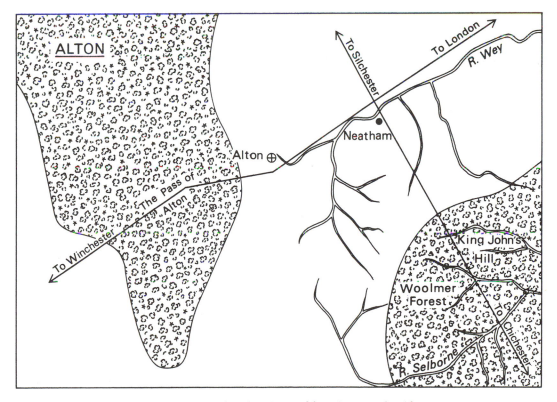

Fig. 3.9 *Mother church siting and location map for Alton.*

No scientific study of the sites and topography of the West Saxon mother churches has yet been made. Nonetheless, it seems clear that the early West Saxons built their mother churches, where possible, near, but not adjacent to, Roman roads – often at the nearest permanent spring to the road (see Figs 3.6, 3.8–10). It is the siting of the church near the spring or stream that caused the Saxon and later town to move away from the Roman towns at Andover, Alton and Wimborne Minster: the Roman towns at these places were at the cross-roads of the Roman roads, the later towns were around the church, a mile or two away.

What is abundantly clear about the West Saxon siting of early mother churches is that sites were normally chosen close to water (see Figs 3.4–13). Several important early churches, including Wimborne Minster and Wilton, are built well within the riverside meadows. Others, including Wells, Basing, Alton, Mottisfont, Bradford-on-Avon and King's Somborne, are built near springs.[43] Romsey, Britford and Wherwell are built on islands between branches of the river. A high percentage of the place-names of early Wessex churches (over half of the Hampshire mother churches) are compounded from place-name components referring to water[44] or from topographical components implying water,[45] or use the stream name, or a compound of it, as the place-name.[46] Very few early West Saxon churches are more than about 150 yards from water.[47]

The reason for this overwhelming preference for sites close to water is that these are, in a chalk country, the optimum sites for modern agriculture and settlement. The siting of the mother churches solely in the zones which recent settlement has favoured, and avoiding almost entirely the High Chalk, makes it clear that the modern settlement patterns of Wessex were established well before the Christianisation of the area: the sub-Roman, Celtic, and early West Saxon central places were in the lowlands, near the streams, as the medieval and modern ones are. It is no accident that the cathedrals of Winchester, Sherborne, Ramsbury and Wells lie at the bottom of hollows in the hills: they share this characteristic with their subordinate churches.

It has been suggested that the early Anglo-Saxons had a preference for siting their mother churches on prominences: hill-tops, spurs jutting out into valleys, or on top of steep river banks at sharp bends in rivers. Once again, however, no matter how much this may be true of other kingdoms, it does not seem to be entirely true of Wessex. A few churches (Malmesbury, Shaftesbury and Odiham, for instance) are in genuinely hill-top and prominent locations, but these examples are rare. In several places, churches were rebuilt on low ground near water, despite earlier foundation on the tops of the hills (Glastonbury, Bruton/Lamyatt Beacon, Congresbury/Henley Wood): it is not yet clear whether this was a seventh-century Celtic development or an eighth-century Saxon one.

More often, the early West Saxon churches were built in a *locally* prominent position, on top of a hillock, such that the church is easily seen from nearby but not from any distance. Thus Mottisfont church is built on top of a small rise which drops steeply away from the church to the spring which gives the place its name, some 100 yards and 30 feet lower than the church, but the hillock on which the church stands is nonetheless still at the bottom of the valley when seen from any of the surrounding hills. Similarly, Andover church stands at the top of the town, with the River Anton at the bottom, but the difference in height is only about twenty feet. Eling, on top of the river bank, near the junction of the Bartley Water and Southampton Water (Fig. 3.4), is another case in point. But most West Saxon mother churches are entirely sited in the bottoms of hollows. Nearness to water was clearly a far more compelling factor in location than prominence.

At the same time, in many cases it was the king's *burh* which was built near the water in the best agricultural location: the church was sited immediately adjacent to the *burh*, and thus came to be sited near the water. Thus, Haslam has drawn attention to the numerous cases (Calne, Warminster, Wilton, Chippenham, and less certainly, Amesbury) where early Wiltshire churches are built close to oval or sub-rectangular street-patterns, which probably represent early defended areas,[48] and adjacent to open market areas used as the district market since records begin. Suggestive street-layouts and, in some cases, street-names suggest a similar situation at Crondall (Hampshire), Farnham (Surrey), Lambourne (Berkshire), Wimborne Minster and especially Sherborne (Dorset), and Crewkerne, Yeovil, and perhaps Milborne Port and South Petherton (Somerset). Some of these oval or sub-rectangular areas are called 'Kingsbury', or 'The Borough', and Haslam assumes, undoubtedly correctly, that these are the sites of the early royal *burh*.

It has been suggested that the oval sites represent early ecclesiastical enclosures, on the lines of the Celtic *lan*, but this is unlikely. Not only are the enclosures larger than any *lans* in the South-West of Britain, but the later churches are, in some cases, clearly built just *outside* the enclosure (e.g. especially Sherborne[49]), or built across the line of the enclosure and thus accessible both from within and without (e.g. especially Lambourne). More significantly, in many cases the bulk of the oval enclosure area was occupied, even in the nineteenth century, with a manor house which can be assumed to descend directly from the early royal *burh* (e.g. Warminster, Lambourne). In no case has archaeology suggested that the early West Saxon church in any of these places occupied a substantially larger site than its late medieval or early modern successor. These places with suggestive topographies should be taken as typical of many: the typical site for an early West Saxon mother church was at the gates of the royal *burh*, facing the district market, in a favourable location near the river or spring.

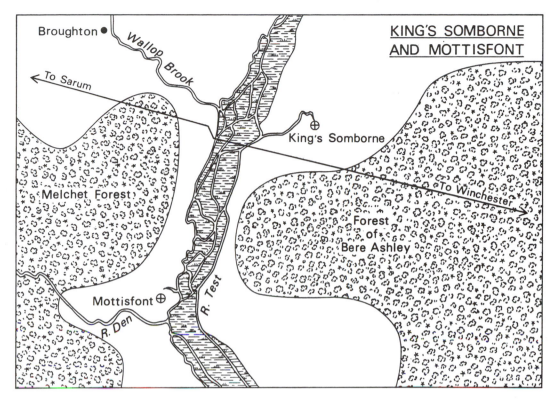

Fig. 3.10 *Mother church siting and location map for King's Somborne and Mottisfont.*

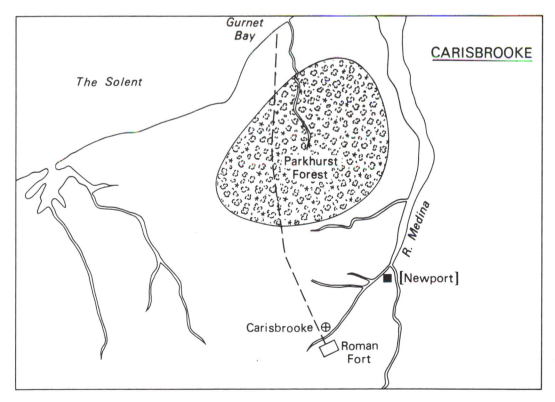

Fig. 3.11 *Mother church siting and location map for Carisbrooke.*

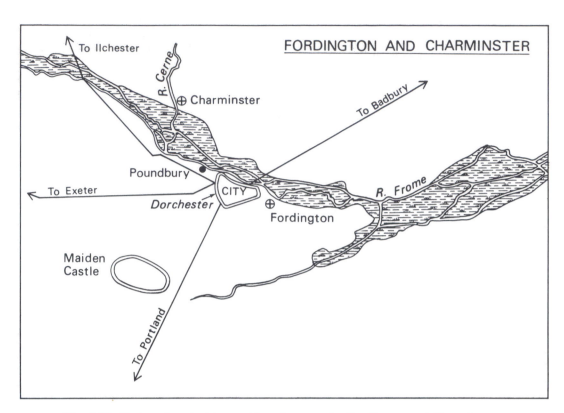

Fig. 3.12 *Mother church siting and location map for Fordington and Charminster.*

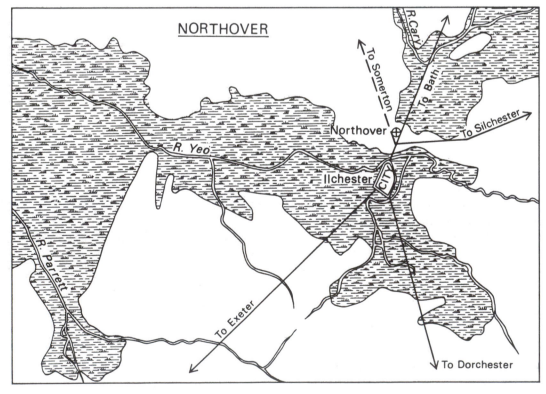

Fig. 3.13 *Mother church siting and location map for Northover.*

(c) Mother Churches, Endowment and Life

The earliest West Saxon churches were generally not outstandingly wealthy. The earliest information we have is in Domesday, but this probably represents in general terms the position three centuries earlier. Most of the major rural churches recorded in Domesday and known or suspected to have been Middle Saxon mother churches have endowments of between one and three hides, with most having either one or two hides. Very few have more than three.[50] A few churches known to be old have very small endowments, but beneficial hidation may be involved here.[51] The reason for the small endowment of the early West Saxon churches must be the small size of the West Saxon *regiones*: if there was to be a mother church every six or eight miles, then they could not be hugely wealthy.

All these churches were designed for communities. They were *monasteria*, 'minsters'. This name should not be read as implying that they were monastic, but the name does imply communal life of some kind. At Christchurch in the early twelfth century a description of life in the church at about the time of the Conquest suggests that a full communal life was practised there, with a Morrow Mass and a High Mass, and with at least the more important of the hours celebrated by the whole community.[52] Christchurch had twenty five virgates of endowment in Domesday, and twenty five 'brethren'. At this one virgate to one 'brethren' rate, most of the West Saxon mother churches can only have held very small communities, of four or five 'brethren', implying, perhaps, only one or two priests. These tiny communities are unlikely to have been 'monastic' in a way that would have been recognised by, say, Bede and they may not have been outstanding centres of learning, but they nonetheless provided a close network of provision for the cure of souls, and brought the Church closer to the places where eighth-century West Saxons lived than was the case, perhaps, in some other kingdoms.[53]

It is interesting to note, in view of Bede's well-known attack on the practice of booking land for the foundation of local monasteries which were in fact not monastic as he saw them, that very few of these early West Saxon churches seem to have had *bocland*. Land was booked freely to the greater churches of the West Saxon kingdom – The Old Minster, Sherborne, Chertsey, Malmesbury, Abingdon, Glastonbury and Muchelney – but not to the local churches. Apart from Farnham,[54] no local West Saxon mother church seems to have been founded on *bocland*, or to have received *bocland* within a century of its foundation – and Farnham seems to have come into the bishop's hands quickly, as may have been intended from the beginning. The small endowments of the West Saxon local mother churches were, it would appear, folkland. The kings of Wessex, apparently, did not want their local churches to be too independent of their and their reeve's control.

The small communities of the West Saxon local mother churches, serving populations which, in the eighth century, were not that large, did not demand very large church buildings. Unfortunately, few early churches have survived in Wessex. The late seventh-century mother church at Titchfield, however, has survived in large measure and can be taken as typical. It consisted of a small, possibly two-storeyed west *porticus*, about 11ft. 6in. square, a nave measuring 53ft. by 22ft. 3in., and a small square chancel: if the church had lateral *porticus*, no sign of them has survived.[55] The only other early West Saxon church of which a good deal is known (apart from the Old Minster and the cathedral at Sherborne[56]) is Wareham, which was larger than Titchfield and had full lateral *porticus*: it is possible, however, that Wareham was rebuilt in the later Saxon period.

Thus, it seems likely that, in the late seventh and eighth centuries, the West Saxon kings founded a network of small, moderately endowed churches, one on each of the royal estates which were the central places of the kingdom at that date. The *parochie* of these churches normally coincided with the secular *regiones* subordinate to those royal estates.[57] These small churches thus formed part of the network of royal social, economic and politi-

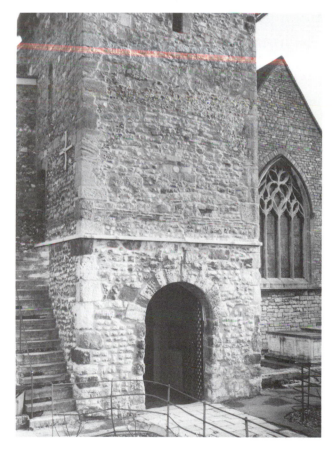

Fig. 3.14 The early Anglo-Saxon porch at St Peter's church, Titchfield, raised c. 1200 to form a tower. (Photo: Michael Hare)

cal control apparatus. These churches were *monasteria* and were served by small communities of clerics. The sites chosen for these churches were, in Wessex, almost invariably in valley-floor sites close to water, in the centre of the best agricultural land, near the *burh* which was the management centre of the *villa regalis* and *regio*. No substantial differences can be seen in these ancient mother churches between the Saxon east and Celtic west of Wessex: as noted already, this suggests that the seventh-century conquest of Dorset and Somerset did not initiate any major religious or social changes, although it may well have lead to additional churches being founded to fill in gaps in the inherited system to ensure that the whole Kingdom was provided with a coherent system of local churches.

However, even though it seems likely that Ine and his ecclesiastical advisers had a clear idea of the system of local churches they wanted, and likely, too, that they took appropriate steps to get it, there can be no doubt that the system of mother churches began to break down shortly after it was in place. If the period 650–850 saw the inauguration and completion of a programme of foundation of a system of mother churches, the following period, from the ninth to the later twelfth century, saw that system slowly distort and break up until the medieval parochial system was established in its place.

From Mother Church to Parish Church: the Establishment of the Medieval Parochial System

There were four factors which caused the Wessex system of mother churches, one to each *regio*, to break down. The first was the difficulty of providing for the cure of souls of a large district from a single centre. The second was the influence of grants of land to the church, particularly in the tenth century. The third was the desire of lay lords for a church of their own at the gates of their own residences. Finally, changes in the character of the mother churches themselves, especially in the eleventh and early twelfth centuries, were of importance.

At Christchurch, documents detail the foundation of Milford within that *parochia*.[58] There, the initiation of the new church was undertaken by the local lay lord about 1090. The lord paid for the construction of the new church and gave half a virgate of land to Christchurch. Christchurch agreed to send a priest from the mother church to serve the new church, at least when the lay lord was resident there. The new church was to have a cemetery, but limited to the slaves of the founder's estate. Boldre and Sopley were almost certainly founded in the same way for the same reasons within the same *parochia* of Christchurch; Sopley at the expense of Earl Godwin, about 1050, Boldre possibly at the direct cost of the mother church, and possibly a hundred years earlier. Foundation of subordinate churches of this sort was probably a common phenomenon: as it became accepted that Christians should attend Mass weekly, pressure to found subordi-

nate churches, to make that commitment easier to meet, would have grown. While such subordinate churches did not imply any break up of the mother church *parochia*, they broke the old equation of single *regio* and single mother church, and possibly made the other types of development easier to introduce.

The question of royal grants to the Church – by which is meant grants to the greater churches of the kingdom – caused problems since there seems to have been a view, at least in the tenth century, that land owned by a greater church depended on that church as its mother church, and so was automatically removed from the control of the local mother church.[59] Tenth-century grants of land to a greater church, therefore, seem to have led, in most cases, almost immediately to the foundation of new local churches on the new estates, free of contact with the old mother churches at the *burh* of the *regiones* from which the new ecclesiastical estates had been cut.

The desire of lay lords to have their own church could lead to establishment of a church subordinate to the mother church, as noted above in the case of Milford. However, where the mother church was more complaisant than Christchurch, or more in need of ready cash, the mother church might be willing to allow a lay lord's church complete independence, if the rights of the mother church were bought off. Where the mother church itself was facing crisis, this sort of buying of complete independence for a new church might occur quite frequently. In the first fifty years after the Norman Conquest this process probably speeded up: Norman lords were not so used to having to take into account the rights of mother churches as their predecessors, and seem to have been more cavalier in their church foundation practices: it seems likely that many parish churches were founded with complete independence in this period by strong lay lords.

The final factor, changes in the nature of the mother church itself, became important particularly in the eleventh and early twelfth centuries. Several West Saxon mother churches were regularised in the tenth century, including the Old Minster, Sherborne, Wherwell, Romsey and Wilton. In every case, this caused stresses in the way the church exercised its pastoral role in the adjacent villages. Some churches, like Romsey, attempted to continue as before,[60] others, like Wherwell, established churches in the outlying villages and to some degree cut themselves off from any need to continue to provide care for them.[61] Wilton moved the nunnery to a new church, leaving the old one to its canons. But in all cases the new regulars took much of the income of the old mother church, and were more likely to be willing to consider lay lords' proposals to buy out their churches from any subordination. Regularisation continued as a problem into the eleventh and twelfth centuries, and even later, with regularisations such as Titchfield at the beginning of the thirteenth century, and Christchurch in the middle of the twelfth. More frequent, however, in the immediate post-

Conquest period, was the donation of mother churches to Norman houses, as alien priories: Andover, Basing, Carisbrooke, Corsham, Wootton Rivers and many others became alien priories in this way.

More insidious was the late-Saxon realisation that, as the numbers of subordinate and independent churches grew, the old mother churches could get by with fewer priests and less income. Both the king and the bishops began to use mother churches as benefices for their clerks. These clerks reduced the number of priests at the mother church to the minimum consonant with the service required, and took half, or more, of the income for themselves, treating this as sinecure income: where mother churches were granted as alien priories the effect was much the same.

At Christchurch, the Post-Conquest documents tell us in detail of what happened there when Ranulf Flambard was granted the church in about 1090: the twenty five canons were reduced to six or seven, and the stipends of the cancelled canonries were appropriated by Flambard. The remaining canons were distributed around the villages served from Christchurch, each receiving the income of one of the village churches as a 'prebend'. Community life at Christchurch was reduced to the barest minimum. To achieve this, the previous Dean of Christchurch was harried into exile by Flambard.[62] This, doubtless, is a tale that could have been told, *mutatis mutandis*, at many mother churches in the last Anglo-Saxon or first Norman century, perhaps, for instance, at Frome, Avebury and Pewsey, all held, clearly *sine cura*, by Reinbald the King's Priest in Domesday. Obviously, mother churches in the hands of absentee priests would be more likely to look favourably on requests to buy independence for cash down.

There was never a concerted effort to provide each vill with its own parish church, except here and there. The four factors discussed above operated erratically and intermittently: one area being powerfully affected by several, others hardly being affected by any. The Anglo-Saxon and Canon Law, indeed, objected to any diminution of the powers and prestige of the mother churches and, where the mother church fought for its rights, the law would support it.[63] The result is that, throughout Wessex, the later parochial system is nothing but a mass of complex anomalies and illogicalities – more so than in the more homogeneous Danelaw – reflecting the accidents of the eleventh and twelfth centuries, as one factor or another was brought to bear on a particular area.[64]

The best way to see how the Wessex parochial system developed in the century either side of the Norman Conquest is to look at a number of particular areas in detail. Four case-study areas are discussed below: they are all from Hampshire, but that county has been chosen since it seems to be entirely typical of Wessex.

Before looking at these case-study areas, however, it is worth pointing out that three grades of local public church existed in England in the Middle Ages,[65] of which the first was the parish church *(ecclesia)*, completely independent of all ties except to the bishop, responsible for the cure of souls within its parish, with its own *personatus*, and its own incumbent, glebe and tithe. The second is the dependent parochial chapel. This also, at least from the later twelfth century, was responsible for the cure of souls within its parish, and had its own incumbent, glebe, parochial boundaries and its own *personatus*, but was usually required to pay a percentage of its tithe to another parish church, often had other formal ties of subordination to that church,[66] and often had only restricted rights of burial. These dependent parochial chapels were sometimes called *ecclesia*, but more often *capella*. The third type were the chapels 'of ease' pure and simple, without *personatus*, without incumbents, but served by salaried chaplains, without glebe, paid from a chantry trust, or from what the lord, or villagers, saw fit to pay, and very rarely with any rights of burial. The chapels of ease were not responsible for the cure of souls, which remained in the parish church. These places are almost always called *capella*.[67] Both the parochial dependent chapel and the chapel of ease are evidence of subordination, but the first type, which is normally the older, represents a different stage in the process of parochial breakup.

The first of the case-study areas is the Andover area (see Fig. 3.15). This is a chalk district, with two streams, the River Anton and the Pilhill Brook. All the villages are strung out along these streams or the dry valleys above their springs. The royal *burh*, and the ancient mother church, was at Andover, at the stream-side near the crossing of the Roman roads. The ancient *parochia* probably covered the whole area shown on the map, apart from Tangley (which was part of the Hurstbourne *regio*) and Goodworth Clatford (which was part of the Wherwell *regio*), and may well have continued west to cover the few parishes between the area shown on the Map and the Wiltshire border. Andover church was granted to the Abbey of Saumur by William I.

Along the Pilhill Brook the original vills seem to have been spaced regularly along the stream. Upper Clatford and Goodworth Clatford seem each to occupy the space of two units. The parish of Amport clearly covers three, since all three survive, Amport itself, East Cholderton and Sarson. Abbotts Ann also seems to cover the space of three, but in this case only one settlement exists: the abbot of the New Minster, who was granted the estate in the early tenth century,[68] may well have consolidated his holding at some stage. Monxton and Little Ann, however, are clearly original single units.

Along the River Anton the same situation exists. Andover occupies the space of two or three units, and then Enham, Charlton, Foxcot and Penton each occupy one: Enham, Charlton and Foxcot were all part of the royal lands. At some stage in the later Saxon period, however, half of Enham was granted out to a lay thegn.

When parish churches began to be founded here,

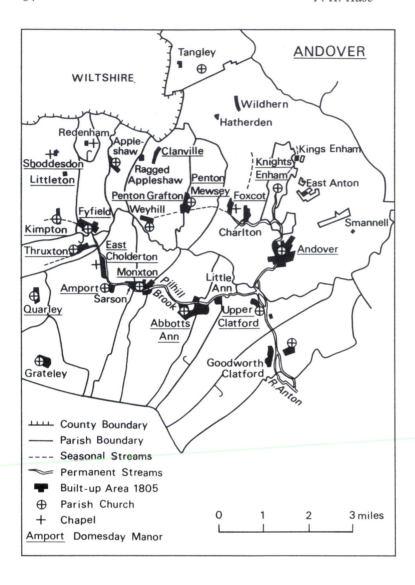

Fig. 3.15 *Parochial structure of the Andover area.*

Amport and Abbotts Ann were probably the earliest after Andover. Amport may originally have been a subordinate church founded to care for the western half of the *parochia*, although it was independent by the twelfth century. Appleshaw, in the forest, remained a parochial chapelry dependent on Amport. The three settlements of Amport parish were held by different lords in and after Anglo-Saxon times: the largest, East Cholderton, established a chapel of ease, probably in the later twelfth century. Abbotts Ann church was probably founded in the tenth century when the New Minster was granted the estate. This estate was all good fertile ground and lacked wood: the original grant therefore included Redenham in the forest – Redenham, with its chapel (of ease), was probably originally a detached part of the parish of Abbotts Ann, but later Redenham became a detached part of the parish of Thruxton, for reasons which are obscure. At Little Ann the pull of lordship was the critical factor in its parochial status. This vill had been part of the tenth-century foundation endowment of Wherwell

Abbey. The abbey, however, rather than establish a separate church for this vill, merely attached it to Goodworth Clatford, of which parish it remained a detached portion thereafter: it never had any chapel.

In the Anton Valley, the thegnly half of Enham (Knight's Enham) established a church for itself, probably early in the twelfth century. The royal half of the vill (King's Enham) remained in the royal *parochia*, so the parish of Knight's Enham remains as a scatter of detached islands entirely surrounded by Andover parish.[69] Of the vills of the royal estate, Foxcot eventually established a chapel of ease, but the inhabitants of Charlton never got any place of worship. To the north and north-east of Andover, the large area of scattered homesteads and little hamlets in the forest never gained any church or chapel either.

Beyond Foxcot, the situation at Penton is interesting. This vill was divided into two manors, Penton Mewsey and Penton Grafton, the latter owned by the abbey of Grestain. The vill lies north-south, and the division between the two manors ran lengthwise through the vill. The Mewsey half established a church, probably in the early twelfth century, but Grestain did not: that half of the vill eventually fell into the parish of Weyhill, a mile to the west, although none of the Grestain homesteads was more than a hundred yards from the Mewsey church. At Penton Mewsey, as at Enham, therefore, the later parish represents only *part* of the vill.

The Andover area shows a number of factors found everywhere in Wessex. The first is the far larger size of the remnant parish of the old mother church than those of the later parish churches cut from it: even when all the break-up factors are considered, a good deal of land, and a significant number of vills, remained within it. The second is that lordship in many places distorted parochial provision, as at Little Ann, Redenham, Knight's Enham, and especially Penton Mewsey. Finally, the older the parish church, the more likely it is to have a wider parish than later arrivals, as shown by Amport, with its dependent vills and dependent forest parish.

The second case-study area is Carisbrooke in the Isle of Wight (see Fig. 3.16). Here the royal manor and mother church stand at the junction of the chalk to the south and the heavily wooded clay to the north. The mother church here was granted to the abbey of Lyre in the reign of William I. Carisbrooke retained a good deal of its ancient *parochia*, however: Northwood and Shorwell remained as dependent parochial chapelries of Carisbrooke throughout: Shorwell, at least, had no cemetery until the middle 14th century.[70]

However, this neat system, with one church and its subordinate dependents occupying the whole block of land, seems to have been interfered with in the early years after the Conquest. The first Norman Lord of the Isle established a castle at Carisbrooke, and built a chapel in it. This chapel he refused to allow to be subordinate to the mother church: the chaplains of St Nicholas-in-Castro therefore held a parish made up of the castle and the numerous tiny detached pieces of land scattered throughout the area, which formed the chapel glebe. Other lands immediately dependent on the royal castle (especially the royal forest of Parkhurst) ended up as extra-parochial places, having fallen between all the available stools.

Chale was founded in 1114 by the lay lord of that vill: Carisbrooke, as the mother church, demanded all the tithe, all the mortuaries, all the alms of the serfs of the estate, half the glebe granted by the lord to the new church, and total freedom from having to care for the new church, either.in its fabric or the souls of its parishioners, as its fee for permitting the church to be built, permitting it to be independent and permitting it to have a cemetery.[71] Gatcombe must have bought its independence at about the same time. Kingston was held by the king in Domesday and it was later a lay manor held of Carisbrooke. Its church is called *capella* in all medieval documents, but without any indication of which church it was a dependent of; it may originally have been dependent on

Gatcombe, in which case this probably represents a short post-Domesday period when it was held with Gatcombe.[72]

The parish of Chale was exactly coterminous with the founding lord's estate. Gatcombe parish was similarly exactly coterminous with the founding estate. Chillerton, a separate lay estate in Domesday, was cut off from Carisbrooke by Gatcombe, but remained as a detached portion of Carisbrooke parish, presumably because the lord of Chillerton was unwilling to pay to build a church for his estate. In these circumstances Chillerton did not fall into the parish of the nearest church – Gatcombe – but remained in the *parochia* from which Gatcombe had been cut out. Chillerton never got any church or chapel. Detached portions of the estates of Brighstone and Wootton near Chillerton became detached portions of the parishes of Brighstone and Wootton as well, respectively four and nine miles away. The main Chillerton area, which was also held together with Wootton from the twelfth century, was probably not made a detached part of Wootton because it was held separately in the critical early twelfth-century period. Since these manorial ties all seem to have developed after the Conquest and before the mid twelfth century, the complex interference they caused with the parochial system in the area must date from the same period. Watchingwell, to the north-west of Carisbrooke, was a detached part of Shalfleet parish, again because of post-Conquest manorial ties.[73]

Outside the *parochia* of Carisbrooke, the forces of lay-lordship also caused problems at Whitwell. This vill was divided into two, both before and after Domesday.[74] Each part was dependent on another vill: Gatcombe, 4 miles to the north-west, or Godshill, 2 miles to the north. The whole of this area was originally part of the *parochia* of, probably, Godshill. However, in the twelfth century the rights of Godshill as mother church seem to have been ignored and the parochial ties treated as an adjunct to the manorial ties. Each half of Whitwell, therefore, was treated as a detached part of the parent manor and parish. However, the two were so intermingled that this became difficult. Disputes between Gatcombe and Godshill, as to which should have the Whitwell area as its dependent parochial chapelry, lead to a unique response: two parochial chapels, each with its own dedication (St Mary, St Radegund), its own nave, and its own chancel, under a single common roof, serving a single common parish jointly, but with two chaplains, one each appointed by the parent churches, and no cemetery, the dead being carried to either Gatcombe or Godshill, depending on who their landlord was.

At Carisbrooke, therefore, the mother church retained much of its *parochia*, but the forces of lay-lordship caused a complexity of parish boundaries that would be amazing, if it was not so common elsewhere in Wessex: within Hampshire, the area between Kingsclere and Sherborne St John is at least as complex. Mother churches with clusters of dependent parochial chapels are common

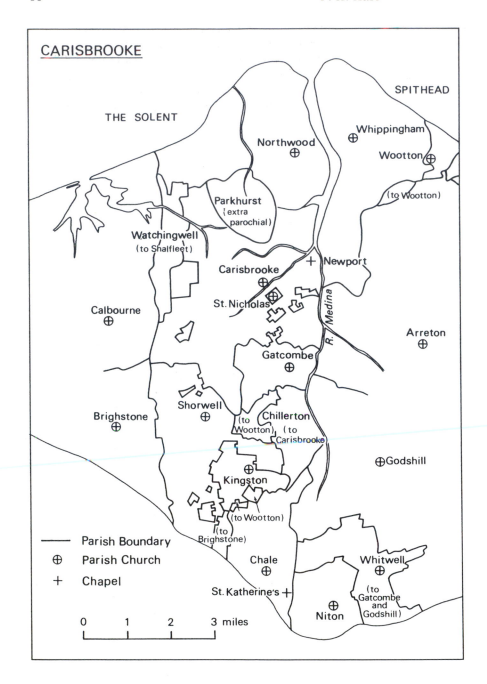

CARISBROOKE

SPITHEAD

THE SOLENT

Northwood ⊕

Whippingham ⊕

Wootton ⊕

(to Wootton)

Parkhurst (extra parochial)

Watchingwell (to Shalfleet)

+ Newport

Carisbrooke ⊕

St. Nicholas ⊕

Calbourne ⊕

R. Medina

Arreton ⊕

Gatcombe ⊕

Shorwell ⊕

Chillerton (to Carisbrooke)

(to Wootton)

Brighstone ⊕

⊕ Godshill

Kingston ⊕

(to Wootton)

(to Brighstone)

—— Parish Boundary
⊕   Parish Church
+   Chapel

Chale ⊕

Whitwell ⊕

St. Katherine's +

(to Gatcombe and Godshill)

Niton ⊕

0   1   2   3 miles

Fig. 3.16 *Parochial structure of the Carisbrooke area.*

throughout Wessex: Christchurch, Alton, Crondall and King's Somborne are among many other examples from Hampshire.

The third case-study area is Titchfield (see Fig. 3.17). Here the ancient mother church (Fig. 3.14) and its community of canons seems to have survived without trouble well into the twelfth century, and possibly even up to the regularisation in 1232. There is no hint in any records that the church was at any date granted to any royal clerk as at Christchurch. As a result, more of the Middle Saxon parochial situation survived here than at Andover, or even, perhaps, than at Carisbrooke, and the influence of lay-lordship was certainly less. The only major problems Titchfield faced were the grants to the Bishop of Win-

chester of Fareham (somewhen probably not long before 963x975)[75] and of Alverstoke, (somewhen probably not long after 948).[76] This removed about a third of the total *parochia* and can be assumed to have been followed shortly by foundation of churches on the two new estates. The loss of Fareham put the Titchfield mother church at the edge of its *parochia*, for the Titchfield/ Fareham parish boundary passes only about twenty yards from the churchyard wall.

After this, however, the *parochia* suffered no further diminution until the twelfth century. Somewhen probably during the early part of that century, the lord of Rowner (the important Hampshire family of Mauditt) managed to establish an independent parish coterminous with his manor, in the extreme south-east of the *parochia*. No records of this foundation, or what it cost the Mauditts, survives.

At Wickham, however, a record of the foundation does survive.[77] Bishop Henry of Blois (probably early in his pontificate) permitted the church, and granted it full independence, but on condition it paid a swingeing pension of 20s a year to Titchfield. Since this was, even at mid twelfth century values, the annual worth of about two virgates, this was a heavy price for the tithe and mortuaries lost to the mother church.

After Wickham there was no further break-up and the parish of Titchfield retained, even into the nineteenth century, a full half of the area it had had in the time of Ine. There were a few chapels of ease, but their rights were always very restricted. Hook Chapel was founded without permission in the mid fourteenth century, and this lead to a dispute lasting over fifty years between the mother church and the executors of the founder's will. The founder's wish for a chapel with a font and grave-

yard here was strenuously opposed by the mother church; a papal licence was secured in 1365 but, after investigation, the bishop interdicted the chapel (1379–1400). A further papal bull lead to further disputes, and an eventual concord papally confirmed in 1437, which permitted Mass to be said at Hook, but forbade a cemetery, and which required the mother church to receive an annual pension of 10 marks.[78] Crofton Chapel, a chapel of ease, was in existence by the time of Domesday, where it is described as *ecclesia*. An ancient chantry provided a chaplain to say Mass and the Hours there: in 1331 a second chantry was to provide for a further priest. No cemetery was ever permitted, however.[79] As to Chark, little is known of it, but it was a chapel of ease with no cemetery.[80] Segensworth was a mere domestic oratory founded in 1347.[81]

Thus Titchfield shows what happened in Wessex where few of the factors favouring break-up of an ancient *parochia* were present. Undoubtedly, in this area, the relatively poor soil (dense woods on clay in the north,

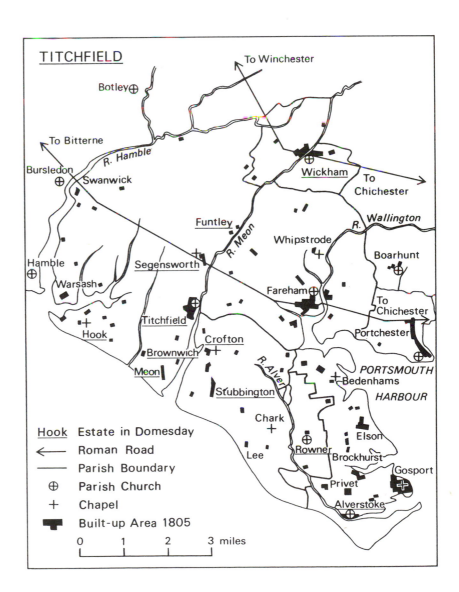

Fig. 3.17 Parochial structure of the Titchfield area.

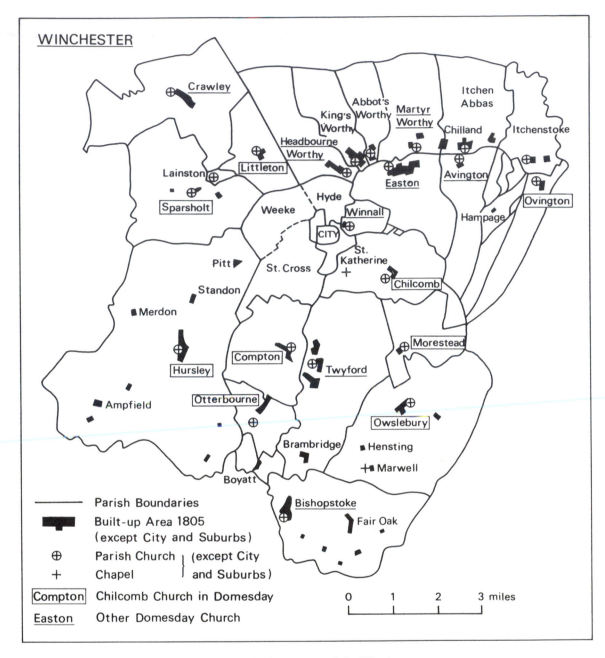

Fig. 3.18 Parochial structure of the Winchester area.

scattered clays and sand in the south, with the royal estate centre and mother church close to the junction between them) played a part. The relatively infertile soil encouraged numerous tiny hamlets and very small manors (eight within the later parish of Titchfield alone at Domesday). There were few strong lay lords with residences here. Massive parishes like Titchfield can be seen in many other places: within Hampshire, Eling, King's Somborne, Kingsclere, Christchurch, East Meon and Crondall are among other very large remnant parishes similar to Titchfield. All these large remnant parishes cover numerous settlements, some of which established chapels of ease, but most not.

The final case-study is the simplest. The Winchester area (see Fig. 3.18) is a very ancient land unit and possibly descends from the Roman *territorium*.[82] Almost all the churches of the area are mentioned in Domesday and the few that are not were almost certainly there then.[83] Almost all the settlements in the area have churches.

In this area, only the parish of Hursley is significantly larger than the others and covers more than one significant settlement: Hursley also had Otterbourne as a dependent parochial chapel. This is probably because Merdon Castle in Hursley was a residence of the bishop's from an early date, and a church at the gates of his residence would have been, at least, a convenience.

Hursley church is, therefore, probably older than the rest and was probably founded as a subordinate church within the *parochia* of the mother church, in this case the Old Minster itself. The next largest vill, Twyford, has Owslebury as a dependent chapelry and may well also be older than the other churches. The others almost certainly all date from the regularisation of the Old Minster and represent a once-and-for-all systematic foundation of churches in all the settlements of the *parochia*, to end problems about the cure of rural souls dependent on Æthelwold's new and observant house. In the whole area only the tiny parish of Lainston is likely to be later than the tenth century in date – this parish, covering only Lainston House and Park, must be twelfth century.

Only two significant settlements, outside the area of Hursley parish, had no church. The first was Chilland, divided lengthwise down the middle between the bishop and Nunnaminster at some unknown Anglo-Saxon date: it may well have been too problematic to decide which house was to pay for any new church there. The other was Hampage, between Avington and Ovington, large in area but sparsely populated, and divided between Easton and Itchen Abbas manors as woodland, and between Easton and Itchen Abbas parishes as detached interlinked outliers.

At Winchester we have a parochial landscape similar to that in much of the Danelaw and evidence of a genuine attempt to provide each settlement, or the majority of settlements, with churches. The area, as a result, has parishes more even in area, with fewer detached portions or anomalies than elsewhere studied. Some other areas within Hampshire are very similar. Mottisfont church, for instance, was granted to the Archbishop of York somewhen in the late Anglo-Saxon period, clearly to provide him with a *pied-à-terre* near Winchester for when the archbishop was at Court in the Wessex heartlands. The archbishop, like Ranulf Flambard, wanted to maximise his income from the estate of the church, since the grant was meaningless unless the church could sustain the Archbishop when he was in the area. The archbishop founded churches on all, or almost all, the settlements of the *parochia*, even the very tiny Bossington and Pittleworth, thus ending any need for him to continue to provide for the cure of souls there. Seven of the ten churches of the area are mentioned in Domesday. Here again a concerted programme of church foundation seems indicated, very probably of the eleventh century.[84]

These case-studies demonstrate at least one thing: that the parochial structure of the medieval period in Wessex was complex and full of anomalies.[85] They show that huge parishes, covering dozens of settlements, like Titchfield, could survive into the medieval period where conditions were right for this, and others equally large could survive in different circumstances, with the remnant parish of the mother church supported by dependent parochial chapelries, as at Carisbrooke. At the same time, the forces of lordship could cause anomalies such as those along the Pilhill Brook and the River Anton, with some vills getting churches, others chapels, and yet others nothing; and with some vills getting churches for the one half of the vill, but not for the other. In yet other places, those same forces could cause the clusters of anomalies that can be seen in areas like that between Gatcombe and Chale. Large settlements with no church or chapel, or attached to churches a good way off, lie next door to minute settlements with churches. In other areas, attempts have been made to give every settlement a church, with nothing left to suggest any lingering mother church influence; in others, the provision of churches seems to have been a matter of pure historical chance. All in all, it is a situation easier to describe than to explain.

Stagnation and Decay, the Parochial System from the late Twelfth to the mid Nineteenth Century

The last phase of the development of the parochial system in England before the modern period is as long as the preceding three phases put together, but there was relatively little development during it. During the twelfth century the development of the Canon Law eventually caused a revolution in thinking on provision of local churches. In the last Anglo-Saxon and the first Norman century, foundation of new churches had proceeded briskly – almost certainly three-quarters of all the later churches of Wessex were founded in this period. In the middle twelfth century this slowed down, and at some point came to an almost total stop. In the Diocese of Winchester it is possible to date the stop to 1171: Bishop Henry de Blois belonged (at least partly) to the old world, Bishop Richard of Ilchester to the new. In the other Wessex dioceses the stop occurs at about the same date.

One of the aims of the Gregorian Reforms was to free the Church from lay domination. At the local level, this aim was manifested by a drive to ensure that all persons responsible for the cure of souls had an indefeasible income, not dependent on the goodwill or charity of laymen or ecclesiastical superiors. Previously, the priests of 'field churches' had often been paid a salary by the lord, or had received the income from land granted by the lord, but on terms which were unclear and which did not necessarily preclude resumption at the lord's will. Further, it was unclear if a priest could sell or otherwise dispose of any land or income that had been granted him.

The reformers introduced three reforms. The first was the concept that all priests with cure of souls must have that cure 'realised', that is, affixed to a defined area of land, which should be land granted to God, indefeasible and sacred. This glebe should be approved by the bishop at the consecration of the church. The glebe formed the *titulus* of the church: priests were not to be ordained unless they had been granted, or granted the reversion, of this *titulus* in full and, once ordained, the priest was to be formally and publicly inducted by the bishop into this land. The tithe, mortuary, alms and other church dues such as church-scot, were steadily more carefully defined, and were to be considered as incidents to the land of the *titulus*. This reform made it difficult for the lord to resume or reduce land granted to the local church. Where churches were held by a monastery, the reform required that the income of the church be formally divided into income which could be held *sine cura* by the monastery, and the land which was to become the *titulus* of the vicar, who was to hold the cure of souls. A major feature of the reform, therefore, was the formal definition of the lands and income to be held by vicars, who were to be inducted into it. The old practice, where monasteries merely used a salaried chaplain, was no longer to be tolerated, except in exceptional circumstances. The local lord was no longer to be the lord, *dominus*, of the church, but merely its defender, *advocatus*, with very tightly defined rights which extended in no way to the glebe.

The second reform was the introduction of the concept of *personatus*. In the eleventh century, the juridical status of the ordinary local church was in doubt. Only the ancient mother churches had a clear legal status, or had held land 'in alms'. Now, all churches with cure of souls were to have juridical status, *personatus*. The local church was, in other words, to be a juridical person, a legal corporation. The inducted holder of the cure of souls, whether rector or vicar, was to be the *persona*, the parson, the holder for the time being of the juridical person: in English law terms, he was to be a corporation sole. As such, the holder of the cure of souls, the curate, had the right to sue in his and his church's name. The *titulus* was placed in the strongest and most difficult to abuse of all legal forms: in an undying corporation holding in mortmain. The implications of this reform were to make it impossible for any priest to alienate, or let on long or unduly beneficial leases, the income of his church: he was only a trustee for his successors as holders of the *personatus*, and would be in danger of his immortal soul if the *titulus* was not handed on exactly as received.[86]

The third reform was to make more clear what the cure of souls was, and where it lay. Essentially, the reform demanded that all places lie in some known parish, and that in each parish there be one and only one holder of the cure of souls. A parochial dependent chapel was, for the future, to be dependent only as to its *sine cura* income, and its inducted *curatus* was to hold the *titulus* and its affixed cure of souls of the bishop direct. No-one was to have two or more churches each responsible for his soul, or each in part responsible. This reform was less fully implemented than the other two, and numerous anomalies remained, but it was enforced to a large degree.

These reforms were extremely successful and the local church operated effectively under them, in England to very recent times. The local churches ceased totally to be subject to the domination of the lord of the vill in question. Although at the end of the eleventh century none of these things was commonly found, by the end of the twelfth century ordained vicarages, inducted *curati*, and local churches with *personatus* were universal in England and were accepted as normal and natural by every class of men.

At the same time, although the success and revolutionary impact for good of these reforms cannot be doubted, they had grave effects on the foundation of new churches. The Canon Law prohibition of founding new churches which harmed any existing church – a prohibition which became steadily more strongly worded during the mid and late twelfth century – had not affected the brisk foundation of new churches in the period 950–1150 because of the doubts as to the juridical status of the new churches. If the new churches were merely chapels, with the cure of souls still juridically lying in the old churches, then the new church did not fall under the prohibition, so long as the older mother church did not object to it. But once every rural church was to be considered juridically to have *personatus*, and once the cure of souls was clearly affixed to the local church and not the mother church, then the prohibition made it difficult for any new churches to be founded with cure of souls. No such church could, in normal circumstances, fail to affect the income of some existing church, and any such church could not be permitted by the *curatus* of the existing church without risking the integrity of the *titulus* he was obliged to hand on to his successor.

Incumbents of existing churches became very jealous of their ecclesiastical income once they were accepted as being merely trustees of it. Even the tiniest of chapels of ease could reduce that income. The week-by-week income from alms for the tiny chapel of Plant in Southwick parish in Hampshire survive for 1392–1394: for 1393, the income from alms was £1.10*s*.7*d*[87] For chapels such as Hook in Titchfield, where the population served would have been ten times as great as that at Plant,[88] the income lost would have been substantial. The objections of Titchfield to the establishment of a chapel at Hook were not unusual: few chapels of ease were granted without a struggle, after the end of the twelfth century, unless there was a grant of income to the mother church to offset the loss, and chapels which were to be in the gift of the founder were usually objected to very strongly (Hook, when eventually agreed, was to be served by a canon of Titchfield). Once the Canon Law reforms were fully in place, new churches or dependent parochial chapels with cure of souls became almost an impossibility; but even new chapels of ease without cure of souls damaged the *titulus* of a church and were, therefore, granted only very reluctantly.

In the Diocese of Winchester Bishops Walkelin and William Giffard had left decisions on church foundation to the heads of the mother churches affected, as their Anglo-Saxon predecessors had also done. They showed no sign of the new, Gregorian, thinking on this issue. The bishop had, of course, to be involved in any church foundation, since the bishop alone could consecrate the new church and the Canon Law had for many centuries forbidden Mass to be said in unconsecrated buildings. However, at Milford in 1090, Walkelin merely noted the concord which the founder and Christchurch had already arrived at, and the church was, it would seem, already built and ready before the bishop was involved. The new church at Milford had no glebe or indefeasible income: the land granted by the founder went to the mother church, which was to serve the church by sending one of its priests there *ad hoc*, or else a salaried chaplain. Clearly, the cure of souls was to remain at Christchurch.

At Chale in 1114 the dispute between the founder and the mother church had to be settled by the bishop's arbitration 'when he arrived to conscrate the church': again, Giffard, despite his reputation as a reformer, and like Walkelin, had not seen fit to intervene or interest himself in the process until the church was built and ready for use. Land was granted to the new church, but the mother church took half of it, and it was still land, it would appear, in the disposal of the lord. Here, however, the cure of souls was transferred to the new church. Neither at Milford nor at Chale were episcopal charters issued: all that survive are notes from memoranda notebooks.

Bishop Henry de Blois took a more lively interest than his predecessors in the local church and local provision for the cure of souls, and was more aware of the trends of thought developing in the church.[89] The first vicarage ordinations in the diocese come from his pontificate, including a very important set covering the churches dependent on Christchurch, from the early part of the pontificate. New churches founded under his supervision were to have adequate endowments and these were to be defined by charter. The foundations in his pontificate, therefore, involve episcopal charters even where, as at Bursledon, private agreements had been reached beforehand between founder and mother church. New churches in this period were to be responsible for the cure of souls: the mother churches were to be bought off by a defined grant of *sine cura* income, as in the pension required to be paid by Wickham to Titchfield. At the same time, Bishop de Blois continued to allow the foundation of churches to go ahead freely: the implications of the juridical independence of the local churches had not yet been fully accepted.

Bishop Richard of Ilchester and his successors and colleagues, however, were aware of the legal implications of the new practices. They accepted that it was impossible for any church to be founded without harming the *titulus* of a pre-exisiting one. The rigid definition and 'realisation' of local parochial income, to defend it against the unscrupulous, had reached its peak, and the negative consequence, the practical impossibility of establishing a new *ecclesia curata,* with it. After 1171 only three or four new parishes were established in Hamp-

shire until the second quarter of the nineteenth century, and much the same is true of all the Wessex dioceses. The king's new town of Portsmouth, granted its charter in 1194, was probably given a parish by Bishop Richard of Ilchester, and its church was permitted to have a graveyard (consecrated 1196), although the new church remained a dependent parochial chapelry of Portsea. The king's new town of Stockbridge also got a parish, but here, although the first certain mention of the town is 1200, the town may in fact have been developed several decades earlier.[90] The bishop's new town at New Alresford (probably founded in the first decade of the thirteenth century) got a parish, as did another episcopal new town at Newton-in-Burghclere (founded 1218). These new town parishes were chapelries dependent respectively on King's Somborne, Old Alresford and Burghclere.[91] Other late twelfth-century new towns, however, founded by less exalted patrons, had to make do with a mere chapel of ease, as at Gosport, or at Newport in the Isle of Wight: the episcopal new town of Newton Francheville in the Isle of Wight only had a chapel of ease, but that new town was only founded in the 1250s, by which time the unalterability of parochial boundaries had become a rigid doctrine.

The same process can be seen in Dorset and Wiltshire: the cathedral, and the other churches in the New Town of Salisbury certainly received parishes (early thirteenth century), but neither Weymouth (?late twelfth century) nor Poole (founded in the 1170s) got a parish, and their chapels remained mere chapels of ease.

Nowhere in Hampshire other than this handful of new towns received a parish after 1171. None of the over-large remnant parishes like Titchfield were divided at a date later than this. No lay lord who had not moved to get himself a church at his gates before then was able to get one hereafter: at best, a chapel of ease, more likely a domestic oratory, if that, was all that was now possible.

A few chapels of ease were founded at all dates, but most were established either at the end of the twelfth century (when they can be understood as a final reflex of the massive wave of parochial foundation of the previous two hundred years) or in the fourteenth century (when they are probably to be seen as a reflex of late medieval piety, since almost all such chapels at this date were established around a chantry). Several date from the eleventh or earlier twelfth centuries: these can be seen as foundations where there was inadequate money to achieve even the circumscribed independence of a dependent parochial chapelry.

Throughout Wessex dozens of tiny eleventh- and twelfth-century churches can still be seen: little one- or two-celled buildings, with tiny wooden bell-cots over the west gable, built of flint or clunch, and seating about forty people. (see Fig. 3.19) In situations such as Mottisfont half a dozen such churches might have been built at one time in a single area: the piety of early twelfth-century lay lords of places like Knight's Enham and

Fig. 3.19 *The Saxon church at Alton Barnes in Wiltshire. (Photo: Mick Aston)*

Penton Mewsey also built churches like this. 250 or 300 years after they were first built, these churches started to become ruinous and to need major repairs. When they were built, there was a great magnate who paid for them, or they came into being on a wave of piety. The rebuilding, however, was the duty of the two or three families of the place, who often could not afford to repair their church.

The fourteenth and fifteenth centuries, therefore, saw a number of minute parishes amalgamated. This was not a development arising from the abandonment of the village: in most cases the parish was far too small ever to have supported a village. It was a retrenchment, reducing the over-enthusiastic parochial provision of the twelfth century down to something closer to what the population could actually maintain. Thus, again taking Hampshire as a typical Wessex county, Cliddesden was amalgamated with Hatch Warren in 1380,[92] Ellisfield All Saints with Ellisfield St Martin in 1383, Kempshott with Winslade in 1393,[93] Wellsworth with Widley in 1426, and West Dean chapelry with West Dean parish (in Wiltshire and Salisbury Diocese) in 1473.[94] Also in the later Middle Ages, but at dates now unknown, Pittleworth chapel became ruinous and was effectively united to Bossington; and Idsworth and Chalton, and King's Worthy and Abbot's Worthy were amalgamated. This process continued after the Reformation with, for example, the amalgamation of Abbotstone and Itchenstoke in 1589, and the

attempted amalgamation of Deane and Ashe in 1591.

By far the most significant retrenchment, however, came at the Reformation. Those many chapels of ease funded from a chantry lost their endowment at the Dissolution of Chantries: a few parish churches, where a chantry provided a substantial part of the income of the incumbent, became unviable at the same time and fell into ruin, or ceased for a time to be used as churches.[95] The majority of domestic oratories also closed: in the later Middle Ages many families of only the most local of significance (e.g. the Waite family at Segensworth in Titchfield) had acquired a domestic oratory: after the Reformation only the greatest of magnates retained one, and even then rarely.

In the Titchfield area, Crofton Chapel survived the loss of its chantry income and was kept in being through the alms of the inhabitants, as did the chapel serving Gosport, but Chark and Hook both disappeared, as well as the domestic oratory at Segensworth, and Whipstrode in Fareham and Bedenham in Alverstoke.[96] Foxcot Chapel survived in Andover in the same way as did Crofton, but East Cholderton and Redenham disappeared, and the domestic oratory at Shoddesden. In Selborne parish, the chapels of Norton, Blackmoor, Oakhanger, Whaddon and Makerel all disappeared, plus two or three domestic oratories. Within the single county of Hampshire some eighty or so places of public worship (i.e. not including domestic oratories, hospitals, etc) disappeared at the Reformation, most, probably, at the Dissolution of Chantries, representing about one fifth of all those that then existed. At most half a dozen rural chapels of ease survived in Hampshire, plus the chapels of ease in Gosport and Newport. It is true that many of the chapels which disappeared at the Reformation were poor and in a run-down condition: nonetheless, the retrenchment in provision for public worship is a feature not always noted as a side-effect of the Reformation.[97] In very large parishes like Titchfield, the disappearance of the public chapels in the mid sixteenth century must have helped in the growth of Dissent in the seventeenth: the Established Church was left just too thinly spread.[98] In the Titchfield area in the seventeenth and eighteenth centuries there were probably no more ministers of the Established Church than had been there in the time of Ine, a thousand years before, and very possibly there were fewer.

This seven hundred year period of stagnation in provision for the local church has often been noted, especially in those areas of the midlands and north where new industrial development led to new towns growing up where previously there had been only waste. In Wessex this did not pose a serious problem. The Wessex towns in the early nineteenth century were much the same as the Wessex towns in the fourteenth century. That part of the parish of St Mary Extra, Southampton, which was separated from the rest of the parish by the estuary of the Itchen was given a new chapel of ease in 1620 (Jesus Chapel, Peartree Green): this area had probably been served before the Reformation by the chapel in the bishop's manor at Bitterne. Portsmouth and Gosport had grown, but not hugely so, and the Commissioners of the Royal Dockyard had exercised their authority to allow foundation of two new churches (plus the dockyard church of St Anne of 1704) to serve the dockyard town of Portsea (St John, of the later eighteenth century, and St George, of 1754), and further new foundations at Portsea were approved in the 1820s. A church was founded to serve the new holiday resort of Cowes in 1816. These were the only new public churches founded in Hampshire between the Reformation and the mid Victorian age. The foundations at Jesus Chapel, Portsea, and Cowes, were legally only chapels of ease, although their ministers seem to have exercised the cure of souls. New parishes at Cowes and Portsea were formally established only in the mid nineteenth century.

Wessex entered the nineteenth century as well served with local churches as it had been two centuries earlier. The Portsea foundations had left Portsmouth noticeably well provided with churches, and Cowes got its chapel very soon after it began to develop as a resort. Nowhere else in Wessex did post-medieval changes in population cause serious stress. When the coming of the railway brought new populations to previously empty places such as Swindon and Eastleigh, or to the heathlands northwest of Titchfield, it brought with it at the same time the Victorian willingness to build new churches.

Thus, from the first coming of the Christian faith to the Wessex countryside in the fourth century to the revolution in the nineteenth century we can see a basically two phase development in provision of local churches. The first was the systematic provision of mother churches at the royal estate centres, a development centred on the late seventh and early eighth centuries. The second was the partial break up of this system, especially during the period from the mid tenth to the mid twelfth century, as the result of a number of forces acting erratically and unsystematically on the mother churches. This development, if it had continued unchecked, would probably have resulted in a situation where every vill, every settlement, had its own church or chapel but, in fact, developments in legal thought led to a seven hundred year long freeze in local church foundation from the later twelfth to the mid nineteenth centuries. The Wessex parochial system, therefore, was inherited by the Victorians in an inchoate form, frozen half-way through a natural process. The system remained anomalous. Economic and social structures continued to develop throughout the period, but the local church, which had been more or less in step with economic and social changes between the eighth and the twelfth centuries, failed to develop with them thereafter.

Notes

1. For Christianity in Roman and sub-Roman Britain see in general Watts (1991) and Thomas (1981); for Poundbury, C. S. Green, 'The Cemetery of a Romano-British Community at Poundbury, Dorchester', in Pearce (1982). It should be noted that almost all the evidence for Roman and sub-Roman Christianity comes from recent archaeological discoveries and significant new finds are being reported almost every year: anything said on this subject, therefore, is liable to become dated quickly. See Fig. 3.12 for Poundbury.
2. Winterbottom (1978), section 10.2.
3. Thomas (1981) p. 169, and Watts (1991) p. 243, n. 9.
4. Bidwell (1978), and C. G. Henderson and P. T. Bidwell, 'The Saxon Minster at Exeter', in Pearce (1982); and for a more accessible treatment, see J. Allan, C. Henderson, and R. Higham, 'Saxon Exeter', in Haslam (1984), pp. 385–394.
5. The most accessible treatment of the Uley evidence is in Woodward (1992).
6. Thomas (1981), Watts (1991), Pearce (1982), Aston (1986), Dunning (1976a), Rahtz (1972, 1982–3), and P. Rahtz, 'Pagan and Christian by the Severn Sea', in Abrams (1991), Costen (1992).
7. See note 6.
8. Thomas (1981) p. 136.
9. Rahtz, in Abrams (1991), Morris (1989), pp. 31–33
10. W. Rodwell, 'From Mausoleum to Minster: The Early Development of Wells Minster', in Pearce (1982).
11. Watts (1991) Rahtz (1972, 1982–3, and in Abrams 1991) *op. cit.*, also P. Rahtz and L. Watts, 'The End of Roman

Temples in the West of Britain', in Casey (1979): Rahtz and Watts suggest that organised pagan worship lasted longer than is suggested here, but give little concrete evidence for this much later than 400.

12. St Patrick, Letter to Coroticus, St Patrick: His writings and Muirchie's life (Hood A. B. E. (ed. and trans.) para 2, 7, 14, 15, 19, pp. 35–38.

13. Colgrave and Mynors (1969), pp. 54–67, esp. p. 54, n. 2, p. 64, n. 1. These statements in Bede are taken from the contemporary Lives of Germanus and Lupus. See Thomas (1981) p. 53–60, 333–335 for an analysis, also p. 203–205 for contemporary rules on admission to baptism of unbelievers.

14. Winterbottom (1978), sections 28–36.

15. Watts (1991) pp. 221–2 discusses the small size of sub-Roman churches in Britain. Woodward (1992) discusses the construction of the successive churches at Uley. Most of the known fourth-century churches were no bigger than the later Irish hermitages, although those found within the *civitates* or other major towns were larger.

16. Discussion of the fifth- and sixth-century religious history of South Wales has been bedevilled by the poor reputation of the hagiographical sources, most of which are very late and demonstrably untrustworthy in many details. However, recent work has shown that the basic structure of the hagiography ties in with archaeological facts on the ground and with the charter evidence that survives (Davies (1982), Edwards and Lane (1992)). It seems reasonable to give credence to the hagiography at least as far as accepting the name, approximate date (to the half century) and church(es) of the saint, and to rather more than that where the saint is mentioned in contemporary or near contemporary written material. The view of W. H. L. Frend ('Romano-British Christianity and the West: Comparison and Contrast', in Pearce (1982)), that Romano-British Christianity was weak and effectively extinguished by the influx of the Anglo-Saxons, and that there was no vigorous early development of monasticism in the sub-Roman church, cannot be sustained.

17. Approximately modern Monmouthshire: Dyfrig was bishop of this area. See Davies (1982) pp. 141–168. There are some half-dozen references to churches from this area founded before 650 in charters surviving from this period: some other similar but undatable charters may also be sixth or seventh century in date.

18. The hagiography for Cornwall is even poorer than for South Wales, but the same basic facts apply. See A. Preston-Jones, 'Decoding Cornish Churchyards', in Edwards and Lane (1992). The recent excavations at Tintagel have demonstrated a fifth-century date for the initiation of Christian uses of this site (most accessible in Thomas (1993), pp. 100–105, and full bibliography at p. 137).

19. Pearce (1978, 1982, 1985), Dunning (1978a). Other 'Celtic' dedications in Somerset are to well-known Celtic saints and should, in the opinion of Pearce, be ascribed to the Celtic sympathies of, in particular, Glastonbury Abbey in the twelfth century. However, Carantoc, Decuman, Kea and Kew are sufficiently obscure to make it unlikely that they would have been chosen as dedicatees in the twelfth century: the Kewstoke dedication, indeed, is mentioned in the eleventh century, and the Celtic form of the place-name Lantocai also suggests a date far ear-

lier than the twelfth century. The fifth-century 'Caratacus' stone, which is clearly Christian, is not far from Carhampton, strongly suggesting that there was a church somewhere in this corner of Somerset before the coming of the Anglo-Saxons, and St Carantoc's is the most likely.

20. Pearce, 'Estates and Church Sites in Dorset and Gloucestershire: The Emergence of a Christian Society', in Pearce (1982); also, Pearce (1978), Taylor (1970). In Wiltshire only West Dean and Cherhill churches are close to villa sites, but both these churches are of late foundation, and the proximity to villas is unlikely to be of significance. West Hulme in Dorset, a late founded church, is also built in close proximity to a major Roman building but this must be considered as arising from different circumstances. For West Dean and Cherhill, see Victoria County History, Wiltshire, Vol. 1 (II), p. 484.

21. Pearce (1978), Taylor (1970).

22. Rahtz in Abrams (1991) *op. cit.* As so often where archaeological evidence is in question, this development is likely, but cannot be proved. The move to the foot of the hill could have come later in the seventh century.

23. Murphy (1991).

24. L. Keen, 'The Towns of Dorset' in Haslam (1984) pp. 205–212, also Gem (1976).

25. Some other early cemeteries in the Isle of Wight and the extreme south-east of the county must represent the first Jutish settlers of that region, rather than the early West Saxons.

26. Anglo-Saxon Chronicle, sub anno 577, the Battle of Dyrham. The date is open to discussion, but the basic fact seems secure.

27. Taylor (1970), suggests that eastern Dorset, including Purbeck, may not have been conquered for some time after *æt Peonnum*. Potts (1976) has suggested that, even down to the 1930s, the populations of Somerset and Dorset were still demonstrably genetically different from those of Wiltshire and Hampshire – i.e. were closer to the genetic norms of the Celtic areas of Britain.

28. Lapidge and Herren (1979), p. 9; (1985), p. 8.

29. Gregson (1985), Jones (1976, 1981, 1985), Faull (1984), Hooke (1988).

30. The essential similarities of the Middle Saxon and Celtic church have recently been the subject of considerable interest: the line adopted here, that the two were, in many ways, very similar, is also the basic finding of the papers in Blair and Sharpe (1992) and of some of those in Edwards and Lane (1992). In only one respect does the Celtic church seem somewhat different from the later Saxon church. The Saxon church was very closely allied to the royal power. The Celtic church was similarly, in practice, tied to the royal power, but seems to have wished to be more detached from it than the Saxon church found desirable. The sort of words St Patrick addressed to King Coroticus, or Gildas to the kings of his day, would have been unthinkable to any Anglo-Saxon cleric. As a result, while the Celtic church, like the Saxon church, built its local churches on the royal estates, the Celtic churches were sometimes built at some distance from the royal hall, rather than, as more frequently with the Saxons, immediately at its gates. St Decuman's, therefore, is even today at an inconvenient distance from Watchet, and

Aldhelm found it desirable to move the church at Sherborne over a mile to a site nearer the *burh* (see above, n. 24). In no other respect, however, does the sub-Roman church seem significantly different from the church in the Saxon east.

31. In Kent, the areas subject to the central places seem larger than those in Wessex, and a hierarchy of central places can be seen. Also, in Kent, the position and lands of the queen seem to be more significant than in Wessex. Early churches are wealthier than in Wessex, reflecting the larger area of the region subject to the central place in question, and the churches were less likely to have been built immediately adjacent to the royal *burh*. The Queen's role in church foundation seems more important than in Wessex. In Mercia, great estates held by noble families seem to be more in evidence than in Wessex: the royal power seems more diffuse. The sizes of areas subject to individual central places in Mercia may have varied from region to region.

32. In two areas of Wessex it has been shown that the *parochiae* of seventh- or early eighth-century churches were contiguous, thus implying strongly that the *regiones* on which they stood were contiguous also. The one is west Surrey, where the *parochiae* of Farnham, Godalming, Woking, and Chertsey are contiguous (see Blair (1991), and J. Blair, 'Introduction: From Minster to Parish Church', in Blair (1988)), the other south-west Hampshire and east Dorset, where Wimborne Minster, Christchurch, Eling, Southampton, Bishop's Waltham and Titchfield are (see P. H. Hase, 'The Mother Churches of Hampshire', in Blair (1988)). Reading and Sonning in Berkshire; Banwell, Congresbury and Cheddar; Watchet and Carhampton; Glastonbury and Wells in Somerset must also have had contiguous *parochiae*.

33. It would be wrong to assume that the king regularly visited all his *villae*. A *burh* which is a busy working farm would have been an uncomfortable place for a court, even temporarily. It is more likely that the king had some specific residences, separated from the farm area, to which the surplus from several *regiones* would be sent as required. Cheddar, where the Saxon palace discloses no sign of a farm, is likely to have been one such. As frequently, the Court met in a hunting lodge in the forest where, doubtless, the bulk of the Court would reside in tented accommodation. Thus, kings were at Andover in Hampshire in 959x963, 980 and 994, but were at Enham in 1006x1011 and Grateley in 924x939. Enham and Grateley were both parts of the royal estate of Andover, and both lay in or near well forested parts of it, where the Roman roads crossed, or came close to, the forest. Similarly, the kings are never recorded at Alton in Hampshire, but are recorded in 898, 970 and *c*. 990 at Woolmer (part of the Alton estate), probably implying Kingsley, where the Roman road across Woolmer Forest crosses King John's Hill. See Figs 3.8, 3.9. The presence of the kings at Woodyates, Dorset (?869, 970/981), and Wellow in Hampshire (934), is probably due to the same factor.

34. See Haslam (with Biek and Littlecote) (1984) for extensive iron working on a royal vill in Wiltshire (Ramsbury). Salt was certainly exacted from all the royal estates along the Solent.

35. See in particular the events following the death of King Alfred, when the revolt by his disappointed nephew, Æthelwold, started with the seizure of the royal *burhs* of Wimborne and Christchurch (Anglo-Saxon Chronicle, sub anno 901), but see also the Anglo-Saxon Chronicle sub anno 733 (Somerton), and possibly sub anno 722 (Taunton), royal assassinations and depositions at such *burhs* (in the general Wessex area) in 758, 765, 786, and 946 (Anglo-Saxon Chronicle, sub anno 757), and the frequent location of battles at or near royal estates in the general Wessex region in 628, 779, 836, 864, 871, 878, 1001 (*bis*) and 1016.

36. Many have survived to become the market towns of today, places like Andover, Alton or Odiham in Hampshire; Chippenham, Calne or Amesbury in Wiltshire; Wimborne or Gillingham in Dorset; Bruton, Frome or Crewkerne in Somerset.

37. It is possible that, in some places, the reeve had no royal estate to manage, but was dependent solely on grain coming in from *vectigal* to meet the king's demands on him, but this is unlikely to have been a frequent situation. There is debate on whether the kings in early and early Middle Saxon times had any 'demesne lands' or were merely possessed of a power to demand *vectigal*, 'hospitality', or other dues from the other land-holders. This last seems unlikely and contrary both to the known facts from later Saxon times, and to what is known of other lands, especially the Welsh lands. *Vectigal* was extremely important, but the system would have broken down if the kings had not had a dependable income from their own lands as well. When the kings granted out broad lands to the Church, covering a hundred hides or so, it is certain that, over most of the area, a right to exact *vectigal* and other dues was what was passing, but in every case, it would seem, at the heart of the grant was an estate which was to be worked directly by the grantee.

38. If for no other reason than that the '-bury' element in the name Shaftesbury implies earthen fortifications. No hillfort is known there, but the name is older than the ninth- to tenth-century fortifications.

39. See J. Haslam, 'The Towns of Wiltshire', in Haslam (1984), pp. 90–94.

40. Knowlton, in Dorset, one of the most famous churches built within prehistoric remains, is a late founded church, in the area originally almost certainly subject to the church at Wimborne Minster.

41. Thus, in Winchester, the Old Minster site occupies about a fifth of the enceinte and does not reach to any of the through roads. The same goes for Exeter, Bath (and for Gloucester, too, even though that was never a Christian West Saxon city).

42. The early church history of the Portchester area is unclear, but there was no early church within the walls.

43. The springs are not within the churchyards, or so close that the church and the spring seem possibly to have had any ritual connection: most frequently, the spring is about 100 yards from the church.

44. E.g. '-æwiell (spring)' (as at Alton), '-wielle (spring)' (as at Wherwell), '-burnan (stream)' (as at Sherborne, Wimborne, Somborne), '-funta (spring)' (as at Mottisfont, Havant), '-ieg (island)' (as at Romsey, Muchelney), '-ford (ford)' (as at Britford, Bradford, Canford), '-dubri/dever (stream)' (as at Andover, Micheldever), etc.

45. E.g. Twynham (Christchurch), '*æt betweonan eam* (between the rivers)'.
46. E.g. (Nether)avon, (Up)avon, (East) Meon, and also Wilton, Bruton, Sturminster, Ilminster (from the rivers Wylye, Brue, Stour, Yeo) and also Downham (the 'downstream settlement') and Overton (the 'upstream settlement').
47. Odiham in Hampshire, Shaftesbury and the Purbeck mother church (whether that was at Corfe or Kingston: see Taylor (1970)) in Dorset, and Tilshead in Wiltshire are among the very few exceptions and, of these, Odiham is within about 250 yards of water, and Tilshead may have been adjacent to a spring when water-tables were higher than they are today.
48. Haslam, in Haslam (1984), *op. cit.*, and maps there, especially p. 135.
49. Barker (1980) and 'The Early History of Sherborne' in Pearce (1982) suggests that the enclosure visible in the Sherborne layout is an old ecclesiastical *lan*, but Keen and Gem (see n. 25) sufficiently demonstrate that this is unlikely. For the size of *lans* in Cornwall see A. Preston-Jones in Edwards and Lane (1992) *op. cit*: for those in Wales see T. James 'Air photography of Ecclesiastical Sites in South Wales', D. Brook 'The Early Christian Church East and West of Offa's Dyke', and H. James 'Early medieval cemeteries in Wales', all in Edwards and Lane (1992).
50. Wealthier churches include Frome (8 carucates), Wells (14 hides), Crewkerne (10 hides), Calne (6 hides), Ramsbury (4 hides), East Meon (6 hides 1 virgate), Mottisfont (4 hides 3 virgates), Alton (5 hides?), Kingsclere (4 hides 1 virgate), Romsey (14 hides), Wherwell (22 hides), Christchurch (6 hides 1 virgate). Of these, Wells, Wherwell and Romsey probably include tenth century additions to an earlier endowment. Some possibly very rich churches (e.g. Andover) are omitted from Domesday. In eighth-century Wessex there were one or two very much wealthier churches in each of the later counties, which quite stand out from the rest: Chertsey in Surrey; the Old Minster in Hampshire; Malmesbury in Wiltshire; Glastonbury and Muchelney in Somerset; Sherborne in Dorset. The special role of these churches in Wessex was important, but is not dealt with here.
51. E.g. Carisbrooke (1 virgate, but worth £4), Eling (½ carucate, 'in alms'), King's Somborne (½ hide, 'in alms'), Congresbury (½ hide, worth 20*s*), Cannington (2½ virgates, worth 30*s*), Chewton Mendip (½ hide, worth 40*s*). Beneficial hidation of mother churches can be seen under way in Domesday, e.g. East Meon (6 hides 1 virgate, previously paying tax for so much, but now paying tax for 3 hides 1 virgate), Mottisfont, (4 hides 3 virgates, but paying tax for 3 hides 3 virgates), Kingsclere (4 hides 1 virgate, but now paying no tax), Romsey (14 hides, now paying tax for 10), etc.
52. Hase, in Blair (1988), *op. cit.*, contains a translation of the document in question, with a discussion.
53. The lack of learning should not, however, be over-stressed. St Boniface lived at the local West Saxon church of Nursling, and his correspondence contains enough letters to and from local West Saxon clerics to make it clear that learning and piety were not unknown there.
54. 685x687, King Caedwalla grants land to Cedde, Cisi and Criswa, for the foundation of a minster at Farnham, Sawyer (1968) no. 235.
55. Hare (1976), (1992).
56. On which last see Gibb (1975).
57. Space does not permit this statement to be demonstrated here, but every detailed study of West Saxon mother churches suggests it, even if it can only rarely be proved. See Hase in Blair (1988) *op. cit.* for a discussion of the evidence for Christchurch, Eling, Southampton, Titchfield and Bishop's Waltham, Blair 'From Minster to Parish Church' in Blair (1988) for Godalming and (1991) for Chertsey, Dunning (1975) for Ilchester and (1976) for Crewkerne, Hinton and Webster (1987) for Wareham, Canford, Wimborne Minster, Bere, Winfrith Newburgh, Corfe/Kingston and Sturminster Marshall, Kemp (1967–68) for Thatcham and (1968) for Berkeley. The articles in Haslam (1984) are also valuable, especially for Wiltshire and Dorset. See also M. Aston 'Post Roman Central Places in Somerset' in Grant (1986). For a general treatment see Blair 'Secular Minster Churches in Domesday Book' in Sawyer (1985), 'Local Churches in Domesday Book and before' in Holt (1987), Blair and Sharpe (1992), Brooke (1982), etc.
58. The documents are discussed in detail in Hase in Blair (1988) *op. cit.*
59. While unequivocal contemporary evidence for such a rule is lacking, the rule can be inferred from the fact that few, if any, of the estates of the bishops or any of the regular monastic houses can be seen in Domesday or later to retain institutional links, such as portions of tithe, or burial restrictions, with the ancient mother church of the *regio*.
60. The later parish church of the very large parish of Romsey occupied the north nave aisle of the abbey church. Two prebendaries supervised the parish altar, a shadow of the old minster arrangement.
61. For the single remainder vill of Wherwell, the parish church was in the Abbey church nave. The Wherwell parish and the parishes of the outlying villages (Longparish and Goodworth Clatford) were held by prebendaries, who continued to form a college at the Wherwell parish church altar, representing a shadow of the old minster arrangement.
62. The documents are given in Hase in Blair (1988) *op. cit.*
63. *Codex Iuris Canonici*, Gratian, Prima, XXX, ii, 'Whoever erects a private church and congregation, with a priest, without episcopal sanction, let him be anathema'. The essential rule governing the episcopal sanction is '*Omnino providendum est episcopo ut alie ecclesie antiquiores, propter novas, suam justitiam aut decimam non perdant, sed semper ad antiquiores ecclesias persolvatur*'. See also *ibid.* XCVI, 'Laymen are not to alienate the church's goods, nor to transfer them from one church to another'; and see also on this *Decretales*, Tit. XIII, C, I, which prohibits bishops and abbots from such alienations as well, and *Decretales*, Tit. XIII. C. V, for a prohibition of alienation of any *rem immobilem* of any church, except in very special and circumscribed cases, also *ibid.*, C. VI, which excommunicates all 'priests and others' who alienate *bona ecclesiastice*, and orders deposition as well as excommunication for both the alienator and whoever receives the alienated lands, and states that such alienations are null *ipso jure*: the parishioners of the injured church

have the right to bring an action, as well as clerics. These laws date from the sixth century onwards, but were greatly strengthened during the eleventh and particularly the twelfth centuries. The question as to whether tithe, mortuaries and alms are *bona ecclesiastice* was settled positively quite early on.

In the secular law, the Laws of Æthelred II and Cnut distinguish between the 'old minsters' and 'field churches' and require that the old minsters continue to receive their rights and dues. Those rights and dues included all villein tithe and all demesne tithe except where the lord of the vill had a 'field church' with a graveyard (Laws of Edgar II), and also plough-alms, church-scot and soul-scot (Laws of Athelstan (I)). The laws do not clearly state how a lord could get a church with a graveyard: probably the consent of the old minster is assumed.

Between the two sets of law, in theory no church could be built if the older church which had previously served the area lost any part of its income, and unless the bishop consented. Under the Canon Law, the bishop was forbidden to consent unless he was satisfied that the new church was adequately endowed for the maintenance of both fabric and pastor (*Decretales*, Cap. VIII), with new endowment, not diverted from the older church. Founding a new church was an expensive business, therefore. In practice, it is clear that where the laws were observed, a new church required the consent of the old church as well as of the bishop.

64. Most of these anomalies were tidied away by the Victorian and later reformers: it is essential, therefore, to work with the earliest available maps of parish boundaries.

65. For a full discussion, see E. Gibson, *Codex Iuris Ecclesiastici Anglicani*, Tit. IX, Cap. XI, p. 209 ff.

66. At Bursledon, when that dependent parochial chapel was founded in the mid twelfth century, for instance, the incumbent had to be presented to the rector of Bishop's Waltham for induction, and swear fealty to him. Bursledon also paid some of its tithe (the tithe on salt) to Bishop's Waltham, Peter's Pence, and a 4s annual pension, and was obliged to collect its chrism from there, rather than direct from the Bishop: the document in question is printed in Voss (1932), pp. 165–66. The rector of bishop's Waltham retained a peculiar legal jurisdiction over Bursledon (e.g. in the proving of wills) to the nineteenth century. Similar indications of subordination were common in the Wessex dependent parochial chapelries.

67. Occasionally *ecclesia* or *ecclesiola* in Domesday.

68. Sawyer (1968), nos 365, 370.

69. An exactly similar position can be seen at Eastrop, surrounded by the royal parish of Basing-Basingstoke.

70. Long (1888), p. 108.

71. Carisbrooke Cartulary, BM Egerton 3667, f. 22b.

72. There was a dispute as to the advowson of Kinsgton between the lord of Gatcombe and the lord of Kingston in 1251, in which the local lord was the victor, on which see the Victoria County History. Little is known about Kingston in the Middle Ages.

73. Gatcombe was held as three manors TRE by three brothers, and only became a unified estate under the first Norman lord, William son of Stur. Chillerton was held by Blacheman TRE, but was divided into two in Domesday (one half held by Jocelyn son of Azor, the other half by William son of Azor) It was probably one of these moieties that was held with Wooton in the twelfth century. Wootton, at Domesday, was a royal manor (Queen Edith held it TRE): it was granted to lay tenants in the early twelfth century. Watchingwell was a property of Wilton Abbey in Domesday: it was alienated to the lay lords of Shalfleet early in the twelfth century.

74. Hence Whitwell does not appear in Domesday, being subsumed under the entries for the two main manors.

75. Sawyer (1968) no. 822.

76. Sawyer (1969) no. 532. Alverstoke may have been cut from a royal estate further to the east, but the topography suggests that Titchfield is more likely. Both Alverstoke and Fareham were later regarded as Liberties, in no Hundred.

77. Goodman (1927) no. 67.

78. Register Edyndon, Vol. 2, f. 59; *Register Wykeham* Vol. 2, (1379); Hampshire Record Office, Wriothesley Deeds 5M53/1294; 5M51/182. See also BM Loan 29/56 (*Register Tychefeld de diversis*) f. 47b (1400).

79. Goodman (1927), nos 70a, b.

80. The rector of the mother church only agreed to repair the chancel of Chark Chapel in 1367 if the inhabitants paid 20s towards the costs, and then not as rector, but as owner of the manor of Mirabel, served from the chapel (see BM Loan 29/55 *Rememoratorium de Tychefeld*, f. 108b).

81. *Register Edyndon*, Vol. 2, f. 8.

82. Bishopstoke and possibly Crawley (or the northern portion of Crawley) were added to the area in 960 and possibly some time between about 900 and 963x975: Sawyer (1968), nos 683 and 381, 827.

83. The churches absent were mostly owned by the New Minster and the Nunnaminster and both houses reported few churches on their manors at Domesday.

84. The parish of Pittleworth covers just one and a third square miles, well over half of which is wood and water-meadows. The parish of Bossington is even smaller – only three-quarters of a square mile. Neither vill can ever have had more than a single farm. Pittleworth church is mentioned in Domesday, but not Bossington: East Dean church and the parochial dependent chapel at West Dean are also not mentioned. These churches may have been founded by the archbishop shortly after Domesday.

85. The range of anomalies is not exhausted by the case-studies here. The development of extra-parochial places, and those – occasionally not insignificant – areas which fell outside the parochial system altogether is a study in itself. Beaulieu, for instance, as the home manor of a great Cistercian house, was extra-parochial: since large numbers of laymen in fact came to live there, a chaplain was funded to provide for the cure of souls, thus causing major legal problems at the Reformation, when the question whether Beaulieu was an extra-parochial place or an anomalous parish, and how to classify the chaplain, was debated for some time. Again, at Pamber, another originally extra-parochial place, the residents took to worshipping at the alien priory in the adjacent parish of Monk Sherborne, and in time a chantry chaplaincy was established. Both at the Dissolution of the Alien Priories, and at the Reformation, the status of this chaplaincy caused problems: at the Reformation the rector (Queens College, Oxford) attempted to cancel the chaplaincy on the grounds

that it was a chantry and so illegal – the bishop had to intervene strenuously to preserve it. Eventually Pamber was classed as an anomalous parish, whose parish church was situated in, but exempt from, a neighbouring parish. At Stratfieldsaye and Stratfield Mortimer, parishes were divided by the county and diocesan boundary, and lay partly in Hampshire and partly in Berkshire: Bramshaw was similarly divided between Hampshire and Wiltshire, and Bramshott between Hampshire and Sussex. Woodhay (East and West), Wellow (East and West), Dean (East and West) and Parley (East and West) were equally once divided by county boundaries (Hampshire/Berkshire; Hampshire/Wiltshire; Hampshire/ Wiltshire; Hampshire/ Dorset respectively) but the original unit was eventually split into two parishes along the border, or, at Dean, into a parish (East Dean) and parochial chapelry (West Dean) on the Hampshire side, and a further parish (West Dean) on the Wiltshire side, and at Parley into a parish on the Dorset side, and a chapelry of ease within Christchurch parish on the Hampshire side.

86. The Canon Law permitted in theory the exchange of glebe land for other land identical in value, or more valuable, but hedged this permission round with so many caveats that in practice even exchange was not possible.

87. Plant served the three or four scattered farms in the eastern part of the parish and in the extra-parochial areas to the east (approximately the modern Purbrook and Waterlooville). This was the heart of the Forest of Bere, and very lightly inhabited. The chapel was served by one of the canons of Southwick. The accounts are in Hampshire Record Office, Daly MSS, 5M50/67. The document is damaged in the section relating to 1394, but that year's income must have been in total as high as 1393.

88. Hook served three small villages or hamlets, Hook Valence, Hook Mortimer and Warsash, and a dozen scattered farms.

89. See Voss (1932) pp. 77–99.

90. The chapel dates from the late twelfth century, Pevsner and Lloyd (1967). For the new towns in general, see Beresford (1988).

91. The new towns of Petersfield, Lymington and Yarmouth all date from the second or third quarters of the twelfth century: all have parishes, as is to be expected.

92. Interestingly, Hatch Warren and Cliddesden are not contiguous parishes, being about half a mile apart.

93. Here, as at Cliddesden and Hatch Warren (which lie between them), Winslade and Kempshott are not contiguous parishes, being about four miles apart. They were, however, in the same lord's hands.

94. For Cliddesden and Hatch see Victoria County History; for Ellisfield *Register Wykeham* Vol. 2, f. 175b; for Kempshott and Winslade, *Register Wykeham* Vol. 2 f. 263; for Wellsworth and Widley, Hampshire Record Office, Borthwick-Norton MSS, *Southwick Cartulary, 3*, 1M54/3, f. 270; for West Dean, *Register Beauchamp*, f. 352a.

95. E.g. South Baddesley, North Charford, Ewhurst and probably Upper Eldon. South Baddesley and Ewhurst were eventually re-established: North Charford disappeared and Upper Eldon was secularised.

96. Hook survived for a generation, but disappeared in the 1570s.

97. The post-Reformation Church of England took over untouched the pre-Reformation Canon Law as to the foundation of churches, and took over with it the feeling that no church foundation was possible without affecting the rights of an existing church. It was only with the Victorian statutes that the foundation of new parishes in the Established Church became practicable.

98. The history of Dissent at the local level is a study in itself, which is not covered here.

References

Alcock, L. 1976–77: 'Her .. gefeaht with Walas: Aspects of the Warfare of Saxons and Britons', in *Bulletin of the Board of Celtic Studies*, Vol. 27, 413–424.

Aston, M., Austin, D. and Dyer, C. (eds) 1989: *The Rural Settlements of Medieval England: Studies Dedicated to Maurice Beresford and John Hurst*, Basil Blackwell, Oxford.

Aston, M. and Bond, J. 1987: *The Landscape of Towns*, Alan Sutton, Gloucester.

Aston, M. and Leech, R. 1977: *Historic Towns in Somerset*, (Committee for Rescue Archaeology in Avon, Gloucestershire, and Somerset, Survey No. 2).

Barker, K. 1980: 'The Early Christian Topography of Sherborne', in *Antiquity*, Vol. 54, 229–231.

Bassett, S. (ed.) 1989a: *The Origins of Anglo-Saxon Kingdoms*, (Studies in the Early History of Britain, ed. N. Brooks), Leicester University Press.

Bassett, S. 1989: 'Churches in Worcester Before and After the Conversion of the Anglo-Saxons', in *Antiquaries Journal* vol 69, 225–256.

Beresford, M. 1988: *New Towns of the Middle Ages: Town Plantation in England, Wales and Gascony*, 2nd ed., Alan Sutton, Gloucester.

Biddle, M. & Hill, D. 1971: 'Late Saxon Planned Towns', in *Antiquaries Journal*, Vol. 51, 70–85.

Biddle, M. 1974: 'The Development of Anglo-Saxon Towns', in *Settimane de Studio del Centro Italiano di Studi Sull' Altro Medioevo*, Vol. 21, 203–230.

Biddle, M. 1983: 'The Study of Winchester: Archaeology and History in a British Town, 1961–1983', in *Proceedings of the British Academy*, Vol. 69, 93–136

Bidwell, P. T. 1979: *The Legionary Bath-House and Basilica and Forum at Exeter*, (Exeter Archaeological Reports, No. 1).

Bidwell, P. T. 1980: *Roman Exeter: Fortress and Town*, (Exeter Museums).

Blair, J. 1987: 'St. Frideswide's Reconsidered', in *Oxoniensia*, Vol. 52, 71–127

Blair, J. (ed.) 1988: *Minsters and Parish Churches: The Local Church in Transition 950–1200*, (Oxford University Committee for Archaeology: Monograph No. 17), Oxbow Books, Oxford.

Blair, J. 1988: 'St. Frideswide's Monastery: Problems and Possibilities', in *Oxoniensia*, Vol. 53, 221–258.

Blair, J. 1991: *Early Medieval Surrey: Landholding, Church and Settlement Before 1300* (Surrey Archaeological Society), Alan Sutton, Stroud.

Blair, J. and Sharpe, R. (eds) 1992: *Pastoral Care Before the Parish* (Studies in the Early History of Britain, ed. N. Brooks), Leicester University Press.

Bourdillon, J. 1980: 'Town Life and Animal Husbandry in the Southampton Area, as suggested by the Excavated Bones', in *Proceedings of the Hampshire Field Club and Archaeological Society*, Vol. 36, 181–191.

Brandon, P. (ed.) 1978: *The South Saxons*, Phillimore, Chichester.

Brooke, C. N. L. 1982: 'Rural Ecclesiastical Institutions in England: The Search for their Origins', in *Settimane de Studio del Centro Italiano di Studi Sull' Altro Medioevo*, Vol. 28, 685–711

Brooke, C. N. L. 1970: 'The Missionary at Home: The Church in the Towns, 1000–1250', in *Studies in Church History*, Vol. 6, 59–84

Brooks, N. (ed.) 1982: *Latin and the Vernacular Languages in Early Medieval Britain*, (Studies in the Early History of Britain, ed. N. Brooks), Leicester University Press.

Brooks, N. 1984: *The Early History of the Church of Canterbury: Christ Church from 597 to 1066*, Leicester University Press.

Bryant, R. and Hare, M. 1990: 'The Lypiatt Cross', in *Transactions of the Bristol and Gloucestershire Archaeological Journal*, Vol. 108, 33–52

Cameron, K. (ed.) 1987: *Place-name Evidence for the Anglo-Saxon Invasion and Scandinavian Settlement*, English Place-Name Society, 1987, (reprints of articles from various sources, originally dated 1965–1973).

Campbell, J. (ed.) 1982: *The Anglo-Saxons*, Phaidon Press, Oxford.

Campbell, J. 1986: *Essays in Anglo-Saxon History*, (reprints of articles from various sources, originally dated 1966–1984), Hambledon Press, London.

Casey, P. J. (ed.) 1979: *The End of Roman Britain: Papers Arising from a Conference, Durham, 1978*, (British Archaeological Reports, British Series, No. 71).

Charles-Edwards, T. M. 1972: 'Kinship Studies and the Origins of the Hide', in *Past and Present*, Vol. 56, 3–34.

Cherry, J. F. and Hodges, R. 1978: 'The Dating of Hamwih: Saxon Southampton Reconsidered', in *Antiquaries Journal*, Vol. 58, 299–309.

Colgrave, B. and Mynors, R. A. B (eds & trans) 1969: *Bede's Ecclesiastical History of the English People*, Oxford University Press.

Constable, G. 1982: 'Monasteries, Rural Churches and the Cura Animarum in the Early Middle Ages', in *Settimane de Studio del Centro Italiano di Studi Sull' Altro Medioevo*, Vol. 28, 349–389

Cunliffe, B. 1972: 'Saxon and Medieval Settlement-Pattern in the Region of Chalton, Hampshire', in *Medieval Archaeology*, Vol. 16, 1–12.

Davies, W. 1982: *Wales in the Early Middle Ages*, (Studies in the Early History of Britain, ed. N. Brooks), Leicester University Press.

Rutherford Davis, K. 1982: *Britons and Saxons: The Chiltern Region, 400–700*, Phillimore, Chichester.

Dumville, D. N. 1992: *Wessex and England: From Alfred to Edgar*, (Studies in Anglo-Saxon History, ed. D.N. Dumville, No. 3), Boydell Press.

Dunning, R. W. 1975: 'Ilchester, A Study in Continuity', in *Somerset Archaeology and Natural History*, Vol. 119, 44–50.

Dunning, R. W. (ed.) 1976: *Christianity in Somerset*, Somerset County Council.

Dunning, R. W. 1976: 'The Minster at Crewkerne', in *Somerset Archaeology and Natural History*, Vol. 120, 63–67.

Edwards, N. and Lane, A. 1992: *The Early Church in Wales and the West: Recent Work in Early Christian Archaeology, History and Place-Names*, (Oxbow Monograph, No. 16), Oxbow Books, Oxford.

Finberg, H. P. R. (ed.) 1972: *The Agrarian History of England and Wales*, Cambridge University Press.

Fleming, R. 1985: 'Monastic Lands and England's Defence in the Viking Age', in *English Historical Review*, Vol. 100 (No. 395), April 1985, p. 247–265.

Foot, S. 1989: 'Parochial Ministry in Early Anglo-Saxon England: The Role of Monastic Communities', in *Studies in Church History*, Vol. 26, 43–54.

Fowler, P. J. (ed.) 1972: *Archaeology and the Landscape: Essays for L. V. Grinsell*, John Baker, London.

Franklin, M. J. 1984: 'The Identification of Minsters in the Midlands', in *Anglo-Norman Studies*, Vol. 7, 69–89.

Fulford, M. and Sellwood, B. 1980: 'The Silchester Ogham Stone: A Reconsideration', in *Antiquity*, Vol. 54, 229–231

Gallyon, M. 1980: *The Early Church in Wessex and Mercia*, Terence Dalton, Lavenham.

Gelling, M. 1992: *The West Midlands in the Early Middle Ages*, (Studies in the Early History of Britain, ed. N. Brooks), University of Leicester Press.

Gem, R. D. H. and Tudor-Craig, P. 1981: 'A "Winchester School' Wall Painting at Nether Wallop, Hampshire', in *Anglo-Saxon England*, Vol. 9, 115–136

Gem, R. G. H. 1985: 'Holy Trinity Church at Bosham', in *Archaeological Journal*, Vol. 142, 32–36.

Gibb, J. H. D. and Gem, R. G. H. 1975: 'The Anglo-Saxon Cathedral at Sherborne', in *Archaeological Journal*, Vol. 132, 71–110.

Goodier, A. 1984: 'The Formation of Boundaries in Anglo-Saxon England: A Statistical Study', in *Medieval Archaeology*, Vol. 28, 1–21.

Goodman, A. W. 1927: *Chartulary of Winchester Cathedral*, Winchester.

Grant, E. (ed.) 1986: *Central Places, Archaeology and History*, (Department of Archaeology and Prehistory, University of Sheffield), Sheffield University Print Unit.

Gregson, N. 1985: 'The Multiple Estate Model: Some Critical Questions', in *Journal of Historical Geography*, Vol. 11, No. 4, Oct. 1985, p. 339–352

Hare, M. 1976: 'The Anglo-Saxon Church of St. Peter, Titchfield' in *Proceedings of the Hampshire Field Club and Archaeological Society*, Vol. 32, 5–48.

Hare, M. 1992: 'Investigations at the Anglo-Saxon Church of St. Peter, Titchfield, 1982–9' in *Proceedings of the Hampshire Field Club and Archaeological Society*, Vol.47, 117–144

Haslam, J. 1984: *Anglo-Saxon Towns in Southern England*, Phillimore, Chichester.

Haslam, J. 1986: 'The Ecclesiastical Topography of Early Medieval Bedford', in *Bedfordshire Archaeology*, Vol. 17, 41–50.

Haslam, J. (with Biek, L. and Littlecote, R. F.) 1984: 'A Middle Saxon Smelting Site at Ramsbury, Wiltshire', in *Medieval Archaeology*, Vol. 24, 1–68.

Heighway, C. 1987: *Anglo-Saxon Gloucestershire*, (County Library Series), Alan Sutton, Gloucester.

Higham, N. 1992: *Rome, Britain and the Anglo-Saxons*, Seaby, London.

Hinchliffe, J. 1986: 'An Early Medieval Settlement at Cowage Farm, Foxley, near Malmesbury', in *Archaeological Journal*, Vol. 143, 240–259.

Hinton, D. A. and Webster, C. J. 1987: 'Excavations at the Church of St. Martin, Wareham, 1985–86, and "Minsters" in South-East Dorset', in *Proceedings of the Dorset Natural History and Archaeological Society*, Vol. 109, 47–54.

Hodges, R. 1989: *The Anglo-Saxon Achievement: Archaeology and the Beginnings of English Society*, Duckworth, London.

Hodges, R. 1989: *Dark Age Economics: The Origins of Towns and Trade, AD 600–1000*, (New Approaches in Archaeology, ed. C. Renfrew), 2nd Ed. Duckworth, London.

Holt, J. C. (ed.) 1987: *Domesday Studies*, (Novocentenary Conference, Royal Historical Society and Institute of British Geographers), Boydell Press, Woodbridge.

Hood, A. B. E. (ed. and trans.) 1978: *St Patrick: His Writings and Muirchie's Life*, (History from the Sources, gen. ed. John Morris), Phillimore, Chichester.

Hooke, D. (ed.) 1985: *Medieval Villages: A Review of Current Work*, (Oxford University Committee for Archaeology: Monograph No. 5) Oxbow Books, Oxford.

Hooke, D. (ed.) 1988: *Anglo-Saxon Settlements*, Basil Blackwell, Oxford.

Huggins, R. H. 1975: 'The Significance of the Place-Name *Wealdham*', in *Medieval Archaeology*, Vol. 19, 198–201.

Jones, G. R. J. 1981: 'Continuity Despite Calamity: The Heritage of Celtic Territorial Organization in England', in *Journal of Celtic Studies*, Vol. 3–1, June 1981, pp. 1–30.

Jones, G. R. J. 1985: 'Multiple Estates Perceived', *Journal of Historical Geography*, Vol. 11, No. 4, Oct. 1985, pp. 352–364.

Keen, L. 1975: 'Illa Mercimonium Qui Dicitur Hamwih: A Study in Early Medieval Urban Development', in *Archaeologia Atlantica*, Vol. 1–2, 165–190.

Keene, D. 1985: 'Introduction to the Parish Churches of Medieval Winchester', in *Bulletin of the Council for British Archaeology, Churches Committee*, No. 23, Winter 1985, p. 1–9.

Kemp, B. R. 1967–8: 'The Mother Church of Thatcham', in *Berkshire Archaeological Journal*, Vol. 63, 15–22.

Kemp, B. R. 1968: 'The Churches of Berkeley Hernesse', in *Transactions of the Bristol and Gloucestershire Archaeological Society*, Vol. 87, 96–110.

Keynes, S. and Lapidge, M. (trans.) 1983: *Alfred the Great: Asser's Life of King Alfred and Other Contemporary Sources*, (Penguin Classics, ed. B. Radice), Penguin.

Lapidge, M. and Herren, M. 1979: *Aldhelm: The Prose Works*, Brewer, London.

Lapidge, M. and Herren, M. 1985: *Aldhelm: The Poetic Works*, Brewer, London.

Leech, R. n.d.: *Small Medieval Towns in Avon: Archaeology and Planning*, (Committee for Rescue Archaeology in Avon, Gloucestershire, and Somerset, Report No. 1).

Leech, R. 1981: *Historic Towns of Gloucestershire*, (Committee for Rescue Archaeology in Avon, Gloucestershire and Somerset, Report No. 3).

Liveing, H. G. D. 1912: *Records of Romsey Abbey: an account of the Benedictine House of Nuns, with notes on the Parish Church and Town (AD 907–1558)*, Winchester.

Long, W. H. (ed.) 1888: *The Oglander Memoirs: Extracts from the Manuscripts of Sir J. Oglander, Kt., of Nunwell, Isle of Wight, Deputy-Governor of Portsmouth and Deputy-Lieutenant of the Isle of Wight, 1595–1648*, Reeves and Turner, London.

Mayr-Harting, H. 1991: *The Coming of Christianity to Anglo-Saxon England*, B. T. Batsford, London, 3rd Ed.

Meyer, M. A. 1977: 'Women and the Tenth Century English Monastic Reform', in *Revue Bénédictine*, Vol. 87, 34–61.

Meyer, M. A. 1981: 'Patronage of the West Saxon Royal Nunneries in Late Anglo-Saxon England', in *Revue Bénédictine*, Vol. 91, 332–358.

Morris, J. (ed. & trans.) 1980: *Nennius: British History and The Welsh Annals*, (History from the Sources, ed. J. Morris), Phillimore, Chichester.

Morris, R. 1989: *Churches in the Landscape*, J. M. Dent, London.

Murphy, E. 1991: 'Anglo-Saxon Abbey Shaftesbury – Bectun's Base or Alfred's Foundation', in *Proceedings of the Dorset Natural History and Archaeological Society*, Vol. 113, 23–32.

Pay, S. 1987: *Hamwic: Southampton's Saxon Town*, (Southampton City Museums Archaeology Series).

Pearce, S. M. 1978: *The Kingdom of Dumnonia: Studies in History and Tradition in South-Western Britain, AD 350–1150*, Lodenek Press, Padstow.

Pearce, S. M. (ed.) 1982: *The Early Church in Western Britain and Ireland: Studies Presented to C.A. Ralegh Radford*, (British Archaeological Reports, British Series, No. 102).

Pearce, S. M. 1985: 'The Early Church in the Landscape: The Evidence from North Devon', in *Archaeological Journal*, Vol. 142, 255–275.

Penn, K. J. 1980: *Historic Towns in Dorset*, (Dorset Archaeological Committee: Dorset Natural History and Archaeological Society: Monograph Series, No. 1).

Pevsner, N. and Lloyd, D. 1967: *The Buildings of England: Hampshire and the Isle of Wight*, Penguin Books, Harmondsworth.

Platt, C. 1976: *The English Medieval Town*, Secker and Warburg, London.

Rahtz, P. A. 1982–3: 'Celtic Society in Somerset AD 400–700', in *Bulletin of the Board of Celtic Studies*, Vol. 30, 176–200.

Ralegh Radford, C. A. 1975: 'The Pre-Conquest Church and the Old Minsters in Devon', in *The Devon Historian*, Vol. 11, 2–11.

Ralegh Radford, C. A. 1978: 'The Pre-Conquest Boroughs of England, Ninth to Eleventh Centuries', in *Proceedings of the British Academy*, Vol. 64, 131–154.

Ridyard, S. J. 1988: *The Royal Saints of Anglo-Saxon England: A Study of West Saxon and East Anglian Cults*, (Cambridge Studies in Medieval Life and Thought, 4th Series, ed. J. C. Holt, No. 9), Cambridge University Press.

Rogers, A. 1972: 'Parish Boundaries and Urban History: Two Case Studies', in *Journal of the British Archaeological Association*, Vol. 35 (3rd Series), 46–64.

Rollason, D. W. 1978: 'List of Saints' Resting-Places in Anglo-Saxon England', in *Anglo-Saxon England*, Vol. 7, 61–94.

Rowley, T. (ed.) 1974: *Anglo-Saxon Settlement and Landscape: Papers Presented to a Symposium, Oxford, 1973*, (British Archaeological Reports, No. 6).

Rumble, A. R. 1977: 'Saxon Southampton', in *Medieval Archaeology*, Vol. 21, 186–188.

Sawyer, P. H. (ed.) 1976: *Medieval Settlement: Continuity and Change*, E. Arnold, London.

Sawyer, P. (ed.) 1985: *Domesday Book: A Reassessment*, E. Arnold, London.

Shennan, S. J. and Schadla-Hall, R. T. (eds) 1981: *The Archaeology of Hampshire from the Palaeolithic to the Industrial Revolution*, (Hampshire Field Club and Archaeological Society: Monograph No. 1).

Sieveking, G., Longworth, I. H. and Wilson, K. C. 1977: *Problems in Economic and Social Archaeology*, London.

Sims-Williams, P. 1990: *Religion and Literature in Western England 600–800*, (Cambridge Studies in Anglo-Saxon England, eds, S. Keynes and M. Lapidge), Cambridge University Press.

Spaul, J. 1977: *Andover: An Historical Portrait*, (Andover Local Archives Committee).

Stafford, P. 1985: *The East Midlands in the Early Middle Ages*, University of Leicester Press.

Tatton-Brown, T. 1986: 'The Topography of Anglo-Saxon London', in *Antiquity*, Vol. 60, 21–28.

Taylor, C. C. 1970: *The Making of the English Landscape: Dorset*, Hodder & Stoughton, London.

Taylor, C. C. 1983: *Village and Farmstead: A History of Rural Settlement in England*, George Philip, London.

Thatcher, A. T. 1982: 'Chester and Gloucester: Early Ecclesiastical Organization in Two Mercian Burhs', in *Northern History*, Vol. 18, 199–211.

Thomas, C. 1981: *Christianity in Roman Britain to AD 500*, University of California Press, Berkeley.

Thomas, C. 1989: 'Christians, Chapels, Churches and Charters – or 'Proto-Parochial Provision for the Pious in a Peninsula' (Land's End)', in *Landscape History*, Vol. 11, 19–26.

Vince, A. 1990: *Saxon London: An Archaeological Investigation*, (The Archaeology of London, eds J. Schofield and A. Vince), Seaby, London.

Voss, L. 1932: *Heinrich Von Blois, Bischof Von Winchester (1129–1171)*, (Historische Studien: 210) Ebering, Berlin.

Watts, D. 1991: *Christians and Pagans in Roman Britain*, Routledge, London.

Welch, M. 1992: *Anglo-Saxon England*, (English Heritage Book), B. T. Batsford, London.

Williamson, T. 1986: 'Parish Boundaries and Early Fields: Continuity and Discontinuity', in *Antiquity*, Vol. 12, No. 3, July 1986, p. 241–249.

Wilson, D. M. (ed.) 1976: *The Archaeology of Anglo-Saxon England*, Cambridge University Press.

Winterbottom, M. (ed. & trans) 1978: *Gildas: The Ruin of Britain and Other Works*, (History from the Sources, ed. J. Morris), Phillimore, Chichester.

Wood, I. N. 1982: 'Roman Britain and Christian Literature', in *Northern History*, Vol. 18, 275–278.

Wood, I. and Lund, N. 1991: *People and Places in Northern Europe 500–1600*, Boydell Press, Woodbridge.

Woodward, A. 1992: *Shrines and Sacrifice*, (English Heritage Book), B. T. Batsford, London.

Wormald, P. (ed.) 1983: *Ideal and Reality in Frankish and Anglo-Saxon Society: Essays in Honour of J.M. Wallace-Hadrill*, Basil Blackwell, Oxford.

Yorke, B. 1982: 'The Foundation of the Old Minster and the Status of Winchester in the Seventh and Eighth Centuries', in *Proceedings of the Hampshire Field Club and Archaeological Society*, Vol. 38, 75–83.

Yorke, B. (ed.) 1988: *Bishop Æthelwold: His Career and Influence*, Boydell Press, Woodbridge.

Yorke, B. 1990: *Kings and Kingdoms of Early Anglo-Saxon England*, Seaby, London.

Yule, B. 1990: 'The "Dark Earth' and Late Roman London', in *Antiquity*, Vol. 64, No. 244, Sep. 1990, p. 620–629.

4. The Administrative and Settlement Framework of Early Medieval Wessex

Della Hooke

This paper examines the territorial framework of Wessex in the later early medieval period. Both British and Anglo-Saxon influence can be seen in the resulting patterns of ecclesiastical and secular administrative organisation. Territorial units were, however, closely linked to land use and settlement patterns, and the evidence for these is reviewed with special reference to two contrasting regions of Wiltshire.

Territorial Boundaries

The archaeological evidence for settlement sites occupied in the early medieval period will accrue slowly, eventually to give a more complete picture of Wessex in a period that was one of the most formative in the region's history. Much is already known, however, about the administrative boundaries of the period. These provide perhaps the earliest secure indicator of the way that the early medieval landscape was exploited, reflecting the social and economic conditions prevailing when territorial divisions were demarcated. Changes occurred as the landscape evolved and in many instances these can still be investigated today. The evidence is derived largely from documents, especially pre-Conquest charters, place-names and Domesday Book, all of which have been subject to intense scrutiny in recent years.

Wessex is of considerable interest at this period for it embodies two cultures which were often in opposition but which both contributed to the subsequent evolution of the country's economic and social development. From the middle of the fifth century the Anglo-Saxon tide rolled westwards, reaching Devon by the mid seventh century (see Eagles, chapter 1). But there it shallowed and the furthest reaches of Dumnonia retained a measure of independence at least into the tenth century, with the Cornish language surviving beneath the weight of the Anglo-Saxon tongue: Old English. It was aided by the resurgence of the British Christian church in Cornwall, especially in the sixth century, with a network of British monasteries and churches and an ordered system of ecclesiastical parishes in place long before the tenth century.

It is Cornwall which provides us with glimpses of a British territorial hierarchy with royal courts suggested by the place-name *lys*, some of them to be identified as later manors. Like the Welsh *llys*, these cannot always be identified as focal administrative sites but were often set within a recognised territory. Lizard, Cornish *lys* with *ardh*, 'court on a height', was a component of the royal lands of Winnianton manor in Kerrier Hundred, located near the southern tip of the peninsula which bears its name. Liskeard, *Lys Cerruyt c.* 1010, is probably 'court of Kerwyd', a manor in Fawton Hundred which became a borough and market town.

With the resurgence of Christianity in Britain it is, however, the early British monasteries which can most clearly be identified. Named after their individual founders, they seem to have become the foci of an early established parochial structure and, although denigrated by Anglo-Saxon church leaders (who owed allegience to the church of Rome), were eventually to be recognised by that church. Several appear in charters, normally with beneficial hidations, and Domesday Book reveals that a number of them had never paid geld to the king, being privileged to collect and retain it for their own purposes (Ravenhill 1967). One grant confirms to the monastery of St Buryan its nuclear lands, effectively re-endowing an existing establishment in the first half of the tenth century (Sawyer 1968; Olson 1989, 80–1); a slightly later grant does the same for *Landochou,* Lanow in St Kew (Sawyer 1968, S. 810).

A further series of tenth-century grants reveals the break-up of a monastic estate in the Lizard peninsula, granting it into secular ownership. These grants involve townships within the original territory of Meneage, the name of which means 'monkish (land)' (Padel 1985). Here a monastery had been established by St Achebrannus at *Lannachebran,* the modern St Keverne, but in AD 967 King Edgar granted Lesneage (another *lys* name) and Pennare to his vassal Wulfnoth Rumuncant (Sawyer 1968, S. 755) and this was followed by grants of Traboe, Trevallack and Grugwith in St Keverne and Trethewey

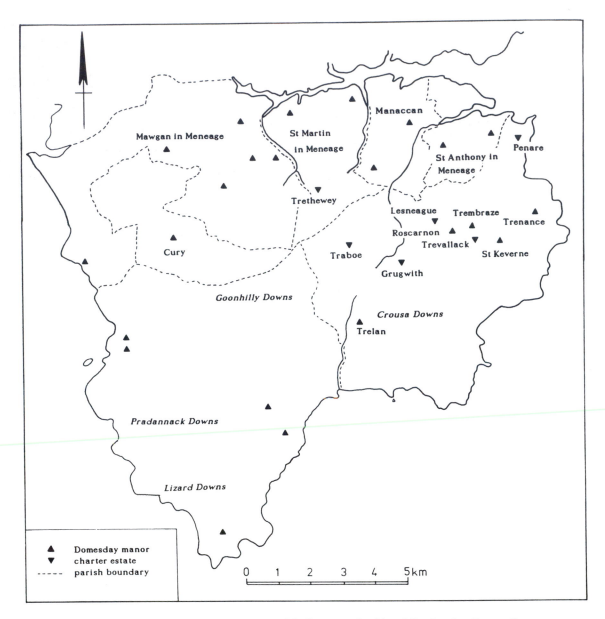

Fig. 4.1 *The pre-Conquest estates of St Keverne, the Lizard Peninsula, Cornwall.*

in St Martin in Meneage to Æthelweard, *comes* (not un-doubtedly an authentic grant) in AD 977, these same estates later granted to Bishop Ealdred in AD 1059 (Sawyer 1968, S. 1027) (Fig. 4.1).

Monasteries were also territorial foci in Anglo-Saxon Wessex. Some were established at the royal vills which emerged as the administrative structure was stabilised; others probably had British antecedents. Their *parochiae* form one group of early territorial units that can be re-constructed, usually from later evidence (Hase 1976). One, however, appears to be represented by a boundary clause accompanying a foundation charter: that of Crediton in central Devon (Fig. 4.2, Fig. 4.3; Hooke 1994, 86–99). The monastery established at the reputed birth-place of St Boniface possessed a foundation (or re-

foundation) charter granted in AD 739 (Sawyer 1968, S. 255) and although the boundary clause is a later addi-tion, it covers rather more land than the 20 hides of Crediton Hundred as it was recorded in Domesday Book. If the boundary clause is a true indication of the lands initially allotted, these extended southwards towards the northern flanks of Dartmoor, to be bounded on the south by the River Teign. Interestingly, they curled around, but did not include, a plateau of land between two deeply dissected streams which was referred to AD 976 as *Hyples eald land* and bore the name of Treable, Cornish *tre*, which Finberg believed was an enclave of land retained by people of Cornish descent (Sawyer 1968, S. 830; Finberg 1953, 27–30). Comparison with the Domesday hundred seems to suggest that the poorer, more marginal

Fig. 4.3 *The Devon countryside near Drewsteignton, within the bounds of the charter of Crediton. (Photo: Della Hooke)*

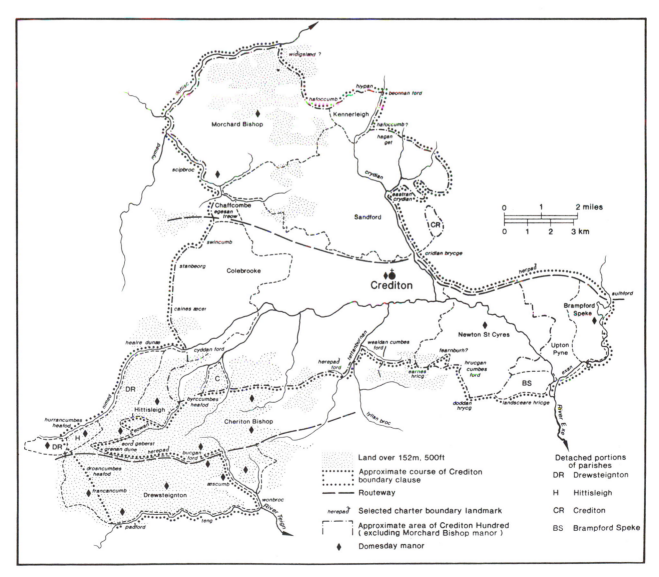

Fig. 4.2 *The boundary clause of Crediton lands.*

manors to the south of this enclave had been granted away to individual thegns by the time of the Norman Conquest. In other *parochiae,* too, it was the marginal lands, often in more backward regions, which were to have the loosest ties to a central mother church or to have no recorded ties at all (Hase 1976).

Under the Roman church, saints' names were not usually maintained as the lasting names of monastic centres. The foundation at Sherborne may have supplanted an earlier British monastery of *Lanprobi* (O'Donovan 1988, 84–7), dedicated to St Probus, but Anglo-Saxon monasteries bore a number of very different types of names. Many bore a topographical-type name, following an early naming tradition already established in Roman times. In Berkshire, for instance, charter evidence records early minsters at Abingdon, Bradfield, Marcham and Cookham. Abingdon is 'Æbba's hill', a reference shown by the charter evidence to have been to Boar's Hill on the ridge of Lower Greensand to the north; Bradfield is 'the broad piece of open land' (Old English *brad, feld*); while Marcham contains Old English *hamm* and is 'riverside meadow where smallage (wild celery) grows' (smallage is a plant which was used for flavouring). Cookham may also be a *hamm* name, hence 'cock's riverside meadow', although a derivation from Old English *ham* is suggested by early forms of the name. The significance of *ham* as an early name form has been discussed by Cox (Cox 1972–3), who compares the incidence of the term with the Roman road pattern.

Abingdon minster was an early foundation sponsored by the kings of Wessex, probably by the later seventh century, although some uncorroborated traditions claim that it was of British origin. It seems that the original endowment included a large estate in *Æaromundeslee*, 'the woodland (or wood-pasture) of Ærmund', a tract of wooded countryside in Hormer Hundred within the great bend of the River Thames, formerly in Berkshire but now in Oxfordshire, and estates centred upon the settlement of Abingdon itself. In the troubled frontier region between Mercia and Wessex, the supremacy of the latter kingdom was not fully regained until the mid ninth century and the monastery was further destroyed by Danish attacks in AD 871 (Stanton 1913). It was not until the house was placed under the authority of Æthelwold of Winchester that it began to play a commanding role in the revival of monasticism in tenth-century England.

Both Abingdon and Cookham were royal vills in pre-Conquest England and, since early minsters were often founded upon such royal estates, there was often a correlation between the *parochiae* of early minsters and early secular territories, although the latter are more difficult to reconstruct. Klingelhöfer has recently attempted to penetrate further back in time in central Hampshire in envisaging valley-based communities, each with "a traditional central place with a large pagan cemetery (later a missionary 'minster' church) and a chieftain's or noble's hall (later a royal vill or 'kingstun'), where tribute

was collected and which often served as the site of the popular 'moot' assembly" (Klingelhöfer 1992, 113–14). He refers to such a territory as an 'archaic hundred' and sees this as the direct forerunner of the eighth- and ninth-century *parochia.* This has much in common with the folk-group territories identified in midland England by Hooke and Ford (Hooke 1983, 1985, 1986; Ford 1976) and in Kent by Everitt (1986) but lacks any early transhumance links similar to those noted in the other regions.

One example quoted by Klingelhöfer is Micheldever Hundred with its centre of the same name situated at the headwaters of the Test and Itchen rivers (Fig. 4.4). The name Micheldever may be derived from Old English *micel,* 'great', or British *micn,* 'bog, quagmire', with British *dubro-,* 'water, river', a topographical toponym of the type discussed above. Micheldever itself, the *caput* of the hundred, was recorded as a king's *tun* or *villa regalis* in AD 862 when the West Saxon council purportedly met there. The church of Micheldever was recognisable as a mother church in the medieval period, retaining authority over the eastern valley but sharing control over the region with Wonston manor to the west. Similar territorial units in Hampshire are suggested for the regions of Somborne, the Middle Test, the Upper Test, the Upper Itchen, Tichborne, Alre and Candover.

Opinions still differ about the date of origin of the links recorded between such nodal regions, often based in riverine locations, and more distant holdings in less developed areas. In the midland region, such links certainly existed in the kingdom of the Magonsaete, the northern part of the Hwiccan kingdom and within Greater Mercia (Hooke 1992; Hooke 1985; Ford 1976) and are evidenced in the earliest charter grants. Land at Ismere, in the Stour valley of north-west Worcestershire, for instance, was granted in AD 736 by King Æthelbald of Mercia to Cyneberht, *comes,* for the construction of a minster and at its donation included an estate at Brochyl some nine miles away in the wooded uplands of Old Swinford (Sawyer 1968, S. 89; Hooke 1990, 61–3). The linkage seem to have been within the folk region of a people known as the *Husmerae* (Hooke 1982). In all cases, the links appear to have arisen out of an early practice of transhumance – the exploitation, in some form, of seasonal pasture, whether the latter was in wooded or upland countryside.

The Kentish charters granting estates with more distant holdings also go back to the early eighth century. Many of these have now been identified and their locations illustrate the great expanse of the common pastures of the Weald, which once extended across the middle of the south-eastern corner of England. The zone corresponds to an area of sandstone and clay formations which lie at the core of an uplifted anticline, reaching almost as far as the sea in the south-east. In early medieval times the area was well wooded and the bulk of the references

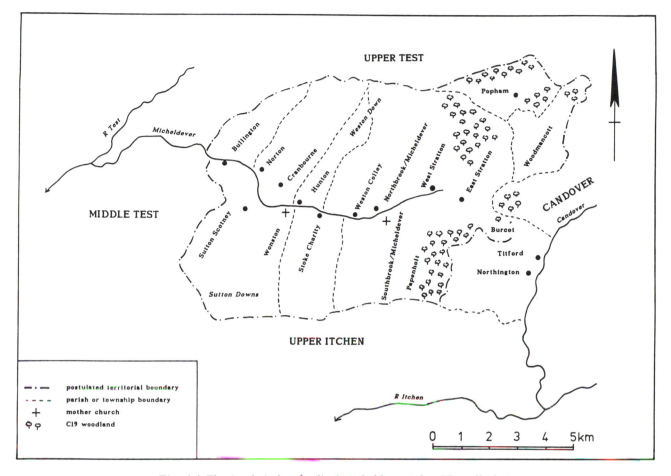

Fig. 4.4 *The 'archaic hundred' of Micheldever (after Klingelhöfer).*

in the charters are to the swine pastures, or 'dens', held in the woodland by the capital estates established in the more heavily developed areas around. In the Weald, it was the use of the land as swine pasture that seems to have been paramount but other domestic stock could also be pastured in the open woodland and the woods themselves were important sources of timber.

Such a system of linked estates appears to have developed as a way of maximising the resources available within a given territory. It was by no means confined to individual estates in different kinds of natural regions for it is often possible to reconstruct a complex pattern of estate linkages involving many different communities. Moreover, the distant pastures recognised in Kent seem to have belonged to communities holding land in common, something which in itself suggests that the arrangement pre-dated the changes in forms of ownership which occurred in the later Anglo-Saxon period. Indeed, the bulk of the central Weald appears to have been regarded initially as commonland: a zone of intercommoning where pastures were only gradually appropriated by particular district groups. An authentic eighth-century charter, for instance, grants swine-pastures in 'the wood of the men of the Lympne district' (based upon the River Limen) – the *Limenwara* – and 'in the

wood of the men of Wye' – the *Weowara* – (Sawyer 1968, S. 1180), referring to the men of the lathes of those areas. Others relate how the inhabitants of Rochester – the *Caesterwara* – and of Canterbury – the *Burhwara* – also had common pasture in the Weald (Sawyer 1968, S. 30, S. 125, S. 157). There is considerable evidence to suggest that the system was of early origin, perhaps even pre-dating the Anglo-Saxon period.

The charter evidence reveals traces of such a system in Wiltshire and northern Hampshire although, admittedly, the references are late in date. The people of the Wylye valley are referred to as the *Wilsaete* c. 800 (Anglo-Saxon Chronicle, AD 800, 878, ed. Plummer, 58) and this may be envisaged as a valley-based territory similar to those reconstructed by Klingelhöfer in central Hampshire. A royal *tun*, Wilton, was established at the eastern entrance to the valley (Fig. 4.5) and a minster was also founded here. It is possible, however, to identify estate linkages beyond the valley region to more distant woodlands. An estate at South Newton, close to the royal centre of Wilton, was granted by King Edmund in AD 943 (Sawyer 1968, S. 492) together with a meadow beside the Wylye and an estate at Frustfield in the south of the county. The latter has been identified as part of the large parish of Whiteparish, later part of the Forest of Melchet

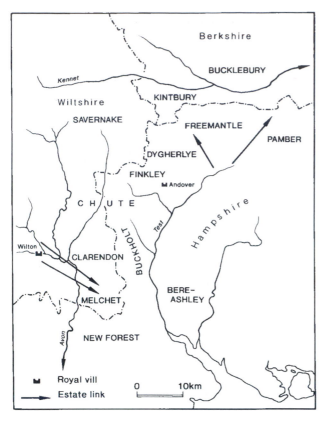

Fig. 4.5 Estate linkages in south-central England.

(Taylor 1964). Wilton still enjoyed timber rights and pasture in Melchet in 1086.

A second example of such an arrangement disclosed by charter evidence is that of Overton in Hampshire, located in the valley of the Test, which was confirmed to the Bishop of Winchester together with its woodland at Tadley, near the northern boundary of the county (later to be included within the Forest of Pamber), in AD 909 (Sawyer 1968, S. 377, S. 824). Whether such links were of ancient origin or whether they stem from the developing territorial arrangements of Anglo-Saxon England once the kingdoms and an established social hierarchy had stabilised (as appears to have been the case by the mid seventh century) remains open for debate, but the system can be identified both within and beyond Anglo-Saxon England. Within the greater territory of Wessex it is as decipherable in Devon, with linkages between coastal estates and holdings on Dartmoor (Hooke 1994, 214–24, citing Fox), as in Kent and Sussex. Jones has also shown that such linkages can be identified between the foci of the multiple estates which developed within such folk regions and their distant holdings (Jones 1976).

It is now widely recognised that community territories, whether they were this type of 'archaic hundred' or 'folk region', or the 'multiple estates' postulated by Jones, were to become fragmented by the ninth and tenth centuries. Within the wider territory, township units became

the basis for local administration in later Anglo-Saxon England, with varying degrees of independence, and were to become grouped together into ecclesiastical parishes as the early *parochiae* also fragmented. The Crediton example seems to show the more distant fringe manors breaking away from central control and the work of Hase (1976) and Franklin (1982) also showed the relatively loose control maintained over the more distant parts of a minster's *parochia* in Hampshire and Northamptonshire. Subdivision of a minster territory occurred as churches were established upon the developing manors, but in remote areas ecclesiastical parishes were often not fully demarcated before the twelfth century.

The smaller units of later Anglo-Saxon England were often closely related to local topographical conditions. Whereas the Micheldever valley, for instance, had been treated as a single economic unit in the early Saxon period, with all inhabitants having common rights in the great arc of woodland which centred on the upper periphery of the valley and in the pasture available at the lower end (Klingelhöfer 1992, 23), division of the valley into separate vills and manors occurred to produce a pattern typical of such valley regions: linear units running from valley floor to the upland rim. This pattern has been examined in some detail in the Wylye valley of Wiltshire and in the Vale of the White Horse (formerly Berkshire but now taken into Oxfordshire), where abundant charter evidence allows the pattern of early townships to be reconstructed in detail and early medieval land use to be identified with considerable precision (Hooke 1986). It is clear that an attempt was made to include within each unit a proportion of valley meadowland, arable land on the sloping hillsides and open pasture above (Fig. 4.6). Such a pattern is readily identified in the chalk regions of southern England where the chalk escarpment drops down to intervening clay vales, but attempts to include land offering different resources are by no means confined to such regions and can be identified in other less obvious township patterns. It will be argued below that the shape and configuration of township and parish boundaries can be related to what is known about the use of the land in the early medieval period to disclose more about the late Anglo-Saxon period than is currently possible from any single source.

Territories and Settlement Patterns

One of the reasons for investigating all the available evidence, however limited it may be, is the lack of knowledge about contemporary settlement patterns. While territorial fragmentation appears to have gone hand in hand with settlement nucleation in some regions, elsewhere the parish pattern was to be established over regions of more dispersed settlement. Archaeological evidence has not yet filled the many gaps in the sequence of settlement development, either because abandoned sites have not been recognised or early sites have been obscured by

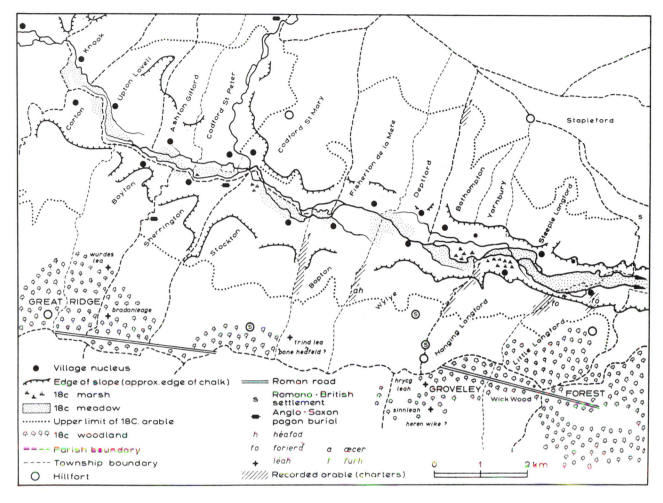

Fig. 4.6 *Estate patterns in the Wylye valley of Wiltshire.*

later development, and use has had to be made, therefore, of the types of evidence mentioned above. These include place-names, Domesday Book, charter and topographic evidence and evidence derived from later historical maps. However indeterminate such sources may be, few previously held ideas have gone unchallenged in recent years.

Doubts have been cast upon the usefulness of place-name data in the identification of settlement sites because the long accepted chronology of certain types of place-name evidence has now been called into question (e.g. Dodgson 1966) and excavation has sometimes failed to identify settlement beneath present-day or medieval villages which undoubtedly bore an Old English place-name (Taylor 1983). Others, however, feel confident that certain types of Old English names referring to local sites may indeed indicate unchanging locations since the date at which the names were given (Gelling 1976). It is well known, also, that Domesday Book refers to manorial names while betraying little about the sites or nature of individual settlements. In Cornwall, however, place-name analysis assisted by the publication of a new Cornish

dictionary (Padel 1985) has been used to considerable effect.

It has long been considered that the present settlement pattern of south-western England, with its isolated farmsteads and scattered hamlets, was of ancient origin (Hoskins 1955). Here, as elsewhere, archaeological evidence remains limited and recourse has had to be made to place-name investigation and topographical analysis. However, even if general settlement patterns did not change there seems to have been little true continuity from the Romano-British period into early medieval times, even in Cornwall where many settlements still bear names of British origin. The British *tre-*, 'farmstead', is common but a discontinuity in relation to earlier Roman sites is detectable (Rose and Preston-Jones, forthcoming). The *tre* settlements continued, however, to occupy the more fertile lowland zones favoured in earlier periods, to be accompanied by gradual colonisation of the moorland fringes.

Whereas today many *tre* settlements are single farms, there is increasing evidence to suggest that the term was often applied to hamlets in the early medieval period. A charter of Trerice in the parish of St Dennis in Cornwall (Sawyer 1968, S. 1019) refers to land held in common within the township, which might infer that several land-owners were present on the half yardland granted in AD 1049 by King Edward to his faithful *minister,* Eadulf, or that this estate shared certain lands with a neighbour (perhaps the other half yardland). The charter notes that 'the enclosures *(worthigas)* and the barley land and the mill and the out-leap are common'; the 'out-leap' seems to have been the common pasture and moor near the bounds of the land unit but the *worthigas* are likely to have been the farmsteads with their fields. Moreover, there is evidence today of a fossilised strip pattern of fields which suggests that fragmented holdings may have been present here even at this early date (Herring and Hooke 1993).

Modern cartographic evidence is of limited use in identifying ancient regions of dispersed settlement. Since the enclosure movement of the eighteenth and nineteenth centuries, outlying farms have been established even within the regions formerly characterised by strong set-tlement nucleation and a closer approximation to the earlier pattern is derived from plotting, and thus discount-ing, regions of large-scale enclosure. It is clearly docu-mented that some other regions, like the Warwickshire Arden and similar woodland regions, were subject to colonisation in the twelfth and thirteenth centuries and here it is likely that many of the outlying farms date only from this period. Marginal lands, too, were subject to fluctuating settlement patterns, with permanent settle-ments replacing seasonal shielings in times of popula-tion pressure or a more favourable climatic regime. Set-tlements of this nature have been identified around the moorland fringes of the South West Peninsula, as at Challacombe on Dartmoor.

It has been suggested that the 'worth' settlements commonly found in south-western England might be the early equivalant of today's outlying farmstead and per-haps even represent survivals of a much earlier farming tradition (Costen 1992). Sadly, even the most modern excavation techniques utilised in the north Devon land-scape of Roadford failed to detect any settlement earlier than the twelfth century at two such excavated sites (Weddell and Henderson 1992). Yet other 'worth' sites lying near parish boundaries are a distinctive feature of the pre-Conquest charters of south-western England (Hooke 1989) and the possibility must remain that they do indeed refer to such outlying farms. In Berkshire, three such sites can be identified in Hormer Hundred and two elsewhere. In Wiltshire eleven different sites are named, the majority in the north-west or south of the county. Of the five Hampshire sites, three occur in the region adja-cent to the Hampshire/Wiltshire border in the north of the county in one charter relating to Ecchinswell but have not been related to known settlement sites. Dorset con-tains three sites and Devon five near boundaries.

What can be substantiated is that a dense pattern of

farming hamlets and farmsteads characterised most low-land regions by the later Anglo-Saxon period but that in some regions there was a strong move towards nuclea-tion by the end of the period. This was apparently most marked in the more fertile regions such as the major river valleys of Wiltshire and Hampshire, where arable farm-ing was predominant, and less marked in more pastoral regions. Yet a degree of nucleation associated with a limited area of open field seems to have been associated with manorial nuclei throughout southern England, a fact that has only been recognised in recent years. The way in which fragmented holdings developed within open com-mon fields has given rise to much speculation but is likely to reflect tenurial methods and landownership patterns as much as economic factors.

Territories and Land Use: Two Case Studies from Wessex

The main source of evidence used here is that derived from Anglo-Saxon charters and primarily from the bound-ary clauses which accompany a substantial number of them. These consist of lists of landmarks which help to demarcate the boundary and, as such, only provide de-tails of the outskirts of particular estates. Occasionally they pick up outlying farmsteads, even hamlets, that were occupied in late Anglo-Saxon times, as noted above, and in this way tell a little about settlement patterns (Hooke 1985) but reveal little about settlement within the core of an estate. The boundaries of such estates can, how-ever, frequently be reconstructed in sufficient detail for their course to be closely followed on the map and on the ground and parish or township shape can be highly sig-nificant. It is usually necessary to refer to historical maps in the identification of specific features, for not only were administrative boundaries surprisingly long lasting, but much later field-names on occasions derive directly from Old English names. In addition, the place-name of the estate itself may be revealing.

Since many of the well-documented charter bounda-ries relating to estates in the Wylye valley have already been discussed in print (Hooke 1988), the charters dis-cussed here are of similarly shaped estates in the Nadder valley, the valley which lies to the south of the Wylye and shares with it a common northern boundary along the Grovely ridge. Jurassic beds of marl and limestone outcrop on either side of the valley and are separated by a band of Gault clay from the overlying Cretaceous beds to the north and south, in which greensand gives way to chalk. The greensand outcrop is considerably wider to the south of the river.

It was alleged that 14 *cassati be Tefunte* were granted by King Æthelred to his *minister,* Osmund, in AD 860 (Sawyer 1968, S. 326). A further grant of 5 *cassati* of land *at Teofunten* was made by King Edgar to Sigestan, his faithful *minister,* in AD 964 (Sawyer 1968, S. 730). On the southern side of the Nadder, 10 *cassati* at Fovant

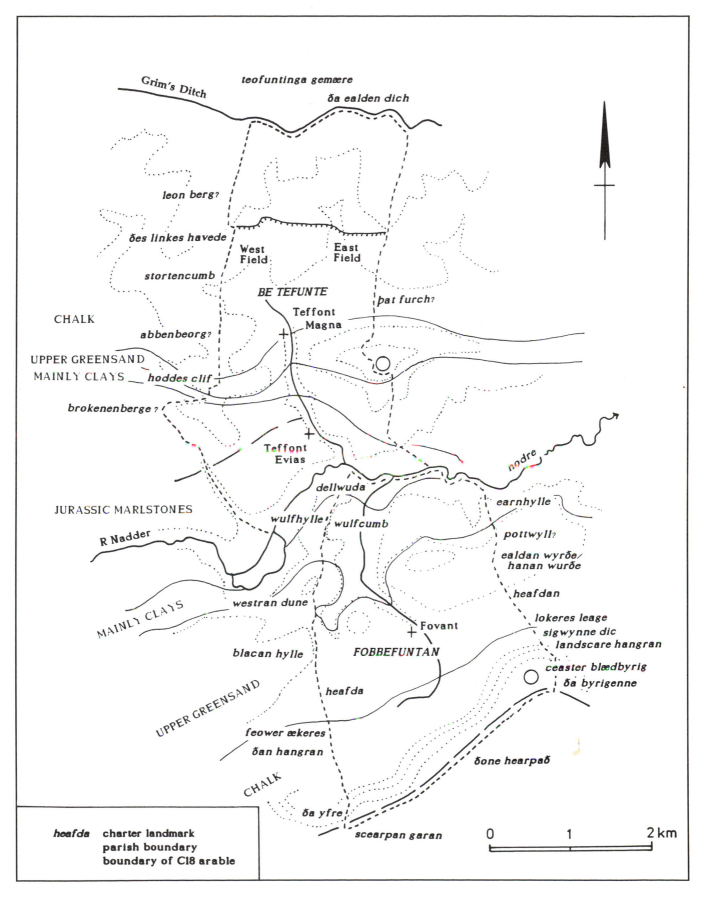

Fig. 4.7 *The pre-Conquest boundaries of Teffont Evias and Teffont Magna, Wiltshire.*

were granted by King Edward to his *minister,* Wihtbrord, in AD 901 (Sawyer 1968, S. 364) and by King Æthelred to St Mary's, Wilton, in AD 994 (Sawyer 1968, S. 881). The river name Nadder is of British derivation.

The place-names of these estates are of interest because both Teffont and Fovant contain the term *funta,* a loan-word from Latin *fons, fontis* meaning 'spring', embodying a word taken directly from the Latin. Gelling has suggested that such springs might have been different in being characterised by Roman building work (Gelling 1978) but this has yet to be substantiated. Teffont means literally 'boundary spring', suggesting a territorial divide, but the spring lies immediately above the present village of Teffont Magna. Teffont Evias lies to the south beside the Nadder. Evidence of substantial Roman occupation has come from both Teffont Evias and Teffont Magna parishes, a building with hypocausts having been located to the south of Teffont Evias in association with a cemetery of over thirty graves, while a second building stood to the west of Teffont Magna; a hoard of 225 coins has been found on the latter site. Additional burials and scatters of pottery sherds have also been found in the parish of Teffont Magna and Saxon pottery has been indentified on the present village site. The church contains a fragment of a ninth-century cross shaft. Fovant, to the south, is 'Fobba's spring', which also rises just above the present village.

The landmarks noted in the mid ninth-century boundary clause of Teffont cannot all be precisely located but the estate obviously ran down from the Grovely ridge to the Nadder, its northern boundary marked by the *ealden dich,* 'old dyke', the Grim's Ditch (or Grovely Dyke) (Fig. 4.7). Its eastern boundary was artificially marked by a furrow which had been driven downhill in the direction of the Nadder. This strongly suggests that the boundary was driven across cultivated ground (Hooke 1981). There was untilled land on the more broken ground of the Jurassic and greensand outcrops on the southern parts of the western boundary, however, because there were references to surviving barrows in this section. Further to the north, however, the western boundary makes a pronounced right-angled bend near 'the head of the linch' which suggests that it was making its way around an existing field system. In later times, Teffont Magna's 'West Field' reached the boundary along this stretch. Further open land on the high chalkland is suggested by reference to *leon berg,* another barrow, perhaps the tumulus surviving near the boundary to the north-east of Chilmark. This was still the open pasture of Teffont Down in historical times. The charter also adds that two meadows belonged to the estate, one beside the Nadder and another beside the Wylye.

The later charter does not have a boundary clause but is of particular interest because it states that there were no fixed bounds of the five hides granted: *nullis certis terminis set iugera iacent ad iugeribus.* The reference to there being 'no certain bounds for the acres adjoin other

acres' is common terminology for the intermingled strips of an open field system and is met with in the tenth century in charters of Charlton in Berkshire and Avon in Wiltshire (Finberg 1972, 489–90). This confirms that the system was in operation in this area by this date. There is a corresponding similarity between the area under the plough in the later Anglo-Saxon period, as suggested by the charter landmarks, and that recorded on post-medieval maps, a corrspondence also noted in the Wylye valley to the north (Hooke 1988).

Grundy (1919, 191–7) includes both the parishes of Sutton Mandeville and Fovant within Edward's grant to Wihtbrord and Æthelred's subsequent grant to St Mary's at Wilton but each grant was only of 10 *cassati,* while Domesday Book records that each of these manors was assessed individually at 10 hides. It is unlikely, therefore, that the boundary encompassed both parishes. That both grants concerned the same area of land is clear from the descriptions of the boundary for at the south-eastern corner of Fovant parish lay Chiselbury Camp, an Iron Age fortification noted as *cester slaed byrg* or *ceaster blaedbyrig* in the boundary clauses. The earlier clause notes that the boundary ran 30 rods to the east of the camp while the later one notes that burials lay upon the boundary at this spot. A road, here referred to by the West Saxon term *herepath,* ran along the whole of the southern boundary following the ridge which separated the valleys of the Nadder and the Ebbesbourne.

The dykes noted on the upper parts of the eastern and western boundaries, *sigewunne dic* and *rugan dic,* suggest that the boundary was passing across open pasture on the high chalkland where archaeological features were the most prominent landmarks available. Headlands, indicating arable land, are noted, however, on the slopes of the shallow valley which separated the greensand escarpment from that of the chalk, noted on the eastern and western boundaries. Four acres to the west of the hanging wood on the lower part of the western boundary may also indicate ploughland.

Several references to woodland indicate that this was present in the parish: *lokeres leage* lay on the upper greensand just before the dyke on the eastern boundary and the hanging woods on the chalk above are noted on the western and eastern boundaries; a further wood lay on the western boundary where it ran down to the Nadder, named in the later Fovant charter as *dellwuda.* The boundary here was crossing bands of Gault clay, lower greensand and Wealden grey loams and today these outcrops are still heavily wooded along the slope extending from Castle Ditches Camp in Tisbury through Sutton Mandeville parish into Fovant. There is, however, another boundary landmark of interest because where the eastern boundary of Fovant drops down the dip slope of the greensand escarpment before climbing the scarp face of the chalk, the boundary clauses record a 'worth' feature: *hanan wurthe* or *tha ealdan wyrthe* but no settlement exists in such a location today. The inference is

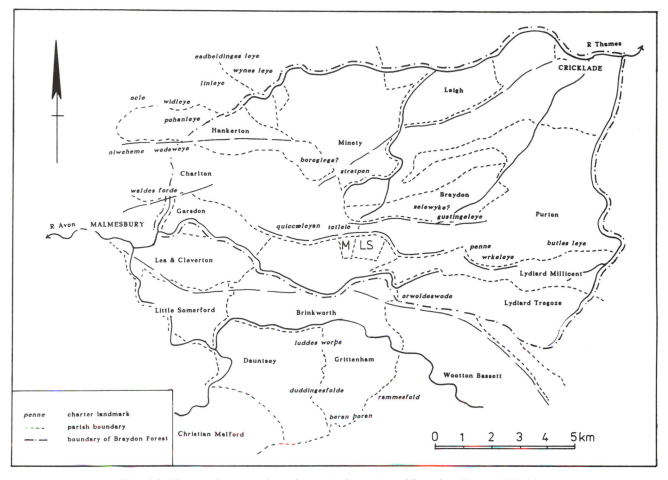

Fig. 4.8 *The pre-Conquest boundaries in the region of Braydon Forest, Wiltshire.*

that total nucleation had not yet taken place in Fovant in the tenth century but that at least some outlying settlements were in existence on the wooded greensand ridge. The evidence is slight and is based upon the interpretation of 'worth' argued above but it is all that is at present available.

Very different parish patterns characterise the area which was to become the Forest of Braydon in northern Wiltshire (Fig. 4.8). Braydon Forest is noted as *siluae Bradon* in a spurious seventh-century charter (Sawyer 1968, S. 149), while an undated charter of Brokenborough refers to *ordwoldeswode quod modo Bradene appellatur*, 'the woodland of Ordweald, which is now named Braydon' (S. 1577). The wood occupied an area of Oxford clay, which drained westwards into the Avon and northwards via tributaries of the Thames. Elongated parishes reach into the woodland core in a shape characteristic of a heavily wooded zone. The fingers of land attached to Purton, Braydon, Lydiard Millicent and Lydiard Tregoze on the east may be especially mentioned but on the west side the parishes of Hankerton, Charlton and Garsdon also show this elongated shape. Detached portions of Malmesbury and Little Somerford parishes in the area of Braydon wood probably represent ancient

rights in the woodland. Through the heart of the wood lay an irregular territorial divide traceable in the boundaries of the parishes between Hankerton and Minety, Charlton and Braydon, Brinkworth and the Lydiards with Wootton Bassett. The eastern boundaries of Grittenham, Dauntsey and Christian Malford seem to continue this line southwards. Many of the estates within this territory were to become incorporated into the estates of Malmesbury Abbey, traditionally a seventh-century foundation.

A number of charter bounds refer to estates extending into the woodland: the undated bounds of a large territory known as 'Brokenborough', and those of Charlton and Purton (Sawyer 1968, S. 1577, S. 1578, S. 1586). Those of Brinkworth (S. 1576, S. 1583) and Crudwell and Chelworth (S. 1579, S. 1584, S. 1582) abut onto the later forest boundary. As in many wooded regions, the boundaries are often difficult to locate because they were less stable in such regions; the Brokenborough clause, in particular, seems to cut through present-day parishes at several places along its course. In addition, many of these bounds survive only in much altered later texts. However, the line taken is sufficiently clear for most of the landmarks to be located within a general area. In addition, many of these bounds survive only in much altered texts. Here, only those bounds running within the forest will be discussed.

Not surprisingly, woodland features are more frequent here. In Charlton *totleie* and *quiccaeleyan* were located near the southern boundary of the parish and upon the boundary of Purton, in the eastern part of the wood, landmarks include *gustingeleye* (this lay near the source of the river Key and the name may be a corruption of Old English *gyte,* 'a pouring forth, i.e. a rushing spring'), *wrkeleye*, either 'Weorca's *leah*' or 'wood where building material is obtained', and *butles leye*, 'Buttel's *leah*'. The *leah* features were obviously individual features and seem to have represented specific patches of wood-pasture or individual woods. Several of the roads leading into the woodland refer indirectly to it, for *waldes forde,* 'the ford of the wood', in Charlton, lay upon the thirteenth-century forest boundary and the *new heme wodeweye* led along the northern boundary of Charlton directly into the forest. Many boundaries followed roads for considerable distances and they must have been one of the most obvious features in such countryside.

Many of these roads must have served as droveways for wood-pasture was clearly a right enjoyed in Braydon by many of the surrounding parishes. It is likely to have been a long established usage and there is no evidence here of the long *haga* boundaries which seem to have demarcated woodland set aside for hunting in later Anglo-Saxon times (Hooke 1989). The only *haga* features noted here related to a small enclosed wood in Christian Malford to the west. In Domesday Book much of the woodland is entered under the names of capital manors, like the woodland measuring 3 by 2 leagues attached to the manor of Brokenborough, revealing this pattern of rights in Braydon. Pasture rights were sometimes contested as boundaries became fixed: part of the woodland belonging to Malmesbury Abbey was obviously taken into the medieval forest and disputes are recorded in the thirteenth century over rights of pasture in Flisteridge Wood which lay in the south-western extension of Crudwell parish. The swine belonging to the Earl of Hereford were impounded by the abbot when they were illegally pastured there (Akerman 1857, 312–13). Two folds are noted on the boundary of Grittenham, one a *rammesfold,* 'rams' fold', and 'pens' or folds lay upon the eastern boundary of Charlton and the boundary of Purton. The latter lay beside a road within the forest and at a later date Summerhouse Farm was established near by. *Stretpen* lay beside one of the boundary roads which ran along the southern boundary of Hankerton. It is not unlikely that the folds were associated with seasonal stock pastures within the woodland.

Named boundary settlements were few: *ele wyke* was a dairying or herding establishment near the northern boundary of Purton, while beyond the later forest boundary *luddes worþe* lay near the Grittenham boundary. *Worð* names are not uncommon in regions which were once well-wooded and in Wiltshire are found most commonly in the north-west of the county on the fringes of Braydon Forest (Gover, Mawer and Stenton 1939, accompanying map). The term seems to describe an enclosed farmstead. The picture presented here is very different to that of the valley regions in the southern part of Wiltshire, implying a region of limited permanent settlement. As a resource, however, the value of its wood-pasture should not be under-estimated.

Charter Evidence: Conclusions

Charter evidence of the type discussed in this paper is particularly plentiful in Wessex and it provides an indication of landuse pre-dating Domesday Book, with which it can then be usefully compared. Although a great deal of preliminary work upon the charters was carried out by G. B. Grundy in the 1920s and '30s, few new county-wide studies have subsequently appeared. Work by the present writer in the West Midlands and the South-West Peninsula and by Costen in Somerset, together with that of numerous other scholars working upon individual boundaries, has shown the potential of such evidence for an understanding of both the territorial arrangements and landuse patterns of early medieval England. The emerging picture clearly reveals the scale of regional differentiation present in the Anglo-Saxon landscape at a time when the regional *pays* of England were becoming established. These landscape regions were to remain dominant throughout the medieval period and can still be recognised today.

Acknowledgements

This paper is based upon research funded by the Economic and Social Research Council whose support is gratefully acknowledged.

References

Akerman, J. V. 1857: 'The ancient limits of the Forest of Braden', *Archaeologia* 37, 304–15.

Anglo-Saxon Chronicle, The, *Two of the Saxon Chronicles Paralleled.* Plummer, C., 1892–9 (Oxford).

Costen, M. 1992: 'Huish and worth: Old English survivals in a later landscape', *Anglo-Saxon Studies in Archaeology and History* 5 (Oxford Univ. Comm. for Archaeol., Oxford), 65–84.

Cox, B. 1972–3: 'The significance of the distribution of English place-names in -*him* in the Midlands and East Anglia', *J. Engl. Place-Name Soc.* 5, 15–73.

Dodgson, J. M. 1966: 'The significance of the distribution of English place-names in -*ingas,* -*inga*- in south-east England, *Medieval Archaeology* 10, 1–29.

O'Donovan, M. 1988: *The Charters of Sherborne* (Royal Hist. Soc., London).

Everitt, A. 1986: *Continuity and Colonization. The evolution of Kentish settlement* (Leicester Univ. Press, Leicester).

Finberg, H. P. R. 1953: *The Early Charters of Devon and*

Cornwall. Univ. Leic. Dept of Engl. Local Hist. Occ. Pap. no. 2 (Leicester).

Finberg, H. P. R. 1972: 'Anglo-Saxon England to 1042', in *The Agrarian History of England and Wales, Vol. LII, AD 43–1042*, ed. H. P. R. Finberg (Cambridge Univ. Press, Cambridge), 385–525.

Ford, W. J. 1976: 'Settlement patterns in the central region of the Warwickshire Avon', in P. H. Sayer (ed.), *Medieval Settlement, Continuity and Change* (Ed. Arnold, London), 274–294.

Franklin, M. J. 1982: 'Minsters and parishes: Northamptonshire studies', unpub. Univ. Cambridge PhD thesis.

Gelling, M. 1978: *Signposts to the Past: Place-Names and The History of England* (Dent, London).

Gelling, M. 1984: *Place-Names in the Landscape* (Dent, London).

Gover, J. E. B., Mawer, A. and Stenton, F. M. 1939: *The Place-Names of Wiltshire*. English Place-Name Society 16 (Cambridge).

Grundy, G. B. ???: 'The Saxon land charters of Wiltshire', *Archaeol. J.* 2nd ser. 26, 143–301.

Hase, P. H. 1976: 'The development of the parish in Hampshire', unpub. Univ. Cambridge PhD thesis.

Herring, P. and Hooke, D. (forthcoming): 'Interrogating Anglo-Saxons in St Dennis', *Cornish Archaeology*.

Hooke, D. 1981: 'Open-field agriculture – the evidence from the pre-Conquest charters of the West Midlands', in T. Rowley (ed.), *The Origins of Open-Field Agriculture*, (Croom Helm, Oxford), 39–63.

Hooke, D. 1982: 'Pre-Conquest estates in the West Midlands: preliminary thoughts', *J. Hist. Geog.* 8, 227–244.

Hooke, D. 1983: *The Landscape of Anglo-Saxon Staffordshire: The Charter Evidence*, Univ. Keele Dept Adult Education (Keele).

Hooke, D. 1985: *The Anglo-Saxon Landscape: The Kingdom of the Hwicce* (Manchester Univ. Press, Manchester).

Hooke, D. 1986: 'Territorial organisation in the Anglo-Saxon West Midlands: central places, central areas', in E. Grant (ed.), *Central Places, Archaeology and History*, Univ. Sheffield Dept Archaeol. & Prehist. (Sheffield). 79–94.

Hooke, D. 1988: 'Regional variation in southern and central England in the Anglo-Saxon period and its relationship to land units and settlement', in D. Hooke (ed), *Anglo-Saxon Settlements*, (Blackwell, Oxford), 123–152.

Hooke, D. 1989: 'Pre-Conquest woodland: its distribution and usage', *Agric. Hist. Rev.* 37, 113–29.

Hooke, D. 1990: *Worcestershire Anglo-Saxon Charter-Bounds* (Boydell Press, Woodbridge).

Hooke, D. (forthcoming): *The Pre-Conquest Charters of Devon and Cornwall* (Boydell Press, Woodbridge).

Jones, G. R. J. 1976: 'Multiple estates and early settlement', in *Medieval Settlement*, 15–40.

Klingelhofer, E. 1992: *Manor, Vill and Hundred. The development of rural institutions in early medieval Hampshire.* Pontifical Inst Medieval Stud (Toronto).

Olson, B. L. 1989: *Early Monasteries in Cornwall* (Woodbridge).

Padel, 0. J. 1985: *Cornish Place-Name Elements*. Engl. Place-Name Soc., Vol. 56/57 (Cambridge).

Ravenhill, W. L. D. 1967: 'Cornwall', in H. C. Darby and R. Welldon Finn (eds), *The Domesday Geography of South-West England*, (Cambridge Univ. Press, Cambridge), 296–347.

Rose, P. and Preston-Jones, A. (forthcoming): 'Changes in the Cornish countryside AD 400–1100', in S. Burnell and D. Hooke (eds), *Early Land Use and Settlement*, Exeter Studies in History, Exeter.

Sawyer, P. H. 1968: *Anglo-Saxon Charters, an annotated list and bibliography* (Royal Hist. Soc., London).

Stenton, F. M. 1913: *The Early History of the Abbey of Abingdon* (Reading).

Taylor, C. 1964: 'The Saxon boundaries of Frustfield', *Wiltshire Archaeol. Mag.* 59, 110–115.

Taylor, C. 1983: *Village and Farmstead* (Book Club Associates, London).

5.   Settlement in Wessex in the Tenth Century: The Charter Evidence

Michael Costen

The purpose of this paper is a very narrow one. It seeks to analyse the material to be found in the boundary clauses of Anglo-Saxon charters of the tenth century, in the modern counties of Wiltshire, Dorset, Somerset and South Avon, in order to extract evidence concerning settlement. Accordingly it avoids the temptation to extrapolate too far or to turn to field-work evidence in order to bolster the charters.

The Charters as Evidence

The corpus of charters used in this study is of course highly problematical as historical material (see Figs 5.2, 5.3, 5.4). Since almost all of the charters exist only in later, post-Conquest copies, the dating of the charters and, even more, of the boundary clauses is extremely difficult. All the charters used in this study have been chosen with the observations of other scholars in mind.[1] Fortunately the worst forgeries are mostly of earlier periods and tenth century charters would seem in most cases to have some basis in fact. Della Hooke's comment about the bounds of charters in Worcestershire would seem to apply here, too; it is normally the body of the charter which has suffered from the attentions of medieval forgers or 'improvers', rather than the boundary clause, which is usually Anglo-Saxon (Hooke 1990, 2–3). Since the purpose of this paper is to use the evidence in 'bulk', the effect of one or two spurious sets of bounds should be minimal.

We first need to consider whether or not the estates for which charters exist are similar to other estates in the region. Will a study of the charter bounds give us an accurate picture of the average sort of settlement in the region in the tenth century?

Statistics suggest that the estates which have charters surviving are not typical of all estates in Wessex and the major difference is in the size of estates with charters. In Somerset the average size of all estates as they were in 1086 was 2.9 hides (Thorn and Thorn 1980). This figure disguises wide variations. The average size of royal estates was probably about 20 hides[2] and the average size of ecclesiastical estates was 10.6 hides. On the other hand, there was a very long 'tail' of very small estates, mostly, though by no means exclusively, in the western part of the shire, which produces the very low average. Almost all of these estates were in private hands – that is non-royal and non-ecclesiastical – in 1086. For properties with tenth-century or eleventh-century charters the average size in 1086 was 11.37 hides.

In Wiltshire the average size of holdings in 1086 was 8.24 hides, reflecting the smaller number of very small estates in the shire. The average size of charter estates in 1086 in Wiltshire was about 17.5 hides. In Dorset the average size of all estates in 1086 was 4.5 hides (Thorn and Thorn 1983). Charter estates averaged 9.3 hides. It is true that the only basis available for comparison is the evidence of the Domesday Survey of the late eleventh century, but it seems likely that these differences are too large to have arisen in the course of a century only. Generally charters deal with larger rather than smaller estates and it is possible that charter estates had a different social and economic history from non-charter estates. Most surviving charters relate to properties which were in the hands of the Church, either as monastic or as cathedral holdings, and it seems highly likely that conservative policies which avoided the breakup of holdings were pursued. The church had no heirs to satisfy. On the other hand the availability of capital and time to plan may have encouraged progressive economic and social policies inside territories (Costen 1992b, 32–36).

Wiltshire has sixty-three identifiable separate estates with charters or with bounds which have become detached from charters, or which perhaps had no charters but were merely surveys of estates. Of these sixty-three, some were direct transfers from the king to the church, others were grants to private individuals who subsequently transferred the property to the church. In Wiltshire there is a difference between the two types of estate. Those which went directly to the church from the crown averaged about 27 hides in size, while those which came from private individuals averaged about 11 hides. Thus, even divided in this way, it is clear that charter grants were not typical of all estates in the county of Wiltshire. In Dorset the distinctions are not quite so clear cut, but even here there are discernable differences. Direct gifts from crown to church averaged just over 12 hides, while gifts from private individuals averaged 7.3 hides each.

Size is a crude measure, but it is the only one available to us. It suggests that the charter estates, whether they had passed directly from crown to church or by gift from some noble family, were not typical of all estates in the region. They were generally bigger and that fact alone probably means that the settlement history of such units was not typical of the region. The information about the early landscape which emerges from the charters may not be as typical as a random sample of places might provide.

The Physical Landscape

Buildings and settlement

The charter bounds contain a mass of detailed information and the problem is to arrange it in a fashion which is meaningful across the landscape of the three counties. The bounds of estates clearly represent the landscape as it was at the edge of the estate, not normally close to its centre. Information about dwellings, buildings and farmsteads is necessarily limited. The church is the building which has survived best from the tenth century into modern times, but it has normally been associated with settlement centres, not with borders and the edges of estates. In a long discussion on the siting of churches Richard Morris (1989, 240–9) shows how frequently churches do not lie in the settlements they serve and explains this in general terms as the result of the movement of the settlement centre. But churches rarely lie on settlement boundaries and in the charters correspondingly the term is rare and all the more interesting for that. At Bemerton (Wi) (S 767) a church is mentioned, not as a boundary point but as an asset on the estate, along with a mill. At West Overton (Wi) (S 784) on the River Kennet, the reference is very precisely to *chiricstede*, a 'church site'. Examination of the charter and of the modern maps (WRO E/A61³) of the estate suggest that the 'church site' lay on the western boundary. It lay between a ford and *lorta lea*, which is probably represented by modern Lurkeley Hill (SU 121665). This is rather over a kilometre to the west of the modern parish church site in the village of West Overton. The charter names not Overton, but 'Cynetun', which has been identified with Kennett (Finberg 1964, 98; Gover, Mawer and Stenton 1939, 297). The church site may have been associated with Kennett at an earlier date. At Bleadon (So) (S 804) there is similarly a reference to *cyrice stede*. The site is on a hillside, distant from any settlement. It seems likely that this was an abandoned church site and one which had little relevance to the settlement pattern of the tenth century.

Ærn, a building, also occurs infrequently, at Corscomb (Do) (S 933) and at Pilton (So) (S 247). Whether or not these were dwellings is impossible to tell. Buildings which were dwellings occur at Chelworth (Wi) (S 1579), where *escote* is represented by the modern Eastcourt (Gover, Mawer and Stenton 1939, 57). Its subsequent development into a settlement suggests that it was already a place of some importance in the estate. At West Knoyle (Wi) a *cytan* stood on the boundary, perhaps the boundary between East and West Knoyle. In Dorset at Portisham the boundary passed the 'western cottage' at Coryates, indicating that there was a settlement at that point at the time of the charter (S 961).

Hus, a house, occurs only once, in Dorset, at Compton Abbas (S630). *Stede*, a site or dwelling place, occurs more frequently. At Hanley (Do) there was *mylen stede*, a mill site (S 630), and also *olde wested* at Sturminster (S 764). In Wiltshire, it occurs as *chiricstede* (see above), *eald treo sted* (S 478) at Beechingstoke and *ealdan ham stede* at Coombe Bisset (S 696). In Somerset the *cyrice stede* has already been mentioned. Also occurring was *humberwe stede* at North Wootton (S 509). The Somerset site is difficult as it may refer to a place beside a stream called the 'Humber', or be a reference to the 'site of Humma's barrow'. Probably only the *ealdan ham stede* and the *olde wested* are significant, describing settlement sites which had been abandoned.

The closely related *ham-steall*, 'the site of a dwelling' was explicitly associated with a former dwelling or farmstead at Weston near Bath (So) (S 508), where there is a reference to *þam ealdan ham stealle þe æþelere ahte*, 'the old dwelling-site that belonged to Æþhelhere'. The *ealdan ham stede* at Coombe Bissett is clearly another example of a deserted building site.

Setl, 'a dwelling place', occurs at East Overton (Wi) as *Æþelferþes setle* (S 449); at Beechingstoke (Wi) as *prestes setel* (S 478); at Broad Chalke (Wi) as *bican setle* (S 582); and at East Pennard (So) as *bulan setl* (S 563). Not surprisingly this term is usually associated with the names or status of individuals and also indicates that the term was used to describe the holding of an individual. These are single household sites.

Individual dwellings on boundaries thus seem to be uncommon and their very rarity probably made them convenient markers. This might suggest that settlement, even when dispersed, was determined by the need to respect boundaries and that where dwellings did occur on boundaries this was probably caused by divisions of property and the creation of new boundaries inside an already settled landscape.

Recent research has shown how common watermills were in Anglo-Saxon England (Holt 1988, 5–16) and Wiltshire and Dorset had a very large number of mills by 1086. In Wiltshire fifty-nine percent of all manors had mills recorded in 1086 and for Dorset and Somerset the figures are fifty and forty-one percent respectively (Darby 1977, 271). As mills are mentioned only infrequently, it might seem chance alone which placed a suitable site for a mill along a boundary, but in view of the frequency with which boundaries follow rivers and streams this seems unlikely. In Somerset no mills were mentioned on boundaries, but there are references to two mill streams, at Ashwick (S 1034) and at Creech (S 345). In Wiltshire a mill is mentioned explicitly at Bemerton (S 767), but was part of the property of the manor rather than being on the boundary. At Ugford the boundary ran along *þa mylen ware*, the 'mill-dam', but at Steeple Ashton only the *milebourne* is mentioned (S 727). In Dorset mills are more numerous. Mill streams are mentioned at Portisham, *mylebroce* (S 961), at Thornford, *mylenburna* (S 516), and the mills themselves at West Orchard, *eadelmes melne* (S 445), and at Cheselbourne, *miliere* (S 955), while at Hanley there is a *mylen stede* (S 630), at Mapperton a *molenhame* (S 490) and at Wyke Regis a *muledich* (S 938). It may be that wherever possible mills were built inside the estate and as close as possible to settlement, to avoid transport problems. The small quantity of water used by early mills would have made this course easier than it became in later centuries as machinery grew bigger. Alternatively, where the boundary simply passed a mill without deviating the mill may not have been mentioned.

A related group of terms refer to small settlements or farm holdings which had land. The references are almost certainly to the territory of these places, not to buildings. Such terms as *wic*, a farm or small settlement, *wyrð*, a farm and *hiwisc*, an individual holding of one hide, occur in all three counties. In Somerset, at Weston near Bath (S 508) there are three separate references to *wics*, two of which lay side by side (*twam wycan*), and at Ditcheat (S 292) *wynewareswik* was mentioned. Two less direct references occur at Taunton (S 311) – *wican mor*- and at Ruishton (S 310) – *wice hrycg*. In Wiltshire there are four direct references to *wics*. The first of these is at East Overton (S 449) –*feoh wicuna gemære*, 'cattle farm boundary'. At Wylye (S 469) was *æt þæm wicum* and at Enford (S 427) was *amwicum* and at Purton there was *appeldore sele wyke* (S 1586). There are also two references to *wic herepað*, one at Stoke (S 400) and the other at South Newton (S 492). In Dorset at Corfe (S 573) there is reference to *wicun* and to an associated stream and ford. While Tarrant Hinton (S 406) and Winterbourne Tomson (S 485) have references to roads associated with *wics*.

In Dorset there are three *wyrðs*. One, *ealdmannes wyrð*, is mentioned in the charters for Fontmell Magna, West Orchard (S 445), East Orchard (S 710) and Thornton (S 656). Fontmell Magna (S 419) also has *beteswirþe sled* and at Horton there is *wænecan wyrð* (S 969). In Wiltshire at Downton there are references to three separate *wyrðes* in two charters (S 540 and S 1518). Two more are mentioned at Fovant (S 881) and two at Bradford (S 899). There was also one at Grittleham in Brinkworth parish (S 1583), and a *wrthwelane* at Chelworth (S 1579). In Somerset *wyrðes* occur at Ditcheat (S 292), at Berrow

(S 793), at East Pennard (S 563) and at Charlcombe. At Lyng (S 432) the reference is to *herworth*, 'the army enclosure', and must be a reference to King Alfred's fort on Athelney Island. From the charter S 1410 of AD 744 it appears that *wyrðes* could be independent units. *Scobbanwirht* near Baltonsborough was probably a separate estate or farmstead. It still stood as a unit in the bounds of Lottisham, a component of the Ditcheat estate (S 292), in the ninth or tenth century.

Hiwisces are represented once in Somerset, at Rimpton (S 441); in Wiltshire at Ford (S 543) – *þæs hiwisces æt winterburnan*; and in Dorset at Fontmell Magna (S 419) and at Cheselbourne (S 955). At Didlington and Uddens (S 609) it is clear that Uddens itself was a one hide unit and functioned as an independent estate, since it was physically separated from the estate centre at Didlington. At Fontmell the reference to '*oþerhalf hewisse*' suggests that the unit had been divided.

It has been suggested that *hiwisces* were individual farmsteads of some importance, created at a time before the introduction of open-field agriculture and sometimes becoming adapted as hamlets or small settlements, but often disappearing as the open fields of communities became all-embracing (Costen 1992). *Wyrðs* in the same period seem to have been smaller farms. The superior survival rate of *wics*, as compared with *hiwisces* or *wyrðes*, suggests that they were far more often small settlements rather than individual farms. The survival of some of the these settlements on or close to boundaries in the tenth and eleventh centuries shows that the process of assimilation of individual units into communal systems was by no means complete. Bearing in mind what has been said already, it is likely also that they display a relationship to an older landscape, rather than the one which emerged in the tenth and the eleventh centuries. Probably such individual holdings were extremely common right across the region.

Of all settlement terms *tun* is the most important and also the most enduring. It continued as a suffix for new settlement names well past the Norman Conquest (Smith 1970, pt II, p. 197).

Many existing settlements with *tun* names are mentioned in boundary clauses, but normally this is because the boundary being perambulated marches with the boundary of the place named. However, some *tun* names do seem to refer to settlements rather than to estates. At Fontmell (S 419) *winteintune* occurs, at Lyme (S442) *werboldiston*, at Mapperton (S490) there was *weritun*. In Wiltshire the reference to the *tune* at East Overton (S 449) suggests that the boundary ran past the settlement of West Overton. The estate map of West Overton (WRO 2203) of 1783 shows that the boundary between East and West Overton passed through West Overton village at that date and presumably close by it in the tenth century. This seems to be clear reference to a settlement rather than an estate. At Clyffe Pypard (S 848) there is a reference to a *tunsteal*, which may have been a farm or settlement centre. The reference to *wudutunnincga gemæro* in the same charter may be to the next-door settlement of Woodhall, now a deserted medieval settlement. At Bradford there were two *tuns*, *cosetun* and *broctune*, neither of which have survived. In Somerset, at Weston near Bath (S 661) the reference to *tune* is probably to the settlement at Weston or to an estate centre. Other *tuns* which were not surviving settlements were *cranhunterston*, at Butleigh (S 270a), *cuttleston* at Long Sutton (S 343), *hentun* at Manworthy (S 709) and *littleton* or *linton* at Pilton (S 247). They were perhaps farmsteads which have not survived, rather than 'villages' or major estate centres.

Evidence for individual settlements is quite sparse, considering the very large number of estates with boundaries, but this is only to be expected if we assume that dwellings or settlements only rarely lay on the edges of the estates. Where individual houses and even hamlets lay close enough to boundaries to be used as boundary points, it is possible that they reflect the drawing of boundaries after the settlements were established. They may be evidence for changes in estate boundaries; for the reapportionment or sub-division of lands; and may well reflect changes which had taken place quite close in time to the survey of the bounds. It is noteworthy how few of the settlements and dwellings mentioned in this way have survived to the present day, pointing to them as remnants of a landscape in the course of change.

Fields and Farming

When looking for evidence of cultivation *æcer, furlang, eorðland, foryrðe* and *furh* are the terms most likely to be of use. In fact they are not common (Figs 5.5, 5.6, 5.7).

In Somerset there is a *crundel æcer* at Bathampton (S 627), *winter acres* at Wrington (S 371), *XXX acres þis kyngge* at High Ham (S 791), *twelfmede acres* at Lottisham (S 292) and a series of references in the charter (S 508) for Weston near Bath. There is a reference to an *oden æcar, ænne æcer, iii æcere* (twice) and to *þa viii æceras þe æþelere ahte*. The *oden æcar* is a 'threshing acre', presumably land where grain was customarily threshed, perhaps to catch the wind. The *crundel æcer* was a quarry site. The single acre, the three acres and the eight acres which Æthelhere owned were possibly arable land, but there is no indication that they were part of a field system. The 'winter acres' at Wrington were perhaps acres which were ploughed during the winter time. The 'thirty acres belonging to the king' near High Ham were in Wearne and can be identified as a small block of land lying on the High Ham side of the stream in Wearne. They probably formed a single block of land.

There are many more references to acres in Wiltshire. Some references are to single acres, as at Ham (S 416) – *anan æcre*; Broad Chalke (S 582) – *anne aker*. At Broad Chalke there is also a reference to *ænne æker innan ælfheages land* – 'an acre in Ælfhere's land'. Other references are to blocks of ploughland: *þreora æcra* at Collingbourne Kingston (S 379) and also at Wylye (S 469). Blocks of acres of different sizes, up to twelve acres, also occur at Fovant, Odstock, Badbury, Rollington, Idmiston and Tisbury. There are references to *akeres heveden* and *swyrd æceras heafod* at Eastcourt (S 1582) and Wanborough (S 1588), the 'top or end of the acres' in each case, suggesting that there were blocks of land. The explicit reference to the *hevedakerende* at Dauntsey (S 1580), clearly refers to the headland at the end of a furlong. The *hevedlonde* (S 1585), at Norton may be a similar reference. Other references are to 'boundary acres' at Grittleton (S 472) and Norton (S1585) and to meadow acres at Bemerton and Broad Chalke (S 767 & S 582). The most telling reference is that in S 719 (Avon farm at Durnford) to *singulis jugeribus mixtum in communi ruri huc illacque dispersis*, 'individual acres dispersed hither and thither mixed among the common land'. Both the reference at Dauntsey and that at Avon Farm clearly suggest open-field agriculture.

In Dorset at West Orchard, *funtmel þry akeres* (S 445) might refer to a detached portion of land and at Didlington (S609) and at Sturminster (S764) there are references to *twegan ærcas* and *sixe acres*. At Hinton St Mary is *akere heueden* (S 502). At Cheselbourne (S 485) was a *forð erthe acre*, a 'fore earth acre'.

In Somerset there was *for yrþe* at Ruishton (S 310). The term has been noted above in Dorset and occurs at Langford (S 1811), Ebbesbourne Wake (S 696) and Ugford (S 586) in Wiltshire. The related term *eorþland* occurs twice at Bemerton (S 767) – *up andlang yrð landes*, and *on yrð land* and at Baverstock in the *wic* which belonged to Wylye there was *forð be þam urþlonde*. Also at South Newton (S 492) there were two references to *yrþland*.

Only one reference to a furlong occurs in Somerset at Marksbury (S 431), but in a boundary clause which can be shown to be twelfth century. In Dorset there is one reference at Chesilbourne (S 763), but in Wiltshire there are references to furlongs at East Overton (S 449), South Newton (S 492), Nettleton (S 504), Moredon (S 705), Eastcourt (S 1582) and Brinkworth (S 1576).

It has been shown that *furh* is a term used to denote a furrow that separated two areas of arable land (Hooke 1981, p. 46). In Wiltshire the term is common, occurring at Stockton, Wylye, South Newton, Nettleton, Idmiston, Enford, Broad Chalke, Winterbourne Monkton, Norton, Sevington and Winterbourne Basset. In Dorset it occurs at Tarrant Hinton (S 406) and Hanley (S 630) but it does not occur in Somerset.

There is plenty of evidence for arable cultivation in the charters of all three counties, but Wiltshire has by far the greatest number of references. The frequency of the references to furlongs and above all to *furhes* suggests that arable agriculture, perhaps in open fields, was well developed in Wiltshire. What we see is arable agriculture affecting the edges of estates, and in many cases parcels of arable land in two different estates abutting one another. This is well illustrated at Stockton in Wylye where Della Hooke has shown that the arable fields were well developed by the tenth century, reaching near the maximum potential even at that early date (Hooke 1988). This suggests that by the mid tenth century some parts of Wiltshire were particularly densely settled and widely cultivated. This is especially noticeable in the river valleys around Wilton and to the west of Wilton, with another smaller concentration in the north-west of the county. It would seem sensible to infer that much of this cultivation was open-field, as it clearly was at Avon Farm, Durnford. But it would not be safe to assume that the open-field system was anything like universal in the shire in the mid tenth century.

Somerset, on the other hand, shows little evidence of arable cultivation, although it clearly existed. There is certainly not enough evidence to suggest widespread open-field agriculture, although lack of documentary evidence does not preclude evidence from other sources (Costen 1991). The most frequent references are on the lands of the Abbey of Bath in the Bath region. On the lands of the Abbey of Glastonbury, which were concentrated in the centre of the shire, the evidence is much less strong. The evidence for Somerset suggests that arable cultivation was not yet as intensive in mid tenth century Somerset as it was in contemporary Wiltshire.

In Dorset evidence is sparse, but what there is suggests that arable cultivation was most intensive in the north-eastern part of the shire, close to Wiltshire. It looks as if the most intensively cultivated areas were to be found in Wiltshire, around Wilton and Old Sarum, with a southward extension into the contiguous part of Dorset and in the north-east of Wiltshire, extending across into the Bath region of North Somerset.

Associated with arable cultivation were special areas set aside for meadow and as agricultural enclosures. Meadow (*mæd*) is of course very common and there is nothing surprising about its appearance in charter bounds. However, meadows which were not within the bounds of the property they served occurred in Wiltshire at Langley Burrell (S 473) and Odstock (S 635). They were *sunder mædes*. They were perhaps the product of a subdivision of land which had left a community without meadow except by provision of distant land, perhaps part of the meadow of a larger estate which had been subdivided. The use of acres to describe the meadow land underlines its importance to communities. At Ashwick (So) there was *twelf æcra mæd* (S 1034). At Fontmell Magna (Do) there was *xxiiii akeres meade* (S 419) and at Swallowcliffe (Wi) *twegan æcras* (S 468). Some meadow was specifically marked as common meadow, as at Wylye (Wi) (S 767) where there was *gemænan mæde*. Most descriptions of meadow refer to physical conditions but a suprising number contain personal names, suggesting private, rather than common use. Thus in Wiltshire there is *bading mede* at Norton (S 1585), in Dorset *brepling*

made at Thornton (S 656) and *babbanmede* at Buckland Newton (S 474) and in Somerset *frisingmede* at Buckland (S 555) and *pendan mede* at Kingsbury (S 1570). Many of these names were not contemporary. Simple names of the type *Babba* cited above do not seem common in the tenth century and *Penda* had long ceased to be fashionable among the West Saxons. These were probably ancient meadow names in the tenth century.

In a landscape which, however it was farmed, was largely open, enclosures for special purposes were important and the number of enclosure names, even on boundaries, suggests that they must have been extremely common. In Somerset there are thirteen *hamme* names. One was a 'bean ham' (*benham*) at Long Sutton (S 343), which survives today as the name of a deserted medieval village site. Two others, one at Henstridge (S 570) and one at Creech Heathfield (S 345), were enclosures for hay. In Wiltshire there were twenty-seven references to *hammes*, most of which have personal names attached to them. In Dorset the seven *hamme* names include two with personal names, *snelles hamme* at Fontmell Magna (S 419) and *breowoldes ham* at Corscombe (S 933), and one which was clearly the site of a watermill – *molen-hamme* – at Mapperton (S 490).

Enclosures used specifically to contain animals were often indicated by *fald*, the modern 'fold'. There are only two in Dorset, one at Uppiddle which was *punfald*, a pinfold or pound specifically intended for straying animals and associated at a later date with common-field agriculture, the other was a *stodfald* at Blashenwell (S 534) – an enclosure for horses. Only two *faldes* occur in Wiltshire, both at Grittleham, one of which was *rammes-fold*, a 'rams' fold'. The three examples in Somerset were all at the western end of the Mendips; a *stodfald* at Bleadon (S 606) and folds at Compton Bishop and at Cheddar, probably both used for sheep.

One other term – *edisc* – occurs in Wiltshire and Somerset. Unfortunately the definition of this word is not at all certain. Smith (1970) shows that the word glosses the Latin *vivarium*, 'a park', and also has the same meaning as the OE *deortun*, 'a deer enclosure'. 'Park' may well be the meaning of the word at Pitminster (So) (S 440), especially since it occurs on the boundary of a well recognised medieval park (Rackham 1988, 27). The *hides edisc* at Norton (Wi) (S 1585) was probably simply an enclosure.

The large range of enclosures suggests the widespread need to control animals or to grow special crops in enclosures, but the overall impression is of the large number of enclosures which have personal names attached to them. It may be that this indicates the extent to which farming was an individual, rather than a communal activity, but it may also tend to indicate the name of the owner of an estate and be a reflection of the extent to which demesne farming was becoming established.

The extensive grazing of animals must have been extremely important to the farmer of the late Anglo-Saxon period. Indications of this in the charters are not, however, very frequent. In Somerset the *wealle* (a wall) at Weston (S 508 and S 661) clearly ran along the edge of the escarpment on Lansdown Hill and may have been intended to keep sheep on the hill out of cultivated land below. It is clear from the charters of the settlements around Lansdown – Weston, Charlcombe and North Stoke – that the flat top of Lansdown was not inside any of the surrounding estates and it may well have been used for sheep. A wall was also mentioned at Stanton Prior and Corston on the southern side of the Avon (S 735 and S 593 and 476), where there is later evidence that the abbey kept a large flock of sheep during the winter. A stone wall, *stanwale*, occurs at Ditchampton (Wi) (S 1010) and at Corfe in Dorset (S 573) and at Portisham (S 961). The most probable explanation for the existence of what must have been expensive items to construct, is probably that they were all intended to control sheep. It is also noticeable that all three shires have references to common (*gemenan*) lands. At Idmiston (Wi) (S 541) there was a *menhulle*, a 'common hill', at Donhead a *gemanen cumb* (S 630) at Edington a *ymananedene*, at Bishopstone *menandene* (S 522). In Somerset there is a *gemenan hylle* at Ruishton (S 310). In Dorset there is a rather doubtful reference to *monnisclive* at Lyme (S 422). The much more frequent occurrence in Wiltshire seems to fit in with the picture of the region as more fully developed, so that controlled common grazing existed in some areas, despite the huge ranges of unstinted grazing which must still have existed on the central plain.

It seems very unlikely that the word *feld* was used to describe agricultural land in the tenth century (Smith 1970). It is clear from the compounds in which it occurs that it indicated an area of open ground in contrast to woodland. In Somerset at Pitminster (S 1066) there was an *oxenafeld*, 'the oxen's field', which may have been used for grazing. Other examples occur in the same area, at Lydeard (S 380) where there was a *fasingafeld*, 'the field of Fasa's men'. With such a proprietorial name this ground, too, clearly had a value, perhaps again for grazing. At Isle Abbots there was *þeodnesfeld*, 'the lord's field', possibly in this case 'God's field'. In Somerset the word is well distributed, with two examples in the Bath area and one at Batcombe as well as the examples already quoted in the Taunton region. In Dorset there are three examples. In Wiltshire there are 13 examples. Some of them clearly refer to rough land, using terms such as *hæpfeld* and *fyrstefelda*, 'heath field and fernfield' and this was probably the normal state of such land. Indeed, the name *clinanfeld*, 'bare field' which occurs at Langley Burrell (Wi) (S 473) and at Weston (So) (S 508), supports this view. These open tracts of rough grazing were probably common on hilltops where boundaries of estates were drawn.

Woodland

Woodland names of all types are very common in the charters of all three counties (see Figs 5.8, 5.9, 5.10). This is not a surprise when we consider the distribution of woodland as it is revealed by the Domesday Book. Dorset and Wiltshire both had about 13% of their area wooded in 1066 and in Somerset the figure was 11%. In Somerset 70% of all settlements had some woodland, in Wiltshire the proportions were much the same at 65% and in Dorset 63% (Rackham 1980, p. 114).

Bearu, a wood, is difficult to distinguish from *bær*, a wood-pasture, in many cases. But for the purposes of this paper the difficulty this causes is not serious. In Dorset the two examples are both at Horton (S 969), *suðbeara* and *ciddesbeara*. Somerset has four examples. Near Taunton lay *dudding bearu* (S 311) and close by at Pitminster was *ac beara* (S440). At Curry (S455) was *hroca beara* and at Rimpton *oaten beares*. This last was a reference to 'Eata's wood', which by 1086, and probably much earlier, was the settlement of Adber (Thorn and Thorn 1980, 19, 74 & 24, 37). However, despite the large number of references to woods the term *bearu* was not used in Wiltshire charters. The word is not mentioned as an element in major or minor place-names and field-names in Wiltshire by Gover, Mawer and Stenton (1939) and so it seems certain that this was a relatively late term and that by the time it became usual the names for woodlands in Wiltshire had already become fixed.

Graf is a much more common word everywhere with thirteen examples in Wiltshire, thirteen in Somerset and five in Dorset. While *bearu* names were often associated with personal names, *graf* names seem either not to have had any other appellative or to have attached to them a term such as *lang*, *middel* or *blac*.

Wudu has twelve examples in Somerset, fifteen in Wiltshire and eight in Dorset, again with topographical rather than personal suffixes. Other less frequently used wood names include *hyrst*, *hangra*, *holt*, *scaga*, *þyrnan* and *þyfel*. There was one *hyrst* in Dorset – *readan hyrstes* at Corscombe (S 975), three in Somerset, at Clifton (S 777), Pilton (S 112) and Compton Bishop and three in Wiltshire, at Ford (S 543) and Grittleham (S 1583). *Hangra* occurs only once, in Somerset at Wellington (S 380). *Holt* occurs twice in Somerset, both times at Taunton (S 311), and at East Orchard in Dorset. *Scaga*, a word which describes a long belt of woodland or a very large and dense hedge, occurs in Somerset and in Wiltshire.

Just as important as woodland names were names associated with woodland, in particular *leah*. This word with its uncertain meaning – a woodland or a clearing in woodland – is so common that it can be found in areas which were not necessarily well wooded by the eleventh century. The distribution of the element in Wiltshire corresponds well with the more general distribution of the element in place-names as recorded by the English Place Names Society survey (Gover, Mawer and Stenton 1939, see distribution map in rear pocket). The only parts of the county where *leah* does not occur in charters are closely around Wilton and Old Sarum and along the northern edge of the Marlborough Downs. In Dorset the element is widely dispersed in the north-eastern and northern part of the county and it is similarly widely spread across Somerset. It is likely that, since the name is so widely spread, sometimes across areas which had little woodland by the eleventh century, this was an early place-name element in the landscape. Its great frequency probably reflects not only the very widespread distribution of woodland but the persistence of names in the landscape, especially where they were on or close to the edges of estates where land-use changes were likely to have been least. Its absence, conversely, points to areas which were open and had no woodland in the period when the term was in active use and landscape names were appearing.

Also associated with woodlands are the terms *hæc*, 'a gate', *hlypgeat*, a device to allow animals such as deer to leave a wood but not enter it. *Haga* 'a hedge or fence', and *gehæg* 'a hedge', may also be connected with woodland on occasions.

Hæc occurs only in Somerset, at Weston (S 508), at Charlcombe, at East Pennard (S 563) and at Pitminster (S 1006). At Weston the gate lay along a boundary in which there was a *hlypgeat* on the western side of the estate. It was almost certainly close to woodland which existed in the neighbouring estate of North Stoke. The *hæc* in Charlcombe nearby also lay close to the later Royal Forest of Kingswood in Gloucestershire. East Pennard lay on the western edge of an area which was still well wooded in 1086 and Pitminster was also in a well forested region on the border of the Forest of Neroche.

Haga, a fence or hedge, is another term associated with woodland elsewhere (Hooke 1981b, 237) and it occurs in all three counties. In many places it is clear that the hedge or fence was built specifically to mark a boundary. In Dorset there is a *landshare hegen* at West Orchard (S 445) two *merhawin* at Buckland Newton (S 474), a *merehawe* at Sturminster (S 764) and a *mearch-agen* at Horton. Other *hagas* occur at Fontmell Magna (S 419), where there were two examples, and at Corscombe (S933), two examples. *Mere haga* occurs in Somerset at Bathampton (twice) (S 627), at Ruishton (S 310) and at Rimpton (S 590). Other *hagas* were at Mells (S 481), Ditcheat (S 292), Pitminster (S 440) (two examples) and at Henstridge (S 570). At Wrington there was a *swynhage* and also a *hagen medewe*, a pig-enclosure and an enclosed meadow (S 371). In Wiltshire *hagas* occurred at South Newton (S 492), at Downton (S 540), three examples at Burbage (S 688) and at Bedwyn (S 756) and at Ashton where there was a *fromesetinga hagen*, the 'hedge of the dwellers around Frome'. This is probably a reference to a hedge or fence which ran along the Wiltshire–Somerset border, where the great royal estate of Frome began. The construction of the phrase suggests that this is a name of some antiquity. Except perhaps for

the example at South Newton, these names occur in areas of Wiltshire where woodland was extensive. It seems likely that the purpose of these hedges was to provide protection for cultivated lands against animals from the woodlands, mostly deer but perhaps also including animals turned out in woodlands to graze.

Hedges (*hecge, gehæg*) also occur quite frequently, but the quite separate use of the word at places where *haga* does not occur suggests that there was a real difference between a *haga* and a *hecge*. That they were constructed or planted rather than simply the result of material left after clearance shows at Langley Burrell, where there was the *hege rewe þat alfric made* (S 473). Hedges are not so specifically associated with woodland and so seem to have had a more generalised use as boundaries, intended to keep the livestock of one estate out of another.

Linear Features

The information so far considered has concentrated on the nature of settlement and landuse, in so far as that can be divined from a study of such a select part of each local landscape. It is worth turning briefly to consider the much more common features of boundary clauses which functioned mostly or even solely as delineators. The most obvious term here is *dic*. A *dic* was nearly always a ditch and a bank. The best known example is Wansdyke, both East and West. Such evidence as there is about the origins of these earthworks shows that they were features which were not related to the estates which used them as boundaries. In Somerset West Wansdyke cuts across the estates at Stanton Prior (S 711 & S 735) and Marksbury (S 431). Here the dyke uses the old hill-fort of Stantonbury as part of its course, ignoring the lands grouped around it (Costen 1983). However, just a little eastwards the dyke does form boundaries for South Stoke (S 694) and Clifton (S 777), showing that the division of territory here took place after the construction of the dyke. In Wiltshire there are over eighty references to *dices*. Wansdyke is well represented in the north-east of the county. Where it occurs as a boundary feature, at Stanton St Bernard and East Overton, it clearly shows that those estates were divided after the construction of the Wansdyke. The same probably holds true for other estates in the district. Although pre-Conquest evidence does not exist, the Wansdyke forms a bound for Box, Corsham, Lacock, Monkton Farleigh, South Wraxall, Atworth and Melksham. It follows the Roman road through these parishes and it is possible that the road was used *as a road* when the bounds were formed, and that it is the road which the bound follows. To the east of Chittoe the dyke/road again forms the boundary between Calne and Heddington, after which dyke and road diverge, with the road used as the boundary for Bishops Cannings. It seems likely that the estates used Wansdyke as a bound almost everywhere in the west. Only Chittoe

Fig. 5.1 *Rimpton on the Somerset–Dorset border. The banks and ditch shown here formed a prominent feature in the two charters for this estate. In S 441 of AD 938 it was a dic. In S 571 of AD 956 it was a beorhtulfes gemær dic, "Beorhtulf's boundary ditch". This feature was therefore in evidence by 938. How much older it may be is impossible to know. (Picture looking north, with Cadbury Castle in the background.) (Photo: Mick Aston)*

Enford (S 427) and Sevington (S 999). In Somerset there are 'old' *dices* at Weston (S 661), Charlcombe, Stanton Prior (S 711), Priston (S 414), East Pennard (S 563), Batcombe (S 462), Bleadon (S 606), High Ham (S 791), Taunton (S311), Pitminster (S440), Rimpton (S590), Henstridge (S570) and Lyng (S432). In Dorset at Bradford Abbas (S422), Buckland Newton (S474), Mapperton (S490), Corfe (S573) and Cheselbourne (S955). The *dices* involved could have been described as 'old' at various points in their history, but it seems most likely that they were 'old' because they were pre-existing, like Wansdyke and Grim's Ditch and that, where convenient, they had been chosen as boundaries.

Some other *dices* have personal names attached to them. In Dorset there was a *cinninces dic* (S490), *chelbrichtes dich* at Hinton St Mary (S502) and *wyndrede dic* at Shaftesbury (S655). In Somerset there was *herces dic* at Bathampton (S627), *offan dic* at Ruishton (S352), *beorhtulfes gemær dic* at Rimpton (S441) and in Wiltshire *sigewunne dic* at Fovant (S364) and *byrdinga dic* at Broad Chalke (S582). At Rimpton (So) *Beorhtulfes dic* is a large bank and ditch which divided an otherwise featureless hillside, with the lands of Sandford Orcas in Dorset on one side and Rimpton on the other (Fig. 5.1). It is a considerable feature even today, with a ditch on the Rimpton side and a bank 2/3 metres wide and almost 2 metres tall from the ditch. The positioning of the ditch in Rimpton suggests that this was the outside of the earthwork and that it was intended to keep animals out of Sandford and was therefore Sandford's bank, not Rimpton's. The personal names attached to these features probably commemorate the owners who had them constructed, but unfortunately tell us nothing about the date of such constructions. However, the use of personal names suggests that such features are related to private ownership and exploitation of estates and might be considered later rather than early in construction.

ignores the presence of the dyke. Its name contains the OW element *ceto*, 'a wood' and its existence as a detached portion of Bishops Cannings Hundred, although it is not mentioned in the Domesday Survey, suggests that this was a detached portion of woodland allocated to Bishops Cannings and containing most of the recorded woodland, 1 league long by 10 furlongs wide (Thorn and Thorn 1979, 3, 2). Here it is likely that the Wansdyke/ Roman road simply disappeared into a dense wood on higher ground, where there was no settlement. The establishment of Chittoe as a separately recognised area – not necessarily a settled estate – was probably part of the break-up of a larger estate long after the road had ceased to be used.

Some *dices* were referred to as 'old'; in Wiltshire at South Newton (S 4920), Moredon (S 705), West Knoyle (S 531), Wylye (S 767 and S 868), Purton (S 1586),

Communications

In 1939 the late Dr G. B. Grundy wrote 'in Saxon times and in the centuries immediately succeeding the conquest, the population of the country was tied to the land it cultivated, land on which it was absolutely dependent for its daily bread' (Grundy 1939, 227).

He went on to suggest that as a result very few people travelled. The users of long distance routes, whom he saw as almost entirely peddlers, salt carriers and packmen, must have been few. Even cattle, he thought, would have been rare. Again, 'For through-intercourse, a feature of life which played but a small part in the lives of communities organised on a basis of individual independence, the great ridgeways met all the needs of the wayfaring public' (Grundy 1939, 227).

This view of communications seems more than a little outdated, especially in view of the number of roads of all types which appear in charter boundaries. The road system can be analysed into three groupings. Firstly there were long distance routes which carried communications between major political, religious and trade centres. Such routes would carry merchants with high value goods and currency who were mostly anxious to pass through the countryside. One might also expect to meet high status individuals, perhaps even the king himself, travelling between estates or to centres of political power, ecclesiastics travelling to court or to the bishop's seat or to a monastery. One might perhaps also meet foreign merchants or emissaries from other kings.

Second level communications might be local routes between central places. Such routes would facilitate local political exchanges as well as providing for the redistribution of high value goods and the exchange of surpluses. At the lowest level local routes provided internal communications and linked smaller dependent and tributary estates, facilitating the movement of goods within the central-place territory and allowing the influence of the central place, both as the site of justice and as a religious centre, to be exercised.

By the mid tenth century towns had begun to grow as the new centres for trade and government and they would have taken over and in places diverted communications. Roads are indicators of economic relationships, of course, but they also express the politico-social relationships within and around the political units they serve.

The evidence that Roman roads were still in use in many places is very strong. The term *stræt* is widely distributed and was commonly used to describe a paved or made road, usually Roman in origin. Figure 5.11 reveals the extent of the recognition of such roads in Wiltshire. The Fosse Way was clearly recognised and in use across north-west Wiltshire, as it was in Somerset (see Fig. 5.12). There are hints that other parts of the Roman system around Swindon and Salisbury were also in use. In Somerset, apart from the Fosse Way, there is little sign in charters that the old system survived and in Dorset, apart from the Badbury Rings to Dorchester road at Mapperton (S 490) (Margery 1967, 108) there is little evidence of use (Fig. 5.13). The distribution of estates makes it unsafe to draw any firm conclusions here, but the continued use of the system in Wiltshire and Somerset points to the continued use of Roman roads in Dorset also, as a means of communication between major centres, especially where, in the centuries before the unification of the English, there was communication between the Old English kingdoms. However, it is noticeable that the survival and use of such roads is more limited in the west of the region, so that the Fosse Way marks the westerly edge of the area within which the Roman roads were recognised. This may point to eastern Somerset as the edge of the area which was most heavily populated and within which most trade took place. The Fosse Way is a north-south road, suggesting that it mostly provided communications between eastern Devon, eastern Somerset and the south of Mercia.

Herepað is a much more common element describing an important road. There is really nothing to suggest that such roads were 'military' roads, built for the purposes of war. It seems most likely that these were the roads where you might meet the warband of a king or nobleman, since they also carried traffic over distances. In Dorset the charters for Uppiddle (S 744) and Cheselbourne both mention a *herepað*. This is probably part of a road which started at Winterbourne Whitechurch and ran via Gallows Corner (ST778005), westward along Streetway Lane in Chesilbourne to Piddletrenthide and thence to Cerne and Maiden Newton, heading perhaps towards Crewkerne. Many other long-distance routes must have existed. In Somerset, at Rimpton (S590) the *herepað* forming the westerly boundary of the estate is still the modern B3184. This road ran from Sherborne and was probably heading towards the Fosse Way. Another *herepað* in the same charter probably ran from Ilchester to Milborne Port and thence eastward towards Wilton.

The impact of major centres of trade and authority in the tenth century becomes apparent when we consider the regions around Wilton (Wi) and Bath (So). The plans of the areas show clearly the influence of major centres on the road system. In the case of Wilton it is clear that some routes, such as the road over Barford Down towards Milborne Port, do run directly, the rest of the road pattern is older than Wilton. The ridgeway which carried communications towards Shaftesbury ran towards Britford ('the ford of the Britons') and was probably an ancient road towards *Venta Belgarum*, while other routes clearly headed towards Old Sarum. In the case of Bath, roads ran into the city from all directions by the late tenth century. In both cases, though, it is clear that the road pattern must have long pre-dated the rise of the centres as *burhs* and trading places. The evidence comes from boundaries which it seems rational to suggest post-date the roads. Even if the bounds were all drawn in the tenth century – a most unlikely conjecture – the roads must be older. The same reasoning can be applied to the more general issue of roads and paths as boundaries. In Somerset references to *herepað*, *lanu*, *pað*, *stræt* and *weg* occur 117 times. In Wiltshire the figure is 178 times and in Dorset 64 times. In most cases the bounds follow rather than cross the roads. In Wiltshire there are 53 sets of bounds where roads are followed. In Dorset the figure is 17 and in Somerset 29. In aggregate many kilometres of boundary follow roads and it must be clear that they were normally used as bounds where convenient. This reinforces the point that the bounds which we see in charters are in large part the result of a process which continued long after the roads had been laid down. Furthermore, by the time these charters were being written, or at least when the bounds were added to them, it is obvious that there was a dense network of roads which fulfilled all the criteria mentioned above.

Bridges were probably a measure of the intensity with which roads were used. In Dorset there were five mentioned in charters. In Somerset there were ten. Of these the one at Stanton Prior (S 735) could be described as *þa ealdan stan bricge*, 'the old stone bridge'. The bridge at West Pennard (S 236), described as *stanenebrugge*, stood on the road from the Fosse Way to Glastonbury Abbey. The site today still has a bridge called 'Stonebow'. In Wiltshire there were only four bridges mentioned. Fords, though, are legion, over fifty being named and almost all having names rather than being anonymous 'fords'. Ford in Laverstock (S 543) had a *chypmanna ford*, 'merchants' ford', probably marking the approach to Old Sarum from Winchester.

There are no ready equations between the estates depicted in the charters of the tenth and the eleventh centuries and the estates as they appear in the Domesday Book. That is as it should be, since it demonstrates the dynamic nature of settlement in this period, as well as owing something to forgery and deception. In Wiltshire about half of the charter estates are recognisably the same in the Domesday Book. The hidages agree. For the other half there is no close match. For example, at Little Langford the holding of six hides (S 612) granted in 956 was probably divided into the Wilton holding of three hides (Thorn and Thorn 1979, 13, 13) with three hides lost to another holding, while the Glastonbury estate at Langford (S 1811) of three hides was divided into two units, one of two hides and one of a single hide. The implication of the Domesday entries (Thorn and Thorn 1980, 7, 12–13) is that these were holdings, not separate economic units. However, there was another hide in Langford (Wi) (Thorn and Thorn 1979, 24, 42) which belonged to Edward of Salisbury but was said to belong in fact to Glastonbury. At Bemerton (Wi) the estate of two hides in 968 (S 767) had been given to Wilton, but may have been alienated to become the two hide estate belonging to Aldred in 1086 (Thorn and Thorn 1979, 67, 34). In addition there was a half hide in Bemerton in 1086 and so it seems likely that the estate at Bemerton, as it had been granted in 968, was already a division of an existing economic unit. At Ditchampton (Wi) (S 1010) the two and half hide estate of the charter had become a two hide estate (Thorn and Thorn 1979, 4, 4) and a half hide estate (Thorn and Thorn, 13, 5) which belonged to Wilton. Again it seems likely that the economic unit had stayed intact, while ownership and jurisdiction had been divided. In other cases the existence of two charters for one named place at Burcombe (S 438 and S 631) suggests that an estate had been divided to make two new units, either at the time of the grant to Æþelstan or earlier.

In Somerset, of the fifty estates which can be identified, from the period under consideration, there is a remarkable stability. Where the bounds of the estates can still be traced with some degree of certainty they are nearly all recognisable as units after 1086 and are often modern parishes. Around Bath only the estate at Weston (S 508) shows signs of strain. Here a single estate of five hides had become an estate of ten hides by 1086. The bounds of the estate seem to contain a conflation of two bounds for two contiguous holdings, suggesting that at some time a copyist had combined two genuine sets of bounds to make a new set. There was probably only one settlement by 1086. Elsewhere some charters described lands which contained many communities, as at Taunton, but normally each estate with a charter was still one unit in 1086.

In Dorset only seven of the twenty-five places with charters correspond exactly with the hidages quoted in Domesday Book. Many changes had clearly occurred. For instance at Didlington the first charter, S 519 of AD 946, was for five hides. The second charter, S 609 of AD 956, granted five hides at Didlington and another one hide unit at Uddens. These two quite separate estates were still grouped together in ownership in 1086, when Didlington was assessed for six hides (Thorn and Thorn 1983, 20, 1). Other cases are much more difficult to understand. At Portisham the charter for eight hides (S 961) does not agree with the single Domesday entry of twelve hides. Both land grants and Domesday Book were concerned with land and jurisdiction, not with economic entities or social groupings.

Conclusion

The charter and the bounds capture the settlement at one instant. Ann Goodier has made a very powerful statistical case for the increasing stability of some parts of boundaries over the course of the Middle Saxon period and her evidence is particularly strong for Wiltshire (Goodier 1985). She makes the point that this study can only apply to those parts of boundaries where pagan Anglo-Saxon burials occur. The evidence presented here – the use of many roads as boundaries, the existence of boundary features with personal names attached – points to a period of division and redefinition of boundaries in many areas. This is almost certainly the result of subdivision either at the time of the grant or at some earlier time. However, the overall picture which emerges is one of stability. Bounds represent the boundaries of property and of jurisdiction, not of communities. What is remarkable is how often, not how rarely the two seem to coincide in this region. The lands which have charters preserved were almost wholly those owned by the church and it is probably the growth of church estates in the tenth century which did much to stabilise settlements, at least those with charters. The question which remains is does this hold true for estates which never belonged to the king, or never passed into perpetual ecclesiastical ownership?

Notes

1. The prime source of information is still H. P. R. Finberg, *The Early Charters of Wessex*, Leicester, 1964, but there are many other scholars who have considered the ques-

tion. Many of them will be found cited by P. H. Sawyer, *Anglo-Saxon Charters: An Annotated List and Bibliography*, London, 1968.

2. Almost all the royal estates in Somerset were assessed only as ploughlands in the Domesday Book. The average size measured in this way is 32 ploughlands.

3. Map of West Overton 2203 of 1783 and also E/A61 of 1802, both at Wilts. Record Office.

Abbreviations

S = charters as catalogued in Sawyer 1968.

References

Costen, M. D. 1992: 'Huish and Worth: Old English Survivals in a Later Landscape', *Anglo-Saxon Studies in Archaeology and History*, vol. 5, pp. 65–84., ed. W. Filmer-Sankey, Oxford University Committee for Archaeology, Oxford.

Costen, M. D. 1992b: 'Dunstan, Glastonbury and the Economy of Somerset in the Tenth Century', in N. Ramsey, M. Sparks and T. Tatton-Brown (eds), *St Dunstan, his Life, Times and Cult*. Boydell, Woodbridge.

Costen, M. D. 1991: 'Some evidence for new settlement and field systems in late Anglo-Saxon Somerset, in L. Abrams and J. Carley (eds), *The Archaeology and History of Glastonbury Abbey*, pp. 39–56, Boydell Woodbridge.

Costen, M. D. 1983: 'Stantonbury and District in the Tenth Century', *Bristol and Avon Archaeology, II*, 25–34.

Darby, H. C. 1977: *Domesday England*. CUP, Cambridge.

Finberg, H. P. R. 1964: *The Early Charters of Wessex*, Leicester U P., Leicester.

Goodier, A. 1985: 'The Formation of Boundaries in Anglo-Saxon England: A Statistical Study', *Medieval Archaeology* 20, 1–21.

Gover, J. E. B., Mawer, A. and Stenton, F. M. 1939: *The Place-Names of Wiltshire*, CUP, Cambridge.

Grundy, G. B. 1939: 'The Ancient Highways of Somerset', *The Archaeological Journal*, 96, 226–297.

Holt, R. 1988: *The Mills of Medieval England*, Oxford.

Hooke, D. 1981: 'Open-field Agriculture – The Evidence from the Pre-Conquest Charters of the West Midlands', in T. Rowley (ed.), *The Origins of Open-Field Agriculture*, Croome Helm, London.

Hooke, D. 1981b: *Anglo-Saxon Landscapes of the West Midlands: the Charter Evidence*, BAR British Series 95, Oxford.

Hooke, D. 1988: 'Regional Variation in Southern England', in D. Hooke (ed.), *Anglo-Saxon Settlements*, Basil Blackwell, Oxford.

Hooke, D. 1990: *Worcestershire Anglo-Saxon Charter Bounds*, Boydell, Woodbridge.

Margery I. V. 1967: *Roman Roads in Britain*, 2nd ed., Baker, London.

Morris, R. 1989: *Churches in the Landscape*, Dent, London.

Rackham, O. 1980: *Ancient Woodland: Its History, Vegetation and Uses in England*, Arnold, London.

Rackham, O. 1988: 'Woods, hedges and forests', in M. Aston (ed.), *Aspects of the Medieval Landscape of Somerset*, Aston, Somerset County Council, Taunton.

Sawyer, P. H. 1968: *Anglo-Saxon Charters: An Annotated List and Bibliography*, Royal Historical Society, London.

Smith, A. H. 1970: *English Place-Name Elements*, 2 vols, nos 25 & 26 of The English Place-Name Society, Cambridge

Thorn, C. and Thorn F. (eds) 1979: *Domesday Book: 6 Wiltshire*, Phillimore, Chichester.

Thorn, C. and Thorn F. (eds) 1980: *Domesday Book: 8 Somerset*, Phillimore, Chichester.

Thorn, C. and Thorn F. (eds) 1983: *Domesday Book: 7 Dorset*, Phillimore, Chichester.

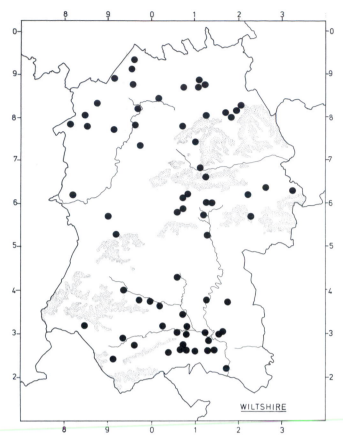

Fig. 5.2 *Places mentioned in charters with bounds in Wiltshire (10th century).*

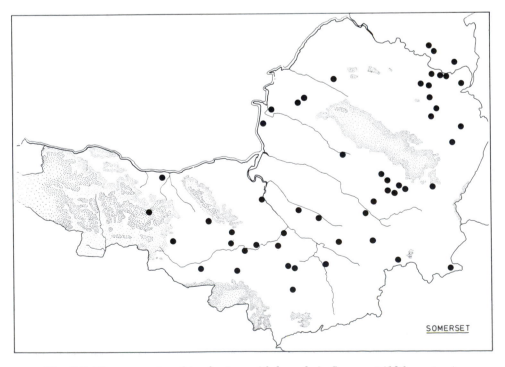

Fig. 5.3 *Places mentioned in charters with bounds in Somerset (10th century).*

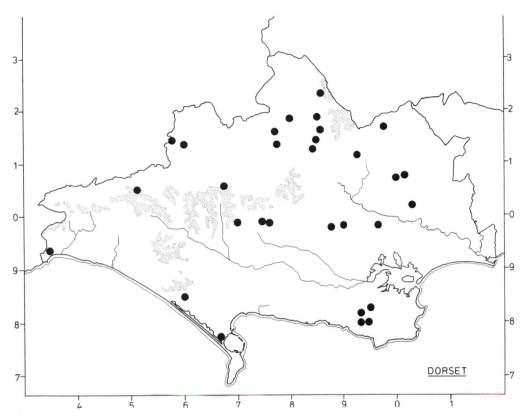

Fig. 5.4 *Places mentioned with bounds in Dorset (10th century).*

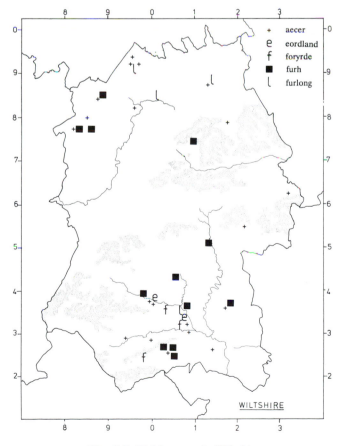

Fig. 5.5 *Field names in Wiltshire.*

Michael Costen

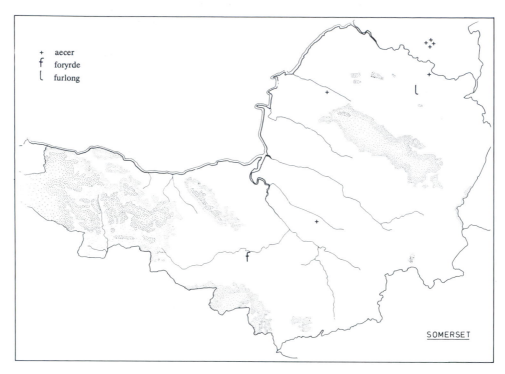

Fig. 5.6 *Field names in Somerset.*

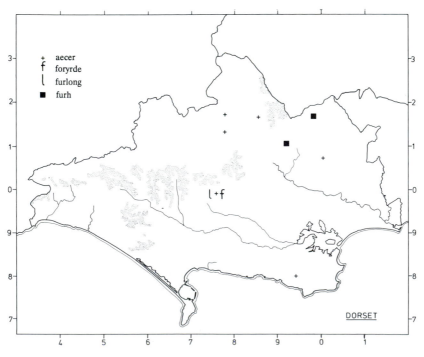

Fig. 5.7 *Field names in Dorset.*

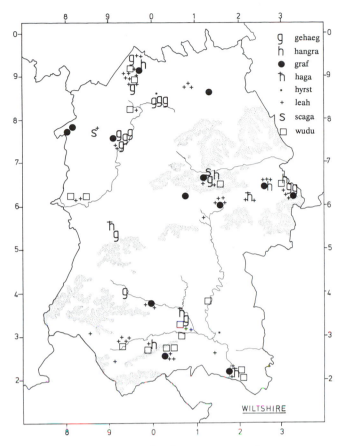

Fig. 5.8 Woodland names in Wiltshire.

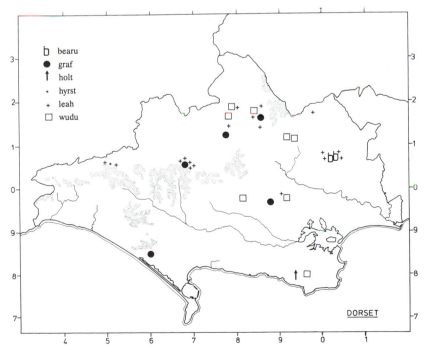

Fig. 5.9 Woodland names in Dorset.

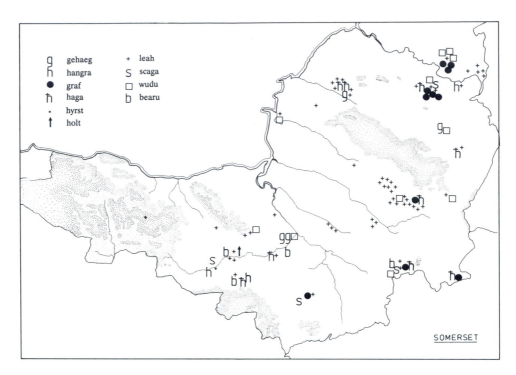

Fig. 5.10 *Woodland names in Somerset.*

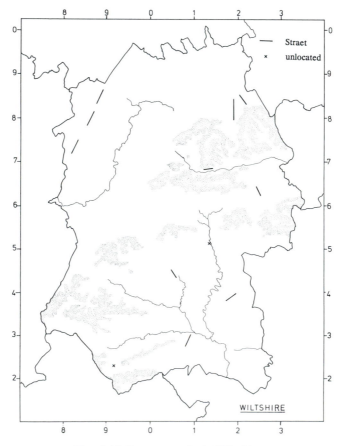

Fig. 5.11 *Roman roads in Wiltshire.*

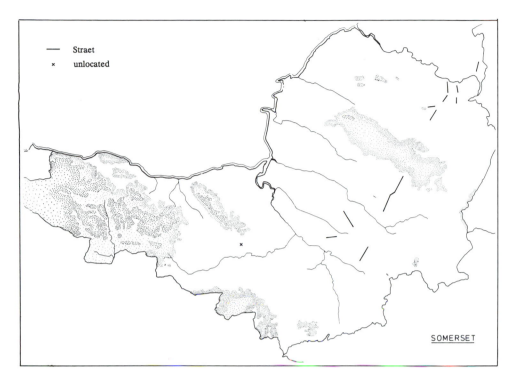

Fig. 5.12 *Roman roads in Somerset.*

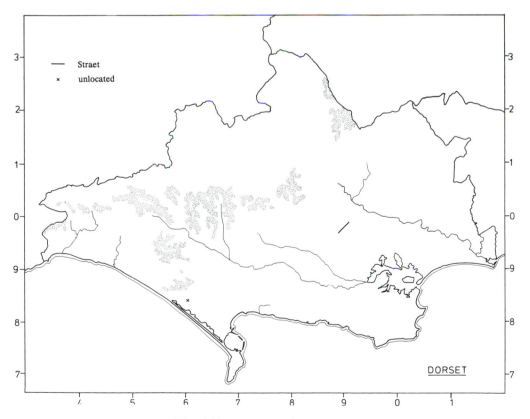

Fig. 5.13 *Roman roads in Dorset.*

6.   Forests, Chases, Warrens and Parks in Medieval Wessex

James Bond

This paper explores the varied environments, origins and purposes of the Royal Forests which covered considerable, but fluctuating areas of the Wessex region during the Middle Ages. As the administrative machinery and the geographical extent of the forests declined, the increasing numbers of private deer parks and warrens came to fulfill some of the same roles. The management of deer, rabbits and other livestock and the exploitation of woodland resources and grazing are considered. The evidence for hunting lodges and other associated buildings is also explored.

Introduction

The title of this paper contains a terminological minefield, and it may be helpful to begin with some definitions. The terms used in this title in modern parlance normally denote areas or features which have some recognisable physical manifestation in the landscape. In the Middle Ages, however, the same words had somewhat different connotations, based more upon concepts of particular legal rights and customs.

The medieval *Forest* was an area circumscribed by defined boundaries and administered by special officials, within which the king reserved for himself the right of hunting certain animals, particularly deer and wild boar; to this end, it was taken out of the rule of common law and placed under the special code of Forest Law (Cox 1905; Young 1979). While most forests had crown estates at their core, they usually included much other land belonging to a multiplicity of holders. There is an extensive literature both on Forest Law (e.g. Manwood 1598) and upon its implications for the inhabitants of the regions affected (e.g. Birrell 1988), and these aspects cannot be explored in detail here. A medieval forest might include extensive woodland within its bounds, as modern usage of the word implies, but it might also include a great deal of open land, pasture, cultivated fields and entire villages and towns. Some medieval forests contained relatively little woodland within their bounds. The precise area of land under Forest Law varied from time to time, reaching its greatest extent under Henry II (1154–89), when it briefly embraced several entire counties, including Berkshire, Devon and Cornwall. From the early thirteenth century the area of royal forest as a whole was progressively reduced in size (Bazeley 1921), and some

individual forests were disafforested. After this period evidence for the extent of many forests is provided by boundary perambulations, which will be discussed further below.

The *Chase* was also an unenclosed but nonetheless firmly delimited hunting preserve; but chases belonged generally not to the king but to great nobles or ecclesiastical magnates, and remained under the remit of common law (Cantor 1982, 70–73). Chases were often former royal forests where the king had granted away his hunting rights to others. Cranborne Chase on the Dorset/Wiltshire border had been granted by William Rufus to Robert Fitzhamon, and long remained in the hands of the Earls of Gloucester, but came back into royal hands in 1470 and remained so until its final disposal by James I to the Earl of Salisbury in 1616 (West 1816; Smart 1841; Poole 1959). Wimbornholt Chase in Dorset, probably the successor to the obscure Forest of Wimborne mentioned in the Domesday survey, was granted by Henry III in 1267 to his second son, Edmund Crouchback, Earl of Leicester (Darby 1967, 103; *C.Ch.R.* ii, 1257–1300, 67–8). Tidenham Chase was part of the Forest of Dean which had come into the hands of the Earl of Pembroke in the early thirteenth century (Cantor 1982, 72). Furches Wood, Kingswood, Keynsham and Filwood Chases, east and south of Bristol, had been taken out of the Forest of Kingswood in the thirteenth century and held in association with the office of Constable of Bristol Castle (Cox and Greswell 1911, 567; Nisbet and Vellacott 1907, 264–5). The Bishop of Winchester held several chases in Hampshire (Roberts 1988, 67), amongst which Waltham, Hambledon and Havant Chases were taken out of the Forest of Bere Portchester, and Highclere Chase out of

Freemantle Forest. In 1284 he also secured by charter rights of chase in all his lands and those of St Swithun's Priory, both within and without the metes of the king's forest, free of interference of the king's forest officials; the only stipulation was that deer should not be taken with nets (*C.Ch.R.* ii, 1257–1300, 274).

The term *Warren* was normally used in the Middle Ages in the legal expression 'rights of free warren'. These were grants by the king permitting local lords to hunt certain small game on their own estates: hare, rabbit, woodcock, partridge and pheasant were hunted for the table; while fox, wildcat, badger, marten, otter and squirrel were hunted as pests, being regarded as harmful to deer, domestic livestock or crops (Cantor 1982, 82). Sometimes, though by no means invariably, the acquisition of rights of free warren appears as a prelude to imparking. One of the modern meanings of the word, a place for raising rabbits for their meat and fur, was covered by various medieval terms such as *coneygarth* and *coneygre*. In one anomalous case in Somerset, the royal warren of Somerton was under Forest Law because there, uniquely, the hare seems to have been treated as a sort of honorary deer (Cox and Greswell 1911, 552–3). Corfe Warren in Dorset was both the nucleus and the remnant of King John's short-lived Forest of Purbeck, and was also noted for its hares (Hutchins 1861–73, iii, 662).

Medieval *Parks* were also very different from the eighteenth-century concept of the manicured landscaped setting of a great house, or the modern idea of lawns, flower beds and gravel paths used for public recreation. In the Middle Ages parks were smaller private game preserves, sometimes created under royal licence, primarily intended for deer, and invariably enclosed by some combination of earthworks, walls, fences or hedges.

Finally, if one wished to be pedantic, the use of the name 'Wessex' in the title is an obvious anachronism, since the Saxon kingdom of that name had ceased to have any separate administrative identity by the time that Forest Law and all its appurtenances had been introduced. Nonetheless, it remains a useful shorthand term for the region, and will here be employed to cover the historic counties of Somerset, Dorset, Wiltshire and Hampshire, together with the adjoining portions of Devon, Gloucestershire and Berkshire.

Location and Environment of the Royal Forests

As indicated above, the number and extent of royal forests varied through the Middle Ages (Fig. 6.1, 6.2, 6.3). Some forests were known by alternative names at different dates, or even at the same time: Mendip Forest, for example, was sometimes referred to as Cheddar Forest from the royal manor at its heart, while Pewsham Forest was also known as Chippenham Forest. The Forest of Whiteingleigh appears to have been an alternative name for part of Freemantle Forest (Colebourn 1983, 21). Some of the larger ancient forests were subsequently divided

into separate forest administrations: for example, parts of Clarendon Forest were divided off in the early thirteenth century to become the separate forests of Buckholt, Melchet and Panshet. Occasionally individual wards or bailwicks, properly administrative subdivisions within a forest, were treated in written sources as separate forests: by the early thirteenth century documents sometimes name the Forest of Alveston and the Forest of Horwood in south Gloucestershire, but these were essentially no more than wooded remnants of the more extensive Forest of Kingswood (Moore 1982, 13). Similarly the Hampshire portion of Chute Forest was divided into the Forests of Digerley and Finkley, while the Hampshire portion of Windsor Forest was divided into the Forests or Bailwicks of Bagshot and Eversley (Bazeley 1921, 161). The Forest of Odiham, frequently named in early thirteenth-century records, appears to have been an alternative name for the Bagshot ward of Windsor Forest in Hampshire. It can, therefore, prove unexpectedly difficult even to determine so basic a question as how many forests the Wessex region contained.

The forests of the west country spanned a wide range of physical environments, but in general avoided prime agricultural land. Some occupied upland areas, particularly in the west of the region. The highest parts of *Exmoor Forest*, on the old red sandstone plateau of west Somerset and north Devon, rise to over 500m above sea level. Much of this forest was bleak open moorland, penetrated towards its margins by narrow wooded valleys. Much of the original extent of *Mendip Forest* in north Somerset was on the high carboniferous limestone plateau, between 230m and 290m above sea level. Here too the land was mostly open pasture. However, woodlands still clung to the steep southern slopes of the hills, and these formed the heart of the forest, the last area to be relinquished by the crown. *Selwood Forest* (Fig. 6.4), on the Somerset/Wiltshire border, spanned the watershed between the streams draining westwards to the Bristol Channel and southwards to the English Channel; the Wiltshire portion rose on the greensand escarpment to nearly 250m, though on the Somerset side it extended onto the lower land of the Oxford clay

Further east in Wiltshire, where the relief is less extreme, some of the forests still occupied relatively high land, but other portions spread over the clay lowlands. *Pewsham Forest* extended over the corallian and greensand hills east of Chippenham, rising to 180m above Bowden Park, but its northwestern portion, along with the neighbouring *Melksham Forest*, lay on the flat land of the Oxford clay vale. The *Forest of Braden* occupied the Oxford clay vale between Malmesbury and Cricklade, but also included part of the corallian escarpment; while achieving no great altitude (mainly between 200m and 380m), it straddled the watershed between the Thames and Avon.

Several other Wiltshire forests occupied parts of the chalk escarpments at heights of between 90m and 260m,

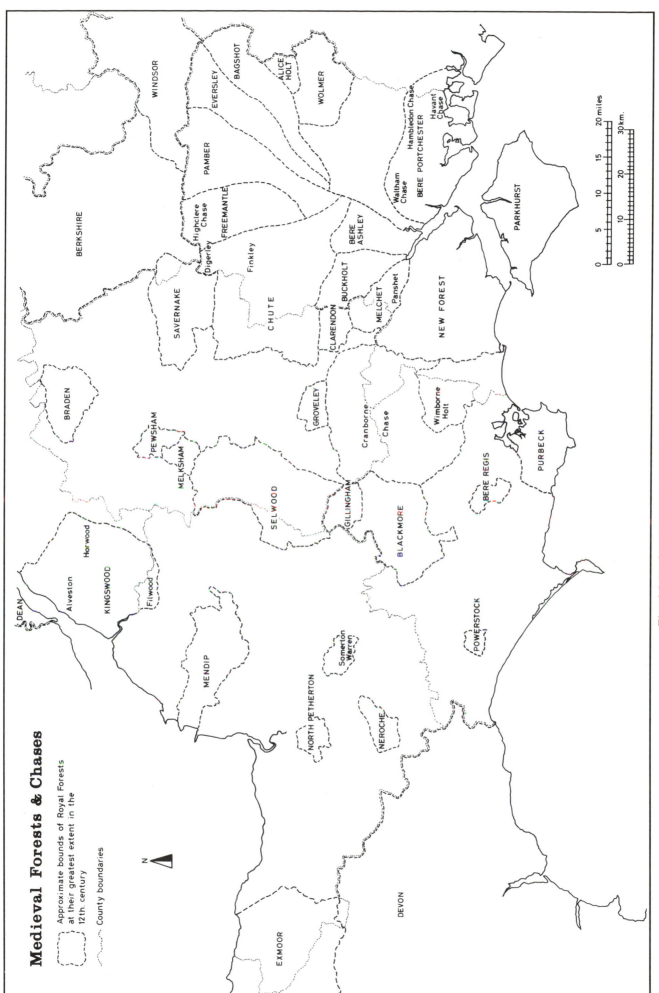

Medieval Forests & Chases

▢ Approximate bounds of Royal Forests
 at their greatest extent in the
 12th. century

⋯ County boundaries

N

Fig. 6.1 Medieval Forests and Chases.

20 miles

15

10

5

0

30 km.

20

10

0

DEAN

Alveston

Harwood

KINGSWOOD

Filwood

WINDSOR

EVERSLEY

BAGSHOT

ALICE
HOLT

WOLMER

PAMBER

Hambledon Chase

Havant
Chase

BERKSHIRE

Highclere
Chase

FREEMANTLE

Digerley

Finkley

Waltham
Chase

BERE PORTCHESTER

PARKHURST

SAVERNAKE

CHUTE

BERE
ASHLEY

BUCKHOLT

CLARENDON

MELCHET

Panshet

NEW FOREST

BRADEN

PEWSHAM

MELKSHAM

GROVELEY

Cranborne
Chase

Wimborne
Holt

SELWOOD

GILLINGHAM

BLACKMORE

BERE REGIS

PURBECK

MENDIP

NORTH PETHERTON

Somerton
Warren

POWERSTOCK

NEROCHE

EXMOOR

DEVON

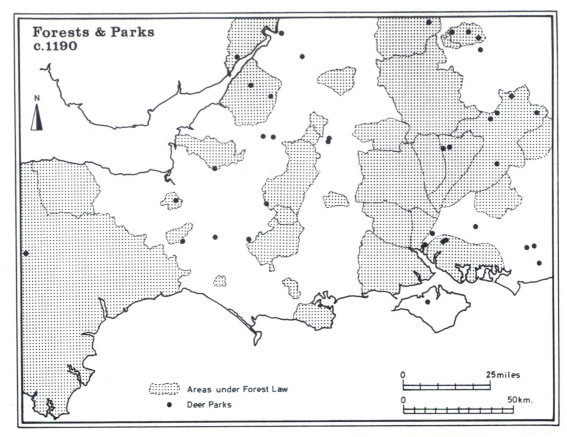

Fig. 6.2 *Forests and Parks, c. 1190.*

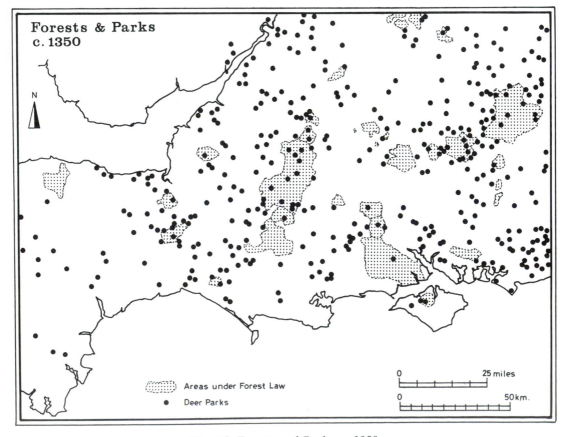

Fig. 6.3 *Forests and Parks, c. 1350.*

Fig. 6.4 *Selwood Forest, view south from Alfred's Tower, Brewham, Somerset. (Photo: James Bond)*

especially where the chalk is mantled with a covering of clay-with-flints. These comprised *Groveley* near Salisbury, and the continuous string of forests straddling the eastern border of the county, including *Savernake*, overlapping into Berkshire; *Chute*, extending from Collingbourne and Ludgershall westwards to the Avon and eastwards into Hampshire; and parts of *Clarendon*, the most important, though not the most extensive of the Wiltshire forests, which included the royal park and palace of the same name. *Melchet Forest* covered the south-eastern corner of Wiltshire around Whiteparish, extending into Hampshire. *Cranborne Chase* spanned the chalk downs on the borders of Wiltshire, Dorset and Hampshire.

Hampshire was by far the most extensively afforested of all the counties, not only in Wessex but also in England as a whole. It included the *New Forest*, arguably the most important of all the royal forests in the region, occupying some 40,000 hectares in the south-west corner of the county. Although this was for the most part relatively low-lying, it lay over an area of infertile Eocene and Oligocene sand, gravel and clay soils which had limited agricultural potential. Apart from the New Forest there were at least ten other forests. *Melchet* extended from across the Wiltshire border into the Blackwater valley, almost to the head of Southampton Water. *Buckholt*, that part of Clarendon Forest included within Hampshire, extended from the Wiltshire border eastwards

to the River Test, including some chalk downland but also overlapping onto the Eocene sands and clays of the Hampshire Basin. The Hampshire portion of *Chute Forest*, sometimes treated as the two separate forests of *Finkley* and *Digerley*, covered much of the chalk downland in the north-western part of the county. South of Chute and east of Melchet the Forest of *Bere Ashley* extended between the Rivers Test and Itchen. The downs east of Chute in north Hampshire were covered by the Forest of *Freemantle* and by *Pamber Forest*, the core of which lay further north on the infertile Eocene sands and clays of the London Basin. East of Pamber, also extending from the chalk downs into the London Basin, were the *Bagshot* and *Eversley* bailwicks of the Berkshire Forest of Windsor, sometimes regarded as separate forests. The small east Hampshire forests, *Alice Holt* and *Woolmer*, separated by a narrow strip of non-forest land but often in practice administered as a single forest, were nonetheless of markedly different character, the former lying mainly on the heavy gault clay, the latter on the infertile greensands of the Wealden Basin. The last of the mainland Hampshire forests, *Bere Portchester*, covered the Eocene sands and clays north of Portsdown (Carter 1968).

The infertile Eocene sands and clays, often remaining as low-lying heaths and bogs even today, also underlie the *Forest of Bere Regis* in Dorset, on either side of the

Piddle valley below Bere Regis. The apparent duplication of name between the Hampshire and Dorset Forests of Bere is accidental, since the earliest recorded forms suggest that the Hampshire name derives from the Old English *baer*, meaning 'swine pasture' and the Dorset example from Old English *bearu*, meaning 'grove' (Ekwall 1960, 38), but it generates much confusion in the documentation. The short-lived *Forest of Purbeck*, or *Corfe*, afforested by King John but largely disafforested after 1217, also included extensive heaths and bogs on the Eocene beds south of Poole Harbour. *Parkhurst*, on the Isle of Wight, seems occasionally to have been regarded as royal forest (e.g. *C.P.R.* 1330–34, 355); it lay on the Oligocene clays in the north of the island.

Other predominantly lowland forests included in south Somerset the *Forest of Neroche*, between Taunton and Ilminster, which extended up to the crest of the Blackdown Hills on its south-western margin, but mostly covered lower, flatter country in the Isle basin, down to 9.5m above sea level (Sixsmith 1958); and the *Forest of North Petherton*, centred on Newton Park in the Keuper Marl lowland of the Parrett valley south of Bridgwater, though possibly a vestige of a once larger upland hunting-ground covering the Quantock Hills. In Dorset *Gillingham Forest* occupied the greensand-rimmed bowl of Kimmeridge clay south-east of the town of Gillingham and abutted the Forest of Selwood, of which it once formed part; and the contiguous *Forest of Blackmore* covered the Oxford clay lowland of Blackmore Vale to the south-west. The remaining Dorset forest, *Poorstock* or *Powerstock*, occupied a more limited area on the liassic and oolitic hills between Beaminster and Bridport.

Important forests on the margin of the region, which can receive only scant treatment in this paper, include the upland *Dartmoor Forest* in south Devon; the still extensive and heavily-wooded *Forest of Dean* in west Gloucestershire; *Kingswood* in south Gloucestershire, occupying the southern part of the Vale of Berkeley between the Bristol Avon and the Little Avon, with its eastern boundary following the crest of the Cotswold escarpment (Braine 1891; Moore 1982); and *Windsor Forest* in east Berkshire.

Although a basic distinction between 'upland' and 'lowland' forests is implied in the above summary, in fact any such view is simplistic: in reality most forests straddled the geological grain of the country and often included a considerable variety of natural topography. The extent to which the medieval forests included woodland cover also varied greatly. The highest upland forests in the west of the region had largely been open moorland and pasture since the Bronze Age or Iron Age; such woodland as survived within their bounds was confined to the deep valleys and coastal slopes of Exmoor and the gorges and steep southern face of Mendip, as is the case today. Botanical and documentary studies have underlined the antiquity of the surviving woodland in a few of these locations: Cheddar Wood in Mendip, which

has a documentary history going back to the tenth century, also contains typical ancient woodland indicator species such as small-leaved lime (*Tilia cordata*) and wild service (*Sorbus torminalis*), and an uncommon ground flora including autumn crocus, tutsan and blue gromwell (Rackham 1988a, 30). The chalkland forests of Wiltshire and Hampshire consisted originally only of scattered woods within great expanses of downland which had been cleared since the Neolithic period, but here too some significant portions survive: Harewood Forest, a mixed oak wood with birch, hazel and ash on clay-with-flints, is today one of the most extensive ancient woodlands surviving in Hampshire, a relic of the Forest of Chute, while Parnholt Wood and Butter Wood are respectively remnants of the Forests of Bere Ashley and Odiham (Colebourn 1983, 20–21, 43). By contrast, other interior forests, especially Selwood, Neroche, Groveley, Clarendon and Melchet, were much more heavily wooded, and in some cases have remained so to the present day.

The woodland of the medieval forests, in so far as it can be reconstructed from documentary records and surviving vestiges, clearly varied considerably in character. Some of the ancient oak/hornbeam/hazel woods in the Oxford clay vale north-west of Swindon represent relics of the medieval woods in the Forest of Braden. Alice Holt included good clay loam soils which supported oak woods, while neighbouring Woolmer Forest was mainly sandy heath, its primary woodland removed in the Bronze Age. Cranborne Chase was noted for its hazel woods, and a map of 1618 (reproduced in Smart 1983 ed.) shows these managed as compartmented coppices. In a few localities beechwoods predominated: Groveley Forest was noted for its beeches in the seventeenth century, and Ebsbury Beeches, with its maple and hazel underwood, represents a surviving fragment of its early beechwood; Buckholt Forest also appears from the documentary record to have been mainly a beechwood, and beeches were also widespread in Clarendon, Alice Holt and Woolmer.

However, of all the forests of the region, it is the New Forest, with its extensive commons, open woodland and old coppice enclosures, which best preserves many of the features of its medieval landscape (Sumner 1925; Tubbs 1986). Many aspects of its history, ecology and management have been the subject of detailed studies (e.g. Barber 1973; Cadman and Manners 1964; Edwards 1985; Edwards and Hollis 1982; Flower 1980; Lascelles 1895; Manners 1988; Manners and Edwards 1986; Spellerberg 1986; Stagg 1989; Sumner 1929; Tubbs 1964, 1968, Tubbs and Dimbleby 1965; Tubbs and Jones 1964). The varied geology and soils provide a range of habitats. The sands and gravels were largely cleared of their primeval woodland in the Bronze Age, and since have supported only heathland with birch and gorse; the heavy clays remain bogland with sedge, cotton grass and alder thickets; only the clay loams support woodland, dominated by oak, beech, yew, holly and thorn, and some of this may represent a continuity of woodland cover which has remained unbroken from the primeval forest (Tubbs 1968). Some unenclosed woods in the New Forest overlie undisturbed acid forest brown earths, indicating that they have never been cleared and farmed (Colebourn 1983, 24). Despite the limitation on the number of species brought about by grazing, many of the old oakwoods retain a distinctive ground flora indicative of ancient woodland, including bluebell, violet, wood anemone, wood spurge, wood sorrel and butcher's broom (Flower 1980). Ancient pollard trees rich in lichen species are widely distributed, and Rose and James (1974) have described it as the nearest approximation to primeval forest suriving anywhere in western Europe, with more than 130 lichen species per square kilometre, including a high proportion of the sensitive ancient woodland indicators.

Despite its antiquity, however, the New Forest has undergone many changes over the centuries. New species have been introduced, while others have declined. Sweet chestnut, probably introduced during the Roman period, formed one entire wood in the forest by the middle of the fourteenth century (Cox 1905, 330). Small-leaved lime, a significant constituent of the primeval forest, survived into the Saxon period to give its name to the forest hamlets of Lyndhurst and Linwood; but lime and elm were both drastically reduced in extent by the early Middle Ages as a result of grazing pressures in the open forest. Hazel, a major constituent of the coppice woods until the seventeenth century, in its turn has been almost eliminated by grazing as coppice management declined. Holly, certainly present before the seventeenth century, has correspondingly increased. Beech has also increased at the expense of oak since the fifteenth century (Rackham 1980, 345–7; Colebourn 1983, 23–5). Despite this long history of management and modification, many features of the medieval forest landscape remain.

What factors determined the location of the royal forests? While it is broadly the case that the medieval forests occupied uplands or areas of heavy clay or infertile sandy soils, country which had not been a prime target of intensive cultivation, they cannot all be regarded as occupying marginal land. Many of them did, indeed, include extensive areas of cultivation, and today it is difficult to see any particular physical disadvantages within the areas of North Petherton Forest, Braden Forest, or Powerstock Forest, which made them significantly more suitable for such a designation than neighbouring unafforested manors. Conversely there were extensive ancient woodlands, heaths or uncultivated upland areas on the Blackdown Hills, the Brendon Hills, Salisbury Plain, the north side of Poole Harbour and elsewhere which were never chosen to become forests. Clearly no simple deterministic explanation can be used to account for their location.

Can historical factors provide any rationale? The continuing role of Winchester as an important seat of Norman government may account for the excessive number of forests in Hampshire (Colebourn 1983, 20). The presence of a royal estate which could serve as a nucleus was clearly a significant factor in some cases: Melksham, which gave its name to one forest; Wootton Rivers and Bedwyn in Savernake Forest; Collingbourne and Amesbury in the Forest of Chute; Westbury, Warminster and East Knoyle in Selwood Forest; Lydiard Millicent in Braden Forest; while Pewsham Forest lay between the royal manors of Chippenham and Calne and included the royal manor of Bromham (Grant 1959, 392). If the estate included an important royal residence, the importance of the forest was correspondingly enhanced. The long association of Clarendon Forest with Clarendon Park and Palace underlines the potential importance of such a relationship, and there can be little doubt here that the development of the palace and the frequent use of the park and forest went hand in hand. The royal lodge at Gillingham similarly provided a base for hunting in the Forests of Gillingham and Selwood. There were no important royal palaces or houses anywhere in the west country which were not located either inside the bounds of, or within easy reach of, a royal forest; even at the royal manor of Somerton, located in densely-populated agricultural countryside, the special status of the hare, protected by Forest Law in its warren, could be interpreted as compensation for the lack of suitable waste or woodland available for designation as forest. Indeed, to some extent the two elements, forest and palace, were interdependent, and the abandonment of the one can be seen to result in the decline of the other. Mendip Forest clearly had a significant role within the hinterland of the royal palace of Cheddar, which was intermittently used by the crown up to the early thirteenth century. When King John sold the manor to the Bishop of Bath and Wells he retained the forest rights, but there is little evidence that these rights were intensively exploited by his successors, and the maintenance of Mendip as a royal forest had in effect been abandoned by 1338. Yet some royal forests, such as Exmoor and Braden, never contained any royal residences, while others, such as Neroche, hardly contained any royal demesne land at all. These were rarely used directly by the king, and their main value to the crown must have come from the perquisites of forest administration and fines from poaching and vert offences.

Origins of Royal Forests

Some of the royal forests were clearly extensively wooded areas in which the crown had important interests well before their formal designation in the Norman period. Many royal estates of the Anglo-Saxon period included extensive demesne woods which provided opportunities for hunting. One of the earliest references occurs in a charter nominally dating from the 680s, though known only from a sixteenth-century transcript, by which King Centwine of Wessex granted to Glastonbury Abbey land at West Monkton and Creech St Michael which was said to lie next to the famous wood which is called *Cantucuudu* (Sawyer 1968, no. 237; Edwards 1988, 17). Despite the late date of the surviving text, there is every indication that this was copied from a genuinely early original, and it clearly indicates woodland on the Quantock Hills. Although there is nothing in later sources to show directly that Quantock was ever regarded as a royal forest, the otherwise anomalous small forest of North Petherton would make sense as a remnant of a much greater tract of wilder countryside.

Asser records that Selwood was known as *Coit Mawr*, Great Wood, by the Welsh in the ninth century (*Life K.Alf.*, 45). Selwood is mentioned as a boundary by the Anglo-Saxon Chronicle in 709, 878 and 893 (*E.H.D.*, i, 158, 180, 187), and the vill of Pendomer in Selwood was held before the Norman Conquest by one Alward, whom the Exon Domesday qualifies as the Hunter (*D.B. Som.*, 19.51). A still more specific reference occurs in the anonymous *Life of St Dunstan*, written around 1000, which records the miraculous escape of King Edmund while riding out from Cheddar Palace on a hunting expedition. The hart which he was chasing plunged to its death over the precipice of Cheddar Gorge, followed by the king's hounds, and he was only able to save himself on the very brink of the cliff by repenting his decision to exile Dunstan from the royal court (*Mem. St.D.*, 23–5, 91, 181, 269–70).

Aelfric's *Colloquy*, compiled around 1000 to teach Latin to the oblates of Cerne Abbey in Dorset by means of a series of contrived dialogues with men of familiar occupations, describes how the king's huntsmen caught harts, boars, roe deer and hare using hounds, nets and spears (*Colloq.*, 23–5).

Further pre-Conquest references occur in the Domesday folios from Somerset and Wiltshire. Three foresters (*forestarii*) are recorded as having held Withypool on Exmoor in the time of Edward the Confessor (*D.B. Som.*, 46.3), though quite what this term implies at this date is not clear. Two of Edward the Confessor's huntsmen held land in the royal manor of Chippenham and in other vills in what became Clarendon and Savernake Forests.

While there is ample evidence for Anglo-Saxon kings indulging in hunting, the concept of Forest Law and the administrative machinery of the forest courts were Norman introductions. Unfortunately the Domesday Survey rarely provides much detail on royal forests, and many are not mentioned at all, since they were not subject to geld and may not even have been under the sheriff's jurisdiction. However, the New Forest forms the subject of a special section in the Hampshire folios (Baring 1910, 1912; Finn 1962, 324–338). Here it is recorded that some forty-six holdings in thirty-two named and five unnamed settlements had been placed entirely under Forest Law. All but two of the names which can be identified lie within the later forest bounds. A further fifty-six holdings in about forty-five settlements were described as having a portion in the forest, and these lie mainly be-

yond the western and eastern fringes of the forest bounds as fixed in 1300 (map in Darby 1977, 200). The impact of the designation of the New Forest upon the local settlement pattern has been much debated. In some cases the record is explicit: at Eling the dwellings of sixteen villeins and three bordars were expropriated in the forest, and at Hordle 'the king holds the woodland in the forest, where six men used to live'. Twelfth-century chroniclers such as Henry of Huntingdon and Florence of Worcester claimed that King William had devastated a flourishing district by the eviction of many of its inhabitants and the removal of villages and churches. The infertile soils of the area and the general lack of solid supporting evidence have led Baring (1901) and others to reject this view, and to suggest that the central area of the forest was probably always sparsely inhabited. Yet, of the names of places listed as located wholly within the forest, fifteen remain unidentified and several others are now no more than single farms. Even if there was little forced depopulation, the creation of the forest probably had some stultifying effect upon the local economy. Clues to this appear elsewhere in the record: the wood of Durley once rendered six swine, but did so no longer, while the value of an estate at Chilworth had fallen from £10 before 1066 to £4 in 1086 because its holder was not permitted to use its woodland. Similarly the values of Holdenhurst had fallen from £44 to £24, Ringwood from £24 to £8.10s, and Christchurch from £19 to £10. Yet the problems of drawing firm conclusions from the survey are underlined by the fact that Brockenhurst, right in the centre of the New Forest, actually doubled in value (Finn 1962, 324–38).

Elsewhere within the Wessex region only the Forest of Groveley in Wiltshire, where the king's foresters held one and a half hides, and the Forest of Wimborne in Dorset, where the king held 'two best of the seven hides' belonging to the Abbot of Horton at Horton, are specifically named as forests (*foresta*). The Forest of Dean and Windsor Forest, on the margins of the region, are also named. Chute is named as a wood (*silva*), one third of which lay in the king's manor of Collingbourne. Melchet is also named as a wood, within which two of Wilton Abbey's manors, South Newton and Washern, had rights to timber and pasture (curiously these two places are some 11–16km distant from Melchet but lie on the very margins of Groveley Forest).

The existence of some of the other forests can be inferred from incidental references. On the Bishop of Winchester's manor of Downton, the king held four hides in his forest (the Geld Rolls later record here 'two hides from which the inhabitants have fled because of the king's forest'), while one quarter of the Wilton Abbey estate at Laverstock is described as being situated within the king's forest. Similar descriptions are applied to half of two separate estates in Milford. Laverstock and Milford were both on the western fringe of Clarendon Forest; Downton was only a few kilometres distant, but closer to Melchet and the New Forest. At Britford, also on the edge of Clarendon Forest, the woodland was said to be in the king's hands. An oblique reference to the Forest of Woolmer or to Alice Holt may be contained in the entry for the Hampshire vill of Oakhanger, where the holder needed the sheriff's permission to have pasture or pannage within the king's wood. A curious entry for Botley in Hampshire, '*silva deest*', may imply that the woodland had been taken out of the manor and placed within the bounds of the Forest of Bere. Some of the royal huntsmen appear as tenants-in-chief or as under-tenants: the fief of Waleran the Huntsman in Dorset, Hampshire and Wiltshire consisted of nearly a hundred hides (Darlington 1955, 103). At Nether Wallop, Over Wallop and Broughton, all in the Forest of Buckholt, whereas the reeve formerly had income from honey, pasture, and timber for building, this income had been transferred to the foresters.

Most of the areas later identifiable as royal forests stand out in the Domesday Survey as areas of relatively low population density with few ploughteams. Some of them included extensive manorial woodlands. The physical existence of Selwood is revealed in the large areas of woodland attached to the manors of Frome and Bruton and in the large numbers of swineherds in Westbury (29) and Warminster (13). The woodlands of 4 x 4 leagues attached to the manors of Chippenham and Melksham no doubt formed the nuclei of the two forests so-named in later records. However, the source is full of pitfalls, and it is dangerous to jump to conclusions without due caution. It would be easy to assume that the exceptionally large 6 x 4 league wood belonging to the Wiltshire manor of Amesbury lay in the nearby forests of Clarendon, Chute or Melchet; but Amesbury at various times held several more distant woodland appurtenances, including Bentley Wood in West Dean, 13km away on the Hampshire border, Lyndhurst in the New Forest, 37km distant, and Hurst by Wokingham, 70km away in east Berkshire (Pugh 1947–8).

For some forests like Savernake and Chute there is no documentation before the twelfth century. Pamber Forest is first recorded in 1164–5 (*Pipe R.*, 11 Hen.II, 41; Stamper 1983, 42), Exmoor Forest in 1204 (MacDermot 1911). In Hampshire Bere Ashley, Bere Portchester, Alice Holt, Freemantle and Eversley all go unrecorded before the early thirteenth century (Colebourn 1983). Nonetheless, although the evidence is often indirect, it seems likely that most of the forests which were to have any lasting significance through the Middle Ages had been defined within the first couple of decades after the Norman Conquest. There is no evidence that Henry I extended the area under Forest Law in the south-west as he appears to have done in parts of the north of England (Young 1979, 11–12; Cantor 1982, 61). Unfortunately the forest records under the early Angevin kings are poor, but it is evident from later sources that Henry II reorganised the forest administration and enlarged the forests to

their maximum extent over vast tracts of private land beyond the royal demesnes, including the entire counties of Devon and Cornwall. This met with considerable opposition, and some disafforestation occurred under Richard I and John, including the lifting of Forest Law from these two counties in 1204 (Young 1979, 19, 21). The Forest Charter of 1217 ordered the disafforestation of all remaining forests created by Henry II and his successors, except for royal demesne woods (Young 1979, 53), and from this time onwards the extent of the royal forests can be documented more fully through boundary perambulations (see further below).

Administration of the Royal Forests

The system by which the forests were administered has been described at length by a number of authors (e.g. Cox 1905; Young 1979; Grant 1991), and can only be summarised here, with a brief definition of terms in order to make intelligible what follows. Various courts dealt with forest pleas. The highest courts were the *Forest Eyres*, circuit courts intended to take place every seven years (though the intervals between them were in practice often much longer), to which all landowners, free tenants and others with interests in the forest were summoned, along with forest officials and representatives of all townships within the forest bounds. These were concerned mainly with pleas of vert (damage and theft of timber and underwood) and venison (poaching of beasts of the forest). A list of Forest Eyres for Wiltshire has been compiled by Grant (1959, Appx. A, 433–4), and some have been extensively summarised (e.g. the Dorset Eyres of 1257 and 1270, described in Cox 1908, 289–90), or published in full (e.g. *Wilts Eyre*, 1249; *For. Pleas Som.*). A trienniel inspection of the forest, the *Regard*, was intended to monitor encroachments such as illegal assarts and purprestures; in practice the regard tended to be made shortly before each Forest Eyre. The Forest Charter of 1217 established the *Swainmotes* or *Swanimotes*, assemblies meeting three times a year to commit offenders for trial at the Forest Eyre and to transact local affairs within the forest, such as arranging for the agistment of pigs in the autumn to forage on the acorns and beechmast and to collect the pannage dues arising. Minor vert offences were sometimes also dealt with at the swanimote. The same term was also applied to the local courts which were supposed to meet in each ward or bailiwick of the forest every forty-two days. Swanimote records have been published for Exmoor (*Exm. Sw.*) and for the New Forest (*New For. Doc.*, ii, nos. 1–55, 56–88, 211–232, 233–246).

The terms applied to the hierarchy of forest officials varied from forest to forest and from period to period, and are discussed more fully by Cox (1905). There were two Justices of the Forest, covering all forests north and south of the Trent. The principal local official in charge of each forest might bear the title of *warden*, *keeper*, *steward*, *bailiff* or *master forester*. This was often an hereditary position: the Esturmy family held the wardenship of Savernake Forest from 1083 to 1427, and were succeeded from 1427 to 1675 by the Seymours (Cardigan 1949), while the Crokes, hereditary wardens of Chute in the twelfth century, were almost certainly descendants of Croc the Huntsman, who held land there in 1086 (Grant 1959, 393). A full list of the wardens of the Wiltshire forests is provided by Grant (1959, Appx. B, 434–442). The office was often linked with the keepership of a royal castle: the wardens of the Forest of Dean also tended to be constables of St Briavels Castle. In some cases it was also associated with the possession of some symbolic hunting artefact, the Savernake Horn being the principal survivor from the Wessex region (Camber and Cherry 1977; Cherry 1989). The *foresters in fee* held lands directly under the warden by serjeanty of keeping particular wards or bailiwicks in the forests: in the thirteenth and fourteenth centuries, for example, there were six such officers in Clarendon Forest and four in Savernake (Grant 1959, 398). Each forest normally had up to half a dozen *verderers*, normally life appointments elected by the local freeholders in the county court, who had to attend the swanimote courts and were responsible directly to the king for the care of the deer covert. The daily work of the forests was carried out by subordinate *foresters*, who were responsible for the preservation of vert and venison within their own bailiwicks. In addition there might be *woodwards* responsible for timber and fuel and for overseeing private woods within the forest and ensuring that their exploitation did not conflict with the king's interests; *agisters*, responsible for controlling the grazing of cattle and pigs; *regarders*, responsible for monitoring the condition of the forest through the regular survey; and *rangers*, charged with the enforcement of the Forest Law.

Early chroniclers such as William of Malmesbury and Eadmer of Canterbury stress the harshness of punishments for offences against Forest Law under the Norman kings, including execution and trial by ordeal. However, by the later twelfth century, as the extent of forest land increased, the Forest Eyres clearly became more geared to producing revenue from fines than to imposing brutal punishments (Grant 1991, 13–14, 17). Despite the Crown's reluctance to relinquish land from the forest, there is little evidence of any concerted efforts to impose the full rigour of the Forest Law beyond those areas traditionally regarded as forest in the early thirteenth century. By the fifteenth century the provincial forests were increasingly neglected as royal hunting preserves. As the forest courts waned in frequency, they did little to protect the traditional resources of the forest, and assarts, purprestures and unrestricted common grazing increased. It is evident by this time that some forests had degenerated to little more than a legal fiction with a bureaucracy of officers; but even if the king had no local residence and never came to hunt there himself, they remained of value as a source of income, and this was the main reason for the Crown's great reluctance to abandon them.

Forest Boundary Perambulations

For the most part the extent of the royal forests at their maximum in the twelfth century can only be estimated retrospectively from the lists of places excluded from Forest Law in subsequent surveys. With a few exceptions there are no detailed topographical records of forest boundaries before the thirteenth century. From that period onwards, however, the pressure upon the forests and the series of rearguard actions taken by the crown to preserve and protect its rights produced a series of perambulations providing precise details of their bounds. It is important to realise that such perambulations do no more than to define those areas which the king wished to see subject to Forest Law or, on occasions, to delimit those areas which he was pressurised into accepting by local juries (Stamper 1983, 44). Other forest records sometimes paint a rather different picture of the precise areas regarded by contemporaries as being within the forest. Only for Wiltshire have the bounds of all the forests been subjected to fairly comprehensive study and accurate mapping (Grant 1959); however, individual perambulations have been transcribed, translated and in some cases mapped by many writers since the eighteenth century (see Appendix 6.1).

Twelfth-century forest bounds are occasionally recited in later documents, but such sources do not present an unbiased view and it is difficult to know how much faith to place in them. The first major series of new perambulations were ordered by Henry III's Council of Regency in the wake of William Marshall's Forest Charter of 1217 (*C.P.R.* 1216–25, 162, 190–1). These put extensive districts outside the forest though the process was quickly reversed. In 1224 Henry III needed money to finance Richard of Cornwall's campaign to recover lands lost to the French in Gascony and Poitou: in exchange for aid, the Forest Charter was reissued and a fresh series of perambulations ordered in fifteen counties, including Hampshire, Wiltshire, Somerset and Dorset (*C.P.R.* 1216–25, 567–70; *Rot.Litt.Claus* 1224–7, 70a, 72b). In effect the bounds described by the local juries represented a renewed demand for the disafforestation of all lands afforested by Henry I, Henry II and Richard I, and the abolition of forest jurisdiction outside the royal demesnes. When Henry III assumed his majority in 1227 he revoked such disafforestations as had been made, partly on the grounds that some of his own demesne woods such as Boreham Wood in Savernake had been put out of the Forest, and attempted to restore the bounds to those of the time of King John. Revised and extended bounds, reafforesting the areas excluded in 1225, were presented in 1228; however, within a few years Henry in his turn was forced to make further concessions to raise revenue. In 1277 Edward I ordered new perambulations of the forests in eighteen counties, including Somerset, Dorset and Wiltshire (*C.P.R.* 1272–81, 237), and there was again an attempt to restore the forest bounds to their greatest extent. Once more this provoked considerable opposition, and in 1297, under pressure to reduce the forest bounds again, a new set of perambulations was ordered by Edward I's regents during his absence in France. Outside this regular series, the metes and bounds of some forests are also recorded in the Eyre Rolls of Henry III and Edward I. Perambulations in eighteen counties were ordered in 1300 (*C.P.R.* 1292–1301, 506) and the last perambulations of the Middle Ages took place under Edward III.

The practice of making boundary perambulations was resumed under the Stuart monarchs as part of a short-lived attempt to re-establish the forest system: perambulations survive for part of Selwood in 1622, Woolmer in 1635 (Rolston 1955) and Bere Portchester in 1688. However, the attempt was soon abandoned and one by one the forests were sold off and the restrictions lifted.

Almost without exception the forest boundaries were defined with reference to pre-existing features – hills, streams, roads, bridges, park and wood boundaries, barrows and other ancient earthworks. In otherwise feature-less areas boundary stones were used: 'Whitestone' appears on the Exmoor bounds of 1218, apparently replaced by the 'Five Stones' of the 1279 and 1298 perambulations; 'Redstone' appears on the Exmoor bounds of 1298. The bounds of Cranborne Chase in 1279 included a 'Horestone'. Crosses are also mentioned in several perambulations, although it is never stated whether they were erected specifically as boundary marks or whether they were already there: the 'Abbess's Cross' on the 1219 bounds of Groveley, the 'Cowled Cross' on the early bounds of Braden Forest, another 'Cowled Cross' on the 1327 bounds of Melchet, and the 'Austin's Cross' also on the 1327 Melchet bounds at least sound like standing structures, though sometimes the word seems to have been used merely to mean 'crossroads'. There are no known examples in the west country of new linear boundaries being constructed specifically to mark the forest bounds, such as Gilbert de Clare's dyke on the west side of Malvern Chase, though in 1330 Edward III ordered the digging of pits along the boundaries of the royal demesnes which were all that remained of the Wiltshire forests defined by the perambulations of 1300 (Grant 1959, 400).

Forest Animals

Four species of animals were normally protected by Forest Law: the native red and roe deer, the wild boar, and the introduced fallow deer. The larger red and fallow deer were the most frequent quarries of the hunt. The small roe deer was excluded after 1338 in some localities because it was believed to frighten off other deer (*Sel. Pleas*, ix). Occasionally other beasts locally came under Forest Law; the case of the hare in Somerton Warren has already been mentioned.

Red Deer were the larger and more widespread of the two native species. Red deer bones have been reported from many prehistoric and Roman sites in the region (Coy and Maltby 1987, 213–6) and they remained important throughout the Middle Ages. Red deer are versatile as regards habitat, being as capable of surviving on open grassland as in wooded countryside. In the Middle Ages they were numerous on the wilder upland forests such as Exmoor (MacDermott 1911) and on the open heaths in the eastern part of the former royal forest on the Isle of Purbeck; they are also recorded from some of the larger royal parks, such as Newton Park in North Petherton, and from two of the Bishop of Winchester's warrens at Marwell and Bishops Sutton (Roberts 1988, 67). In the lower-lying forests such as Clarendon, Melksham and Pewsham, however, their numbers may have dwindled to near-extinction by the end of the Middle Ages. They still survive on Exmoor and in the New Forest today.

Roe Deer are also attested from prehistory, and their bones have been reported from several Saxon sites in the region (Coy and Maltby 1987, 216). After the Norman Conquest they remained in some numbers in the Dorset forests of Bere, Blackmoor, Gillingham and Powerstock (Cox 1908, 297), and in the Wiltshire forests of Groveley and Chute (Grant 1959, 392 n. 20; *C.Cl.R.* 1254–6, 70–71), and were also recorded on Exmoor (MacDermot 1911, 32, 80). They were also occasionally found in parks. In 1232, for example, Godfrey de Crocombe was given six roebucks from Powerstock Forest and six more from Newton Park for stocking the park of Beercrocombe (*C.Cl.R.* 1231–4, 15). Hazel forms an important part of the diet of the roe deer, and the species may have been affected adversely by the spread of coppicing during the Middle Ages, since it cannot thrive on low-quality browsing. Its exclusion from the protection of Forest Law in 1338 may also have contributed to its decline. Whatever the reason, roe deer had become scarce in southern England by the fifteenth century, and the present stock is a result of reintroduction in the early nineteenth century.

Fallow Deer are native to southern Europe, and evidence for its presence in Britain before the Norman Conquest is slender. Although a few fallow deer bones have been recorded from Roman sites elsewhere, they do not seem to appear in Wessex until the Saxon period, and then only in very limited quantities. They have been reported from Saxon deposits at Portchester (Grant 1976, 284) and at Cheddar Palace (Higgs *et al.* 1979, 354–362), but are absent from other Saxon sites such as Southampton. Early documentary evidence is inconclusive: the dialogue with the hunter in Aelfric's Colloquy, for example, uses the Latin word *dam(m)ae* (fallow deer) along with *cervi* (stags = mature male red deer) and *capreae* (roe deer), but the Old English gloss translates *dammae* as *rann* (roebuck) (Aelfric, *Colloq.*, 24).

While fallow deer remain such a small proportion of the overall faunal record before the Norman Conquest, it seems best to view them primarily as a Norman introduction. They were well established in the New Forest and in Savernake by the twelfth century, and in Petherton Forest by the thirteenth century (Lever 1979, 162, 165); by this time they also made up a quarter of all the deer poached in the Forest of Dean (Birrell 1982, 21); however, they failed to colonise the bleaker upland forest of Exmoor. Fallow deer were especially suited to being kept in parks: they are gregarious by nature, adaptable, able to fatten on poor land, need little attention, breed readily, are less dangerous than red or roe deer in the rutting season, will graze alongside cattle, and produce excellent venison.

Faunal remains from kitchen middens in the region underline the increasing importance of fallow deer in the aristocratic diet. Deer bones are relatively common at castles and similar high-status sites, but much less so in towns and villages. At Southampton Castle remains of fallow already outnumber red deer by the thirteenth century, while roe deer is absent (Bourdillon 1986, 75). Although the overall number of deer bones from Portchester Castle is relatively low, it may be significant that the proportion of fallow to red deer is four times greater in the period 1320–1400 (Grant 1985, 246). At Okehampton Castle in Devon red deer is present in deposits before 1300, but during the fourteenth century venison was eaten in increasing quantities, and it was the fallow deer which came to contribute more than half of the main mammalian bones, outnumbering cattle, sheep and pig (Maltby 1982).

Wild Boar had once been sufficiently widespread to influence a number of place-names in the region, such as Eversley in Hampshire, Everley in Wiltshire and Evercreech in Somerset (Old English *eofer* = boar; Ekwall 1960, 170). However, boars had been deprived of much of their natural habitat by the early Middle Ages, and survived only in the most remote and densely-wooded areas. Their main stronghold was in the Forest of Dean, but they were also still present in Clarendon Forest into the fourteenth century. A single wild boar was taken at Bishopstoke in Hampshire in 1355–6, the only known reference from the Bishopric of Winchester pipe rolls (Roberts 1988, 72); and as late as 1456 the vicar of Iwerne in Dorset was presented for killing four wild boar with bow and arrow in Iwerne Wood in Cranborne Chase (Cox 1905, 30–31). The household book of Edward Seymour also attests their survival in Savernake as late as 1539–43 (Jackson 1875, 148, 173). Archaeologically it is not always easy to distinguish their bones from those of the domestic pig, but possible wild boar bones have been reported from Romsey in Hampshire (Coy and Maltby 1987, 217). There were attempts to reintroduce wild boar to the New Forest in the seventeenth century and to Alice Holt and Woolmer Forest in the eighteenth century (Harting 1880, 94–5).

Manwood (1598) also lists the *Wolf* as a protected beast of the forest, but there is no evidence that it ever held this status in England. The wolf had been abundant before the Norman Conquest and, indeed, gave its name to Wolmer Forest (= 'Wolf's mere', Ekwall 1960, 533). In 1156 Henry II's exchequer allowed the sheriff of Hampshire 100*s* for livery for the king's wolf-hunters, and the charter of liberties granted to the inhabitants of Devon by John, while Count of Mortain, included the right to hunt wolves. A sum of 5*s* was paid for the capture of a wolf at Freemantle in 1212 (Harting 1880, 136–9). Bones identified possibly as wolf have been excavated from a pit in the outer bailey of Portchester Castle (Grant 1977, 232). In the 1280s there were concerted attempts to exterminate wolves from a number of royal forests, though they remained numerous in the Forest of Dean. They did not finally become extinct in England until the late fifteenth or early sixteenth century (Cox 1905, 32–4).

The Management and Exploitation of Deer

An assured, regular and copious supply of deer was required by medieval kings, (i) for normal domestic consumption, (ii) for banquets on feast days, (iii) for hunting, both for personal recreation and for the entertainment of guests and (iv) as gifts to others as a sign of favour, either live for stocking parks or in the form of venison. Venison was valued as a prestigious element of the aristocratic diet, proclaiming the high social status of its consumer. It was probably more important as a special item for feast days than as regular fare. The Bishop of Salisbury's household accounts for October 1406 to June 1407 record the serving of twenty-one deer carcasses, thirteen fresh, eight salted, at the four great feasts of All Saints, Easter, Christmas and New Year, when guests were entertained (*Ho. Accts.*, i, no. 14, pp. 301, 303, 313–4, 316–7, 319, 360). However, deer bones of all three species represented no more than two per cent of the mammalian bones from the baileys of Portchester Castle in the thirteenth and fourteenth centuries (Grant 1985, 244–256). Venison was regularly packed in barrels and salted and sent to the king or to other feudal magnates over considerable distances: in 1238 and 1239, for example, venison from Taunton Park was sent to the royal larder at Winchester for the Christmas feast (*C.L.R.*, i, 1226–40, 355, 431), while in 1247 twenty-five does taken in Bridgwater Park were carried to Westminster for the feast of St Edward (*C.Cl.R.* 1247–51, 11–12). By contrast, the Bishop of Winchester's venison seems more frequently to have been eaten fresh (Roberts 1988, 73).

There is an extensive literature on the conventions and techniques of medieval hunting, and records of seignurial hunting for recreation and entertainment do occur. Red and roe deer were normally hunted on horseback across the open country of forests, chases and warrens, but as their numbers began to dwindle during the

Fig. 6.5 Depiction of deer on late medieval church bench-end at Monksilver, Somerset. (Photo: James Bond)

Forest with dogs to take ten harts and fifteen bucks (*C.Cl.R.* 1227–31, 546). Occasionally very large quantities were involved: in 1254 the king sent an order for a hundred fallow does from Braden Forest (*C.Cl.R.* 1254–6, 10), and over the following two years fifty does from Melksham and Pewsham Forests were ordered on two occasions (*C.Cl.R.* 1254–6, 244, 335) and around 100 does from Savernake Forest for the queen's stay at Marlborough (*C.Cl.R.* 1254–6, 265, 332). Normally the venison was then salted down, packed in barrels and despatched ready for the next feast day. In 1248 the keeper of Newton Park received an order to allow the king's huntsmen to take five stags to be salted and sent to Winchester for Whitsuntide (*C.L.R.*, iii, 1245–51, 183), the first of a string of similar orders over the next twenty-five years. Conspicuously the king often failed to use the nearest source to the point of consumption: in 1266, for example, twenty buck carcasses from Savernake and Chute were carried all the way to Kenilworth and Windsor (*C.L.R.*, v, 1260–7, 226). This may hint at increasing difficulties in ensuring a satisfactory supply from the forests.

Harts and bucks were usually taken between June and September, when at their fattest before the autumn rut, while hinds and does were usually taken in the winter. The Bishops of Winchester's hunt was sometimes conducted by knights attached to his household, but there was also a permanent staff of professional huntsmen, including fewterers (keepers of the greyhounds), berners (keepers of the brachet hounds, running dogs which hunted by scent) and falconers (Roberts 1988, 70–73). Other landowners employed huntsmen only for part of the year: in 1406–7, for example, the Bishop of Salisbury's accounts include payments to a huntsman, page and fewterer only for the winter season, between October and February (*Ho. Accts.*, 416–7).

Presents of deer from the royal forests were frequently bestowed as a favour by the king. Sometimes such gifts were made specifically for the purpose of stocking private parks. In 1223 Henry III gave John de Erleigh eight does and two bucks or brockets from Blackmoor Forest to stock his park at Duston (Cox 1908, 291). In 1229 the Earl of Pembroke received twenty does from Clarendon to stock his park at Hamstead Marshall (Cox 1905, 314). In 1230–1 Bishop Jocelin was allowed eleven does and one buck from Selwood and further deer from Cheddar for his park at Bath (*C.Cl.R.* 1227–31, 459, 572). In 1252 Robert de Musgrove received five bucks and ten does from Selwood to stock Brewham Park (*C.Cl.R.* 1251–3, 144). In 1280 Roger de Amery was granted five bucks from Mendip Forest to replace five bucks which had escaped from his park at Ubley (*C.Cl.R.* 1279–88, 32). Less frequently transfers were made from park to park. Bridgwater Park on occasions supplied considerable numbers, including fifty bucks and twenty-five does destined for the various parks of Richard of Cornwall in 1234 (*C.Cl.R.* 1231–4, 494). In 1281 Edward I granted

course of the thirteenth century, the focus of attention fell increasingly upon fallow deer reared in parks. A few parks were themselves sufficiently large to permit full-scale hunting, such as Blagdon in Dorset (*C.P.R.* 1494–1509, 188; Cantor and Wilson 1964, 165–170). In smaller parks alternative techniques had to be devised. By the late thirteenth century parkland deer were more regularly culled by being driven by beaters and shot by hunters standing at butts. By the sixteenth century deer coursing had even become a spectator sport, and a feature labelled as the 'Standing' on a map of Clarendon Park of *c.* 1640 may have been a vantage for watchers (Musty 1986). The lord's enjoyment of the chase, while far from negligible as a reason for the creation of deer preserves, was secondary to their purpose as live larders.

More frequently hunting was carried out by professional servants charged with the duty of supplying their employers with venison as and when required: in August 1215, for example, King John sent his huntsman, Albert de Capell, with two horses and fourteen buckhounds, to take bucks in Blackmoor Forest (Cox 1908, 291), while in August 1231 Henry III sent his huntsman to Braden the Bishop of Bath and Wells twenty bucks and does from Neroche Forest to stock his park at Buckland St Mary, but the keeper of Neroche failed to comply with the order, and on learning of this later in the year, the king granted him instead fifteen does and five bucks from Dunster Park for the same purpose (*C.Cl.R.* 1279–88, 97, 143).

Such grants often involved the transport of live deer, caught in nets and carried by cart, over considerable distances. King John had deer sent to replenish the depleted herd in Taunton Park from Hereford (Greswell 1905, 9, 38), a distance of over 180km by road. Windsor Great Park was stocked on several occasions from Chute Forest, 70km to the west (Cantor and Hatherly, 1979, 73). In 1234 Walter Beauchamp received ten bucks and three does from Savernake Forest for his park at Elmley Castle, nearly 80km away to the north in Worcestershire (*C.Cl.R.* 1231–4, 529). Even more remarkably, in 1225 Henry III granted William de Marisco ten live does and two bucks from Cheddar to take to the island of Lundy (Cox and Greswell 1911, 559), a minimum of 16km overland and 120km by sea, or more than 100km overland for the shortest sea crossing of 40km; there is no evidence as to whether this transfer was ever actually achieved.

Forest officials also received venison as a customary perquisite, often recorded in the Forest Pleas. In 1487 the keeper of Clarendon received two bucks, the verderers of Melchet one buck and the regarders one buck, while in 1490 the regarders of Melksham and Pewsham were entitled to one buck between them, the justices' deputy to a pricket (a two-year-old male fallow deer) and the sheriff of Wiltshire to one buck (Cox 1905, 318, 323–4).

It is almost impossible to guess the total number of deer in the forests at any given period. Some forests never seem to have been particularly productive: the maximum yield from Pamber Forest, for example, was never more than 140 deer in any one decade, and more frequently averaged only about thirty per decade (Stamper 1983, 48). However, documents recording the numbers of deer legitimately hunted and poached probably consistently underestimate the true quantities involved. The records of deer found dead through disease in some years imply a large total population: the catastrophic epidemic which hit Clarendon Forest in 1470 resulted in the discovery of 2209 carcasses, while 560 deer died in the Forests of Melksham and Pewsham in 1485–8 (Cox 1905, 28–9). The overall numbers, especially of red deer, may have declined during the thirteenth century as their habitat contracted through agricultural encroachment into the waste and woodland; fewer royal gifts of deer from the forests are recorded, and the king's huntsmen were unable to meet their orders with increasing frequency. However, this shortfall may have been balanced by increasing numbers of private deer parks.

Deer eat voraciously all year round, grass forming their staple diet. In hard winters they were especially vulnerable to cold and starvation. Given the relatively mild climate of the south-west of England, there was probably less need for the deer-houses sometimes encountered in the midlands, east and north of England (Cf. Birrell 1992, 117). Nonetheless, the Bishop of Winchester's accounts record some expenditure on the building of deer-houses in the later fourteenth century in the parks of Hambledon, Fareham and Merdon, which appear to have been substantial timber-framed thatch-roofed structures (Roberts, 1988, 79). In the Forest of Dean it was the custom to exclude other stock in order to safeguard the feed between November and April; in Cranborne Chase this was only done in exceptionally hard winters (Birrell 1992, 117). Fodder was stored for supplementary use, particularly in those parks and forests most frequently used by the king. Accounts for the reigns of Edward III and Richard II show considerable expenditures on hay for the deer in Clarendon Forest, and in 1483 the Sheriff of Wiltshire was required to buy in each summer £10-worth of hay to be stored in the barn in Clarendon Park for winter feed (Hoare 1837–45, 128–9) while the sheriff of Hampshire similarly had to provide winter feed for the deer in Freemantle park (Brown *et al.* 1963, ii, 940–1). The park of Bishop's Sutton in 1375–7 contained four cribs 68 feet (20.7m) long, from which the deer were fed (Roberts 1988, 79). Browse-wood, clippings taken in summer from forest trees and stored until needed, provided a cheaper alternative to hay or oats. In 1391–2 wages were paid to one man for cutting brushwood for wintering deer in Badbury Park in Dorset (Papworth 1989), while cutting of browsewood is mentioned in the Braden Forest swanimote courts into the early seventeenth century (Grant 1959, 397).

Although it is clear that deer were farmed quite effectively for consumption in privileged households, venison seems not to have reached the open market in any significant quantity, perhaps because that would have devalued it as a high-status food. However, poachers supplied a considerable black market. The small ports along the Severn estuary witnessed a regular illicit traffic in venison from the Forest of Dean being smuggled to Bristol and elsewhere (Birrell 1982, 14, 20). The records of the Forest Eyres record numerous instances of poaching. Presentments at the Forest Pleas for the New Forest for the period 1284–1300 were concerned with the slaughter of twenty-two does, ten bucks, three hinds, two harts and six fawns, in addition to several cases where the quantity of game poached was unknown; fines imposed ranged from 12*d* to 20*s* (Cox 1905, 306). All ranks of secular and clerical society were involved in poaching, but the identity of the perpetrators still sometimes occasions surprise. The Somerset Pleas of 1270 include a case against a monk and others from Witham Priory, a house of that most austere and strict of all the monastic orders, the Carthusians, for poaching a hart ten years earlier in an enclosure in Mendip Forest, and for hunting another with mastiffs in Cheddar Wood. It was alleged that the brother concerned captured deer by fixing wooden stakes with fire-hardened points in a gap in the enclosure (Cox and Greswell 1911, 559–60). Many other poaching offences are recorded by commissions of oyer and terminer enrolled in the Patent Rolls. Archaeological evidence for poaching may be represented by deer bones from peasant house middens: for example, fallow deer bones have been recovered at the deserted village of Gomeldon in Wiltshire (Harcourt 1986, 166–8).

Timber and Wood Production

The Domesday Survey gives a somewhat imperfect impression of the general distribution of woodland within the region, both inside and outside the royal forests, but hints at some variety of woodland types and management practices which is endorsed by later sources. High forest may still have survived in some places, but in the more open countryside there is evidence of coppicing. Underwood (*Silva minuta, silva parva, silva modica*) occurs in many localities in Somerset, particularly on the Cotswolds south of Bath and on the Polden Hills, and also occurs less frequently in Wiltshire and west Dorset (Finn and Wheatley 1967, 177–8; Finn 1967, 36; Darby 1967, 102). As the overall extent of woodland contined to contract, an ever greater proportion of surviving woods were managed by coppicing, and this more intensive style of exploitation expanded at the expense of high forest and wood-pasture. One of the earliest detailed formal records of coppice management occurs in the Beaulieu accounts of 1269–70. Beaulieu Abbey's estates were concentrated in the New Forest, and the account book includes a 'forester's table', giving production figures from its woods: one acre of coppice cut every twenty years yielded 4,800 bundles of firewood, 500 bushels of vine-stakes or fencing-rods and 4,000 oven-faggots, with the waste going for charcoal, making a total of some two tons of wood per acre per year. While sales from coppicing produced an annual income of a little over 2s per acre, timber sales varied from 5s to 10s (*Beaul. Acct.*, 198–201; Rackham 1980, 140–2). Returns from sales of underwood in Clarendon Park and Groveley Forest in 1330–32 clearly indicate the practice of a coppice rotation here (Hoare 1837, 173–4). New coppice-woods were still being formed out of old wood-pasture in the New Forest in the late Middle Ages (Tubbs 1968), where miles of wood-banks remain.

Throughout the Middle Ages there was a demand for massive oaks for the roofs of great churches, halls and barns. Tracts of high forest and wood-pasture provided timber for the works at royal houses like Clarendon and Winchester. Timber from the royal forests was also regularly awarded by the king as gifts, particularly to religious houses. The Domesday survey records that two Wiltshire manors, South Newton and Washern, both belonging to the nuns of Wilton; each took a customary due of eighty cartloads of timber from Melchet Forest for repairing their houses and fences (Finn 1967, 34–6).

The Forest of Dean, of all south-western woodlands perhaps the one which most closely resembled a tract of surviving primeval forest, was particularly important as a source of outsize oaks (Hart 1966; Rackham 1980, 153). By the 1250s, however, great oaks were in increasingly short supply, and many forests were becoming so depleted that the king suspended benefactions (*C.Cl.R.* 1256–9, 131).

Medieval documentary records of timber production from royal forests, of which only a random selection can be quoted below, may give a misleading impression of the constituents of the woodlands within them, since they naturally throw most emphasis upon the commercially useful species. Oak emerges almost universally as the most important tree for building timber. Considerable quantities were sometimes carried over long distances, and Rackham (1980, 151) has pointed out that transport was cheap, and the location of skilled sawyers could be as important as that of the trees. In 1395 great oak timbers 15m long, probably from Alice Holt, were prefabricated at Farnham, carted overland to the Thames at Ham, and then carried downriver for the roof of Westminster Hall (Salzman 1967, 350–1). Clarendon Forest was the source of numerous grants of oaks for ecclesiastical and other buildings: six oaks for Gilbert de Lacy's new chapel at Britford in 1222, five oaks in 1230 for the Greyfriars in Salisbury, four oaks for Mottisfont Priory in 1275, and then in the following year four oaks for rebuilding the king's mill below Old Sarum which had recently been thrown down by a flood, thirty oaks for the church of Wilton Abbey, forty oaks to make shingles for roofing buildings at Clarendon Palace, and sixty beams for rafters (*chevrones*) at Queen Eleanor's buildings at Lyndhurst (Cox 1905, 313–5). One oak from Blackmore Forest went for the repair of the bridge at Corfe Castle in 1230 (*C.Cl.R.* 1227–31, 452). In 1251 Henry III gave twenty oaks from four different forests, Melksham, Chippenham, Digerley and Finkley, to make ten couples (i.e. twenty rafters) for the roof of Salisbury cathedral (*C.Cl.R.* 1247–51, 462). Melchet Forest provided four oaks for the church of Mottisfont Priory along with twenty oaks for joists (*gristas*) and eight oaks for shingles for Clarendon Palace in 1275 (*C.Cl.R.* 1272–9, 146, 155). In 1278 thirty oaks from Pamber and thirty oaks from the New Forest were sent for the rebuilding of Winchester Castle, while Alice Holt provided thirty oaks the following year (*C.Cl.R.* 1272–9, 471, 525). Timber from Pamber Forest was granted to the nuns of Godstow in Oxfordshire (*C.Cl.R.* 1247–51, 409), to the Oxford Blackfriars (*C.Cl.R.* 1288–96, 211), and in 1298 eighty oaks from Pamber were granted to Westminster Abbey for repairs after a fire (*C.Cl.R.* 1296–1302, 251). In 1363 820 oaks were cut in Combe Park and 120 in Pamber Forest for building works at Windsor Castle (Salzman 1952, 237). The Prioress of Amesbury received from Chute Forest twenty oaks for the repair of the cloisters in 1231 and sixteen rafters three years later for the church roof (*C.Cl.R.* 1227–31, 486; 1231–4, 370). Twenty oaks from the same forest were granted in 1231 to the Countess of Pembroke for the repair of her mills at Newbury (*C.Cl.R.* 1227–31, 527). Oaks from Chute Forest were also bestowed upon the Abbess of St Mary's, Winchester, (*C.Cl.R.* 1227–31, 169). In 1230 Henry III ordered the sheriff of Dorset to assign twenty oaks from Bere Forest to Henry FitzNicholas for building his manor-house at Fordington (*C.Cl.R.* 1227–31, 348).

Oak was also much in demand for fittings and furnishings. In 1230 the Prioress of Amesbury received three oaks from Clarendon Forest, and two more the following year, for making and repairing the stalls in the church (*C.Cl.R.* 1227–31, 310, 486). In 1231 the Abbess of Romsey received five good oaks from Melchet for planks for the dormitory (*C.Cl.R.* 1227–31, 483). The Blackfriars of Oxford were granted six oaks from Pamber Forest for the repair of their stalls in 1291 (*C.Cl.R.* 1288–96, 211).

Beech is mentioned in some New Forest records, as in 1330 when the vert presentments include a case of three beeches worth 3*s* being illegally felled (Tubbs 1968, 174, 177, 180, 187, 241, 319), though it was probably less widespread there in the Middle Ages than it is now. Twenty beeches from Buckholt Wood, along with thirty oaks from Clarendon Forest and thirty oaks from Melchet, or sixty oaks from Chute, were felled for further repairs to the king's water-mills below Old Sarum in 1320–1 (*C.Cl.R.* 1318–23, 193, 195, 309). In 1442 the king sent instructions to fell 400 beeches in Buckholt, along with 200 oaks in Melchet Forest, for repairs to sundry manor-houses, lodges and park pales; the beeches were valued at 2*s*–2*s*.6*d* each (Cox 1905, 317). The same tree also figures among the perquisites of the officers of Bere Forest in Hampshire in 1490, the deputy of the justices being entitled to six beeches, the two sessional clerks to four beeches, the regarders to two beeches, and the deputy keeper, ranger and each verderer one beech each (Cox 1905, 311). Beech was used particularly for tables and other furniture, and for the fittings and centrings of arches. The building accounts for Winchester Castle in 1222–3 record two purchases of 100 and 175 beech boards for 1*s*.8*d* and 5*s*.3*d* respectively (*Bldg. Acct. H.III*, 140–1, 142–3).

Elm was used in the early Middle Ages mainly for piling and in damp situations, but as large oak became increasingly scarce after the middle of the fourteenth century, it was increasingly pressed into more general service, particularly for floorboards and roof timber. Elm boards cost 2*s* per 100ft at Devizes in 1460 (Salzman 1967, 250). The churchwardens of St Michael's Church in Bath accounted for four elm planks for the 'punyon' (?gable) in 1460 (*Bath Chw. Accts.*, 56), and in 1521 a 'false roof of elm' was set over the unfinished buildings of Thornbury Castle in Gloucestershire, perhaps as an emergency measure (*L. & P. Henry VIII*, iii, 1286). Ash forms a pliant and resilient wood which was also occasionally used in building: in 1292 one ash was cut for

studs at Corfe (Salzman 1967, 251). It had the drawback of vulnerability to worm, however, and was not extensively favoured.

It is clear that the forests, woods and parks of the west country were able to supply much of the local demand for timber, but certain specialised needs had to be met by imports from outside the region, particularly of long straight knot-free boards for wainscotting and for certain fittings. 'Walschborde' (?walnut or timber from Wales) appears in the churchwardens' accounts of St Michael's Church, Bath, in 1370 (*Bath Chw. Accts.*, 8). Fir from Scandinavia and the Baltic was regularly imported from the 1230s. In 1238 shutters were made of fir for a new window in the gable of the queen's chamber at Marlborough (Salzman 1967, 257). In 1252 Henry III ordered the bailiffs of Southampton to buy 200 Norway boards of deal (*sapino*) for the wainscotting of Prince Edward's room in Winchester Castle (*C.L.R.*, iv, 1251–60, 86–7). In 1292 200 *estrichboards* (by the long hundred of six score, making a total of 240) were imported for doors and shutters at Corfe (Salzman 1967, 245).

'Wood for fencing' (*silva ad clausarum*) is recorded in a number of localities in the Domesday folios for Hampshire and Wiltshire (Finn 1962, 320–1; Finn 1967, 36). This may imply that the grazing was reserved for demesne livestock and that the commoners had only rights of hedgebote, i.e. to remove wood only for making fences. In 1233 the king ordered 3000 hurdles from the wood at Cheddar (Rackham 1988a, 23). One poplar and one ash were used in making wicket-gates at Carisbrooke Castle in 1353 (Saltzmann 1967, 250).

Fuel was a regular product of manorial woodland throughout the region, and the taking of wood from the royal forests for this purpose is often recorded as a customary right. The nuns of Wilton had a right to four score loads of firewood from Melchet Forest. On many occasions it was granted by the king as a favour, particularly to the heads of religious institutions. In 1224 the Bishop of Salisbury received forty loads of fuel from Clarendon Forest (Cox 1905, 314). When Thomas de Sampford, one of the king's chaplains, became Warden of Cricklade Hospital in 1231, the king gave him and his successors way-leave for their horses and carts to take fuel from Braden Forest without hindrance from the foresters or verderers (*C.Cl.R.* 1227–31, 487). The following year the king gave a similar general dispensation to the Maiden Bradley Hospital to take horses and carts to collect any wood, charcoal or timber that they might be given or purchase in Selwood Forest (*C.P.R.* 1225–32, 468). In 1231 the nuns of Amesbury were permitted six *robora* (dead trees or the bollings of pollards) from Buckholt, six from Chute and three from Groveley for their fire; two years later they received five loads of firewood from Clarendon Forest in addition to their customary privilege of estover there (*C.Cl.R.* 1231–34, 3; Cox 1905, 314). In 1232 the hospital of St John outside Wilton received thirty cartloads of underwood from

Groveley for fuel, with another twenty cartloads two years later (*C.Cl.R.* 1231–4, 46, 370). In 1246 the monks of the alien priory of Monk Sherborne were allowed two cartloads of dead wood a week from Pamber Forest, 'so that they take no greenwood' (*C.Cl.R.* 1232–47, 475). In 1276 the Dominican Friars of Wilton received ten cartloads of brushwood from Clarendon Forest (Cox 1905, 315). The Close Rolls of the thirteenth century record many grants of beech from Clarendon Forest for firewood.

In addition to domestic fuel, woodland also supplied industrial needs. Oak bark was in demand for tanning. Charcoal burners were active in the New Forest throughout the Middle Ages (*New. For. Doc.*, i, no. 148, p. 85; no. 503, pp. 187–8; no. 521, p. 194). The Domesday survey records rents paid in blooms of iron in six places in Somerset, of which five were in or near the Forests of Neroche and North Petherton (Finn and Wheatley 1967, 211). A similar render is recorded from Alvington in the Forest of Dean (Darby 1954, 49), where there were later numerous iron forges. In 1235 forty acres of wood at Cheddar was allotted for the smelting of ore from the bishop's iron and lead mines in Mendip Forest (*C.Cl.R.* 1234–7, 86, 92–3). In 1276 Thomas Foxcote, forester of fee in the New Forest, had a customary right to burn beech and other trees in his bailwick to make potash for dyeing cloth (*New For. Doc.*, i, no. 148, p. 85). Excavation of the Laverstock pottery kilns recovered charcoal of oak, willow, hazel and birch in the stoke pits (Musty *et al.* 1969). The pottery kilns of Donyatt could have drawn their fuel from the Forest of Neroche, but the presence of charcoal of poplar and willow as well as oak, ash and elm, suggests that part of the supply was coming from hedges and open commons rather than woodland by the sixteenth century (Rackham 1988b). Limekilns producing mortar for building operations also required much fuel: in 1220 the king gave sixty great *robora* for the limekiln at Wells Cathedral, and five years later gave another thirty oaks from his wood at Cheddar for the same purpose (Rackham 1988a, 23).

Grazing Rights

The designation of a tract of land as royal forest, or its enclosure within a park, did not automatically extinguish all common rights, many of which were of considerable antiquity. While the removal of timber trees and the enclosure of land were not normally permitted, most of the standard rights of common – herbage or pasturage for domestic cattle and horses, pannage for pigs, estover and turbary – were entirely compatible with the maintenance of a wood-pasture regime. The practice of grazing in the forests, both for those with customary rights and for outsiders who purchased agistments, was at first strictly regulated by the forest officers: in 1280, for example, it was reported that the Abbot of Beaulieu and the Priors of Christchurch and Breamore had an excess of livestock grazing in the New Forest, damaging the pasture of

the king's deer (*New For. Doc.*, i, no. 191, p. 93). Later on in the Middle Ages, however, with the decline of the administrative machinery of the forest, stinting arrangements often became more laxly observed.

The pasture resources of many forests were shared by a ring of neighbouring communities, an arrangement often dating from before the first legal designation of the forest. Manors all around the Forest of Bere Portchester had common rights of pasture in it for cattle and ringed swine from the early Middle Ages right up to its final disafforestation and enclosure in 1814, when it still comprised over 4000ha of open forest grazed by deer and cattle (Munby 1985, 271–4; Colebourn 1983, 21).

The income from agistments for grazing cattle fluctuated considerably, and on occasions ceased altogether. There were no agistment sales in Clarendon Forest between 1298 and 1337 because the king had ordered all the oaks to be cut and sold, and grazing livestock could not be readmitted until the replacement trees had reached sufficient maturity (Young 1979, 129).

Pigs were normally allowed into the forest between 14th September and 18th November to feed upon fallen acorns and beechmast, in exchange for which a pannage fee was payable at the Martinmas swanimote court. The Domesday survey records that at their two Wiltshire manors of South Newton and Washern the nuns of Wilton had customary rights in Melchet Forest which included the pasturage of a total of 160 pigs (Finn 1967, 34–6). The canons of Ivychurch had rights of pasturage in Clarendon Forest, and in 1248 Henry III allowed them to put twenty swine with their litters into the forest to feed, free of pannage dues, provided that they were ringed, each year that the forest was agisted; but no pigs were to be allowed in the forest in years when agistments were not permitted (*C.Cl.R.* 1247–51, 88; Grant 1959, 289). In *c.* 1300 the Abbot of Beaulieu had fifty pigs and the Abbot of Netley forty pigs in the New Forest (*New For. Doc.*, i, nos. 405–6, pp. 147–8).

Cattle were also allowed to graze in the forest so long as they were branded for identification. The Abbot of Beaulieu had 200 head and the Abbot of Netley sixty head of cattle and oxen in the New Forest around 1300 (*New For. Doc.*, i, nos. 405–6, pp. 147–8). In 1317 Edward I allowed the canons of Ivychurch pasturage for forty oxen and cows in Clarendon Park in exchange for their grazing rights in the forest, for a rent of 56s. (*C.Cl.R.* 1313–18, 507; *C.P.R.* 1313–17, 628). By the middle of the fourteenth century Dartmoor Forest had become more important as cattle pasture than as a deer preserve.

Sheep, by contrast, were generally excluded under Forest Law because it was believed that their grazing habits placed them in direct competition with the deer. Despite this the Abbot of Beaulieu had 1300 sheep and the Abbot of Netley 300 sheep in the New Forest around 1300 (*New For. Doc.*, i, nos. 405–6, pp. 147–8). This regulation seems increasingly to have been relaxed towards the end of the Middle Ages as the forest administration declined, and by the sixteenth century the admission of sheep to graze in the forests had become more widespread.

Disafforestation

Forest Law, even when not enforced to its extremes, still inhibited agricultural expansion and economic growth during a period of population expansion, while abuses perpetrated by individual forest officials caused much resentment. The restrictions imposed upon landowners and commoners alike remained a source of grievance throughout the early Middle Ages. The legal process of disafforestation, the returning of the tracts to common law (a process entirely unrelated in the Middle Ages to any physical contraction in the extent of woodland), can be seen partly as a response to pressures brought to bear upon the king, and partly as an opportunity for the king to raise revenue by imposing substantial fines for the lifting of restrictions from some of the less valuable forests. It took place in three main stages.

The first important wave of disafforestations took place during the thirteenth century (Bazeley 1921; Grant 1991, 133–159). In 1204 King John, financially embarrassed by the cost of his war against the French and in desperate need of new revenue, lifted Forest Law from the greater part of the counties of Cornwall and Devon in exchange for considerable fines. The disafforestation of Cornwall, saving only two moors and two woods which were disafforested eleven years later, cost its landowners the equivalent of 2,200 marks; the disafforestation of Devon, apart from Dartmoor and Exmoor, cost 5000 marks (*Pipe R.*, new ser., 18, 1204, 40, 85; *Rot. Chart.*, 122b, 132, 206; *Rot. Litt. Claus.* 1204–24, 197; *C.Ch.R.*, ii, 1257–1300, 247). Concessions wrung from John through Magna Carta were reinforced by the Forest Charter of 1217, which eased the burdens imposed by Forest Law and promised the disafforestation of all private lands outside the royal demesne taken into the forest by Henry II and his sons. Part of Purbeck Forest was an immediate casualty (though a plan of 1585, reproduced in Cantor, 1982, 58, still shows the whole peninsula adorned with deer). Elsewhere the effects were somewhat delayed: demands for disafforestations from local jurors in Somerset in 1218 were refused, and a decision on similar demands from Berkshire in 1221 was shelved by the regents until Henry III reached his majority. While Henry III's initial impulse seems to have been to repudiate the concessions and he did in fact take back some disafforested parts of Savernake, Gillingham and Bere in Dorset, financial necessity soon compelled him to relinquish further rights. In 1227 he granted a charter for the disafforestation of all Berkshire, except for the eastern portion which remained within Windsor Forest (*C.Ch.R.*, i, 1226–57, 39), and in the following year he disafforested most of Gloucestershire east of the Severn, including the Forest of Kingswood (*C.Cl.R.* 1227–31, 58, 293; Moore 1982).

The Dorset Forest of Bere, having been reafforested in 1227 and 1250, was then granted along with the manor of Bere Regis to Simon de Montfort in 1259 (Cox 1908, 292). After de Montfort's fall it was granted in 1269 to Edmund, Earl of Lancaster, and ceased to be royal forest (*C.Ch.R.*, ii, 1257–1300, 277–8; Hutchins 1861–73, i, 136). Edward I also attempted to restore some of the Crown's lost rights after 1272, but met with considerable opposition throughout the west country, and was forced to make further concessions, including the disafforestation of much of Blackmoor, the most extensive of the Dorset forests, in 1277 (Cox 1908, 292; Grant 1991, 155), and the reduction of the Forest of Dean in 1300. Eversley, Bere Ashley and Buckholt also appear to have been disafforested at a relatively early date. By the 1330s the area under Forest Law in England as a whole had contracted to around two-thirds of its extent in the mid-thirteenth century, while what remained was administered with decreasing effectiveness (Cantor 1982, 66).

The second major phase of disafforestations occurred in the second half of the sixteenth and early seventeenth centuries, beginning with grants of Groveley in the mid sixteenth century to the Earl of Pembroke (Grant 1959, 432) and Savernake and Purbeck to Edward Seymour, Duke of Somerset, in 1547–50 (*C.P.R.* 1549–51, 430–2; Cardigan 1949, 148–9). By this time, although the forests were still valued for their deer, their function as a source of timber was becoming more important. Moreover the Tudor monarchs were less peripatetic than their medieval predecessors, preferring to settle near London, so that many of the royal palaces in the provinces were neglected and abandoned. Those forests which were remote from any current royal residence or which had little game or sparse or poor-quality timber were leased out or sold and disafforested: Melchet, Clarendon and Panshet between 1577 and 1610 (Grant 1959, 431); Odiham and Freemantle under James I (Colebourn 1983, 22); Pamber Forest in 1614 (*C.S.P.Dom.* 1611–18, 247); Chippenham and Melksham Forests in 1618–23 (saving Bowood park, which remained in royal hands) (Grant 1959, 401, 412–14, 431); Gillingham in 1625–30 (Hutchins 1861–73, ii, 620–4, 649; Bettey 1976); Selwood in 1627–9 (*C.S.P.Dom.* 1627–8, 232, 242; *ibid.* 1629–31, 141); Neroche in 1627–34 (*C.S.P.Dom.* 1625–9, 336, 344; *ibid.* 1629–31, 141); Braden in 1630 (Grant, 1959, 401, 405–7); and Chute in 1639–61 (*C.S.P. Dom.* 1638–9, 592; Grant 1959, 426–7). Even the royal park of Clarendon, the last relic of the once extensive royal forests in Wiltshire, was finally disparked in 1664, its palace having been derelict since the middle of the previous century (*C.S.P. Dom.* 1660–61, 285–86; *ibid.* 1663–4, 275, 502; Grant, 1959, 401, 431; James and Robinson 1988, 45).

The final phase of extinction came in the nineteenth century, when most of the remaining forests were disafforested and enclosed by Act of Parliament: Bere Portchester in 1810 (50 Geo.III, *c.* ccxviii), Alice Holt in 1812 (52 Geo.III, *c.* 72), the remaining parts of Exmoor in 1815 (55 Geo.III, *c.* 138), and Woolmer in 1855 (18 and 19 Vict. *c.* 46). Only the New Forest and the Forest of Dean retain some vestiges of their ancient administration, including their verderer's courts, and ancient customary rights of common, though in 1923 the crown lands within them were transferred to the Forestry Commission (Hart 1971, 135–69, 190–202; Grant 1991, 214–7).

Origins and Chronology of Park Creation

Deer parks, like forests, are usually held to be a product of Norman feudal society (Cantor and Hatherly 1979, 71; Stamper 1988, 140), but the point has already been made that enthusiasm for hunting and the enjoyment of venison were nothing new. There is clear evidence of some provision for trapping and enclosing deer in the pre-Conquest landscape. A charter of Athelstan granting land at Pitminster (Somerset) in 938 has attached to it a boundary perambulation which includes features described as *haga* ('game enclosure') and *ealden haga* (the 'old game enclosure' – whether 'old' in the sense of 'ancient' or 'disused' is a moot point). *Hagas* are frequently mentioned in Hampshire charters, being especially concentrated in what later became the Forests of Bere, Chute and Woolmer. Elsewhere in England several pre-Conquest records of game enclosures, deerfolds or leapgates can be located in or near medieval parks, which may be seen as their successors. At Closworth the county boundary follows the park boundary, taking a piece of land on the Dorset bank of the stream into Somerset (Wilson and Cantor 1969): was this a boundary adjustment made after the creation of the park, or could the park already have been in existence at the time when the county boundary was first defined?

Few parks are recorded in the Domesday Survey. In Somerset Drogo held a park at Donyatt from the Count of Mortain (*D.B. Som.*, 19.24; Finn and Wheatley, 1967, 177, 213). In Hampshire the Bishop of Winchester held what is described as a 'park for beasts of the chase' (*parcus bestiarum*) at Bishop's Waltham, while at Soberton there are two references to a park held by Earl Roger of Shrewsbury (though, since he held no land in Soberton itself, this may have been located in one of his neighbouring manors, Hambledon or Chalton). On the Isle of Wight the king's park of Watchingwell included an unspecified extent of meadow. Reductions in hidage recorded at Soberton and Watchingwell may imply that these parks were of recent creation (Finn 1962, 355–6). On the margins of the Wessex region there were Domesday parks at Old Sodbury in Gloucestershire and Winkleigh in Devon (Darby 1977, 201–3). Finally, what has sometimes been claimed as a remarkable record of twenty park-keepers (*parcarii*) at North Petherton in Somerset derives from a misreading of the word *porcarii*, meaning swineherds; however, a royal servant named

Ansketil the Parker held land in Newton (*D.B. Som.*, 46.17), so there is a case for including the important royal park of Newton in North Petherton amongst the Domesday parks.

The total number of medieval deer parks in England will probably never be known. It was, in theory, necessary to obtain royal permission to enclose a park, since deer were held to be the property of the king; and it was especially advisable to do so if the park lay within or near an area designated as royal forest and protected under Forest Law. Here emparking represented, in effect, a release of a small tract of land from the restrictions: in 1231, for example, Henry III permitted the Bishop, Dean and Chapter of Bath to disafforest the manor of North Curry so that its inhabitants should be quit of forest pleas, and to enclose its woods as parks (*C. Wells MSS*, i, 8; *C. Ch. R.*, i, 1226–57, 104). It is no accident that the highest proportion of licensed parks in the region occurs in Hampshire, the most heavily forested county. Many emparking licences were enrolled in the Pipe Rolls and Close Rolls. In practice, however, there were also large numbers of unlicensed parks which have been identified only through chance references in later documents, or by the evidence surviving in the landscape today. In 1246, for example, Geoffrey de Zeals was called to account at the Forest Eyre for enclosing without licence a park at Zeals (Wi), the bounds of which can still be traced today (*C.P.R.* 1232–47, 490; inf. Jon Byron). Emparking and disparking went on throughout the Middle Ages, and if it is difficult to determine the overall total, it is even more so to ascertain the number in use at any one time. An invaluable provisional checklist of earliest known references to medieval parks drawn from a wide variety of documentary sources has been published by Cantor (1983), but detailed study of any county will certainly produce further examples. In Wessex the county which has been subjected to the fullest examination is Dorset (Cantor and Wilson 1961–1969; Wilson, 1970–1974). There are earlier surveys for Somerset and Dorset by Batten (1896), and for Somerset by Greswell (1905), and several later local studies (e.g. Iles 1978; Lay and Iles 1979; Williams 1988; Franklin 1989).

Increasing numbers of park creations are recorded through the twelfth century, but the peak period of creation fell within the second half of the thirteenth century, continuing up to the disruption of the Black Death in the middle of the fourteenth century (see Figs 6.2 and 6.3 for recorded parks in *c.* 1190 and *c.* 1350). The increase to some extent corresponds with a contraction in the extent of countryside under Forest Law. The number of new parks then tails off to the beginning of the sixteenth century. Sometimes the acquisition of grants of free warren can be seen as a prelude to emparking: in 1256, for example, a charter of free warren for Wiveliscombe in Somerset was obtained by Bishop William Bitton, followed in 1330 by an emparking licence granted to the prebend of Wiveliscombe (Greswell 1905, 249; *C.P.R.*

1330–34, 6). Elsewhere in Somerset emparkment followed grants of free warren at Castle Cary (Phelps 1839, i, 379; *C.I.P.M.*, ix, no. 665), Huish Episcopi (*C.Ch.R.*, i, 1226–57, 469), Chaffcombe (*C.Ch.R.*, ii, 1257–1300, 76; Bush 1978, 121), Aley (*C.Ch.R.*, iii, 1300–26, 388; *C.P.R.* 1354–8, 616), Nettlecombe (Cox and Greswell 1911, 570; Greswell 1905, 246–7) and Staple Fitzpaine (*C.Cl.R.* 1231–4, 212; *C.Ch.R.*, i, 1226–57, 391; Sixsmith 1958, 7, 9–10, 14).

Emparking licences form only a minority of first records, and even these need to be used with caution as dating evidence. Sometimes they are clearly retrospective attempts to legalise a park already in existence, as at Nether Stowey in Somerset, where Peter de Columbariis received permission to have a park in 1248, which other sources show was already there by 1222 (*C.Ch.R.*, i, 1226–57, 330; Dunning 1981, 126). Conversely, sometimes the licence represents a declaration of intent which might be long delayed in its fulfilment. When the manor of Cheddar was disafforested in 1337, Bishop Ralph and his successors were given licence to enclose its woods and to hold them as a park 'at their will' (*C.Ch.R.*, iv, 1327–41, 428). Emparking licences are most frequently encountered within the royal forests because they represent, in effect, a form of local disafforestation: in 1237 Henry de l'Orti acquired a licence to empark his woods of Curry Rivel in order to be exempt from the regard of the foresters of Neroche (*C.Cl.R.* 1234–7, 433). They also provided a source of revenue to the Crown: in 1251 when Robert de Musgrove acquired a licence to enlarge Brewham Park within Selwood Forest by the addition of two acres, which was to be enclosed by a hedge and ditch 120 perches long, the charter records that William de Montacute had held this park in the time of King John, but had allowed it to fall into decay because the price asked for the licence was too expensive (*C.P.R.* 1247–58, 107; *C.Ch.R.*, i, 1226–57, 357; the bounds of this park are discussed by McGarvie 1974). Royal parks, of course, did not require a licence at all.

In the late Middle Ages some of the less viable parks were abandoned, but others were extended as the reduced population allowed more land to go down to pasture. In the immediate aftermath of the Black Death high labour costs may have restricted new emparking activities to the wealthiest landowners such as the Bishop of Winchester (Roberts, 1988, 69). However, as economic and demographic recovery developed, park ownership also began to spread lower down the social scale.

Distribution and Ownership of Parks (Figs 6.6–6.9)

While few parts of the Wessex region were devoid of parks, their distribution was far from uniform. They were particularly numerous in west Dorset, in south Somerset and in the region between the Quantock Hills and the River Parrett, also in those parts of Hampshire facing the Weald and the London Basin. By contrast there were few examples on the open uplands of Exmoor, the Brendon Hills, Mendip, Salisbury Plain and the Hampshire Downs, or on the flat lands of the Somerset Levels or the heaths around Poole Harbour. On a regional scale it was the intermediate land in the vales, below the uplands and above the coastal marshes, particularly where there were also significant extents of woodland and wood-pasture, which tended to attract the greatest concentrations of parks. The legal restraints of Forest Law are sometimes said to have inhibited park creation (Cantor 1982, 81), and some forests did indeed contain few parks or none at all, such as Groveley, Purbeck, Blackmore, or the Forest of Dean. In North Petherton, Gillingham, Pewsham, Clarendon and the New Forest the only parks were those belonging to the king. However, in less intensively used forests with more private demesnes such as Pamber and Neroche, the density of park distribution was not markedly inhibited.

At parochial level the parks were often located on the most marginal land available, on the edge of the estate, where they did not conflict with the needs of agricultural production; they were, therefore, often at some distance from the palace, castle or manor-house to which they belonged. There were, however, some conspicuous exceptions, such as the park of the Bishop of Bath and Wells at Westbury-sub-Mendip, which occupied much of the better-quality land on the manor, forcing the inhabitants of the village to create terraced cultivation strips high on the south face of Mendip. Ultimately the power and resources of their creators and owners were a more significant element in the location and distribution of parks than any deterministic preconceptions.

The crown owned around ten per cent of the parks in the region, though the precise total fluctuated. The largest and most important royal park was Clarendon. Other important royal parks included Newton Park in North Petherton, the largest in Somerset, with a circuit of 4 miles (6.5km) (Shirley 1867, 97), and Gillingham Park in Dorset. Other parks in royal hands for significant periods included Bridgwater and Queen Camel (So), Blagdon, Marshwood and Rampisham (Do). Royal parks tended to be located within the royal forests, though not exclusively so. In addition to their direct use, they could also be seen as a means of ensuring that deer were available when the king wished to hunt in the forest, with individual specimens being released as needed (Cantor and Wilson 1961, 110). The crown also had intermittent custody of many other parks, through confiscation, minority of heirs and other factors.

Episcopal owners were also prominent, accounting for about fourteen per cent of the total. The Bishop of Winchester had at least twenty-three parks, most of which were in Hampshire (Roberts 1988), but which also included Downton in Wiltshire and Poundisford Park in his Somerset manor of Taunton. The Bishop of Bath and Wells had at least ten parks in Somerset, in addition to others in neighbouring counties, such as Dogmersfield

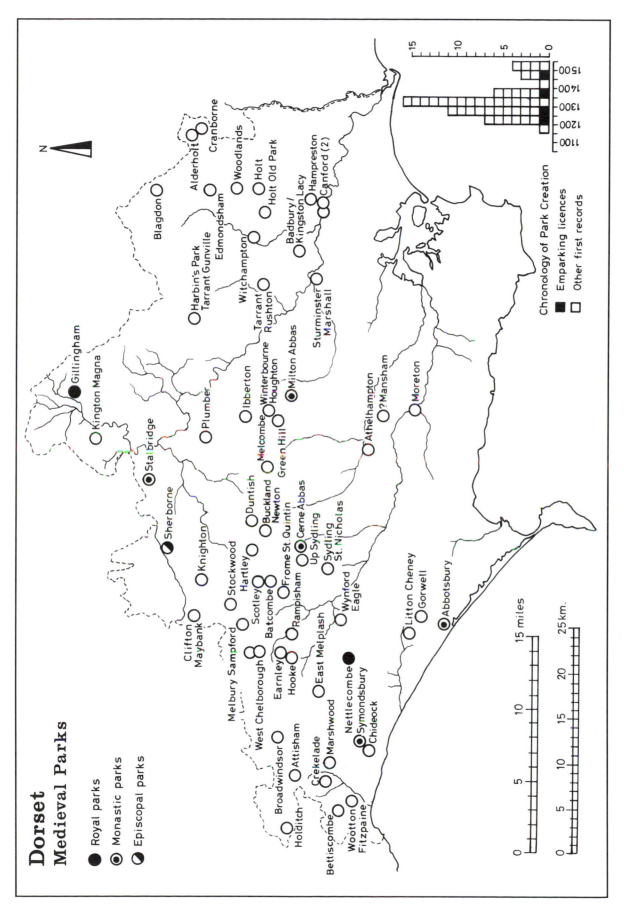

Dorset
Medieval Parks

● Royal parks

◉ Monastic parks

◑ Episcopal parks

Chronology of Park Creation

■ Emparking licences

□ Other first records

Fig. 6.6 Dorset, Medieval Parks.

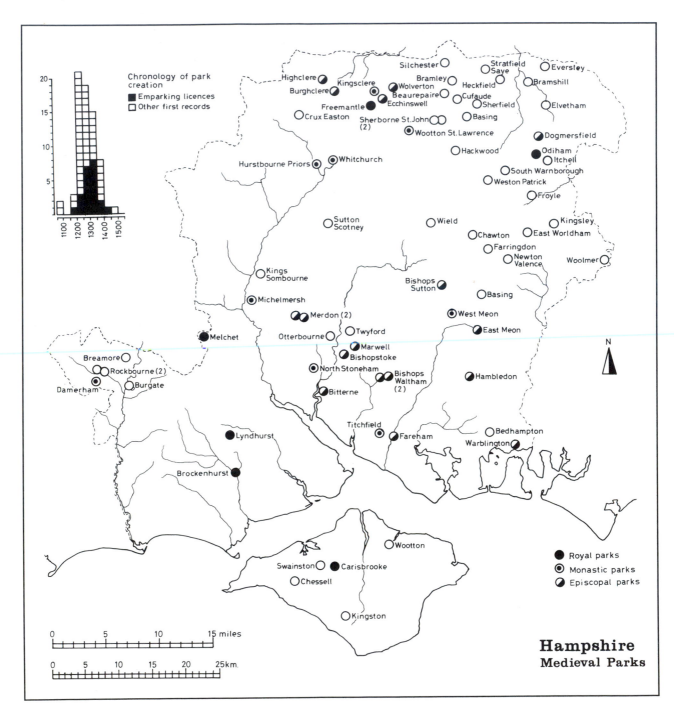

Fig. 6.7 *Hampshire, Medieval Parks.*

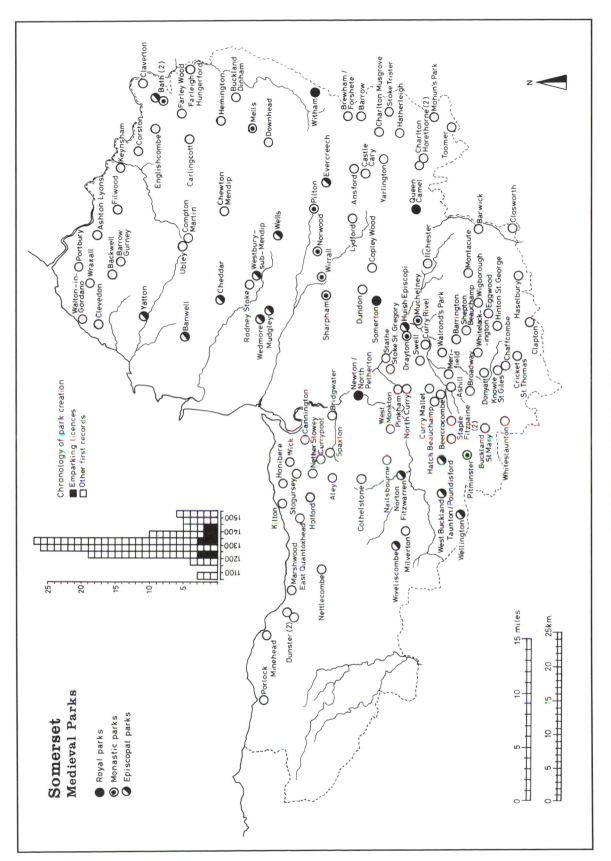

Fig. 6.8 Somerset, Medieval Parks.

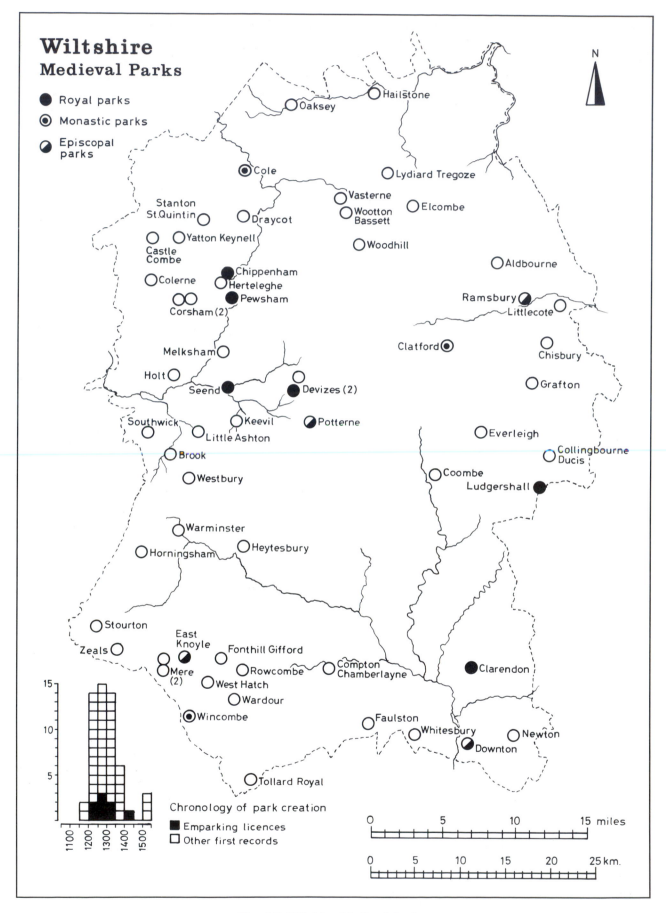

Fig. 6.9 Wiltshire, Medieval Parks.

in Hampshire. The Bishop of Exeter had parks at Norton Fitzwarren in Somerset and Farringdon in Hampshire. The Bishop of Salisbury had parks at Sherborne in Dorset and Ramsbury and Potterne in Wiltshire (*C.P.R.* 1345–8, 307; *C.Cl.R.* 1237–42, 268).

Glastonbury Abbey was the major monastic owner, holding at least seven parks on its estates in Somerset, Hampshire and Berkshire. The Prior of St Swithun's, Winchester, had six parks in Hampshire. The heads of several other monastic houses, including the Benedictine Abbots of Cerne, Hyde, Malmesbury and Muchelney, the Prior of Frampton and the Premonstratensian Abbot of Titchfield had at least one park on their west country estates (Cantor, 1983), monastic owners holding some eight or nine per cent of the regional total. There is little doubt that most of these were genuine deer parks. The involvement of clergy and monks in hunting was frowned upon by the church authorities, and venison in theory found no place upon the monastic table. The justification put forward by such institutions for owning parks was that they provided entertainment for important visitors, but it is evident that many abbots kept their own hawks and hounds and were not above indulging in the chase themselves. However, in some cases the passing of a park into monastic ownership may have led to the cessation of its original function: at Montacute the park enclosed by the Count of Mortain before 1100 was granted to the Cluniac priory in 1192, but is not mentioned in a survey of 1302–3 (Dunning 1974, 210, 216). An inquisition into the lands of the Abbot of Cerne in 1356 recorded an annual income of 6s.8d from the herbage of Symondsbury Park, but it contained no deer (Cantor and Wilson 1963, 151–2).

The secular nobility also owned numerous parks. When Edmund, Earl of Cornwall, died in 1300, his extensive estates contained some 35 parks, including two at Corsham and two at Mere in Wiltshire (*C.I.P.M.*, iii, no. 604, pp. 456–489; *Wilts I.P.M.*, i, 256, 263). John de Warenne, Earl of Surrey and Sussex, in 1347 held two parks in Charlton Horethorne, also Ley, Canford and Knighton Parks, all on Canford manor in Dorset (*C.I.P.M.*, ix, no. 54, pp. 47, 49) The Earls of Salisbury had parks at Donyatt, Knowle St Giles and Yarlington in Somerset and Swainston on the Isle of Wight. The properties of the great barons had less stability, as their lands were more liable to change through marriage, confiscation and other factors. Canford Park in Dorset, for example, belonged in succession to the Earl of Lincoln (1309), the Earl of Surrey and Sussex (1347) and the Duke of Somerset (1462–3) (Cantor and Wilson 1963, 142), while Alderholt Park was successively in the hands of the Earl of Gloucester (1315), the Earl of March (1398) and the Earl of Pembroke (1583) (Wilson 1974, 47–8). The majority of parks, however, were held by local lords with much smaller estates, particularly in the later Middle Ages as the threshold for park ownership crept down the social scale.

Size and Shape of Medieval Parks (Fig. 6.10)

By far the largest park in the region was the royal park at Clarendon, occupying 1,737 hectares in 1650 (Grant 1959, 429). A few other examples ranged between 350 and 500 hectares, such as Marshwood and Crekelade in Dorset (Wilson 1973, 76–9). The vast majority were of the order of 40–120 hectares. At the lower end of the scale there were some examples of ten hectares or less: Iwerne Courtenay Park in Dorset, for example, occupied only eight hectares in 1554 (Cantor and Wilson 1962, 147). The larger parks were clearly more economical in terms of maintenance costs per head of deer, and some authors see parks of twenty hectares or less primarily as status symbols (e.g. Rackham 1980, 195); yet even a very small park could, with careful management, contain a sizeable herd. Early this century the 3.4 hectares of Hatch Beauchamp park in Somerset, which had been much bigger in the Middle Ages, still supported forty head of fallow deer (Cox and Greswell 1911, 570). The smaller parks could at least have a significant practical role as live larders, if not as hunting preserves.

Many parks were enlarged during their lifespan, some of them on more than one occasion. In 1228 Henry III gave Jocelin, Bishop of Bath, six acres of pasture outside the southern limits of his Hampshire park of Dogmersfield for its enlargement (*C.Cl.R.* 1227–31, 23). At least three of the Bishop of Winchester's parks were enlarged during the fourteenth century (Roberts 1988, 69). Vastern Park near Wootton Bassett was extended by twenty hectares in 1267, by over 240 hectares in 1320, by about fifty hectares in 1363, and by a final addition of twenty-two hectares in the early fifteenth century, till it covered most of the parish north and west of the town (Crittall 1970, 189–190). The park at Minehead, only twenty hectares in extent in 1383, was enlarged by the Luttrells to thirty hectares in 1428, and was estimated at eighty hectares in 1551 (Lyte 1909, i, 159–60, ii, 344; Binding and Stevens 1977, 31, 44). The enlargement of parks, not unnaturally, often led to conflict. In 1516 the tenants of Rodney Stoke brought a case in Star Chamber against Sir John Rodney who, they claimed, had added part of their common pasture to his park, enclosed eighty hectares from the Royal Forest of Mendip, pulled down tenements and enclosed them within his park, blocked up the common road, and had then installed red deer in the park and killed the hounds of any of his tenants who tried to drive the deer off their crops. For his part, he claimed that the case against him had been brought out of malice by certain ill-disposed persons who had already broken down his park pale and attacked him with a pitchfork; he claimed that his deer did little harm, and that he was within his rights to enclose a park on his own ground, provided that he left sufficient common for his tenants (*Proc. Star Ch.*, 34, 73–5, 79).

The creation or enlargement of deer parks not infrequently interfered with the course of pre-existing roads.

In 1207, for example, Bishop Jocelin of Bath was permitted to enclose two parts of the king's highway within his park at Wells (Greswell 1905, 249). In 1386 Thomas West received pardon on payment of one mark for his father's action seven years earlier in enclosing within his park at Fonthill Gifford part of the highway from Marlborough to Shaftesbury without royal licence, on condition that he make a new road round the northern and western sides of the park (*C.P.R.* 1385–9, 242). The evidence of such diversions can often clearly be seen in the present landscape, as at Lytchett Matravers in Dorset, where the creation of the former park clearly cut across the line of the old road to Morden. They might also have a significant impact upon the local settlement pattern: Dunning (1981, 126) has pointed to the creation of Nether Stowey park in Somerset as a likely reason for the isolation and decline of the Domesday vill of Budley.

Archaeologically the most striking remains of deer parks are likely to be their boundary earthworks (Fig. 6.11). Deer are capable of leaping considerable obstacles, so the park fences needed to be up to 2–3m high, depending upon the slope of the ground, and needed to be well-maintained to prevent escapes. The maintenance of fencing was expensive. In older parks this was sometimes carried out by tenants as a labour service. In the early thirteenth century, for example, various tenants of Glastonbury Abbey had to put in so many days' work each year on repairing the ditch and palings of the abbot's park at Pilton, or had specific responsibility to keep in repair 2- to 4-perch lengths of the pale, the local perch being 16ft. or 4.9m (*Rent. & Custum.*, 7–8, 36–7, 45–7, 49, 148, 150–3, 157, 163). Tenants of the Bishop of Bath and Wells owed similar services for the maintenance of the park of Westbury-sub-Mendip in the same period (*C.Wells MSS*, i, 62, 78–9, 100, 104, 136, 144–5). In both cases the services were owed, not just by tenants in the immediate vicinity, but by the inhabitants of widely scattered villages up to 30km distant. Similar arrangements applied at Duntish Park in Dorset (Cantor and Wilson 1962, 147–9).

The classic form of deer-proof boundary consisted of cleft-oak palings set in a bank and fastened to a rail, with a ditch inside the bank to inhibit deer inside the park from leaping the fence. In 1289, for example, Queen Eleanor obtained a grant of twenty oaks from Selwood Forest in order to make palings to enclose her park at Queen Camel in Somerset (*C.Cl.R.* 1288–96, 3). In 1419–20 twenty-seven oaks and one aspen were felled in Seend Park (Wiltshire) to make palings (Chettle and Tillott 1953, 101). The costs of making such a boundary were considerable. The accounts of the Bishop of Winchester for 1252–3 record the costs of making the relatively modest boundary of the park at Bishop's Sutton: over £31 for digging twelve furlongs (2412m) of bank outside and ten furlongs (2010m) inside the park, representing nearly 6000 days' work, plus twenty carts with two men each fetching wood for the palings, a further ten carts bring-

ing timber, wages of two sawyers for three weeks preparing the timber, and wages of five carpenters for twelve weeks making two park gates and two deer-leaps (Roberts 1988, 69–70). Remains of the banks and ditches can still be seen in many west country parks: at King's Sombourne (Hampshire) the banks still remain up to 3.6m high in places, while the southern bank of Cerne Abbas Park (Dorset) still stands 2–3m high and 6m wide. Few examples have been examined by excavation, although a section of the Poundisford Park boundary in Somerset recorded in a water pipe trench revealed a severely truncated bank 6–8m wide and 0.8–1.2m high (Hawkes 1991).

However, massive boundary earthworks were by no means universal, and probably became less common in the later Middle Ages as costs of labour increased: in 1546 the pales of Melbury Sampford Park in Dorset were set in a strip only 0.6m broad (Cantor and Wilson 1963, 142). The natural contour of the ground and the fact that some parks were converted from enclosed woods also often resulted in the omission of the bank or ditch or both. Emparking licences sometimes permit lesser forms of boundary: Marshwood Park in west Somerset was enclosed partly by a ditch and hedge and partly by a paling fence in the mid-sixteenth century (Lyte 1909, i, 160), while ditch and hedge were specified in the licences for Chisbury Park in Wiltshire and Ashton Lyons in north Somerset (*C.Ch.R.*, ii, 1257–1300, 28; Greswell 1905, 261). In October 1254 the king ordered the removal of some of the palings of Clarendon Park and their replacement with a hedge (*C.L.R.*, iv, 1251–60, 180).

Deer-proof barriers were also needed to keep wild deer off islands of cultivated land in the forest, the effect being something like a park in reverse, with the ditch outside the bank. In 1256 Henry III gave Netley Abbey special licence to enclose 300 acres of land in the New Forest against the king's deer, confirmed in 1461 (*C.P.R.* 1461–67, 158).

Sometimes the pale was set back from the boundary of the property, leaving a narrow band, often about one perch (*c.* 5m) wide, known as a freeboard, which was used to give access for inspection and repair. In 1279 a strip 7.5 feet (2.3m) wide between the parks of Huish Episcopi and Drayton was the subject of a dispute between their respective owners, Bishop Burnell of Bath and the Abbot of Muchelney; this was resolved by an agreement that the strip was owned by the bishop, with rights of access to repair his park wall, but that the abbot's beasts would be permitted to graze there (*Much. Cart.*, no. 21, pp. 56–7). The 1687 map of Marshwood Park in west Somerset notes the owners' rights to a 'verge' of 18 feet (*c.* 5.5m) outside the park (Somerset C.R.O., DD/L1/10/35A), while the freeboard outside Marshwood Park in Dorset was the subject of a dispute as late as 1849 (Batten 1896, 86). Such a strip of ground can still be seen between the park bank and neighbouring woodland on the western boundary of Draycot Park in Wiltshire.

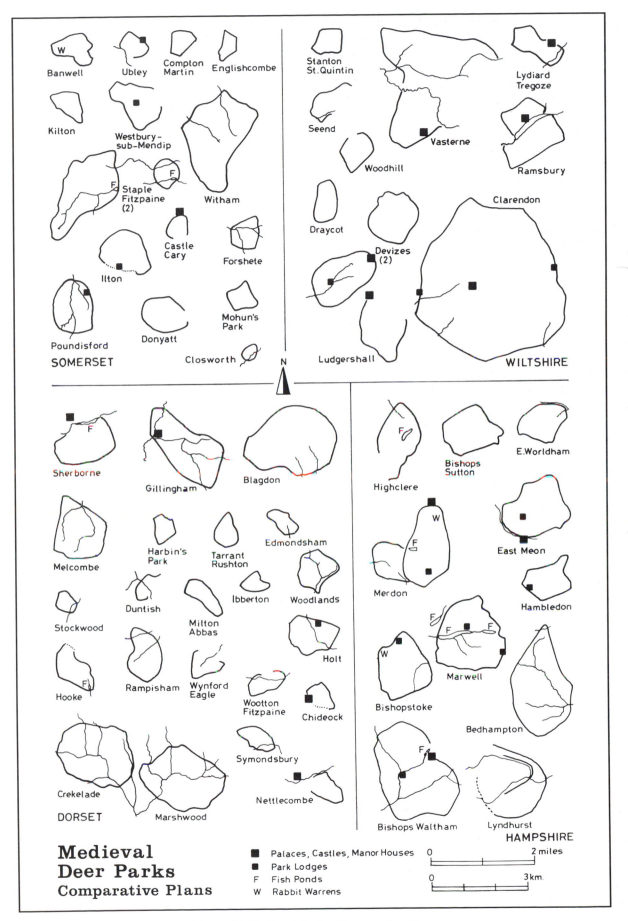

**Medieval
Deer Parks**
Comparative Plans

- ■ Palaces, Castles, Manor Houses
- ▪ Park Lodges
- F Fish Ponds
- W Rabbit Warrens

0   2 miles

0   3 km.

Fig. 6.10 Medieval Parks, Comparative Plans.

Fig. 6.11 *Staple Fitzpaine, Somerset: The Great Park, southern boundary. (Photo: James Bond)*

Park or Poundisford Park were first created, the lord had sufficient control at least to create an elliptical outline. Extensions to the original circuit are often betrayed by sharp changes of direction in the boundary, clearly seen at Merdon in Hampshire, where the Inner Park and Out Park of the Bishops of Winchester maintained a degree of separate identity (Roberts 1988, 76–7, 83). Examples with a more rectilinear outline are often lesser manorial parks, created at a later period and fitted into an existing framework of agricultural boundaries.

Deer-leaps allowed deer to enter a park from the surrounding countryside, but not to leave it again. They took a variety of forms, including an earthen ramp from the exterior up to the top of the wall, or a lowering in the paling fence coinciding with a widening and deepening of the interior ditch. Their possession was a special privilege for which royal permission was normally required. In 1324 the Bishop of Bath and Wells received confirmation of an earlier charter permitting him two deer-leaps in each of his parks of Evercreech and Wellington, both of which lay outside the royal forest (*C.Ch.R.* iii, 1300–26, 474). Deer-leaps were rarely permitted in private parks within or even near royal forests. When in 1267 Philip Bassett was permitted deer leaps in the old park of Vastern and the new park of Wootton Bassett, both within the bounds of Braden Forest, it was only for the term of his own life (*C.P.R.* 1266–72, 177). An interesting case is recorded in 1367, when William Montagu, Earl of Salisbury, was requested to take deer from Neroche Forest for the king's table, and during the hunt one buck escaped from the forest and entered Matthew Gurney's park at Curry Mallet, where there were two deerleaps. The forester followed it into the park to take it for the king, but was prevented from doing so by five local men, including the parson, who carried off the venison for their own use (Cox and Greswell 1911, 562–3).

The Management of Parks

Parks, if properly managed, were able to support large herds of deer, and produced venison far more efficiently than the forests. Shirley (1867) recommended two bucks and one doe to three acres of parkland, though in practice ratios of a half to two head per acre were commonly used. The numbers could be increased by a variety of means: reducing the woodland cover, improving the quality of the grass, bringing in supplementary feed, regular restocking with deer imported from elsewhere. While fallow deer were the normal parkland species, both red and roe deer were sometimes kept in parks (Shirley 1867, 230, 236). The species do not mix well, and this sometimes explains the existence of two parks on the same manor. In 1244 Henry III ordered the making of a smaller second park at Freemantle to keep the roe deer separately from the fallow (*C.L.R.*, ii, 1240–5, 220), while Leland records two parks at Nether Stowey for fallow and red deer (*Itin.*, i, 164).

Stone walls, already noted at Huish Episcopi, were a more ostentatious form of boundary, and they were particularly favoured by the crown and by episcopal and monastic owners. However, they were even more costly to build and maintain, and did not become at all common in the region until late in the Middle Ages. The expenses of the communar of Wells in 1448–9 included the hire of a labourer for three days and three waggonloads of stone to make two ropes (1 rope = 20 feet, *c.* 6m) of park wall at Westbury-sub-Mendip (*C.Wells MSS*, ii, 76). John Leland saw several park walls on his travels in the sixteenth century, including the two derelict parks of the Bishop and Prior outside Bath, both then with their stone walls ruinous and without any surviving deer (*Itin.*, v, 86).

The labour and expense involved in making and maintaining any sort of boundary meant that the optimum shape for the deer park was a perfect circle, thereby maximising the area of grazing within while minimising the length of boundary. While no examples actually achieved this ideal shape, it was possible for those laid out on the waste to approach it: for example, it is clear that when Devizes

The parks' primary purpose of raising deer was not incompatible with other forms of exploitation. Domestic livestock such as cattle and pigs could share the feed with the deer, provided that overgrazing did not occur, and income could therefore be obtained from agistments and pannage. In 1378 Rowcombe Park in Wiltshire was feeding fifty or more cattle (Crowley 1987, 228), while the bailiff's accounts for Hooke manor in Dorset in 1510–11 record an income of £4.12*s*.6*d* from agistments within the park (Cantor and Wilson 1964, 164–5). Elsewhere in Britain, notably at Chillingham in Northumberland and Chartley in Staffordshire, there are distinctive strains of white cattle thought to be descended from native wild herds which had become confined to parks by the thirteenth century. At Leigh Court in north Somerset a white or fawn breed claimed to be descended from a herd owned by the canons of St Augustine's Abbey in Bristol survived up to 1806. The beasts were so savage that the owner then had them all shot, exterminating the only known herd of wild park cattle known from south-west England (Shirley 1867, 99; Harting 1880, 239–240; Kirby 1974, 126). Part of the royal stud was maintained at various periods between the thirteenth and fifteenth centuries in Odiham Park and Vastern Park (Moger *et al.* 1911; Crittall 1970, 194).

Despite the demand for grazing, timber production from parks appears to have increased in importance during the thirteenth century. As the extent of unmanaged woodland diminished through clearance and as coppice management became characteristic of surviving woodlands, it was increasingly only under the wood-pasture regime of parks that very large trees could be found. Newton Park in North Petherton was the source of much timber granted away by the king: six *furcas* (? pairs of cruck blades) to Godfrey de Crocombe for building a barn in 1230 (*C.Cl.R.* 1227–31, 308); a total of seventy oaks to the sisters of the Order of St John at Minchin Buckland in 1234 and 1236 to help with the rebuilding of their house after its destruction by fire (*C.Cl.R.* 1231–4, 402; 1234–7, 282); a total of eighteen oaks to the Blackfriars of Ilchester in 1261 (*C.L.R.* v, 1260–67, 18, 48); three oaks for the townspeople of Somerton to repair their belfry in 1278; in the same year five oaks to the Greyfriars of Bridgwater towards the building of their dormitory (*C.Cl.R.* 1272–9, 451) Timber was also supplied for fine woodwork: two oaks in 1232 for choirstalls at Cleeve Abbey (*C.Cl.R.* 1231–4, 77), three oaks for making images for the abbey church of Glastonbury in 1250 (*C.Cl.R.* 1247–51, 312). Dead trees, windfallen wood and undergrowth provided fuel: in 1229, for example, the sisters of Minchin Buckland received a series of grants of dead wood, thorn, buckthorn and maple from Newton Park for this purpose (*C.Cl.R.* 1227–31, 166, 176, 211–12, 214), grants often repeated in later years. Similar grants of timber and wood could be documented from many other parks. Gillingham Park in Dorset provided sixty oaks in 1234 for the repair of the roof of the tower of Corfe Castle (*C.Cl.R.* 1231–4, 537). Melchet Park in Hampshire provided twenty oaks in 1277 to make laths (*latas*) for the queen's manor-house at Lyndhurst, and ten oaks in 1278 for repairing the church of Breamore Priory (*C.Cl.R.* 1272–9, 370, 452).

Vestiges of the ancient wood-pasture regime can still be identified in many former deer parks. Massive old pollard oaks with girths of 7m or more, such as survive in Mells Park in Somerset (Cox and Greswell 1911, 571) are particularly characteristic. Parkland trees were often pollarded at fifty to eighty–year intervals, a process which not only produced a regular crop of wood while allowing new shoots to grow out of range of grazing livestock, but also had the effect of prolonging the life of the tree, sometimes to a great age. Another distinctive feature is their richness in lichen species: 122 different epiphytic lichen taxa have been recorded in Mells Park, 123 in Lulworth Park (Dorset), 150 in Nettlecombe Park (Somerset), 161 in Longleat Park (Wiltshire) and no less than 213 species in Melbury Park (Dorset). By contrast, parks dominated by eighteenth- or nineteenth-century planting, such as Montacute or Orchardleigh, have fifty to sixty different species of lichens while an average coppice-wood may contain only forty or fifty species. Age of trees is not the only factor influencing the number of lichens found; range of habitat within the park and level of pollution are also important. However, if examination is restricted to thirty taxa known to be widely distributed throughout the country but restricted to 'ancient' woodlands, parks like Melbury still emerge with high totals, while parks more heavily modified by later post-medieval planting like Montacute and Orchardleigh, score much lower totals (Rose and Wolseley 1984).

While wood-pasture was the characteristic form of land use in early parks, it was not necessarily the only one. The Bishop of Winchester's Hampshire parks included pasture for horses, cattle and sheep, hay meadows, arable land, a vineyard and fishponds, in addition to woodland providing forage for pigs and producing timber and charcoal (Roberts 1988, 73–7). Since the early fourteenth century, when income from rents had been much reduced as a result of famine and plague, many landowners had been forced to reappraise the ways in which their estates were managed. The preservation of tracts of wood-pasture solely for deer may increasingly have seemed an unaffordable luxury, and more varied and flexible forms of land use were sought, which might include some pasture for fattening stock and even some arable (Stamper 1988, 146). Rackham (1980, 195) estimates that about half the parks of medieval England included some form of compartmentation, reserving some areas for pasture and others for woodland. In 1330–33 sales of underwood from coppices of 25–40 acres in Clarendon Park yielded around £20–35 per annum (Hoare 1837, 173–4). In late medieval parks this is sometimes implicit in the original licence, as in 1448 when William Carent was permitted to impark 80 acres of wood and

300 acres of land in Toomer and Henstridge (Somerset) (*C.Ch.R.*, vi, 1427–1516, 101). The surveys of some of the Glastonbury Abbey parks at the Dissolution imply that they were compartmented: Northwood Park contained 800 deer and 172 acres of wood felled and sold on a sixteen-year rotation, while Sharpham Park included 160 deer, pasture for horses, 80 acres of oak, ash and maple coppice felled on a fourteen-year rotation, and 200 timber oaks (*Mon. Angl.*, i, 10; Cox and Greswell 1911, 568). The 1588 map of Merdon Park shows the Out Park reserved as wood-pasture, while the Inner Park is compartmented into coppice, meadow, launde and rabbit-warren (Roberts 1988, 76–7).

Contrary to earlier opinions which viewed woodland plantations as an innovation of the sixteenth century, John Harvey has been able to document examples from a much earlier date, including two plantations of oak and nut trees on the estates of the Prior of St Swithun's, Winchester, in the thirteenth century, and a purchase of 700 young 'poplars' (possibly aspen rather than the native black poplar, which is a tree of open commons rather than woodlands) on the Bishop of Winchester's manor of Bishopstoke in 1327 (Harvey 1981, 13–16). Trees were sometimes planted in parks. The Bishop's pipe roll of 1210–11 records the expenditure of 2*s* on wages for 12 weeks' work in planting brook willows in Taunton Park (Harvey 1981, 72).

Deer needed water, and watercourses were often diverted to feed fishponds within the park. In 1250 Henry III, temporarily holding the manor of Taunton after the death of Bishop Peter des Roches, ordered forty bream and ten pike from the ponds in its park for his Christmas feast at Winchester (*C.Cl.R.* 1247–51, 381). Many other examples are documented, for example at Lyndhurst Park in the New Forest (Brown *et al.* 1963, ii, 984), and in Dunster Park (Lyte 1909, i, 97). The earthwork remains of fishponds can be seen in many other parks, for example at Staple Fitzpaine in Somerset and at Zeals in Wiltshire.

What part did parks play in the medieval economy? There are two schools of thought. On the one hand, the maintenance of parks – salaries of parkers, purchase of winter feed, repairs to boundaries and lodges – tended to be costly, whereas the income from sales of timber, wood and pasture were intermittent. The welfare of the deer took precedence over the exploitation of the park in other ways, yet even in aristocratic households venison represented less than ten per cent of the total quantity of meat consumed. Many parks had non-resident owners who can only have enjoyed hunting there on an occasional basis, and there seems to have been no attempt to produce venison commercially for the open market. The numerous commissions of oyer and terminer concerning park-breaking recorded in the Patent Rolls encourage the suspicion that the greatest benefit was derived by poachers. This has led many authors to dismiss parks as mere status symbols, an expensive luxury typifying the philosophy of conspicuous consumption (Platt 1978, 47; Stamper 1988, 146).

This view has been challenged by Birrell (1992), who has argued that, far from locking up land unprofitably, deer parks were fully integrated with other agricultural and woodland activities, that considerable care and skill was lavished upon the active farming of deer, that they produced venison efficiently in a way which was quite compatible with other forms of land use, and that owners derived considerable benefits from them.

There is, in fact, little doubt that deer parks were managed more efficiently and more flexibly as the Middle Ages progressed. However, the extent to which they made a recognised aesthetic contribution to the landscape has also probably been underestimated. We tend to think of conscious landscape design as a new idea of the eighteenth century, and fail to realise how much the medieval park with its great trees and open glades could have been valued for its scenic qualities in the Middle Ages. Taken in combination with fishponds, plantations, orchards and gardens, it is becoming increasingly evident that deer parks did have an ornamental function as well as a practical and prestige value. In cases where the park lodge itself developed as an important residence, they begin to anticipate the role of the Georgian park in providing a setting for the great house.

Warrens and Coneygres

As defined earlier, the term 'warren' implied the right held by a lord to hunt certain small game on his own estates, and the acquisition of warren rights was sometimes, though not always a prelude to emparking. The Bishops of Bath and Wells had an important warren at North Curry from 1280 (*C. Wells MSS*, i, 313; *C.Ch.R.*, ii, 1257–1300, 219), and on one occasion in the late fourteenth century a claim was made that 2000 hares, 10,000 rabbits, 1000 pheasants and 1000 partridges as well as an unspecified quantity of fish had been poached from here by persons unknown (Greswell, 1905, 250). Beasts and fowl of the warren were frequently by-products of deer parks: when the see of Winchester was vacant after the death of Bishop Peter des Roches, and its properties temporarily in the hands of Henry III, the king sent an order for as many pheasants, partridges, 'witecocks', plovers, larks and other game as could be despatched from the manor of Taunton for his Christmas feast at Winchester (*C.Cl.R.*, 1247–51, 385). Four cranes were also ordered (*ibid.*, 387) - probably the true crane (*Grus grus grus* L.), which was still relatively common in England and was regarded as a great delicacy, rather than the heron.

The hare was the principal beast of the warren, and in the royal warren of Somerton it uniquely acquired the protection of Forest Law; verderers' presentments at the 1257 Forest Eyre include a case where four hares had been killed there. The bounds of Somerton Warren are recited in a perambulation of the time of Edward I, just as if it were a normal royal forest (Cox and Greswell 1911, 552–3). Warrens devoted specifically to hares are also occasionally recorded elsewhere: at Everleigh, in part of the Forest of Chute which had been disafforested by 1300, the hare warren extended for nearly 5km across the south-western part of the manor in the fifteenth century, at the opposite end from the deer park and rabbit warren (Crittall 1980, 139).

Unlike hares, which are a species native to Britain, rabbits were almost certainly introduced after the Norman Conquest. While small quantities of rabbit bones have been recorded from a number of Roman sites, these have not been securely stratified and appear to be a result of intrusive burrowing at a later date. One perambulation, attached to a charter with a nominal date of AD 936, describing the bounds of Marksbury in Somerset, appears to imply the presence of rabbits by its mention of a landmark '...*on Conigrave*'; but the extant copy of the survey may be as late as the fourteenth century, and it does not provide secure evidence for the pre-Conquest period. On balance there is still no reliable evidence for the presence of rabbits before the late eleventh or twelfth century (Veale 1957; Sheail 1971; Bond 1988).

Rabbits are first mentioned in the documentary record on the offshore islands of south-western Britain. The earliest known reference occurs in a charter of 1176, whereby the Abbot of Tavistock successfully claimed a tithe of rabbits on the Scilly Isles (*Tavist. Ch.*, xxxiii, 365). Some time between 1183 and 1219 the tenant of Lundy was authorised to take 50 conies per annum (Veale 1957, 86), and an inquisition of 1274 recorded the export of 2000 skins a year from Lundy to the mainland, fetching £5.10s.0d, or 5s.6d per hundred skins, though the carcasses were not sold - probably because they had gone bad before reaching the market (Sheail 1972, 70; Lever 1979, 69). Rabbits appear to have been settled on Steep Holm in the Bristol Channel by the Berkeleys, who were leasing the island after the late thirteenth century (Rendell and Rendell 1993, 60–64). By 1492 there was also a rabbit-warren on neighbouring Flat Holm (Matheson 1941, 373).

Rabbits were a particularly important commodity on the Isle of Wight. The Bishops of Winchester had warrens at Swainston, first recorded in 1219–20, from which they received an annual income of 6s.8d by the end of the thirteenth century (Roberts 1988, 77). The accounts of the Earl of Devon's manor of Bowcombe in Carisbrooke in 1225 record the wages of the warrener and receipts from the sale of 200 rabbit skins (Hockey 1982, 206). In 1292 Christchurch Priory obtained the tithe of rabbits from the manor of Thorley (Hockey 1982, 207). Quarr Abbey had warrens on its estates at Arreton, Combley, Newnham, Shalcombe, Redway and Claybrook, which were regularly leased out in the fifteenth and early sixteenth centuries (Hockey 1970, 164, 177–8, 189, 194; Hockey 1982, 208–9). References in the Liberate Rolls

show the king's provisioners taking full advantage of the island's resources when opportunity offered. During the vacancy of the see of Winchester in 1243 the king ordered 100 rabbits to be despatched to Westminster from the bishop's estates on the Isle of Wight, together with 40 from Meredon Warren and 40 from Bitterne (*C.L.R.*, ii, 1240–5, 196). Similarly in 1248 the keeper of the lands of the recently-deceased Earl of Devon was ordered to send 100 rabbits to Westminster for the king's Christmas feast (*C.L.R.*, iii, 1245–51, 215). Leases of the late fourteenth and fifteenth centuries frequently mention rights to take rabbits (Hockey 1982, 208–10).

Rabbits were an attractive proposition for many landowners. They were valued for their flesh and their fur, and trade in both began early in the Middle Ages, though it was not until the early fifteenth century that records of the Dorset ports such as Poole began to produce evidence of any significant export of skins and furs (Sheail 1971, 69). They could be raised on a wide variety of terrain, including calcareous downland, acid upland moors, and above all, poor sandy soil which was fit for little else. However, throughout the early Middle Ages their viability remained precarious, and they remained largely restricted to artificial coneygres where they were carefully tended by warreners who grew gorse, sow-thistles, dandelions, groundsel and parsley for feed.

The earliest securely stratified deposits of rabbit bones in the west of England occur in twelfth-century levels in Exeter (Maltby 1979, 61). However, evidence for the raising of rabbits on the mainland, as opposed to their consumption, remains slender before the end of the twelfth century. From the middle of the thirteenth century the quantity of references to coneygres increases. In 1236–7 the Bishop of Winchester attempted to transfer rabbits from his Bitterne warren to Bishopstoke Park, though this may not immediately have been successful (Roberts 1988, 77). Just like deer, rabbits were sometimes transported considerable distances across country to establish new warrens: in 1241 the keepers of the bishopric of Winchester were required to take 100 live rabbits to the Bishop of Hereford's manor of Sugwas (*C.L.R.*, i, 1240–45, 54). Rabbit meat increasingly figured at banquets: in 1240 the lands of the bishopric of Winchester had to supply 100 rabbits for the king's Christmas feast, and in the following year the sheriff of Hampshire had to supply 100; the bishop's three warrens of Meredon, Bitterne and Swainston again provided 180 rabbits in 1243 (*C.L.R.*, i, 1240–45, 196; Roberts 1988, 77).

Rabbits continued to command a high price throughout the thirteenth century, but they began to come down in price during the later Middle Ages as the number of warrens increased and individual warrens became more efficiently managed. The park at Everleigh contained a rabbit warren valued at 60s in 1297 (*Wilts I.P.M.*, i, 217–8), but by the 1360s its value had declined to 40s (*Wilts I.P.M.*, ii, 288, 305). During the fourteenth century rabbit numbers continued to increase, and more warrens were developed outside parks. In 1361–2 one man and his horse made eighteen journeys from Overton Warren to the Bishop of Winchester's house at Farnham carrying 632 rabbits, while in 1400–1, 322 rabbits from Longwood Warren were sent to Wolvesey Palace for St Giles's Fair (Roberts 1988, 77–8). Records of poaching became increasingly common, although the plaintiff's case sometimes inflated the numbers - the complaint mentioned above concerning the theft of 10,000 rabbits from the North Curry warren sounds distinctly suspect. The rabbit warrens within Clarendon Forest were of special value, being frequently mentioned in the accounts through the fourteenth and fifteenth centuries, and a Bohemian traveller named Schasek saw 'rabbits and hares without number' in Clarendon Park in 1465 (Lever 1979, 73). In 1495 the revenue assigned to the king's household included £100 received from the farmer of the conies in Clarendon (Hoare 1837, 129; Cox 1905, 37, 316–7). The warrens of Aldbourne Chase yielded around £40 per annum from sales of rabbits or from leases between 1390 and 1430, sometimes amounting to half the total profits from the demesne of Aldbourne manor. In 1434 nearly 1000 rabbits, valued at £14, were supplied to the royal household, and 66 couples sold to other purchasers; but exceptionally hard winters in the following two years virtually wiped out the rabbit population (Freeman 1983, 78; Scott 1959, 18).

Rabbit bones have been reported from a number of medieval sites around the region. The archaeozoological evidence bears out the view that, as an introduced species, the rabbit did not become sufficiently well-established to contribute much to the general diet before the late Middle Ages. In Exeter, despite the early appearance of the rabbit in the twelfth century, it did not begin to surpass the hare as a regular souce of food before the sixteenth century, and even then it remained a luxury item (Maltby 1979, 61). At Okehampton Castle rabbit bones do not appear before the fourteenth century (Maltby 1982). The proportion of both rabbit and hare bones increases significantly in the later medieval phases of the inner bailey at Portchester Castle, but even then made up only a small part of the diet (Grant 1985, 247–8).

By the later Middle Ages depictions of rabbits in illustrative sources were becoming more common, reflecting their increasing familiarity in the countryside. The ground of the memorial brass to Bishop Robert Wyville (1330–75) in Salisbury Cathedral includes several rabbits, possibly in commemoration of the bishop's recovery of Bere Chase in Dorset from the Earl of Salisbury. Rabbits also figure on several late medieval church bench ends, notably at Bishop's Lydeard and Lyng in Somerset.

The most characteristic archaeological feature of the coneygre is the so-called 'pillow-mound', more widely known in the west country by the name 'rabbit buries' (see Fig. 6.12). Examples are particularly widespread on Dartmoor (Linehan 1966), the Mendip Hills (e.g. Russett 1986) and the chalk downs. Pillow-mounds frequently

occur in groups, but they also occur singly: there is a particularly prominent example at Bruton in Somerset (Fig. 6.13). They vary considerably in form: those within the hill-fort of Dolebury in Somerset are unusually long (Hollinrake and Hollinrake 1986), while less than 5km to the west there is a cruciform example in Banwell Park (Iles 1984, 57). Few examples can be dated precisely, but probably only a minority of them are medieval. Medieval illustrations show that the rabbits were normally taken from the burrows by means of ferrets and nets – the domestic ferret, like the rabbit itself, seems likely to be a medieval introduction into England (Coy and Maltby 1987, 217). In 1405–6 accounts of Bishop's Sutton manor in Hampshire record the purchase of a large net called a 'haye' and twelve purse nets for catching rabbits (Roberts 1988, 77–8). Coneygres were sometimes enclosed, in an attempt to prevent escapes. In 1280 the abbot of Keynsham acquired a licence to enclose with a stone wall a pasture called 'Wynterleye' within Filwood Chase, and to convert it to a rabbit warren (*C.P.R.* 1272–81, 371).

Occasionally the remains of the warrener's isolated dwelling may also be seen. At Dolebury the footings of a small rectangular stone building survive within a small circular garden enclosure in the midst of the warren (Hollinrake and Hollinrake 1986) (Fig. 6.14). Excavations on Steep Holm have shown that the buildings of the Augustinian priory, abandoned in 1265, were repaired and adapted in the following century to provide accommodation for Lord Maurice Berkeley's warreners. Fourteenth and fifteenth century midden deposits associated with this building contained numerous rabbit bones (Rendell and Rendell 1993, 60–63).

Despite attempts to confine them, rabbits not infrequently escaped from the warrens, and from the thirteenth century onwards there are occasional complaints about their destructiveness from neighbouring proprietors. A charter of Reginald de Mohun to the burgesses of Dunster in *c.* 1250 permitted anyone who found rabbits causing damage to kill them (Ballard and Tait 1923, 107), while in 1378 the abbess of Lacock received confirmation of an allowance of four dozen coneys a year from Aldbourne Warren in compensation for the damage done to her lands adjoining (*Lacock Chart.*, no. 306, p. 78). However, the number of rabbits in the wild was kept firmly in check, partly by the much greater number of natural predators (foxes, badgers, stoats, weasels, polecats, martens, rats, buzzards, owls) and partly by the lack of winter feed. In contrast to the mainland, escaped rabbits fared somewhat better on the Isle of Wight, since there were no foxes on the island before 1845 (Bonnett 1912, 535). Elsewhere, it was generally not until the eighteenth and nineteenth centuries that the widespread introduction of fodder crops in place of winter fallows, coupled with the onslaught upon the rabbit's predators by gamekeepers becoming interested in rearing pheasants, first allowed rabbits to survive in large numbers in the wild; and it was only then that the rabbit ceased to be

Fig. 6.12 *Ashey Down, Isle of Wight: pillow mound. (Photo: James Bond)*

Fig. 6.13 *Bruton Priory, Somerset: pillow mound. (Photo: James Bond)*

Fig. 6.14 *Dolebury Warren, Somerset: remains of warrener's lodge and garden enclosure. (Photo: James Bond)*

regarded as a carefully cossetted resource and became instead an over-prolific pest.

Amongst the commonly-mentioned wildfowl of the warren, the woodcock and the common or grey partridge are both native species. However, the common pheasant (*Phasianus colchicus*), originally from the Caucasus region, is another exotic which made its first appearance in Britain in the early Middle Ages. It may have been brought from Sicily by the Normans and could have been introduced from the continent in the time of Edward the Confessor. The earliest mentions from the west country, in the records of the Benedictine abbeys of Amesbury and Malmesbury, around 1100, are suspect, but it is recorded with increasing frequency after the later twelfth century, and soon seems to have become naturalised as a feral breeding bird. It is sometimes mentioned in poaching cases, as in that at North Curry described above. Unlike deer, it sometimes appeared on the open market, though it was very expensive; however, in contrast to both deer and rabbit, there seems no evidence in the Middle Ages for any systematic breeding and management of pheasants (Lever 1977, 336; Rackham 1986, 50).

Palaces in Royal Forests, Hunting-Lodges and Park Lodges

Most of the royal forests and some of the more important

parks included related domestic buildings, and at their most elaborate these ranked as full-scale palaces. At least one of the royal palaces in the region shows clear continuity from a pre-Conquest site. Cheddar had been held by the Crown since the ninth century and, as the near-fatal incident involving King Edmund mentioned earlier demonstrates, it provided a base for hunting in the Anglo-Saxon period. After the Conquest it continued to serve as a royal residence within Mendip Forest. Excavations in the early 1960s revealed a long ninth-century timber hall with associated buildings, enclosures and drains. This was replaced in the tenth century by a new timber hall with new agricultural buildings and a small stone chapel, implying a stronger royal interest in the site. This hall and chapel were reconstructed in the late tenth or early eleventh century. Then, in the early twelfth century, a much grander new aisled hall was added to the east with some further reconstruction of the older hall. This phase represents the palace complex at its most elaborate: Henry I is known to have stayed here with his court on at least two occasions, in 1121 and 1130. The older western hall was then abandoned, and the eastern hall rebuilt on a smaller scale in 1209–11 at a cost of £40, using timber imported from Wales. This may represent a diminution of function under King John, from palace to hunting-lodge. After 1213 John was forced to surrender the manor, and it came into the hands of Bishop Jocelin of Bath.

The hall and chapel were rebuilt again under episcopal ownership in the later thirteenth century, but the chapel was the only building to survive beyond the fourteenth century. Curiously, despite the location of the palace within Mendip Forest, the bone evidence indicates that venison formed a very limited proportion of the diet on the site, cattle being the principal livestock represented, followed by sheep and pig (Rahtz 1979).

Gillingham in Dorset had also been a royal estate before the Conquest, though there is no evidence of a royal residence here before the late eleventh century, when a lodge was begun on the western margins of the park. King John, who seems to have been particularly fond of hunting in the west country, undertook considerable building activity there between 1199 and 1211, including the construction of a bank and ditch around the completed buildings in 1211. Henry III rebuilt the old chapel and added a new one for the queen in 1249–52, also ordering the building of a new wardrobe, kitchen, almonry and chamber for the chaplains. These buildings were to be enclosed within a rubble wall in 1252, but this seems not to have been built, and instead in 1260 a hedge was planted; this was replaced in its turn by a fence of oak palings 3m–3.5m high in 1269–70. Intermittent repairs are recorded through to the middle of the fourteenth century, but in 1369 Edward III ordered the demolition of the buildings and the sale of the lead, stone and timber (Brown *et al.* 1963, ii, 944–6). The site is now represented by a prominent rectangular moated earthwork known as the King's Court, on the eastern outskirts of the town. The moat island measures about 90m by 50m, with an internal bank, and the moat itself is up to 18m wide and 1.5m deep, with external banks on the downslope side. The original entrance was at the southwest corner, facing the Gillingham-Shaftesbury road, where there are traces of possible gate towers (RCHME 1962, 51–2).

By far the most important of the royal residences in the region was Clarendon. Both documentary and archaeological evidence point to some sort of building complex here in the Norman period. It became a favourite residence of Henry II, and he enlarged the Norman huntinglodge into a palace, which included a great aisled hall built of flint with stone dressings on the north side of the courtyard, a chamber to the east, and a wine-cellar further east dug into the solid rock; by 1178–9 there was also a chapel, the site of which is still unidentified. Henry III also stayed there, and there were numerous additions during his reign. The hall was altered, with new gothic windows, a new porch was added on the south, and a new kitchen, larder and salsary on the north. A series of new private chambers was built east of the hall. The winecellar was doubled in length. The remaining sides of the courtyard were taken up by a rambling series of rooms for Prince Edward, chambers for various knights and chaplains, rooms for the baliff of the manor, and the almonry, bakery, napery, chancellery, toolshed, stables and priv-

ies. Both the documentary record and the evidence from excavation point to Clarendon being amongst the most magnificent of Henry III's country palaces, rivalled only by Woodstock and Guildford. The palace continued in regular use throughout the fourteenth and fifteenth centuries, and there are many records of repairs, though few major alterations took place (Brown *et al.* 1963, ii, 910–18; Borenius and Charlton 1936; James and Robinson 1988). Clarendon was the last royal palace to survive in the west country, as the resources of the Crown contracted and the distribution of royal houses became more concentrated around the fringes of London.

Of the smaller hunting lodges, little is known of those built by the Norman kings, but the establishment of the Angevin dynasty marked the beginning of a proliferation of forest and park lodges on the royal estates. The hunting-lodge at Freemantle in Hampshire was begun in 1180–83 under Henry II, and was frequently visited by King John. After a period of neglect in the early thirteenth century, a new hall, chapel, chambers, tower, cellar, kitchen and stables were built in 1251–6. Freemantle was alienated by Edward I in 1276 and the buildings dismantled, but it reverted to the crown ten years later, and by the later fourteenth century a new lodge consisting of several tiled and thatched buildings had appeared (Brown *et al.* 1963, ii, 940–1). Henry II also had a lodge in the deer-park at Wolverton between Pamber and Freemantle Forests, another at Tidgrove in Freemantle Forest, and another at Hurstbourne in the Forest of Chute; these all seem to have been abandoned by the end of the twelfth century (Brown *et al.* 1963, ii, 963, 1005, 1009).

King John's predelection for hunting in the region is reflected by the number of sites and buildings within the forest districts to which his name is attached, though the authenticity of many of these associations is suspect. Nonetheless, he did have an important hunting-lodge in the New Forest at Beaulieu until 1204, when he gave it to the community of Cistercian monks transferred from Faringdon in Berkshire. In its place he made use of a building in Romsey, but this in its turn was granted by his successor to the Abbess of Romsey in 1221, either for use as, or to provide materials for, her infirmary. The stone and flint house now known as 'King John's Hunting Box' in Romsey is a first-floor hall which appears to date from *c.* 1230–40, though it may contain the skeleton of an earlier structure disguised by alterations carried out by the Abbess (Wood 1950, 24–26). Subsequently there seems to have been no royal lodge maintained in the New Forest until the later thirteenth century (Brown *et al.* 1963, ii, 922). In Dorset a hunting-lodge at Cranborne came into the king's hands through his marriage with Isabel de Clare, co-heir to the Earldom of Gloucester, and in 1207–8 it was much enlarged (Brown *et al.* 1963, ii, 922). King John also built a house at Bere Regis in 1201–4, which included a chamber, chapel and kitchen, and used it on his frequent visits to hunt in the Forest of Bere. Subsequently, however, it fell into disuse, and its exact site is unknown (Brown *et al*. 1963, ii, 900). In 1205 John obtained the castle of Powerstock from Robert of Newburgh, and this was occasionally used by the crown until Edward I released it back into private hands (Brown *et al*. 1963, ii, 987–8). Brewcombe Lodge in Selwood was also reputedly used by King John; the site has produced an ancient key (Phelps 1839, i, 231–2, Plate V). The medieval building known as 'King John's Lodge' at Tollard Royal in Cranborne Chase consists of a first-floor hall with a ruined tower at the south-western angle. It appears to be later than John's time, and was probably built around 1240–50 by the Lucys, tenants of the Earls of Gloucester (Wood 1950, 96–7). 'King John's Hunting Lodge' in Axbridge (Somerset) is a late medieval town house with no known royal connection.

The double ringwork castle of Ludgershall in the Forest of Chute, first built during the Anarchy and refortified by Henry II, was converted to a hunting-lodge by Henry III. During his reign considerable expenditure upon the improvement of the royal apartments is recorded, including the wainscotting of the king's and queen's chambers in 1234–5 and 1241–2, the building of a new hall with buttery and pantry in 1244–5, the rebuilding of the kitchen and salsary in 1250, and the rebuilding of the stables in 1261. Three separate chapels are documented (Brown *et al*. 1963, ii, 729–731). Excavation has revealed a complex sequence of defensive and domestic timber and stone buildings with occupation from the eleventh century to the early Tudor period. Deer bones have come from a rubbish-pit (interim reports in *Med. Archaeol*., Vols 9 (1965) – 14 (1970) and 16 (1972)).

Edward I had a hunting-lodge built in Woolmer Forest in 1284–5. It consisted of a timber-framed hall and kitchen roofed with shingles, and a stone-built chamber above an undercroft. Regular repairs are recorded up to the end of the fourteenth century, but then no more is heard of it (Brown *et al*. 1963, ii, 1017–18).

After Edward III had retrieved custody of the New Forest from Queen Philippa in 1358, he began the construction of an important group of royal residences and hunting-lodges there, comparable with the group in Windsor Forest and Park. The old manor-houses of Lyndhurst and Brockenhurst were rebuilt, and four new lodges built in or near Lyndhurst Park, each timber-framed and plastered, with roofs of Purbeck and Cornish slate, each including a kitchen, and enclosed with a ditch. The most important of these was Hatheburgh, within Lyndhurst Park, which included a great gate and postern, a great chamber, a chapel, and a long range containing the kitchen, larder, granary and stables. Most of the New Forest lodges were still maintained in repair into the fifteenth century (Brown *et al*. 1963, ii, 983–6).

Lodge Farm at Badbury, on the southern edge of Cranborne Chase, is a stone-built hunting-lodge erected in the late fourteenth or early fifteenth century over the causewayed entrance of an older ditched and pallisaded deer park boundary. There is a record of two locks and

keys purchased for the park gate and lodge door here in 1391–2. Samples from the floor of the lower southern room revealed a high concentration of chloride salts, probably due to the use of the room for curing meat (Keen and Papworth 1987, 135; Papworth 1989, 112–4). Other lodges are recorded in the royal forests in the fifteenth century, including Groveley, Buckholt and Melchet, but little is known of them. Groveley Lodge is shown on a plan of 1589 as a small T-shaped building within a rectangular pasture enclosed by a paling fence (Crawford 1954, 193). A lodge in the Finkley bailiwick of Chute Forest was extensively repaired early in the reign of Henry VII, including purchase of 7000 shingles for the roof at 20*s* and 500 shingle nails at 8*d* (Cox 1905, 328).

There is a distinction between those hunting lodges, which were used on appropriate occasions by the king or lord, and the smaller forest and park lodges which provided domestic accommodation or served as temporary bases for officals charged with the management of the deer and their protection against poachers. The Black Prince required his Dartmoor foresters to 'stay continually on the moor while the does are fawning and fawns are tender' (*B.P.R*., ii, 71), and lodges were provided for the keepers during the 'fence month' (the fortnight either side of Midsummer Day). The parker or keeper, as a relatively minor manorial official, rarely had a very elaborate dwelling. Edward III built a couple of new lodges for keepers in the royal parks: at Clarendon he provided a hall with two chambers, a garderobe, cellar, pantry, kitchen, larder and stable to serve as a residence for the keeper (Brown *et al*. 1963, ii, 917). When he acquired the manor of East Worldham near Wolmer Forest in 1374, he enlarged the park and also built a new lodge there (*C.P.R*., 1374–7, 183–4; Brown *et al*., 1963, ii, 929).

Many such lodges were built in private parks, usually sited either at the entrance or in the centre of the park or on the highest point within it, wherever it would provide the most effective safeguard against poachers. At Bishop's Sutton the parker's lodge in 1355–6 contained only two rooms, set within a small hedged enclosure. At East Meon the lodge consisted simply of a hall and chamber with a stable in 1376–7 (Roberts 1988, 77). The keeper's lodge in Devizes park was moated, and in *c*. 1543 included four chambers, a parlour, buttery and kitchen alongside a stable and dairy house (Pugh 1975, 246). The remains of park lodges can sometimes be identified as moated earthworks, as at Merifield and Forshete in Somerset (Fig. 6.15).

Parker's lodges could themselves be taken over by the lord to become elaborated into more sumptuous residences. In the fourteenth century Ralph, Bishop of Bath and Wells, built a palace within the park at Evercreech (Hembry 1967, 22). Similarly Abbot Beere of Glastonbury rebuilt the lodges of Sharpham and Norwood Parks and used them as country residences (Leland, *Itin*. i, 290; Phelps 1839, i, 560–1). Shortly after Poundisford Park was leased out by the Bishop of Winchester in 1534, the

Fig. 6.15 *Forshete Park, Brewham, Somerset: The moated park lodge site, aerial view. (Photo: Mick Aston)*

keeper's lodge there appears to have been rebuilt on a grander scale by one of the lessees, a Taunton merchant named Roger Hill (Vivian-Neal and Gray 1940, 78).

Several other types of buildings associated with forests and deer parks are recorded. Prisons for the confinement of forest offenders are documented at a number of royal castles and lodges, including Lyndhurst in the New Forest and Clarendon. There were kennels for hunting dogs at Woolmer, enclosed with high palings in 1336 and repaired in 1364 (Brown *et al.* 1963, ii, 1018). Sheds for the shelter of hay and browsewood were often attached to park lodges: repairs to 'a certain long house for storing hay' are recorded at Woolmer in 1387 (Brown *et al.* 1963, 1018). Mews for hawks are recorded at Clarendon in 1156–8 and 1186 (Brown *et al.* 1963, ii, 911; James and Robinson 1988, 4) and at Bere Regis in 1201–4 (Brown *et al.* 1963, ii, 900). In 1181–2 Henry II bought a house outside Winchester's Westgate which he converted to a mews for his falcons; this use continued until about 1250 (Brown *et al.* 1963, ii, 1006). King John was importing Norwegian gerfalcons for use at Clarendon (James and Robinson 188, 8). The structural details of these minor park and forest buildings still await archaeological investigation, but there is some reflection in the archaeozoological record. At Portchester Castle there is a significant increase in the quantity of dog remains after the Conquest, including bones of some large dogs which may have been bred for hunting (Grant 1977, 216, 232;

Grant 1985, 248, 255). Bones of goshawks and sparrowhawks have also been recorded from twelfth and thirteenth century levels in the outer bailey of Portchester Castle (Eastham 1977, 234), while medieval pits in Ilchester contained remains of goshawk, sparrowhawk and peregrine falcon (Levitan 1982, 280–1). Unfortunately it is not possible to distinguish the bones of captive birds from the wild species, but whereas sparrowhawk and peregrine falcon appear to be native, the goshawk may have been introduced from continental Europe by falconers (Lever 1979, 18–19).

Footnote

The preparation of this paper has suffered severe disruption through unexpected and prolonged illness and other difficulties outside my control, and as a result I have not been able to revise my first draft as thoroughly as I would have wished, nor had opportunity to edit it down to a more manageable length. In the interests of comprehensive coverage within the volume, the editors have been prepared to accept it 'warts and all', and I am grateful to them for their tolerance of its excessive length and late delivery. However, I would like to offer my apologies to readers for all errors and misjudgements surviving in the paper, some of which might have been eliminated by further revision. The selection and presentation of data on the accompanying maps in particular required more careful consideration than was possible in the circumstances, and they should therefore be regarded as provisional rather than definitive.

Appendix 6.1: Forest Boundary Perambulations (for sources see references at end of paper)

	1218/19	1225	1227–32	temp. Henry III	1277–80
DORSET Bere Regis	—	—	—	—	—
Blackmore	Hutchins, 1861–73, iv, 516–7	—	—	(1247) Hutchins, 1861–73, iv, 79	—
Cranborne Chase	(1220)	—	—	(1245)	(1280) Hutchins, 1861–73, ii, 149; Smart, 1841, 170, 285–9; Dayrell-Reed, 1932
Gillingham	Hutchins, 1861–73, iii, 662–3	—	—	—	—
Powerstock	—	—	—	—	—
Purbeck	—	—	—	—	—
HAMPSHIRE Alice Holt	—	—	—	(1269)	—
Bagshot	—	—	—	—	—
Bere Ashley	—	—	—	—	—
Bere Portchester	—	—	—	(pre-1226)	—
Buckholt	—	—	—	—	—
Chute	—	—	—	(pre-1241)	—
Digerley	—	—	—	(pre-1241)	—
Eversley	—	—	—	—	—
Finkley	—	—	—	(pre-1241)	—
Freemantle	—	—	—	—	—
New Forest	Stagg, 1974	—	—	—	(1280) Wise, 1863, 40; Moens, 1903; New For.Doc. i, no. 196
Pamber	—	—	—	—	—
Woolmer	—	—	—	(1269)	—
SOMERSET Exmoor	MacDermot, 1911, 116–120	—	—	—	MacDermot, 1911, 129–131
Mendip	Gough, 1930	—	—	—	Gough, 1930
Neroche	—	—	—	—	—
North Petherton	—	—	—	—	—
Selwood	Chart.Glaston. i, 177	—	—	—	—
Somerton Warren	—	—	—	—	Cox & Greswell, 1911, 552
WILTSHIRE Braden	—	Grant, 1959, 444	(1228) Akerman, 1857, App. 1, 310–11; Grant, 1959, 444	—	Grant, 1959, 444
Chippenham	—	—	(1228) Grant, 1959, 446	—	—
Chute	—	—	—	Grant, 1959, 452–3	—
Clarendon	—	—	—	—	—
Groveley	Grant, 1959, 456–7	—	—	—	Hoare, 1822–45, iv, 184–90; Grant, 1959, 456–7
Melchet	—	—	—	—	Hoare, 1822–45, v, 77
Melksham	—	—	—	—	—
Savernake	—	—	(1228) Grant, 1959, 448–51	(1238x1252, 1244) Grant, 1959, 448; (1259) Brentnall, 1942	(1280) Jackson, 1879
Selwood	—	—	(1228) Grant, 1959, 448	—	—
SOUTH GLOS. Dean	—	—	(1228) Hart, 1971, 80	—	—
Kingswood	—	—	(1228) Moore, 1982	—	—

1297–8	1299–1300	temp. Edward I	temp. Edward III	Late Medieval & Post Medieval	
—	—	—	—	—	
—	Hutchins, 1861–73, iv, 517; Som. & Dors. N&Q, 14, cviii, 156; Mayo, 1915	Hutchins, 1861–73, iv, 519	—	—	
—	—	—	—	—	
—	Hutchins, 1861–73, iii, 620–1, 656	—	(1330) Hutchins, 1861–73, iii, 657	(1568) Hutchins, 1861–73, iii, 621	
—	Hutchins, 1861–73, ii, 317	—	—	—	
—	—	—	—	—	
—	Southwick Cart., i, no. II.42	—	—	—	
—	Southwick Cart., i, no. II.44	—	—	—	
—	Southwick Cart., i, no. II.43	—	—	—	
—	Southwick Cart., i, no. II.54–5	—	—	(1688)	
—	Southwick Cart., i, no. II.52–3	—	—	—	
—	Southwick Cart., i, no. II.50	—	—	—	
—	Southwick Cart., i, no. II.57	—	—	—	
—	Southwick Cart., i, no. II.46	—	—	—	
—	Southwick Cart., i, no. II.49	—	—	—	
—	Southwick Cart., i, no.II.48	—	—	—	
—	Moens, 1903; Southwick Cart., i, no.II.45	—	—	—	
—	Southwick Cart., i, no. II.47	—	—	—	
—	Southwick Cart., i, no. II.42; Rolston, 1955	—	—	(1635) Rolston, 1955	
Collinson, 1791, ii, 19; iii, 57–8, n. iii; Phelps, 1839, i, 46–7; MacDermot, 1911, 137–142	MacDermot, 1911, 143–50	—	—	(1815) MacDermot, 1911, 419–23	
Collinson, 1791, iii, 55–9, n. iv, 373; Phelps, 1839, i, 43–4; Hobhouse, 1891, 82–4; Gough, 1930	Gough, 1930	—	—	—	
Collinson, 1791, i, 16; iii, 57, n. ii; Phelps, 1839, i, 45–6	Som. For. Peram., 265–6	—	—	—	
Collinson, 1791, iii, 59–60, n.v., 58–61; Phelps, 1839, i, 44–5	Som. For. Peram., 264–5	—	—	—	
Collinson, 1791, ii, 195, iii, 56, n. i; Phelps, 1839, i, 42; Hobhouse, 1891, 79–81; Greswell, 1905, 266–8; Robinson, 1918, 17–18	McGarvie, 1978	—	—	(1622)	
—	—	—	—	—	
—	Wilts. For. Peram., 200–1; Grant, 1959, 444	—	(1330) Grant, 1959, 444; (1355) Akerman, 1857, App. 1, 311; App. 2, 311–12	(1426) Akerman, 1857 (c.1635) Akerman, 1857, App. 6, 314–5	
—	Wilts. For. Peram., 206; Grant, 1959, 446	—	—	—	
—	Wilts. For. Peram., 205–6; Grant, 1959, 452–3	—	—	—	
—	Hoare, 1822–45, ii, 116–8; Wilts. For. Peram., 197–8	—	(1327) Grant, 1959, 454 (1356)	—	
—	Wilts. For. Peram., 200; Grant, 1959, 456–7	—	—	—	
—	Wilts. For. Peram., 199–200	—	(1327) Grant, 1959, 455	—	
—	Wilts. For. Peram., 206–7; Grant, 1959, 446	—	—	—	
—	Wilts. For. Peram., 201–5; Grant, 1959, 450–1	—	(1330) Brentnall, 1942	—	
—	Wilts. For. Peram., 207	Grant, 1959, 448	—	—	
—	—	(1282)	—	—	
—	—	—	—	—	

References

1. Published Documentary Sources

Ælfric, *Colloq.*: *Ælfric's Colloquy*, ed. Garmonsway, G. N. (Methuen's Old English Library, London, 1939).

Asser, *Life K.Alf.*: *Asser's Life of King Alfred*, ed. Stevenson, W. H. (Oxford, 1904).

B.P.R.: *Register of Edward the Black Prince*, ed. Dawes, M. C. B. (4 vols, H.M.S.O., London, 1930–33).

Bath Chw. Accts.: 'The Churchwardens' Accounts of the Church and Parish of St Michael without the North Gate, Bath, 1349–1575', ed. Pearson, C. B., in *Proc. Somerset Archaeol. & Nat. Hist. Soc.*, 23.iii (1877), 24.iii (1878), 25.iii (1879), 26.iii (1880).

Beaul. Acct.: *The Account Book of Beaulieu Abbey*, ed. Hockey, S. F. (Royal Hist. Soc., Camden 4th ser., 16, 1975).

Bld. Acct. H.III: *Building Accounts of King Henry III*, ed. Colvin, H. M. (Clarendon Press, Oxford, 1971).

C.Ch.R.: *Calendar of Charter Rolls* (P.R.O., London, commencing 1903).

C.Cl.R.: *Calendar of Close Rolls* (P.R.O., London, commencing 1892).

C.I.P.M.: *Calendar of Inquisitions Post Mortem* (P.R.O., London, commencing 1904).

C.L.R.: *Calendar of Liberate Rolls* (P.R.O., London, commencing 1917).

C.P.R.: *Calendar of Patent Rolls* (P.R.O., London, commencing 1891).

C.S.P. Dom.: *Calendar of State Papers, Domestic Series* (P.R.O., London, commencing 1856).

C.Wells MSS.: *Calendar of the Manuscripts of the Dean and Chapter of Wells*, ed. Bird, W. H. B. (Historical Manuscripts Commission, London, 12.i, 1907; 12.ii, 1914).

Ch. Glaston.: *The Great Chartulary of Glastonbury*, ed. Watkin, A. (3 vols, Somerset Record Soc., 59, 1944; 63, 1948; 64, 1949–50.

D.B. Som.: *Domesday Book, 8: Somerset*, ed. Thorn, C. and Thorn, F. (Phillimore, Chichester, 1980).

E.H.D., i: *English Historical Documents, Vol. i: c. 500–1042*, ed. Whitelock, D. (Eyre and Spottiswoode, London, 1955).

Exm. Sw.: *The Swainmote Courts of Exmoor, and the Devonshire Portion and Purlieus of the Forest*, ed. Chanter, J. F. (Rept. and Trans. Devonshire Assocn. for Advancement of Science, Literature and Art, 39, 1907, 268–301.

For. Pleas, Som.: *Forest Pleas, Somerset*, ed. Thompson, E. M. (Somerset and Dorset N. & Q., 5, 1897, xxxvii, 210–213, xxxviii, 270–273, xxxix, 296–298; 6, 1898, xli, 24–26, xlii, 69–73, xlvi, 259–262, xlvii, 295–299.

Ho. Accts.: *Household Accounts from Medieval England*, ed. Woolgar, C. M. (2 vols, British Academy, Records of Social and Economic History, new ser., 17, 1992; 18, 1993).

L. & P. H.VIII: *Letters and Papers, Foreign and Domestic, of King Henry VIII* (P.R.O., London, commencing 1864).

Lacock Chart.: *Lacock Abbey Charters*, ed. Rogers, K. H. (Wiltshire Record Soc., 34, 1978).

Leland, *Itin.*: *The Itinerary of John Leland, c. 1535–1543*, ed. Toulmin Smith, L. (5 vols, Centaur Press, London, 1964 edn.).

Mem. St.D.: *Memorials of St Dunstan*, ed. Stubbs, W. (Rolls Series, 63, London, 1874).

Mon. Angl.: Dugdale, W., *Monasticon Anglicanum*, ed. Caley, J., Ellis, H. and Bandinel, B. (6 vols, London, 1817–30).

Much. Cart.: *Two Cartularies of the Benedictine Abbeys of Munchelney and Athelney in the County of Somerset*, ed. Bates, H. E. (Somerset Record Soc., 14, 1899).

New For. Doc.: *A Calendar of New Forest Documents, i: 1244–1334*, ed. Stagg, D. J. (Hampshire Record Ser., 3, 1979); *ii: The Fifteenth to the Sixteenth centuries*, ed. Stagg, D. J. (Hampshire Record Ser., 5, 1983).

Pipe R.: *The Great Roll of the Pipe* (Pipe Roll Soc. publications, commencing 1884; new series commencing 1925).

Proc. Star Ch.: *Proceedings in the Court of Star Chamber in the Reigns of Henry VII and Henry VIII*, ed. Bradford, G. (Somerset Record Soc., 27, 1911).

Rent. & Custum.: *Rentalia et Custumaria Michaelis de Ambresbury, 1235–1252, et Rogeri de Ford, 1252–1261*, ed. Elton, C. J. and Hobhouse, E. (Somerset Record Soc., 5, 1891).

Rot. Chart.: *Rotuli Chartarum in Turri Londinensi asservati, 1199–1216*, ed. Hardy, T. D. (Record Commission, London, 1837).

Rot. Litt. Claus.: *Rotuli Litterarum Clausarum in Turri Londinensi asservati*, ed. Hardy, T. D. (2 vols, Record Commission, London, 1833, 1834).

Sel. Pleas: *Select Pleas of the Forest*, ed. Turner, G. J. (Selden Soc., 13, 1901).

Som. For. Peramb.: 'Perambulations of the Somerset Forests', ed. Turner, G. I., in *Somerset and Dorset N. &. Q.*, 6, xlvi (1899), 264–266.

Southwick Cart.: *The Cartularies of Southwick Priory*, ed. Hanna, K. A. (2 vols, Hampshire Record Ser., 9, 1988; 10, 1989).

Tavist. Ch.: 'Some Early Tavistock Charters', ed. Finberg, H. P. R., in *English Hist.Review*, 62, (1947), 352–377.

Wilts. Eyre, 1249: *Crown Pleas of the Wiltshire Eyre, 1249*, ed. Meekings, C. A. F. (Wiltshire Archaeol. & Nat. Hist. Soc., Records Branch, 16, 1961).

Wilts. For. Peramb.: 'Perambulations of Forests in Wiltshire', ed. Jackson, J. E., in *Wilts Archaeol. & Nat. Hist. Mag.*, 4 (1858), 195–207.

Wilts I.P.M., i: *Abstracts of Wiltshire Inquisitiones Post Mortem, AD 1242–1326*, ed. Fry, E. A. (British Record Soc., London, 1908).

Wilts I.P.M., ii: *Abstracts of Wiltshire Inquisitiones Post Mortem, AD 1327–1377*, ed. Stokes, E. (British Record Soc., London, 1914).

2. Secondary Works

Akerman, J. Y. 1857: 'Some Account of the Possessions of the Abbey of Malmesbury ... with Remarks on the Ancient Limits of the Forest of Braden', in *Archaeologia* 37.i, 257–315.

Ballard, A. and Tait, J. 1923: *British Borough Charters, ii: 1216–1307*.

Barber, K. 1973: 'Vegetational History of the New Forest: a preliminary note', in *Proc. Hants Field Club & Archaeol. Soc.* 30, 5–8.

Baring, F. H. 1901, 1912: 'The Making of the New Forest', in *English Hist. Review* 16, 427–438; 27, 513–515.

Batten, J. 1896: 'Deer Parks in Dorset and Somerset', in *Somerset and Dorset N. & Q.* 5, 83–87.

Bazeley, M. 1921: 'The Extent of the English Forest in the

Thirteenth Century', in *Trans. Royal Hist. Soc.* 4th ser., 4, 140–172.

Bettey, J. H. 1976: 'The Revolts over the Enclosure of the Royal Forest at Gillingham, 1626–1630', in *Proc. Dorset Nat. Hist. & Archaeol. Soc.* 97, 21–24.

Binding, H. and Stevens, D. 1977: *Minehead: a New History* (Exmoor Press/Floyds, Minehead).

Birrell, J. 1982: 'Who Poached the King's Deer? a Study in Thirteenth-Century Crime', in *Midland History* 7, 9–25.

Birrell, J. 1988: 'Forest Law and the Peasantry in the Later Thirteenth Century', in Coss, P. R. and Lloyd, S. D. (eds), *Thirteenth-Century England, II: Proceedings of the Newcastle-upon-Tyne Conference, 1987* (Boydell Press, Woodbridge).

Birrell, J. 1992: 'Deer and Deer Farming in Medieval England', in *Ag. Hist. Review* 40.ii, 112–126.

Bond, C. J. 1988: 'Rabbits: the Case for their Medieval Introduction into Britain', in *The Local Historian* 18.ii, 53–57.

Bonnett, F. 1912: 'Fox-hunting', in *The Victoria History of the County of Hampshire* 5, 513–535.

Borenius, T. and Charlton, J. 1936: 'Clarendon Palace: an Interim Report', in *Antiq. Jnl.* 16, 55–84.

Bourdillon, J. 1986: 'The Animal Bones', in Oxley, J. (ed.), *Excavations at Southampton Castle* (Southampton Archaeological Monograph, 3).

Braine, A. 1891: *The History of Kingswood Forest* (facsimile edn, Kingsmead Bookshop, Bath, 1969).

Brentnall, H. C. 1942: 'The Metes and Bounds of Savernake Forest', in *Wiltshire Archaeol & Nat. Hist. Mag.* 49, 391–434.

Brown, R. A., Colvin, H. M. and Taylor, A. J. 1963: *The History of the King's Works: The Middle Ages* (2 vols, H.M.S.O., London).

Bush, R. 1978: 'Chaffcombe', in *The Victoria History of the County of Somerset* 4, 121–128.

Cadman, W. A. and Manners, J. G. 1964: 'Land Use and Silviculture in the New Forest', in Monkhouse, F. J. (ed.), *A Survey of Southampton and its Region* (British Association for the Advancement of Science), 140–147.

Camber, R. and Cherry, J. 1977: 'The Savernake Horn', in *British Museum Year Book* 2, 201–211.

Cantor, L. M. 1982: 'Forests, Chases, Parks and Warrens', in Cantor, L. M., *The English Medieval Landscape* (Croom Helm, London), 56–85.

Cantor, L. M. 1983: *The Medieval Parks of England: a Gazetteer* (Dept. of Education, Loughborough University of Technology).

Cantor, L. M. and Hatherly, J. 1979: 'The Medieval Parks of England', in *Geography* 64, 71–85.

Cantor, L. M. and Wilson, J. D. 1961: 'The Medieval Deer Parks of Dorset, Part 1', in *Proc. Dorset Nat. Hist. & Archaeol. Soc.* 83, 109–116.

Cantor, L. M. and Wilson, J. D. 1962: 'The Medieval Deer Parks of Dorset, Part 2', in *Proc. Dorset Nat. Hist. & Archaeol. Soc.* 84, 145–153.

Cantor, L. M. and Wilson, J. D. 1963: 'The Medieval Deer Parks of Dorset, Part 3', in *Proc. Dorset Nat. Hist. & Archaeol. Soc.* 85, 141–152.

Cantor, L. M. and Wilson, J. D. 1964: 'The Medieval Deer Parks of Dorset, Part 4', in *Proc. Dorset Nat. Hist. & Archaeol. Soc.* 86, 164–178.

Cantor, L. M. and Wilson, J. D. 1965: 'The Medieval Deer Parks of Dorset, Part 5', in *Proc. Dorset Nat. Hist. & Archaeol. Soc.* 87, 223–233.

Cantor, L. M. and Wilson, J. D. 1966: 'The Medieval Deer Parks of Dorset, Part 6', in *Proc. Dorset Nat. Hist. & Archaeol. Soc.* 88, 176–185.

Cantor, L. M. and Wilson, J. D. 1967: 'The Medieval Deer Parks of Dorset, Part 7', in *Proc. Dorset Nat. Hist. & Archaeol. Soc.* 89, 171–180.

Cantor, L. M. and Wilson, J. D. 1968: 'The Medieval Deer Parks of Dorset, Part 8', in *Proc. Dorset Nat. Hist. & Archaeol. Soc.* 90, 241–8.

Cantor, L. M. and Wilson, J. D. 1969: 'The Medieval Deer Parks of Dorset, Part 9', in *Proc. Dorset Nat. Hist. & Archaeol. Soc.* 91, 196–205.

Cardigan, Earl of, 1949: *The Wardens of Savernake Forest* (Routledge and Kegan Paul, London).

Carter, D. J. 1968: 'An Historical Geography of the Forest of Bere, Hampshire', in *South Hants Geographer* 1, 72–100.

Cherry, J. 1989: 'Symbolism and Survival: Medieval Horns of Tenure', in *Antiq. Jnl.* 69.i, 111–118.

Chettle, H. F. and Tillott, P. M. 1953: 'Melksham', in *The Victoria History of the County of Wiltshire* 7, 91–121.

Colebourn, P. 1983: *Hampshire's Countryside Heritage, 3: Ancient Woodland* (Hampshire County Council).

Collinson, J. 1791: *The History and Antiquities of the County of Somerset* (3 vols, R. Cruttwell, Bath).

Cox, J. C. 1905: *The Royal Forests of England* (Methuen, London).

Cox, J. C. 1908: 'Forestry', in *The Victoria History of the County of Dorset* 2, 287–298.

Cox, J. C. and Greswell, W. H. P. 1911: 'Forestry', in *The Victoria History of the County of Somerset* 2, 547–572.

Coy, J. and Maltby, M. 1987: 'Archaeozoology in Wessex', in Keeley, H. C. M. (ed.), *Environmental Archaeology, a Regional Review*, Vol. 2 (Historic Buildings and Monuments Commission for England, Occassional Paper 1), 204–251.

Crawford, O. G. S. 1954: *Archaeology in the Field* (3rd edn, Phoenix House, London).

Crittall, E. 1970: 'Wootton Bassett', in *The Victoria History of the County of Wiltshire* 9, 186–205.

Crittall, E. 1980: 'Everleigh', in *The Victoria History of the County of Wiltshire* 11, 135–141.

Crowley, D. A. 1987: 'Tisbury', in *The Victoria History of the County of Wiltshire* 13, 195–248.

Darby, H. C. 1954: 'Gloucestershire', in Darby, H. C. and Terrett, I. B., *The Domesday Geography of Midland England* (Cambridge University Press), 1–56..

Darby, H. C. 1967: 'Dorset', in Darby, H. C. and Finn, R. W., *The Domesday Geography of South-West England* (Cambridge University Press), 67–131.

Darby, H. C. 1977: *Domesday England* (Cambridge University Press).

Darlington, R. R. 1955: 'Introduction to Wiltshire Domesday', in *The Victoria History of the County of Wiltshire* 2, 42–112, 169–177.

Dayrell-Reed, T. 1932: 'Notes on the Outer Bounds of Cranborne Chase', in *Proc. Dorset Nat. Hist. & Archaeol. Soc.* 53, 215–227.

Dunning, R. 1974: 'Montacute', in *The Victoria History of the County of Somerset* 3, 210–224.

Dunning, R. 1981: 'The Origins of Nether Stowey', in *Proc.*

Somerset Archaeol. & Nat. Hist. Soc. 125, 124–6.

Eastham, A. 1977: 'The Animal Bones: Birds', in Cunliffe, B. W., *Excavations at Portchester Castle, Vol. III: Medieval, the Outer Bailey and its Defences* (Soc. of Antiquaries of London, Research Report, 34), 233–239.

Edwards, H. 1988: *The Charters of the Early West Saxon Kingdom* (British Archaeological Reports, British Series, 198, Oxford).

Edwards, P. J. 1985: 'Some Effects of Grazing on the Vegetation of Streamside Lawns in the New Forest', in *Proc. Hants. Field Club & Archaeol. Soc.* 41, 45–50.

Edwards, P. J., and Hollis, S. 1982: 'The Distribution of Excreta on New Forest Grassland used by Cattle, Ponies and Deer', in *Jnl. Applied Ecology* 19, 953–964.

Ekwall, E. 1960: *The Concise Oxford Dictionary of English Place-Names* (4th edn, Clarendon Press, Oxford).

Finn, R. W. 1962: 'Hampshire', in Darby, H. C. and Campbell, E. M. J., *The Domesday Geography of South-East England* (Cambridge University Press), 287–363.

Finn, R. W. 1967: 'Wiltshire', in Darby, H. C. and Finn, R. W., *The Domesday Geography of South-West England* (Cambridge University Press), 1–66.

Finn, R. W. and Wheatley, P. 1967: 'Somerset', in Darby, H. C. and Finn, R. W., *The Domesday Geography of South-West England* (Cambridge University Press), 132–222.

Flower, N. 1980: 'The Management History and Structure of Unenclosed Woods in the New Forest, Hampshire', in *Jnl. of Biogeography* 7.

Franklin, P. 1989: 'Thornbury Woodlands and Deer Parks, Part 1: the Earls of Gloucester's Deer Parks', in *Trans. Bristol & Gloucs. Archaeol. Soc.* 107, 149–169.

Freeman, J. 1983: 'Aldbourne', in *The Victoria History of the County of Wiltshire* 12, 67–85.

Gough, J. W. 1930: *Mendip Mining Laws and Forest Bounds* (Somerset Record Soc., 45).

Grant, A. 1976: 'The Animal Bones', in Cunliffe, B., *Excavations at Portchester Castle, Vol. II: Saxon* (Soc. of Antiquaries of London, Research Committee Reports, 33), 262–287.

Grant, A. 1977: 'The Animal Bones: Mammals', in Cunliffe, B., *Excavations at Portchester Castle, Vol. III:Medieval, the Outer Bailey and its Defences Medieval* (Soc. of Antiquaries of London, Research Committee Reports, 34), 213–233.

Grant, A. 1985: 'The Large Mammals', in Cunliffe, B. and Munby, J., *Excavations at Portchester Castle, Vol. IV: Medieval, the Inner Bailey* (Soc. of Antiquaries of London, Research Committee Reports, 43), 244–256.

Grant, R. 1959: 'Royal Forests', in *The Victoria History of the County of Wiltshire* 4, 391–457.

Grant, R. K. J. 1991: *The Royal Forests of England* (Alan Sutton, Stroud).

Greswell, W. H. P. 1905: *The Forests and Deer Parks of the County of Somerset* (Barnicott and Pearce, Athenaeum Press).

Harcourt, R. 1986: 'Animal Bones', in Musty, J. and Algar, D., 'Excavations at the Deserted Medieval Village of Gormeldon, near Salisbury', in *Wilts Archaeol. & Nat. Hist. Soc. Mag.* 80, 166–168.

Hart, C. 1966: *Royal Forest: a History of Dean's Woods as Producers of Timber* (Oxford).

Hart, C. 1971: *The Verderers and Forest Laws of Dean* (David & Charles, Newton Abbot).

Harting, J. E. 1880: *British Animals Extinct within Historic Times, with Some Account of British Wild White Cattle* (Trübner & Co., London).

Harvey, J. 1981: *Mediaeval Gardens* (B.T. Batsford Ltd, London).

Hawkes, J. 1991: 'Poundisford Park Pale, ST.21762035', in *Proc. Somerset Archaeol. & Nat. Hist. Soc.* 135, 158.

Hembry, P. M. 1967: *The Bishops of Bath and Wells, 1540–1640: Social and Economic Problems* (University of London Historical Studies, 20).

Higgs, E., Greenwood, W. and Garrard, A. 1979: 'Faunal Remains', in Rahtz, P., *The Saxon and Medieval Palaces at Cheddar* (British Archaeological Reports, British Series, 65), 354–362.

Hoare, R. C. 1822–45: *The History of Modern Wiltshire* (4 vols, J. B. Nichols and J. G. Nichols, London).

Hobhouse, Bp. 1891: 'Somerset Forest Bounds', in *Proc. Somerset Archaeol. & Nat. Hist. Soc.* 37.ii, 76–91.

Hockey, S. F. 1970: *Quarr Abbey and its Lands, 1132–1631* (Leicester University Press).

Hockey, S. F. 1982: *Insula Vecta: The Isle of Wight in the Middle Ages* (Phillimore, Chichester).

Hollinrake, C. and Hollinrake, N. 1986: 'Survey of Dolebury Hill-Fort and Dolebury Warren', in *Bristol & Avon Archaeol.* 5, 5–11.

Hutchins, J. 1774: *History and Antiquities of the County of Dorset* (3rd edn, ed. Shipp, W. and Hodson, J. W., 4 vols, J. Nichols, Westminster, 1861–73).

Iles, R. 1978: 'The Medieval Deer Parks of the Bristol Region', in *Bulletin of Bristol Archaeol. Research Group* 6, 116–119.

Iles, R. 1984: 'Avon Archaeology, 1983', in *Bristol & Avon Archaeol.* 3, 54–65.

Jackson, J. E. 1875: 'Wulfhall and the Seymours', in *Wilts Archaeol & Nat. Hist. Mag.* 15, 140–207.

Jackson, J. E. 1881: 'Savernake Forest', in *Wilts Archaeol. & Nat. Hist. Mag.* 19, 26–44.

James, T. B. and Robinson, A. M. 1988: *Clarendon Palace: the History and Archaeology of a Medieval Palace and Hunting Lodge near Salisbury, Wiltshire* (Soc. of Antiquaries of London, Research Reports, 45).

Keen, L. and Papworth, M. 1987: 'Lodge Farm, Pamphill', in *Proc. Dorset Archaeol. & Nat. Hist. Soc.* 109, 135.

Kirby, D. P. 1974: 'The Old English Forest: its Natural Flora and Fauna', in Rowley, T. (ed.), *Anglo-Saxon Settlement and Landscape* (British Archaeological Reports, Oxford, 6), 120–130.

Lascelles, G. W. 1895: 'A Brief History of the Arboriculture of the New Forest', in *Trans Royal Scottish Arboricultural Soc.* 14.

Lay, S. and Iles, R. 1979: 'Medieval Deer Parks in Avon', in *Avon Past* 1, 5–12.

Lever, C. 1979: *The Naturalised Animals of the British Isles* (Granada, St Albans).

Levitan, B. 1982: 'Bird bones', in Leach, P. (ed.), *Ilchester, Vol. 1: Excavations, 1974–1975* (Western Archaeological Trust, Excavation Monograph 3), 280–284.

Linehan, C. D. 1966: 'Deserted Sites and Rabbit-Warrens on Dartmoor, Devon', in *Medieval Archaeol.* 10, 113–144.

Lyte, H. C. M. 1909: *A History of Dunster and of the Families of Mohun and Luttrell* (2 vols, St Catherine Press, London).

MacDermot, E. T. 1911: *A History of the Forest of Exmoor* (revised ed. Sellick, R. J., David & Charles, Newton Abbot, 1973).

McGarvie, M. 1974: 'Brewham: a Lost Park', in *Somerset and Dorset N. & Q.* 30, 60–63.

McGarvie, M. 1978: *The Bounds of Selwood* (Frome Historical Research Group, Occasional Papers 1).

Maltby, M. 1979: *The Animal Bones from Exeter, 1971–1975* (Exeter Archaeological Reports, 2; Dept. of Prehistory and Archaeology, University of Sheffield).

Maltby, M. 1982: 'Mammal and bird bones', in Higham, R. A., Allan, J. P. and Blaylock, S. R., 'Excavations at Okehampton Castle, Devon, part 2: The Bailey', in *Proc. Devon Archaeol. Soc.* 40, 114–135.

Manners, J. G. 1988: 'The Fungi of the New Forest', in *Proc. Hants Field Club & Archaeol. Soc.* 44, 5–10.

Manners, J. G. and Edwards, P. J. 1986: 'Death of Old Beech Trees in the New Forest', in *Proc. Hants Field Club & Archaeol. Soc.* 42, 155–156.

Manwood, J. 1598: *A Treatise and Discourse of the Lawes of the Forrest* (London).

Matheson, C. 1941: 'The Rabbit and the Hare in Wales', in *Antiquity* 15, no. 60, 371–381.

Mayo, C. H. 1915: 'Perambulation of the Forest of Blackmore, Dorset', in *Somerset & Dorset N. & Q.* 14, cx, 251–3.

Moger, O. M., Kennedy, F. and Upcott, K. M. 1911: 'Odiham', in *The Victoria History of the County of Hampshire* 4, 87–98.

Moens, W. J. C. 1903: 'The New Forest: its Afforestation, Ancient Area and Law in the time of the Conqueror and his Successors', in *Archaeol. Jnl.* 60, 30–50.

Moore, J. S. 1982: 'The Medieval Forest of Kingswood', in *Avon Past*, 7, 6–16.

Munby, J. 1985: 'Portchester and its Region', in Cunliffe, B. and Munby, J. (1985), 270–295.

Musty, J. 1986: 'Deer Coursing at Clarendon Palace and Hampton Court', in *Antiquaries Jnl.* 66.i, 131–132.

Musty, J. W. G., Algar, D. J. and Ewence, P. F. 1969: 'The Medieval Pottery Kilns at Laverstock, near Salisbury, Wiltshire', in *Archaeologia* 102, 83–150.

Nisbet, J. and Vellacott, C. H. 1907: 'Forestry', in *The Victoria History of the County of Gloucester* 2, 263–286.

Papworth, M. 1989: 'Lodge Farm and Badbury Park, Pamphill', in *Proc. Dorset Archaeol. & Nat. Hist. Soc.* 111, 112–114.

Phelps, W. 1839: *The History and Antiquities of Somersetshire* (2 vols, London).

Platt, C. 1978: *Medieval England: a Social History and Archaeology from the Conquest to AD 1600* (Routledge and Kegan Paul, London and Henley).

Poole, E. H. L. 1959: 'Cranborne Chase', in *The Victoria History of the County of Wiltshire* 4, 458–460.

Pugh, R. B. 1947–8: 'The Early History of the Manors in Amesbury', in *Wiltshire Archaeol. & Nat. Hist. Mag.* 52, 70–110.

Pugh, R. B. 1975: 'The Borough of Devizes', in *The Victoria History of the County of Wiltshire* 10, 225–314.

Rackham, O. 1980: *Ancient Woodland: its History, Vegetation and Uses in England* (Edward Arnold, London).

Rackham, O. 1988a: 'Woods, Hedges and Forests', in Aston, M. (ed.), *Aspects of the Medieval Landscape of Somerset* (Somerset County Council, Taunton), 13–31.

Rackham, O. 1988b: 'The Forest of Neroche and the Fuel Supply of the Donyatt Kilns', in Coleman-Smith, R. and Pearson, T. (eds), *Excavations in the Donyatt Potteries, Somerset* (Phillimore, Chichester).

Rahtz, P. 1979: *The Saxon and Medieval Palaces at Cheddar* (British Archaeological Reports, British Series, 65, Oxford).

Rendell, S. and Rendell, J. 1993: *Steep Holm: the Story of a Small Island* (Alan Sutton, Stroud).

RCHME 1962: *An Inventory of Historical Monuments in the County of Dorset, Vol. iv: North Dorset* (Royal Commission on Historical Monuments (England), HMSO, London).

Roberts, E. 1988: 'The Bishop of Winchester's Deer Parks in Hampshire, 1200–1400', in *Proc. Hants Field Club & Archaeol. Soc.* 44, 67–86.

Robinson, J. A. 1918: 'The Foundation Charter of Witham Charterhouse', in *Proc. Somerset Archaeol. & Nat. Hist. Soc.* 64, ii, 1–28.

Rolston, G. R. 1955: 'Wolmer Forest and a New Roman Road North of Milland', in *Proc. Hants Field Club & Archaeol. Soc.* 19.i, 12–19.

Rose, F. and James, P. W. 1974: 'Regional Studies on the British Lichen Flora, i; The Corticolous and Lignicolous Species of the New Forest, Hampshire', in *Lichenologist* 6, 1–72.

Rose, F. and Wolseley, P. 1984: 'Nettlecombe Park: its History and its Epiphytic Lichens: an Attempt at Correlation', in *Field Studies* 6, 117–148.

Rudder, S. 1783: *A New History of Gloucestershire* (Cirencester, revised edn).

Russett, V. 1986: 'Three Rabbit Buries (Pillow-mounds) at Shute Shelve Hill, Axbridge', in *Proc. Somerset Archaeol. & Nat. Hist. Soc.* 130, 107–113.

Salzman, L. F. 1967: *Building in England down to 1540: a Documentary History* (2nd edn., Clarendon Press, Oxford).

Sawyer, P. H. 1968: *Anglo-Saxon Charters: an Annotated List and Bibliography* (Royal Historical Soc. Guides and Handbooks, 8).

Scott, R. 1959: 'Medieval Agriculture', in *The Victoria History of the County of Wiltshire* 4, 7–42.

Sheail, J. 1971: *Rabbits and their History* (David & Charles, Newton Abbot).

Shirley, E. P. 1867: *Some Account of English Deer Parks, with Notes on the Management of Deer* (Murray, London).

Sixsmith, R. A. 1958: *Staple Fitzpaine and the Forest of Neroche* (Privately published, Taunton).

Smart, T. W. W. 1841: *A Chronicle of Cranborne and the Cranborne Chase* (2nd edn, Dovecote Press, Wimborne, 1983).

Spellerberg, I. F. 1986: 'Ecology and Conservation of Reptiles in the New Forest', in *Proc. Hants Field Club & Archaeol. Soc.* 42, 5–14.

Stagg, D. J. 1974: 'A Perambulation of the New Forest, 1217–1218', in *Hants Field Club & Archaeol. Soc., New Forest Section Rept.* 13, 26–27.

Stagg, D. J. 1989: 'Silvicultural Enclosure in the New Forest to 1780', in *Proc. Hants Field Club & Archaeol. Soc.* 45, 133–146.

Stamper, P. 1983: 'The Medieval Forest of Pamber, Hampshire', in *Landscape History* 5, 41–52.

Stamper, P. 1988: 'Woods and Parks', in Astill, G. and Grant, A. (eds), *The Countryside of Medieval England* (Basil

Blackwell, Oxford), 128–148.

Sumner, H. 1925: *A Guide to the New Forest* (2nd edn, C. Brown and Sons, Ringwood).

Sumner, H. 1929: 'J. Norden's Survey of Medieval Coppices in the New Forest, AD 1609', in *Proc. Hants Field Club* 10.ii, 95–117.

Tubbs, C. R. 1964: 'Early Encoppicements in the New Forest', in *Forestry* 37, 95–105.

Tubbs, C. R. 1968: *The New Forest: an Ecological Study* (David & Charles, Newton Abbot).

Tubbs, C. R. 1986: *The New Forest* (Collins New Naturalist Ser., London).

Tubbs, C. R. and Dimbleby, G. W. 1965: 'Early Agriculture in the New Forest', in *Adv. Sci.*, June 1965, 88–97.

Tubbs, C. R. and Jones, E. L. 1964: 'The Distribution of Gorse (*Ulex europaeus* L.) in the New Forest in relation to former Land Use', in *Proc. Hants. Field Club & Archaeol. Soc.* 23.i, 1–10.

Veale, E. M. 1957: 'The Rabbit in England', in *Agricultural Hist. Review* 5, ii, 85–90.

Vivian-Neal, A. W. and Gray, H. St. G. 1940: 'Materials for the History of Taunton Castle', in *Proc. Somerset Archaeol. & Nat. Hist. Soc.* 86.ii, 45–78.

West, W. 1816: *A History of the Forest or Chace of Cranborne*.

Williams, R. 1988: 'Deer Parks in Sutton and West Chelwood', in *Bristol & Avon Archaeol.* 7, 11–13.

Wilson, J. D. 1970: 'The Medieval Deer Parks of Dorset, Part 10', in *Proc. Dorset Nat. Hist. & Archaeol. Soc.* 92, 205–211.

Wilson, J. D. 1971: 'The Medieval Deer Parks of Dorset, Part 11', in *Proc. Dorset Nat. Hist. & Archaeol. Soc.* 93, 169–175.

Wilson, J. D. 1972: 'The Medieval Deer Parks of Dorset, Part 12', in *Proc. Dorset Nat. Hist. & Archaeol. Soc.* 94, 67–69.

Wilson, J. D. 1973: 'The Medieval Deer Parks of Dorset, Part 13', in *Proc. Dorset Nat. Hist. & Archaeol. Soc.* 95, 47–50.

Wilson, J. D. 1974: 'The Medieval Deer Parks of Dorset, Part 14', in *Proc. Dorset Nat. Hist. & Archaeol. Soc.* 96, 76–80.

Wilson, J. D. and Cantor, L. M. 1969: 'A Medieval Park Site at Closworth', in *Somerset and Dorset N. & Q.* 29, pt. 289, 49–51.

Wise, J. R. 1863: *The New Forest: its History and Scenery* (Gibbings, London).

Wood, M. E. 1950: *Thirteenth-Century Domestic Architecture in England* (Archaeol. Jnl., 105, Supplement).

Young, C. R. 1979: *The Royal Forests of Medieval England* (Leicester University Press).

7. Agriculture and Rural Settlement in the Chalklands of Wiltshire and Hampshire from *c*. 1200 – *c*. 1500

John Hare

The chalklands of Wessex provide a distinctive core to the landscape of Hampshire and Wiltshire. This essay examines how the agriculture and settlement of this area was influenced by the land itself, by demographic changes, by the work of the lord and of the tenant, and by late medieval commercial growth. It considers the role and dating of such landscape features as: sheep houses, strip lynchets, rabbit warrens, and of growing and declining villages.

Agriculture and Settlement

Wiltshire and Hampshire shared much in common during this period particularly in their physical geography, but they also showed substantial and growing contrasts. Both were dominated by the chalklands that had for so long provided the social and economic backbone of Wessex and of central southern England; and both incorporated contrasting regional variations beyond. This essay seeks to focus on the chalkland core of these two counties, but reference will be made to some of the areas immediately around in order to establish the distinctiveness of the chalklands themselves. It attempts to provide an historical background to the study of the landscape of this central part of Wessex, based on the study of a large amount of manorial documentation, particularly for Wiltshire. The period chosen for study allows an examination of the state of agriculture and settlement at the end of a long period of sustained population growth, and then of the impact of demographic fall and industrial expansion in the later fourteenth and fifteenth centuries.

In Wiltshire, the regional contrasts between the chalklands and elsewhere have been well documented. Thomas Davis, writing at the end of the eighteenth century (1794), wrote clearly of the different agricultural regions emphasising the distinctiveness of the chalklands. His analysis has been extended to the sixteenth and seventeenth century by E. Kerridge (1959), who contrasted the chalk country (with its dependence on arable farming and sheep, large-scale farming units and wage labour) and the cheese country of the clay vale (with its emphasis on pastoral farming and on family units), as well as referring to other less crucial distinctions, such as the islands of lighter soils within the clay vale and the lower slopes of the Cotswolds to the west. More recently,

some of these contrasts have been carried back and been seen evolving in the later Middle Ages (Hare 1976 and 1981; see also Lewis, this volume).

In the chalklands, settlement was concentrated in the river valleys or at the foot of the scarp slopes of the downs, with settlements lying along the spring lines or just above the meadow, and with parishes that ran back in long narrow strips from the river or lowland to the downland heights. Thus each settlement had a portion of the different types of land, contrasting soils but interlinked in the operation of the local agricultural economy. Each settlement had a portion of the meadowland in the valley bottom, whose rarity (and the need for hay) was such that it was worth much more per acre than good arable land. Above this lay the linear settlement and then came the arable, the fertile soils around the village and the poorer downland arable beyond. Although parts of the downs were cultivated, the land was essentially prized for the sheep pastures. It was an area largely devoid of settlement, although an important point of contact between the settlements that lay around, both for the movement of people and of livestock. It was the need to use these various soil types that had led to the long thin parishes so typical of the chalklands. But the pattern of parishes partially conceals this development, since it lumps together a group of tithings each of which had the characteristic long thin shape. Thus in the early fourteenth century, the parish of Enford was subdivided into seven tithings, all of the settlements being strung along the banks of the River Avon and all with associated downland behind them. The varying soil types are reflected in the *Inquisitions post mortem*; thus at Steeple Lavington, the lord held 88 acres of sandy soil worth 3*d* per acre, 20 acres of deepland worth 8*d* per acre, and 374 poor acres upon the hill worth 2d per acre (*Wilts IPM,* i, 192). The poorer downland soils were generally sown with oats as at Enford (Hare 1976, 45–49). Arable cultivation took place in open fields that largely survived until the eighteenth century. The strips were incorporated in a number of fields but tended to operate within a two course rotation, with half the land left fallow each year (Hare 1976, 41–4; Scott 1959, 12–8). This was less wasteful than might appear given that the fallow provided pasture for livestock, particularly for the sheep that were such a key feature of the local agricultural economy.

Elsewhere, and beyond the chalklands, were different patterns of settlement, in areas of woodland that offered greater scope for colonisation. To the west lay the clay vale and the vales of Pewsey and Tisbury, to the east lay areas of chalk covered by a clay capping. Parts of these clay woodlands were used for hunting and recreation, particularly the area to the east dominated by the royal residences of Clarendon, Marlborough and Ludgershall, where the woodland had become used for hunting. This was particularly the case under Henry III who regularly stayed for a substantial time at these places (*Itinerary Henry III*). Within these areas some settlements comprised open-field nucleated settlements, others were much smaller: isolated farmsteads or groups of squatters. Here the estates were not long and thin and sheep farming was less important. Here too the role of the lord and of the manorial structure became less noticeable: manors being generally smaller, more poorly documented, with more transient demesne agriculture.

Such variations in settlement patterns have in part been concealed by the taxation records. Those from 1334 (Beresford 1959) seem to provide a realistic impression of the structure of chalkland settlement, but this was frequently not the case elsewhere (Hare 1976). Forest records make it clear that many settlements existed by the thirteenth century but were not separately taxed, being included with the mother settlements which lay around the forest, thus giving an inflated population to such places as Chippenham and concealing the extent of more dispersed settlement (Hare 1976, 22–24). This same oversimplification was to be found in much of non-chalk Wiltshire. Thus at Bremhill in north-west Wiltshire on the ridge of corallian limestone, the tax assessments were made under the headings Bremhill, Foxham and Avon, but the late thirteenth century rental shows that there were four other settlements (Brewer 1879–90, 162–9; Hare 1976, 23). Again at Nettleton in the Cotswolds, the taxation figures point to one settlement, but the early sixteenth-century rental of Glastonbury Abbey shows that there were four (BL Harl Mss 3961 f.16v–), and Malmesbury and Glastonbury provide similar examples at Crudwell and Grittleton (Brewer 1879–90, 144–53; BL Harl Mss 3961 f.4–). Something of the complexity of settlement away from the chalk has been revealed in the detailed study of Whiteparish, in the far south-east of the county (Taylor 1967).

The situation in Hampshire shows many similarities, but the picture is more sketchy as published research has been more limited (Thirsk 1967; Miller, 1991). Here, as in Wiltshire, the chalklands were dominated by the long narrow downland units and the great landlords. Agriculture, throughout this period, was characterised by the open fields, and by the importance of mixed farming and large sheep flocks. By contrast, to the north in the Thames basin and in the south in the Hampshire basin there were a variety of smaller nucleated, open green, or dispersed settlements. Some of these variations were clearly evident to contemporaries, as Leland showed in his travels in the 1530s and 1540s, when he noted the contrasts between the open-field champion landscape of the chalklands, as between Salisbury and Winchester, and the enclosed fields elsewhere, as in the areas of south Hampshire (around Portsmouth, Southwick, Wickham and Bishop's Waltham, or between Winchester and Southampton) (*Itinerary*, pp. 275, 284–5, 269–).

While the emphasis was on mixed farming, the large sheep flocks offered a characteristic element in the chalkland economy. They provided a means of extracting wealth from the poor downland pastures, both from meat and from wool, but in addition they provided a means of boosting arable production. The sheep who had eaten on the downland grasslands during the day could be taken down to the arable fields for nightfall, where their manure would be left to fertilise the soil. It is unlikely that this had yet reached the late eighteenth-century situation, when the most valuable product of the downland sheep was reputed to be its manure (Davis 1794), but medieval farmers were clearly aware of the value of such manure. Thus in the fifteenth century, lords rented out their flock as manufacturers of manure, at Kingston Deverill, Warminster and Aldbourne; in both the latter cases such renting generated over £5 per year (WRO/192/32; WRO/845/ Warminster accounts; PRO/ DL29/730/12007; Hare 1976, 72–74).

Lords frequently maintained very large flocks, as a few examples from the thirteenth century should show. On the estates of the bishopric of Winchester in 1211 there were 2,365 sheep at Knoyle and 1,238 at Downton, and numbers were to grow. Thus in the thirteenth century flocks of over 2,000 sheep were to be found in peak years at the manors of Knoyle, Downton, Twyford, Meon and Crawley, and of over 1,000 at Overton, Hambledon and Bishop's Waltham (Pipe Roll 1211; Titow 1962, 49, and table IV). Although flocks were kept under 20,000 from the late 1270s to the Black Death (Titow 1962, 50), they were on an exceptional scale. But in a more modest fashion the large flocks were characteristic of the area. In 1282/3, Hyde Abbey, Winchester had 4,869 sheep on its various manors, mainly in the chalklands and of which Collingbourne, Chisenbury, Pewsey and Micheldever produced over 2,800, and numbers are likely to have subsequently grown (WCM 12192). Elsewhere on the great lay manors, there were over 1,300 sheep at Aldbourne

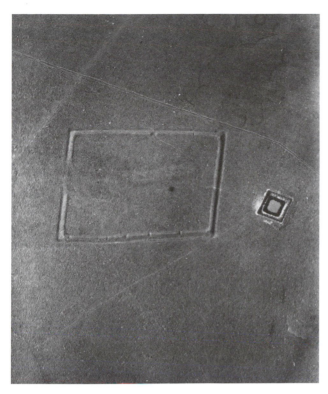

Fig. 7.1 *Earthwork remains of a probable sheep pen and dewpond on Morton Down in Bishops Cannings, Wiltshire. Traces of a possible structure are visible as a faint elongated dark rectangle within the large enclosure. (Crown copyright RCHME)*

and Merc and 1,511 at Amesbury (Hare 1976, 54). Other flocks were much smaller, but it was clear that those of many hundreds were a familiar part of the agriculture of this area in the thirteenth century and afterwards (Hare 1976, 54–5), and that then and later the flocks were to be organised within the great estate in a highly centralised fashion (Scott 1959, 21–5; Hare 1976, 59–63).

Such large flocks were kept and sheltered in winter time in permanent sheep houses, or *bercaria*, whose earthwork remains provide a characteristic downland feature, a large and often rectangular enclosure (Fig. 7.1). On the great estates, the various parts of the main flock were separated and given distinct pastures as well as their own sheep house. Thus at Chilbolton there were three such houses, one for the wethers, one for the ewes and one for the hogasters (the young sheep), while at Michelmersh there was one for the ewes and one for the hogasters. At Silkstead the more labour intensive ewe flock was kept in a sheep house outside the gate of the main farm complex, while the wethers were kept much further off at Newbury. Often the accounts do not give an indication of where the sheep houses would be, but occasionally this can be resolved. Thus at Overton (Wi) there was a sheep house at Raddon, and others at Hackpen and Attele (Audeley's Cottage, south of River Kennet), and neighbouring Wroughton had one at Wyke (Kempson 1962,

114; WCL Box VI J). At Barton, near Winchester, the priory kept its ewes at Chilcombe, the wethers at Morestead and the hogasters at Wyke (WCL/8/24; Goodman, 1934, 42–3), and at Overton (Ha) there was a sheep house at Willesley (HRO 11M59 B1/129).

The sheep house was usually surrounded by a ditch and bank with surmounting hedge as at Crawley, Chilbolton and Raddon (Gras and Gras 1930, 298; Drew 1945, 281; WCL Box VI/J]. Occasionally, references to a stone wall may apply to the enclosure or the sheep house, as at Enford and Michelmersh (BL Harl Rl/X/7; Drew 1943, 33) so that in some cases there may have been a stone enclosure wall. The more typical hedge growing on a bank would have offered a much cheaper alternative. The sheep shed itself, in which the sheep were housed, was usually timber-framed with timber or stone footings and wattle and daub infill, as at Chilbolton, Michelmersh and Silkstead. These would have been substantial buildings, of several bays, and with two or more doors. Thus at Michelmersh a new eight bay house was built in 1280 at a cost of 42*s*6*d* (Drew 1943, 125). Occasionally stone was used, as at Enford (BL Harl Rl/X/16). The buildings were almost always roofed in thatch, whose advantages would have included its insulating qualities, as also at All Cannings and Kingston Deverill (WRO/192/28/1451; WRO/192/32/1419), but at Barton one of the buildings had a slate roof (Goodman 1934, 43; WCL Box 9/36). Occasionally it proved necessary to extend the sheep sheds, thus in 1299 a four-bay building (with five pairs of forks) at Silkstead was lengthened by an additional three, and enlargement also took place at one in Michelmersh (Drew 1947, 160; 1943, 160). Wooden racks and mangers were purchased; hay and straw were brought for winter feed.

By the mid nineteenth century these enclosure or pennings were apparently a thing of the past, but still part of the folk memory, and Dean Merewether's description may provide a suitable starting point. He noted that the term 'the Pennings' was not a farmyard and adjacent fold, but '... belongs to disused enclosure adjoining, of a double square in form, and of some extent, surrounded by a slight ditch and mound, on which still grow many stunted whitethorn bushes. The term pennings is applied by husbandmen to other similar enclosures and earthworks (RCHM 1979, xxi). By their very nature such earthworks are going to be difficult to date, but there are a group of large rectangular enclosures, often in sheltered or south facing combes, that would seem likely to belong to such a category. Few have been excavated, and with disappointing results: the timber structures would have left ephemeral remains, easily missed by narrow trenches or limited excavations (Cunnington 1910, 590–8; Passmore 1943, 50, 194–5; Fowler, Musty and Taylor 1965). That near Morgan's Hill had an outer enclosure which originally had a continuous bank and ditch before both were interrupted with a series of openings, and a small inner enclosure (Cunnington 1910, 591–

6). That at Barbury provided evidence of stone walls (Passmore 1943, 194).

Large-scale agriculture, open-field settlements and the emphasis on the sheep flock within a regime of mixed farming were all features of the downland rural economy that had been inherited from an earlier period, but all were to continue for long afterwards. Thus large-scale agriculture was to continue beyond the withdrawal of the lord from direct cultivation: when lords leased their chalkland demesnes they usually leased them to a single tenant, whereas elsewhere, as in the north of the county at Oaksey and Poole, the demesne might be broken up into multiple occupation (Hare 1981b, 2; 1976, 127). Moreover, the tenant lands in the chalkland were increasingly concentrated in fewer and fewer hands (Hare 79/80, 145–7; Hare 1981b, 13–15).

Colonisation and Agricultural Expansion

The chalklands of the early fourteenth century had reached their demographic peak, after a sustained period of population growth (e.g. Scott 1959, 9–12; Titow 1962). The impact of such growth varied from region to region. In the chalklands, the pattern of settlement had already been long established and there was little scope for the formation of new villages and hamlets, but in areas of woodland there were opportunities for the development of new settlement. Thus in the chalkland valleys the demand for land was met by the growth of existing centres: extending the open fields or creating a new cottage, group of cottages, or other tenancy. Here one of the most obvious surviving features of this expansion are the strip lynchets which line so many of the valley sides on the downland river valleys (Fig. 7.2), as in those of the Wiltshire Avon, Ebble or Wylye, or the chalk scarp slope. People were being forced by population pressure to cultivate steep and unsuitable hillsides (Taylor 1966; Wood and Whittington 1960, 335–338). The considerable distance which these extended from the main settlement, as in Chalke, is a testimony to the acuteness of the population pressure.

The growth of chalkland settlements can be established from the rentals and accounts of the medieval manors, but they may also be represented by some of the regular additions to settlements whose later decline has thus left evidence of their earlier expansion frozen in the

Fig. 7.2 *Bishopstone, Wiltshire. Oblique air photograph showing the regular alignment of abandoned tofts and crofts. The earthwork remains of the neighbouring hamlet of Throope are visible in the top left-hand corner of the photograph. Post-medieval water meadows occupy the area above Bishopstone. (Photo: Roy Canham)*

landscape. Here in the chalkland valleys, the strength of the manor and the limited opportunities for new colonisation meant that the lord would often have been in control of such expansion. Thus on the estates of the bishopric of Winchester, the Wiltshire manors of Bishopstone, Knoyle and Fonthill showed no, or virtually no, colonisation by the tenants. There was some at Downton, although this manor stretched far beyond the chalkland proper (Titow 1962).

Sometimes the expansion of agriculture can be ascribed to the manorial lords investing in agricultural expansion. Thus the prior of St Swithun created a new manorial farm on the woodlands south of Winchester, at Silkstead (Drew 1947). The exceptional surviving documentation of the bishopric of Winchester provides a clear picture of the lord's activity in expanding cultivation. At Downton, he created two new farms or granges: at Timberhill and at Loosehanger (or Cowyk). During the first two years the bishop spent over £45 to create the latter great assart, and this figure does not include any of his stocking expenses (Titow 1969, 198–201). The bishop was also active in the assarting or enclosure of land in Hampshire: in the north at Ashmansworth, the Cleres (Highclere and Burghclere), and Overton; and beyond the southern edge of the chalklands at Merdon, Twyford, Bishop's Waltham and Stoke; and to the east at Meon (Titow 1962, 74–5, 77–82).

It is not always clear whether expansion was for the lord or for the tenant, and land might be first taken over by the lord and then subsequently let to tenants (Titow 1962, 72–3). The bishopric shows evidence of considerable tenant colonisation on some manors, particular at Merdon, Burghclere and Highclere, and above all (in our counties at least) at Woodhay, where the bishop added a substantial tenant population onto a small group of customary holdings, the rental rising from £4.4s.10d in 1209 to over £29 in 1255 (Titow 1962, 72–3). Such expansion of agriculture could take place through small irregular assarts of the heath and woodland, as has been shown on other estates on the fringes of the chalk at Whiteparish (Taylor 1967).

Such population growth affected different manors and regions in contrasting ways, but such variety could also occur within an individual manor, as at Bromham, just beyond the chalklands. Here the core of settlement was represented by the three tithings of Netherstreet, Hawkstreet and Westbrook, which all fringed the upper greensand plateau. To these may have been added the present village with its parish church. To the north lies an area with small irregular enclosures suggesting piecemeal activity of the tenants, and subsidiary settlements at Stockwellstreet and Slapperton. But there was also a large enclosed field, le Cley, where the manorial lord seems to have cultivated continuously. Demesne cultivation also stretched to the chalklands to the east and the cultivation of oats (Hare 1976).

In the two counties under consideration, as elsewhere,

the thirteenth century was to be a period dominated by a growth of population and consequent high food prices. It was probably its immediate impact rather than the general trends that varied, a reflection of the different influences on settlement and the countryside: the geographical influences, the relative availability of easily colonised land, the relative intensity of the demand for food and land, the strengths of the lord's control, and individual seigneurial policies.

Population Decline

The fourteenth century was to see a dramatic downturn in population. It may have begun in the early part of the century, but the death of probably between 40% and 50% of the population in the Black Death of 1348/9 inaugurated a new phase in the development of agriculture and settlement in Wiltshire and Hampshire (Titow 1969, 68–72; Hare 1966, 247–8). Further outbreaks of plague, such as the second in 1362, and other factors led to a prolonged period of demographic decline, or stability at a new and lower level.

Such a development was general throughout the country and provided one of the main influences of the period on rural life. The balance of bargaining between lord and tenant and employer and employee had been changed. The would-be tenant or labourer could increasingly choose his terms. Such a development was not, however, uniform within these two counties, any more than it was throughout the country. For some areas, the demographic decline was accentuated by migration away, while in other parts the economic growth or attractive agriculture led to an immigration that would have done something to compensate. At a generalised level these contrasts may be seen in the taxation ranking of the two counties, by comparison with the other counties of England. Whereas Wiltshire was one of the counties that were rising in the rankings of taxable wealth per acre, during the period from 1334 to the early sixteenth century, Hampshire increased its taxable wealth but slipped overall: Wiltshire moved up from 14th to 5th, while Hampshire fell slightly from 21st to 23rd (Schofield 1965, 504). In Wiltshire the period was to see the enormous growth of the cloth industry in the late fourteenth and fifteenth centuries in and around such centres as Bradford, Trowbridge, Castle Combe, Devizes, Warminster and Salisbury (Carus-Wilson 1959; Hare 1976). Such industrial expansion produced a direct increase in the demand for food, wool and labour, but it would also have generated the demand for food and manufactured goods required by a flourishing industry, its organisers and operatives, and those who serviced them. Thus in the fifteenth century the demand for land, as represented by rent totals, varied within the county: those areas well away from the cloth industry showed falling rents, by contrast to the stable and sometimes rising rents elsewhere. In the latter areas, where rentals had been underpinned by the prosperity of the cloth industry, the period of mid century industrial depression produced falling rent totals (Hare 1992, 25–30). In Hampshire industrial expansion seems to have been less applicable, but here too there were regional contrasts. We have for long been familiar with the remarkable resilience in the later fourteenth century of the rich riverine manors of the bishopric of Winchester (Levett 1916), compared to the condition of downland manors in the north of the county where the signs of demographic decline were more evident (Shillington 1912, 422).

It was to be a period of growing contrasts between the chalklands and beyond. Elsewhere, the open fields and the traditional holdings were already being eroded (Hare 1981, 9–10). On the lands of Glastonbury, enclosure was taking place at Grittleton in the Cotswolds and at Christian Malford in the clay vale, but not on its chalkland river valley manors. On the Titchfield Abbey estate in south Hampshire enclosure had been pushed ahead by 1381 when all the arable, meadow and pasture of Crofton had been enclosed, as was the vast majority of land at Funtley, Warde and Barton (Shillington 1912, 421). But it was also to be a period of growing contrasts within the chalklands: between those areas where the pattern of farming remained much as before, and those depressed areas where new uses for and organization of the land became seen.

The fall in population opened up new opportunities for a more varied and less intense use of land. Arable could shrink and open up opportunities for pastoral farming. Sheep farming was already on a very extensive scale, but this could be enlarged still further. Here, on the downlands of Wessex, the later fourteenth century showed the seigneurial sheep flocks at their peak, as on the estates of St Swithun's Priory, Winchester and the bishopric of Winchester (Hare 1976; Miller 1991, 144). In the fifteenth century numbers were gradually in decline but this may represent a shift from the demesne to the tenants' flock rather than a decline in sheep farming itself. Even when the great lords leased their flocks (which frequently occurred long after they had given up demesne agriculture), the large-scale structure of sheep farming and the sheep house would have continued. Thus a lease of the manor of Overton (Wi) in 1496, includes among the stock ten carts of good hay in the lord's sheep house in the grange at Raddon, while the maintenance of a sheep house at Old Alresford is also specified in a lease of 1492 (Greatrex 1978, 190 and 167).

Another use for poor downland pastures was in the rearing of rabbits. The presence of rabbit warrens within parks was nothing new, but in the later fourteenth century, as the sandy soils of the East Anglian breckland (Bailey 1988, 1–20), lords developed very different large downland warrens. Nowhere was this more evident than in east Wiltshire and north Hampshire, on the great expanses of downland distant from the richer river valleys. Here, the industry was on a particularly large scale at Aldbourne, where in some years the warren produced over 5,000 rabbits for sale, and when the warren was leased it still generated the very large sum of £30 per year. In the fifteenth century between one third and a half of the revenue of this great manor came from the proceeds of rabbit sales (PRO DL29 728/11991 – 734/12044; 710/11456; 687/11134, 11137; 737/12073, 76, 78, 86; DL28/12A f.34a) Other large warrens on the downlands of east Wiltshire were to be found at Everleigh, Mildenhall and Marlborough, producing £6.13s.4d and £4.13s.4d and £14 per year (PRO DL29/732/12034; SC6 1056/14; Scott 1959, 18). Further west and south on the chalklands were warrens at Heytesbury, Amesbury, Winterbourne Stoke and Teffont (Scott 1959, 18; PRO SC6/1062/6). In Hampshire the bishopric of Winchester had warrens on the northern and central expanses of downlands at Highclere and Ashmansworth (e.g. HRO Eccl. 2 159422; Greatrex 1978, 193) and above all at Overton and Longwood Warren. At Overton the warren was located near the sheep house at Willesley (Willardesle), and by the end of the fourteenth century was producing over 1,000 rabbits per year, including 1,448 in 1421. It was leased in 1433 with a lodge and 2,000 rabbits (HRO Eccl. 2 159384, 159500, 159422, 155846). Longwood Warren, to the south-east of Winchester, operated on a similar scale in the fifteenth century, producing over 1,100 rabbits in 1402 and being leased for an annual rent of £10 from 1441 (HRO Eccl. 2 159436 f.25). Other downland warrens have been documented from this period from King's Somborne, Micheldever and Littleton (PRO DL29 728/11991; Redstone 1908, 391; Greatrex 1978, 135). Such warrens provided a means of converting the poor downland soils and difficult terrain into a valuable and easily produced crop, and with low labour running costs. The precise chronology of the process is unclear, but it was underway at Overton by the 1360s and at Aldbourne by the previous decade (Roberts 1988, 78; *Wilts IPM* 1327–77, 181, 299).

Such large-scale production would have left its mark on the landscape. The medieval rabbit would seem to have been less tough than its more recent descendants (Rackham 1987, 47); it was therefore kept in artificially protected warrens with disturbed and well drained soils and built-in burrows. The management of the warren might also involve the roofing of the rabbit holes with scrub and bushes as at Merdon (Greatex 1978, 180), and the management of the burrows or *les buryes* is also referred to in a lease of Longwood Warren (Greatex 1978, 150). The warrens would also have served to make the catching of stock easier. They remain on the chalk downlands as pillow mounds, or as groups of banked ridges as at Gander Down on Longwood Warren, and have occasionally been excavated as at Danebury and Mount Down (Cunliffe 1984, 4–5, 13–4; Clark *et al.* 1983, 122–4; see also Williamson and Loveday 1989). It is difficult, however, to date such landscape features. Some overlie evidence of medieval ploughing of ridge and furrow and have been described as post-medieval. But this relationship merely suggests that the ridges post-date the peak period of medieval cultivation, and so could as easily be of late fourteenth and fifteenth century date as post-medieval. These warrens would cost some money to build and maintain, the bigger ones such as Overton and Longwood had their own lodges (Brough 1911, 213; Greatrex 1978, 150), and the production of the warren might vary considerably from year to year, as at Aldbourne. But they provided a use of poor soils and a means of catering for the growing demands for meat and rabbit skins from an increasingly prosperous population. Such warrens were also far off from the main arable fields, but new waste-land nearer to the village and the arable could also be used. Thus a lease of the manor of Michelmersh in 1496 included the profits of a warren inside the park and outside 'at le lynche which is called Typcliffe'. The description suggests some of the strip lynchets on a steep hillside, created in a period of population pressure and now no longer needed as arable, but where the lynchet provided disturbed, easily drained and easily burrowed soil. Encouraging the rabbit might have had its dangers and it is not clear whether the requirement that the tenant would both look after and add to the rabbit stock, and ensure that they did not multiply to the detriment of the tenants, was effective (Greatrex 1978, 189).

The Shrinkage and Desertion of Settlements

Another earthwork feature that should be examined in the context of such demographic decline is the deserted village. In both Wiltshire and Hampshire, particularly in the chalklands, there were areas where such villages were widespread. In Wiltshire there are over 100 deserted village sites known. Some of these were villages that might more appropriately be described as shrunken rather than deserted, and the material in the Wiltshire Sites and Monuments Record suggests that 28% of deserted villages and 30% of deserted and shrunken villages were in the chalklands (pers. comm. Carenza Lewis, see also the maps in Aston 1982, 11; 1983, 11; and 1989, 109). In Hampshire there are 120 known deserted villages, with 34 additional settlements deserted as a result of the formation of the New Forest, and approximately half are found in the high chalklands (Hughes 1981, 72). Here as in neighbouring Dorset (Taylor 1970), they were largely found in the river valleys where most chalkland settlement had been located. But it is easier to list, than to establish a precise chronology, and the latter is an essential basis for explaining why such desertion occurred. How far did they result from late medieval demographic decline as in C. Dyer's work in the west Midlands (Dyer 1982)? How far did they result from late fifteenth- or early sixteenth-century replacement of arable by sheep; or by post-medieval enclosure for parkland (e.g Hughes 1981, 72)?

Such questions are difficult to resolve in a quantifiable fashion. We are endlessly restricted by the limitations of the evidence, and by the problems of when a village should count as being deserted: how many farmsteads on its site still prevent us from using this description? Taylor (1968) has discussed the difficulties of dating desertion in areas of dispersed settlements, but it is not much easier in the very different world of the chalklands (see also Aston 1989). Two general comments may usefully be made. Desertion cannot be treated in isolation from village shrinkage or of other changes in the rural economy of the surrounding areas. Moreover, it could be the product of long-term developments or a succession of changes that weakened and only ultimately resulted in desertion. It is thus clear from the post-medieval evidence that on some villages it was later developments that led to the end of the village. Michael Hughes has emphasised the importance of emparking as a factor in Hampshire, although, as he noted, this could occur at the end of a long period of decline. But such a development might also occur after a village had been deserted. Thus Barford (Downton) has been treated as a victim of emparking (e.g. Bettey 1986). But other evidence suggests that it was declining substantially in the fourteenth century (by 1377), that by 1500 it was restricted to two farmsteads and by about 1567 to only one (Crowley 1980, 54). In short, emparking was easy, because the village had been deserted long before. How often did such a situation occur?

Other post-medieval developments would also help cause depopulation. Away from the chalklands the growing development of the family farm economy may have helped to produce the decline of the existing small open field settlements (Kerridge 1959), replacing them by a more dispersed pattern of farmsteads. Within the chalklands the growing emphasis on the gentleman farmer may have helped to reduce some villages to the big house and a farm. By 1826, William Cobbett could notice the contrast between the large number of churches and manor houses in the valley of the Avon and its present population, 'It is manifest enough that the population of this valley was at one time, many times over what it is now; for, in the first place what were the 29 churches built for?' (1830, 311). Yet he noticed the process continuing with the disappearance of some of the gentry houses (1830, 311–4). Cobbett rightly thought that the population had once been much larger, but it would continue to decline here in the late nineteenth century (except where this was counterbalanced by the growing tentacles of suburban growth or the emergence of the army as a major source of employment). This was a rural depression that was to continue to drive people away from the land, as at Snap (Freeman 1973, 80; Smith 1960, 389–90).

The difficulties of establishing convincing conclusions on the scale of and explanation for late medieval desertion can usefully be seen by looking at the evidence of two parishes in south Wiltshire. At Bishopstone (Table

7.1), the three deserted settlements of Bishopstone, Flamston and Throope (Fig. 7.3) might suggest a classic example of settlements in narrow chalkland valleys being left for more prosperous lands elsewhere and being deserted in the later Middle Ages. Throope as the poorest of the settlements in 1334 and the least populated in 1377 might seem an obvious candidate for the desertion that was indeed to come. Bishopstone was still a substantial settlement in 1377 despite its later desertion; but Faulston, the third of the deserted villages, provides the most interesting contrast. Although it was the poorest settlement in 1334, it had become one of the most populous of the six settlements of Bishopstone by 1377. It and Flamston seem to be settlements that were growing, and not declining, in the fourteenth century (Beresford 1959, 299, 308).

Downton, by contrast to Bishopstone, included both river valley settlements and more dispersed ones, particularly on the clays and gravels to the east. It contained twelve taxable settlements of which five were to be subsequently deserted. Of the latter only two (Walton and Standlynch) were amongst the poorest in 1334, but they had sunk well to the bottom in the comparative population figures for 1377. None of the other three (Barford, Pensworth and Witherington) seem to have been particularly poor in 1334, and only one was well to the bottom of the ranking in terms of population in 1377, when Walton with only five taxpayers had the second smallest population in the county, and was almost already deserted. Barford and Standlynch would also seem to have been in decline by 1377, although Witherington with 34 taxpayers still seemed secure. Pensworth in the east of the parish had even more (53 taxpayers), but this figure may have been inflated by the inclusion of a number of smaller scattered settlements. In the fifteenth and sixteenth centuries Barford, Witherington and Standlynch saw the merger of customary holdings into single farms although the chronology has yet to be convincingly established (Beresford 1959, 299, 308; Crowley 1980, 54, 71–76). At Witherington, the decline in rent in the later Middle Ages seems to have been particularly substantial. Despite this the traditional pattern of rents and tenements still seemed apparent in 1473. But a year later the documentation reveals a changed and deserted world, although the reality may have changed long before. The village was now leased out to a single tenant, and the account explained that the changes had resulted from the tenants having died or left the township (HRO Eccl.2 155837, 155840). Here, however the lord was actually able to increase his rent as a result of the change. Bishopstone and Downton thus remind us of the dangers of generalising about the chronology and causation of desertion. There were both variations between the two parishes, and between settlements within the same parish.

Occasionally, a clear dating of desertion can be established. One such village was Northington, near Overton (Ha). The lease from the Bishop of Winchester to William

Table 7.1

	1332 tax payer	1334 tax- ation	1377 poll tax	1445 tax reduction	1525 lay subsidy
Bishopstone	15	32s	47	5s	£5.4.6d
Croucheston	10	56s.8d	73	6s.4d	
Faulston	4	18s	60	2s.6d	£4.18.2d
Flamston	8	25s	75	2s.6d	£2.10.6d
Netton	7	34s	44	2s	
Throope	5	16s	26	1s.8d	

Sources: figures taken from
1332 The Wiltshire tax list of 1332
1334 and 1377 Beresford (1959)
1445 PRO E179/196/112
1525 Sheail (1968)

The absence of a reference in the 1525 figures may represent a regrouping of taxation units rather than the desertion of a village.

Ayliff, husbandman, in 1485 makes it clear that the village had now become deserted and that this was not merely the replacement of the four previous lessees by a single tenant. The instructions for the construction of a new hall, chamber, kitchen and grange are more detailed than would be provided in any usual lease requirement to rebuild, while in addition Ayliff was required to divide all the arable land into four fields with ditches and new hedges. This enclosure was to be completed within six years, showing that it represented a change (Greatrex 1978, 145–6). What had once been a substantial village of 28 virgates and 7 half virgates, representing 35 households or more, had shrunk by 1485 to the four tenants (HRO Eccl. 2 155846). Now the remains of open field agriculture and the village tenements were replaced by a new enclosed landscape. The development of Northington represented in an extreme form some of the difficulties faced in the surrounding manor of Overton, where the shrinking demand for land was reflected in the declining rent income from £25 in 1347 to £22 in 1396, and near £20 in 1446. The bishop was also unable to maintain the existing income from pasture rents. By 1396, seven of Northington's virgates were in the lord's hands (HRO Eccl. 2 159500). When the life of the village was formally ended in 1485, it may have been a sensible rationalisation to new conditions, but the bishop had been the loser, and he had lost almost half his income. His tenants at Northington had yielded a rental of £16.10s.8d, but now his new tenant produced only £9.6s.8d (HRO Eccl. 2 155846)

Northington provides us with the model of a settlement in severe decline, that ultimately led to desertion in the later Middle Ages. It appears to be particularly appropriate to conditions in the chalklands of north Hampshire. Around Overton, some of the neighbouring de-

Fig. 7.3 *Well-preserved medieval strip lynchets at Mere, Wiltshire. (Photo: Mick Aston)*

serted villages would seem to have been victims of the period: Quidhampton, Assh, Tadelegh and Oakley and Deane all seem to have been poor in 1334, and continuing poor in 1524 (except for Quidhampton and Oakley which may well have disappeared), but Pollhampton, a future deserted village, remained one of the most highly taxed settlements (Glasscock 1975; Sheail 1968). Elsewhere, at Abbotstone the later Middle Ages seem to have been a period of considerable change, from a substantial settlement of eighteen taxpayers in 1327, to one with fewer than ten households in 1428 and only two taxpayers by 1544 (Sanderson 1971, 64–5). At Lomer, effective desertion probably took place in the later fifteenth century (Collins and Oliver 1971, 73–5). There is also evidence of considerable later medieval shrinkage at Burghclere and Highclere (Shillington 1912, 422; Greatrex 1978, 19–20). What all these Hampshire villages have in common is that they belong not to the wide fertile river valleys of the south Hampshire chalklands, but to areas away from the rivers or in their upper reaches. The high downland hamlet of Shaw in north Wiltshire, which was deserted in the early fifteenth century, may fit into this pattern (Crowley 1975, 10–11).

In the chalkland valleys of Wiltshire, desertion seems to have been of less significance than shrinkage, and some villages were even expanding. The landscape of this area still provides much evidence of settlement shrinkage and

desertion, some of which probably comes from this period, particular concentrations having been demonstrated in the valleys of the Avon and the Till (Aston 1982, 11; 1983, 11). Certainly, the documentary evidence shows considerable evidence of decline in tenant numbers in parts of this area, and also fewer and fewer tenants for the main arable tenant blocks. Durrington, in the valley of the Salisbury Avon, provides a good example of these developments. The number of customary tenant families fell from thirty in the mid fourteenth century to nineteen at the end of the fifteenth, and instead of the thirteenth-century pattern whereby each virgate was held by a different person, by 1506, five tenants between them held twelve virgates (Hare 1979/80, 144–6). At Durrington and Winterbourne Stoke declining demand for land probably led to the wholesale rent reductions in 1461 and by 1465, respectively (Hare 1979/80, 141; 1992, 28). In the Avon valley, the difficulties of comparing the taxation records of wealth in 1334 with population of 1377 are reinforced by the lack of consistency in linking together some of the settlements between the two assessments. But a study of the returns for the area between Upavon and Amesbury, excluding these two marketing centres, suggests that the future deserted villages of Knighton, Syrencot, Alton and Choulston were in groups of settlements that showed, by comparison with their neighbours, a particularly sharp drop between the assessments. Here the settlements seem to be in decline and vulnerable by 1377 (calculations from figures in Beresford 1959). In the Bourne valley, Gomeldon showed evidence of dramatic shrinkage (Musty and Algar 1986, 129–30).

The Wiltshire chalklands suggest a very varied pattern with some settlements shrinking faster than their neighbours and moving towards desertion, but where agriculture and settlement remained characterised by traditional patterns (Hare 1981). In general, the lord did not seem to have difficulty in leasing out the virgate holdings, and the inherited pattern of virgates and demesne remained a regular feature of agricultural life. Nor were these areas characterised by a decline in rent rolls, other than during the recession of the mid fifteenth century (Hare 1992, 27). The demand for agricultural produce from the neighbouring textile areas may have helped to maintain this continuity.

Such a cursory survey can do little more than to reinforce the need for further study. We need to know more about comparisons between the chalklands and elsewhere, and within the chalklands themselves, between those areas closer to, and those more distant from expanding markets. The evolution and desertion of settlement needs to be seen within the context of developments in agriculture and in rural industry. The later Middle Ages must take a prominent role in this continuing evolution and decay of rural settlement, but the Wiltshire evidence might suggest that it was more important in making settlements vulnerable to future desertion than in producing desertion itself.

Conclusions

The study of the agriculture and settlement in this period reinforces the impression of a continuity of response to the geographical conditions. It was this that gave the chalklands much of their distinctive character, whether several centuries before or several centuries later. But these regional patterns of agriculture were also being dramatically affected by short-term developments, of which the demographic decline was merely one. Here in later medieval Wessex we have also to consider the impact of the prosperity generated by the growing cloth industry in the Salisbury and west Wiltshire areas. This was to superimpose an additional set of regional factors. There were chalkland areas in close contact with the growing market of the west of England cloth industry, where prosperity cushioned the area against the impact of the general demographic decline. By contrast, there were the more distant and less well endowed areas of the east Wiltshire and North Hampshire downlands. In these latter areas, the continued loss of population to more prosperous centres increased the impact of the period on the landscape and the rural economy. Here amongst the shadowy evidence available we seem to be seeing an area where the breakdown of demesne agriculture was earlier and more substantial, where land was driven to

new uses, and where village desertion would seem to have been greater. It is perhaps a reminder of the need to integrate the study of the landscape and of the market.

Acknowledgements
I am grateful to the archaeologists, historians and archivists who have over many years enabled me to attempt to link landscape and documents.

Abbreviations
BL   British Library
HRO   Hampshire Record Office
PRO   Public Record Office
WRO   Wiltshire Record Office
WCL   Winchester Cathedral Library
WCM   Winchester College Muniments

References

Aston, M. 1982: *MVRG Report*, 30, 11.
Aston, M. 1983: *MVRG Report*, 31, 11–2.
Aston, M. 1989: 'A regional study of deserted settlements in the west of England', in Aston, M., Austin, D. and Dyer, C. (eds), *The Rural Settlements of Medieval England* (Oxford).
Bailey, M. 1988: 'The rabbit and the medieval East Anglian economy', *Agric. Hist. Rev.* 36, 1–20.
Beresford, M. W. 1959: 'Fifteenths and tenths: quotas of 1334'; 'Poll tax payers of 1377'; 'Poor parishes of 1428'; in *VCH Wilts* IV, 294–314.
Bettey, J. H. 1986: *Wessex from AD 1000*.
Bowen, H. C. and Fowler, P. J. 1962: 'The archaeology of Fyfield and Overton Down, Wilts', *Wilts Archaeol. Mag.* 58, 98–115.
Brough, F. 1911: 'Overton Hundred', in Page, W. (ed.), *VCH Hants* IV.
Carus-Wilson, 1959: 'The woollen industry before 1550' in *VCH Wilts* IV (Oxford).
Brewer, J. S. (ed.) 1879/90: *Registrum Malmesburiense*, J. S., Rolls Series, 1879/90.
Clark, A. J., Hampton, J. N. and Hughes, M. F. 1983: 'Mount Down Hampshire, the reappraisal of the evidence', *Antiq. Jn.* 63.
Collins, F. and Oliver, J. 1971: 'Lomer: a study of a deserted medieval village', *Proc Hants Field Club* 28, 67–76.
Crowley D. A. 1975: 'Alton Barnes' in *VCH Wilts* X.
Crowley D.A. 1980: 'Downton' in *VCH Wilts* XI.
Cunliffe, B. 1984: *Danebury, An Iron Age Hillfort in Hampshire*.
Cunnington, M. E. 1910: 'A medieval earthwork near Morgan's Hill', *Wilts Archaeol. Mag.* 36, 590–8.
Davis, T. 1794: *General View of the Agriculture of the County of Wiltshire*.
Drew, J. S. (ed.) 1943: *Michelmersh: The Manor of Michelmersh*, ed. Drew, J. S., typescript 1943 (copies in Institute of Historical Research, London and W.C.L.)
Drew, J. S. (ed.) 1945: *Chilbolton: The Manor of Chilbolton*, typescript 1945 (copies in Institute of Historical Research, London and W.C.L.).
Drew, J. S. (ed.) 1947: *Silkstead: The Manor of Silkstead*,

typescript 1947 (copies in Institute of Historical Research, London and W.C.L.).

Dyer, C. C. 1982: 'Deserted Medieval Villages in the West Midlands', *Econ. Hist. Rev.* 35, 19–34.

Freeman, J. A. 1983: 'Aldbourne' in *VCH Wilts* XII.

Glasscock, R. 1975: *The Lay Subsidy of 1334.*

Goodman, F. R. 1934: *Winchester – Valley and Downland* (Winchester).

Greatrex, J. (ed.) 1978: *Common Seal: The Register of the Common Seal*, Hants Record Series, II.

Fowler, P. J., Musty, J. W. G. and Taylor, C. C. 1965: 'Some earthwork enclosures in Wiltshire', *Wilts Archaeol. Mag.* 60, 1965, 52–74.

Gras N. S. B. and Gras E. C. 1930: *The Economic and Social History of an English Village* (Harvard).

Hare, J. N. 1976: *Lord and Tenant in Wiltshire, c. 1380 – c. 1520, With Particular Reference to Regional and Seigneurial Variations* (unpublished PhD thesis, University of London).

Hare, J. N. 1979/80: 'Durrington, a chalkland village in the later Middle Ages', *Wilts Archaeol. Mag.* 74/5, 137–47.

Hare, J. N. 1981: 'Change and continuity in Wiltshire agriculture in the later Middle Ages', in Minchinton, W. (ed.), *Agricultural Improvement: Medieval and Modern*, Exeter papers in Economic History.

Hare, J. N. 1981b: 'The demesne lessees of fifteenth century Wiltshire', *Agric. Hist. Rev.* 29, 1–15.

Hare, J. N. 1985: 'The monks as landlords: the leasing of the monastic demesnes in Southern England', in C. Barron and C. Harper-Bill (eds), *The Church in Pre-Reformation Society* (Woodbridge).

Hare, J. N. 1992: 'The lords and their tenants: conflict and stability in fifteenth century Wiltshire', in B. Stapleton (ed.) *Conflict and Community in Southern England* (Stroud).

Hughes, 1981: Settlement and landscape in Medieval Hampshire, in Shennan, S. J. and Schadla Hall, R. T. (eds), *The Archaeology of Hampshire* (Hants Field Club, 1981).

Itinerary of Henry III: typescript in PRO Round Room.

Kempson, E. G. H. 1962: 'Wroughton Mead: a note on the documentary evidence' in Bowen and Fowler 1962.

Kerridge, E. 1959: 'Agriculture 1500–1793', in *VCH Wilts* IV (Oxford).

Leland, J. *Itinerary*, Toulmin Smith, L. (ed.) 5 vol., 1906–8.

Levett, A. E. 1916: *The Black Death on the Estates of the See of Winchester* (Oxford Studies in Social and Legal History).

Miller, E. (ed.) 1991: *The Agrarian History of England* III, 1348–1500 (Cambridge).

Musty, J. and Algar, D. 1986: 'Excavations at the Deserted Medieval Village of Gomeldon near Salisbury', *Wilts Archaeol. Mag.* 80, 127–169.

Page, W. 1908: *VCH Hants* III.

Page, W. 1911: *VCH Hants* IV.

Passmore, A. D. 1943: 'Medieval enclosures at Barbury and Blunsdon', *Wilts Archaeol. Mag.*, 194–5.

Pipe Roll, 1211; The Pipe Roll of the Bishopric of Winchester, 1210–11, ed. N. R. Holt, Manchester, 1964.

Rackham, O. 1987: *The History of the Countryside.*

RCHM 1979: *Stonehenge and its Environs*, Edinburgh.

Redstone, L. J. 1908: 'Micheldever Hundred', in Page, W. (ed.), *VCH Hants* III.

Roberts, E. 1988: 'The bishop of Winchester's Deer parks in Hampshire'. *Proc. Hants Field Club* 44, 67–86.

Sanderson, I. 1971: 'Abbotstone: a deserted medieval village', *Proc. Hants Field Club*, 28, 57–66.

Schofield, R. 1965: 'The distribution of wealth in England 1334–1649', *Econ. Hist. Rev.* 18, 1965.

Scott, R. 1959: 'Medieval Agriculture', in *VCH Wilts* IV (Oxford).

Sheail, J. 1968: *The Regional Distribution of Wealth in England as Indicated in the 1524/5 Lay Subsidy Returns* (unpublished PhD thesis, University of London).

Sheail, J. 1971: *Rabbits and Their History* (Newton Abbot).

Shillington, V. 1912: Social and Economic History, in *VCH Hants* V.

Smith, M. W. 1960: 'Snap – a modern example of depopulation', *Wilts Archaeol. Mag.* 57, 386–90.

Taylor, C. C. 1966: 'Strip Lynchets', *Antiquity* 40, 1966, 277–83.

Taylor, C. C. 1967: 'Whiteparish: a study of the development of a forest-edge parish', *Wilts Archaeol. Mag.* 62, 79–102.

Taylor, C. C. 1968: 'Three deserted medieval settlements in Whiteparish', *Wilts Archaeol. Mag.* 63, 39–45.

Taylor, C. C. 1970: *Dorset.*

Thirsk, J. 1967: *The Agrarian History of England and Wales* IV (Cambridge).

Titow, 1962: Land and Population on the Bishop of Winchester's estates (unpublished PhD thesis, University of Cambridge) (copy in HRO).

Titow, J. Z. 1969: *English Rural Society, 1200–1350.*

Williamson, T. and Loveday, R. 1988: 'Rabbit or Ritual: artificial warrens and the neolithic long mound tradition', *Archaeol. Jn.* 145, 290–313.

Wilts IPM, i, *Abstracts of the Inquisitiones Post Mortem Relating to Wiltshire from the Reign of King Henry III*, ed. Fry, E. A. (Wilts Archaeol. Soc., and Index Soc.)

Wilts IPM, ii, *Abstracts of the Inquisitiones Post Mortem Relating to Wiltshire from the Reign of King Edward III*, (Wilts Archaeol. Soc., and Index Soc.)

The Wiltshire Tax List of 1332, ed. D. A. Crowley, Wilts Record Society, 45 (1988).

Wood, P. and Whittington, G. 1960: 'Further examination of strip lynchets north of the vale of Pewsey in 1958', *Wilts Archaeol. Mag.* 28, 332–338.

VCH Hants Victoria County History of Hampshire.

VCH Wilts History of Wiltshire: IV (1959); X (1975); XI (1980); XII (1983) (Oxford).

8.   Patterns and Processes in the Medieval Settlement of Wiltshire

Carenza Lewis

This paper examines the nature of the medieval settlement pattern in Wiltshire using archaeological, histori-cal and topographical evidence. The first part of the paper describes what can be ascertained about the pattern and nature of settlement in the medieval period and summarises briefly the evidence for various historical and natural phenomena which may have a bearing on the development of settlement in the medi-eval period, including settlement form, moated sites, land-use, demography, and settlement contraction. The second part will consider the problems of ascertaining the origins of the observed contrasts in settlement pattern.

Introduction

Wiltshire (Fig. 8.1) is in many ways an ideal county for the study of the medieval rural settlement pattern. It com-bines good pre- and post-Conquest historical documen-tation with an up to date computerised Sites and Monu-ments Record, a comprehensive place-name survey (Gover *et al.* 1939), a well advanced Victoria County History series and a wide variety of distinct landscape types. The nucleated settlement pattern on the north-western extremity of the county contrasts with the riverine settlement pattern of the chalklands and the highly dis-persed landscapes of much of the rest of the county. The first map of the county to show the extent and arrange-ment of settlement in any detail was produced by An-drews and Davy in 1773 (WRS 1952) and is of a use-fully high standard. Although the rich pre-medieval ar-chaeology of the county has tended to concentrate the minds of those working in the area on the earlier periods, to the disadvantage of the medieval, this has produced the spin-off benefit that it is possible to speak with more confidence about the pre-existing settlement framework than in the midland heartland of medieval settlement stud-ies. It is thus perhaps surprising that the medieval settle-ment pattern of the county has been the subject of so little detailed attention.

The Historic Landscape of Wiltshire

Topography

Wiltshire's distinctive natural topography forms a basic background for the settlement pattern. It has long been

Fig. 8.1 *Wiltshire, showing larger towns and location of settlements discussed in detail in text.*

divided by commentators into two regions, as John Aubrey commented in the seventeenth century:

"In the dirty claey country they feed mainly on milke meates which cools their brains too much and hurts their inventions. These circumstances make them melancholy, contemplative and malicious ... they are generally more apt to be fanatiques"; on the chalk, on the other hand "'tis all apon tillage, or shepherds and hard labour, their flesh is hard, their bodies strong; being weary after their hard labour they have not the leisure to reade, and contemplate religion"

These contrasting areas are commonly known as the 'Chalk' and the 'Cheese' (essentially 'not-the-chalk'), loosely based on the perceived differences in agricultural base (Fig. 8.2). The chalklands are dominated by arable and sheep farming; other regions have a more mixed economy, a substantial component of which is dairy and cattle farming. Regional variation within the county is, inevitably, rather more complex and subtle than this simple division (see Fig. 8.3). Much of the south and east of the county is indeed dominated by the rounded hills and sharply defined valleys of the chalklands. These are divided into two blocks, defined by their drainage. The southern, lower-lying area around Salisbury (*South Wiltshire* on Fig. 8.3) is drained by the Hampshire Avon and its tributaries which flow south into the Solent, while the more elevated central-eastern block of the *Marlborough Downs* is drained by the Kennett which flows east into the Thames. The chalklands are characterised by light freely-draining soils which are easily cultivated

although prone to loose their fertility. Remains of field systems dating from the Iron Age and probably earlier are found across much of these areas, where they have not been destroyed by later ploughing. Those areas where the chalk is capped by clay-with-flints (Grovely Ridge, Chute Forest) are today still extensively wooded, although there is some evidence that this may have regenerated after pre-medieval clearance. Alluvial deposits are present in all but the uppermost reaches of the stream valleys. These two chalkland expanses are separated by the high, dry expanse of *Salisbury Plain*, bounded on its north by a lower-lying tongue of upper greensand comprising the *Vale of Pewsey*. In the south of the county the expansive arable chalkland is intersected by the sharply contrasting *Vale of Wardour*. Although this, like the chalklands to the east, is drained by tributaries of the Hampshire Avon, geological irregularities have produced a sharply contrasting region of steep slopes and deeply incised lanes. Like the Cotswolds in the north, this part of the county retains extensive woodland broken by small fields of pasture and arable. In the far south-east of the county the tertiary gravels are also still heavily wooded.

Much of the west and north of the county is dominated by a broad swathe of lowlying claylands (*Northern Clay Vale*), comprising the western extremity of the Upper Thames Valley and the eastern part of the valley of the Bristol Avon. Here the landscape is dissected by numerous small streams which drain north into the Thames

Fig. 8.2 *Chalk' and 'Cheese'. This photograph is taken from the edge of the 'chalk' of the Marlborough Downs, looking down on to the 'cheese' of the north Wiltshire clay belt. In the top of the left-hand corner can be seen the dark wooded band of the corallian ridge, beyond which the landscape drops into the northern clay vale of Wiltshire. (Photo: Carenza Lewis)*

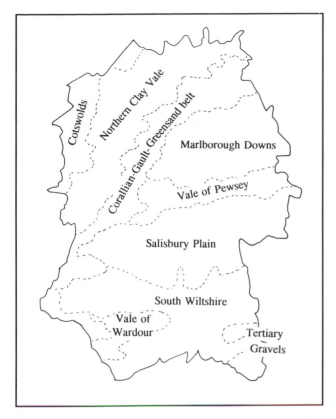

Fig. 8.3 *Wiltshire, showing the major topographical divisions in the county.*

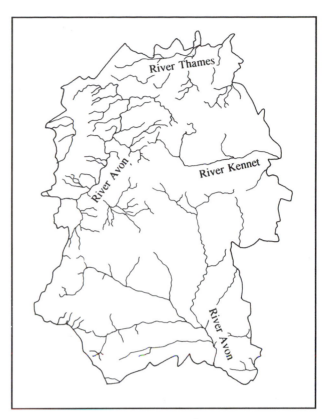

Fig. 8.4 *Wiltshire drainage pattern.*

or west into the Bristol Avon. The watershed between the valleys of the upper Thames and the Bristol Avon extends across the vale just north-east of Malmesbury, but is not a noticeable feature in the landscape. The predominantly heavy Oxford clay derived soils are difficult to plough and prone to waterlogging after even fairly short episodes of cultivation. Although extensive ridge and furrow attests to the fact that they have been ploughed in the past, they are more commonly areas of pastoral farming. The clay vale is bounded on its north-west by the Oolitic limestones and clays of the *Wiltshire Cotswolds*, where deeply incised 'V' shaped valleys are drained by the upper reaches of the Wiltshire Avon and the Bybrook. The clay vale is bounded on its south-east by an elevated band of corallian limestone, gault clay and upper greensand which extends in an almost continuous line from Mere to Highworth. The corallian is characterised by mixed wood pasture with some good arable land and is flanked on its south by a band of predominantly pastoral Kimmeridge clay, which is itself flanked on the south by a band of porous upper greensand with its characteristic deeply carved lanes and reliable springs on the junction with the Chalk.

Settlement Form

The eighteenth-century map of Andrews and Drury (WRS

1952) provides the earliest complete, reliable and detailed evidence for settlement form across the whole county. It has been demonstrated through fieldwork to be reasonably accurate, it covers the whole county at a scale of slightly more than one inch (2.75cm) to the mile, and it pre-dates most of the changes in the landscape which occurred with enclosure and nineteenth-century industrialisation. The distribution map of settlement forms in figure 8.5 has been created using the evidence for settlement arrangement as depicted on this map, following the principles outlined by Brian Roberts (Roberts 1987) and developed in the Leverhulme Trust funded research into medieval settlement patterns in the east midlands (Lewis *et al.* forthcoming). The categories used are a simplification of those used by Roberts, and focus on the basic characteristics of agglomeration, linearity, regularity and irregularity of plan, as follows:

(1) Nucleated cluster settlements where the tofts were clustered together in a compact grid, radial or agglomeration plan;

(2) Regular rows where the contiguous tofts were arranged as a row with property boundaries of a largely uniform length extending perpendicular to an axial street;

(3) Irregular clustered settlements where a number of single tofts lay too close together to be depicted

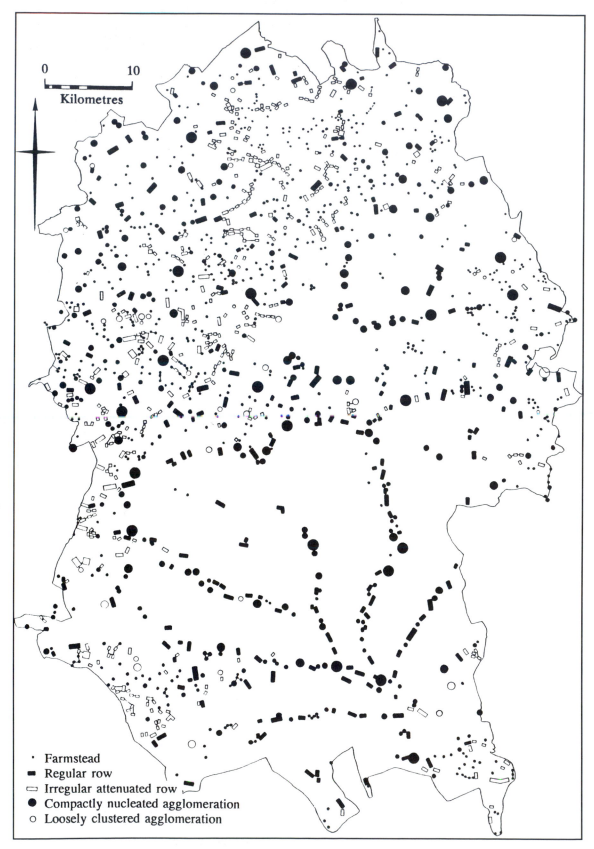

Fig. 8.5 *Wiltshire, showing the settlement pattern in 1773 (drawn from Andrew and Drury's map of Wiltshire, 1773, WRS vol. 8).*

Fig. 8.6 *Shrunken medieval settlement of Chilhampton in Wiltshire, showing the regular parallel arrangement of tofts and crofts within the chalkland valley of the river Wylye. (Photo: RCHME Crown Copyright)*

individually as single isolated farmsteads but were too dispersed to be classified as nucleated clusters;

(4) Irregular or interrupted rows where a number of tofts, separated from one another by small paddock or field, formed an attenuated string along a lane or on the edge of an area of common land;

(5) Single isolated farmsteads.

The size or length of the symbol used for (1)–(4) gives an indication of the extent and disposition of the settlement. Although these five categories can, of course, be subdivided into a large number of variant types based on various plan-structural attributes (see Roberts 1987), this would, for the purposes of this paper, be counter-productive as it would serve only to cloud the pattern with details of doubtful relevance to the medieval period. It is of course difficult to assign some of the settlements recorded by Andrews and Drury to these categories, and inevitably, the selecting and ascribing of settlements to categories is a subjective exercise, with some blurring at the edges. It is possible to argue that, for example, a string of single farmsteads widely spaced along an irregular track may be structurally and functionally identical to an irregular or interrupted row arranged along a similar lane, or along the edge of a common, the presence or absence of which in 1773 is likely to be due to post-medieval factors.

Notwithstanding these caveats, some significant observations can be made. The traditional division between the 'Chalk' and the 'Cheese' is at once startlingly evident. In the chalk downlands, for many the classic Wiltshire landscape, settlement was densely crowded into the river valleys, generally at the point where the valley side met the flood plain. These settlements almost invariably took the form of regular rows along streets running parallel with the valley axis. Archaeological investigation in south Wiltshire (Lewis 1992; RCHME forthcoming) has demonstrated that this pattern was even more uniform than previous fieldwork and the evidence of Andrews and Drury suggest: here, settlements such as Bishopstone, Norrington, Chilhampton and Little Langford, all reduced by 1773 to single farmsteads or tiny clusters of three or four cottages, were arranged as regular rows in the medieval period. As in Dorset (see Taylor, this volume), the common standardisation of toft size or width suggests that these settlements were subject to strict control in their organisation and layout. Although this regularity was an important element in most of these settlements, evidence of a greater dynamism is also present. Many extended for considerable distances along the valleys, and were made up of regular 'planned' sections interspersed with more informal arrangements which often appear to represent small nuclei around churches or manor houses. These appear to belong to different phases of development. These chalk valley settlements, although often classified as 'nucleated' (Roberts 1990, 52), were very different to the compact agglomerated villages which characterise much of the nucleated village landscapes of the midlands and the north of England. In Wiltshire, these types were present only in the far north of the county, on the lias formations of the Wiltshire Cotswolds and in parts of the adjacent northern clay vale.

Settlement in the area between Malmesbury and Swindon was, in contrast, highly dispersed, with nearly all settlement taking the form of isolated farmsteads or cottages strung out along winding lanes (Fig. 8.7) or on the fringes of irregularly shaped commons. The siting of these is clearly topographically determined in many cases, with settlement favouring the more elevated ridges: at Brinkworth the entire settlement straggled for more than a kilometre along such a raised area, while at Christian Malford the church lies on a slightly raised area, while the attenuated row extended away from this core. Much of the unoccupied centre of this region of dispersed settlement lay within Braydon Forest, and the relationship of this distinctive form of settlement with the presence of the forest has interesting implications for the process of colonisation and settlement formation in the later medieval period, which will be considered in more detail later (see below p. 188).

The area between Bradford-on-Avon and Swindon, essentially the area of the corallian-gault-greensand belt, had a dense confusion of settlement of widely varying size and form. Interrupted rows, common edge and hamlet/farmstead settlements were all present, interspersed with other settlements which were larger and more compact. The overall pattern was generally highly dispersed. A similar pattern was present in the south-west of the

Fig. 8.7 Brokenborough in north Wiltshire, showing the dispersed nature of the settlement pattern in much of the north of the county. (Photo: Roy Canham)

county, in the same corallian-gault-greensand region. Around Trowbridge and Bradford-on-Avon, on the edge of the clay vale, there was, however, slightly more coherence of settlement, with a larger number of small clusters and several fairly regular rows. This was part of the most populous area of the county in 1086 and had a considerably higher number of recorded plough teams than the chalkland manors. It is an area that was prominent in the cloth industry from the fourteenth century onward, and a large number of fulling mills made use of the fast-flowing Bybrook. The wealth generated by these activities is clearly indicated in the fourteenth-century tax returns (see below, Figs 8.8, 8.9).

In the south-east and south-west the presence of dispersed settlement forms also appears to correlate strongly with changes in soils and topography. The Vale of Wardour and the forest fringe parishes of Landford, Redlynch and Whiteparish were all essentially devoid of nucleated settlements. While the exact development of settlements in this area is hard to ascertain with confidence (Taylor 1967 and 1989; Austin 1989), the strong contrast of the dispersed end product to that of neighbouring chalkland parishes is undeniable.

In contrast, in the central-eastern part of the county the settlement pattern was less distinct. The greensand of the Vale of Pewsey was characterised by a mixture of nucleated and dispersed settlements and, interestingly, the linear settlements in the Vale were commonly aligned across the river, rather than along it, as was usually the case in the southern chalk valleys. The clay and chalk parishes of the Kennett Valley around Marlborough also displayed a mixture of settlement forms, with a firmly riverine distribution to the west and a less structured arrangement to the east as the valley widens out and becomes dominated by London clays.

We can thus identify in Wiltshire at least four basic patterns of settlement. These are:

(1) Agglomerated nucleated patterns, as seen in parts of the northern clay vale and the Cotswold area;
(2) Constricted riverine row settlement in the chalkland valleys;
(3) Irregular string development along lanes or common land fringes across parts of the northern claylands and the corallian-gault-greensand belt; and
(4) Dispersed farmstead and hamlet settlement intermittently present away from the chalk.

These categories are by no means always clear cut, which is not surprising as the evidence available merely reflects one fossilised time-slice in an ongoing process. However, the distinctions are sufficiently marked, both on the regional scale (between the chalklands and the 'cheese') and locally (between some neighbouring settlements which display different plans), to justify seeking a historical context for these differences, and in so searching, to look first to the medieval period, the end of which is a *terminus ante quem* for the existence of the vast majority of settlements in the county.

Historical Land Use

The Domesday Book evidence for Wiltshire has been mapped and discussed (Darby and Welldon Finn 1967) and need only be summarised here. The evidence contained within it for land type and use across the county provides a useful context for medieval settlement studies, although it is frequently difficult to interpret.

Considering that the county, particularly the chalklands, is now commonly thought of as extensively arable, with its wealthy 'barley barons' and vast expanses of undifferentiated cornfield, it is by no means nationally prominent in Domesday Book as an arable area (Darby 1977). Indeed, the chalklands have generally a low density of both plough teams and woodland, with moderately large areas of meadow and pasture. Given that archaeological, topographical and historical evidence all point to the chalk valley slopes as prime arable land even in the pre-conquest era (see also Costen, this vol-

ume) this is perhaps unexpected, although the largish extents of meadow and pasture fit well with existing notions of land use in this region. The distribution of plough teams shows that much of the northern clay vale, between Warminster, Bradford and Calne, had the highest density. Ridge and furrow in parts of the clay vale points to its use as arable land in the medieval period despite the fact that it is difficult land to cultivate in this manner, better suited to pasture. (Certainly, in both the sixteenth century and more recently, it was an area of cattle and dairy farming, hence the adoption of 'Cheese' as a moniker for the region.) The high number of plough teams recorded in Domesday Book in this area appears to suggest that this land was cultivated in the eleventh century. It may possibly also reflect the difficulty of ploughing the heavy land, necessitating a larger number of ploughs. Indeed, the fact that this area is also one with very high levels of recorded woodland and moderately large areas of pasture may bear out this suggestion that a high density of plough teams may not necessarily imply a large area of cultivated arable here. In contrast, in the Cotswold region – plough teams, meadow and woodland are all under-represented.

The northern extent of the gault-greensand belt has slightly lower densities of plough teams than the chalk, and larger areas of meadow and pasture, although as the latter have been recorded in acres rather than the more commonly used furlongs it is difficult to compare directly. It does, however, bear out the traditionally accepted mixed nature of the rural economy of this area. The corallian ridge itself has extensive woodland in Domesday Book, as do the areas of historical royal forest, with the rather surprising exception of Melchet Forest in the south-east, which has virtually none. Much of the east and west of the county lay within royal forests in 1086, and indeed the Saxon forest of *Sealwudu* appears to have once extended unbroken from the Thame Valley in Buckinghamshire to the Vale of Blackmore in Dorset. Post-Conquest royal forests such as Chippenham and Melksham were carved out of this great area as it gradually broke up. Records of assarts are common in many of the manors fringing the royal Forests (VCH 4, 1959).

Demography

John Hare in this volume reviews the evidence for changes in population over time in the Wessex chalklands; the following section is intended to consider and map only the evidence for changing *relative* levels of population across the regions of Wiltshire from 1086 to the early fifteenth century. Domesday Book provides us with the earliest written evidence for population. The highest recorded population densities were then in the Warminster-Bradford-Calne area and also in the Avon Valley, both around Salisbury and in the area north of the Plain around the Cannings. Other parts of the county, particularly in the forest areas on the eastern, western and northern borders of the county, had low levels of population re-corded in 1086. The Cotswolds were very low despite the regular spread of recorded holdings across the area: by contrast, other areas of low population (namely the forest fringes) have a much more erratic and sparse distribution of recorded named holdings.

Useful later medieval taxation data across the whole of Wiltshire is available in 1332 (WRS 1989), 1334 and 1377, supplemented by a list of places exempted from tax because they contained fewer than ten households in 1428 (VCH 4, 1959). The 1332 Lay Subsidy (Fig. 8.8), naming each taxpayer, has been published in full (WRS 1989) but as it was a tax levied only on those deemed capable of paying (i.e. those with moveable goods worth ten shillings or more), rather than per capita, and was also, of course, subject to much evasion, it must be treated with considerable caution. Some comparison of relative values across the county may be valid, if only because it is the only evidence we have at this date and we must perforce make the best of a bad job. Notably, a higher density of people were taxed in the Trowbridge-Devizes area (which may well reflect money made in the thriving cloth industry) and in the northern clay vale south of Malmesbury and around Swindon. The chalk valleys north and west of Salisbury also had a generally higher than average *number of people eligible for tax*. The pattern for the *amount of tax actually paid* contrasts with this in one notable respect, namely that the chalk valleys north and west of Salisbury were generally significantly lower than average. Those who were being taxed appear to have paid considerably less than those in other area of high proportions of payers, which may indicate that they were less wealthy and (or, perhaps alternatively) that the primarily arable economy meant that individuals owned fewer taxable animals in these areas.

The 1377 returns for the 1377 Poll Tax (Fig. 8.9) can be used with slightly more confidence as they attempted to record all individuals over the age of fourteen and thus give an indication of the distribution of population rather than prosperity. They can be compared (with caution) with both Domesday Book and the 1332 Lay Subsidy. Compared with Domesday Book, there appear to be some marked changes. The Warminster-Bradford-Calne area still had a generally higher than average level of population, as did the area around and to the south of Salisbury, but the upper reaches of the Avon Valley are distinctly lower by 1377. The chalklands west of Salisbury show little change. While much of the east of the county was still thinly populated, other areas, notably around Potterne north of the Plain and on the clay vale around Sutton Benger and Swindon, show a marked rise in relative population levels, which may be associated with colonisation or expansion involving assarting. It is notable that areas with high or greater than average rises in recorded population are generally those with dispersed settlement patterns.

Because of the differences between the recorded sources, it is very difficult to use demographic information from Domesday Book and fourteenth-century tax returns to suggest levels of population growth between the eleventh and fifteenth centuries, at any level above that of individual manors. Many manors show a substantial rise in the number of tenants recorded from 1086 to the late twelfth century (see Scott 1959, 10; and Hare, this volume), but it is difficult to ascertain how much is due to the rise in population and how much to an increase in manorial and state bureaucracy. It is, however, notable that in many estate records, there is an apparent stagnation in numbers of tenants from the late twelfth century onward.

If relative rather than absolute changes in recorded population densities are considered, the overall impression is more of a steady state in many areas, particularly in the chalklands, whose population appears to have been rising no faster than the rest of the county. This can be contrasted with the northern claylands, where population rose relatively faster during these centuries. While it is impossible, for the reasons given above, to confidently use a comparison of the evidence from 1332 and 1377 to assess the impact of the Black Death and general fourteenth-century economic decline on population levels, it is notable that the areas of greater numbers of taxpayers and highest sums collected in 1332 do generally correlate well with those of higher recorded population in 1377. A profound and sustained catastrophic decline in population resulting from the Black Death might be expected to produce more changes in the demographic pattern in 1377, rather than something essentially similar to 1332. It is notable that at Durrington, for example, most of the tenements which had fallen vacant by 1350 had been retaken by 1354 (Hare 1981, 140–1).

Desertion and Shrinkage

These fluctuating patterns of wealth and population can be compared to the recorded evidence for desertion and shrinkage, although it is often difficult to find any direct correlation. Smaller settlements of the fourteenth and fifteenth centuries (Fig. 8.10) are sometimes later deserted or shrunken but there is little overall useful correlation across the county. Earthwork remains of settlement shrinkage and desertion are visible in most parts of the county (see Aston 1989, for distribution of deserted and shrunken settlements in Wiltshire), but has interesting regional patterning. The map of archaeological evidence for desertion and shrinkage (Fig. 8.11) is based upon the records held in the county Sites and Monuments Record and on fieldwork carried out in the south of the county by RCHME. By and large, earthwork evidence of former occupation is very common around chalkland settlements. However, the rarity of large areas of shrinkage or desertion suggests that it is more commonly the result of settlement shift or replanning rather than substantial contraction. The evidence from Domes-

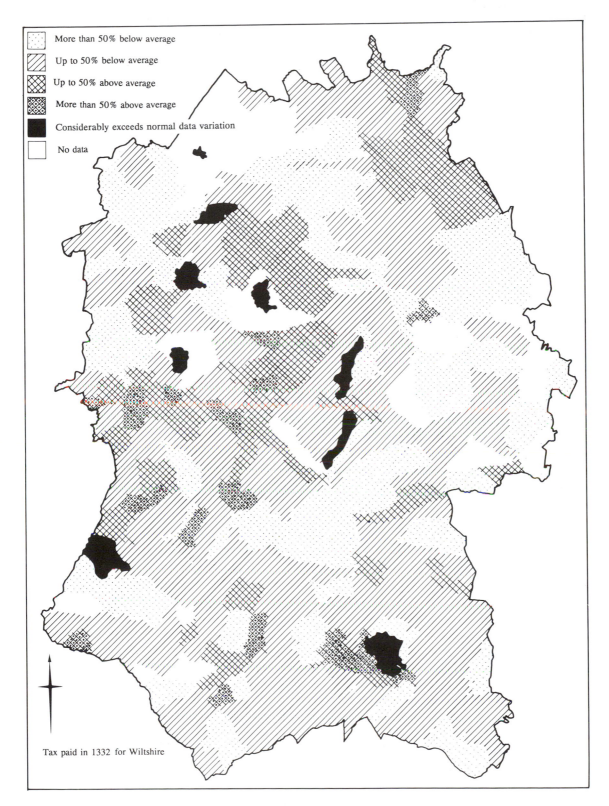

Fig. 8.8 *Taxable wealth in 1332, calculated in shillings per square kilometre.*

Legend:
- More than 50% below average
- Up to 50% below average
- Up to 50% above average
- More than 50% above average
- Considerably exceeds normal data variation
- No data

Tax paid in 1332 for Wiltshire

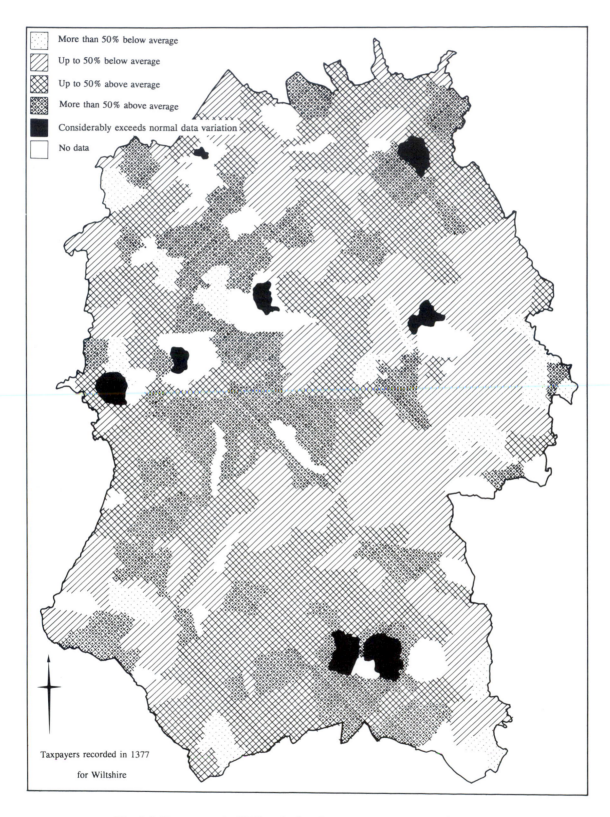

Fig. 8.9 *Tax payers in 1377, calculated as persons per square kilometre.*

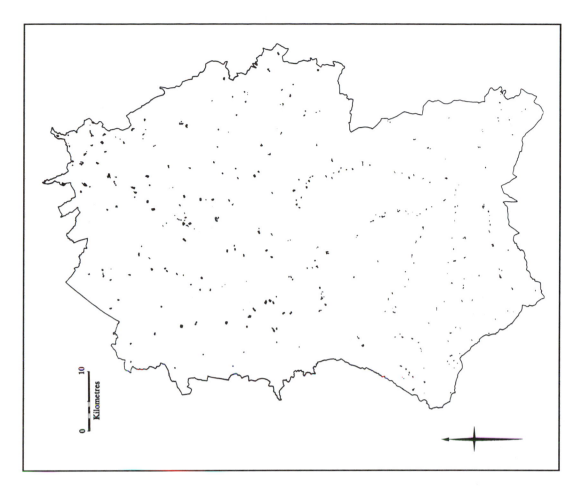

Fig. 8.11 *Settlement earthworks in Wiltshire (plotted to scale showing extent).*

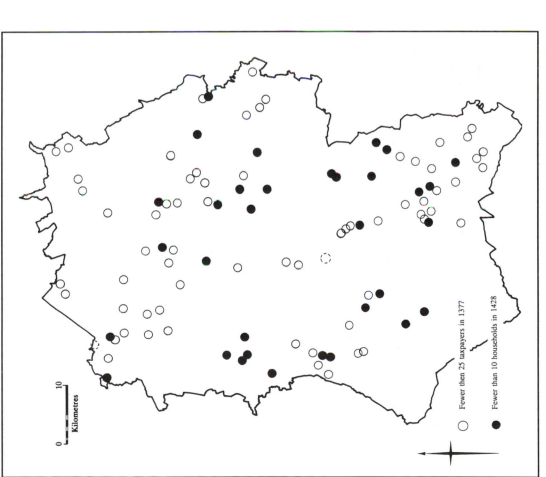

○ Fewer then 25 taxpayers in 1377

● Fewer than 10 households in 1428

Fig. 8.10 *Smaller settlements of the late fourteenth and early fifteenth century, according to taxation return.*

Fig. 8.12 *Shrunken settlement of West Leaze near Swindon. (Photo: Roy Canham)*

Fig. 8.13 *Deserted settlement south of Brinkworth in north Wiltshire. (Photo: Roy Canham)*

Fig. 8.14 *Deserted settlement of Woodhill in Clyffe Pypard, north Wiltshire. (Photo: Roy Canham)*

day Book; wealth in the early fourteenth century; population in the late fourteenth century and exempt settlements in the early fifteenth century, fails to indicate any dramatic rises or falls in general terms compared with the rest of the county. A significant number of the very shrunken or deserted settlements are not named geld centres in Domesday Book, appear only later in the documentary record, and have subsidiary place-names: one example is Norrington in Alvediston, called 'Norkington' in 1198, which refers to its situation north of the main settlement (Gover *et al.* 1939, 199). A late appearance in the documentary record does not indicate that it was not in existence at an earlier date, and indeed it probably was (Desmond Bonney (1979) has suggested that many of the smaller townships may well have existed as settlements within the larger pre-Conquest estates), but these various factors together suggest that it may have been less important, and perhaps a subsidiary foundation. Many other very shrunken chalk valley settlements may have been small foundations or expansions which had a relatively short occupancy. Gomeldon, one of the few Wiltshire chalkland settlements which has been excavated (Musty and Algar 1986), perhaps demonstrates this: it is unnamed in Domesday Book, with occupation in the excavated area spanning only a couple of centuries and abandonment occurring by the mid fourteenth century. It

appears that settlement may have been really quite mobile within the valley bottoms.

The pattern of desertion and shrinkage is very different away from the chalk. Across the northern clay vale and the gault-greensand belt, earthwork sites are typically larger, and are more frequently completely deserted than in the chalk valleys (Figs 8.12, 8.13, 8.14). This is perhaps surprising in an area where wealth and population was rising relative to the rest of the county in the period 1086–1377. It is possible that an economic downturn may have been later in this area and perhaps harder hitting on an over-expanded rural economy. The fact that so many of these deserted sites take the form of regular villages, which are generally uncommon in this part of the county, is also very interesting: furthermore, very few *dispersed* settlements have recorded evidence for shrinkage around them. It may be that a brief period of village creation during a period of rapid expansion was followed by contraction and a general return to the earlier pattern of dispersed settlement, with only a few settlements retaining a nucleated form. It is possible that this pattern of settlement change may occur in repeated cycles as it is noticeable that many of the settlements which have a highly dispersed form in 1773 had taken on a more regular and nucleated form a century later, and even more so by the present day: it is frustrating that so

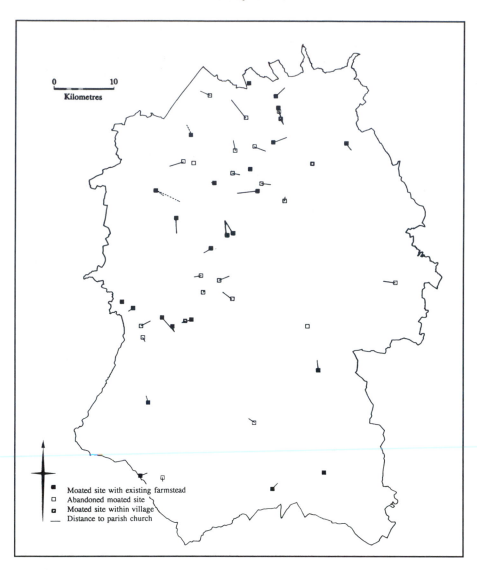

Fig. 8.15 *Moated sites in Wiltshire.*

little detailed work has been carried out on most of these settlements.

Moated Sites

Moated sites are uncommon in Wessex generally, and correspondingly fairly rare in Wiltshire, with only 48 definite examples recorded. The map (Fig. 8.15) shows their distribution, indicates whether they are abandoned or occupied, and where the parish church is sited relative to each moated site. It is immediately evident that there are very few moated sites on the chalk. Those that are known tend either to incorporate streams or rivers and may well not be habitative in function (e.g. West Chisenbury, Little Langford), or to have originated in the post-medieval period as garden features (e.g. Britford). There is certainly no convincing evidence of moats being used as status indicators at manorial *caputs* in this part of the county. Away from the chalk the pattern is

different. Most striking is the string of parishes on the fringes of the clay vale which each have a single moat (Bremhill, Hilmarton, Lyneham, Tockenham, Clyffe Pypard, Wootton Bassett, Lydiard Tregoze). This is quite different to the pattern in areas of dispersed settlement in other parts of the country, for instance Bedfordshire and Buckinghamshire, where veritable strings of moats occur within some parishes. Assuming that most were constructed between the twelfth and fourteenth centuries, as is usually found to be the case in examples which have been excavated (Le Patourel and Roberts 1978, 51–2), it is also interesting that so few are recorded around Bradford and Melksham, apparently one of the wealthiest parts of the county at that date. Although superficially the swathe of moated sites south of Trowbridge could be assumed to correspond with that part of the county paying the most tax, and having the largest number of taxpayers in 1332, careful examination shows that in fact parishes with moats in them are generally below

Fig. 8.16 Moated site at Woodhill, Clyffe Pypard in north Wiltshire. (Photo: Mick Aston)

average on both counts, and that there is furthermore no consistent pattern of very wealthy individuals in parishes with moats. (The 1332 taxation lists are, of course, very unreliable as they were subject to high levels of evasion, and also only relate to this specific date.)

Origins of the Settlement Pattern in Wiltshire

While the above combination of archaeological and historical evidence can provide us with a picture of the likely pattern of settlement in the medieval period, and with glimpses of how settlements evolved and contracted in the later medieval period, it provides us with fewer clues as to why these different types of settlement pattern occur as they do. Furthermore, by emphasising, as it does, the importance and antiquity of the contrasts between these areas, it underlines how much we need to understand their origins. Most theories as to the origin of variation in settlement pattern have focused on the appearance of nucleated settlement in some areas and not in others: they have looked only at this most obvious bipartite division, and it is now admitted that they have not produced a satisfactory answer (Dyer 1990; Lewis *et al.*

forthcoming). In Wiltshire also, the presence of four distinct settlement pattern types, and numerous local variations, suggests that this may be unduly simplistic.

Some earlier explanations can be disproved using the evidence discussed above. The idea that population pressure could have acted as an impetus towards nucleation is certainly not borne out by the evidence for the eleventh century and later in Wiltshire, as areas of high and/or rising population in this period are in fact commonly areas of dispersed settlement. A similar pattern has been noted by Tom Williamson in Norfolk (Williamson 1993, 110–114). In addition, the most distinct area of more classically nucleated settlement pattern (the Cotswold fringe) retains low levels of recorded population throughout the medieval period. The role of lords in founding villages has also been discussed recently (Dyer 1985; Harvey 1989). Certainly in Wiltshire there are large numbers of manors held by powerful ecclesiastical lords, including the abbeys of Glastonbury, Shaftesbury, Wilton and Malmesbury which kept comprehensive records from the twelfth century onward which attest to the fervour with which they managed and maximised returns from their resources. However, there is no correlation readily apparent between these holdings and any particular form of settlement. Earlier, it is apparent that the manors in Domesday Book of the Church and the Crown, lords who might be thought to be particularly strong and capable of reorganising settlement into villages if they so desired, in no way correlate with the observed variations in settlement pattern.

Variations in landuse and topography are clearly important in determining some of the broad characteristics of the settlement pattern in Wiltshire; dispersed settlement is common in areas of former royal forest or high levels of recorded woodland, and these are mostly on on the chalk. Landuse and topographical contrasts do not, however, readily provide an adequate explanation for the more detailed variations in settlement pattern. Areas of dispersed settlement, for example, are commonly characterised by a varying combination of hamlet/farmstead and irregular row dispersed settlement, and not all dispersed settlement areas lie within forest or woodland areas, such as the Vale of Wardour and parts of the eastern Kennett Valley. Conversely, nucleated riverine settlements are common in areas which lay within the forests of Chute, Grovely and the south of Selwood (Grant 1959, 391–460).

The fact that historically observable factors cannot provide an adequate explanation for variation in the settlement pattern suggests, despite the fact that many excavated villages have little or no evidence for settlement pre-dating the Norman Conquest, that the causes may lie in the historically opaque earlier centuries. Early ideas indeed focused on this period and suggested that villages were founded by pagan Saxon immigrants in the south and east, leaving the native Britons occupying dispersed settlements in the north and west. This simple and superficially persuasive idea cannot account for the more localised contrasts in settlement pattern present in Wiltshire, and have in any case long been confounded by archaeological evidence in various parts of the country, which has shown that many excavated villages have no evidence of planned early post-Roman occupation, and that settlements of this date tend in fact to be small dispersed hamlet or farmstead units (e.g. Millet 1983; Hall and Martin 1979; Hall 1988). The idea that planned villages appeared as part of the Danish occupation and the subsequent Wessex 'Reconquest', while possibly applicable in parts of the east midlands is evidently not relevant in Wiltshire. (It is perhaps worth noting that if this were indeed the case in the east midlands, we might expect that planned villages of this type should feature more strongly in the settlement pattern of the heartland of Wessex.)

An alternative explanation is that the broad foundations of the in settlement pattern existed even earlier. The Roman period is the prologue for the development of settlement in the centuries 400–1500 AD. There is extensive, though patchy, evidence for Roman activity across all of Wiltshire and it is clear that most of the county was settled and occupied at the height of the Roman era. Numerous villas are known across the north of the county from the Cotswolds to the Kennett chalklands and are turning up with increasing frequency in the southern chalk valleys. They are likely to have been the centres of estates exploiting the arable and extractive wealth of these regions. The widespread distribution of Roman pottery along the valley bottoms noted during RCHME fieldwork in south Wiltshire, and in excavation around Avebury (Evans *et al.* 1993), combined with the presence of large buildings which may in some cases be villas (Mark Corney, pers comm), indicates that these areas were favoured for occupation in this period, but we are less certain as to the form of these settlements. They may have been nucleated settlements, but ironically, medieval and later occupation has destroyed or obscured much of the evidence for this. Extensive settlements of Romano-British date do indeed survive, as earthworks (often strikingly similar in plan to medieval nucleated villages), on the highly inhospitable downland crests of Salisbury Plain, where they are commonly associated with extensive arable field systems. In some cases they cover a large area and display two or three phases of replanning. There is little evidence for higher status buildings on these settlements, and they may be planted settlements created to facilitate the farming of the upper slopes. If this is the case, they eloquently underline the power and sophistication of the villa estate system in this area.

In contrast, several low-lying Roman 'villages' have been recorded in the north of the county (e.g. Ashton Keynes, Water Eaton, Stratton St Margaret). The identification of this type of site has certainly been facilitated in this area by the presence of both development threats

prompting fieldwork and intensive recording of sites through air photography (Canham 1982), which has filled in many of the gaps in distribution maps such as that produced by Desmond Bonney in 1979 (Bonney 1979, 46). It is clear from work in the upper Thames Valley in neighbouring Oxfordshire (Miles 1978; 1982, 53–79) that this area was intensively settled in the Roman period with a hierarchy of settlements including villas, farms and villages (see also Hingley 1993). It is notable that this area where Roman nucleated village-type settlements occur is also one where nucleated villages occur in the medieval period. In contrast, evidence for settlement in the Roman period is thinner in the corallian-gault-greensand region. This area was clearly not devoid of settlement at this date, as a distribution map of settlements and findspots in the county SMR shows that Roman material turns up regularly, albeit rather more thinly spread. This may be a result of the lesser amount of fieldwork carried out in these areas and the difficulty of retrieving archaeological material from pastoral landscapes (see Gingell and Harding 1983), but may also reflect a less intensive exploitation of this area. Work that has been carried out a short distance away in the Vale of the White Horse in Berkshire (Tingle 1991) suggests that Roman settlement in this region was indeed less dense than on the chalk or in the Thames Valley and may have reached its apogee later, in the late second or third centuries AD. A number of small settlements at intervals of one or two kilometres were indicated by field-walking. Might this be evidence of a dispersed settlement pattern in this area in the Roman period?

On balance, it seems plausible that the contrast in the recorded distribution of Roman material in Wiltshire represents at least a partial truth: it is possible to suggest from the existing evidence that the Roman settlement of Wiltshire at its height may indeed have displayed a clear division between, on the one hand, the chalklands and much of the upper Thames and Avon Valleys, with a dense and extensive settlement pattern of villas, villages and small towns based on a primarily arable economy; and on the other, the more mixed pastoral economy and settlement which was characterised by less intensive small-scale farming. However, while the archaeological evidence does not disprove this theory, it cannot be said to prove it either, and we are left once again with a need for more evidence.

From this uncertainty, we are next faced with the problem of the extent to which the Roman settlement and tenurial pattern might have continued and influenced settlement in the post-Roman era. Evidence directly relating to settlement is very limited in Wiltshire. Charter evidence, if used alone, would suggest that settlement was concentrated in the Cotswolds and the chalklands, but archaeological evidence amplifies this picture in other parts of the county, suggesting that there were few areas which were not settled at this date; even the intractable claylands have produced evidence of occupation in the pre-Norman era. Beyond this it is, however, very difficult to ascertain either the nature of Saxon settlement in Wiltshire, or the relationship between the late Roman and Saxon occupation. The distinctions between the 'Chalk' and the 'Cheese' are once again apparent in the form and distribution of evidence and merit separate discussion.

'Chalk'

Evidence for settlement in the Saxon period is very sparse in the chalklands as elsewhere in Wiltshire, and much of the recorded evidence comes from place-name references in charters, which are obviously limited in the areas to which they allude. Most progress has been made in looking not at settlements themselves but at their territories or estates. Previous writers (Bonney 1979; Goodier 1984; Hooke 1988; 1989) have suggested convincingly that many parish and township boundaries in the chalk valleys may have been in use as boundaries of, or within, estates of the pagan Saxon period and later, and the distribution of Roman settlements and villas with regard to these boundaries suggests that they may also represent earlier estate boundaries or subdivisions. Other factors, including the use of the iron age Grims Ditch in south Wiltshire and Roman roads in the north as parish boundaries, reinforce the suggestion that some of the basic land boundaries which evolved or were in use in the Roman period may have survived into and through the Saxon period. Although there is scope for disagreement as to the date at which these boundaries were fixed exactly (Ann Goodier, looking at parish boundaries, favours the seventh and eighth centuries, but ignores the coincidence of township boundaries and Saxon inhumations which may suggest a different conclusion), it seems that boundary *zones* at the very least, on the downland above the valleys, were established very early, perhaps even in the pre-Roman period.

The continued use of specific settlement sites across these centuries is, however, another matter. Some Roman settlements, notably the downland villages, were clearly abandoned by the fourth or early fifth century. On the other hand, we can probably assume that valley bottoms continued to be occupied from at least the Roman period onwards. We have little direct evidence for this in Wiltshire, particularly between the fifth and ninth centuries AD, but examples such as Winterbourne Gunner where the earthworks around the church have produced Roman, early and late Saxon and medieval pottery seem to support the argument. At what stage this valley bottom occupation adopted, or re-adopted, the form of nucleated villages is even more difficult to ascertain. If settlement was indeed nucleated in the Roman period, it is likely that any reduction in population or change in economic organisational requirements might lead to the fragmentation of these nucleations into smaller settlement units in the post-Roman era. A similar process can

be observed in the reduction of some medieval riverine villages to mere farmsteads in the late or post-medieval period. A rise in population or a change in organisation could, in the later pre-Conquest era, lead to the infilling once again of the gaps between these settlements and the consequent compaction of settlement into villages.

The arrangement of settlements into such characteristically regular rows may have occurred at this date or later, as part of an ongoing process. Many of these rows display such regularity of plan, evident even in the dimensions of the individual properties, that their laying out must have been subject to strict regulation. Whether this implies planning by lords or merely adherence by peasants to some customary practice is difficult to ascertain (see Dyer 1985, 27–32; Harvey 1989, 31–43; RCHME 1991, 13–30 for recent discussions of this vexed subject). It is clear that many of the chalkland manors were in royal or ecclesiastical hands at Domesday and had previously formed parts of large units which were in the process of being broken up. This is clearly demonstrated by the place-names of many of the settlements. It is common to see groups of adjacent places bearing the same name, identified only by adjunctive elements which are usually manorial or descriptive: examples include the Chalkes, the Deverills, the Winterbournes and the Langfords. The Chalke estate, in particular, is thought to have earlier been much larger even than the parishes which bear the name today, originally including nearly all of the Ebble Valley, due west of Salisbury (Freeman 1987, 3ff). These large estates were progressively broken up into their smaller component parts (probably along long-established fault-lines demarcating the lands of the smaller settlements within the estates) in a process which was clearly already under way at the Conquest, as the large number of separate holdings bearing the same names attests, and probably continued into the twelfth and even thirteenth centuries. A significant minority of the place-names of the smaller manors are not recorded until this time, but their distribution is uneven, suggesting that the process of subdivision and replanning occurred at different rates. At Shrewton, for example (see Aston 1985, 79–80), and between Durrington and Figheldean, several of the eponymous settlements of the Domesday manors are crowded together, each occupying a classic chalkland unit comprising meadowland, arable and pasture extending up from the valley floor on to the downs (see Bonney 1979). In contrast, in parishes such as Enford, Bishopstone and Woodford, several named units are not recorded until the twelfth or thirteenth century, and do not even appear in Domesday as 'silent' holdings, recorded but not identified by name. The siting of the unnamed Woodford settlements, lying between Great and Little Durnford named in 1086, is particularly striking.

There is no significant correlation between the record of a name in Domesday Book and the regularity of layout of the eponymous settlement. While most of the manorial settlements of Domesday are rigidly linear, so are others such as Norrington and Bishopstone. Planning does not correlate with any differences in status which might be implied by the naming of the settlement as a geld centre in Domesday Book. There does appear to be some geographical variation within the chalk valleys: most of the settlements in south Wiltshire are very regularly linear, and even those places which have a more confused plan in 1773 retain elements strongly suggestive of an underlying earlier linear plan. By contrast, other chalkland settlements on the northern edge of Salisbury Plain appear not to display such a remorseless regularity of layout. It is difficult to be categorical about this, because the area has not been the subject of detailed fieldwork, but it is nonetheless apparent that many of the settlements do not follow the pattern of those in the south of the county. Places such as Bratton, Edington, East Coulston, the Cheverills and Urchfont, although mostly occupying linear parishes extending up on to the downs, do not have such regularly linear settlements. The regular planned settlements seem, within Wiltshire, to be geographically limited to the southern chalklands and, to a less marked degree, the Marlborough Downs. Although most medieval settlements were clearly (from pottery finds and place-name evidence) also occupied in earlier periods, it is likely that the planned form of these settlements which we see in the archaeological evidence is the result of subsequent and repeated phases of reorganisation. Some of this, such as at many of the smaller, later recorded settlements whose regular plan survives intact, may have occurred in the post-Conquest period, others, to judge from the subsequent confusion of the plan, may have occurred earlier. Essentially, the emergence of the so very regularly planned, so-called 'nucleated' settlements in these valleys is likely to be not the result of any major shift in settlement, but merely a continuation of a settlement pattern that had been in existence, albeit probably in a less regular form, for several hundred years. By the late Saxon period, occupation had probably reached saturation point, and expansion in the post-Conquest era was perhaps limited. Although the Avon valley has a high recorded population at Domesday, the western chalklands are only marginally above average for the county, and by 1377 the whole area was only average, indeed, the population of the upper reaches of the Avon had fallen noticeably.

It is plausible, then, that the chalkland medieval settlement pattern had its origins in the Roman period, with dense occupation of the river valleys which may or may not have taken the form of nucleated villages, within small tenurial units which extended up to the boundary zone on the downs. Subsequent de-intensification of settlement (in the late and post-Roman centuries) is likely to have produced a more dispersed pattern along the valley bottoms accompanied by an abandonment of less favoured downland sites. Later intensification of settlement (probably from the ninth century to the eleventh) accompanied by changes in agrarian and organisational structure

with the break-up of the large Saxon estates, led to the appearance (or perhaps re-appearance) of nucleated settlements, largely as a result of coalescence of the smaller discrete units. These may not have achieved a planned layout until later, perhaps in the twelfth and thirteenth centuries, when many small settlement units certainly displayed the highly regularised plan seen in many medieval riverine chalkland settlements in Wessex (see Taylor, this volume).

'Cheese'

Other parts of the county are even more problematical, mainly because we have less idea of what the settlement pattern looked like at any period and thus it is difficult to find a known point from which to build a hypothesis. We also lack archaeological evidence which might enable us to hypothesise about the siting and antiquity of estate boundaries, as we can in the chalklands, and which can provide a starting point for discussion about settlement siting and continuity. Dispersed settlement, which predominated in this area, is often thought to be the result of late, generally post-Conquest, colonisation of previously unoccupied areas. Certainly, in one part of northern Wiltshire a pattern of dispersed irregular or interrupted row settlements can be dated with reasonable confidence to this late period: this is the area occupied before the thirteenth century by Braydon Forest. This formed part of the great forest of *Sealwudu* and is first named in 796 AD (Grant 1959, 402ff). It was a royal forest by 1135. The bounds of Braydon were described in a perambulation of 1228 and defined the greatest known extent of the medieval forest. This was contested and in 1279 a total of eleven square miles on the east and west of the forest was agreed to be disafforested, which apparently correlated with an earlier perambulation in 1225. In 1300 the majority of the remainder of the forest was disafforested, leaving only seven square miles west of Purton Stoke.

The correlation between the patterning of settlement and the bounds of the forest are very striking indeed: a distinct pattern of attenuated irregular row settlements ranged along the outer edge of the thirteenth century forest bounds. What is particularly interesting is the fact that the contested area around Hankerton, Charlton and Garsdon, which was disafforested in 1279, also contains some small dispersed settlements arranged along the new boundary, in contrast to the rest of the area which remained within the forest bounds until 1300, which remained devoid of settlement. This seems to date the formation of these settlements firmly to the late thirteenth century. The fact that settlement is so evidently affected by the forest indicates that it was still evolving up to and during the thirteenth century, but the absence of similar settlement within the areas disafforested in the fourteenth century suggests that this evolution had halted by that date. While it is frustrating to know so little about the pre-medieval pattern of settlement in this area, it is clear that the characteristic irregular interrupted row settlement can be reasonably securely dated to the post-Conquest era, around Braydon at least. It is interesting to contrast the attenuated irregular row form of these settlements with those of the chalk valley, where settlements replanned, probably at a similar date display, as we have seen, very regular row plans.

Other settlements, however, displaying a morphology very similar to those around Braydon Forest, lie away from the forest and must have had their form determined by different factors. Also in contrast to the imputed late date for the Braydon settlements is the evidence in other areas of dispersed settlement for occupation on the same site in the Roman, Saxon and medieval periods and, even more tellingly, evidence that some places which were high status in the Roman and even iron age were still so in the middle Saxon period.

One such place is Tisbury, lying on the Greensand ridge west of Salisbury. Here there is a large multi-vallate hillfort (Castle Ditches), a large Roman site that may even be a villa (Mark Corney, pers. comm.), a possible middle Saxon monastery and a medieval market town. The monastery is known from references to the Abbot of Tisbury in the eighth century, and as Tisbury was held by Shaftesbury Abbey at the conquest it has been suggested that Tisbury was the earlier site of a monastery (Crowley 1987, 195, 208, 239). It has also been suggested that Tisbury was also a *burh*, listed between Wilton and Shaftesbury in the Burghal Hidage as 'Cisanbyrig', but this has been the subject of some dispute.

The parish, derived from the abbey estate, contains numerous small dispersed hamlets and isolated farmsteads, mostly tucked into the narrow valleys. The wood pasture landscape makes it difficult to carry out fieldwork and the soil is not conducive to the recovery of pottery. It is unlikely that either a villa, or a *burh*, or even a monastery, would have existed in isolation, and there must have been other settlement around the centre. From what is known about both Roman and Saxon rural settlement in such areas, it is likely that this would have comprised small scattered hamlets and farms. It is thus possible to suggest that Tisbury itself existed as a focal place from the Roman period through to the medieval, and that the medieval dispersed settlement pattern, most of whose elements only appear in the documentary record around the thirteenth century, is likely to have been very similar to that of the Saxon and even the later Roman period. The individual settlements may have shifted site, become more or less numerous, expanded or contracted, but the nature of the pattern may well have been established in the Roman period (see Leech 1982 for discussion of a similar pattern in south Somerset and north Devon).

Another example can be found in north Wiltshire at

Fig. 8.17 *Place Farm, Tisbury – outer gatehouse of a grange of the nunnery of Shaftesbury, one of a series of high status sites including an iron age hillfort, Roman site, possible Saxon monastery and burh, and medieval market town that lie together in the centre of this highly dispersed parish. (Photo: Carenza Lewis)*

Fig. 8.18 *This pond at Tockenham in north Wiltshire is the remains of a moat which lies in the centre of the parish, close to the thirteenth-century church (centre background) and a Roman villa. (Photo: Carenza Lewis)*

Bradenstoke in the parish of Lyneham (see Stevenson 1970a, 90–104). Settlement in this parish was dispersed, made up of a number of scattered hamlets and farms. It is extensively wooded and may once have been within the bounds of Braydon Forest. Lyneham itself is not named in Domesday, but was doubtless included in the manorial holding named 'Stoche', later Bradenstoke, where a priory was founded in the twelfth century. A Roman presence at this site is indicated by finds of coins, and an earthwork enclosure called Clack Mount, of supposed Norman date, lies a few metres from the priory site (information from county SMR). This has also been known as 'lousy clack' (Stevenson 1970a, 91), derived from the Old English *hlaew*, which in this area generally refers to burial mounds (Gelling 1984, 162–3). This might seem rather circumspect were it not for the name 'Barrow End' referring in 1773 to that part of Lyneham closest to Bradenstoke. As at Tisbury, it seems possible that a focal place may have lain on the same site in the Roman and medieval periods.

Close examination of the evidence shows that other dispersed settlements may also have early origins. Little more than a mile from the priory site at Bradenstoke is the small hamlet of Tockenham (see Stevenson 1970b, 168–174), sited astride the present Lyneham parish boundary. It is named in a charter of AD 757 which grants ten hides of land "*iuxta siluam quam dicunt Toccan*

Sceaga (Tockenham) *habens in proximo tumulum ...*" to Malmesbury Abbey (Edwards 1988, 125). (The reference to a nearby tumulus is interesting; it may be the one recorded near Bradenstoke (above), or another nearer Tockenham itself.) A coin of Cuthred (740–756 AD) has also been found somewhere in the parish. More precisely located is a substantial moated manor house adjacent to the parish church of St Giles (formerly St John) and a fourth-century Roman villa or shrine which lies nearby (*c.* 300m from the church and 250m from the centre of the moat). A Roman stone relief of a household genius, now set into the wall of the church (Stevenston 1970b, 168), and a stone water pipe carved to resemble a fish presumably both came from this site. It is noteworthy that, in addition to copious Roman material, several sherds of early Saxon pottery were recovered from the villa in the course of trial excavation on the site (Harding and Lewis forthcoming). Coins and pottery ranging in date from the second to the fourteenth centuries AD have been found during fieldwork in and around the village (*ibid*). Thus Tockenham has yielded evidence for occupation in the second, fourth, fifth/sixth, eighth and eleventh centuries onward: this would appear to be a strong case for continuity of occupation of settlement. Furthermore it is clear that the Roman and medieval high status estate foci (i.e. the villa and the moated site) both occupied this same site within the landscape.

The settlement around the church at Tockenham thus appears, like Tisbury and Bradenstoke, to have been the medieval focal point for an area of dispersed settlement which appears likely to have been similarly important in earlier periods. This still leaves us with the question of the origin and antiquity of the lesser elements within the dispersed pattern of settlement. In some places, evidence for early occupation of such sites can be imputed. For example, several of the small scattered hamlets and farmsteads within the parish of Hilmarton, immediately south of Lyneham and Tockenham, have produced material including a Roman pavement at Hilmarton itself, a well close to the moated site at Corton in the south-east of the parish and coin hoards at Goatacre in the north and elsewhere (Crittal 1970, 51). (Hilmarton is named in a grant of 962, but neither Corton nor Goatacre appear in the written record until after Domesday Book.)

The existing evidence, inadequate as it is, can plausibly be used to suggest that most dispersed settlement regions in Wiltshire were occupied in the Roman period; that the nature of the settlement pattern may have been established then; that many of the same sites may have also been occupied then; and that settlement nuclei frequently continued in occupation. It emphasises also that different dispersed settlement types may have different origins and history, although to tackle this question properly we really need much more evidence, both for the earlier and the medieval periods. In particular, perhaps, we still need to know more about the distribution of Roman and Saxon material, both within later settlements and away from them, and to be confident that we have identified all retrievable medieval settlements. We know much less about estate organisation or continued use of boundaries in these areas than on the chalk and we are ignorant of much of the basic framework of settlement in the Saxon period. It is apparent, however, that a number of 'central places' certainly did continue to be occupied, probably from at least the later Roman period onward. These continued in most cases to be occupied thereafter, while appendant and subsidiary settlement may have ebbed and flowed around them. It is in fact likely, from the limited evidence as yet at our disposal, that many other smaller places also often continued in occupation. The basic geographical structure of settlement cores or nuclei thus appears likely to have been established early, probably by the late Roman period. It is apparent that many of these dispersed areas saw considerable growth in settlement between the eighth and twelfth centuries, which may have caused many settlements to develop or expand as irregular ribbons along boundaries or tracks. As with the planned row settlements of the chalklands, various of these dispersed settlements may have developed differently at different dates, achieving much of their local morphological homogeneity only in the later medieval period, perhaps in the centuries either side of the Norman Conquest. The basic process behind this model is not so very different from that suggested for the chalklands, but clearly produced a very different resultant settlement pattern.

Conclusion

In Wiltshire, variations in the settlement pattern correspond broadly with topographical regions, with dispersed settlement on the clays and sandstones and nucleated and riverine patterns elsewhere. This generalisation masks a considerably more complex variety of settlement form which topography alone cannot adequately explain. Other explanatory frameworks, such as population, landuse and lordship also fail to provide the key. In Wiltshire, and probably in most of Wessex, the evolution of settlements between 400–1500 AD is part of a process rather than a single event, with its origins set firmly in preceding patterns of settlement and boundaries. This process is constantly ongoing, and some aspects, such as nucleation, may even be cyclical. There are clearly several periods in the medieval millennium at which changes in settlement organisation are likely to have been particularly widespread and comprehensive, including the fourth to sixth centuries following the breakdown of the Roman economy and market system; the ninth and tenth centuries with the breakdown of large administrative units into smaller townships; the eleventh and twelfth centuries, accompanying economic expansion and the rise in the power and sophistication of both the state and the market place; and another accompanying the economic and demographic upheaval of the late thirteenth and fourteenth centuries. These are unlikely to have been clear-cut across the county, and inevitably produce an idiosyncratic layering of consequent changes in settlement form which may be complex and difficult to untangle. (Further developments in the post-medieval period will, of course, confuse the pattern still further.) However, the accumulating evidence for continuity of settlement, and, perhaps more importantly, continuity of occupation of high status centres, appears to transcend these fluctuations in economic and social fortunes and provide a considerable stabilising influence in the settlement pattern across the landscape. This processual palimpsest characterises the evolution of dispersed and nucleated settlement alike, and neither should be studied in typological, or chronological, isolation.

This is not to say that an understanding of settlement forms is of no help in the study of the development of the rural landscape. Indeed it is only by starting with as detailed a picture as possible of the later medieval landscape that we can appreciate the historical complexity of both the pattern and the process, and develop a framework for unravelling the earlier periods. It is clear, for example, that the difference between the interrupted row dispersals of the Braydon area and the nearby hamlet/farmstead settlements of the corallian/gault ridge does represent a real difference in historical circumstances, although both could easily be lumped together in a 'dispersed settlement' category where the distinction would be lost. To understand more clearly the development of settlement, dispersed and nucleated areas must not be studied rigidly, or in isolation, but in a manner where ideas about one can inform the other. Wiltshire, with its varied settlement and landscape types, its good evidence from earlier periods and its abundance of historical evidence, has considerable further potential for this sort of work.

Acknowledgements

I have benefitted greatly from lengthy discussions with numerous colleagues at the Royal Commission on the Historical Monuments of England and the School of History at Birmingham University, including Christopher Dyer and Chris Taylor who have read and commented on earlier drafts of this paper, and David McOmish and Mark Corney who discussed aspects of the prehistoric and Roman settlement of Wiltshire with me. I am grateful to Mick Aston and John Hare who also read and commented on earlier drafts of this paper, and staff at the Wiltshire Sites and Monuments Record who have been unfailingly generous and helpful in providing access to the records they hold.

References

Aberg, A. (ed.) 1978: *Medieval Moated Sites* (CBA Res. Rept. 17).
Aston, M. 1985: *Interpreting the Landscape* (London).
Aston, M., Austin, D. and Dyer, C. C. (eds) 1989: *The rural settlements of medieval England* (Oxford).
Aston, M. 1989: 'A regional study of deserted settlements in the West of England' in Aston *et al.* (eds).
Austin, D. 1989: 'The excavation of dispersed settlement', in Aston *et al.* (eds).
Bonney, D. 1979: 'Early boundaries and estates in southern England', in P. Sawyer (ed.), *English Medieval Settlement*, 41–51 (London).
Canham, R. 1982: 'Aerial photography in Wiltshire 1975–81', in *Wiltshire Archaeological Magazine* 76, 3–19 (Devizes).
Crittall, E. 1970: 'Hilmarton', in *VCH* 9, 49–64.
Crowley, D. A. 1987: 'Tisbury', in *VCH* 13, 195–248.
Darby, H. and Welldon Finn, R. 1967: *The Domesday Geography of South-West England* (Cambridge).
Darby, H. C. 1977: *Domesday England* (Cambridge).
Dyer, C. C. 1985: 'Power and conflict in the medieval village', in Hooke (ed.), *Medieval Villages*, 27–32 (OUCA Monog. 5, Oxford).
Dyer, C. C. 1990: 'Past, present and future in medieval history', in *Rural History, Economy, Society, Culture*, Vol. I, no. I.
Edwards, H. 1988: *The Charters of Wessex* (BAR).
Evans, J. *et al.* 1993: 'An environmental history of the upper Kennet valley, Wiltshire, for the last 10,000 years', in Proceedings of the Prehistoric Society.
Freeman, J. 1987: 'Chalke Hundred', in *VCH* 13, 3–88.
Gelling, M. 1984: *Place-names in the Landscape* (London).
Gingell, C. and Harding, P. 1983: 'A fieldwalking survey in the Vale of Wardour', in *Wiltshire Archaeological Magazine* 77, 11–25 (Devizes).
Goodier, A. 1984: 'The formation of boundaries in Anglo-Saxon England: a statistical study', in *Medieval Archaeology* 28.
Gover, J., Mawer, A. and Stenton, F. 1939: *The place-names of Wiltshire* (Cambridge).
Grant, R. 1959: 'Royal Forests', in *VCH* 1959, 391–434.
Hall, D. N. and Martin, P. W. 1979: 'Brixworth, Northampton: an intensive field survey', in *Journal of the British Archaeological Association* vol. 132, 1–6.
Hall, D. N. 1988: 'The late Saxon countryside – villages and their fields', in Hooke (ed.), *Anglo-Saxon Settlement*, 99–122 (Oxford).
Harding, P. and Lewis, C. (forthcoming): Archaeological investigations at Tockenham, Wiltshire.
Hare, J. N. 1981: 'Durrington: A chalkland village in the later middle ages', in *Wiltshire Archaeological and Natural History Magazine* 74/75, 137–147 (Devizes).
Harvey, P. D. A. 1989: 'Initiative and authority in settlement change', in Aston *et al.* (eds).
Hingley, R. 1993: *Rural Settlement in Rural Britain.*
Hooke, D. 1988: 'Regional Variation in southern and central England in the Anglo-Saxon period and its relationship to land units and settlement', in Hooke (ed.), *Anglo Saxon Settlements*, 123–152 (Oxford).
Hooke, D. 1989: 'Early medieval estate and settlement patterns: the documentary evidence', in Aston *et al.* (eds).
Le Patourel, J. and Roberts, B. K. 1978: 'The significance of moated sites', in Aberg, A. (ed.) 46–55.
Leech, R. 1982: 'The Roman interlude in the south-west: the dynamics of economic and social change in Romano-British south Somerset and north Dorset', in Miles (ed.), *The Romano-British Countryside*, 209–267 (BAR 103, Oxford).
Lewis, C. 1992: 'Medieval rural settlement in south Wiltshire', in Aberg and Mytum (eds), *Medieval Europe 8, Rural Settlement*, 181–186 (York).
Lewis, C., Mitchell Fox, P. and Dyer, C. C. (forthcoming): 'Settlement and landscape in the East Midlands' (Manchester).
Miles, D. 1978: 'The Upper Thames Valley', in Bowen and Fowler (eds), *Early Land Allotment*, 81–8 (BAR 48, Oxford).
Miles, D. 1982: 'Confusion in the countryside: Some comments from the Upper Thames region', in Miles (ed.), *The Romano-British Countryside*, 53–79 (BAR 103, Oxford).
Millett, M. 1983: 'Excavations at Cowdery's Down, Basingstoke, Hampshire 1978–81', in *Archaeological Journal* 140.
Musty, J. and Algar, D. 1986: 'Excavations at the deserted medieval village of Gomeldon, near Salisbury', in *Wiltshire Archaeological Magazine* 80, 127–169 (Devizes).
RCHME 1991: *Change and Continuity – Rural Settlement in North-West Lincolnshire* (London).
RCHME (forthcoming): A Wessex Landscape.
Roberts, B. K. 1987: *The making of the English Village* (Harlow).
Roberts, B. K. 1990: 'Rural settlement and regional contrasts: Questions of continuity and colonisation', in *Rural History* 1.1, 51–72 (Cambridge).
Scott, R. 1959: 'Medieval Agriculture', in *VCH* 1959.
Stevenson, J. 1970a: 'Lynehan', in *VCH* 1970.
Stevenson, J. 1970b: 'Tockenham', in *VCH* 1970.

Taylor, C. C. 1967: 'Whiteparish: a study of the development of a forest-edge parish', in *Wiltshire Archaeological and Natural History Magazine* 62, 79–102 (Devizes).

Taylor, C. C. 1989: 'Whittlesford: the study of a river edge village', in Aston *et al.* (eds).

Tingle, M. 1991: The Vale of the White Horse Survey (BAR 218, Oxford).

VCH 1959: A History of the County of Wiltshire vol. 4 (London).

VCH 1970: A History of the County of Wiltshire vol. 9 (London).

VCH 1983: A History of the County of Wiltshire vol. 11 (London).

VCH 1987: A History of the County of Wiltshire vol. 13 (London).

Williamson, T. 1993: *The Origins of Norfolk* (Manchester).

Wilts Archaeol. and Nat. Hist. Soc. Records Branch vol. 8. 1952: *Andrews and Dury's Map of Wiltshire, a reduced facsimile* (Devizes).

Wilts Records Soc. Branch vol. 45, 1989: *The Wiltshire Tax Lists of 1332* (Devizes).

9. Towns and Villages in Medieval Hampshire

Michael Hughes

This paper is concerned with the archaeology, history and development of the medieval townscape and landscape of Hampshire between the tenth and sixteenth centuries. These six centuries saw tremendous changes take place in the topography and layout of the county's large and small market towns, their growth in status and their burgeoning populations. In the countryside villages and hamlets experienced mixed fortunes. Some waxed and waned due to various economic, social and climatic factors, whilst others grew in stature and sometimes rivalled neighbouring, often similarly sized, small market towns, which somehow had acquired 'official' urban status in the middle ages.

Urban Expansion in the Middle Ages

In Hampshire before the ninth century only Southampton displayed evidence of what we would now recognise as an urban settlement. In the late ninth or early tenth century, King Alfred and his son Edward the Elder had established a network of centres of refuge or *burhs* which was a stimulus to the development of many English towns. Of the original four Hampshire *burhs*, Winchester, Southampton, Portchester and Christchurch, *Twyneham* (Christchurch) is now in Dorset. Only at Winchester are the effects of this stimulus supposedly apparent, although perhaps not quite in the planned way envisaged twenty years ago (Biddle and Hill 1971). Recent excavations in the western part of the city have shown, for example, that some of the late Saxon streets in this area are a later addition to the town's tenth-century layout, which suggests that 'town planning' may have been implemented to a greater or lesser extent in a piecemeal fashion (Hughes 1986b). Portchester does not appear to have developed as a trading centre before the Conquest and Southampton's fortunes do not seem to have significantly developed, during the late Saxon period.

Of the other centres which probably developed during the late Saxon period, only Basingstoke, Titchfield and Neatham (Alton) are specifically mentioned in the Domesday Survey as having a 'market', although a 'toll' is recorded at Kingsclere which may suggest the presence of an eleventh-century market place. There may have been small market centres serving the needs of the tenth-century Abbey at Romsey, of royal estates at Andover, possibly Alton (Neatham) and Odiham, and of the bishop of Winchester's estate and residence (mentioned in the Anglo-Saxon Chronicle in 1001) at Bishop's Waltham. Romsey is probably the only one of these which offers the opportunity of identifying any evidence of the deliberate 'planning' of a smaller late Saxon centre, as has been argued for Winchester, and other larger urban centres.

After a temporary setback in the disturbed period following the Norman Conquest, the twelfth and thirteenth centuries was a flourishing period for towns large and small, with the development of trade and commerce, both at home and abroad. In Hampshire many market towns were located by major roads – routes along which kings and bishops travelled frequently – a factor which must have influenced the creation of new markets and towns and the growth of existing centres. A number of towns are known to have been accorded borough status by the middle of the thirteenth century (Fig. 9.1).

Southampton

Medieval Southampton originated on the western side of a neck of land between the rivers Test and Itchen. Its predecessor was the Anglo-Saxon town of *Hamwic*, which appears from archaeological evidence to have been abandoned some time during the ninth century, but during its heyday was possibly the largest urban settlement in Wessex, if not in southern England, and important enough to give its name to the shire before it was attacked by the Danes in the ninth and tenth centuries. Recent excavations have revealed evidence for late Saxon occupation of the site of the later medieval town, including impressive defensive ditches, which argues strongly for a slow but sure revitalisation of the town in the tenth and eleventh centuries.

Southampton played a major part in the extensive cross-channel trade which grew after the Conquest and rose to become one of the country's leading ports in the twelfth and thirteenth centuries. This status is reflected

Fig. 9.1 *Market towns in medieval Hampshire.*

in the town plan, based on the rectangular framework of its defences; a north-south street, the present High Street (English Street in the middle ages); the building of a royal castle, partially demolished in the thirteenth century and rebuilt in the mid- to late fourteenth century; and the change from timber to stone buildings in the late twelfth century, especially those belonging to the wealthy, often foreign merchants (Fig. 9.2), who settled mainly in the western half of the town (Hughes 1981).

Southampton was the first town in Hampshire to show renewed interest in urban defence in the early thirteenth century with the construction of earthwork fortifications, which in the north-east corner of the town had been built over existing properties of late Saxon or early medieval date. In the late thirteenth century the earthen banks were strengthened by stone walls. As a result of the French raid on the town in 1338, further construction work was undertaken on the walls in the mid- to late fourteenth century. Of the gates, only the Bargate survives, built sometime towards the end of the twelfth century. Contrary to previous suggestions that these gates were inserted later into the earthen defences, it is possible that they were originally constructed as free-standing symbols of urban pride rather than for defensive reasons (Hughes 1994).

The loss of Normandy in 1204 had some effect on the

Fig. 9.2 *Twelfth-century merchants house, Southampton.*

fortunes of the town, compensated by the port's participation in the growth in the Gascon wine trade and in the expanding wool trade with Flanders and Italy. The wars with France from the thirteenth to the fifteenth century, however, reduced the importance of the town for some time. The French raids on the town, and on other places on the Hampshire and Isle of Wight coastline in the fourteenth century, which are demonstrated vividly in the archaeological record in Southampton, did not help the struggling fortunes of the townspeople. However, towards the end of the fourteenth century and the beginning of the fifteenth, an upsurge in trade with the Italian markets helped the town to regain some of its former prosperity (Hughes 1981; 1994). The sixteenth century finally saw an end to Southampton as an important centre of European commerce. Although the town continued to be of local importance as a coastal trading port, it never regained its former status until the late nineteenth and twentieth centuries.

Winchester

By 1066 Winchester had become a major commercial settlement, the ancient centre of the kingdom of Wessex, the site of a royal residence and the administrative centre of one of the most powerful bishoprics in England. During the eleventh and twelfth centuries further changes took place in the town's topography: the building of a castle, which destroyed streets and late Saxon properties; the construction of a new Norman cathedral; the re-establishment of the late Saxon New Minster at Hyde in the northern suburbs of the city and the rebuilding of the bishop's palace of Wolvesey. These and other undertakings boosted the city's economic status as never before or since; the suburbs extended to half a mile or so beyond the walls. Merchants flourished – some of the fifty-odd parish churches in the city were enlarged and St Giles' Fair, by then international in status, reached its peak towards the end of the twelfth century (Hughes 1981).

However, by 1200 Winchester had been overtaken by London as the centre of royal administration and began to decline in importance especially in relation to other provincial centres. Towards the end of the thirteenth century, St Giles' Fair declined rapidly, and by 1400 international trade in the city had almost ceased. By this time the bishop's palace at Wolvesey was falling into disuse and the king seldom visited the city. Some parts of the town were abandoned or in decline by the end of the fourteenth century. The fourteenth century plagues had further serious effects on the city's importance, reducing the population by nearly a third. A temporary revival in Winchester's fortunes occurred at the turn of the fifteenth century as a result of its cloth industry. However, by the first quarter of the fifteenth century this too suffered competition from the West Country. The continuing influence of the See of Winchester, one of

Fig. 9.3 *Winchester College, founded by William of Wykeham in the fourteenth century.*

the wealthiest in England, prevented the city from worse decline, but in spite of this the population was reduced in size and the suburbs shrank in comparison with their extent in the middle ages. Winchester simply became a county town with new and splendid buildings erected under the patronage of the bishops. However, the construction of the new college by Bishop William of Wykeham (Fig. 9.3), for example, gave Winchester a new status, that of an educational centre (Hughes 1981).

Smaller Market Towns in Hampshire

Apart from the expansion and later contraction of the existing major urban centres of Southampton and Winchester during the middle ages, there was similar growth in some of the smaller market centres, like Alton, Andover, Basingstoke, Odiham and Romsey, whilst a number of 'new' towns were founded by both lay and ecclesiastical land owners seeking to increase their revenue by rents and tolls.

By 1087, Alton consisted of two manors. The first, Alton Westbrook, belonged to the king, whilst the other, Alton Eastbrook, which had prior to the Conquest be-

Fig. 9.4 *Charity Street and St Mary's Church, Andover.*

longed to the Crown, now belonged to the Old Minster, Winchester. Neatham, Holybourne and Anstey, all suburbs of the modern town of Alton, were also royal manors by the late eleventh century. Neatham was by far the largest in terms of hides and population. Domesday Book records that it possessed a market. Excavations undertaken in the early 1980s on the corner of the High Street and Market Street revealed a series of thirteenth-century rubbish pits below later High Street properties which indicated that plots in this part of the town, on the slope down to the river Wey, were occupied at this time (Millett 1983). Martin Millett consequently argues that this evidence implies expansion in Alton in the thirteenth century, since a flat terrace further to the north would have been a preferable location. The investigations also demonstrated that in the late fifteenth century or early sixteenth century much of the same area had been terraced, which may have destroyed any positive evidence of buildings, but left the remains of the thirteenth-century rubbish pits. In addition a series of cess-pits (as distinct from rubbish pits) were recorded along the frontage of Market Street, which were in use until the late sixteenth century. This suggests that in contrast to the High Street, Market Street may have been comparatively unimportant until the beginning of the seventeenth century (Millett 1983). This may be borne out to some extent by the first recorded mention of *le Market strete* in 1554 (Hughes 1976).

Andover was an important royal late Saxon estate and

references in charters, wills and the Anglo-Saxon Chronicle suggest that there may have been a royal residence and royal staging post in the vicinity. Its borough status and consequent expansion was probably associated with its position on the route from London to Salisbury and the West Country and the establishment of a priory in the town in the late eleventh century (Fig. 9.4). In 1175 a grant of a merchant guild was made to the burgeoning market town by Henry II (Hughes 1976).

A town whose growth is closely associated with the increase in importance of its nunnery is Romsey, on the River Test. The small market centre almost certainly originated around the gate of the tenth-century abbey, and by the early twelfth century Henry I had granted the town a market and fair. By the first half of the thirteenth century it was legally recognised as a borough (Hughes 1976). A series of archaeological investigations in the town over the past ten years has begun to reveal something of the nature of the medieval town and will enable the excavators to build up a picture of the growth and changing pattern of the town's topography. Already evidence from the town centre suggests that both the late Saxon and the twelfth- to fourteenth-century occupation was far more extensive and intensive than previously considered (Hughes 1985b). The publication of the results of these excavations are awaited with interest as, of all the small towns of Hampshire, Romsey is to date the most studied.

New Towns

The majority of the speculative urban developments that took place in Hampshire in the twelfth and thirteenth centuries seem to have been successful. New Alresford and Overton were new urban market centres created by the bishops of Winchester on the opposite sides of rivers (the Itchen and the Test), from existing pre-Conquest rural settlements. New Alresford was probably the most successful of the six new towns founded by the bishops of Winchester during the thirteenth century. In the pre-Conquest period the main London to Winchester road ran along the northern boundary of Tichborne parish. The bishop's new foundation, however, attracted this road northwards to form a new main east-west route through the planted town. Today one can still recognise the simple planned medieval layout of the small town with its wide, aptly-named Broad Street, where the markets and fairs were held. Bishop Godfrey de Lucy (who was also responsible for the construction of the retro-choir at Winchester Cathedral) obtained a charter for a market in 1200. Within forty years of its foundation the population was growing, including forty burgesses and market stall holders. The bishop had meanwhile provided a fulling mill, a market hall, a communal oven and a house for sifting flour. By the fourteenth century New Alresford was one of the country's ten greatest wool markets, a collecting centre for the downland east and north-east of Winchester (Hughes 1976).

Newtown, founded in *c.* 1218, was a completely new borough, located on the Hampshire–Berkshire border close by the main route from Oxford to Southampton. The new town and its parish were created out of the larger episcopal parish of Burghclere. By the seventeenth century, however, all documentary references to the town had ceased, and by the eighteenth century virtually all vestiges had disappeared under the parkland that was laid out around Newtown House (Hughes 1981).

Other medieval new towns in Hampshire were Stockbridge (Fig. 9.5), founded *c.* 1200 by William de Briwere, the owner of nearby Ashley Castle; Whitchurch, a rural settlement converted to borough status by charter from the Winchester Cathedral monks; Lymington, Petersfield, and Portsmouth. At Lymington and Petersfield existing rural settlements were extended by planned development during the last quarter of the twelfth century. Lymington was accorded borough status by Earl William de Redvers (Fig. 9.6), whilst Petersfield received its charter from the Countess of Gloucester. In both towns the new developments were simple in plan. At Lymington it consisted of a new wide market street, leading northwards from the older area of settlement by the river, whilst at Petersfield the planned element consisted of a new main street linking the original settlement clustered around the early twelfth-century church with the main road to London (Hughes 1981).

Excavations undertaken in Petersfield in 1976 prior

Fig. 9.5 *Aerial photograph of Stockbridge.*

Fig. 9.6 *Quay Hill, Lymington.*

Fig. 9.7 *Fifteenth-century defences, Portsmouth.*

to the construction of a small housing development in Sheep Street gave an important insight into the town's development from the late twelfth century onwards (Fox and Hughes 1994), while in 1990 and 1992 limited investigations were undertaken as part of a planning application to redevelop an area of the town centre (Torrance and Ford 1994). Both investigations demonstrated that the archaeological evidence closely accorded with the documentary evidence for a late twelfth-century development of the town after it had received borough status, in the Sheep Street and High Street areas. However, there is a cautionary tale for those who use street names to demonstrate the previous use of the area without checking their interpretation fully! In 1976 I claimed that Sheep Street referred to the use of the area as a sheep market, as 'Sheep' may have also been derived from 'cheap' meaning market (Hughes 1976). In his documentary research on the history of Sheep Street, Nicholas Cahill found that in fact the street name was derived from an inn (first recorded in 1653) called the Ship! A reference to a Ship Street also existed in 1710 (Cahill in Fox and Hughes 1994).

At Portsmouth, John de Gisors founded a new town *c.* 1180. He was believed to have been a merchant of Norman origin and already held estates in the area, including the manor of Buckland, on Portsea Island, which he had acquired from the de Port family (sheriffs of the county) in 1170. He laid out streets, gave land and endowments for St Thomas' church and let out 'places' for what was thereafter called Portsmouth. However, within a few years de Gisors had forfeited all his estates, including his new town, to the Crown. Richard I granted Portsmouth borough status towards the end of the twelfth century (Hoad and Wells 1989). The first dock was also laid out around this time and although the town had connections with the victualling and supply of royal and mercantile shipping in the thirteenth and fourteenth centuries, it was not until Portsmouth's strategic importance was recognised during the Hundred Years War that its potential as a naval base was realised. The early fifteenth century saw the construction of stone walls for the town (Fig. 9.7), whilst in the latter half of the same century Henry VII constructed the first dry dock, thus ensuring Portsmouth's future prosperity (Hughes 1994).

Town Plans

New foundations or new additions soon acquired a town plan from their owners, and in settlements of pre-Conquest origin an existing and often irregular street pattern would be modified during the middle ages by the addition of a planned element. The larger, proto-urban pre-Conquest settlements of Hampshire, especially those in royal or monastic hands, such as Alton, Andover, Basingstoke and Romsey, appear, however, to have continued to expand in a more organic way, although such towns may well contain later planned streets. The planned

element in other Hampshire towns consisted of a well-defined grid plan, as within the town walls of Southampton and Winchester, the provision of a large market or fair place (as for example at Wickham – although its earliest reference as a borough is of sixteenth-century date), or merely the laying out of a wide market street with burgage plots on each side for the new townspeople. This pattern of medieval property boundaries is still a distinctive feature of some of the smaller planned towns like Overton, Alresford, Fareham, Petersfield and Lymington. However, without further results of archaeological investigations in the county's smaller historic towns (although it is less likely in the 1990s that archaeology will shed much light on this subject because of the restrictions placed on development inside historic conservation areas), more detailed documentary research and a house by house survey, it is very difficult to date accurately the laying out of the streets or their plots.

Town plans are more than just planned streets. A number of other aspects are important when attempting to understand the way a particular town plan has originated and developed: the relationship of streets to one another; individual plots and their relationship to the street pattern and the siting and relationship of domestic and public buildings to the street layout, in addition to an understanding of their status and function. Important historical precincts such as churches, manor houses, market places and monastic houses may also have affected the urban topography at some time in the town's development. For example, some limited research has been carried out on the development of Fareham, in south Hampshire, another of the bishops of Winchester's boroughs (probably founded in late twelfth or early thirteenth century), which had a simple planned layout, very similar to Alresford and Overton, of a wide market street joining a major through-road. It has been shown that this market street, present-day High Street (North Street until the nineteenth century), was a planned element of the town (Hughes 1976). It has clear distinctive property boundaries on either side of the street, which back on the west side onto what were at one time medieval open fields. High Street, however, cannot be dated by architectural evidence or from documentary research to be earlier than the sixteenth century, and apart from a few fragments of medieval pottery from the area around the church, no earlier archaeological evidence has been found. However, in view of what occurred in Alton, it is possible that the late medieval and Georgian building or terracing programme in the High Street may have destroyed any earlier structural evidence.

Further possible support for a late date for the development of Fareham comes from government documentary records: the Lay Subsidy Rolls for 1334 (Glasscock 1975) and 1524/25 (Sheail 1968), and the Hearth Tax Assessment of 1665 (Hughes and White 1992). In the first case the returns for Fareham were extremely low in value, whilst the 1524/25 return records seventy-one taxpayers for the town (suggesting a population of around 2–300), of which approximately two thirds were engaged in agricultural activities. By the late seventeenth century the Hearth Tax returns suggest that the total population was in the region of 300–400, but by the beginning of the nineteenth century the first Census returns record a population of just over 3000.

Population, Size and Structure

The population figures as extrapolated from the Lay Subsidy Rolls of 1524/25 would seem to indicate that even by the first half of the sixteenth century the size of some of the smaller boroughs in Hampshire, and elsewhere in Wessex, did not exceed 100 taxpayers or 3–400 head of population. In the county those smaller boroughs included all the bishop of Winchester's new towns as well as Stockbridge, Basingstoke, Andover, Alton, Whitchurch, Petersfield, Romsey and Lymington. Even towns like Portsmouth had only 124 taxpayers recorded. These figures, even if used with some caution, do suggest that many medieval boroughs and market towns may only have been of village size, or contained village-sized populations. However, even though they may have been 'village' in size or population they were clearly differentiated, both by their appearance and topography (although some villages have planned layouts similar to those in the smaller towns) and by the occupation of some of their inhabitants. A fifteenth-century court roll for Basingstoke, for example, records a list of tradesmen from the town, which included fullers and dyers of cloth, tanners and wool traders, whilst for Newtown, the bishop's 'failed' borough, there is evidence for butchers, bakers, ironmongers and shoemakers (Hughes 1976).

By the beginning of the fourteenth century, fourteen market towns in Hampshire had received borough status, either by royal, aristocratic or episcopal charter, or were included in parliamentary or taxation returns as having borough status. Other market places such as Kingsclere, Ringwood (strangely, this is one of the wealthiest places in Hampshire in the middle ages according to the taxation returns yet was never accorded borough status), Fordingbridge, Havant and Emsworth remained important local market villages, and did not develop any real urban qualities until the nineteenth century. Titchfield, one of the few places in the county to have a market and toll recorded in Domesday, was referred to as a *villa mercatoria* during the fourteenth century. However, due to the strong domination of the abbey (a Premonstratensian house founded in 1232 by Peter des Roches, Bishop of Winchester), Titchfield never achieved true urban status. Bishop's Waltham, another of the bishop's manors and the site of an episcopal palace, contained a simple grid pattern of streets in its layout but, as far as is known, never achieved borough status (Hughes 1981).

Other settlements that may represent failed medieval urban sites are Botley, near Southampton, for which documentary evidence exists for 'burgesses' in the fourteenth century, and Southwick, near Portsmouth, where there is some semblance of a simple, laid out street plan outside the gate of the twelfth-century priory.

Economic decline, plagues and wars with France marked the end of new town foundations in Hampshire until the eighteenth and nineteenth centuries, when military needs and the laying out of the railway network dictated the need for new urban centres and gave rise to towns like Portsea, Gosport, Aldershot and Eastleigh.

The Pattern of Rural Settlement

The problems involved in the study of the origins, development and, in some cases, demise of rural settlements in Hampshire between the medieval and early modern periods are both large and complex. Apart from my limited attempts (Hughes 1979, 1981, 1984a, 1984b and forthcoming) a synthesis of any real merit is still lacking, even though there has been a small number of isolated studies of deserted rural settlements. There has also been a small number of excavations in recent years which have aided the understanding of how certain settlements have developed.

The Norman Conquest of 1066, which resulted in such dramatic changes in political, religious and social life, appears to have affected the rural landscape far less. The Domesday Survey is an invaluable document for describing much about the landscape, including that of Hampshire. This information must, however, be treated with extreme caution. By no means all the settlements, or more correctly 'places', that existed in the late eleventh century are recorded, nor is much light shed on the patterns of the newly evolving parishes and their constituent churches (Fig. 9.8). Some of the settlements the Survey mentions were already in the process of decay or depopulation, as were a number of those recorded for the New Forest (Hughes 1984a).

Although the distribution of eleventh-century 'places' across the county does not differ markedly from that of the middle ages or the sixteenth century, the number of settlements does. There are approximately 320 places recorded in Domesday, nearly 500 recorded in 1334 (Glasscock 1975) and around 600 in the first half of the sixteenth century (Sheail 1968). While this may be indicative to some extent of the pitfalls of using Domesday 'statistics', it does suggest the growth of new settlements in Hampshire. Because so much of the fertile soil was already being exploited during the twelfth and thirteenth centuries, new settlements were created on what today would be called marginal land, such as the higher downland, the heathlands of the New Forest and northeast Hampshire and the often clayey lands of the royal forests of Bere, Alice Holt, Woolmer, Chute and Pamber (Hughes 1981).

The broad distribution of rural settlement in the county

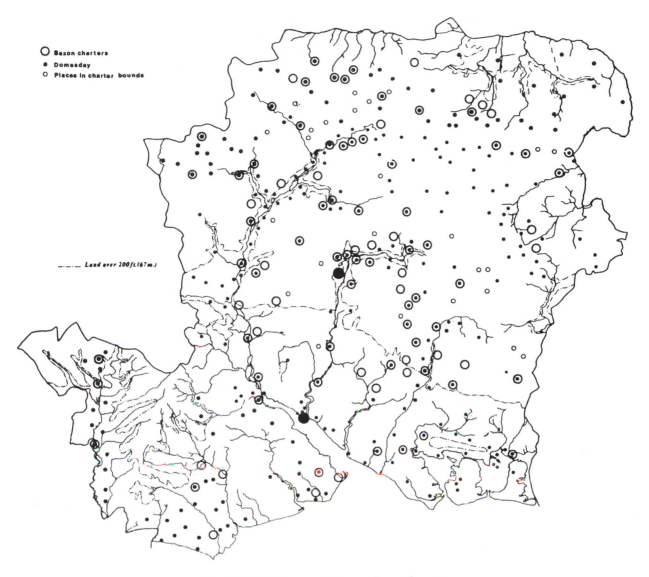

Fig. 9.8 *Late Saxon and Domesday settlement.*

during the middle ages consisted in general of nucleated villages on the central chalklands and in the west, while in other parts, such as the south-eastern coastal plain, the south-west and the north and east, the pattern was a combination of villages, satellite hamlets and dispersed farmsteads. Concentrations of settlements occurred in the area between Southampton and the Sussex border, around Basingstoke and Odiham, between Andover, Stockbridge and the Wiltshire border, around Winchester and in the Avon Valley. These areas were amongst the wealthiest in late medieval Hampshire (Hughes 1981).

Nucleated villages, some large some small, one in each ecclesiastical parish, normally contained the parish church, a manor house and a cluster of farms and dwellings. Some were important enough locally to be granted market and fair rights and some have evidence of 'planned' streets like East Meon, a bishopric manor and village. Many villages, especially some of those along the banks of the rivers Avon, Test and Itchen and their

tributaries, are one-street villages with the occasional side street, as for example at Martin, Rockbourne, Longparish, Leckford, Itchen Stoke and Kingsworthy. A number of villages exhibit evidence of possible settlement mobility over the past millennium – medieval churches and manor houses located away from modern village centres as, for example, at King's Somborne, Meonstoke, Twyford, Monk Sherborne, Bramdean, Otterbourne, Sherfield-on-Loddon, Blendworth and Hartley Wintney.

Recent archaeological investigations at King's Somborne, in the Test Valley, seem to confirm some form of settlement mobility. It would appear that there was middle Saxon occupation adjoining the site of the later medieval palace of John of Gaunt and around the area of the church (possibly a late Saxon minster or mother church). This occupation later expanded as the nucleus of a royal and aristocratic estate within which the village grew, and the borough of Stockbridge was established in the twelfth century (Hughes 1986a).

Another example of settlement mobility comes from the Meon Valley. A mid- to late Saxon settlement, discovered from recent excavations and field survey to the north of Meonstoke, appears to have shifted to one of three possible new sites – Meonstoke, Exton or Corhampton – by the eleventh century, if not earlier. All three present-day settlements are within half a mile of each other, and on opposite sides of the river. Domesday records that Meonstoke was a royal manor, whilst Exton belonged to the Bishop of Winchester. Corhampton, the only village to still have a late Saxon church, belonged to the de Port family, sheriffs of Hampshire (Hughes 1985a).

Hamlets appear to be ubiquitous in Hampshire, with the exception of the central chalklands and some areas to the west of the county. Many almost certainly originated as isolated farms and probably attracted further settlement during this period of growth (Hughes 1981). Some were originally served by chapels under the jurisdiction of the mother church. They are often found as 'satellites' to larger villages in the same parish. In the area north of Basingstoke, for example, a number of settlements carry the "-end" place-name element (e.g. Mortimer West End and Pamber End), which normally indicates that they started life as a hamlet in the middle ages, situated at the edge of the parish away from the major settlements (Hughes 1984b). Some hamlets flourished while others were short-lived due to economic and social factors, both during medieval times and later. Examples of deserted hamlets are Lainston, west of Winchester (the site is now in the grounds of Lainston House, where the ruined chapel is part of a landscaped garden), Westbury, near West Meon, Quidhampton and Polhampton, near Overton and North Fareham. Some hamlets that originated close to an existing settlement, especially a town or larger village in the process of expansion, were eventually encompassed within the boundaries of the latter. This is recognisable at Bishop's Waltham, where a small hamlet based around Shore Lane had been incorporated into the larger village's boundaries by the seventeenth century, if not earlier (Hughes 1976). Fareham eventually incorporated the hamlets of Wallington and Cams, Hurstbourne Tarrant incorporated Ibthorpe, whilst Longparish took East Aston under its wing after the hamlet had shrunk considerably in size as the result of the building of a country house and the consequent shifting of the local road around its new small park. The earthworks of the deserted plots are visible alongside the former road line, together with evidence of possible ridge and furrow in fields close by (in Hampshire there is little evidence for medieval ridge and furrow, possibly because the lighter chalkland soils did not require these techniques of cultivation).

Contraction and Change

The difference between the number of rural settlements recorded in the Lay Subsidy Rolls for 1334 and 1525/25 (see page 202) is reflected in the hundred or so deserted and shrunken sites that have been identified for Hampshire by Beresford and Hurst in their survey, including more than thirty in the New Forest, possibly depopulated to make way for the laying out of the new royal forest (Beresford and Hurst 1971). However, in that survey they were all described as 'deserted medieval villages', whereas over half the number recorded are hamlets or manorial settlements and the majority were depopulated or shrunken after the end of the middle ages (Hughes 1979 and 1981). Although many of these smaller settlements were in decline by the end of the medieval period, they were nevertheless still considered worthy of record by the taxation clerks. There is no basis for other simplifications like "along the chalkland valleys of Hampshire ... whole villages were abandoned or reduced to single farms during the thirteenth and fourteenth centuries" (Bettey 1986).

In the 1980s a series of excavation programmes took place on three of Hampshire's medieval settlements, two hamlets, Foxcotte and Popham, and the small village of Hatch. In the fourteenth century the fortunes of these three settlements was very different. Foxcotte was a small but thriving hamlet whose gradual depopulation took place in the sixteenth and seventeenth centuries. Popham, another thriving fourteenth-century manorial settlement, possibly due to the importance of its tenants and owners, appears to have gradually shifted its focus away from the older centre towards a new one to the east of the medieval hamlet sometime from the fifteenth century onwards. It would appear provisionally from the interim excavation reports that the village of Hatch was in decline even before the onset of the fourteenth century-plagues, for reasons as yet unclear.

Foxcotte

Excavations at Foxcotte, near Andover, have shown that the decline of the hamlet, like many others in the county, was not a case of medieval desertion but a gradual depopulation throughout the sixteenth and seventeenth centuries (Fig. 9.9). The settlement appears to have been divided into rectangular plots, with post-built houses, by the thirteenth and fourteenth centuries, in a somewhat planned fashion. In the fifteenth century a new rectangular timber-framed house and two outbuildings were erected across earlier plots; towards the end of the century these had burnt down and were never rebuilt. By the sixteenth century the Foxcotte family which had given its name to the settlement had disappeared from records, and although the 1524 Lay Subsidy Rolls recorded thirteen householders, by 1546 the number had been reduced to four. This evidence could indicate either a mobile population, a shift in wealth between the inhabitants, or a gradual depopulation due to the attraction of the nearby town of Andover (Russel 1993).

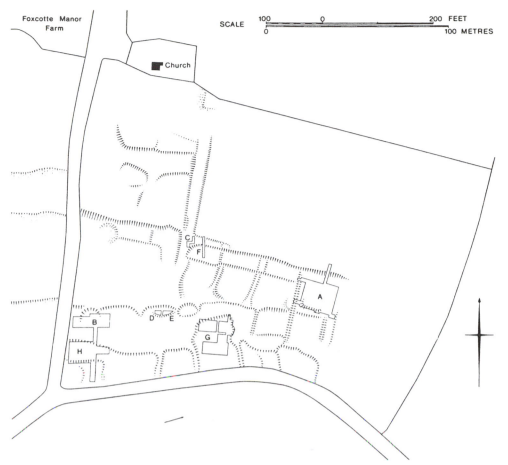

Fig. 9.9 *The Foxcotte earthworks in 1981. The letters A–H denote the positions of the excavated areas, which ranged from narrow trenches to whole house structures. (From Russel, 1993)*

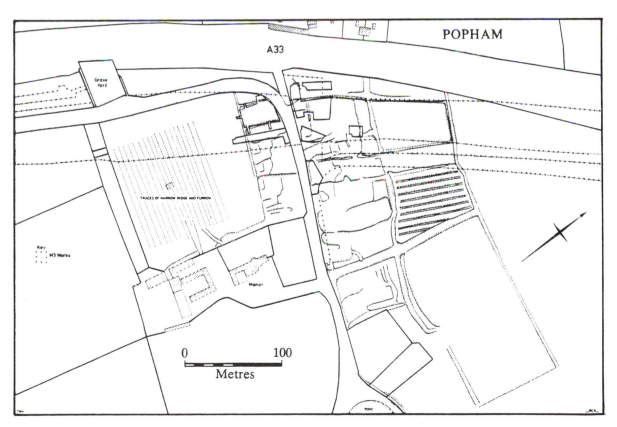

Fig. 9.10 *Popham: Survey of part of the earthworks showing the excavations of 1975 and the investigation of 1983. (After Fasham, 1987)*

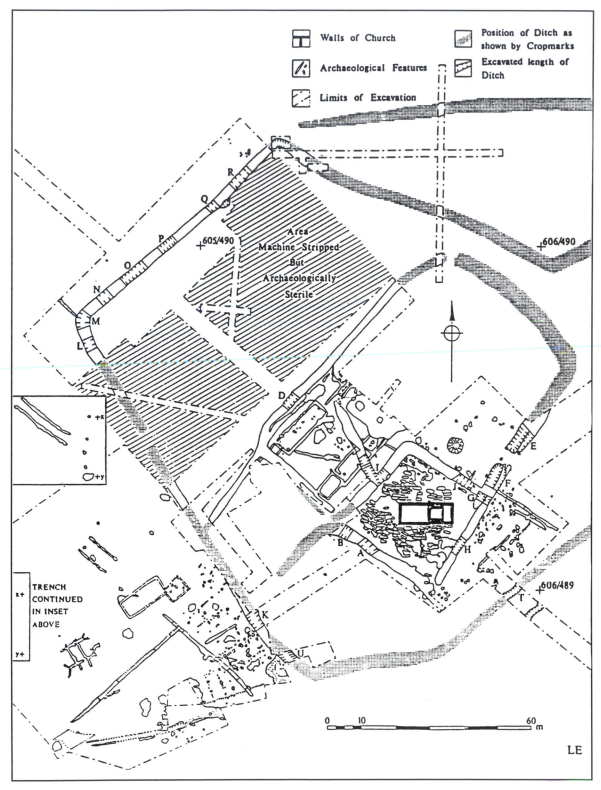

Fig. 9.11 *The medieval village at Hatch showing excavated areas and features (from Hughes (ed.) 1987a).*

Popham

Popham was a Domesday manor linked with Micheldever, a major estate of Hyde Abbey (before 1110, the New Minster, Winchester), a link that remained throughout the middle ages. There is a reference to a chantry chapel in 1300, which survived until the mid-nineteenth century when a new church was constructed on a new site in 1875–78. A chaplain's house also existed from 1308 until the sixteenth century. The manor was tenanted by the de Port family, periodically sheriffs of Hampshire in the twelfth, thirteenth and fourteenth centuries; they were then succeeded in the fifteenth century by the St Johns (Page (ed.), VCH Hants 1908). The Popham family were also important 'county' people – Robert de Popham was abbot of Hyde from 1281 to 1292, whilst in 1340 another Robert de Popham was Sheriff of Hampshire (Cahill in Fasham 1987). There is no evidence from documentary sources for shrinkage or desertion during the fourteenth century and the manorial settlement appears to have been stable or even growing economically in the fifteenth century. Excavations of part of the medieval settlement took place in advance of the construction of the two sections of the M3 motorway in 1975 and in 1983 (Fig. 9.10). Although Saxon pottery was found it could not be related to any contemporary features. From the range of pottery (after the 1320s to early fifteenth century) it would appear that the part of the settlement excavated was flourishing in the fourteenth century. Some of the buildings had stone footings, although these were not numerous. The majority were aligned with an east-west street. Other timber-framed buildings were scattered around the settlement. There is no evidence for periods of intense occupation and repeated rebuilding (apart from one house), as might be expected from research elsewhere in the country. There are also no indications from the investigations as to why the settlement was reduced in size in the mid- to late fifteenth century, although it is possible that the focus of settlement moved to an area further east. The scattered, perhaps irregular layout of the settlement as revealed by the excavations, contrasts with the apparent regularity of the surviving earthworks that appear to overlie the earlier settlement remains. It has been suggested that the earthworks are of a later date and did not involve the construction of buildings (Fasham 1987). It is possible that the earthworks represent enclosures or paddocks and are related to a different landuse associated with the shift in settlement focus. This change in the landscape of Popham may have been due to a change in the fortunes of later owners, possibly the Ashburton family who took over the manor in the late eighteenth century.

Hatch

In 1984, excavations in advance of a major housing development at Hatch Warren on the south-west fringes of Basingstoke unexpectedly revealed the lost medieval settlement of Hatch, almost in its entirety (Fig. 9.11).

The ceramic evidence from the site concurs with the documentary sources and shows a village in decline in the first part of the fourteenth century – a decline that appears to have started before the plagues affected the area (Fasham 1987). *Heche*, first recorded in Domesday, later became a detached tithing of Cliddesden, a parish and village nearby. A church is also recorded in the Domesday Book. The parish of Hatch became the property of the lord of Cliddesden in the fourteenth century because of its poverty and depopulation and because the church was in ruins. Also during the first half of the fourteenth century it was recorded that 300 acres of land in Hatch were untilled and unsown and a petition was made to Edward III asking that the church might be exonerated from the payment of the tenth because there was no one at the time living within the parish (Page (ed.), VCH Hants 1911).

The excavated site showed that the village was contained within an outer and inner enclosure, the latter with an enclosed church and churchyard. Until the excavation report is published the chronological relationship of the remains of the enclosures is unclear. From within the inner enclosure re-deposited material, almost certainly from the church, was discovered in a back-filled terrace connected with some timber buildings, which may relate to the demolition of the church once the settlement was in decline. The outer enclosure contained no features but was bounded by a substantial ditch and may have been a stock enclosure. The settlement contained a number of timber buildings, the largest of which has been tentatively interpreted as a farm building. The churchyard contained over 250 burials, although this number does not represent accurately the total number of individuals, as it was clear that the graves frequently intersected and some graves contained more than one body. More graves were revealed within the church itself (Hughes 1987a).

Shrinkage and Desertion

A significant number of medieval settlements, small villages and hamlets in Hampshire were depopulated or shifted due to the emparking movement and the building of country houses between the fifteenth and eighteenth centuries (Fig. 9.12). This process was almost certainly a gradual one, the decay in the wealth of a settlement or its owner taking place over a number of generations. Settlements of few inhabitants and dwellings were easier to shift than a thriving village or hamlet. Furthermore, the dissolution of the monasteries created opportunities for a new class of landowner in the county who acquired former monastic and episcopal property, which in many cases included declining settlements and their fields.

In the case of the twelfth-century settlements of Dogmersfield, near Basingstoke and Hartley Mauditt, near Alton it was not until the eighteenth century that their final demise took place when the owners decided to lay out new parks. The remains of the medieval village of

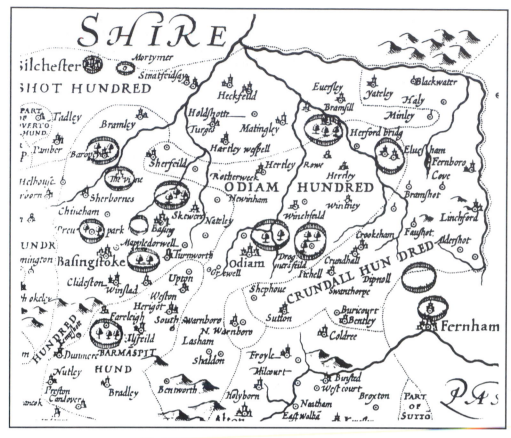

Fig. 9.12 *Settlements and parks in north-east Hampshire c. 1600. (Reproduction of part of a map of Hampshire by John Speed 1610)*

Idsworth on the Hampshire-Sussex border, whose origins lay in late Saxon times, can still be identified as earthworks somewhat eroded by ploughing, and by the isolated, but attractive, surviving twelfth-century church of St Hubert (Fig. 9.13). The settlement was depopulated in the seventeenth century when the new owner of the manor house wanted to create a landscaped park around his house. Other examples of settlements deserted in the late sixteenth to eighteenth centuries for the same reasons are Herriard (where Humphrey Repton, the eighteenth-century landscape designer had the settlement moved), Hackwood near Basingstoke, Bramshill, Elvetham, and Deane, in north Hampshire, and Hinton Ampner near Cheriton. Ashe, near Overton, finally depopulated in 1580, was recorded in 1428 as having fewer than ten inhabitants, as were nearly fifty other settlements (Hughes 1981).

Fieldwork undertaken by the Avon Valley Archaeological Society in the vicinity of Breamore House and the nearby late Saxon 'minster' church (Fig. 9.14), near Fordingbridge, has shown that the buildings of the earlier village of Breamore were grouped around the present driveway to Breamore House and to the east of the church. To the east of the village field-walking has revealed an additional settlement, probably a hamlet grouped around a nearby cross-roads, whose occupation seems to have

occurred, from the date of the pottery finds, from the twelfth to the fourteenth centuries. It would appear that a number of properties, both on the village site and that of the hamlet, were abandoned before or during the fifteenth century as the pottery scatters have produced few, if any, sherds of a later date. This evidence of shrinkage is borne out by documentary sources which record a number of abandoned holdings in the 1420s. Consequently William Doddington, the new, late sixteenth-century owner of Breamore, had few problems when constructing his new house and laying out his park as by then most of the abandoned village properties had probably disappeared (Hughes 1987b).

Westbury, near West Meon, a small medieval settlement whose thirteenth-century owners had one of the few licences to crenellate in Hampshire and which has produced evidence of late Saxon occupation, was emparked, probably in the late seventeenth century when the new manor house was built (nine taxpayers in 1524/25). The chapel, now in ruins, was not in ecclesiastical use at the end of the seventeenth century but used only as a family mausoleum (Hughes 1981).

Fieldwork and air photography at Little Somborne (Fig. 9.15), near King's Somborne, have revealed evidence of a settlement in the grounds of Little Somborne House. The remains consist of rectangular plots on each side of what appears to be a 'street' leading to the church. This settlement was almost certainly demolished to make way for the creation of a small park, possibly in the seventeenth or eighteenth century. The decline of Little Somborne is reflected in the evidence from archaeological excavations around and inside the late Saxon church (now vested in the care of the Redundant Churches Fund) in the late 1970s (Webster and Cherry 1976). The Saxon church had been enlarged in the fourteenth century by the addition of a side chapel, an indication possibly that the village was flourishing and could afford to make additions to the church. However, by the late sixteenth century the chancel had been reduced in size and the side chapel demolished.

Not all parks were created in the post-medieval period, however. There were nearly eighty deer parks in Hampshire by the end of the 1400s, many of which belonged to the powerful and wealthy bishops of Winchester. The original laying out of these parks or of later extensions could have caused the depopulation or shifting of small older settlements, or formed the focus of new settlements when the owners moved from their town houses to new country estates on land which previously had been under cultivation. It would appear that by the fourteenth century the impressive manor house of the bishop of Winchester at Highclere (Fig. 9.16), details of which are contained within the episcopal Pipe Rolls (Dunlop 1940), consisted of a number of buildings which served the needs of the bishop and his large estate. A deer park, first recorded in the thirteenth century, was greatly extended within a hundred years to include land to the south. Field survey inside the medieval deer park boundary in 1992 revealed the earthworks of a deserted settlement which may be associated with the running of the bishop's house and his estate, or may represent the earlier village of Highclere, now situated one and a half miles to the north-east. Whatever the status and function of the settlement, it may have been depopulated either as a result of the parkland extension or because of the decline of the bishopric lands in the mid-sixteenth century.

The medieval village of Burghclere (now called Old Burghclere), also owned by the bishop, which lies immediately south-east of Highclere Castle and on similar geology, is an example of depopulation and desertion influenced by the change from arable to pasture farming that occurred especially on estates owned by prelates and monastic houses in the later middle ages. Today the shrunken village consists of the surviving earthworks of house platforms and those of individual 'closes', together with a twelfth-century church and a manor house which encapsulates a fourteenth-century aisled hall. In the early fifteenth century the bishop was annexing most of the arable land that belonged to the church at Burghclere and giving permission for a local landowner to pasture his and the bishop's sheep on all pastures within the parish boundaries. The process of shrinkage was gradual, however, for even in 1524 a population of over forty was recorded for the village (Hughes 1981).

The change of agricultural regimes from arable to pastoral farming, as profits to be made from the wool increased and attracted more landowners to convert their land, brought misfortune and misery to the inhabitants of

Fig. 9.13 *St Hubert's church and site of deserted village, Idsworth.*

Fig. 9.14 *Aerial photograph of Breamore House, late Saxon church and site of former village between house and church.*

Fig. 9.15 *Aerial photograph of village of Little Somborne with late Saxon church in centre foreground – Little Somborne House right.*

Fig. 9.16 *Highclere Castle (nineteenth century), possibly a site of former medieval palace of bishops of Winchester.*

other settlements whose houses and plots were given over to sheep pastures. In his book '*Speculum Brittaniae*', the Elizabethan cartographer and traveller, John Norden, makes an explicit statement that "one John Fisher, deceased, depopulated this place (Chilton Candover, north of Alresford) extirpating the inhabitants and pulling down the houses. Only remains the churche and a ferme". This event must have taken place sometime between 1562, when John Fyssher acquired the manor and 1595 when Norden wrote his text (Hughes 1984b).

Another settlement that eventually became completely deserted possibly due to a change from an arable to a pastoral economy was Lomer, in the central chalklands of Hampshire. Lomer, first recorded in a tenth-century charter and in Domesday, was another of the bishop of Winchester's manors and later parish. The depopulation of the village is reflected in the records of the parish church, which was still undergoing diocesan visitations in the first quarter of the sixteenth century, although the chancel was stated to be in disrepair. The parish name, however, had disappeared from the Visitation Books by the end of the sixteenth century. Another, or additional, explanation for the desertion of Lomer is the gradual loss of its fresh water supply. On the higher chalklands of the county, where approximately fifty percent of the known deserted settlements are located, there is evidence that the water table in the chalk was much higher in the late Saxon period than it is now (Hughes 1984a). Falls of between thirty and sixty metres have occurred (Aldsworth 1973–4). Access to water was one of the major factors in

siting any settlement and its gradual loss would have been without doubt one of the major factors in that settlement's decline.

A contraction in settlement was hastened in some cases by the effects of high mortality rates due to the recurring mid- to late fourteenth-century plagues and a deterioration in climate. The Bishop of Winchester's records suggest that the plagues were sporadic in their devastation and the mortality rate appears to have varied across the county. The district around Winchester and Alresford and around Basingstoke was affected to some extent, whilst in other areas around Fareham and in the northeast there were comparatively few traces of its effects on the population. Some of the changes wrought by the plagues were a greater emphasis on the enclosure of smaller fields, a reduced labour force and higher agricultural wages and prices for farming products. This was accompanied by a surplus of land in those areas more badly affected by the epidemic, and a subsequent decline in land values. However, some communities which were reduced in size had, by the 1350s, recovered in economic terms.

According to documentary sources population decline occurred (for example) at the village of St Anastius-by-Weeke, on the outskirts of Winchester (Hughes 1981). Abbotstone, near Alresford, was a flourishing settlement until the early fourteenth century, and eighteen householders were recorded in the 1327 Lay Subsidy. By 1428, eighty years after the first plague epidemics, fewer than ten households remained in the village, and in the six-

teenth century all the holdings belonged to one landowner. The Bishop of Winchester agreed to amalgamate
the two parishes of Abbotstone and Itchen Stoke in 1589
because the church at Abbotstone was in a ruinous state
(Sanderson 1973).

Other factors contributed to the gradual decline in
settlements. For example, competition from a neighbouring burgeoning community occurred at Netherton in north-
west Hampshire where, from the fourteenth century, after
the demise of the manor house, the village shrank due to
the rising importance of nearby Faccombe. Hordle on
the coast near Lymington shrank gradually due to a late
medieval decline in the local salt industry (Hughes 1981).
Although documented elsewhere in the country, there is
no evidence for the depopulation of small settlements
due to the foundation of Cistercian houses in Hampshire
– the monasteries of Beaulieu and Netley and the nunnery at Hartley Wintney. It is possible, however, that
some of the eleven 'lost' places in the New Forest, recorded in Domesday, may have been destroyed by the
establishment of the abbey at Beaulieu in the early thirteenth century. This is an area worthy of further research
and field survey.

There are other factors affecting the waxing and wan-
ing of settlements in Hampshire as well as elsewhere in
Wessex which I have not attempted to cover in this paper. The study of village plans has not been discussed, let
alone studied, nor the relationship of rural settlements to
their landscapes. What was the influence, if any, of the
bishops of Winchester or the abbots of Titchfield on the
pattern of early enclosure on rural settlement, especially
during the fourteenth and fifteenth centuries? All these
aspects of the medieval landscape need further attention.
However, it is only through more field survey and more
documentary research that we can begin to provide an
academic framework upon which we can base further
excavation programmes of rural settlement in the county.

References

Aldsworth, F. 1973–4: *A pre-Domesday geography of Hamp-
shire* (unpublished B.A. dissertation, University of South-
ampton).
Beresford, M. and Hurst, J. G. 1971: *Deserted Medieval
Villages* (London).
Bettey, J. H. 1986: *Wessex From AD 1000* (London).
Biddle, M. and Hill, D. H. 1971: 'Late Saxon planned towns',
Antiquaries Journal 51, 70–85.
Cahill, N. J. 1987: 'Historical Background', in Fasham, P. J.
'The Medieval Settlement at Popham, Excavation 1975 and
1983', *Proceedings of the Hampshire Field Club and
Archaeological Society* 43, 87–90.
Cahill, N. J. forthcoming 1994: 'Historical Summary', in Fox,
R. and Hughes, M. 'Excavations at Sheep Street, Peters-
field', *Proceedings of the Hampshire Field Club and
Archaeological Society* 49 (1993).
Dunlop, G. D. 1940: *Pages from the History of Highclere*
(Oxford).
Fasham, P. J. 1987: 'The Medieval Settlement at Popham,

Excavation 1975 and 1983', *Proceedings of the Hamp-
shire Field Club and Archaeological Society* 43, 83–124.
Fox, R. and Hughes, M. 1994: 'Excavations at Sheep Street,
Petersfield, 1976', *Proceedings of Hampshire Field Club
and Archaeological Society* 49, 159–174..
Glasscock, R. E. (ed.) 1975: *The Lay Subsidy of 1334* (London).
Hoad, M. and Webb, J. 1989: 'From the Norman Conquest to
Civil War', in Stapleton, B. and Thomas, J. H., *The Port-
smouth Region*, 45–58 (Gloucester).
Hughes, M. F. 1976: *The Small Towns of Hampshire* (Win-
chester).
Hughes, M. F. 1979: 'Hampshire', in *Medieval Village
Research Group Report* 26 (1978), 7.
Hughes, M. F. 1981: 'Settlement and Landscape in Medieval
Hampshire', in Shennan, S. J. and Schadla-Hall, R. T. (eds),
The Archaeology Archaeology of Hampshire, 66–77
(Winchester).
Hughes, M. F. 1984a: 'Rural Settlement and Landscape in
Late Saxon Hampshire', in Faull, M. L. (ed.), *Studies in
Late Anglo-Saxon Settlement*, 65–80 (Oxford).
Hughes, M. F. 1984b: *Man and the Landscape* (Winchester).
Hughes, M. F. 1985a: *Excavations at Meonstoke, 1984*
(Winchester).
Hughes, M. F. (ed.) 1985b: *Archaeology in Hampshire:
Annual Report for 1983*, 35–6 (Winchester).
Hughes, M. F. (ed.) 1986a: *Archaeology in Hampshire:
Annual Report for 1984/5*, 31–2 (Winchester).
Hughes, M. F. (ed.) 1986b: *Archaeology in Hampshire:
Annual Report for 1984/5*, 36–7 (Winchester).
Hughes, M. F. (ed.) 1987a: *Archaeology in Hampshire:
Annual Report for 1986*, 23–4 (Winchester).
Hughes, M. F. (ed.) 1987b: *Archaeology in Hampshire:
Annual Report for 1986*, 36–8 (Winchester).
Hughes, M. F. 1994: 'The Fourteenth-Century Raids on Hamp-
shire and the Isle of Wight', in Curry, A. and Hughes, M.
(eds), *Arms, Armies and Fortifications in the Hundred Years
War* (Woodbridge).
Hughes, M. F. (forthcoming): The Origins of Hampshire (Man-
chester).
Hughes, E. and White, P. (eds) 1992: *The Hampshire Hearth
Tax Assessment 1665* (Southampton).
Millett, M. 1983: 'The History, Architecture and Archaeology
of Johnson's Corner, Alton', *Proceedings of the Hamp-
shire Field Club and Archaeological Society* 39, 77–109.
Page, W. (ed.) 1908: *Victoria County History of Hampshire
and the Isle of Wight*, 397 (London).
Page, W. (ed.) 1911: *Victoria County History of Hampshire
and the Isle of Wight*, 147 (London).
Russel, A. D. 1993: *Foxcotte The Archaeology and History of
a Hampshire Hamlet*, Test Valley Archaeological Trust
Report 1 (Romsey).
Sanderson, I. 1973: 'Abbotstone: A Deserted Medieval
Village', *Proceedings of the Hampshire Field Club and
Archaeological Society* 28, 57–66.
Sheail, J. 1968: The Regional Distribution of Wealth in
England as indicated in the 1524/25 Lay Subsidy Returns
(unpublished Ph.D. thesis, University of London).
Torrance, L. J. and Ford, S. 1994: 'Archaeological Investiga-
tions in Petersfield, 1992', *Proceedings of the Hampshire
Field Club and Archaeological Soceity* 49, 149–158.
Webster, L. E. and Cherry, J. (eds) 1976: 'Medieval Britain in
1975', in *Medieval Archaeology* 20, 182.

10.   The Regular Village Plan: Dorset revisited and revised

C. C. Taylor

More than thirty years ago, in its Dorset Inventories, the Royal Commission on the Historical Monuments of England pioneered the field recording and analysis of medieval settlement remains. Since then the Commission's Dorset work has, in some respects, been overtaken by advances in the subject. This paper re-examines the material to see if it can be used to answer questions which were not even conceived of at the time of the original surveys.

Between 1955 and 1965 the Archaeological Field Staff of the RCHME office in Salisbury worked on the archaeological sites of south, north and east Dorset, later published as Dorset II–V (RCHME 1970–75a). Most of the work was concerned with prehistoric and Roman monuments for, in those days, medieval field archaeology had hardly begun. Nevertheless, considerable numbers of settlement sites broadly datable to the medieval period were recorded, although seldom planned in detail. By present standards the level of recording, documentary research and even interpretation was minimal, though at the time it seemed, and was probably true, that the Royal Commission was at the forefront of scholarship in this discipline.

Since the publication of the Dorset Inventories the study of medieval settlement has developed and expanded far beyond the confines of those early Commission volumes. Thus, perhaps not surprisingly to judge by the rare references to those books, few scholars have made use of the medieval settlement information contained within them. Perhaps the most valuable contribution of those Inventories has been to the development of the Commission Investigators who worked on them.

One problem with the material is that it was written at a time when objectivity was regarded as the primary aim and little or no subjective interpretation was permitted. The fact that the 'evidence' was almost all subjective was something that was not considered. The problem of this lack of ideas on and interpretation of medieval settlement in Royal Commission Inventories has been corrected since the 1950s, a little in Cambridgeshire (RCHME 1968), more in Northamptonshire (RCHME 1975b–82) and especially so in Lincolnshire (RCHME 1991).

But need we write off or ignore the medieval material in the Dorset Inventories as so many people seem to have

done? Can we not return to it and see if it can help in understanding some of the problems that bedevil the study of medieval rural settlement today? The purpose of this paper is to attempt to reassess one particular aspect of the material in the Dorset Inventories in the light of new knowledge. After all, this can be done most easily by someone who wrote most of the original accounts!

One of the most widely used methods of approach in English medieval landscape studies has been the analysis of settlement morphology in order to explain the origins of villages. The work now has a respectable history, the most notable achievement of which is perhaps the recognition of the so-called regulated villages which in turn have led on to the development of the concept of village planning (Sheppard 1976; Taylor 1983, 133–48). However, though regulated villages are now known from almost every part of England, they still remain difficult to identify in many places. In almost every area of England, except perhaps in the north-east, the greater proportion of villages which exist actually show little or no evidence of regularity and thus can play no part in the discussion on regulated settlements except in a negative sense. It is particularly difficult to assess how common regulated villages once were in any particular region, although this information is crucial to the understanding of their origin.

There are two possible reasons for the lack of regularity in any given existing village: first, that the village was never regulated anyway, or second, that the regularity has been obliterated by later changes. One solution to this problem is to look at the evidence from abandoned or shrunken settlements. With the exception of the very late desertions and the deliberately cleared examples which leave very little in terms of analysable remains, most abandoned or reduced settlements retain, in their earthworks or even crop or soil marks, elements of their

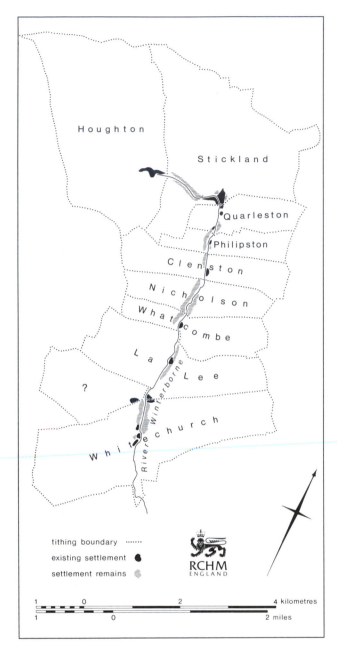

Fig. 10.1 Medieval settlement, tithings and parishes, North Winterborne valley, Dorset. RCHME Crown Copyright.

isting Dorset villages are examined for evidence of regularity there are few that are readily convincing. Of the 300 or so places in the county that can be called 'villages' by the broadest definition some, such as Abbotsbury, Cerne Abbas and Cranborne, stand out as probably once regulated settlements. However, all these also had minor monastic or baronial market functions which may have made them special. Even places such as Bere Regis and Puddletown might be considered as semi-urban settlements. Others such as Chideock and Charmouth, both exceptionally fine regulated double-row settlements, seem to have had a higher than normal economic and social status. On the other hand some quite large villages, such as Shillingstone, have markedly regular elements within them and a number of relatively small villages, such as Puncknowle, Swyre and Cattistock, can be considered to have regulated plans. Nevertheless, of all the 300 or so villages in Dorset, only between twenty-five and thirty can readily be suggested as perhaps having regulated plans, that is between eight per cent and ten per cent of the total. The conclusion to be reached from these figures is that regular villages are, or were, rare in Dorset and other explanations must be sought for the arrangement for the vast majority of the others.

However, if all the known deserted settlements of large hamlet size and above recorded by RCHME are examined in the same way, a very different picture emerges. A large proportion of these have regular layouts and some are extremely well preserved. The best is perhaps Holworth (RCHME 1970a, Chaldon Herring (20)), a superb single-row village, but others such as the double-row examples of West Ringstead and East Hemsworth are almost equally impressive (RCHME 1970a, Osmington (27); 1975a, Witchhampton (27)). Even very mutilated sites were still just recognisable enough in the 1950s for the Commission to note their form and these can thus now be interpreted as having regular forms, as at West Woodsford (RCHME 1970a, Woodsford (4)).

The Royal Commission Inventories list just under fifty places, by no means identical to the forty-two places listed by Beresford and Hurst (1971), which are now deserted. Only a few sites have detailed plans but the rest are described and, more importantly, can be checked against the excellent RAF vertical air photographs that were available to the Commission. Of these fifty places just over half have or had forms that would be described as reasonably regular. The rest either did not or there is not clear evidence either way. This means that at least fifty per cent of the deserted settlements in Dorset may have once had a fairly regular plan.

Though the figures for existing and deserted settlements are not necessarily accurate and certainly not comparable, they do suggest, if no more, that in Dorset in late medieval times regulated villages and hamlets were perhaps much more common than they are now. It is possible to look more closely at some places and even to see where the change from a regular to an irregular plan

form which are likely to be much closer to their early layout than in any existing village. The average deserted medieval village which was perhaps abandoned in the fourteenth, fifteenth or sixteenth centuries will, in effect, show the form of that village at that date, that is 400 to 600 years earlier than any existing village, and without the accumulated changes of those later centuries. This is not, of course, a new idea, and indeed the Royal Commission itself has been detailing and analysing such evidence for decades (RCHME 1968–91). But can we use evidence of this type from a county such as Dorset when the only body of information is now nearly thirty years old and defective by modern standards? Certainly if ex-

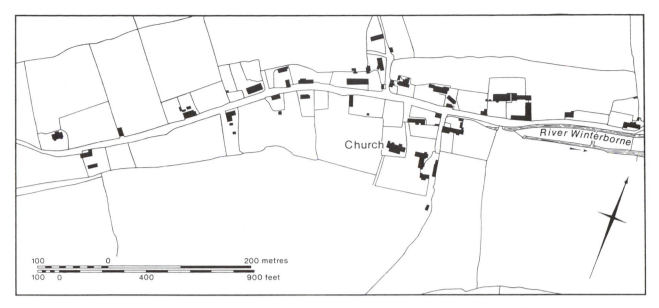

Fig. 10.2 *Winterborne Houghton village. Based on OS 1st edn 25 inch map, 1888.*

actually takes place. One of the best areas to see this is in the valleys of the chalk dip-slope. There, in the valleys of the Rivers Tarrant, Allen, Piddle, the North and South Winterbornes and the Gussage Brook, the modern villages rarely have indications of a regular form, though an exception is Piddletrenthide. Most are, or were until the late nineteenth century, irregular lines of large farmsteads interspersed with groups of cottages with a resulting ragged pattern of plots and closes. On the other hand there are, or rather were, between these villages both deserted and shrunken settlements where the earthwork remains were extremely regular. A completely deserted example is Rew in Winterborne Abbas parish in the South Winterborne valley, which the Royal Commission did not plan but which has subsequently been surveyed (Bond 1989). Among examples of shrunken villages with associated regular patterns of former closes and house sites, reduced to earthworks, are those at Cheselbourne, Long Crichel and Tarrant Rawston, not all of which now survive (RCHME 1970b, Cheselbourne (19); 1972, Long Crichel (4); 1975a, Tarrant Rawston (3)).

Perhaps the best and certainly the most remarkable area, however, is that of the upper reaches of the North Winterborne valley to the west of Blandford Forum (Fig. 10.1). The area comprises four parishes, Winterborne Houghton, Winterborne Stickland, Winterborne Clenston and Winterborne Whitechurch. Within them are the villages of Houghton, Stickland and Whitechurch, and the hamlet of Whatcombe in Whitechurch. None of these villages, nor the hamlet, have any indication whatsoever of regularity in their plan. Indeed the principal feature of their nineteenth-century arrangements is the existence of large compact farmsteads and associated cottages (Figs 10.2 and 10.3).

However, between and around all these existing settlements are, or were, extensive earthworks representing

former settlements, which can be variously identified as parts not only of the three villages and the hamlet but also of other settlements. All have been either completely abandoned or reduced to one or two farmsteads, but all were formerly places of village status and lay within their own economic units or tithings (townships elsewhere), whose boundaries can be reconstructed from post-medieval cartographic evidence or other sources. These were Quarleston in Stickland parish, Philipston, Nicholson and Clenston in Clenston parish and La Lee in Whitechurch.

A large portion of the remains had already been destroyed by the early 1960s when the Royal Commission investigated the area and more has gone since. Nevertheless enough survives, recorded on air photographs or was planned and/or described by the Commission for certain features to be quite clear (Figs 10.1 and 10.4).

In detail, from north to south, in Winterborne Houghton only fragments of three adjacent near-rectangular closes 30m across survive at the west end of the village (not recorded by RCHME). Even so, nothing in the existing village plan comes close to the regular form of those closes (Fig. 10.2). To the east, in Winterborne Stickland parish, the valley of the Winterborne has settlement remains on both sides of the stream between the Houghton boundary and the present Stickland village (RCHME 1970b, Winterborne Stickland (15)). On the south side of the stream are seventeen regular closes, ranging in width from 15m to 30m. On the other side of the stream is another group of seventeen almost identical closes. The Commission described these as destroyed, but in fact they are still visible even today as slight earthworks. A further three closes existed to the north and west of Stickland church but had already been destroyed by 1960. They are visible only on air photographs. The existing village of Stickland has, or had before the extensive expansion of the 1950s and later, a reversed L-shaped

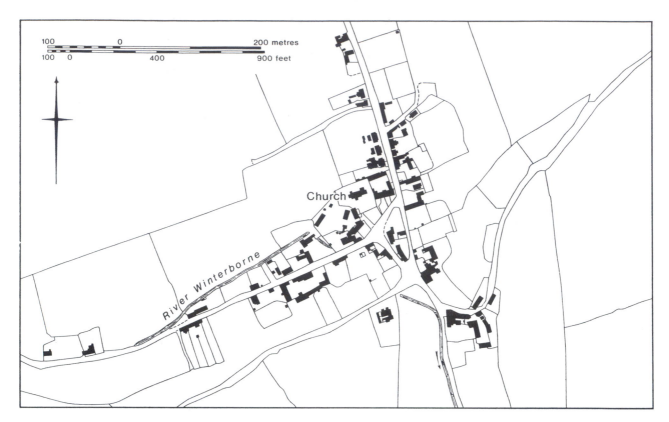

Fig. 10.3 *Winterborne Stickland village. Based on OS 1st edn 25 inch map, 1888.*

plan with no recognisable regularity (Fig. 10.2).

Occupying the extreme south end of Winterborne Stickland parish was the tithing of Quarleston whose associated settlement, Winterborne Quarleston, once lay along the valley, immediately to the south of Stickland village. On the west of the stream are some very disturbed earthworks which appear to be the result of post-medieval desertion. On the east there were, before destruction in the 1950s, six of the by now familiar parallel closes, 80m long and 28m to 30m wide. Pottery of the eleventh to thirteenth centuries is recorded from this site (RCHME 1970b, Winterborne Stickland (16)).

To the south of Quarleston lies the parish of Clenston. In medieval times this was divided into three tithings, Philipston, Clenston and Nicholson, each with its settlement along both sides of the Winterborne. All three are now deserted. Philipston, the northernmost settlement, has only slight traces of earthworks on the east side of the brook, due at least in part to the presence of a large farmstead there. These, however, seem to have been of the usual regular pattern of closes. To the west of the brook is the only block of settlement earthworks in the valley that the Royal Commission recorded in detail (RCHME 1970b, Winterborne Clenston (7); Fig. 10.4). These consist of eleven rectangular closes of varying length but of 13m to 15m wide, all with traces of former buildings at their lower, east, ends. The southernmost close is twice as wide as the rest.

The next settlement to the south was Clenston, now

represented by a major farmstead, Clenston Manor, a remarkable sixteenth-century structure (RCHME 1970b, Winterborne Clenston (2)). The only settlement remains noted in the 1960s by the Commission were four of the usual rectangular closes 29m across on the west of the stream opposite the manor house (RCHME 1970b, Winterborne Clenston (5)).

The rest of the parish was occupied by the tithing of Nicholson, which also included the parish church of St Nicholas, which still stands. Settlement remains once lay on both sides of the stream here, though most had already been damaged or destroyed when the Commission visited the site. Enough remained or were visible on air photographs to indicate that there had once been twelve or thirteen, perhaps more, rectangular closes on the west side of the stream and certainly four, perhaps more, on the east. House sites or debris from former occupation sites was visible at the lower ends of all of them (RCHME 1970b, Winterborne Clenston (6)).

The next parish to the south is Winterborne Whitechurch. Its north end was formerly the tithing of Whatcombe whose settlement, now called Higher Whatcombe, is made up of two farmsteads and some associated cottages. The Commission recorded at least six rectangular closes 30m across on the west of the stream and an unknown number on the east. All were destroyed in 1966 (RCHME 1970b, Winterborne Whitechurch (16)). The tithing to the south was known as La Lee and seems to have included a triangle of land in its south-west cor-

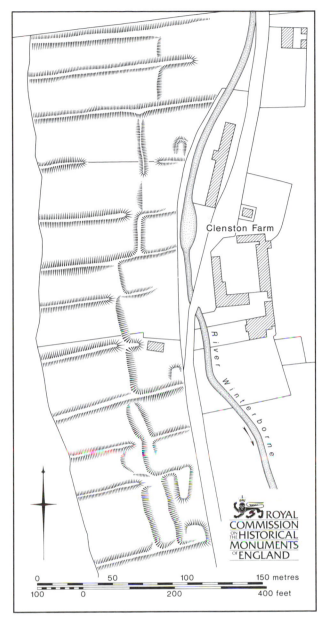

Clenston Farm

River Winterborne

ROYAL
COMMISSION
ON THE HISTORICAL
MONUMENTS
OF ENGLAND

| 0 | 50 | 100 | 150 metres |
| 100 | 0 | 200 | 400 feet |

*Fig. 10.4 Settlement remains, Winterborne Philipston.
(RCHME Crown Copyright)*

ner that was formerly in Milton Abbas parish (see fig. on p. xlv in RCHME 1970b). This and the unusual name has resulted in its being one of the few Dorset Winterborne settlements to be directly identified in Domesday Book when it was held by Milton Abbey. The present hamlet, Lower Whatcombe, comprises only one farm and some former estate buildings of Whatcombe House, a mid eighteenth-century seat, erected on a new site to the west. Because of the associated emparking and the estate buildings, no settlement remains were recognised by the Commission to the west of the stream. On the east, nine closes were recorded by the Commission, all in poor condition (RCHME 1970b, Winterborne Whitechurch (17)).

To the south again lay the tithing of Whitechurch itself. The present village has spread north into what was

part of La Lee and east along the main Dorchester to Blandford road which crosses the Winterborne at this point. In the nineteenth century it consisted of a church, only two or three farms and a handful of cottages. A detached hamlet, made up of two farmsteads and five cottages and known as Lower Street, lay close to the Winterborne in the extreme south of the parish. Between the village and the hamlet, on both sides of the stream, the Commission recorded twenty-seven long rectangular closes, ten on the west and seventeen on the east, a number clearly amalgamations of earlier narrow ones, all of which appear to have measured around 15m, 30m or 45m in width. Most have evidence of occupation at their lower end. Some are now destroyed (RCHME 1970b, Winterborne Whitechurch (15)).

Here, then, in the North Winterborne valley, there is extensive evidence for a repetitively regular layout of former settlement on a grand scale. Though the overall lengths of the settlement closes vary considerably, due largely to the width of the valley into which they were placed, their width is remarkably consistent in that they are all 15m wide or multiples of 15m, that is 30m or 45m. Yet the associated existing settlements show little or no sign of any similar regularity except where the occasional large farmstead might be interpreted as occupying two, three or more former closes, presumably following amalgamation. Even here, without the evidence of the adjacent earthworks it is unlikely that any possibility of regularity ever having existed would have been suggested.

What is the date of this regularity of settlement in the North Winterborne valley? Without excavation this is almost impossible to ascertain, not least because of the difficulty, already mentioned, of identifying most of the numerous documented Winterbornes with places on the ground, particularly before the thirteenth century.

Because of its name and tenure Winterborne La Lee can be identified in Domesday Book but this is the only certain one, and even then it is not clear whether the land included part of what is now Whitechurch village. In 1086 it was held by Milton Abbey with a recorded population of only three, one serf and two bordars. By the early fourteenth century only eleven taxpayers are listed for La Lee and Whatcombe combined and by the late seventeenth century the population of La Lee was down to six households (RCHME 1970b, Winterborne Whitechurch (17); Mills 1971). This suggests that, even taking into account all the difficulties of non-comparable figures, the great expansion of population at La Lee, and thus by implication the rest of the valley, took place between 1086 and 1300. Certainly by 1332 the taxpayers listed in the Subsidy Roll for the North Winterborne settlements do not suggest that the areas of the earthworks are likely to have been fully occupied. Even allowing for massive evasion, the twenty-five taxpayers and their families at Winterborne Stickland could not have occupied all the thirty-seven closes and house sites that survive as well as the area covered by the existing village. Quarleston, with thirteen taxpayers in 1332, could just have included the six earthwork closes at that time, but the twelve taxpayers at Clenston, Philipston and Nicholson combined could not have fully occupied the minimum of thirty-one closes known to have existed there, quite apart from other land which was probably built over as well. Even at Winterborne Whitechurch, the twenty-four taxpayers in 1332 seem too few to have filled the twenty-seven recorded closes, the hamlet of Lower Street and the area of the present village (Mills 1971). The conclusion that the period of major population expansion occurred between 1086 and 1300 is hardly surprising and indeed by analogy with elsewhere, a closer dating of 1100 to 1250 might be postulated. For what it is worth, the date of the pottery found from the occupation areas in the 1960s, and indeed subsequently by the present writer from empty plots within the village of Winterborne Houghton in 1989, would agree with this.

The evidence for similar regular layouts of settlement closes is, as has already been noted, widespread in Dorset. The Royal Commission's more recent, but as yet unpublished, large-scale survey work in south Wiltshire has indicated that the same phenomenon of regular settlement plans represented in earthwork form is extremely common, as is the lack of regularity in the associated existing settlements (Lewis 1992). Unsystematic and limited fieldwork by the author in Hampshire has also produced similar results, all of which show that regularity of settlement form was perhaps once very common at least in the chalkland parts of Wessex. It is thus perhaps necessary to reassess ideas on the origin of settlement forms in this region.

One other point, not hitherto discussed in any great detail, emerges from the above analysis. Overall regularity of planning on a limited scale is one thing, provision of numerous almost identical closes in a repetitive pattern over a distance of more than ten kilometres is quite another. Any overall desire to produce a new area of settlement needed for an actual or anticipated rise in population, whether carried out as part of lordly commercial aims or by cooperative peasantry (Harvey 1989) may well produce a general regularity of settlement form. But what lies behind the provision of relatively large numbers of similar sized closes or apparently carefully designed multiples of a unitary width, be they planned at one instant or possibly, but less likely, resulting from gradual expansion? One answer is that such regular closes were intended to be, or perhaps were, occupied by people of a carefully organised and already fixed social hierarchy and/or economic status. That is, their existence poses a further question as to whether these regular closes are the result of contemporary demands of existing medieval social or tenurial structure, or were merely a planned intention or even the preparation for a piecemeal development. Whatever lay behind it, an even and fairly simple social or tenurial structure is implicit in the form of the earthworks. The limited evidence that is available does not indicate that such a social structure ever existed.

Even if the identification of the North Winterborne holdings in Domesday Book are not absolutely certain, it is clear that in 1086 the area had the full range of occupiers usually recorded therein and there is no sign of any unified or regular social structure. By the early fourteenth century the surviving taxation assessments again reflect considerable economic variation in the local society (Mills 1971). With regard to tenurial structure, it would be useful to know what the pattern of peasant holdings was in the manors of the North Winterborne valley. It might then be possible to see if the numbers and the sizes of the holdings were in any way comparable to the numbers and plot sizes within the settlements. Unfortunately such evidence does not appear to exist. Nevertheless, this is a subject which might well repay further research elsewhere (Brown and Taylor 1989).

Once this repetitive pattern of closes, related to multiple units of width, is recognised, then it is possible more clearly to understand the pattern within the existing villages. There are, too, suggestions of 30m or 45m wide closes still occupied in the nineteenth century by farmsteads, while some of the even wider ones may be interpreted as later amalgamation by engrossing of the earlier arrangement. More detailed work elsewhere in Dorset on both abandoned and existing settlements might give additional support to such ideas. In the end, however, even this limited re-evaluation of thirty year old fieldwork still shows how little we understand of the background to settlement form in Dorset and perhaps beyond.

References

Beresford, M. W. and Hurst, J. G. 1971: *Deserted Medieval Villages*, 186.

Bond, J. 1989: 'Winterborne Rew, Martinstown', *Proc. Dorset Natur. Hist. Archaeol. Soc.* 111, 112.

Brown, A. E. and Taylor, C. C. 1989: 'The Origins of Dispersed Settlements, Some Results from Fieldwork in Bedfordshire', *Landscape History* 11, 61–81.

Harvey, P. D. A. 1989: 'Initiative and Authority in Settlement Change', in Aston, M., Austin, D. and Dyer, C. (eds), *The Rural Settlement of Medieval England*, 31–43.

Lewis, C. 1992: 'Medieval Settlement in South Wiltshire', in Aberg, A. and Myten, H. (eds), *Medieval Europe 1992–8 Rural Settlement*, 181–6.

Mills, A. D. 1971: 'The Dorset Lay Subsidy Roll of 1332', *Dorset Rec. Soc.* 4.

RCHME 1968: *Cambridgeshire* I.

RCHME 1970a: *Dorset* II.

RCHME 1970b: *Dorset* III.

RCHME 1972: *Dorset* IV.

RCHME 1975a: *Dorset* V.

RCHME 1975b: *Northamptonshire* I.

RCHME 1979: *Northamptonshire* II.

RCHME 1981: *Northamptonshire* III.

RCHME 1982: *Northamptonshire* IV.

RCHME 1991: *Change and Continuity*.

Sheppard, J. A. 1976: 'Medieval Village Planning', in Northern England, *J. Hist. Geogr.* 2, 3–20.

Taylor, C. C. 1983: *Village and Farmstead*.

11. Medieval Settlement Studies in Somerset

Michael Aston

This article reviews recent and current research into the development of rural settlement in the historic county of Somerset. Following a review of the archaeological evidence for Anglo-Saxon rural settlement sites in the county comes a survey of work currently being carried out by a variety of researchers in different parts of Somerset. The case study of Shapwick, the subject of a long term research project, is outlined. A general model for settlement origin, growth, decline and persistence from the late Roman period to the end of the middle ages for Somerset is put forward based on research so far. Recommendations for further research and discussion of further problems are also included.

Introduction

Rural settlement in the medieval period in Somerset has been the subject of considerable research in the last twenty years. There has been little excavation as most attention has been focused on historical, topographical and field archaeological research.

Research began in the 1970s on the deserted medieval settlements of the county, (rather later than work in the neighbouring counties of Wiltshire and Gloucestershire). These sites have been mapped and discussed (Aston 1982, 1985b and 1989b) and some reasons advanced for their disappearance (Aston 1988). For the surviving medieval villages in the county there has been some preliminary work on their morphology (Roberts 1987) and the reasons for their development (Aston 1985b, Costen 1991). In contrast moated sites have been studied only superficially and there is little in print as yet. Dispersed farmsteads, particularly in the west of the county, have been examined, both those deserted sites of medieval and later date and those surviving farmsteads that can be shown to be at least medieval in origin (Aston 1983). Many of these were probably once hamlets, rather like those in Hartland parish in Devon (Fox 1983) but have waxed and waned over the centuries to end up as single farms today, if they have survived at all. In fact, hamlet settlement can be shown to have been the normal pattern in the county in the middle ages. In the west it is accompanied by large numbers of isolated farmsteads, while in the south, centre and east of the county, parishes with numerous hamlets predominate; there are few early parish units with a single nucleated village (Aston 1989c). Other aspects of the medieval settlement pattern, particularly the places higher up in the settlement hierarchy engaged in trading and exchange activities have also been examined (Aston and Leech 1977, Aston 1986b, Gerrard 1987.

While the research so far has resulted in perhaps inadequate information to answer many of the questions which interest us, and settlement studies have often seemed somewhat divorced from research into other aspects of the contemporary landscape (Rippon 1993), a general model has nevertheless been developed from research in Somerset and elsewhere which can now be tested against further work in the county, including archaeological excavation. This began in 1988 with the research project based on the parish of Shapwick (Aston 1989a, 1990, Aston and Costen 1992, 1993).

Pre-Medieval Settlements 400–900 AD

Pre-medieval settlement patterns have been investigated by Burrow (1979) for hillfort and hill top settlement from the first to the eighth centuries AD and Leech (1977) for Romano-British settlements over much of the county. These have demonstrated the likelihood of considerable continuity of settlement pattern and land units from the late Roman period onwards with little detectable disruption in the sub-Roman, post-Roman and Anglo-Saxon periods, aspects reinforced by Costen (1992b) looking at the place-name and estate evidence, and Rahtz (1991) reviewing the archaeological evidence for cemeteries and religious sites. Late Roman Somerset, although an anachronistic concept, has a fully exploited and well-developed landscape with a clearly defined hierarchy of settlements from major towns such as Ilchester and Bath, through small towns or market villages, villages and hamlets to single farmsteads. Within this there were large numbers of well appointed villas which must represent

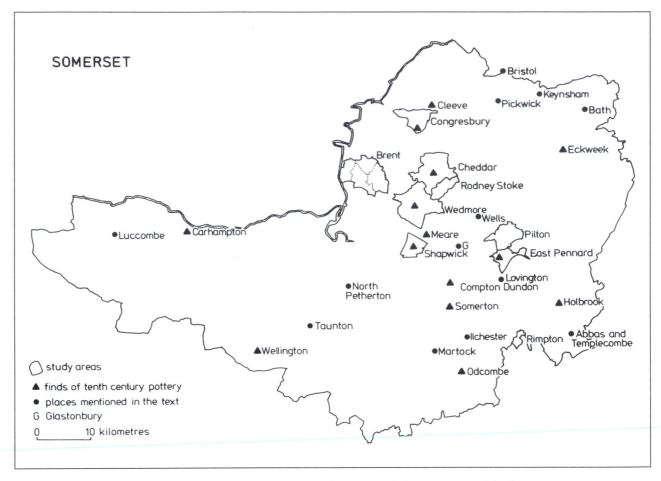

Fig. 11.1 *Somerset, historic county, study areas and places mentioned in the text.*

either individual country houses for the wealthy or the equivalent of manor houses in village-like settlements. The west of the county seems to have remained more native and less Romanised with many farms based on 'hill slope enclosures' and 'ringworks'; a fully developed and integrated Romano-British society is best represented in the east and south of the county.

How much of this society survived into the seventh century is still not clear. Generally it is assumed both nationally and locally that the population levels fell between the late Roman period and the tenth century and that over the same period intensively cultivated land was abandoned and there was much woodland regeneration as communities became more self-sufficient and the market-orientated commercial economy collapsed. Some of these concepts have been challenged however by recent research. Esmonde Cleary (1989) sees little evidence for major population decline, while Bell (1989), arguing from environmental evidence, cautions that there is no overwhelming evidence for forest regeneration everywhere.

In Somerset a start has been made on identifying the make up of estates, their secular and ecclesiastical arrangements and likely settlement patterns in the period seventh to tenth centuries from the abundant charter evi-

dence and a fresh examination of place-names (Aston 1986a and b, Costen 1992a and b). Quite how this material relates to the late Roman situation is not clear in detail though it does seem likely that some seventh and eighth century blocks of land could have been estates attached to Roman villas and other settlements; examples could include Brent (Aston 1985a), Keynsham (Prosser forthcoming) and Bath (Aston 1986a). Rather clearer, perhaps, is the relationship of these Saxon estates to the later patterns of land units and settlements in the middle ages, although there is a danger of circular argument here, as much of the earlier organisation is extrapolated from later evidence.

Costen (1992b) has argued that many settlements of the pre-medieval period are represented by certain habitative names, particularly those associated with the place-name elements 'huish', 'worth' and 'wick', as well as the more familiar 'ton', 'cote' and so on. In general these are taken to represent farm sites rather than nucleated settlements; indeed in the west of the county many are still attached to individual isolated farmsteads. Elsewhere, and particularly in the east of the county, such names are found attached to fields and furlongs in areas which were once common field or at least open country. In such cases the suggestion is that individual settlements were abandoned as common fields were laid out, perhaps attached to villages which were being planned and planted at the same time (Aston 1985b). The '*wic*' names bear a close relationship to known Romano-British settlements suggesting that they are in some way a reflection of the Roman settlement pattern.

Few of these sites have been looked for on the ground, indeed a cursory examination of maps and air pictures suggests that there is little field evidence for them. In view of the likely date for them, presumably some time between the fourth/fifth century and the eleventh century, it is clearly a very important objective for settlement research to locate some of them, and even to excavate one or two, if progress in settlement studies in this period is to be advanced.

Field Evidence for Anglo-Saxon Settlements in Somerset

Three cases can be cited from fieldwork (Fig. 11.2). In the west a case has been made for continuity of land use for a group of settlement sites in Luccombe parish (Aston 1989c). One of these, Sweetworthy, with the 'worth' element in its name, is represented either by the reused

probable prehistoric ringwork or the earthwork site of the medieval settlement nearby or by some as yet unlocated settlement in the near vicinity. The second, in Lovington parish, is associated with the name '*huish*' (Costen 1992b). The early air photographs of this area show a roughly circular enclosure, now largely ploughed out (Fig. 11.3). Field-walking across the site produced no finds of any date. The third site is in Kingsdon parish, in an area well researched by the editors of the Victoria County History. A '*huish*' group of field names are found on the borders of Somerton and Kingsdon parishes. Air pictures taken in the drought of 1976 show a series of rectangular buildings. There is no documentary evidence for a medieval settlement in this area and a subsequent field visit failed to retrieve any pottery of Roman date. Could it be that each of these sites represents a post-Roman/pre-Conquest farmstead or hamlet?

The Evidence from Archaeological Excavations of Anglo-Saxon Settlements in Somerset

At Eckweek in Peasedown St John a settlement has been excavated by Andrew Young and the Avon Archaeological Unit which may well represent one of these early farm

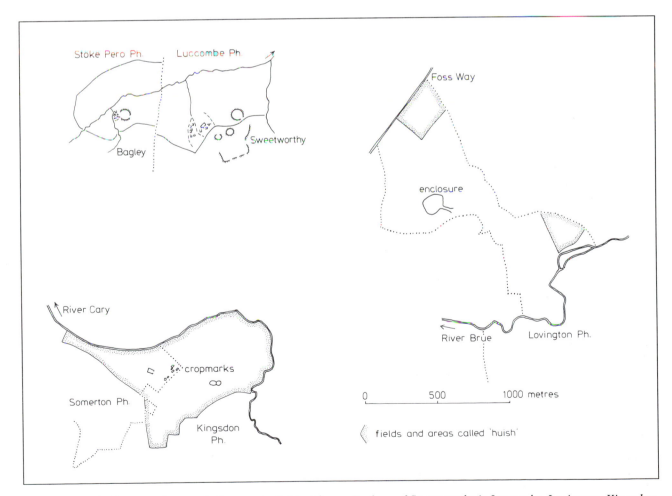

Fig. 11.2 *Anglo-Saxon settlements in Somerset – field evidence; Bagley and Sweetworthy in Luccombe, Lovington, Kingsdon.*

Fig. 11.3 *Aerial photograph of ploughed out enclosure at Lovington, Somerset, which may be the site of 'huish'. (Photo: Mick Aston 18511)*

sites, in this case represented by a place-name with the 'wick' element (Fig. 11.4). Two estates called 'Ecewiche' are listed in the Domesday Survey and occupation continued all through the middle ages; there is still a farm on the site today. Excavation, field survey and geophysical survey of the site has shown a sequence from the tenth to the fourteenth centuries with occupation continuing in one area from the fifteenth to the eighteenth centuries. For much of the middle ages, Eckweek was a scattered hamlet of two and three farmsteads; it had a small common field system with two fields – west and east.

A similar site to Eckweek was excavated some years ago at Pickwick on Dundry Hill by Kenneth Barton (1969) who demonstrated that the site was occupied in the later prehistoric, Roman and medieval periods with what he describes as a 'gap in the ceramic sequence' from the fifth to the twelfth centuries. Indeed the site was only abandoned in 1850 when occupation was moved to a planned farm, New Model Farm, in a lower situation near the village, Norton Malreward. The earthworks of the site suggest at least two farmsteads; it is likely that the site has been continuously occupied since the late prehistoric period although pottery, as dating evidence, is lacking, as is usually the case in the west country, for the Anglo-Saxon period (K. Barton, pers. comm.). The site at Cheddarford in Cheddar probably represents a similar sort of development (see below).

Anglo-Saxon Pottery in Somerset

This last point is critical for the discussion of settlements in Somerset in the period 400–900 AD. As settlement archaeologists we rely on pottery sherds to locate and date settlements (it is usually all we have!) and with careful consideration this is often adequate to demonstrate the rise and decline of settlements within broad limits. In eastern parts of England study of the relatively well-developed Saxon pottery industry there has enabled us to locate pre-Norman settlements from fieldwork (Hall 1988, Taylor 1983) and the detailed phasing of excavated sites to be attempted (Cadman 1983). In Somerset there is apparently little pottery being made or used between the fifth and the tenth centuries. By about 900 AD small quantities of pottery are being produced and this enables us to recognise settlements for the first time for many centuries. Most of our knowledge of the pottery in use at this time derives from the important excavations at the Saxon palaces at Cheddar (Rahtz 1979) and subsequent research on urban and high status sites (Taunton – Pearson 1984, Ilchester – Pearson 1982); the most distinctive ware in 'Cheddar E', associated with early tenth century coins.

Little pottery of this date has been recognised on rural sites so far in Somerset although recent excavations and fieldwork have produced small but significant quantities of it (Fig. 11.1). No doubt more will be found now

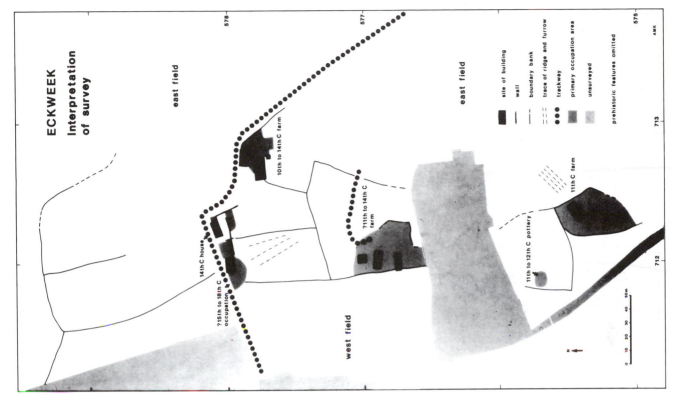

ECKWEEK
Interpretation
of survey

east field

578

577

east field

575

AMK

10th to 14th C farm

?11th to 14th C
farm

11th C farm

14th C house

?15th to 18th C
occupation

11th to 12th C pottery

west field

- site of building
- wall
- boundary bank
- trace of ridge and furrow
- trackway
- primary occupation area
- unsurveyed
- prehistoric features omitted

N

0 10 20 30 40 50m

713

712

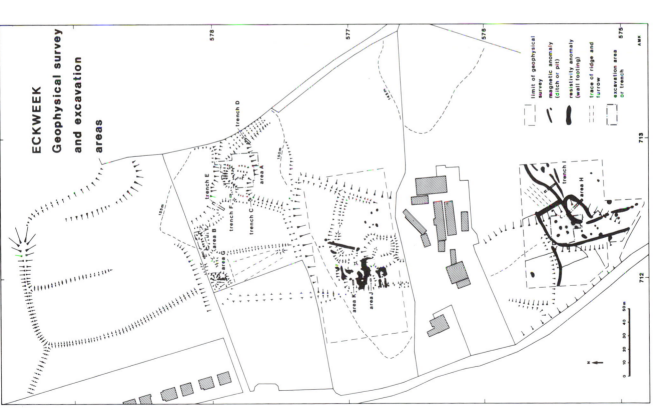

ECKWEEK
Geophysical survey
and excavation
areas

578

577

576

575

AMK

trench D

185m

150m

trench E

area A

trench F

area B

trench C

area G

area K

area J

- limit of geophysical survey
- magnetic anomaly (ditch or pit)
- resistivity anomaly (wall footing)
- trace of ridge and furrow
- excavation area or trench

trench I

area H

N

0 10 20 30 40 50m

713

712

Fig. 11.4 Eckweek in Peasedown St.John. *Geophysical survey and excavation areas; interpretation of survey (after Andrew Young).*

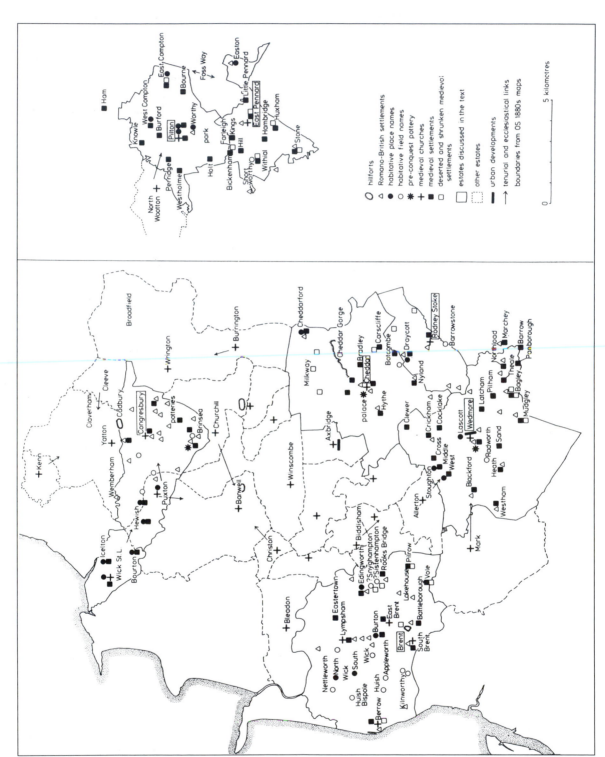

Fig. 11.5 Parish Studies: Brent, Cheddar, Congresbury, Rodney Stoke, Wedmore, East Pennard and Pilton.

that its significance is appreciated and re-examination of pottery material from older excavations (those before the 1970s perhaps) would surely produce more of this material and help us to identify settlement sites in use by at least the tenth century. In recent years late Saxon pottery has been found at a site on the Wincanton by-pass (at Holbrook) (Ellison and Pearson 1981), at the bulldozed deserted hamlet of ?Barrow in Odcombe (Pearson 1978) and more recently at Wedmore, Meare and Shapwick.

At Wedmore (Hollinrake and Hollinrake 1992) trial trenches located a scatter of this early medieval pottery associated with gulleys and ditches. The site is at the west end of the village within a probable earthwork enclosure and may represent a pre-village farmstead on the Wedmore estate (Fig. 11.5). By contrast the pottery from Meare was found associated with the rectilinear pattern of village properties and may well be an indication that the very regular plan of Meare was established as a planted village by the tenth century (Hollinrake and Hollinrake 1993). The same may be true of Dundon in Compton Dundon parish where late Saxon pottery has been found within what appears to be a planned village between two common fields (C. and N. Hollinrake pers. comm.).

Settlement in the Middle Ages

A considerable amount of fieldwork and documentary research is underway at the moment in the county, mainly undertaken by part time groups and individuals compiling parish surveys and studies of the landscape developments of individual parishes. Much of this work is of a very high standard although perhaps inevitably the data generated are variable reflecting the different interests and abilities of the researchers and the quality and quantity of the archaeological and historical material available to them. It has not been possible to include such studies as individual contributions in this volume so what is attempted here, with the permission and cooperation of the individual researchers, is an edited summary of the work in progress at the moment in Somerset. Only from the overall view obtained from a comparison of the detailed study of individual places like this will it be possible to test the models and hypotheses that are being developed generally.

In order to assess the extent of medieval settlement, its variety of forms, its relationship to earlier and later settlement and its subsistence base it was decided to gather information under a number of headings from the researchers studying individual parishes in the county. These headings were based on the following questions:-

1. How much pre-medieval settlement is there in the area, particularly Roman, and what do we know of its form (villas, farmsteads, villages) and its field system?
2. What was the medieval settlement pattern of the land unit (parish, tithing, manor) – village, hamlets, farmsteads? What evidence is there for change through time and how much was subsequently deserted?
3. What was the field system of this/these settlement(s)? If open field – how many common fields – two, three or more; is there any evidence of change through time?
4. Is there any evidence of the settlement pattern after the Roman period and before the medieval? From field names with habitative elements, pottery scatters, or other evidence.
5. Is there any evidence for the field system before the one evident in the middle ages?

The following areas and parishes were examined in this way – Brent, Cheddar, Congresbury, East Pennard, Pilton, Rimpton, Rodney Stoke, Shapwick, and Wedmore (Figs 11.5 to 11.7).

Pre-Medieval Settlement Patterns

Prehistoric and Roman settlement sites are widespread in Somerset and therefore it is not surprising that in most of the parishes under investigation there is some evidence of pre-medieval activity.

At Cheddar for example a large Roman villa has been known for some time situated between the later church which was a minster and the Saxon royal palace. Recent watching briefs in the vicinity have shown a scatter of Romano-British pottery over a wide area under the present village suggesting perhaps a village-like settlement contemporary with the villa. Elsewhere in the large parish there are at least a dozen scattered farmstead sites of Roman date. These are represented by pottery scatters and none seems to be of high status. Most sites seem to loosely correlate with later sites, being no more than fifty metres away, and they are widely distributed from the fen edge, across the lower slopes to the top of the Mendips (Fig. 11.5).

In the adjacent smaller parish of Rodney Stoke extensive Roman settlement on the levels has been recognised from earthworks on Stoke Moor. These must represent a major phase of Roman drainage and utilisation of the Axe valley. However, although there is probably a Roman settlement near the church and manor house at Rodney Stoke and there seems to be one north of Draycott, nothing else is known for the parish (Fig. 11.4).

Congresbury shares the important hillfort of Cadbury with the parish to the north, Yatton. This site was occupied in the pre-Roman period, was in use in the Roman period together with an adjacent temple in Henley Wood, and most significantly was reoccupied as an occupation and probable cult site in the post-Roman centuries to about 600 AD (Rahtz *et al.* 1992). Little is known so far of its contemporary iron age farmsteads but at least eight (though there may be as many as sixteen) Romano-British sites are known in Congresbury. There was also a

Roman villa at Wemberham. These sites are only about seven hundred metres apart, representing a considerable density of farmsteads. There was also a Roman pottery-making industry, centred in the area at the south end of the present village (Fig. 11.5).

The estate of Brent, or Brentmarsh as it was often called, was also centred on a hillfort, which has produced iron age and Roman material, probably contained a late Roman temple, and was almost certainly reoccupied in the post-Roman centuries (Burrow 1981). This estate was granted to Glastonbury Abbey in the late seventh century and remained with the abbey until the Dissolution. A number of Roman sites are known from the four later parishes of South Brent (now Brent Knoll), East Brent, Lympsham and Berrow – well over a dozen – and at least one of these, Lakehouse Farm, has produced wall plaster, heating flue tile and so on, which might suggest it was a villa. The exact relationship of these sites to the surrounding marshy areas is still the subject of much speculation (Rippon 1993). The juxtaposition of hillfort to villa and the early date of the grant of the estate to Glastonbury Abbey has led to the suggestion that this is an early estate which survived intact through to the middle ages (Aston 1985a) (Fig. 11.5).

Little is known of the pre-medieval settlement and field pattern in Rimpton parish although it is in an area with a very high density of Romano-British sites and can perhaps be expected to produce evidence of a villa or farmsteads in future field survey work. In East Pennard about ten percent of the parish has been field surveyed in the ploughed fields. A new Roman villa has been located at Lower Easton and Romano-British material recovered from the church suggesting it is on a villa site. Elsewhere there are a number of pottery and finds scatters suggesting a series of farmstead or small hamlet sites. Some of these seem to have areas of fields attached surviving in later field remains (Fig. 11.5). In the adjacent parish of Pilton only one Roman site seems to have been located so far and this does not seem to have been a villa. One scatter of Romano-British finds at Worthy farm is associated with the slight earthworks of an early field system (Fig. 11.5).

Finally within the large parish of Wedmore research over a number of years has located at least nineteen Roman sites, many associated with medieval settlements (Fig. 11.5). One of these may be a villa, at Shortlands above the village of Wedmore, while the scatter of finds from Wedmore itself suggests a village-like settlement as at Cheddar. All of the other sites are probably rural farmsteads or hamlets, at least one of which has produced burials.

Medieval Settlement Patterns and Field Systems

Fully developed individual nucleated villages with their own common fields inside a parish unit are rare in medieval Somerset. Much more common are parishes with settlement patterns made up of hamlets and farmsteads with irregular field systems. There are few major desertions with piecemeal small scale and generally unaccountable shrinkage and desertion being most common. The parishes being studied show this diversity very well.

The medieval settlement pattern in Cheddar consisted of a scatter of hamlets. Three of these – The Hall, The Green and the Kings Head – provide the foci for the later village while the others are hamlets first recorded from the tenth to thirteenth centuries – Nyland (959), Batcombe (1189), Hythe (1120); Lower Farm (11th cent – the earlier Cheddarford), Carscliffe (1247), Milkway (1247), Bradley Cross (1463) and Piney Sleight (12th cent). Little of this pattern was later deserted. Carscliffe, which may well have developed from an iron age site since earthworks of round houses and square fields have been recognised there, grew into a substantial hamlet across the hillside. This is now deserted, represented by fine earthworks and house remains. Milkway has also disappeared, only a barn remains, and there is slight shrinkage elsewhere. There are also several deserted post-medieval farmsteads on the top of the Mendips.

None of these settlements had a well-developed common field system. Cheddar itself had two fields, east and west, but either the system was not well developed or it had collapsed early on. Strips are recorded elsewhere but usually in closes. All the farms and hamlets had their own land with shared moorland on the levels. On the hilltop the extensive pasture was shared but with specific areas traditionally allocated to individual places; these were retained at enclosure.

The settlement pattern in the adjacent parish of Rodney Stoke was sharply divided between an irregular scatter of farms down the street and along the side of the moor in Rodney Stoke and the well planned nucleated village of Draycott. The latter was probably developed by the Augustinian canons of Bristol sometime in the late 1200s based on twelve farmsteads, six tenements on each side of the street. It had a regular two field system, east and west, with holdings apparently evenly scattered within it. There are a few deserted farmsteads on the hill above; these have produced thirteenth century pottery but nothing earlier. One of the marsh-edge farms, Barrowstone, was probably a 'tun' – a Saxon farmstead.

The manor of Congresbury included the settlements of Wick St Lawrence, Puxton and Huish out in the moors in the pre-Conquest period. Within the present parish of Congresbury there was a series of farmsteads, some clustered around the church and some under the present village with the rest scattered across the parish. These seem to relate in part to earlier Roman sites but also the records of landholding in the early middle ages and in a survey of 1567. Thus yardlands of eighty acres, half yardlands (forty acres), fardel lands (twenty acres) and so on can be related to later farmsteads and to sites on the ground. Land Farm, Honey Hall, Brinsea Batch and Brinsea Farm are all early medieval farm sites and there are earthworks

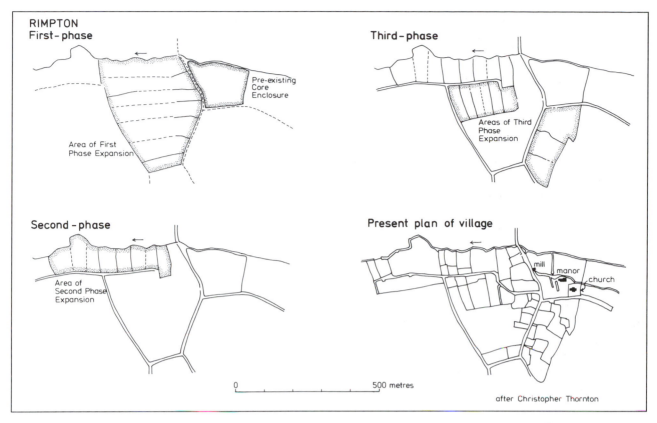

Fig. 11.6 Rimpton – possible phases of development of the village plan as suggested by Christopher Thornton.

of a few others. There was no proper common field system; most settlements had fields in severalty with shared areas of moorland.

The settlement pattern on the Brent estate was one of dispersed hamlets and farmsteads with the only appreciable nucleation being along the moor edge in South Brent and associated with the church at East Brent. Even so at these centres there was no fully developed common field system judging from the surveys of the early fourteenth and early sixteenth centuries. Medieval hamlets can be recognised at Berrow, Lympsham, Edingworth, Wick, Southwick, Burton and Battleborough with other likely centres at Ham, Batch, Rooks Bridge, the lost settlements of Sistenhampton and Snyghampton and at many of the scattered farms. Little of this pattern was subsequently deserted; it is possible but perhaps unlikely that Sistenhampton may be another name for Rooks Bridge and Snyghampton part of Edingworth.

In the middle ages Rimpton had one nucleated village at the centre of the parish with a small hamlet of probable twelfth century origin at Woodhouse to the north. The village itself, following extensive research on the abundant documentation, is suggested to have developed as a result of several phases of planning of crofts adjacent to the manorial enclosure (Fig. 11.6). This has been related to both inheritance customs and the tenurial system in existence in the late Saxon and early medieval periods.

Christopher Thornton (1988) suggests that a pattern of dispersed peasant farmsteads, cultivated in severalty and passed on by partible inheritance, was replaced sometime in the Anglo-Saxon period by a nucleated settlement, farming a common-field system with regular sized holdings passed on by impartible inheritance. The village may have been developed as seven or so tenements, located opposite an earlier enclosure, originally for *coliberti* working the estate when it was in royal ownership before 938 AD. These first holdings may be associated with the bordars listed in Domesday Book (1086) and the ferling tenants who served as estate *famuli* in the thirteenth century. Some of the these properties were later partially redeveloped, either by two tenth century lay owners of the estate or by the monks of Winchester to whom the estate had passed by 964x980 AD, perhaps to accommodate local people displaced from their several holdings by the new common-field system. These second and third phases of the village were apparently occupied by the villein tenants of 1086 and the customary tenants holding virgated tenements in the thirteenth century. This analysis represents the most advanced attempt so far to unravel the plan of a Somerset village.

The fields at Rimpton in the middle ages were run as an irregular common field system, but its core may have comprised two fields lying to the south-east and south-west of the village which were laid out at the time of settlement nucleation. This field system was subsequently expanded by extending southwards and also northwards towards Woodhouse. By the thirteenth century the rotation was by individual furlong, with demesne land and peasant land intermixed in some areas and separate in others.

East Pennard is made up of a series of medieval hamlets; East Pennard, Little Pennard, Withial, Huxham, Stone, Hembridge, Farleigh and Easton, with several others of later date, and medieval farm sites at Hill and Kingshill. Some desertion of these took place in the later middle ages so that there are earthworks at East Pennard, Withial and Easton and some lost cottage sites at Huxham. There is little evidence for fully developed common fields in the parish but what there is in the sixteenth century suggests two fields attached to each of the hamlets at East Pennard, Withial, Easton and Stone. There seems to have been much reorganisation of the fields after the dissolution of Glastonbury Abbey, the medieval owner, in 1539.

The settlement pattern of Pilton is similar with hamlets at West and East Compton, Westholme and Holt. The latter is called West Holt so presumably there was an East Holt at some stage. This may have been in the area of the vast medieval Pilton Park belonging to the abbots of Glastonbury situated in the south west of the parish where the landscape is relatively empty of settlement. The village of Pilton itself is a series of farms strung out along the valley without any obvious centre to it. Ham was a detached hamlet to the north and was also a tithing. Other tithings were Pilton, East and West Compton (two), Westholme or Fulbrook and Holt; North Wootton to the west was a chapelry of Pilton. Little of this pattern was deserted. East Holt is a possibility before the thirteenth century and ruined buildings suggest that West Holt was once more than a single farm. East Compton seems to have shrunken village earthworks.

Wedmore is the only one of the parishes included in this discussion which had any 'urban' attributes. Around 1200 or a little earlier the dean of Wells seems to have laid out forty or so plots at the east end of the small village of Wedmore to create a 'new borough'. Otherwise there are about eighteen medieval settlements in the later parish of Wedmore. Many of these were large hamlets and several of them have a regular rectilinear layout suggesting that they may have been planned settlements. The most obvious from eighteenth century and modern maps are Mudgley, with fifteen or so units along an east-west street, Sand, Blackford with a moated manor house of the bishops of Bath and Wells, Westham, West and Middle Stoughton, Theale, Clewer and Cocklake. Irregularly laid out hamlets include Panborough, Heath, Northload, and Stoughton Cross, and there were farmsteads at Perrow, Pilham, Latcham and Martins Close. Interestingly some of the settlements in the parish can be shown definitely to be of post-medieval date; Bagley, which is now deserted and moved up to a main road, and Oldwood, now largely disappeared, were newly planned

settlements of the 1580s. From the nineteenth century Gooseham, four houses from the 1800s, has now gone while New Town of the 1830s, laid out in an area of wood and scrub, has also largely disappeared. Little of the medieval settlement pattern has disappeared.

Wedmore seems to have had a rather more obvious common field system than the other places discussed here. This was based perhaps originally on an east and west field but was shared with several other hamlets in the parish such as Cocklake. The same situation existed with the hamlets of Blackford and Mudgley. Each had its own common field system, based on two fields but these were shared with other hamlets; Blackford east and west fields with Westham and the Stoughtons, and Mudgley with Sand and Heath. Other hamlets had their own single field as at Clewer and Theale, or fields as at Crickham. There is at least the suggestion that single fields or infield/outfield systems may have been more typical before the common fields were developed; Wedmore may have had the single field of Erdeland in earlier times while the site at West End may have had its arable in the field called Whatley.

Anglo-Saxon Settlement Patterns and Field Systems

The picture that seems to be emerging in Somerset in the pre-medieval period, as for other areas, is of a predominantly scattered settlement pattern with little evidence of fully developed common fields. Sometimes Anglo-Saxon settlements are indicated by habitative type place-names, either attached to existing settlements or as field or furlong names in open country, or more rarely by pottery scatters or other archaeological evidence (Fig. 11.5). Many of the parish studies demonstrate these aspects.

Cheddar was a large royal estate centred on the palace which has been discovered and excavated (Rahtz 1979). Charter evidence suggests that at least one farm (Lower farm, the earlier Cheddarford, now Longwood Grange) was there by the mid eleventh century; it has pottery from the Roman period to the present day so has probably been continuously occupied over the last two thousand years. The site is referred to as a 'separate worth' with a wood in 1068. There are other habitative names recorded for fields – Calcott on the boundary with Draycott, Brinton, Buckleston, Donston, Knightcott, Middleton and Shelliton. Pre-conquest pottery, which was found at the palace, has not been found at any of the hamlets in the parish in fieldwork so far. Nevertheless it is felt that many of the hamlets in existence in the twelfth and thirteenth centuries, and which have produced Roman pottery, were probably in existence as farmsteads in the Anglo-Saxon period, often with rounded field boundaries suggesting original infields – Hythe, Bradley Cross, Cheddar, Nyland, Carscliffe, and Cheddarford. Other sites, on the hilltop, may well represent seasonal steadings of the pre-conquest period which developed into permanent farmsteads later on.

Next door in Rodney Stoke no pre-conquest pottery has been found, nor are there apparently any habitative field names other than 'worthyland'. Presumably the 'cott' of Draycott was a farm before the village was developed there, and Barrowstone is probably another (see above).

Congresbury was probably an early estate based on the hillfort and later possibly the monastery referred to in Alfred's will. Much early material has come from the excavations at the hillfort (Rahtz *et al.* 1992). Elsewhere grass or chaff-tempered pottery of fifth or sixth century date has come from the churchyard, a possible indication of the early religious site associated with St Congar. Much later Saxon pottery has been found in Brinsea. A few habitative field names are recorded which may indicate other dispersed farm sites. There is a worthy in the Honey hall area, wick and enwick, a worth (or warth) near Stepstones and a Greenworthy at East Huish. A '*wickham*' furlong name in the dole moors of Congresbury is near to a Roman site in Puxton moor and is a rare example of this type of name in Somerset (Gelling 1967).

Many of the settlement names on the Brent estate indicate Anglo-Saxon settlements; Edingworth, Burton, Wick and Southwick. Field names likewise suggest other sites. There are a number of '*worth*' and '*huish*' names for example – kilnworthy, kyllyngworth, drowsenworth, holleworth/holworthy, sakeworth, huish and kemyshewys, lytle huysh – and on the hill a field with the name Galhampton where there are enigmatic earthworks. In Lympsham the names Norton and Muttomworth occur. No late Anglo-Saxon pottery has been found so far but the impression is that the scatter of settlement is much as it would have been in the pre-conquest and early medieval periods.

Rimpton was in royal ownership before 938 AD, perhaps as part of the large estate of Lanprobi based at Sherborne. During the tenth century it was 'booked' to two royal thegns, the second of whom left it to the monks of Winchester (964x980). It has been argued (Costen 1985 and 1992b) that the land unit which became the medieval parish had been constructed from the five hides of Rimpton itself with the addition of two one-hide units to the immediate north, one originally a separate family unit '*huish*' and the other an additional hide added in the tenth century (later the site of Woodhouse hamlet). It has also been suggested by Michael Costen (1985) and Christopher Thornton (1988) that the earlier pattern of settlement within Rimpton was one of dispersed farmsteads, as indicated by later field names such as Hamstedemede and Worthemede/Wicmede and by names indicating fields once held individually rather than in common. Although the core enclosure and the first phase of the village may be pre-tenth century, the later phases of nucleation and the accompanying common field system are likely to have been laid out by the estate's new feudal landowners, lay or ecclesiastical, between 938 and

1086 AD (Fig. 11.6). In this case the settlement pattern was drastically altered from one of dispersed farmsteads to a single nucleated village, apparently planned in several stages.

In East Pennard there is the place-name 'Shortworthy' attached to a field near Withial and possible tenth century pottery has been recovered from field-walking in the parish. East Pennard and Stone have estates in Domesday Book (1086) and it is thought likely that Withial, Farleigh, Easton and Huxham were also in existence by 1066. Interestingly all these hamlets occupy the best soils in the parish and at least one, Stone, may have had an infield/outfield system indicated in the field name 'oldfield'.

A probable villa, followed by an estate centre with a minster, seems to have developed into the parish centre at East Pennard. To the east, a 'tun' developed at Easton from another Roman villa site while to the south a Romano-British farm site became Stone. There is here no evidence for drastic replanning of the landscape or of the settlements within it.

Within Pilton village there is a farm with the name Old Worthy, while to the south is another farm, the site of the Glastonbury pop festival, called Worthy. Otherwise there seem to be no other habitative field names (though perhaps kinton and kintons are) and so far no pre-medieval pottery has been found. The scatter of hamlets is felt to represent the Anglo-Saxon settlement pattern.

Recent excavations at West Close in Wedmore have produced tenth century pottery indicating perhaps at least one of the farm units dating from before the nucleation of the village and its development as a small town. Elsewhere eleventh century pottery has been found under the new town and at Mudgley, which has produced a lot of pottery of all dates. There are few habitative field names; to the west of the village there is Red or Rad worth. Also the names whittington, damaston, warrinton and wallington occur on the title map. It is suggested that most of the medieval hamlets were probably in existence in the pre-Conquest period and many had been continuously occupied since the Roman period. Some may have been newly planned or replanned in the late Saxon period, perhaps when common fields were developed, but persistence rather than dramatic change seems to have been the typical pattern.

A good case can be made out from the work carried out so far in these parishes for considerable continuity from the Roman, through the Anglo-Saxon to the medieval periods with little evidence generally for disruption or major upheaval (as in Wiltshire, see Lewis this volume). In such places a persistence of earlier dispersed patterns of settlement with poorly developed common field systems (if at all) seems to be the norm. In some cases actual settlement sites seem to have been continuously used presumably farming the land around; elsewhere it was probably the land unit which was continuously worked with the farmstead being placed at different sites on the land at various periods. However in a few cases there was complete transformation of the settlement and field pattern from dispersed farmsteads to nucleated villages with common fields. Such examples as Rimpton (Fig. 11.6) and Shapwick (Fig. 11.7) mirror developments seen in other parts of the country.

The Example of Shapwick

Rural settlements with pre-Conquest archaeological evidence, other than those sited above, remain elusive however because of our reliance on finds of pottery to indicate sites. As can be seen from the parish studies there still remains the general problem of recognition of rural settlements in the Somerset landscape before the tenth century. How are we to recognise traces of settlements whose buildings were constructed using organic materials with little use of post holes or wall trenches for timbers and inhabited by people who apparently did not use pottery and who possessed little in the way of inorganic equipment that could be recognised later by archaeologists? In order to locate such sites archaeologists require a fresh approach with different methods; conventional archaeological methodology is clearly incapable of retrieving evidence of people and their settlements at that time. In future a strategy based on geophysical surveying and geochemical sampling will be needed to locate such sites. This should perhaps be carried out without reference to what is known already of settlements in the area although habitative names might be used to narrow down the areas to be sampled. Excavations should then be undertaken where concentrations of features and/or soil chemicals occur; the main purposes of these excavations would be to find material which can be absolutely dated and to retrieve plans of settlements (Aston 1992).

At Shapwick in the centre of the county many of the strands of the above arguments are coming together in a ten year research project designed to investigate the origins of the medieval village and its common field system in the parish (Fig. 11.7). Attention was drawn to the parish by the research of Nicolas Corcos (1982, 1983) who suggested that the village had been planned together with a very regular field system and that these had replaced an earlier scattered settlement pattern of farms. These ideas were based on furlong names with habitative elements recorded in the middle ages in the two common fields – west and east.

Furthermore he suggested these developments took place in association with the break-up of a large estate on the Polden Hills belonging to Glastonbury Abbey – called in the pre-Conquest period 'Pouholt' (Fig. 11.8). Names in the medieval documents included the elements 'wick' – Sladwick, and Shapwick itself, 'worth' – Langenworthy, Shortenworthy, Shortgoldworth, worthie, nutherworthe, overworthe and emmyngewurth, and 'hay' – an enclosure – Abofehaies, Bosehaies and grasshaie.

Other names might also indicate early settlement or at least a different and non-open field system – Manycrofte, Purycrofte and the Borgh names for example. The exact location of many of these names is not known yet.

Fieldwork undertaken since 1989 over ploughed fields in Shapwick has already located a scatter of tenth century pottery in some fields which may indicate pre-village settlement sites. As yet there is no apparent correlation between early pottery scatters and habitative field names, mainly because of the difficulty of precisely locating the areas of the furlongs with habitative names, recorded in the documents, within the later field patterns. Similarly the small amount of geophysical work undertaken has failed to locate features even in those areas where habitative names are known to have existed. Nevertheless it is still felt that geophysical and geochemical methods offer the best chance of locating and recording farmsteads of the period 400–900 AD in the fields of Shapwick.

At Shapwick present indications are that the village and its two medieval common fields may have replaced three or four hamlets rather than a scatter of ten to a dozen farmsteads. It is always possible of course that there were more stages of settlement evolution than were formerly envisaged with perhaps up to a dozen scattered farmsteads at one stage and fewer hamlets at another. The village itself may have been developed with several extensions and the open fields may not always have been as extensive as they later came to be. Current ideas of these possible stages of development are shown here as a model, which to a large extent the project is seeking to test (Fig. 11.7).

A Model for Pre-Medieval Settlement Development in Somerset (Fig. 11.9)

Research so far then suggests discrete blocks of land in the Somerset landscape some of which may be the descendant of Roman estates and which were centred on a Roman villa or some other substantial settlement. These centres were probably replaced in the sub-Roman and post-Roman periods by refortified hillforts. In later times these centres had themselves been replaced by lowland foci which were the centres of estates belonging to royal, episcopal or monastic owners, although they were presumably run by reeves or bailiffs. No such site has been excavated in Somerset, and few elsewhere for that matter, and so what they looked like in detail is not known. Cheddar provides an interesting royal example from later times with its halls, bowers and ancillary buildings, all in close proximity to a minster church. Nothing is known of any contemporary accompanying lay settlement or of the surrounding field system.

Such a 'focal place' would have been supported by surrounding settlements many of which are probably now represented by the characteristic pattern of hamlets in Somerset while others only exist as habitative field names.

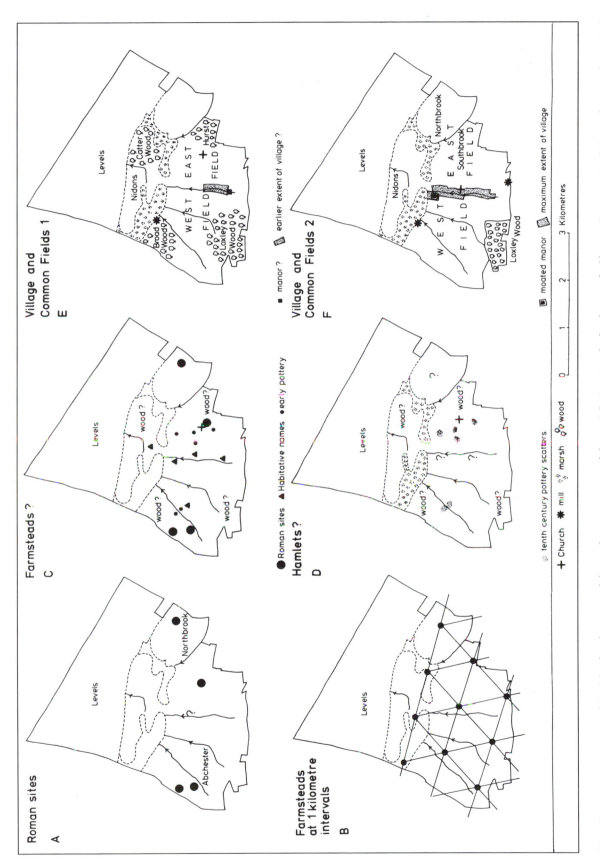

Fig. 11.7 *Shapwick – a model of the development of the settlement pattern of the parish. Against the background of known Roman sites (A) are shown a theoretical distribution of ten farmsteads one kilometre apart (B) (see Chisholm 1979, 127), habitative field names and tenth century pottery scatters (C). Before the village there could have been farmsteads (B and C) and/or hamlets (D). Following replanning of the landscape the village and its common fields may have developed by planned stages (E and F) in the middle ages. No definite dates can be attached to each of these stages but the following may indicate the way thoughts are going – A to 400 AD, C seventh to tenth century?, D by the tenth century?, E circa 1100, F circa 1350.*

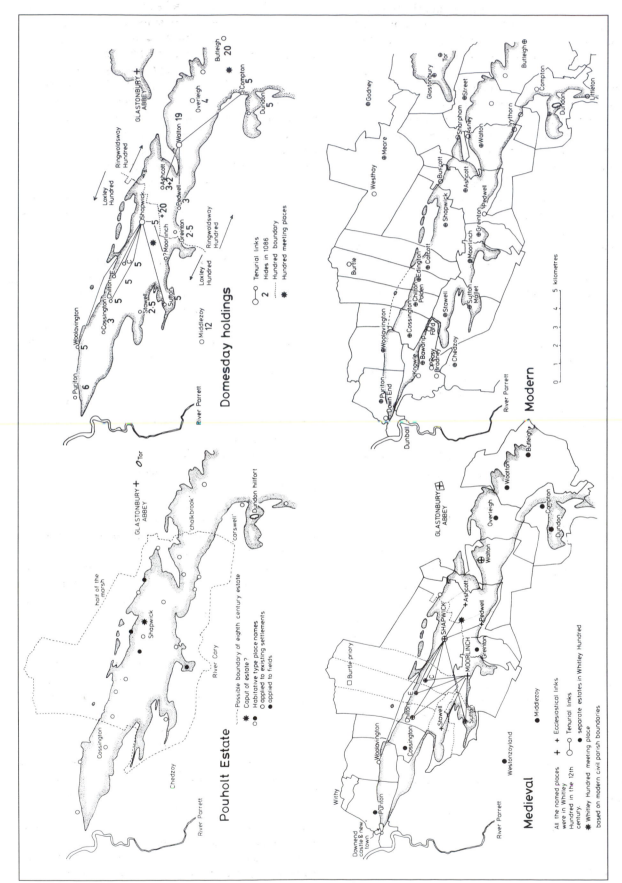

Fig. 11.8 *Settlements on the Polden Hills. An example of how the break up of the Pouholt estate may have led to the creation of a series of nucleated villages with common fields. Their relationships in the ecclesiastical and tenurial hierarchy and to hundredal arrangements can be demonstrated in the early middle ages.*

Most of these settlements were presumably not extensive, and were certainly not villages, judging by the types of names used to describe them. It is at least possible that in Somerset there were several stages of development and settlement change in the pre-conquest period with a wider scatter of farmsteads, many of which are indicated by the habitative field names which are so widespread in the county, being replaced in many areas by a fewer number of larger hamlet settlements, even before the larger more nucleated villages were developed (as in Fig. 11.7C and D for example).

Research elsewhere in the country (Jones 1979, Fox 1981) and for Somerset (Corcos 1983, Costen 1988) suggests the break up of these relatively large estates in late Saxon times into smaller independent units which we recognise as the parishes, tithings and townships of the middle ages and later times. The small units based on individual settlements, especially hamlets, were nevertheless the original economic units within the larger estate and as such would have been readily identifiable to folk at the time. The process of fragmentation was certainly happening in the tenth century and later and seems to have been associated with parish (Gerrard 1987) and village development (Taylor 1983, Aston 1985b, 1988, Costen 1991), common field origins (Fox 1981) and the beginnings of parish churches (Blair 1988). Many aspects of these processes were never fully developed in Somerset. There are for example still many large parishes which were formerly royal or ecclesiastical estates such as Wells (St Cuthbert Out parish), North Petherton, Wedmore and Martock where the fission to smaller parish units was never completed and which have within them numerous large village-like hamlets with their own field systems. In general in Somerset the fission of larger units did not result in single settlements surrounded by a common field system in a discrete parish unit. Neither did the classic midland type of common field system develop everywhere in the county. It is evident in the centre, south and east of the county (Aston 1988) but elsewhere very mixed and varied field systems were in use in the middle ages, often with extensive areas of woodland and common pasture available to the local farmers. The settlement pattern in many parishes remained in the form it had been before the break up of the estates, small hamlets or scattered farmsteads.

There are few deserted medieval villages in Somerset of the type studied so extensively in the midlands; there were few strongly nucleated settlements existing singly in their parish units to be deserted. Much more common are the abandoned or severely shrunken hamlets within parishes where other very similar hamlets and more important village centres have survived. This is particularly the picture in the south and east of the county.

Conclusions

From the research described above a persistence of ham-let settlement or farmsteads from at least the Roman period to the middle ages can be taken as the 'normal' model for settlement development in Somerset. The hamlet sites may have grown from single farms and indeed may at some stage have shrunk back to the single farms which are often all that remain today following population increase, decline and economic changes. Such settlements tend to be associated with non-common field systems based on perhaps infield/outfield arrangements in earlier times and with land held in severalty in the middle ages, although still with some shared arable and common access to upland and lowland grazing areas.

In some places more typical strongly-nucleated villages were developed usually associated with common field systems based on two, or occasionally in Somerset three, open fields. Not many of these have been discussed in the examples cited above (Shapwick, Draycott in Rodney Stoke and Rimpton) but they occur in some numbers across south-eastern Somerset and along the Polden Hills (Fig. 11.8). In some (most?) cases they seem to have replaced the more scattered settlement pattern of either hamlets or farmsteads and to have been deliberately planned and laid out closely associated with the development of more classic common field systems. They are nevertheless the exception to the more typical hamlet pattern. The research by Christopher Thornton at Rimpton suggests interesting links between tenurial and inheritance customs and these are characteristics which ought to be looked for and examined elsewhere. Otherwise the research on Shapwick offers perhaps the best opportunity to examine some of the changes and developments discussed here.

Any fieldwork elsewhere in the county may produce archaeological evidence, in the form of pottery for example, which would extend our knowledge of developments in the critical late Saxon period, while further rigorous examination of the documentary evidence of, for example, place-names, early estates or detailed manorial surveys like those for the estates of Glastonbury Abbey, is bound to be fruitful.

Acknowledgements

Clearly this article could not have been written without the full cooperation of the many scholars and researchers working on the various places mentioned in the text – Jem Harrison (Brent), Vince Russet (Cheddar), Richard Broomhead (Congresbury and Rodney Stoke), Charles and Nancy Hollinrake (Meare, Wedmore), Richard Raynsford (Pilton), Penny Stokes (East Pennard), Christopher Thornton (Rimpton), Frances Neale and Hazel Hudson (Wedmore) and Andrew Young (Eckweek). To all I am most grateful; I hope they find their specific research is adequately reflected in this general survey and that I have not misrepresented information either sent to me or conveyed in personal conversations by the people working on the various areas and parishes of the county.

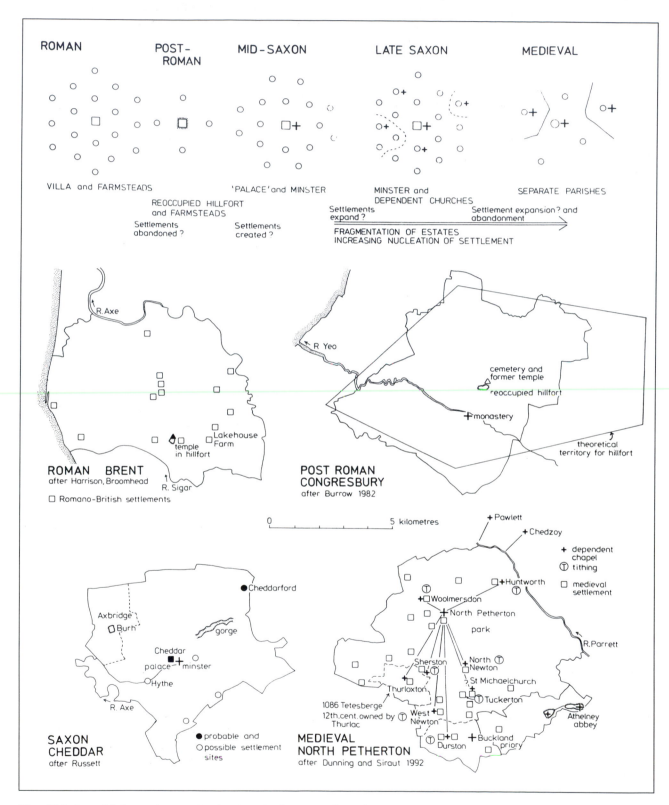

Fig. 11.9 *A model for settlement development in Somerset, from the Roman period to the early middle ages. Examples of each stage of development fossilised in the Somerset landscape are also shown.*

More generally I am grateful to David Bromwich of the Local History Library, Taunton Castle, Christopher Webster of the Somerset County Sites and Monuments Record and the staff of the Somerset County Record Office for all their assistance. My colleagues Carenza Lewis and Michael Costen provided useful criticism and advice.

Gazeteer of Archaeological Evidence for Pre-Conquest Rural Settlements in Historic Somerset

(See Fig. 11.1, information up to late 1993; note that other than Cheddar, finds from urban or high status sites are not included)

Abbas and Templecombe
A cemetery of at least eleven burials was found in a pipeline trench on the parish boundary with Horsington. Two radiocarbon dates of 681–974 AD and 794–1026 AD centre on *c.* 850 AD. Residual pottery is said to be 'Iron Age' as well as Roman and medieval. There is no known contemporary settlement in the area and it is unlikely that the earthworks nearby are pre-conquest (Newman 1992).

Bratton Seymour, Holbrook
A site indicated by a scatter of pottery found in roadworks associated with the Wincanton by-pass. The report says 'The settlement at Holbrook is not mentioned in Domesday Book ... but the archaeological assemblage from this site indicates that there was a settlement here in the eleventh century and the find demonstrates how important it must be to amplify historical evidence with that deriving from archaeological fieldwork' (Ellison and Pearson 1981).

Carhampton, Eastbury
Evaluation excavations in advance of roadworks located a few pre-conquest sherds in an area where burials have been found in the past and where there may have been a pre-medieval religious site (Chris Webster and C. and N. Hollinrake).

Cheddar, Saxon Palace site
Pottery from the excavations of the Saxon palace site (Rahtz 1979).

Cleeve, Bickley
Tenth century pottery found at the small scale excavations at this farm site (Rippon 1993 p. 28).

Compton Dundon, Dundon
Tenth to fourteenth century occupation has been located at Court Orchard (pers. comm. C. and N. Hollinrake).

Congresbury, Brinsea
See text above (pers. comm. R. Broomhead).

East Pennard
See text above (pers. comm. P. Stokes).

Meare, Meare Hospital/The Laurels
Although the summary of evaluation work at the site says that pottery of the eleventh to the fourteenth centuries was found, the finds included 'late tenth' to fourteenth century sherds associated with various features. The plot within which the features were found is one of a number of regular tenements on the north side of the road which probably represent a planned village (C. and N. Hollinrake 1993).

Odcombe, ?Barrow
Finds from the ploughing of a deserted medieval hamlet which may have been called Barrow ranged from the late tenth-early eleventh century to the fourteenth century (Pearson 1978).

Peasedown St John, Eckweek
Extensive excavations in advance of road building have revealed the best evidence in the county so far for a series of farmsteads and hamlets dating from the pre-conquest period to the eighteenth century, with a surviving farm on the site. There were three phases of late Saxon and earlier medieval timber structures on the site dated by ceramic and radiocarbon dates to between the later tenth and the later twelfth centuries (pers. comm. Andrew Young).

Somerton, St Cleers
Tenth century occupation has been located in archaeological evaluations which, if they are not associated with the royal 'palace' site could relate to a farmstead (pers. comm. C. and N. Hollinrake).

Wedmore, West End
An archaeological evaluation at The Close revealed numerous features associated with pottery of tenth to fourteenth century date (forty sherds of the tenth century and ?earlier). Magnetometry suggested numerous features in a roughly square enclosure bounded by earthworks and a stream (C. and N. Hollinrake 1992).

Wellington
In evaluation excavations near the church tenth and eleventh century pottery was found indicating domestic occupations (pers. comm. Chris Webster and Mark Horton).

References

Aston, M. 1982: 'The Medieval Pattern 1000–1500AD', in M. Aston and I. Burrow, *The Archaeology of Somerset: a review to 1500AD*. Somerset County Council, Taunton.

Aston, M. 1983: 'Deserted Farmsteads on Exmoor and the Lay Subsidy of 1327 in West Somerset', *Somerset Archaeology and Natural History* 127, 71–104.

Aston, M. 1985a: *Interpreting the Landscape: Landscape Archaeology in Local Studies*. Batsford, London.

Aston, M. 1985b: 'Rural Settlement in Somerset: some preliminary thoughts', in D. Hooke (ed.), *Medieval Villages: A Review of Current Work*. Oxford University Committee for Archaeology Monograph 5, 81–100.

Aston, M. 1986a: 'The Bath Region from Later Prehistory to the Middle Ages', *Bath History* 1, 61–89.

Aston, M. 1986b: 'Post-Roman Central Places in Somerset', in E. Grant (ed.), *Central Places, Archaeology and History* Department of Archaeology and Prehistory, University of Sheffield, 49–77.

Aston, M. 1988: 'Settlement Patterns and Forms', pp. 66–81 and 'Land Use and Field Systems', pp. 82–97, in M. Aston (ed.) *Aspects of the Medieval Landscape of Somerset: contributions to the landscape history of the county*. Somerset County Council, Taunton.

Aston, M. 1989a: *The Shapwick Project: A Topographical and Historical Study* 1988 Report, University of Bristol.

Aston, M. 1989b: 'A Regional Study of Deserted Settlements in the West of England', in M. Aston, D. Austin and C. Dyer *The Rural Settlements of Medieval England: Studies dedicated to Maurice Beresford and John Hurst*. Basil Blackwell, Oxford, 105–128.

Aston, M. 1989c: 'The development of medieval rural settlement in Somerset', in R. Higham (ed.), *Landscape and Townscape in the South West*. Exeter Studies in History 22, University of Exeter, 19–40.

Aston, M. (ed.) 1990: *The Shapwick Project: A Topographical and Historical Study* 1989 (2nd) Report, University of Bristol.

Aston, M. 1992: 'The Shapwick Project, Somerset: A study in need of remote sensing', in P. Spoerry (ed.), *Geoprospection in the Archaeological Landscape*. Oxbow Monograph 18, Oxford, 141–154.

Aston, M. and Leech, R. 1977: *Historic Towns in Somerset Archaeology and Planning*. Committee for Rescue Archaeology in Avon, Gloucestershire and Somerset. Bristol.

Aston, M. and Costen, M. D. (eds) 1992: *The Shapwick Report: A Topographical and Historical Study*. The Third Report (1990), University of Bristol.

Aston, M. and Costen, M. D. (eds) 1993: *The Shapwick Report: A Topographical and Historical Study*. The Fourth Report (1991 and 1992), University of Bristol.

Barton, K. 1969: 'Pickwick farm, Dundry, Somerset', *Proceedings of the University of Bristol Spelaeological Society* 12 (1), 99–112

Bell, M. 1989: 'Environmental Archaeology as an Index of Continuity and Change in the Medieval Landscape', in M. Aston, D. Austin and C. Dyer, *The Rural Settlements of Medieval England: Studies dedicated to Maurice Beresford and John Hurst*. Basil Blackwell, Oxford, 269–286.

Blair, J. (ed.) 1988: *Minsters and Parish Churches: The Local Church in Transition 950–1200*. Oxford University Committee for Archaeology Monograph 17, Oxford.

Burrow, I. 1979: *Aspects of Hillfort and Hilltop Settlement in Somerset in the First–Eighth Centuries AD*, unpublished PhD thesis, University of Birmingham.

Cadman, G. E. 1983: 'Raunds 1977–1983: An Excavation Summary', *Medieval Archaeology* 27, 107–122.

Chisholm, M. 1979: *Rural Settlement and Land Use: An Essay in Location*. Hutchinson, London.

Corcos, N. 1982: *Shapwick: The Enclosure of a Somerset Parish 1515–1839*, unpublished MA dissertation, Department of English Local History, University of Leicester.

Corcos, N. 1983: 'Early Estates on the Poldens and the Origin of settlement at Shapwick', *Somerset Archaeology and Natural History* 127, 47–54.

Costen, M. 1985: 'Rimpton in Somerset – a late Saxon Estate', *Southern History* 7, 13–24.

Costen, M. 1988: 'The Late Saxon Landscape', in M. Aston (ed.), *Aspects of the Medieval Landscape of Somerset*. Somerset County Council, Taunton, 33–47.

Costen, M. 1991: 'Some Evidence for New Settlements and Field Systems in Late Anglo-Saxon Somerset', in L. Abrams and J. Carley, *The Archaeology and History of Glastonbury Abbey*. The Boydell Press, Woodbridge, 39–55.

Costen, M. 1992a: *The Origins of Somerset*. Manchester University Press.

Costen, M. 1992b: 'Huish and Worth: Old English Survivals in a later Landscape', in W. Filmer-Sankey (ed.), *Anglo-Saxon Studies in Archaeology and History* 5, 65–83.

Dunning, R. W. and Sirant, M. 1992: 'North Petherton', *Victoria County History for Somerset* VI, 278–315.

Ellison, A. and Pearson, T. 1981: *The Wincanton By-pass – A Study in The Archaeological Recording of Road Works*. CRAAGS Occasional Papers 8, Bristol.

Esmonde Cleary, A. S. 1989: *The Ending of Roman Britain*. Batsford, London.

Fox, H. 1981: 'Approaches to the Adoption of the Midland System', in T. Rowley (ed.) *The Origins of Open Field Agriculture*. Croom Helm, London, 64–111.

Fox, H. 1983: 'Contraction, desertion and dwindling of dispersed settlement in a Devon parish', *Annual Report of the Medieval Village Research Group* 31, 40–2.

Gelling, M. 1967: 'English place-names derived from the compound wicham', *Medieval Archaeology* 11, 87–104.

Gerrard, C. 1987: *Trade and Settlement in Medieval Somerset: An Application of some Geographical and Economic Models to Historic Data*, unpublished PhD thesis, Department of Classics and Archaeology, University of Bristol.

Hall, D. 1988: 'The Late Saxon Countryside: Villages and their Fields', in D. Hooke (ed.), *Anglo-Saxon Settlements*. Basil Blackwell, Oxford, 99–122.

Hollinrake, C. and Hollindrake, N. 1992: The Close, Wedmore, An Archaeological Evaluation, unpublished typescript.

Hollinrake, C. and Hollindrake, N. 1993: An Archaeological Evaluation at 'The Laurels' Meare Hospital, Meare, near Glastonbury, unpublished typescript.

Jones, G. 1979: 'Multiple Estates and Early Settlement', in P. Sawyer (ed.), *English Medieval Settlement*. Edward Arnold, London, 9–34.

Leech, R. H. 1977: *Roman-British Rural Settlement in South Somerset and North Dorset*, unpublished PhD thesis, University of Bristol.

Newman, C. 1992: 'A Later Saxon Cemetery at Templecombe', *Somerset Archaeology and Natural History* 136, 61–72.

Pearson, T. 1978: 'Late Saxon and Early Medieval Pottery from the Deserted Village of Barrow(?) in Odcombe Parish', *Somerset Archaeology and Natural History* 122, 79–82.

Pearson, T. 1982: 'The Post-Roman Pottery', in P. Leach (ed.), *Ilchester Volume 1 Excavations 1974–1975*. Western Archaeological Trust, Excavation Monograph 3, Bristol, 169–217.

Pearson, T. 1984: 'Medieval and Post-Medieval Ceramics', in P. Leach (ed.), *The Archaeology of Taunton: Excavations and Fieldwork to 1980*. Western Archaeological Trust, Excavation Monograph 8, 142–144.

Prosser, L. forthcoming: *The Keynsham Hundred: A Study of the Evolution of a North Somerset Estate, 350–1550*, unpublished PhD thesis, University of Bristol.

Rahtz, P. 1979: *The Saxon and Medieval Palaces at Cheddar*. British Archaeological Reports, British Series 65, Oxford.

Rahtz, P. 1991: 'Pagan and Christian by the Severn Sea', in L. Abrams and J. Carley, *The Archaeology and History of*

Glastonbury Abbey. The Boydell Press, Woodbridge, 3–37.

Rahtz, P. *et al.* 1992: *Cadbury Congresbury 1968–73: A late/ post Roman hilltop settlement in Somerset*. Tempus Reparatum, British Archaeological Reports, British Series 223, Oxford.

Rippon, S. 1993: *Landscape Evolution and Wetland Reclamation Around the Severn Estuary*, unpublished PhD thesis, Department of Archaeology, University of Reading.

Roberts, B. K. 1987: *The Making of the English Village*. Longman, Harlow, Essex.

Taylor, C. 1983: *Village and Farmstead: A History of Rural Settlement in England*. George Philip, London.

Thornton, C. C. 1988: *The Demesne of Rimpton, 938 to 1412: A Study in Economic Development*, unpublished PhD thesis, Department of English Local History, University of Leicester.

12. Medieval Wetland Reclamation in Somerset

Stephen Rippon

This paper presents a history of wetland reclamation on the Somerset Levels. The subject was first examined in detail by Williams (1970), based upon documentary sources, but a wider range of evidence allows the modification and expansion of some of his conclusions, and the examination of a much greater area. Attention will focus on the neglected coastal claylands, as opposed to inland peat moors, and consider the period from around the ninth century, when recolonisation of the Levels began after a period of marine transgression. The role of the great monastic houses will be explored, and the changing patterns of landuse considered. Finally, the marginal nature of this environment will be questioned.

Introduction

The Somerset Levels consist of a series of broad valley basins with their axes perpendicular to the Severn Estuary (see Fig. 12.1). The various Levels are divided by narrow peninsulas of land such as the Polden Hills, which divide Sedgemoor and the Parrett Valley to the south, and the Central Levels to the north, comprising the Brue and Axe Valleys. The North Somerset Levels are divided from the Axe Valley by the western extension of the Mendips, the 'Bleadon Hills'. Finally, to the north of another ridge at Tickenham, lies the Gordano Valley.

These valleys were flooded during the post-glacial rise in sea-level, which deposited a deep sequence of peat and alluvium forming the Levels (Kidson and Heyworth 1976). Inland, peat continued to form as late as the tenth century (Beckett and Hibbert 1979; Cox 1992), and is exposed on the modern ground surface (see Fig. 12.1). Towards the coast, peat growth ceased towards the end of the second millennium bc, and is sealed by a thick layer of alluvium deposited during the last major marine transgression (Housley 1988; Murray and Hawkins 1976, 391). As areas closest to the sea or tidal rivers are flooded most often, more sediment will be deposited in these locations than inland. Thus, the coastal parts of the clay belt are higher than the inland moors. Along much of the coast, the Levels are fringed by a belt of sand-dunes, that may well date back to the bronze age, and almost certainly the Roman period (Bell 1990; Rippon 1992).

All the coastal areas of alluvium were extensively settled in the Roman period (Rippon 1991; 1992; 1993).

Some areas appear to have been protected by sea-walls and river floodbanks and were subsequently drained, but from the end of the Roman period, water levels appear to have risen and settlements were abandoned. In Central Somerset there was a substantial marine transgression that reached up to 10km inland, sealing the Roman landscape with around 0.5–0.7m of estuarine alluvium (Rippon 1991). However, the North Somerset Levels appear to have escaped major inundation, though flooding may have become a problem (Rippon 1992).

This paper will concentrate on the recolonisation of these areas, and is a summary of more detailed research (Rippon 1993). It aims to suggest certain areas in which conventional wisdom is in need of modification, rather than attempting a review of the whole history of reclamation. Particular attention will be paid to the initial late Saxon reoccupation, continued early medieval reclamation, and late medieval adaptation to changing economic circumstances.

Process of Reclamation

Before we can piece together the history of this landscape, we must understand the process of reclamation. In the Somerset Levels, there were two main sources of flooding; the sea, and inland freshwater run-off from the surrounding uplands. Much of the coastline was protected by natural sand dunes, so only the tidal rivers needed imbanking. The only areas of open coastline, where sea-walls were required, lay between the Rivers Parrett and Brue, and Middlehope and Wains Hill (see Fig. 12.1). However, though the combined effect of sand dunes, sea-

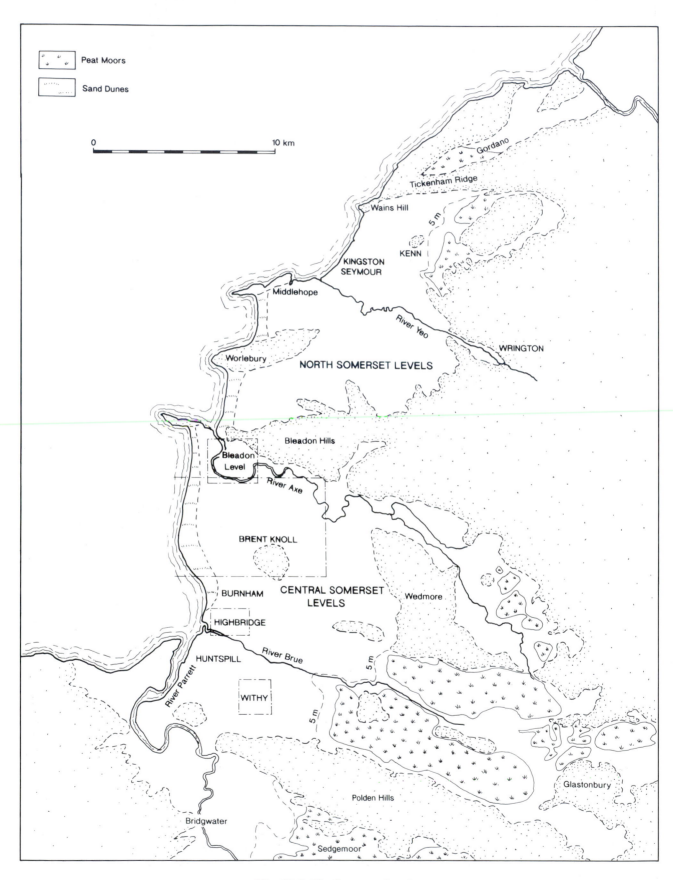

***Fig. 12.1** The Somerset Levels.*

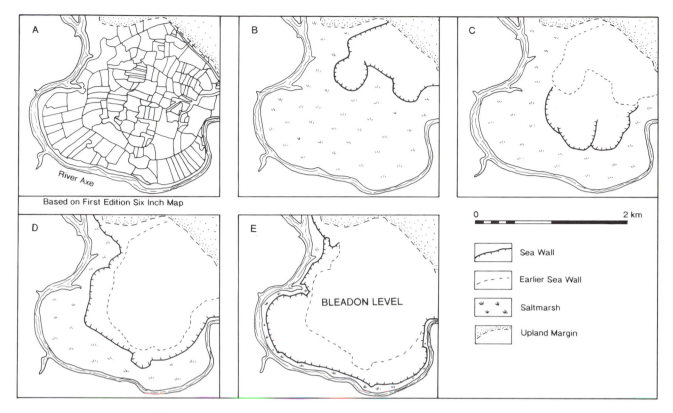

Fig. 12.2 *Reclamation of Bleadon Level based upon documentary, cartographic, earthwork and field-boundary evidence.*

walls and river embankment kept the sea at bay, they could cause flooding by disrupting freshwater discharge. To prevent this, a network of drainage ditches is required with sluice gates, to allow ground water to flow into tidal rivers at low tide.

Reclamation can be regarded as two distinct processes. Firstly, the construction of sea-walls and river flood-banks to prevent inundation. A wall was built on the active saltmarsh, consisting of a line of stakes and brushwood with a bank made of mud dug from a dyke behind the wall (Williams 1970, 91–2). On the Bleadon Level, the pattern of field-boundaries shown on the earliest surviving map of 1658 (S.R.O. T/PH/sfy 1) and surviving earthworks reveals a series of concentric sea-walls, representing a gradual expansion of reclaimed land (Fig. 12.2). The earliest reclamation was of "three great hammes" documented as existing in *c.* 1221 (Naish 1968), which can be located through field-names on the 1658 map (Fig. 12.2.B.). The next documented sea-wall is that of the early seventeenth century (Fig. 12.2.D.), when the sea was "kept from overflowing by a windmill built at the same time as the said enclosure" (Havinden 1981, 51). Between this, and the "three great hammes", there is the line of another, undated, sea-wall, the second to be constructed (Fig. 12.2.C.). All these reclamations form a series of 'lobe' shaped enclosures, probably representing several intakes of saltmarsh. The fourth sea-wall in the sequence dates to *c.* 1800 (Fig. 12.2.E.)

Interestingly, there is no such pattern of concentric

sea-walls over most of the Levels, for example around the islands of Huntspill, Brent Knoll (see Fig. 12.3) or Kenn. The only sea-walls appear to have been within a few hundred metres of the coastline and tidal rivers, enclosed virtually all the Levels (Fig. 12.3).

Because such a huge area was enclosed, does not mean that it was all drained at the same time. The second stage of reclamation involved lowering the water-table within an enclosed area through the digging of drainage ditches, to upgrade rough pasture into meadow and even arable land. This could be undertaken for the whole of an enclosed area, or in a more gradual, piecemeal fashion.

On the Somerset Levels as a whole, the higher coastal zone has a distinctive landscape, characterised by small irregular fields often incorporating the courses of natural drainage channels, long sinuous droveways with wide tracts of roadside waste, and occasional patches of common (see Fig. 12.3, e.g. Huish Bispole). A gradual and piecemeal approach to reclamation is suggested, as seen in Bleadon. In contrast, some parts of the higher coastal clayland have a rather more regular pattern of fields, with blocks of strips between roughly parallel sinuous boundaries (Fig. 12.3, e.g. Appleworthy). These landscapes are more common in lower lying, inland areas and represent a more co-ordinated approach to drainage; they generally appear to be rather later in date than the 'irregular' landscapes.

The Late Saxon Recolonisation

A wide range of indirect evidence can be used to show that major drainage works were already underway by the Norman conquest and not just on the extensive estate of Glastonbury Abbey at Brent. The Domesday Book shows that extensive reclamation had already taken place, as several vills, with numerous ploughteams, are located wholly on the alluvium; Biddisham, Edingworth, Huish (two manors), Lympsham, and Tarnock in Central Somerset, and Kingston Seymour in North Somerset. These areas must have been protected by flood defences, but as described above, there is no evidence for their having been individually defended by sea walls. This suggests that the whole of the coastline/tidal rivers must have been embanked by this time, a situation reminiscent of the Fenland (Hallam 1965; Silvester 1988). However, it does not necessarily mean that the whole area enclosed was drained.

Hidage and Ploughlands

Further evidence for extensive reclamation and drainage is in the nature of the Domesday assessments. A curious phenomena is that in Somerset generally, and on the Levels in particular, 'ploughlands' often exceed hides (Welldon-Finn and Wheatley 1969, 350). Both of these can be regarded as assessments of agricultural potential, but their nature is unclear. Harvey (1985; 1987) suggests that 'ploughlands' may have included a wide range of resources, but Higham (1990) has forcibly argued that the assessment was based primarily on arable potential. It is not known when the hidage was calculated, but it may not have been reviewed since the tenth century (Stenton 1971, 271). The ploughland assessment appears to have been carried out shortly before 1086 (Harvey 1985). The hypothesis presented here, is that where the eleventh-century ploughland assessment exceeds the older hidage, there may have been an increase in the agricultural productivity of that area, most obviously, an expansion of the cultivated area. This in turn implies late Saxon reclamation. Table 12.1 compares the hides and ploughlands for three areas; the coastal clay belt of the Levels, and two adjacent areas of upland; Wedmore, and the Poldens.

This analysis shows that the Polden Hills appear to have seen little improvement in the agricultural potential or productivity between the hide and ploughland assessment and Wedmore Island faired little better. However, the difference on the clay belt was considerable. Interestingly, the greatest improvement was not in Brent, owned by Glastonbury Abbey, but on manors in lay hands, notably Huntspill and Kingston Seymour. This impression is supported by the relative distribution of wealth at Domesday, reflected for example in ploughteams; the North Somerset Levels had around 3.0 per mile^2, whereas the Central Somerset Levels only had 2.4 (Rippon 1993, 245–9; Williams 1970, 75–9).

Saxon Documentary Sources

Therefore, the location of Domesday vills, presence of arable testified by the ploughteams, and difference between hides and ploughlands, suggests extensive reclamation by the mid eleventh century. It is more difficult to say when this recolonisation began. The earliest indication is a charter for Hamp beside the Parrett near Bridgwater, dated to AD 794 (Bates 1899, 144–145; Finberg 1964, No. 398). The boundary clause describes a field called "Ham", a "ditch" called "Candeldich", and a "trench". Landmarks in the boundary description of the Bleadon charter of AD 956 (Finberg 1964, No. 519), mostly suggest an unreclaimed marsh, though reference to an "Old Meadow Ditch" indicates at least limited improvement. The boundary clause of Berrow (Finberg 1964, No. 516), dated AD 993, suggests a totally unreclaimed landscape (translations by Grundy (1932) and more recently by Michael Costen pers. comm.).

Table 12.1 Domesday Hides and Ploughlands

Central Somerset	Hides	Plough-lands	Ploughlands/Hides
Clay Belt			
Brent	20	30	1.5
Burnham	4	12	3.0
Huntspill	1.75	15	8.6
Huish	0.5	2	4
Edingworth	2	5	2.5
Pawlett	0.25	1	4
Tarnock	2	5	2.5
Brean	2	8	4
Average = 3.8 (3.1 excluding Huntspill)			
Wedmore			
Allerton	17	8	-0.5
Badgworth	2	2	0
Alston Sutton	4.5	6	1.3
Blackford	4	6	1.5
Wedmore	11	36	3.3
Clewer	0.75	2	2.6
Average = 1.4 (1.0 excluding Wedmore)			
Polden Hills			
Shapwick	5	5	0
Ashcott	5	3	-0.6
Stawell	2.5	2.5	0
Cossington	3	6	2
Greinton	2.5	2.5	0
Average = 0.28			
Average for all areas = 1.8			
North Somerset			
Kingston Seymour	5.5	2.5	4.5

Fig. 12.3 *Brent: Late nineteenth century field-boundaries and interpretation of landscape morphology.*

Unfortunately, there are just two relevant charters with boundary clauses in North Somerset; Wrington dated AD 904 (Finberg 1964, No. 423) and Banwell *c.* AD 1030 (Finberg 1964, No. 424). Only the Banwell boundary extends onto the Levels, and the only topographic features recorded are natural watercourses and a withy bed. Grundy (1932, 169) translates one word as "balk", but Michael Costen (pers. comm.) reads this as "lake". The Wrington boundary extends into the Vale of the River Yeo which feeds into the North Somerset Levels. There are references to "East" and "Enclosed" meadows, suggesting that some drainage had taken place.

Burnham is first recorded in King Alfred's will in the late ninth century (Whitelock 1979, 534–7). The reference is to "land at" Burnham and does not specifically mention a settlement, or the condition of that land. However, the place-name supports a reclamation; 'Burn' is derived from stream, and 'ham' refers to an enclosed piece of land (M. Costen pers. comm.). Burnham currently lies at the southern end of the sand-dunes. It is possible that the village was founded on the dunes, or alternatively, the location may originally have been a saltmarsh reclamation which was only later partly buried by the sand.

Finally, and most speculatively, there is the life of St Congar, founder of the monastery at Congresbury during the reign of King Ine (688–726). Congar's 'Life', written in the medieval period, attributes to him the ability to convert marshland into fields and flowering meadow;

"The following was the first miracle performed through the divine mercy by the most holy Congar. Places covered with water and reeds, which surrounded his dwelling, and at that time no use to man, were converted into fields most suitable for cultivation, and into flowering meadows. The people acknowledged Congar's miracle by saying 'we see clearly fields and meadows where the reeds of the marsh used to grow'" (Cran 1983, 2).

Some small-scale reclamation may have occurred around the fen-edge in Congresbury at this time, but field-boundary morphology suggests most of the Moor was not drained until the medieval period and later.

Worths and Huishes

Other evidence for late Saxon settlement of the Levels are the place-names, and those field-names which indicate the existence of an abandoned settlement. '*Huish*' is derived from 'hide', a pre-conquest term for the area of land required to support a family; it is unlikely to have been used to name settlements after the Norman conquest (Costen 1992, 65). Several occur on the Levels as field-names, indicating abandoned settlements, while two were recorded in Domesday and survive as settlements today (Huish near Highbridge in Burnham (Fig. 12.4), and Watchfield a detached tything of Huish). Costen (1992, 73) has suggested that '*huishes*' may have been "pioneering units", often occurring in areas peripheral to

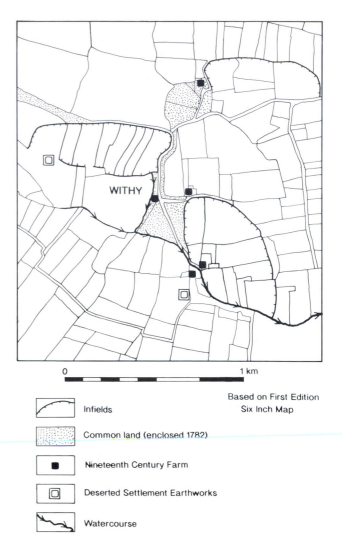

Fig. 12.4 '*Infields*' *at Withy, East Huntspill.*

older settled areas; this certainly applies to those on the Levels.

'*Worth*' refers to some form of enclosure, originally forming a very common element in a dispersed settlement pattern (Costen 1992, 73–4). Like '*huish*', they appear to be of late Saxon origin (Costen 1992, 74, 80). There are numerous examples on the Levels usually surviving only as field-names (Costen 1992, 74–7; Rippon 1993, 470–1, 493) and occurring in the same broad area as the '*huishes*' and other Domesday settlements, that is the higher coastal claylands with their 'irregular' landscape.

Several of these possible late Saxon settlements are associated with marked oval areas in the pattern of field boundaries, often around thirty acres in size (e.g. Huish, now called Withy in Huntspill; see below). It is tempting to see these 'infields' as slightly raised areas, representing some of the primary colonising settlements on the Levels. Post-medieval settlements, as shown on cartographic sources (e.g. Day and Masters 1782; Greenwood 1822), show a marked tendency to cluster around the edges of these areas, as if the enclosed area was some form of arable 'infield'. Elsewhere, medieval settlements appear to occur more centrally, such as at Huntspill Court. Vole for example, south-east of Brent Knoll, contains the earthworks of a deserted settlement of unknown date, though the modern farm lies on the eastern edge of the 'infield'.

Unfortunately, none of these sites have been surveyed. However, detailed mapping of slight changes in relief along the corridor of the M5 motorway covers a particularly fine group of oval shaped 'infields' at Withy in eastern Huntspill (Fig. 12.4). This is a documented holding of Glastonbury Abbey (Keil 1964), possibly associated with the eighth-century legend of St Indract. Lapidge (1982) assumes that the '*huish*' referred to was Huish Episcopi, eight miles south-west of Glastonbury, but Costen (1991, 55) has convincingly argued that it was the Huish, later part of Withy, in Huntspill. The earthworks of deserted farmsteads and documented post-medieval farmsteads all cluster on the edges of the Withy 'infields', one of which is covered with long narrow fields with reversed-S profiles (Fig. 12.4). The M5 data shows the enclosed areas to be very slightly higher than the surrounding areas, on average one foot (0.348m).

In North Somerset, many of the 'infields' lack 'gripes', corrugation of the field surface to aid drainage, possibly indicating once again that these areas were higher than the surrounding areas. Many are associated with Roman and medieval pottery scatters. For example, at Puxton, the roads from Congresbury and Sandford make diversions around the 'infield', which is slightly higher than the surrounding area, and contains the faint earthworks of rectangular platforms. When ploughed, around 250 medieval sherds were recovered including several possibly eleventh century or earlier pieces (Clarke 1980). Interestingly, there were just three post-medieval sherds, possibly indicating that the marked tendency for post-medieval settlement to occur around the edges of 'infields', was a relatively late phenomena.

Around seventy sherds of Roman pottery were also recovered from the Puxton 'infield' (Clarke 1980). In North Somerset especially there is a strong correlation between 'infield' sites, finds of Roman material, and *worth/huish* place-names (Rippon 1993, Table 3.9). This raises the question of possible continuity in occupation. Though post-Roman flooding on the North Somerset Levels appears not to have been as severe as in Central Somerset, localisation flooding of low lying areas is likely. The infields, as slightly raised areas, would have been the obvious foci for settlement, if only seasonal though surprisingly few appear to have 'eg' place-names, since corrupted to 'sea' (e.g. Hillsea in Yatton), meaning island (Gelling 1984, 33–9). More work is clearly required on this important class of settlement, which possibly represent some the earliest colonist settlements on the Levels.

Aston (1989, 122–3) has stressed the importance of another class of deserted settlement earthworks, often formed by rectilinear raised platforms, no more than a metre or so above the level of the surrounding land. Most have seen no archaeological work, though as several can be identified with documented settlements, including Domesday manors. These presumably late Saxon sites are also a high priority for future work.

The River Siger

Before leaving the Saxon period, we must consider the fate of the River Siger, which flowed to the south of Brent Knoll in central Somerset (Fig. 12.3B). This major river channel is recorded in the boundary clause of the Brent charter (AD 693; Finberg 1964, No. 364), in a form that suggests it was still an extant watercourse. However, the Berrow charter of AD 973 (Finberg 1964, No. 516) follows the line of the Siger for about 1km, but does not refer to it by name. Therefore, the Siger may have largely silted up between the seventh to tenth centuries. Now, the channel is only evidenced by the pattern of field-boundaries (cf. Fig. 12.3A–B), and a slightly lower elevation perceptible when flooded (Aston 1985, Fig. 54).

There are a number of possible causes of its disappearance. Firstly, the belt of sand-dunes may have migrated south, blocking its course. Secondly, the inland source of water may have stopped, causing the tidal pill to become clogged. This could have been caused by reclamation and drainage, as early as the eighth or ninth century, the diversion of water courses, and/or peat cutting; all of which lower the water table (I would like to thank Mick Aston for raising this possibility). The buried channel of the Siger is likely to preserve an important palaeo-environmental sequence that needs investigation.

The Eleventh-Century Landscape

As mentioned above, the lack of sea-walls around islands such as Brent Knoll or Kenn, or documented eleventh-century settlements such as Lympsham and Kingston Seymour, suggests that the bulk of the Somerset Levels were protected by sea-walls along the open-coast and tidal rivers by that date. The area that was actually drained is unclear, but large areas of unreclaimed waste certainly survived into the twelfth and thirteenth centuries (see below). Therefore, the eleventh-century landscape was probably a patchwork, with small areas of arable, meadow and pasture, all recorded in Domesday, and extensive areas of increasingly freshwater moor in the lower lying areas.

Though not listed in Domesday, these moors would still have been a valuable resource, providing pasture and wild resources such as fish. In Domesday, the Wedmore Moors were described as valueless (Round 1906, 425), but this is probably because the assessment of 'value' was heavily weighted towards arable. The fact

that unreclaimed moor is not usually listed is probably
due to its abundance, and common ownership; large areas of moor continued to be exploited through inter-com-
moning into the medieval period (Williams 1979, 33).

Late Saxon settlement appears to have been fairly dispersed, especially if the 'huish' and 'worth' sites were
mostly contemporary. The extent to which there were
larger nucleations around the ecclesiastical and manorial
centres can only be tested through archaeological survey.

The Early Medieval Period

It has been shown that there was certainly extensive reclamation of the Somerset Levels by the time of Domesday. Williams (1970, 43) has argued that because records
of the great monastic estates, dating from the twelfth
century, do not refer to reclamation, drainage of the
coastal claylands was largely complete by this date.
However, a wide range of evidence indicates that reclamation, or at least drainage and improvement of already
enclosed land, was continuing throughout the early medieval period.

'Enclosure' of common pasture

The simplest form of improvement was the enclosure of
common pasture. Though most of the Levels appear to
have been protected from marine inundation by Domesday, extensive areas were still regularly inundated by
freshwater, especially the lower lying backfens. In the
following centuries these moors became highly valued
as pasture was gradually converted to arable on the high
coastal areas (Williams 1970, 33). References to the 'enclosure' of common pasture must be examined with care,
as they do not necessarily mean actual drainage was taking place. For example, Blackford Moor was enclosed in
1308 (Williams 1970, 72), yet this extremely low lying
area was not drained until 1781 (S.R.O. Q/RDe 136).
Here is the distinction between medieval enclosure, which
merely defined boundaries, and reclamation, which actually drained the land.

Reclamation and Drainage

Specific references to actual acts of reclamation are few,
but clearly show that reclamation was proceeding throughout the early medieval period. The twelfth century saw a
general decline in monastic authority over their estates,
when much land was alienated (e.g. Postan 1952–3;
Lennard 1955–6). Thus, the twelfth century, though
poorly documented, probably saw considerable reclamation on the initiative of individual tenants. This is paralleled elsewhere, for example, on Romney Marsh (Brooks
1988) and in the Fenland (Hallam 1965).

There is one twelfth-century reference to drainage in
Somerset (Williams 1970, 71). Adam of Domerham
records that Abbot Herlewin of Glastonbury (1100–1118)

granted a piece of land 'besides the Axe' to Ralph de
Santa Barbara without any rent as it was of no value.
However, Abbot Henry of Blois (1126–76) found it surrounded by a wall on one side, and bounded by the river
on the other. It was under cultivation, and Blois revoked
the grant. Clearly a successful reclamation had taken
place, and this was probably the only one of many to be
documented.

Reclamation was also proceeding in the thirteenth
century. A reference in 1235 to Eastmere in East Brent
includes "land recently brought into cultivation there"
(Harrison 1987, 99). Some tenants of Brent did a considerable amount of labour service "in mora", and only a
small service at harvest time (Williams 1970, 43, 69). If
this indicates the active conversion of moor into meadow,
certain areas must have remained unreclaimed until this
time. Even if the work on the moors was simply collecting fenwood and peat, then this also suggests that part of
the Brent estate were still unreclaimed.

Overall, there are few direct references to continued
reclamation in the post-Norman conquest period. However, indirect evidence does suggest that improvement
was continuing. The best evidence comes from comparing the relative values and densities of ploughs on the
Levels with the surrounding uplands in 1086 and 1327
(Rippon 1993, 145–9; Williams 1970, 75–9). This shows
that prosperity on the Levels, particularly Central Somerset, improved dramatically during this period.

As the exploitation of the Levels became more intense, so the need for improved communications increased. In several places raised causeways were built,
rivers were canalised and artificial waterways cut (Helm
1949; Rippon 1993, 165–7; Williams 1970, 65–6) illustrating major investment of resources in the management
of this volatile landscape.

Therefore, the great ecclesiastical landowners and their
tenants were certainly intensifying the exploitation of their
estates in the early medieval period. Unfortunately we
lack comparable sources for the lay manors to the south
of Brent, and the whole of North Somerset. However,
various fragments of evidence can be pieced together to
show that reclamation was proceeding, reflected in the
increased relative wealth of the claylands between 1086
and 1327 (Rippon 1993, 145–9; Williams 1970, 75–9).
The excellent documentary sources for the minority
monastic estates must not lead us to see the lay estates as
in the least bit backward.

The Expansion of Settlement

The expansion of settlement is another indication of
continuing reclamation, but is poorly understood on the
Levels. As described above, knowledge of the late Saxon
settlement pattern is limited, but it has a distinctively
dispersed character, as seen elsewhere in Somerset (e.g.
Aston 1988, 71–3). The development of nucleated settlements do indeed appear to have been an "aberration"

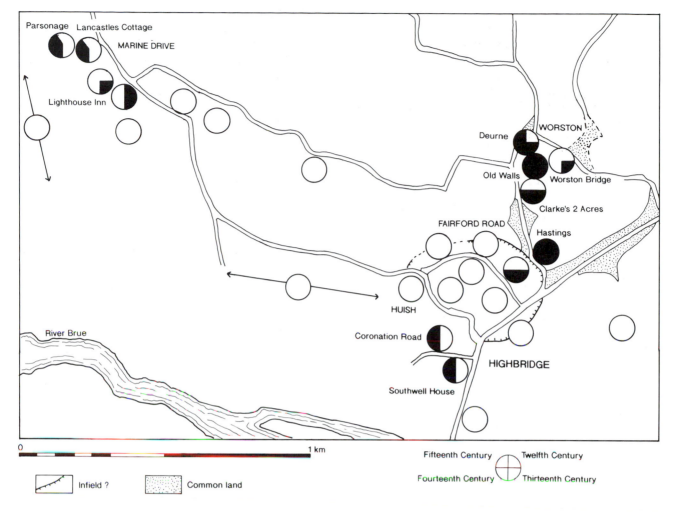

Fig. 12.5 *Burnham: Ceramic evidence for medieval settlement based upon the fieldwork of Sam Nash.*

(Hurst quoted in Aston 1988, 71), starting in places in the late Saxon period.

In order to trace the development of the settlement pattern archaeologically, a good ceramic sequence is required. In Somerset, pottery generally appears to have been in common use on rural sites from the twelfth century, possibly a little earlier in the north of the county (Gerrard 1987; Ponsford 1987; Vince 1984). Recent fieldwork on the Poldens at Shapwick has suggested that a little pottery may have been in use on rural sites as early as the tenth century (Gerrard and Gutierrez 1993). Thus, if a settlement around Brent Knoll has a pottery assemblage dated from the twelfth century, it may have been founded at that date, or earlier. If however, the pottery assemblage starts in the thirteenth century, then the lack of twelfth-century material can be taken to indicate that the site was a recent foundation.

The collection of dated pottery assemblages from several areas of the Levels (e.g. Clarke 1973, 1979, 1980; Nash 1972–3) allows the expansion and contraction of settlement to be examined (see Rippon 1993, 151–4, 194–8, 249–54). The best evidence is around Burnham

(Fig. 12.5). During the 1960s, local archaeologist Sam Nash observed building works, service trenches, road building and quarrying throughout the parish, especially in the Highbridge district (see Rippon 1993, Appendix 2.A.). Though the distribution of findspots is largely determined by the location of these developments, important patterns do exist. Figure 12.5 shows the locations of all sites where Nash carried out work. It can be seen that those locations producing medieval material fall into three clusters; Marine Drive, Highbridge and Fairford Road/ Worston. Nash's pottery dating must be used with care, but the following pattern appears to emerge.

The earliest material was from Worston, where a slight scatter of twelfth-century pottery was focused at Old Walls and Hastings. The name Worston may be derived from a 'worth' place-name indicating a possible late Saxon origin. Other possible twelfth-century sherds came from Marine Drive (Lighthouse Inn). Only a little work has been carried out around the modern site of Huish near Highbridge, but interestingly, no twelfth-century material has been recovered, suggesting the Domesday settlement was elsewhere.

In the thirteenth century, there was an expansion of settlement at Worston and Marine Drive. The Edithmead Moat further north may have been occupied from this time. The fourteenth century saw continued growth at Worston, the major expansion at Edithmead and Marine Drive, while a new settlement was established at Coronation Road in southern Highbridge. There was a decline in the density of settlement in the fifteenth century, with a number of sites occupied in the fourteenth century being abandoned, including several around Worston. At Marine Drive, occupation ceased by the mid fifteenth century. However, this was the only settlement foci to be totally abandoned, and occupation here was never extensive, possibly just one farmstead that moved over time. This pattern of shifting settlement may also apply to Huish, explaining the lack of medieval occupation at its present location.

The one possible exception to the general picture of early medieval settlement expansion appears to be around Brent. The widespread distribution of 'huish' and 'worth' names has been described above, and the fact that many are now only preserved as field-names is noted above. Costen (1991) argues that in many parts of Somerset, dispersed settlements such as these may have been extinguished during the creation of open fields and nucleated villages in the tenth century. This certainly seems to have occurred on the nearby Polden and Wedmore Hills (Aston 1988, 73–6; Corcos 1983; Costen 1988, 53; Rippon 1993, 180–3) However, on the Levels there is another possible context. It may have been that these small isolated settlements originated in an essentially unreclaimed landscape, and as drainage proceeded and the open-fields were laid out, had to be abandoned as settlement was nucleated into the major villages.

The Late Medieval Period

The late-medieval period appears to have been one of consolidation and adaptation within areas already reclaimed, rather than contraction. Though it must be born in mind that the documentary sources are poor, and not comparable in their nature to the early medieval period, there appears to have been little new reclamation, and the material we have suggests that it was increasingly difficult to maintain existing works. The evidence for a climatic deterioration in the Severn Estuary is summarised in Table 12.2. This shows there was certainly an increased incidence of flooding from the late thirteenth century (for similar evidence in the east of England see Bailey 1991).

From the mid fourteenth century there are other signs of strain. In 1358, two sluices in Mark, Northpound and Southpound were said to be "broken" and the Dean of Wells was ordered to have them repaired (Flowers 1923, 131–2). In the same year, the Dean was ordered to repair a common watercourse as it was "stopped up" (Flowers 1923, 131). In 1385, the Commissions of Sewers heard a complaint against the Abbot of Glastonbury, that the watercourse called "Wythyrne" was choked with sand and weeds at "Wythies" [Withy] and Huntspill (Dugdale 1662, 106). In 1425 lands of Cannington Priory to the north-west of Bridgwater were flooded, and in 1475 the Bleadon sea-walls were destroyed (Havinden 1981, 118; Williams 1970, 83). In 1485, the clyce at Highbridge was said to be "now by the great rage and tempest of water and also for the non-repairing, broken and fallen great decay; so the great substance of Country thereabouts be overflowed and likely to be destroyed" (Williams 1970, 70).

In the light of these cases the decreasing frequency of

Table 12.2 *Documented floods around the Severn estuary.*

1253	Edingworth (Central Somerset)	Helm 1949, 44
1259	Pawlett (Central Somerset)	Ross 1959, xxvii
late C13	Huntspill (Central Somerset)	Williams 1970, 43
late C13/early C14	Goldcliff (Gwent)	Williams 1970-8, 44
pre 1312	Avonmouth	Coles 1912, 6
1316	Pawlett (Central Somerset)	Ross 1959, xxvii
1326	Pawlett (Central Somerset)	Ross 1959, xxvii
1336	Margam (near Port Talbot)	Williams 1970-8, 278
1383	Margam (near Port Talbot)	Williams 1970-8, 244-6
1425	Central Somerset	Havinden 1981, 118
1440	Margam (near Port Talbot)	Williams 1970-8, 278
1475	Central Somerset	Williams 1970, 83
late C15	Avonmouth	Coles 1912, 19
1515	Margam (near Port Talbot)	Williams 1970-8, 278
1520	Llanwern (Gwent)	Courtney 1983, 291-2
1563	Avonmouth	Green 1959, 177
1606	Whole Estuary	Coles 1912, 19
1687	Avonmouth	Coles 1912, 24
1703	Avonmouth and North Somerset	Coles 1912, 24

Commissions of Sewers is curious; 1304 to 1352 there were thirteen Commissions, 1359 to 1401 there were nine, and 1405 to 1455 only four (Dugdale 1662). Perhaps the break down of this, the only regional administrative mechanism for the maintenance of drainage work, is in itself indicative of a worsening situation.

However, there was some continued reclamation, though in a piecemeal fashion, from the later fifteenth century. For example, in 1452 a watercourse was diverted, and two acres in "Saltemare" [Huntspill ?] enclosed with a dyke (May 1966, 1). The field-name 'wharf' refers to land taken from riverside marshes. There are a few possible thirteenth-century examples; in 1262, a 'Wart' is recorded in East Brent, and in 1272 at Edingworth there is "a pasture called Warth" (Nash nd., 34). The term does not appear again until 1404 (Ross 1959, 133–5), 1471–4 (Nash 1972–3, 101) and then relatively frequently.

In North Somerset efforts were made to control flooding through the construction of a bank, known as the "Wowwall", in the late fourteenth/early fifteenth century (Coward 1980). The Wowwall was constructed by local communities "to bar the flooding of fields between the manor of Banwell on the one side [east], and manors of Worle, Hutton, Ashcombe, Weston [Super Mare], Uphill, Oldmixon, and Locking [to the west]" (Coward 1980, 151).

It is worth observing that in the Wowwall document, the Commissions of Sewers are not mentioned once. The institutions responsible appear to have been the Hundred Court, local tythings and manors. The lack of evidence for a regional body responsible for co-ordinating drainage and sea-defence could only have had a detrimental effect on flood prevention, especially as this came at the same time as manorial authority was weakening, demesne was leased out and tenant labour services were being commuted to cash payments (e.g. in Brent: Stacey 1972, 21–2).

From the early sixteenth century, individual parishes assumed increasing responsibility for drainage matters. This is well illustrated in the Yatton Churchwardens accounts, published for the period 1440–1560 (Hobhouse 1890). These give an interesting insight into local government, and the considerable effort required to maintain drainage works. Some expenses relate to isolated events, such as the construction of new sluices in 1528 and 1547. More frequent expenses were incurred in the maintenance of dykes and sluices, as was the case in 1521, 1543, 1558, and 1559. By the 1540s, scouring the River Yeo was an annual cost. It is significant that the burden of sea-defence and drainage had fallen on the parish, suggesting, once again, that the traditional institutions, such as the Commissions of Sewers, had become obsolete.

Therefore, late-medieval and early post-medieval evidence suggests increasing difficulty in maintaining existing drainage works, and occasional floods. As would be expected, there are some signs of settlement contrac-

tion, for example at Fairford Road and Marine Drive in Burnham, but little evidence of settlements being totally abandoned. This is in sharp contrast to the surrounding uplands where several villages and hamlets were deserted (Rippon 1993, 145–9, 249–54). The only part of the Levels where this occurred was around the Parrett Estuary when the hamlets at Crook, Horsey, and Pigness were abandoned, while Chislett contracted. Without excavation, the date of these desertions is unknown and so cannot at present be attributed to the late medieval period. This area can also be regarded as untypical of conditions elsewhere on the Levels, for they lie close to a region, around Bridgwater and Cannington, that suffered some settlement contraction in the late and post-medieval period (Rippon 1993, 145–9).

The pattern on most of the Levels in the late medieval/early post-medieval period, appears to have been one of settlement dispersion, associated with the break-up of the open-fields and disintegration of manorial authority. This allowed the growth of independent farmsteads on reclaimed riverside wharfs, the edge of roadside waste and the unreclaimed moor. Newly created sub-manors also became the focus for small hamlets, for example Rooksbridge and Grove in East Brent (Croot 1981, 53–5).

Discussion: The Changing Patterns of Land Management

After a major period of flooding that certainly affected Central Somerset and possibly the north, recolonisation of the Levels appears to have begun by the ninth century. The very considerable reorganisation of upland landscapes around the Levels in the tenth century (see p. 248) suggests that period may also have seen expansion on the Levels. However, all that can be said with any certainty is that major advances had been made by the mid eleventh century. Reclamation continued thereafter, and by the early fourteenth century, most of the higher, coastal part of the clay belt was probably reclaimed, creating a patchwork of irregular and regular landscapes.

In common with other British wetlands, such as the Fenland (Hallam 1965), North Kent (Neilson 1928; Smith 1940), and Romney (Brooks 1988; Neilson 1928; Smith 1940), documentary sources indicate a strong monastic involvement in reclamation in Central Somerset. However, other wetlands saw equally extensive reclamation yet no monastic ownership; Gwent (Rippon 1993, 323–32) and North Somerset (Rippon 1993, 254–9) are good examples, as is the Pevensey Level in Sussex (Brandon 1974, 113). In Somerset as a whole, Glastonbury does not appear to have been any more active than other lay or ecclesiastical owners in the late Saxon period. This is best illustrated by the greater relative wealth of the North Somerset Levels compared to Central Somerset at Domesday, and the difference between ploughlands and hidage (see p. 242).

A notable aspect of the Levels today is their distinctive landscape and pastoral economy. However, this may not always have been the case, and the difference in landuse strategies between the higher parts of the Levels and the surrounding uplands in the early medieval period may not have been so stark as was the case in the late and post-medieval period (see below). Economic specialism is likely to be most pronounced on those parishes whose land lay entirely on the Levels, and when the Levels were in an unreclaimed state being exploited for natural resources such as fish and wildfowl. Unlike the Roman period, there is no evidence for medieval salt production in Somerset, though this was widespread during the early medieval period in the coastal Levels of Sussex (Brandon 1974, 111) and the Fenland (e.g. Silvester 1988, 165). Rather, the Levels appear to have supported purely agricultural communities.

Domesday shows that large areas of the reclaimed Levels were turned over to arable. This situation continued until the early fourteenth century testified by the well developed ridge and furrow, and manorial accounts. The survey of Glastonbury demesne land in *c.* 1330 shows that in Brent, over three quarters of the demesnes was arable (Keil 1964; Rippon Fig. 2.E.21.). Beans and barley each comprised nearly 40% of that arable, with wheat providing a relatively small part of the annual crop. Thus, patterns of landuse, while showing some local variations, appear to conform to the regional picture of a mixed economy.

However, not all areas would have seen the same balance of arable and grassland, as some more specialised settlements still existed, especially in the lower lying locations. At Withy in Huntspill, 79% of the demesne was meadow, compared to 15% at Brent and 17% at Shapwick (Keil 1964, 25). Even the arable at Withy was specialised, with a predominance of legumes. Also, equally large areas were still unreclaimed moors, providing a rich pasturing resource, exploited by numerous upland communities through intercommoning (Williams 1970, 33). Indeed, a high proportion of the Levels were exploited by fen-edge settlements whose territory extended onto the surrounding uplands forming part of an integrated economy.

The same picture can be seen in the pattern of animal husbandry. Domesday gives the first detailed insight into livestock regimes (see Table 12.3). Shapwick is included for comparison, as a predominantly upland manor. The percentages exclude horses.

These figures support the hypothesis of a generally mixed agricultural regime. Horses appear to represent one of the few economic specialisms on the Levels at this time, though only certain manors took part, notably Burnham and Tarnock. The predominance of cattle appears to have increased in the twelfth and thirteenth centuries (Keil 1964, 110; Stacey 1972, 114), though large pig herds are still found on the Levels into the fourteenth century (Keil 1964, 120). The true extent of sheep farming is difficult

Table 12.3 *Domesday livestock*

	Cattle	Sheep	Pigs	Horses
Brent/Edingworth	28 (26%)	65 (61%)	13 (13%)	0
Burnham/Huish	16 (12%)	110 (79%)	13 (9%)	12
Others	73 (28%)	58 (50%)	131 (22%)	17
(Brean, Crook, East Bower, Hamp, Pigness, Tarnock)				
Kingston Seymour	20 (12%)	120 (70%)	31 (18%)	0
Shapwick	31 (22%)	100 (70%)	11 (7%)	0

to determine because of the importance of inter-manorial grazing, though in Brent there appears to have been a decline during the twelfth century (Postan 1952–3, 363). This is in accord with continued reclamation.

Regional agricultural specialism in Britain started to develop in the late twelfth and thirteenth centuries, which the late medieval population decline accentuated, as falling demand for bread and a rise in real wages increased the demand for meat (Campbell 1990; Dyer 1981). There was a shortage of labour, weakened manorial authority, growth of the land market, and increased size of holdings. Tenants and small yeoman farmers were increasingly free to specialise and innovate, allowing them to adapt quite successfully to the changing economic conditions. This is seen on most British coastal wetlands (Rippon 1993, 378–82), but also inland areas such as Breckland (Bailey 1989) and the Arden of Warwickshire (Dyer 1981). Access to urban markets was particularly important in all these areas.

A distinctive regional economy based on pastoralism appeared on the Somerset Levels, and indeed on most British coastal wetlands, from the late medieval period. Late medieval probate records for the Brent area suggest arable declined significantly in importance (see Table 12.4), and was replaced by a very flexible pattern of animal husbandry dominated by cattle, with some farmers involved with fattening animals for beef, and others in dairy production (Croot 1981, 163–5). The whole region benefited from its proximity to a large number of market and port towns, notably Bristol. However, the critical variable in terms of the Levels appears to have been the tenurial and social structure, dominated by small family farmers relatively free from manorial controls, allowing specialisation in livestock in a way to which the Levels were physically suited. By contrast, many upland vills, such as Shapwick had a more rigid manorial and open-field structure, and the shift to pastoralism was not as marked.

Similar trends in agriculture are seen in other British coastal wetlands. By the early fourteenth century, the Fenland was an extremely prosperous area based upon rich arable land, and relatively plentiful pasture and meadow. The proportion of arable depended on the area of flood free land; thus Kirton and Skirkbeck in the higher northern Lincolnshire Fens had a slightly higher propor-

Table 12.4 Changes in landuse on the levels.

Manor	% Demesne Arable (and date of survey)			
	c.1300	Early C16	Late C16	Early C17
Berrow	92%	38% (1516)		
East Brent	79%	34% (1516)		33% (1607)
Edingworth				23% (1624)
Lympsham	84%	32% (1516)	26% (Eliz. I)	
Northgrove (E. Brent)			20% (1572)	
South Brent	80%	44% (1516)	32% (1568)	
Tarnock		37% (1540)	27 (Eliz. I)	
Shapwick	70%	53% (1515)		

Based on : Rippon 1993, Table 2.16

tion of arable than Elloe to the south (H. Hallam 1965, 174–96). By the seventeenth century, there had been a shift towards pastoralism. In the late thirteenth century, Elloe was 66% arable, and Skirkbeck 76%. By the early-seventeenth century, the amount of arable dropped to 13% and 40% respectively (Hallam 1965, 195; Thirsk 1953). Like the Somerset Levels, this economic specialisation in the late medieval period, along with the weakness of manorial authority and high proportion of free small-holdings, enable the region to maintain its prosperity in the late and post medieval period.

Conclusion: A Marginal Environment?

Coastal wetlands would, traditionally, be regarded as 'marginal' as expressed in Postan's 'population-resource model' (e.g. Postan 1972, 16–19). This sees marginal land as consisting of areas of poor quality soil, only exploited for arable when existing agricultural land was no longer sufficient to support the growing population. The Postan model makes several important assumptions, and has several important flaws (see Bailey 1989; Dyer 1990; Rippon 1993, 12–15, 387–95).

Firstly, the model assumes that the margins are only exploited when population expands and that the use of the margins was primarily for arable agriculture. Soil fertility is seen as easily exhaustible, which is not the case on the Levels, and that by the medieval period, agricultural communities had established which were good/bad soils and which were the best crops to grow in different areas. However, land was not always judged in terms of its arable potential, as some areas may also have had non-agricultural resources that encouraged their exploitation. For example, in their natural state, peat moors provide fish, wildfowl, peat for fuel and withies for basketry. Unreclaimed saltmarsh is less ecologically diverse, but does provide the potential for salt-production, wild fowling and sheep grazing. Even when reclaimed in the medieval period, meadow land was often more highly valued than arable.

Secondly, the Postan model assumes a low level of agricultural technology, which did not improve significantly during the medieval period. This appears to have underestimated man's ability to adapt his agricultural methods to preserve or even improve soils (e.g. Langdon 1990). Reclamation of the Levels certainly represents a major alteration of the natural environment, and an improvement in soil quality, from the point of view of arable farming.

Another major flaw in the Postan model is that it assumes medieval agriculture was at a subsistence level. This was not the case, and the impact of markets on the exploitation of different soils may have been significant; poor soils close to a market may have been exploited, whereas good soils without market access may not (e.g. Bailey 1989). The Severn Estuary Levels are a good example of this, being so close to Bristol. Social and political factors could also effect the exploitation of land. For example in the Somerset Levels, the irregular pattern of open-fields, high proportion of enclosed land and weakness of manorial authority allowed a far greater degree of adaptation and innovation in the late medieval period, than was possible in the more rigidly controlled regular open-field systems on the adjacent uplands.

The factors described above are "endogenous", that is controlled from within society (Bailey 1991, 184–6). An "extraneous" prime mover was the environment. As described above, there was a marked increase in storminess all around Britain from the late thirteenth/early fourteenth century, making the maintenance of sea-defence and drainage works increasingly difficult. However, despite this, the Levels continued to be exploited, and even appear to have faired better than some upland settlements that were abandoned.

Therefore, we have four major types of 'margin'; physical, environmental, locational, and socio-political. The importance of these different perspectives can be seen in the Somerset Levels. In its unreclaimed state, the Levels are 'marginal' in a physical sense with regard to arable farming. Once drained, the soils are fertile and crop yield were very high (Keil 1964, Table A), but sea-walls and drainage ditches need constant attention and investment of resources. Locationally, however, the Levels are ideally situated in a region with a large number of markets, and close to the major port of Bristol. There was a weak manorial system, and no rigid open-field system, which gave farmers a relative freedom in their agricultural practices not seen on the adjacent uplands. Hence the region was able to adapt to the demographic and economic crisis of the fourteenth century despite the deteriorating natural environment, through new agricultural techniques, diversification and specialisation, particularly in cattle rearing and dairy production. Therefore, the Levels overcame their physical disadvantages due to locational and socio-political advantages, to see the emergence of a distinctive economy, and the distinctive landscape we see today.

Acknowledgements

I would like to thank Dr Grenville Astill and Professor Michael Fulford both of Reading University, and Mick Aston and Michael Costen both of Bristol University Department for Continuing Education for all their help and encouragement in my research. I am also grateful to Dr Roger Leech for his assistance and for supplying the M5 data, and J. Harrison for discussing his research on the manorial records of Brent.

References

Aston, M. 1985: *Interpreting the Landscape*. Batsford, London.

Aston, M. 1988: 'Settlement Patterns and Forms', in Aston. M. (ed.), *The Medieval Landscape of Somerset*, 67–81. Somerset County Council, Taunton.

Aston, M. 1989: 'A Regional Study of Deserted Settlements in the West of England', in Aston, M., Austin, C. and Dyer, C. (ed.), *The Rural Settlements of Medieval England*, 105–28. Blackwell, Oxford.

Bailey, M. 1989: *A Marginal Economy?: East Anglian Breckland in the Later Middle Ages*. Cambridge University Press.

Bailey, M. 1991: 'Per Imperetum Maris'; Natural Disaster and Economic Decline in Eastern England, 1275–1350', in Campbell, B. M. S. (ed.), *Before the Black Death: Studies in the Crisis of the Early Fourteenth Century*. Manchester University Press.

Bates, E. H. 1899: *Two Chartularies of the Benedictine Abbeys of Muchelney and Athelney*. Somerset Records Society 14.

Beckett, S. C. and Hibbert, F. A. 1979: 'Vegetational Change and the Influence of Prehistoric Man on the Somerset Levels', *New Phytologist* 83, 577–600.

Bell, M. 1990: *Brean Down Excavations 1983–7*. English Heritage, London.

Brandon, P. 1974: *The Sussex Landscape*. Hodder and Stoughton, London.

Brooks, N. 1988: 'Romney Marsh in the Early Middle Ages', in Eddison, J. and Green, C. (ed.), *Romney Marsh: Evolution, Occupation, Reclamation*. Oxford University Com-

mittee for Archaeology Monograph 24, 90–104.

Campbell, M. S. 1990: 'People and Land in the Middle Ages', in Dodgson, R. A. and Butler, R. A. (ed.), *A New Historical Geography of England and Wales*, 69–121. Academic Press, London.

Clarke, M. 1973: 'East Rolstone Fieldwork', Banwell Soc. for Arch. Newsletter, July 1973, 1–2.

Clarke, M. 1979: 'Kingston Seymour, Part 1', *Axbridge Archaeological and Local History Society Newsletter* 34, 1–3.

Clarke, M. 1980: 'Puxton', *Axbridge Archaeological and Local History Society Newsletter* 38, 1–2.

Corcos, N. 1983: 'Early Estates on the Poldens and the Origin of Settlements at Shapwick', *PSANHS* 127, 47–53.

Costen, M. D. 1988: 'The Church in the Landscape: Part 1: The Anglo Saxon Period', in Aston M. (ed.), *The Medieval Landscape of Somerset*, 49–53. Somerset County Council, Taunton.

Costen, M. D. 1991: 'Some Evidence for New Settlements and Field Systems in Later Anglo-Saxon Somerset', in Abrams, L. and Carley, J. (ed.), *The Archaeology and History of Glastonbury Abbey*, 39–55. Boydell Press, Woodbridge.

Costen, M. D. 1992: 'Huish and Worth: Old English Survivals in a Later Landscape', in W. Filmer-Sankey (ed.), *Anglo-Saxon Studies in Archaeology and History* 5, 65–83. Oxford Committee for Archaeology.

Coward, H. 1980: 'The Wowwall: Some Aspects of the Government and Land Drainage Early in the Fifteenth Century', *PSANHS* 124, 151–7.

Cox, M. 1992: *A Palaeoenvironmental Investigation of a Field off White's Drove, Godney Moor, Near Wells, Somerset: Interim Report*. Planning Department Somerset County Council, Taunton.

Cran, J. 1983: *The Story of Congresbury*. Local Publication, copy in Taunton Local Studies Library.

Croot, P. E. C. 1981: Aspects of Agrarian Society in Brent Marsh, Somerset 1500–1700. Unpublished PhD, Leeds.

Day and Masters 1782: Map of Somerset in Hartley, J. and Dunning, R. (ed.) 1981, *Somerset Maps; Day and Masters 1782, and Greenwood 1822*. Somerset Records Society 76.

Dugdale, W. 1662: *The History of Imbanking and Draining*. Reprinted 1772, ed. by Coles, C. N. Bowyer and Nichols, London.

Dyer, C. 1981: *Warwickshire Farming 1349–c.1520*. Dugdale Society Occasional Papers, 27, Oxford.

Dyer, C. 1990: 'The Past, The Present and the Future in Medieval Rural History', *Rural History* 1(1), 37–50.

Flower, C. (ed.) 1923: *Public Works in Medieval Law*, Volume 2. Seldon Society 40.

Finberg, H. P. R. 1964: *The Early Charters of Wessex*. Leicester University Press.

Gelling, M. 1984: *Place Names in the landscape*. Dent, London.

Gerrard, C. 1987: *Trade and Settlement in Medieval Somerset*. Unpublished Thesis, Bristol.

Gerrard, C. and Gutierrez 1993: 'Summary of Field-walking Results in 1991', in Aston, M. and Costen, M. D. (ed.), *The Shapwick Project : A Topographical and Historical Study*. Fourth Report. University of Bristol, Department For Continuing Education.

Grundy, G. B. (ed.) 1932: 'The Saxon Charters of Somerset', *PSANHS* 78, Appendix.

Hallam, H. E. 1965: *Settlement and Society: A Study of the Early agrarian History of South Lincolnshire*. Cambridge University Press.

Harrison, J. 1987: *The Composite Manor of Brent 1189–1307*. Unpublished M.A. Dissertation, Leicester University.

Harvey, S. P. J. 1985: 'Taxation and the Ploughland in the Domesday Book', in Sawyer, P. (ed.), *Domesday Book: A Re-Assessment*, 86–103. Edward Arnold, London.

Harvey, S. P. J. 1987: 'Taxation and the Economy', in Holt, J. C. (ed.), *Domesday Studies*, 249–64. Boydell Press, Woodbridge.

Havinden, M. 1981: *The Somerset Landscape*. Hodder and Stoughton, London.

Helm, P. J. 1949: 'The Somerset Levels in the Middle Ages', *J. Br. Arch. Ass.* XII, 37–52.

Higham, N. 1990: 'Settlement, Landuse and Domesday Ploughlands', *Landscape History* 12, 33–43.

Hobhouse, B. 1890: Churchwardens Accounts of Croscombe, ..., and Yatton. S.R.S. 4.

Housley, R. 1988: 'The Environment of Glastonbury Lake Village', *Somerset Levels Papers* 14, 63–83.

Keil, I. J. E. 1964: The Estates of Glastonbury Abbey in the Later Middle Ages. Unpublished PhD Thesis, Bristol.

Kidson, C. and Heyworth, A. 1976: 'The Quarternary Deposits of the Somerset Levels', *Quarterly Journal Engineering Geology* 9(3), 217–35.

Langdon, J. 1988: 'Agricultural Equipment', in Astill, G. G. and Grant, A. (ed.), *The Countryside in Medieval England*, 86–107. Blackwells, Oxford.

Lapidge, M. 1982: 'The Cult of St Indract at Glastonbury', in Whitelock, D., McKitterick, R. and Dumville, D. (ed.), *Ireland in Early Medieval Europe*, 179–212. Cambridge University Press.

Lennard, R. 1955–6: 'The Demesne of Glastonbury Abbey in the Eleventh and Twelfth Centuries', *Econ. Hist. Rev.* VIII, 255–303.

May, D. R. 1966: *Drainage Authorities on the Somerset Levels*. Unpublished Typescript in Somerset Local Studies Library.

Murray, J. W. and Hawkins, A. B. 1976: 'Sediment Transport in the Severn Estuary During the Past 8000–9000 Years', *Journal of the Geological Society of London* 132, 385–98.

Naish, R. B. 1968: 'Thirteenth Century Customary Services Relating to Sea-Defences in Bleadon', *Somerset and Dorset Notes and Queries* 28, 135–40.

Nash, S. (n.d.): *Notes Relating to the Coastal Area of Somerset*. Unpublished Typescript; copy held by Somerset Archaeology and Natural History Society. Brief published summary in Nash 1972–3.

Nash, S. 1972–3: 'A Deep Water Inlet at Highbridge: A Precis of a Paper', *P.S.A.N.H.S.* 117, 97–101.

Neilson, N. (ed.) 1928: *The Cartulary and Terrier of the Priory of Bilsington, Kent*. British Academy Records of Social and Economic History, London.

Ponsford, M. W. 1987: 'Evidence for the Production of Medieval Pottery in the West Country *c*.930–*c*.1750', in Vyner, B. and Wrathmell, S. (eds), *Studies in Medieval and Late Pottery in Wales*, 75–91.

Postan, M. 1952–3: 'Glastonbury Estates in the Twelfth Century', *Econ. Hist. Rev.* 5, 358–66.

Rippon, S. 1991: 'The Somerset Levels in the Roman Period', *SELRC Annual Report* 1991, 43–6.

Rippon, S. 1992: 'The Exploitation of the North Somerset Levels in the Roman Period', *SELRC Annual Report* 1992, 35–8.

Rippon, S. 1993: Landscape Evolution and Wetland Reclamation Around the Severn Estuary. Unpublished PhD, University of Reading.

Round, J. H. 1906: 'The Domesday Survey', in Page W. (ed.), *The Victoria County History of Somerset* Vol. 1, 383–426.

Ross, C. D. 1959: *Cartulary of St Marks Hospital Bristol*. Bristol Records Society XXXI.

Silvester, R. J. 1988: *The Fenland Project: Marshland and the Nar Valley, Norfolk*. East Anglian Archaeology 45.

Smith, R. A. L. 1940: 'Marsh Embankment and Sea Defence in Medieval Kent', *Econ. Hist. Rev.* X(I), 29–37.

Stacey, N. R. 1972: *The Estates of Glastonbury Abbey c. 1050–1200*. Unpublished PhD Thesis, Leeds.

Stenton, F. 1971: *Anglo-Saxon England*. Third Edition. Oxford, University Press.

Thirsk, J. 1953: *Fenland Farming in the Sixteenth Century*. Dept. Eng. Local History Occ. Paper 3. University Press, Leicester.

Vince, A. 1984: *The Medieval Ceramic Industry of the Severn Valley*. Unpublished PhD, Southampton.

Welldon-Finn, R. and Wheatley, P. 1969: 'Somerset', in Darby, H. C. and Whelldon Finn, R. (ed.), *The Domesday Geography of South West England*, 132–222. Cambridge University Press.

Whitelock, D. 1979: *English Historical Documents. Vol. I c. 500–1042*. Eyre Methuen, London.

Williams, M. 1970: *The Draining of the Somerset Levels*. Cambridge University Press.

13. Protecting Medieval Settlement Sites in Somerset

R. A. Croft

The aim of this paper is to examine how medieval settlement sites in Somerset, both rural and urban, are protected from operations and development which would damage them.

Recent work in Somerset has shown that heritage strategies linked in with planning policies are one of the most effective ways of securing the preservation and management of medieval settlement remains. Examples will be given of the ways in which Somerset County Council has joined with other authorities to protect, preserve and interpret important medieval settlement sites. It will look at local authority heritage policies used as part of the planning process and assess their value as a research and predictive tool in providing a better picture of the true nature of medieval settlement in the county.

Introduction

The preservation of any archaeological site requires a range of factors to coincide which make it possible to secure its long term protection. It has only been in relatively recent years that the concept of preservation *in situ* rather than excavation has been the approved government policy (DOE 1990). The protection of a site as a scheduled monument requires the use of the 1979 Ancient Monuments and Archaeological Areas Act. Each site is assessed against a range of nationally recognised criteria which look at several linked factors. These are period, rarity, group value, documentation, and survival; condition and fragility; and vulnerability, diversity and potential.

In Somerset there are currently 29 medieval settlement sites which are scheduled as ancient monuments. These were identified and scheduled to reflect their national importance and they include the remains of village earthworks, castles and parts of towns. Recent efforts by English Heritage have redefined many of the monument descriptions as part of their Monument Protection Programme. These definitions do not cover all settlement sites of the medieval period and further work is currently being undertaken to finalise settlement definitions on a national basis. Somerset, like many other counties in Wessex, has numerous classes of medieval settlement sites.

In recent years the concept of a planning-related preservation strategy has appeared and, with the influence of County Archaeological Officers, all county councils have revised their conservation strategies to take account of archaeological matters (Baker 1993). Somerset has been fortunate in having a County Archaeological Officer in post since 1974 and this has resulted in the development and implementation of wide-ranging archaeological and heritage strategies, examples of which are given in the appendix. Where medieval settlement sites survive as visible earthworks, such as moated sites or motte and bailey castles, it is relatively easy for the general public to appreciate what is being saved and protected. It is much more difficult to seek to protect and preserve buried and invisible archaeological remains in the middle of an existing village or small town. An increasing awareness of the archaeological heritage coupled with the issue of local distinctiveness, has made the conservation of rural settlements and historic landscape features an important issue both at a county and parish level. The identity of a particular place is the result of the interaction of a variety of factors which have shaped and influenced the development of an area through time. Modern planning practice controls development and it is therefore essential that the conservation of medieval settlement sites should be closely allied to the planning system. The concept of protecting important architectural and historic buildings by including them in a parish list which is monitored by the local planning authority and controlled by the Department of the Environment is widely accepted as an efficient way of influencing what happens to our stock of listed buildings. No such lists or legal protection exists for the vast majority of archaeological sites in Somerset or any other county. The role of the local authority archaeologist, particularly at county level, is therefore essential if our archaeological and his-

Fig. 13.1 *Cheddar: excavations between 1960 and 1962 by Philip Rahtz revealed the remains of several Saxon palaces. The plans of these timber halls have been laid out in concrete blocks adjacent to the main kings of Wessex school buildings. (Photo: Aerofilms)*

toric landscapes are to be conserved and managed for future generations.

The protection of a site is only part of the story. If archaeological remains are to be conserved then some attempt must be made to present and interpret them to the landowner and the local community. The innovative presentation of the Saxon palaces at the Kings of Wessex School Cheddar has unfortunately been poorly appreciated by most visitors to the site (Fig. 13.1). There is a need for local awareness and responsibility towards the ownership and care for our visible past. Archaeological remains are a finite resource and are being looked after by this generation. Current thoughts and opinion as to what is archaeologically important and in need of conservation often reflects the fashionable interests of countryside conservation. The concept of historic landscapes had been increasingly defined by cultural resource managers in recent years and it frequently identifies areas of well preserved medieval landscapes. The protection of such landscapes has yet to achieve a statutory basis, and English Heritage takes the view that scheduling is an inappropriate form of legislation to protect such areas. The use of an Historic Landscapes Register is proposed but to date little detailed work has been carried out in Somerset.

The split between the curator's role to protect and preserve archaeological sites *in situ* and the digging and research archaeologists' need for information has focused attention on several important medieval settlement sites in Somerset such as Milborne Port. The conflict between conservation and development is complicated by the concept of 'preservation by record'. This concept, which is seen as the last resort by all responsible archaeological curators, is only applicable to sites which 'on balance' do not require their preservation intact. Such sites will be excavated and recorded rather than preserved for this and future generations. The decision making process which decides which medieval settlements are to be preserved and which are to be excavated is frequently made at county level. Those decisions are frequently made with minimum information and within a very short timetable. Local planning authorities have the right to ask for additional archaeological information where it is justified and this has been used with considerable success in Somerset. There are few county, regional or national research objectives available to the County Archaeological Officer (CAO) which enable an academic argument to be made (MSRG 1984; Croft and Williamson 1988). The national perspective set by English Heritage refers to:

'Medieval rural settlement: settlement patterns are the key to understanding the economic, social and political structures of rural England, and in extending our knowledge of change. We now appreciate the importance of regional differences, broadly between the areas of nucleated and non-nucleated settlement... All types of settlement and landscape sites should be investigated – peasant farms, moats, seigneurial sites, churches, mills, ponds and fields. The result will throw light on the special characteristics of the region, and, through comparisons,contribute to the national picture.' (English Heritage 1991, 39).

The guidance given by English Heritage in conjunction with the specialist interest groups (such as the Medieval Settlement Research Group) helps to provide the context in which wider strategic decisions can be made to protect and preserve medieval settlement remains in Somerset. This collection of papers should in turn help to set the regional context for many aspects of the preservation of medieval settlement sites in the Wessex region.

How can medieval settlement remains be best presented and interpreted? There is a growing need for the archaeological curators to work closely with the local community to encourage local awareness and understanding of what is significant and what is relatively commonplace. Much evidence available in the archaeological records is unreliable and sampling strategies to obtain further information often require up to approximately two percent of a site to be examined. This concept was used originally on such sites as green field areas where crop marks and other features may have indicated earlier settlement activity. Using the same figures for assessing the cores of historic settlements may not be adequate and experience of work within medieval settlements in Somerset would suggest a larger figure of five percent may be more appropriate. Local planning authorities in Somerset are now familiar with the need to adequately assess the implications of a planning application prior to its determination. This approach has secured the preservation, conservation and recording of several medieval settlement sites in the county.

The extent of the site, the nature of the archaeological remains and the access opportunities for the general public are all relevant factors which need to be taken into consideration in deciding which medieval settlement sites are to be interpreted and presented to the public. English Heritage has guardianship of a number of sites in the county, but these represent the classic examples of medieval ruins in the form of abbeys and castles. One of the smaller more typically vernacular medieval buildings which is protected by English Heritage is the medieval fish house of Glastonbury Abbey at Meare. It is associated with a range of fishponds and other earthworks on the eastern edge of Meare village but only the fish house enjoys statutory protection, and the landscape within which it lies is not covered by any legal restrictions.

Several medieval settlement sites, particularly earth-works and buildings, are looked after and managed by sympathetic owners and these include English Heritage, The National Trust, local authorities and various conservation minded owners.

Policy Framework

For many years scheduling sites as Ancient Monuments was the only way in which important medieval settlement remains in Somerset could be protected. In the latter half of the 1980s the use of conservation-minded heritage strategies enabled many sites to be protected by local planning policies. Those policies had their origins in the rapid archaeological surveys which were carried out by the Western Archaeological Trust and the Committee for Rescue Archaeology Avon, Gloucestershire and Somerset, and include the pioneering survey of Somerset Historic Towns in 1977 by Michael Aston and Roger Leech (Aston and Leech 1977) and the archaeological survey of the Medieval Villages in South East Somerset by Ann Ellison in 1983 (Ellison 1983).

Those reports have continued to be the only assessment surveys published for the medieval towns and villages in the county and they are still in regular use by conservation groups, and archaeological contractors and curators. They are used for reference and contain brief archaeological details on the extent of the known and likely areas of archaeological interest and potential both in and around the villages and towns.

There is a considerable gap in the coverage and analysis of the rural settlements in the county and further comparative work is needed if the contrasting picture of scattered and nucleated settlement is to be identified and recorded. Only when this detailed analysis has been completed will it be possible to start to interpret the patterns and assess their relative importance. Following on from this it may then be possible to argue for the protection of the more important medieval settlements which occur in Somerset.

In the 1980s there was a steady growth in the use of specific policies in the planning system to protect, preserve and assess the archaeological potential of historic settlement sites. There are several examples of this approach characterised in Local Plans such as the Wells Area Local Plan (Mendip District Council 1987). In 1987 when this plan was published the emphasis was on permitting access to development sites to undertake watching briefs and similar recording exercises at the expense of the local authorities. This approach was a legacy of the 1970s and early 1980s idea of Rescue archaeology. It was largely a reactive approach to archaeological data collection and several small areas of medieval settlement sites, particularly in towns such as Taunton or Ilchester, were recorded in this way, often with limited financial resources. The concept of developer funding had a limited affect upon excavation costs in small towns and villages in the 1980s and the principal source of finance was from English Heritage or through the efforts of the County Archaeological Officer and local volunteers.

County Council Planning Policy

The main planning policy document which seeks to use the planning system to protect medieval settlement remains is the County Structure Plan. The first county archaeological policy and conservation policies date from 1982 and these have subsequently been modified and altered several times, the most recently approved policies being given the approval of the Department of the Environment in June 1993 (SCC 1993).

The first archaeological conservation policies were principally concerned with ensuring that sites of national or county importance were protected from development. Such aims were most commendable but the policy gave no guidance as to how archaeological sites were to be protected. It was not until the influence of predictive archaeological assessment work developed in the late 1980s that an assessment and mitigation strategy was adopted in Somerset. This assessment concept, which is used in PPG 16 (DOE 1990) and the adopted Somerset Structure Plan, has an explicit policy which seeks to protect archaeological sites from damaging developments by undertaking some form of assessment and evaluation. The success of this strategy is still being measured, but in the last four years an increasing number of medieval settlement sites have been evaluated as part of the assessment process. One archaeological conservation policy which has been developed in Somerset is the identification of Areas of High Archaeological Potential (AHAPs) which was developed originally for parts of the Somerset Levels and Moors (SCC 1984). This concept was used to identify areas which by virtue of their soil conditions, topographic setting, archaeological context, water table and other physical factors were likely to contain waterlogged archaeological remains. In the mid 1980s the identification of areas was primarily aimed at ensuring that some form of rescue archaeological monitoring was undertaken in areas which were to be affected by agricultural activity. It was not directly related to the planning process and relied upon voluntary notification from the farmer to the CAO of the intention to carry out works in an AHAP. The idea was further developed in the later 1980s with several Local Plans such as the Frome and Wells area plans and was extended to include the similarly historic cores of medieval settlements, in both towns and villages. The main difference between using the voluntary AHAP concept in the Somerset Levels and Moors and the AHAP within settlements was the change in emphasis to enable the local planning authorities to ask for further information which could then be used to assess and protect sites where archaeological factors are thought to be a significant consideration. The use of the AHAP designation is under review in the light of the widespread ability to use PPG 16 and the County Sites

and Monuments Record to ensure that archaeological matters are taken into consideration prior to the determination of a planning application. The planning system is much more effective than it once was to secure the assessment of medieval settlement sites, and planning permissions have been granted on several medieval sites in Somerset with a condition or legal agreement which requires the applicant to secure an appropriate mitigation strategy and programmes of archaeological work. Largely due to the economic recession many developments which have received planning permission are currently on hold and the programme of archaeological works have yet to be agreed with the local planning authority. A large scale programme of archaeological work has yet to be agreed in relation to very extensive stone quarry applications at Halecombe on the Mendip Hills. Here the application will remove Rookery Farm which is a listed building of largely late seventeenth, or early eighteenth-century date. In spite of the land having planning permission for quarrying this building is currently protected by listed building legislation which has prevented it from being demolished.

Milborne Port

The small medieval market town of Milborne Port (Fig. 13.2) in the eastern part of the county has become something of a case study in Somerset and will serve as an example of what can happen if the process of assessment and evaluation is taken through to achieve statutory protection of a medieval settlement site.

In 1989 a development proposal was submitted to build a sheltered housing scheme in a 0.4ha garden plot on the eastern side of St John's church in the historic core of Milborne Port. An archaeological assessment was requested by the local planning authority using the policy guidance of the Wincanton Area Local Plan (SSDC 1987). As a result of this assessment extensive archaeological deposits were found which dated from the tenth to the fourteenth century (Fig. 13.2, 13.3). The quality of the deposits located here in the form of pits ditches, post hole structures and substantial quantities of artefacts clearly demonstrated that this was a well preserved archaeological site (Wessex Archaeology 1989 and Oxford Archaeological Unit 1991).

The local planning authority and English Heritage were involved in extensive discussions with the developer and the application in its original form was refused planning permission. English Heritage confirmed that the site was of national importance and in May 1990 the garden plot and the land underneath the existing bungalow was scheduled as an ancient monument. Negotiations and discussions have continued over the past three years to decide on an appropriate mitigation strategy for this nationally important monument and a compromise was reached between English Heritage and the applicants to permit a revised form of development which will destroy only a

Fig. 13.2 Milborne Port: the historic core of the medieval settlement. (Photo: Aerofilms)

Fig. 13.3 Milborne Port, Somerset. The historic core of the town with the scheduled monument area shown shaded.

Marston Magna Moated Manor

In this field are the remains of a medieval Moated Manor house. It is likely that at one time the island contained buildings, probably including stables, servants quarters, kitchens, barns and the Manor house itself. The date of the moat is unknown but was probably dug in the 13th or 14th century. The earliest documentary reference to Marston Magna is in the Domesday Book of 1086 which refers to two manors at "Merstone" one of which was probably Marston Magna. The manors were held by the Beauchamp family of Hatch Beauchamp may be descended. The Marston Magna Manor was in use by the lords of the Beauchamp estate in the 13th century but by 1327 a tenant may have occupied the site. No one knows when the moated site fell out of use or when the site was definitely occupied.

The moat may have been dug as a defensive ditch although some moats were dug as status symbols. The south side is very wide and is linked to a rectangular hollow which was probably a fish pond. Fish formed an important part of the medieval diet as an additional source of protein during the winter months and on religious fast days such as Fridays and during Lent.

The area around the moat shows traces of further buildings, paddocks and gardens now reduced to grassy "humps and bumps". The field south of the moat is covered by regular ridge and furrow caused by medieval ploughing. A slight curve on each ridge was caused by plough-teams starting to turn as they reached the headland.

SCHEDULED MONUMENT
This site is a Scheduled Monument and it is an offence to damage or disturb it, or to use a metal detector on the site.

FOOTPATH
There is a public right of way across the field. Please keep your dog on a lead if animals are grazing here.

This site is owned by Somerset County Council. It was purchased with the help of English Heritage and donations from the villagers of Marston Magna. Should you require further information about the site please contact the Department for the Environment, County Hall, Taunton, Somerset. TA1 4DY.

This map shows the main earthworks. Based upon a survey by the Royal Commission on the Historic Monuments of England.

Fig. 13.4 *Information panel erected at Marston Magna moated site, Somerset.*

small percentage of the site (less than five percent is estimated). A series of design measures has been adopted for the site, including the use of small piling-type foundations in conjunction with structural concrete rafts and ring beams to support the buildings rather than traditional cut and fill trenches which would be wholly inappropriate here. In addition to redesigning the type of foundations and service trenches a recording programme has been agreed to permit the development to go ahead. The responsibility and funding for this archaeological work and the protection of the site has fallen upon the developer who has somewhat reluctantly taken on the archaeological dimension of this planning application. As a direct result of the discoveries at Milborne Port there was considerable questioning of the preservation policies being implemented, and the concept of Heritage Blight was used to describe the planning situation here. (Cadogan, *Financial Times* 19 May 1990). To date no development has taken place on the site.

The publication of PPG 16 in November 1990 clarified much of what was already happening in many counties, including Somerset, and gave official recognition of 'best practice' which was being used by local planning authorities to protect and preserve archaeological sites of all periods. The use of statutory scheduling legislation rather than the planning system alone makes Milborne Port an exceptional case study but it does illustrate the policy thinking concerning preservation *in situ* which was being developed in Somerset between 1989 and 1991 at a time when PPG 16 was being implemented for the first time.

There have been numerous examples of archaeological assessments on medieval settlement sites since the publication of PPG 16. Each application is examined individually by Somerset County Council to determine the approach needed to assess the impact upon the archaeological resource. In the majority of cases these assessments have shown how it is possible to evaluate an area of archaeological potential quickly and efficiently and then use that information to advise local planning authority when it makes a decision on a planning application. There are four main options open for local planning authorities:

(i)   to preserve *in situ*
(ii) to record by excavation and survey
(iii) to undertake a watching brief, or
(iv) to carry out no further archaeological work on the
      site.

Combinations of the above are used depending upon the nature and extent of the remains, and it is unusual for a development proposal within a medieval settlement site of county importance to be refused purely on archaeological grounds. The situation is rather different on sites of national importance and the planning authorities are usually advised to refuse an application until the applicant has obtained scheduled monument consent for the proposed work.

Management and the Protection of sites

Somerset County Council has established a policy of acquiring archaeological sites which are in need of protection and management. This has been very successful in securing the long term protection and management of several nationally important medieval settlement remains. The following case studies represent this approach and expand upon the reasons for the protection of medieval settlement sites.

Marston Magna moated site

On the southern side of St Mary's church in Marston Magna are the earthwork remains of an extensive medieval moat and fishpond complex. An exact date for the earthworks is not known and no detailed archaeological excavation has been undertaken. In 1985 the sale of the scheduled monument described by English Heritage as 'Moated site with related earthworks' resulted in a potential development threat and Somerset County Council in conjunction with the parish council bid for and acquired the site. The site was purchased with grant aid from English Heritage, the County Council and the parish council. The initial acquisition did not include the total scheduled area which included the large fishpond to the east and which was subsequently bought in 1990. A management plan has been drafted for the site which seeks to protect the main areas of earthworks by stock grazing, ideally using sheep. Due to lack of local interest, sheep grazing has proved difficult and currently a grazing regime using cattle has been running fairly successfully for five years. The area of the earthworks is also open to the public and an interpretation panel has been erected on the site giving details of the history of the moat and a description of the earthworks. A detailed survey of the earthworks has been undertaken by RCHME and this drawing forms the basis of the interpretation panel (Fig. 13.4). The archaeological field survey clearly shows the position of the moat and fishpond in relation to the surrounding ridge and furrow field system (Fig. 13.5). Site management is carried out by the county council in consultation with the parish council and the earthworks are now in reasonably good condition. An increasing number of people are visiting and looking at the moat field both for recreational and educational purposes. Sites such as this are integral to the modern village community and provide valuable open spaces which can be managed for the benefit of the community and the archaeological resource.

Nether Adber Deserted Medieval Village

The earthworks of the former medieval village site of Nether Adber are one of the best examples of a deserted medieval village site in Somerset (Fig. 13.6). The site was purchased in 1987/8 by the county council with a

R. A. Croft

Fig. 13.5 An aerial photograph of Marston Magna.

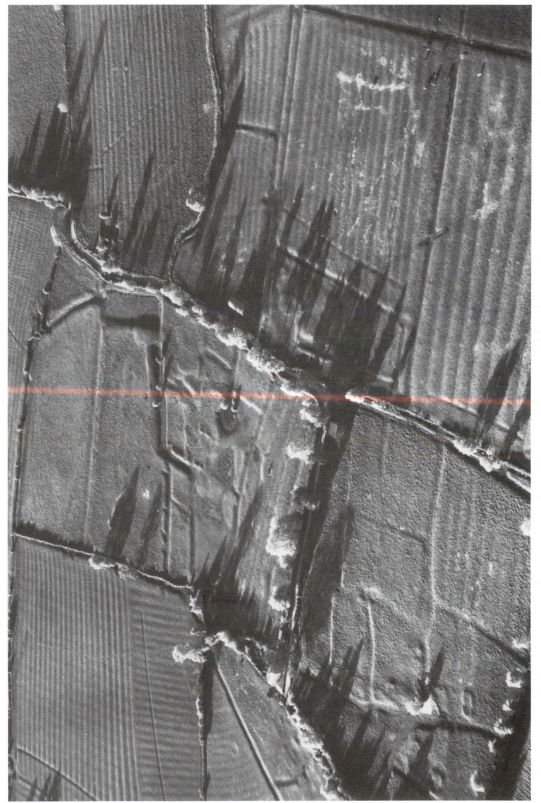

Fig. 13.6 *An aerial photograph of the earthworks at Nether Adber deserted medieval village, Somerset. This photograph was taken in 1966 and clearly shows the extent of the surrounding village earthworks and the associated ridge and furrow fields which were destroyed in the late 1960s and early 1970s. (Copyright: Cambridge University Collection)*

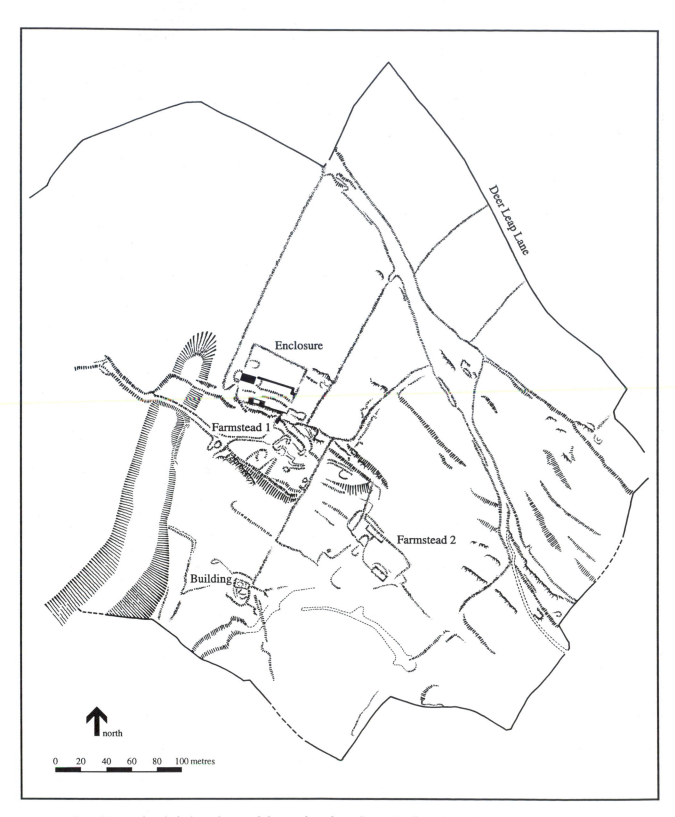

Fig. 13.7 *A detailed plan of part of the earthworks at Ramspits, Deer Leap, Somerset. (after RCHME)*

substantial grant from English Heritage. A detailed survey of the earthworks was carried out by the RCHME and this survey was used as the basis for the management plan for the site. In common with Marston Magna, which is less than 2km to the north-east, Nether Adber is currently grazed by cattle and careful monitoring is needed to ensure that they do not overgraze and poach the earthworks.

A programme of hedge laying and replanting of the boundaries of the site is being carried out and this has helped to make the fields stock proof and to increase the wild life and nature conservation interest in the site. There is also limited on-site interpretation which gives visitors information on the origins and nature of the earthworks. Both Marston Magna and Nether Adber are linked by public footpaths and these paths are used by an increasing number of people on longer walks or as part of an organised heritage trail.

Deer Leap

In contrast with the low lying clayland sites of Marston Magna and Nether Adber a third site, known as Deer Leap or Ramspits, on the Mendip Hills, was purchased by the county council in conjunction with the Countryside Commission and English Heritage. The earthworks at Deer Leap are some of the best preserved medieval settlement remains on the Mendip hills. This is a most picturesque part of the Mendip limestone landscape with fine views to the south. The protected area includes two medieval farmstead sites and several other archaeological features including building remains and a late eighteenth- or early nineteenth-century cattle shelter and stock watering pond. A plan of the earthworks and analysis of the site and its history recently published by the RCHME has identified the complex nature of the archaeological remains within the scheduled area and illustrates how they continue along the side of the Mendip escarpment (Fig. 13.7). The scheduling at this site covers a substantial part of the associated field system, this being one of the few medieval sites and fields in Somerset so protected. It is obvious from detailed surveys such as this one that medieval settlement sites of this type are set within a contemporary field system which may overlie an earlier one. Where such field systems exist they should be seen as part of the monument in its wider historic landscape and efforts should be made to ensure their preservation *in situ*. In recent years farm diversification schemes and changes in traditional agricultural practices have brought new threats to these landscapes through tree planting and extensive pig farming, and these are not encouraged from an archaeological and historic landscape viewpoint.

This site is perhaps one of the best preserved and most visited deserted medieval farmstead sites in the county, but the fragmentary nature of the earthworks make it difficult for many people to imagine and interpret these remains. To help with this interpretation, a self guiding trail leaflet was published by the county council in 1990 with the aim of explaining the context of the site within the Ebbor Gorge valley. On site interpretation was erected in 1994 giving details of the history of the site and the importance of the earthworks.

The management plan for this site involves cattle grazing in the summer and some limited sheep grazing in the winter, but problems can arise where the thin soils on the Mendip limestone are liable to poaching by cattle in wet weather and the grazing of stock is strictly controlled each season. As part of the wider conservation of this historic landscape the county council has carried out repairs to the dry-stone enclosure walls which surround the site and to the former cattle shelter. Limited visitor interpretation and an area of car parking and picnic facilities have been constructed on the eastern side of the earthworks next to the main road. This area is the focus for the interpretation of the site and takes advantage of the splendid views to describe the setting of Deer Leap within the Mendip Hills. A detailed panel describing the archaeological remains of the farmsteads has been erected on the interior of the repaired cattle barn. In common with many sites owned by the county council on the Mendip Hills the current policy is not to advertise and encourage visitors to the area which would result in increased erosion, but to advise and inform the existing visitors to use the countryside with due care.

Deer Leap has some nature conservation interest but does not have sufficient diversity of species for it to be designated as a Site of Special Scientific Interest (SSSI). Some small scale replacement of trees has occurred on parts of the site but the emphasis is on keeping an open landscape with a good limestone grassland sward. Recent initiatives by the Countryside Commission to introduce Countryside Stewardship have had some effect on securing the protection of medieval settlement sites across the county. Stewardship agreements last for 10 years and they provide an agreed programme of landscape management which will not damage archaeological remains, and such an agreement has been secured for Deer Leap.

The Future of Policy and the Protection of Medieval Settlement Sites in Somerset

The protection of medieval settlement sites is a key part of the wider debate of the conservation of our countryside and the wise use of a sustainable landscape. Archaeology has firmly entered the Green debate and cultural resource management is one aspect of the issues facing national and local government policy makers (Macinnes and Wickham Jones 1992). There are many questions relating to the preservation of medieval settlement sites such as where is all this identification and interpretation of medieval settlement sites leading to and how effective is statutory protection in preventing the damage or destruction of the archaeological resource? Clearly the pro-

Fig. 13.8 Areas of High Archaeological Potential and Conservation Area boundaries for Wedmore (AHAP). (Copyright: Sedgemoor District Council).

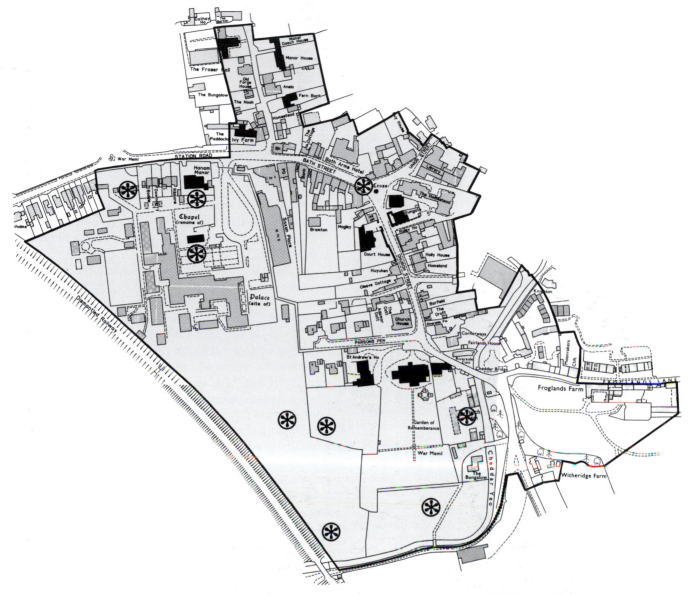

Fig. 13.9 *Area of High Archaeological Potential and Conservation Area boundaries (AHAP) for Cheddar. (Copyright: Sedgemoor District Council)*

tection polices for isolated and deserted farmstead sites such as Deer Leap or Nether Adber are not the same as those needed for the protection of our existing lived in heritage settlements such as Wells or Wiveliscombe. The link with other statutory planning constraints such as Conservation Areas and Special Landscape Areas in the countryside needs to be developed over the next few years.

In towns and villages the concept of a linked designation has been developed with some success in Somerset in recent years with the lines of Conservation Areas and AHAPS coinciding in several small towns and villages such as Wedmore and Cheddar (see Figs 13.8 and 13.9). Several Local plans with this designation have now been subjected to a public inquiry and the plans have been endorsed by the Department of the Environment. Further guidance has been given by English Heritage on devel-

opment plan policies for archaeology (English Heritage 1992).

Any decisions now made to excavate or preserve settlement remains will be judged against current research strategies, frequently set by specialist groups such as the Society for Medieval Archaeology and the Medieval Settlement Research Group. The very nature of such research strategies clearly means that there is a constant need for revision and review of the archaeological resource and the way in which it is both managed and conserved.

The development threats affecting many medieval settlement sites are wide ranging. Within historic settlements both at the small town or village level the threats are similar: frequently housing schemes, infilling gardens, closes, paddocks and orchards, or relatively large schemes such as schools, leisure complexes and industrial or commercial developments. Where development is proposed within the AHAP then it is usually possible to arrange for an archaeological assessment of the development proposal in line with the guidance given in PPG16. The incomplete nature of AHAP designation within historic settlement cores across the county and its occasional and erratic use by local planning authorities can be seen as a valid criticism of the concept of AHAPs. Reasonable and justifiable use of PPG 16 and the county SMR could make the plan based AHAP policy outdated and unnecessary if the planning control system were working effectively. This is accepted, in part, but experience has shown that in Somerset the concept of an AHAP has been successful in ensuring that archaeological assessments of several medieval settlement sites have been carried out at the request of the local planning authority. In one instance the AHAP around the medieval chapel site at Beckery near Glastonbury was extended after the local planning inspector recommended an extension of the boundary (Mendip District Council 1991).

Why should we concentrate on medieval sites? What is special about them and should they receive more attention than any other settlements of an earlier or later period? It is true that medieval settlement remains are relatively common in Somerset but our understanding of how and when our towns and villages grew up is poorly understood. It is my opinion that workable policies to assess and understand our medieval settlement sites are essential if we are to protect and preserve the sites important for this and subsequent generations. This in turn will allow us to appreciate the origins of our more recent past and how the current settlement pattern and land-use of the county has developed. In this way we will be better informed when making decisions about the conservation of the wider historic environment which makes up our towns, villages and countryside.

Scheduling to Protect Medieval Settlement sites

The use of Scheduling to protect important medieval settlement sites is very limited in Somerset and the graph given in Fig. 13.10 clearly shows how few sites are protected by statutory legislation. The boundaries of many of the medieval settlement sites which are currently Scheduled are largely based upon the earlier assessment of the standing and visible earthworks rather than the series of interlinked criteria which are currently used by English Heritage. The large number of deserted and shrunken medieval rural sites identified in the county is largely due to research which was carried out in the 1970s and early 1980s, principally by Mick Aston who identified a range of sites, particularly farmsteads in the west (Aston 1983), and Ann Ellison, and the Western Archaeological Trust working in the south east.

It is becoming apparent that Scheduling is not necessarily the most appropriate way to protect all medieval settlement sites. English Heritage has indicated on many occasions that Scheduling of the interiors of existing towns and villages is not necessarily the best way to ensure their long term preservation (Startin 1993). A revision of the national and regional criteria used for the Monument Protection Programme is currently in progress and this will have a marked affect upon the identification and a protection of the medieval sites in all counties. Somerset will particularly benefit from this study because it is a boundary between two distinctive settlement patterns with a largely dispersed settlement pattern in the west and a more nucleated one in the east.

The identification of new sites of county or national importance is happening all the time, although the measures which can be implemented to protect them are largely associated with the planning system rather than with Scheduling legislation. If local planning policies are used effectively then it is sometimes possible to protect the

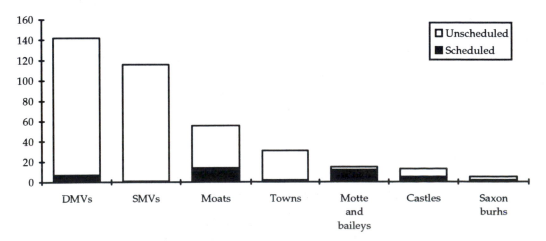

Fig. 13.10 Medieval settlement sites recorded in Somerset SMR.

historic and archaeological cores of medieval settlements from developments which will destroy them. This system relies upon the County Archaeological Officers and the county SMRs providing adequate advice and recommendations to the local planning authorities. In most instances in Somerset the local planning committees do take full account of archaeological matters but it must be remembered that the planning system relies upon the local councillors to make the decisions rather than the planning officers and the specialist advisors. Leaving the protection of nationally important archaeological sites to individual planning authorities has few advantages and the use of Scheduling should be used particularly where the planning authorities are uncertain about their role.

Conclusion

The protection of important medieval settlement sites in Somerset is progressing in a positive and academically justifiable way. The use of countryside initiatives to protect rural sites and their associated landscapes through management agreements in Environmentally Sensitive Areas, such as the Blackdowns or Exmoor, should help to protect a range of sites without the need for statutory scheduling.

Planning policies are in place which enable the local planning authorities to obtain further information on the significance of sites and this assessment process will ensure that nationally important sites receive appropriate protection. Integrated landscape management plans for the interpretation and presentation of the important medieval settlement sites is happening with some success in Somerset. Co-operation and communication between all interested parties will ensure that the initiatives outlined here will move forward and have a more positive role to play in the wise use of the historic environment.

References

Adkins, L. and Adkins, R. 1992: *A Field Guide to Somerset Archaeology* (Dovecote).

Aston, M. A. 1977: 'Deserted Settlements in Mudford Parish, Yeovil', *PSANHS* 122, 11–18.

Aston, M. A. 1982: 'The Medieval Pattern AD 1000–1500', in Aston and Burrow 1982, 122–33.

Aston, M. A. 1983: 'Deserted Farmsteads on Exmoor and the Lay Subsidy of 1327 in West Somerset', *PSANHS* 127, 71–104.

Aston, M. A. (ed.) 1988: *Aspects of the Medieval Landscape of Somerset.* Somerset County Council, Taunton.

Aston, M. A. and Burrow, I. C. G. (eds) 1982: *The Archaeology of Somerset*, County Council, Taunton.

Aston, M. A. and Leech, R. H. 1977: *Historic Towns in Somerset – Archaeology and Planning*, CRAAGS, Bristol.

Baker, D. 1993: 'Managing England's local heritage, in Heyworth, M. (ed.), *Archaeology in Britain 1992* (CBA, York).

Brown, K., Croft, R. and Lillford, R. 1988: 'Preserving the Historic Landscape of Somerset', in Aston, M. (ed.) 1988.

Cadogan, G. Heritage Blight, Financial Times 19 May 1990.

Croft, B. and Williamson, T. 1988: Medieval Settlement Research Group: Statement of Excavation Policy, *MSRG Annual Rep 3*, 8. London.

Croft, R. and Lillford, R. 1989: *Protecting the Historic and Architectural Heritage of Somerset.* SCC, Taunton.

Darvill, T. C. 1987: *Ancient Monuments in the Countryside: An archaeological Management review.* London: HBMC.

Darvill, T., Saunders, A. and Startin, B. 1987: 'A Question of National Importance: Approaches to the Evaluation of Ancient Monuments for the Monuments Protection Programme in England', *Antiquity* 61, 393–408.

Darvill, T. C. 1993: *Valuing Britain's Archaeological Resource* (Bournemouth University Inaugural Lecture).

DoE 1990: *Planning Policy Guidance Note 16: Archaeology and Planning.* (PPG 16) London: HMSO.

English Heritage 1991a: *Exploring Our Past: Strategies for the Archaeology of England.* London: HBMC.

English Heritage 1991b: *The Management of Archaeological Projects.* London: HBMC 2nd edn.

English Heritage 1992: *Development Plan Policies for Archaeology: Advice note for Local Planning Authorities.* London: HBMC.

Ellis, P. 1992: *An Archaeological Survey of the Mendip Hills*, AONB, Somerset County Council Taunton.

Ellison, A. 1983: *Medieval Villages in South East Somerset*, CRAAGS, Bristol.

Havinden, M. 1981: *The Somerset Landscape*, Hodder and Stoughton, London.

Hughes, M. and Rowley, T. (eds) 1986: *The Management and Preservation of Field Monuments.* Department of External Studies, University of Oxford, Oxford.

Hunter, J. and Ralston, I. 1993: *Archaeological Resource Management in the UK – An Introduction.* Alan Sutton, Stroud.

Medieval Village Research Group 1984: The Preservation of Deserted Medieval Village Sites and The Excavation of Medieval Settlement Sites: Memoranda submitted by MVRG to the Historic Buildings and Monuments Commission for England. MVRG London.

Mendip District Council 1987: Wells Area Local Plan.

Mendip District Council 1991: Glastonbury and Street Local Plan.

Oxford Archaeological Unit 1991: Church Street, Milborne Port, Somerset – Archaeological Evaluation.

Pattison, P. 1991: Settlement and Landscape at Ramspits, Deer Leap Westbury sub Mendip: A new survey by the Royal Commission on the Historical Monuments of England. *Proc. Somerset Archaeol. and Nat. Hist. Soc.* Vol. 135, 95–111.

Sedgemoor District Council 1993: *The Conservation Areas of Sedgemoor – Appraisal and Audit.* Sedgemoor District Council, Bridgwater.

Somerset County Council 1984: *Somerset County Structure Plan.* SCC, Taunton.

Somerset County Council 1984: *Somerset Levels and Moors Strategy, Framework for Implementation.* SCC, Taunton.

Somerset County Council 1993: *Somerset County Structure Plan Approved written statement.* SCC, Taunton.

South Somerset District Council 1987: Wincanton Area Local Plan.

Startin, W. 1991: 'Protecting the Archaeology of our Historic Towns', *Conserve. Bull.* 13, 14–15.

Wessex Archaeological Unit 1989: *Church Street, Milborne Port, Somerset – Archaeological Assessment.*

Index